Tempted for Us

Theological Models and the Practical Relevance
of Christ's Impeccability and Temptation

Tempted for Us

Theological Models and the Practical Relevance of Christ's Impeccability and Temptation

John E. McKinley

Foreword by Gregg R. Allison

WIPF & STOCK · Eugene, Oregon

Wipf and Stock Publishers
199 W 8th Ave, Suite 3
Eugene, OR 97401

Tempted for Us
Theological Models and the Practical Relevance of Christ's Impeccability and Temptation
By McKinley, John E.
Copyright©2009 Paternoster
ISBN 13: 978-1-60608-876-0
Publication date 6/19/2009
Previously published by Paternoster, 2009

This Edition published by Wipf and Stock Publishers by arrangement with Paternoster

PATERNOSTER THEOLOGICAL MONOGRAPHS

Series Preface

In the West the churches may be declining, but theology—serious, academic (mostly doctoral level) and mainstream orthodox in evaluative commitment—shows no sign of withering on the vine. This series of *Paternoster Theological Monographs* extends the expertise of the Press especially to first-time authors whose work stands broadly within the parameters created by fidelity to Scripture and has satisfied the critical scrutiny of respected assessors in the academy. Such theology may come in several distinct intellectual disciplines—historical, dogmatic, pastoral, apologetic, missional, aesthetic and no doubt others also. The series will be particularly hospitable to promising constructive theology within an evangelical frame, for it is of this that the church's need seems to be greatest. Quality writing will be published across the confessions—Anabaptist, Episcopalian, Reformed, Arminian and Orthodox—across the ages—patristic, medieval, reformation, modern and counter-modern—and across the continents. The aim of the series is theology written in the twofold conviction that the church needs theology and theology needs the church—which in reality means theology done for the glory of God.

PATERNOSTER THEOLOGICAL MONOGRAPHS

Series Editors

† David F. Wright, Emeritus Professor of Patristic and Reformed Christianity, University of Edinburgh, Scotland, UK

Trevor A. Hart, Head of School and Principal of St Mary's College School of Divinity, University of St Andrews, Scotland, UK

Anthony N.S. Lane, Professor of Historical Theology and Director of Research, London School of Theology, UK

Anthony C. Thiselton, Emeritus Professor of Christian Theology, University of Nottingham, Research Professor in Christian Theology, University College Chester, and Canon Theologian of Leicester Cathedral and Southwell Minster, UK

Kevin J. Vanhoozer, Research Professor of Systematic Theology, Trinity Evangelical Divinity School, Deerfield, Illinois, USA

To Becky

Contents

Foreword by Gregg R. Allison	xvii
Acknowledgements	xix
Abbreviations	xxi
Introduction	1
Tempted *and* Unable to Sin?	3
Scope and Sequence	8

BIBLICAL EVIDENCE

Chapter 1
The Temptation and Sinlessness of Jesus — 15

Biblical Evidence for Christ's Temptations in His True Humanity	15
Jesus' Temptations in Hebrews 2:17-18	16
Jesus' Temptations in Hebrews 4:15	18
Jesus' Temptations in the Wilderness	22
Jesus' Temptations in Gethsemane	27
GOSPEL ACCOUNTS	27
HEBREWS 5:7-8	32
Jesus' Temptation during the Crucifixion	34
The Relational Setting of Christ's Temptations	36
Conclusion	41
Biblical Evidence for the Sinlessness of Jesus	41
Luke-Acts	42
The Gospel of John	43
2 Corinthians	44
Hebrews	44
1 Peter	45

1 John	46
Conclusion	46

Chapter 2
The Relevance of Temptation and Sinlessness — 49
Empathy and Help — 49
The Pattern to Copy — 50
   Jesus: The Pattern to Copy in Hebrews 12:1-3 — 50
   Jesus: The Pattern to Copy in 1 Peter 2:21-25 — 54
The Sufficient Sacrifice — 58
Conclusion — 59

Chapter 3
Jesus and the Holy Spirit — 61
Old Testament Promise of the Messiah — 62
   Pneumatological Christology in Isaiah 11:1-5 — 63
   Pneumatological Christology in Isaiah 42:1-9 — 67
   Pneumatological Christology in Isaiah 61:1-3 — 68
   Conclusion — 69
New Testament Fulfillment of the Messiah — 70
   The Holy Spirit and Jesus' Conception, Birth, and Early Life — 70
   The Holy Spirit and Jesus' Baptism — 72
   The Holy Spirit and Jesus in the Wilderness — 73
   The Holy Spirit and Jesus' Ministry — 74
Conclusion to the Biblical Evidence — 76

THEOLOGICAL MODELS

Chapter 4
Patristic Models (Part 1) — 81
Background to the Patristic Models — 82
   Common Presuppositions — 84
      THE NICENE FAITH — 84
      SOTERIOLOGICAL REQUIREMENTS — 84
      OPPOSITION TO HERESIES — 85
      THE HELLENISTIC PHILOSOPHICAL SETTING — 88
         Divine Impassibility — 88

The Knowledge of God Incarnate	91
Stock Theories of Physical Union	92
Divergent Theological Tendencies	93
Geopolitical Setting	96
Four Models in the Patristic Period	97
M1: Sinless by Inherent Impeccability	97
DESCRIPTION OF M1	97
REPRESENTATIVES OF M1	98
EVALUATION OF M1: SINLESS BY INHERENT IMPECCABILITY	100
M2: Sinless by Deification	102
DESCRIPTION OF M2	102
REPRESENTATIVES OF M2	104
EVALUATION OF M2: SINLESS BY DEIFICATION	112

Chapter 5
Patristic Models (Part 2) — 117

M3: Sinless by Divine Hegemony	117
DESCRIPTION OF M3	117
REPRESENTATIVES OF M3	118
EVALUATION OF M3: SINLESS BY DIVINE HEGEMONY	128
M4: Sinless by Empowering Grace	131
DESCRIPTION OF M4	131
REPRESENTATIVES OF M4	132
EVALUATION OF M4: SINLESS BY EMPOWERING GRACE	140
Conclusion	143

Chapter 6
The Medieval Model — 145

Background to the Medieval Model	145
Description of M5: Sinless by Created Grace	149
First Part: The Impeccability of Christ	150
TRANSFORMED BY GRACE	151
The Grace of Union	152
Created Grace	152
The Beatific Vision	154
Grace and Normal Human Weaknesses	156
IMPECCABLE BY HEGEMONY OF THE DIVINE WILL	157

IMPECCABLE BY MORAL NECESSITY	159
Second Part: The Temptability of Christ	160
EXTERNAL TEMPTATIONS	160
FREEDOM	161
MERIT	162
THE EXAMPLE FOR HUMANITY	163
Evaluation of M5: Sinless by Created Grace	164

Chapter 7
The Reformation Model — 169

M6: Temptable by the Human Eclipse of Divine Power	171
Description of M6	171
Recycled Elements	173
INHERENT IMPECCABILITY	173
EMPOWERING GRACE	174
PURIFICATION FROM ORIGINAL SIN	175
New Elements in Luther	176
TEMPTATION IN BODY AND SOUL	176
HUMAN EXPERIENCE IN THE FOREGROUND	177
New Elements in Calvin	179
HUMAN EXPERIENCE IN THE FOREGROUND	179
THE INTEGRITY OF HIS TEMPTABLE HUMANITY	181
THE HELP OF THE HOLY SPIRIT	184
Evaluation of M6: Temptable by the Human Eclipse of Divine Power	185

Chapter 8
Modern Models (Part 1) — 189

Background to the Modern Models	189
Reassertion of the Traditional Models (M1-M6)	192
M1: SINLESS BY INHERENT IMPECCABILITY	193
M2: SINLESS BY DEIFICATION	193
M3: SINLESS BY DIVINE HEGEMONY	195
M4: SINLESS BY EMPOWERING GRACE	197
M6: TEMPTABLE BY THE HUMAN ECLIPSE OF DIVINE POWER	200
Innovation: Did Jesus Possess a Fallen Human Nature?	202
M7: Temptable by the Humanization of Divine Impeccability	205
Description of M7	205
TRUE HUMANITY REQUIRES PECCABILITY	208

TRUE TEMPTATION REQUIRES PECCABILITY	209
Evaluation of M7	211
CONTRA: TRUE HUMANITY REQUIRES PECCABILITY	212
CONTRA: TRUE TEMPTATION REQUIRES PECCABILITY	215
CONCLUSION	216

Chapter 9
Modern Models (Part 2) — 219

M8: Temptable by Kenotic Restriction	219
Description of M8	219
Evaluation of M8	222
M9: Temptable by Psychological Restriction	227
Description of M9	227
Representatives of M9	229
THOMAS V. MORRIS	229
GERALD O'COLLINS	231
RICHARD SWINBURNE	232
DONALD MACLEOD	232
WILLIAM LANE CRAIG	233
Evaluation of M9	235
NOT KNOWING IS NOT ENOUGH FOR *US*	236
HOW COULD JESUS *NOT* HAVE KNOWN HE WAS IMPECCABLE?	236
IF JESUS BELIEVED HE COULD SIN, THEN JESUS BELIEVED A LIE	240
THE EPISTEMIC POSSIBILITY OF SIN?	241
THE TWO-MINDS MODEL IS NESTORIAN	242
CONCLUSION	243
Conclusion to the Theological Models	243

SYSTEMATIC FORMULATION

Chapter 10
Jesus Could not Fail — 247

Jesus Christ, the Impeccable Godman	247
Why Impeccable But Not Omniscient, Omnipotent, etc.?	250
IF IMPECCABILITY, THEN WHY NOT OTHER ATTRIBUTES?	251
WHY THE EXCEPTION FOR IMPECCABILITY?	252

If He is Impeccable, How is Jesus Free?	254
THE POSSIBILITY OF BEING IMPECCABLY FREE AS A MAN	255
DIVINE IMPECCABILITY AND FREEDOM	256
If He is Impeccable, How is Jesus Praiseworthy?	259

Chapter 11
Tempted as We are Tempted — **261**

How We are Tempted	262
Temptation on Five Fronts	263
TEMPTATION UNDER GOD	263
TEMPTATION IN THE CREATED WORLD	266
TEMPTATION WITH OTHER PEOPLE	267
TEMPTATION AND THE SELF	268
TEMPTATION AND SUFFERING	269
CONCLUSION: HUMANITY, JESUS, AND TEMPTATION	270
How Temptation Works	272
The Dual Purposes of Temptation	273
The Person-Variability of Temptation	275
Internal Factors of Temptation	277
BELIEFS	278
DESIRES	279
WHAT ABOUT CORRUPT DESIRE IN JAMES 1:12-15?	282
External Factors of Temptation	285
Definition of Temptation	287
Jesus was Tempted for Us	288
The Holy Spirit and the Temptation of God's Son	290
The Dual Life of God Incarnate and Pneumatological Veiling	291
The Holy Spirit as the Unifying Bond	294

Chapter 12
The Perfect Human Life — **299**

The Implausibility of Sinlessness by His Divine Power	299
The Plausibility of Sinlessness by Empowering Grace	302
Six Signs of Empowering Grace	305
FILLING BY THE HOLY SPIRIT	305
ENGAGEMENT WITH GOD THROUGH PRAYER	306
VISIBLE DIVINE HELP OF ANGELS	308

ENGAGEMENT WITH GOD THROUGH SCRIPTURE	308
THE COMMUNITY OF FELLOW BELIEVERS	309
THE MOMENTUM OF MATURING CHARACTER	310
Conclusion: A Human Triumph of Righteousness for Us	312

Conclusion   315

Bibliography   321

General Index   343

FOREWORD

People in our postmodern society are intrigued by many different kinds of Jesus: a good teacher of morality, the man for others, the leader out of exile, a peasant Jewish cynic, the founder of a historic religion, an eschatologically-deluded revolutionary, the husband of Mary Magdalene, a prophet, a way to God for some Christians, and the like. In order to create these different images of Jesus, the presentation of him by the New Testament writings has largely been dismissed as an early church invention, corrected by additional sources (e.g., the *Gospel of Thomas*) that were squelched by the early orthodox Christian party, or reinterpreted in light of existentialist or Marxist or feminist or other types of philosophy; thus, it carries little weight today. Jesus has been deconstructed, then reconstructed, according to the imagination that best suits people and their worldview.

Having so removed themselves from the biblical presentation of Jesus, should they return to it for a moment, people might be shocked by one peculiarity that the New Testament writings claim for him: he was sinless. Though Jesus is presented as a real and fully human being, tempted like all the rest of humanity, the New Testament underscores the extraordinary fact that he never once sinned. Tempted, yes; sinned, no. Moreover, when the church has paid close attention to the sinlessness of Jesus in the face of temptation, it has often wondered: Does the fact that Jesus *did not sin* though tempted indicate that he *could not sin*? One can only imagine how consideration of this matter would affect people's construal of Jesus today.

Given this context, John McKinley has given us a wonderful gift—he has set himself to think hard about the temptations, temptability, peccability, sinlessness, and impeccability of Jesus. His disciplined thinking encompasses exegesis of key biblical texts (to find out what Scripture affirms about this matter), biblical theology (to note, for example, the intersection of the themes of pneumatology and Christology), historical research (to find out what key patristic, medieval, and Reformation theologians believed about this matter), contemporary theology (to consider recent developments on this matter), and systematic theology (to synthesize Scripture so as to articulate a coherent, intelligible, contemporary model for this aspect of Christology). In addition, he traces the practical relevance of his proposal for those who hope for concrete help in facing their temptations. Accordingly, both in content, methodology, and practicality, John has distinguished himself as a key theological contributor on this matter of Christ's impeccability and temptation.

I had the special privilege of supervising John McKinley in his work on the PhD dissertation that is the basis for the book you now have in your hands. As my first PhD supervisee at the institution where I now teach, Dr. McKinley set the bar high for all those who follow him. I am delighted to introduce this book and this young theologian to you. If you wish to rebuff the contemporary caricatures of Jesus and consider instead a historically-aware, biblically-grounded, well-developed theological presentation of him as the God-man facing and overcoming temptations, this book will deliver exactly that.

Gregg R. Allison
Associate Professor of Christian Theology
The Southern Baptist Theological Seminary
Louisville, Kentucky

ACKNOWLEDGEMENTS

Many people have helped me in many different ways to bring this book to completion first as a dissertation, and then as a major revision into the present form. Gregg Allison supervised my dissertation and helpfully directed me to follow a models approach to the topic. He contributed many suggestions in the course of reading and re-reading the dissertation. Robert Saucy and Bruce Ware have also been influential teachers for me, and I am indebted to their guidance in listening to Scripture. I am also grateful to Bruce for suggesting the topic. As an independent reviewer of the dissertation, Oliver Crisp alerted me to several weaknesses and suggested many helpful changes that are reflected in the book.

I am grateful for the school where I now teach, Biola University. One of the deans of my school, Michael J. Wilkins, provided the guidance I needed to get my dissertation to a publisher. Three of my colleagues, Ashish Naidu, Rob Lister, and Matt Jenson, were kind enough to read the entire revised manuscript and offer valuable suggestions. They also caught dozens of errors that my tired eyes did not see, and their encouragement to see the book through has helped me to stick with it. Of course, all the errors that remain in the book are my own responsibility. Biola University also provided me with a research grant in 2007 for this project. Without the support of extra time to complete research and writing, finishing this book would have come much later.

Outside the two seminaries where I have been blessed to study theology, God has provided two allies for me. Keith Poppen has walked with me regularly as a brother disciple seeking the transformation of life in Christ. Keith is ever challenging me to think theologically and practically in ways that are reflected in this book. I could not have done this book without my dear wife Becky. She has been my constant friend and encouragement to rally my enthusiasm for the project. She is a gift to me, and I dedicate this book to her.

Finally, I am thankful for the frequent help of Anthony R. Cross, editorial consultant for Paternoster's Academic Monograph Series, and to Jeremy Mudditt, Robin Parry, and Paternoster for bringing this book for publication.

John McKinley
Talbot School of Theology, Biola University
January 2009

ABBREVIATIONS

Books and Series

CSEL	Corpus scriptorum ecclesiasticorum latinorum (Vindobonae: F. Tempsky, 1866-)
CO	*Ioannis Calvini Opera quae supersunt omnia*, ed. W. Baum, E. Cunitz, E. Reuss (Halle: C. A. Schwetschke & Sons, 1834-1900; reprint, New York: Johnston Reprint, 1964)
CCSL	Corpus Christianorum Series Latina (Turnhout: Brepols, 1953-)
FOC	Fathers of the Church (New York: Fathers of the Church; Washington DC: The Catholic University of America Press, 1947-)
LW	*Luther's Works*, American Edition, ed. Jaroslav Pelikan and Helmut T. Lehmann (Philadelphia: Muhlenberg, 1955-76)
NPNF[1]	A Select Library of the Nicene and Post-Nicene Fathers of the Christian Church, First Series, ed. P. Schaff (New York: Christian Literature Co., 1886; reprint, Grand Rapids: Eerdmans, 1980)
NPNF[2]	A Select Library of the Nicene and Post-Nicene Fathers of the Christian Church, Second Series, ed. P. Schaff (New York: Christian Literature, 1887-94; reprint, Grand Rapids: Eerdmans, 1975)
OS	*Johannis Calvini Opera Selecta*, ed. P. Barth and W. Niesel (Munich: Chr. Kaiser, 1926-62)
PG	Patrologia Graeca (Paris: J. –P. Migne, 1857-66)
PL	Patrologia Latina (Paris: J. –P. Migne, 1841-64)
ST	*St Thomas Aquinas Summa Theologiae* (London: Eyre & Spottiswoode; New York: McGraw-Hill, 1965-74)
WA	*Weimarer Ausgabe*. D. Martin Luthers Werke: Kritische Gesamtausgabe (Weimar: Hermann Böhlaus Nachfolger, 1883-)

Abbreviations for the Theological Models

M1   *Sinless by Inherent Impeccability*
Jesus was unable to sin because of his deity, so he never sinned

M2   *Sinless by Deification*
Jesus' human nature was energized by his divine nature to resist sin perfectly

M3   *Sinless by Divine Hegemony*
The Logos led all his human actions perfectly

M4   *Sinless by Empowering Grace*
Help for resisting temptation was provided to Christ in his humanity by various means and the Holy Spirit

M5   *Sinless by Created Grace*
Grace enables and transforms Christ's humanity to be impeccable and yet able to earn merit, be tempted, and provide an example of right living for Christians

M6   *Temptable by the Human Eclipse of Divine Power*
God the Son veiled his deity with the vulnerable humanity he assumed to become temptable as a man while remaining unable to son

M7   *Temptable by Humanization of Divine Impeccability*
Jesus could be truly tempted as a man because he had surrendered his divine impeccability

M8   *Temptable by Kenotic Restriction*
Jesus remained impeccable, and he was truly tempted because he temporarily gave up his omniscience regarding his inability to sin

M9   *Temptable by Psychological Restriction*
Jesus remained impeccable, and he was truly tempted because his full knowledge of his inability to sin was veiled from his consciousness as a man

INTRODUCTION

How much is Jesus just like us? Was he a true man tempted in all the same ways that we are? Does he truly understand what it feels like to be tempted to sin? Was he able to sin? Nikos Kazantzakis has given one answer to these questions in his notorious novel, *The Last Temptation*.[1] Kazantzakis reconstructs Jesus as a man tortured by his lifelong and sexually charged desires to marry his cousin, Mary Magdalene. The lustful temptations assail Jesus frequently, and he is just as frequently diverted to his loner path by the piercing pain as of a great bird's pinions driving into his skull. He is tempted to lust, fear, and doubt, but he does not sin in the struggle to obey God's will. The *spirit* (the divine within him?) triumphs over the desires of his *flesh* (his humanity). Even in the ultimate temptation that comes to Jesus through a vision in his last moments on the cross, the savior finally refuses the appeals of marital bliss (and polygamy!) and chooses instead to embrace his role in salvation.

Kazantzakis has been praised and condemned for contradicting the traditional view that Jesus was asexual.[2] Nonetheless, *The Last Temptation* expresses a trend that has become common in recent centuries: Jesus was a normal man with ordinary desires and temptations shared by all of us.[3] The popularity of this just-like-us view of Jesus also shows in the bestselling success of Dan Brown's novel, *The Da Vinci Code* (2003), in which Jesus is the

---

[1] Nikos Kazantzakis, *The Last Temptation: a novel* (Oxford: B. Cassirer, 1960). This is the first English edition of the Greek original (1951). A Martin Scorsese film, *The Last Temptation of Christ* (1988), popularized the book. Paperback editions continue to be published, as recently as 1998.

[2] An ancient example is Augustine, who claimed in *Contra Iulianum* V, 7, 27 (PL 44, 801) that Jesus had no sexual desires (since all sexual desires are sinful, so Christ willed not to have any sexual sense), cited by Roland J. Teske, "St. Augustine on the Humanity of Christ and Temptation", *Augustiniana* 54 (2004): 276. After many centuries, the trend is changing. Bernard L. Ramm, *An Evangelical Christology: Ecumenic and Historic* (Nashville: Thomas Nelson, 1985), 84, observes approvingly that several contemporary theologians such as Norman Pittenger are affirming Jesus' sexuality as part of his authentic humanity.

[3] Cf. Kathryn Tanner, *Jesus, Humanity and the Trinity* (Minneapolis: Fortress, 2001), 7-8.

father of Sarah, his daughter by union with Mary Magdalene.[4] These examples illustrate that modern authors and readers celebrate a just-like-us view of Jesus instead of the Godman of the Scriptures and Christian theology. These modern authors and their audiences embrace the bare humanness of Jesus who was merely one historical man among others. Many theologians have not been far behind, as in the nineteenth-century proliferation of lives-of-Jesus studies that stripped Jesus of either his divinity, or his historicity as a real man, or both.[5]

This modern view of Jesus is a rehearsal of the ancient Ebionite heresy of adoptionism (Jesus was merely a remarkable man adopted and empowered by God to be the Messiah), and recalls the early struggle in the church to explain the biblical evidence for Jesus. Following the apostolic testimony in the New Testament, the teachers of the Christian faith affirmed that Jesus deserves worship as the exalted Lord and Savior who is able to save humanity because he is God incarnate. Early claims about Jesus established his deity and humanity despite many competing proposals that diminished both truths. In the first few centuries of the church, Docetism and Apollinarianism diminished Christ's humanity, and Ebionitism and Arianism diminished his deity. Other proposals construed the teaching about Christ in ways that were unacceptable, as in Nestorianism (the separation of his two natures into two personal subjects) and Eutychianism (the confusion of his two natures into one incarnate nature).

Christian theology progressively excluded these heresies as unacceptable interpretations of the biblical evidence for Jesus of Nazareth. Church teachers defended the New Testament teaching that Jesus is fully divine and fully human, two natures joined by union in one person, and that he possesses the two natures without confusion, change, separation, or division. This decisive clarification of the New Testament teaching occurred at the Fourth Ecumenical Council (Chalcedon, 451). The boundaries defended there are commonly known as Chalcedonian Christology and have served to this day as the basic framework for understanding Jesus properly.[6]

Nonetheless, Chalcedonian Christology did not address further problems stemming from the basic intuition that humanity and divinity seem vastly incompatible. The Chalcedonian Definition (a creedal summary of what the participants discerned as orthodox teaching about Christ) described the basic truth of God incarnate, but many questions remained concerning how this

---

[4]Dan Brown, *The Da Vinci Code* (New York: Doubleday, 2003).
[5]Fisher H. Humphreys, "The Humanity of Christ in Some Modern Theologies", *Faith and Mission* 5 (1988): 3-13. Humphreys notes that Ernest Renan, *The Life of Jesus* (1863), is typical of the emphasis on Jesus' humanity and historicity to the diminution of his divinity, and D. F. Strauss, *Life of Jesus* (1835), is typical of the critical scholarship that dispensed with historicity and divinity.
[6]Some have questioned the adequacy of Chalcedon for doing Christology today. It is not my purpose here to defend Chalcedonian Christology. Others have addressed these critiques and I accept the basic boundaries as adequate and useful starting points.

doctrine of Christ's two-natured, divine-human existence could be coherent. How can one person be both omnipotent and weak? How can the Creator and source of life take up creaturely existence and die? How can one individual person function with two wills in two natures? Chalcedon cleared the stage of heretical pretenders, but the Chalcedonian Christology also set the stage anew for disputes about these and other questions that were pressed as part of understanding the ways and means of God incarnate.

Theologians have been able to explain the many incongruities of divinity and humanity more or less satisfactorily by maintaining the distinction between Jesus' two natures in two conditions of existence (or, frames of reference).[7] According to his condition of existence as the divine Son, Jesus is omniscient and omnipotent; according to his existence as a man, Jesus is limited in knowledge and subject to the normal human weaknesses—even death. While these explanations have not convinced all that the traditional Christological doctrine is coherent,[8] many theologians and Christian believers are satisfied with this foundational patristic interpretation of Scripture. Despite this satisfaction with the tradition, many Christological problems have proven to be difficult to explain adequately. One of these was the center of the novel by Kazantzakis.

Tempted *and* Unable to Sin?

The traditional account of Jesus is that he was truly tempted to sin as a man, but he was unable to sin because he was God. Several moral and theological problems have been raised against this traditional view that Jesus was both tempted and impeccable. I will set out the relevant definitions and support for their meanings.

Impeccability refers to the absolute inability of a person to commit sin or, alternately, the person cannot fail to do right. An impeccable person has never sinned, cannot sin in any state of affairs that exists (i.e., in no possible world), and will never be able to commit sinful action or even intend to do so. An impeccable person is essentially and immutably good (or, necessary goodness). Impeccability is thus a form of ethical immutability, the moral fixedness of the person to be unchangeably good and righteous.

The antithetical term, *peccability*, means that a person is vulnerable to sin (he may fail to do right acts). A peccable person is mutable, but may be contingently good while remaining sinless. A peccable person possesses the

---

[7]Gerald O'Collins, *Christology: A Biblical, Historical, and Systematic Study of Jesus* (New York: Oxford University Press, 1995), 233-34.
[8]Thomas V. Morris, *The Logic of God Incarnate* (Ithaca, NY: Cornell University Press, 1986), reviews and addresses the contemporary philosophical objections to the Incarnation, among which are the incoherence of the numerical identity of Jesus and God, and the incongruence of divinity and humanity.

susceptibility to turn away from right and good to commit sin (*posse peccare*). We should remember also that Scripture does not affirm Christ's impeccability as theologians have articulated the doctrine (any more than the doctrine of the Trinity), but the traditional claim is an entailment from the evidence for his deity. Most Christians have recognized that God is impeccable, so, being fully God, Jesus is impeccable.

Sinlessness means the person has never sinned, but he has always done right. Sinlessness is an entailment of impeccability, but sinlessness does not entail impeccability since mutable beings (e.g., angels, Adam and Eve before the fall) can be potentially sinless and then cease to be so if they should sin. A peccable person *may* be sinless, but an impeccable person *must* be sinless. The attribute of sinlessness means positively that the person is pure and unstained in relation to evil.

Temptation (and the related terms *tempted*, *tempting*, and *temptable*) will be used with the specific sense of an enticement to sin. So, temptation involves a sinful target (whether the target presented is an intention or an action) and a path leading to that sin. Temptation is experienced as the pull or draw towards the evil action. A prior state of sin is not necessary for temptation, as in the case of Adam and Eve in Eden, and for Christ's temptations. Temptation seems to require the presence of needs or wants if there is to be any appeal to an agent (thus, God, who has no needs and is immutably perfect in every way, cannot be tempted in the sense I have specified here, temptation to evil, as declared in Jas 1:13).

What is the support for these traditional definitions? Scripture indicates that God cannot sin (e.g., the inability to lie in Titus 1:2; Heb 6:18) or even be tempted to sin (Jas 1:13).[9] By contrast, God incarnate was tempted to sin on many occasions (cf. Heb 4:15), particularly in direct confrontation with Satan (Mark 1:12-13 par.). The divine inability to be tempted seems to contradict Christ's human vulnerability to temptation: how could God incarnate experience the moral struggle of temptation if God cannot be tempted to sin? A common answer is that Jesus was able to be tempted according to his humanity. Thus, temptation is regarded as a marker of his real humanity. By contrast, his sinlessness indicates his real divinity.

How has this topic been discussed? First, many theologians in recent centuries assume that temptability entails peccability (the ability to sin, *posse peccare*).[10] They argue that the possibility of choosing sin is a necessary

---

[9] But notice that God can be tested by humans in the sense that they can challenge his character and will, e.g., Ananias and Sapphira (Acts 5:9) and the issue of circumcising Gentiles (Acts 15:10). This sort of testing is not a temptation to sin. W.R. Baker, "Temptation", in *Dictionary of the Later New Testament and Its Developments*, ed. Ralph P. Martin and Peter H. Davids (Downers Grove, IL: InterVarsity, 1997), 1166.

[10] In addition to contemporary theology, Herman Bavinck, *Reformed Dogmatics: Sin and Salvation in Christ*, trans. John Vriend, ed. John Bolt (Grand Rapids: Baker, 2006), 314,

condition for a real experience of temptation. If God incarnate is impeccable, then how can he have had any sort of struggle when he immutably chooses the good? Thus, impeccability and temptability seem to be mutually exclusive attributes. Because Scripture is clear that Jesus was tempted, how can the theology be right that he is also impeccable in any sense that fits together with his temptability? Common answers are (1) that Christ's temptation was the struggle to choose among many good options (but never among evil choices), (2) that Christ's human peccability limited his divine impeccability so that he became able to sin, or (3) that he simply did not know for sure that he could not sin when tempted (while he remained impeccable and was unaware of it). The variety of answers to this question demonstrates the confusion, troubling proposals, and need for a clear statement in contemporary theology. Providing such a statement of explanation is my goal in this book.

Second, contemporary philosophers have objected that the supposed sinlessness of God incarnate is not a praiseworthy accomplishment because he could not sin. The claim that Jesus possesses the divine attribute of necessary goodness (or, impeccability) disqualifies him from the praise that is due to someone who has never sinned. Critics charge that the claim of Christ's impeccable sinlessness is nonsense—how can Jesus be praised for not having done what he could not do? A common solution to the problem is that Jesus (and God) must be able to sin.

Third, a difficulty related to the conjunction of temptation and impeccability is the disagreement about *how* Jesus is impeccable.[11] Scripture does not say how Christ could not sin in an explicit way (as we might wish). Christ's impeccability remains a theological opinion, though one that has a firm and long tradition, as the historical chapters to follow will bear out. We will see in the history that many different arguments arrive at the same conclusion of impeccability. On the surface, the fact that historical theology has generated a succession of models indicates that many believed that the models they received were theologically inadequate. Part of my goal is to sort through these models, evaluate them for an adequate explanation of Christ's impeccability (and temptation) in our contemporary setting.

A fourth problem with the traditional claim is that the orthodox faith includes the affirmation that Christ's impeccability as God extends to his humanity, but otherwise he is not omnipotent, omniscient, or immortal according to his humanity. These last three (and other) divine attributes seem

---

observes that there has been a minority of theologians in the tradition who argued that Jesus was able to sin. Bavinck lists as examples the Arians, Pelagians, and nominalists (Duns Scotus, Biel, Durandus, and Molina).

[11]Cf. Jean Galot, *Who is Christ? A Theology of the Incarnation*, trans. M. Angeline Bouchard (Chicago: Franciscan Herald, 1981), 385. "The impeccability of Jesus has been generally accepted in Catholic theology, but there has been no agreement as to the reason why."

inconsistent with authentic human existence; indeed, the Gospels report that Jesus was vulnerable to the common human weaknesses of hunger, thirst, fatigue, limited knowledge, and death. The exception is impeccability; theologians have traditionally argued that Jesus was not vulnerable to sin in the way that is common to humanity. Theology makes the exception because of the problem that peccability entails possible sin, and sin is impossible for God and even God incarnate. Nonetheless, the exception seems to undermine the full humanity of Jesus because many contemporary theologians assume that peccability is essential to human freedom (cf. Adam and Eve before the Fall, and all fallen humanity). The problem of special pleading for impeccability seems to undermine the coherence of the orthodox doctrine. Moreover, until recently, theologians have traditionally affirmed that Jesus' sinlessness—declared many times in the New Testament as a redemptive necessity (e.g., 1 Pet 1:18-19)—is an expression of his divine impeccability. Thus, the overriding moral strength of his divine attribute seems to have canceled the humanness of Jesus' temptations in a way that is inconsistent with, and separates Jesus from common human experience.

Fifth, problems arise from the biblical evidence for Christ's temptations as experiences that are redemptively relevant for the church. Scripture exhorts Christians to copy Christ's pattern of life in humble obedience to God (Phil 2:5-11) and particularly with reference to his exemplary refusal to sin when he suffered unjustly (1 Pet 2:21-24). Because Jesus is the example for others to follow in resisting temptation to sin, and he is uniquely impeccable despite his assumed humanity, then how can he be a credible and relevant pattern for others who are not divinely immune to sin as he is? The exhortation seems plainly unrealistic and misapplied to those who are mere human beings because they possess all the common human susceptibility to sin—which Jesus apparently lacked—without possessing his advantage of the divine immunity to sin. Thus, Christ's relevance as an example in resisting temptation seems to be nullified by his impeccability. As a solution, some contemporary theologians seek to save Jesus' relevance by denying his impeccability.

Finally, a related problem of relevance is that Scripture reassures Christians that Jesus is empathetic for others who are tempted (Heb 2:17-18). His ability to sympathize with others and his readiness to offer help are constituted by his own experiences of having been tempted as a man as others are tempted. His temptations are the proof that he understands what others experience and consequently has help to give them that is relevant to their situation of temptability. The problem with the affirmation of Christ's impeccability is that this seems to undermine his relevance to be empathetic: his innate immunity to sin implies that he does not understand the strain of temptation as a personal, internal experience of struggle against enticement to sin. Accordingly, the author of the book of Hebrews addresses the possible misgivings of his readers by elaborating the claim that Jesus was tempted significantly to the same extent that they are (Heb 4:15), and then he illustrates this claim by recalling Jesus' struggle in Gethsemane (Heb 5:7-8). Right on the point of the readers' possible objection to Jesus' ability to empathize with their experience of temptation, the author writes that Christ's struggle to obey God in the setting of his suffering and temptation was not mitigated by his divinity: "Although he was the Son, he learned obedience through what he suffered" (Heb 5:8). Thus, Scripture is clear that Jesus was tempted, and, because of his temptations, he can empathize with and help other people resist their temptations. Against this biblical evidence, the claim of Jesus' impeccability seems to invalidate Jesus' relevance as priest for the people because his immunity to sin prevents him from being able to experience temptation the ways they do.

These several problems illustrate the complexity and difficulty of the traditional affirmation of Christ's impeccability and temptation. This difficulty is a subset of the basic Christological problem of how to reconcile coherently the biblical evidence for Jesus' full divinity and full humanity. Because of the clear entailments from biblical evidence for Jesus' two natures, and because of the further evidence for his sinlessness and temptation, the orthodox faith includes the paradoxical claim that Jesus, in his earthly life, was both impeccable and temptable. In answer to the question of how this paradox can be true and not self-defeating, many wise and pious theologians such as Augustine of Hippo have affirmed plainly that Jesus triumphed over his temptation because he was God.[12] In other words, Jesus remained sinless because as God he was unable to sin. Others throughout the tradition have offered an alternate explanation that Jesus, to be an example for others, resisted temptation entirely as a man, not at all by relying on his divine power of immunity to sin.

Moreover, some innovative contemporary proposals seek to reconcile the difficulties by explaining that Jesus' divinity must have been modified to be peccable according to the peccability of his true humanity. Christ's triumph against temptation is thereby a real achievement of sinlessness and model of moral fortitude that can inspire Christians in their efforts against sin. On this view, the certainty of redemption is stripped away because the Savior may have voided the entire project (and, if he could possibly sin even now as the glorified mediator, he may yet forfeit his role as the perfect priest and king if he sins tomorrow).

A serious practical problem shows up when we consider how Jesus' temptation experiences are relevant for us. In the local church, an explanation will sometimes be heard that Jesus could have sinned (hence his real temptation) but he overcame temptation because he was God. Aside from the problem of saying that Jesus was peccable despite his divinity (presumably on parallel with his capability to be weak despite his divine omnipotence) and the troubling implication for reformulating the doctrine of God to include peccability, the paradox remains unresolved. Worse still, Jesus' relevance in

---

[12]See M1, below in ch. 4.

this second peccability proposal remains invalid because of his recourse to the special advantage of inherent divine powers in his earthly life as a man. The Christian might protest: "What would Jesus do in my life situation? Does it even matter? For Jesus it was easy to turn away from temptations and refuse to hit back when others abused him—he's God. *I'm* not God. *I* can't live like Jesus did." Thus, following the example of God incarnate seems no more reasonable than imitating the eternal, immutable, and infinite Creator. God, despite having made human beings in his image and likeness, is vastly different from his creatures (cf. Isa 55:8-9). Apparently, in the popular view, divine incarnation has not advanced God's assistance for humanity to have an example and priest who wrestled through a human life within human limitations and thus understands our human difficulty firsthand in temptation. These proposals have no doubt discouraged many Christians from taking solace in Jesus' empathy and courage by his example with the promise of support in the time of need (Heb 4:16). Jesus is not perceived as a fellow-sufferer, and his means of help seem largely irrelevant to human needs.

Therefore, the difficulties of understanding Christ's impeccability and temptation (as in the traditional affirmations) have practical implications for the life of the church. Christians need a contemporary explanation of the biblical and theological evidence that will clarify and illuminate Jesus' experience of temptation and impeccability, and inspire their own faithfulness after his pattern of righteous human life.

Scope and Sequence

This is a theological study within the broader topic of Christology with significant doctrinal overlap with sanctification. This study, however, will not propose a Christology or develop a distinct model of sanctification. Furthermore, this study will not emphasize psychological and philosophical accounts of temptation. I will seek assistance from these disciplines as they have proven helpful, but I am not assuming the burden of drawing significantly from or contributing to the way our topic is understood in those disciplines.

Although this study will include both historical theology and biblical exegesis, my goal is neither to recount a history of the doctrines nor to formulate a biblical theology of Christ's impeccability and temptation. The purpose of using these materials is to draw from the main stream of orthodox theology and the biblical source. For the historical portion, I endeavor to excavate models of Christ's impeccability and temptation in patristic theology, and then trace the Western developments of models in the medieval, Reformation and modern periods to the present day. To my knowledge, this scope does not omit anything theologically significant that bears upon the topic.

I accept Chalcedonian Christology as the profound and accurate boundary statement about Christ's constitution, one person in two natures, fully God and fully man, etc. With the majority of those who accept Chalcedonian

Christology, I affirm that Christ was impeccable and truly tempted. My specific burden is to explain the difficulty that results when we say Jesus was tempted but he could not have sinned. For the sake of taking on a reasonably sized task, I do not assume the burden of defending the claim for Jesus' impeccability. Others have done this ably (though a contemporary explanation and defense would be worthwhile).[13]

In recent centuries, the impeccability of God has been questioned as inconsistent with divine freedom, praiseworthiness, and the divine attribute of omnipotence. Similar charges may be raised against the claim of Christ's impeccability. Most theologians readily accept Jesus' sinlessness, but some contemporary scholars have questioned Jesus' impeccability and others have affirmed his peccability instead. Nonetheless, I will limit this study to the traditional affirmation of Christ's impeccability and the way it fits with the evidence for his temptation. The majority of theologians have recognized this, and most evangelical theologians continue to affirm this position in the present day. Accordingly, and despite some contemporary alternative proposals, I do not adopt a position on the topic that has no defense or long tradition in theology. Moreover, having accepted the specific dilemma of Christ's impeccability and temptation, my goal will be to clarify and provide a better

---

[13] Among evangelical scholars, the traditional claim of Christ's impeccability remains the majority view, as the list below shows, and has been ably defended by many. An older, focused defense of Christ's impeccability has been done by Howard C. Zabriskie, "The Impeccability of Christ" (ThD diss., Dallas Theological Seminary, 1938), in which he elaborates some of the same arguments that are presented vigorously in the eighteenth century by Jonathan Edwards, *Freedom of the Will*, ed. Paul Ramsey, vol. 1 of *The Works of Jonathan Edwards* (New Haven: Yale University Press, 1957), 281-94. More recently, the doctrine of Christ's impeccability has been affirmed explicitly by Louis Berkhof, *Systematic Theology*, 4th ed. (Grand Rapids: Eerdmans, 1939), 318, Loraine Boettner, *The Person of Christ* (Grand Rapids: Eerdmans, 1943), 125, Lewis Sperry Chafer, *Systematic Theology* (Dallas: Dallas Seminary Press, 1948), 5:77, G. C. Berkouwer, *The Person of Christ*, trans. John Vriend (Grand Rapids: Eerdmans, 1955), 262, Karl Barth (as recorded in) *Karl Barth's Table Talk*, ed. John D. Godsey, Scottish Journal of Theology Occasional Papers 10 (Edinburgh: Oliver and Boyd, 1963), 68-69, Thomas V. Morris, *The Logic of God Incarnate* (Ithaca, NY: Cornell University Press, 1986), ch. 6, Wayne A. Grudem, *Systematic Theology* (Grand Rapids: Zondervan Publishing House, 1994), 538, Richard Swinburne, *The Christian God* (New York: Oxford University Press, 1994), 208, John S. Feinberg, "The Incarnation of Jesus Christ", in *In Defense of Miracles*, ed. R. Douglas Geivett and Gary R. Habermas (Downers Grove: InterVarsity, 1997), 245, Donald G. Bloesch, *Jesus Christ: Savior and Lord* (Carlisle, UK: Paternoster, 1997), 73, Donald Macleod, *The Person of Christ* (Downers Grove: InterVarsity, 1998), 229-30, Gerald O'Collins, "The Critical Issues", in *The Incarnation*, ed. Stephen T. Davis, Daniel Kendall, Gerald O'Collins (New York: Oxford University Press, 2002), 15, and Michael S. Horton, *Lord and Servant: A Covenant Christology* (Louisville: Westminster John Knox, 2005), 45. More could be listed.

understanding of the biblical and theological evidence. Some additional presuppositions should be mentioned.

First, I accept the starting points provided by Chalcedonian Christology, that Jesus is God the Son who preexisted his incarnation.[14] Jesus is the Godman, one person in two natures, fully God and fully man. Accordingly, my Christological presuppositions include the traditional claims that Jesus could be tempted but he could not sin. I will offer some explanations to understand how this and other apparent paradoxes can be understood, but in advance of those arguments, I affirm with the orthodox tradition that such is the case for Jesus, whether or not we can satisfactorily understand the biblical-theological paradox.

Second, I presuppose five assertions about Christ's authentic human nature.

(1) Jesus was not in a condition of spiritual death that is the consequence of Adam's guilt for original sin (corporate alienation of the human race from God because of guilt for sin). Jesus came in the *likeness* of sinful flesh (Rom 8:3), that is, his human nature was not physically pristine as Adam before the fall, but Jesus was not himself sinful, fallen, corrupted or implicated with Adam's guilt. Not having originated from Adam (being the eternal Logos before incarnation), Jesus does not depend on Adam for his existence or share in Adam's guilt for sin.

(2) Jesus lacked corrupt human desires that result from personal sin and spiritual death. According to his human existence, Jesus was not in a state of alienation from God (as are the rest of fallen humanity), and so he did not possess the disordered, corrupt desires such as lust, greed, pride, self-centeredness, etc.

(3) Jesus was voluntarily susceptible to the sufferings of sickness, pain, and death that accrued to Adam's race as consequences of original sin in the world.[15]

(4) Jesus was not able to sin but could be tempted to it just as we are.

(5) His assumed human nature (a created body and soul) was created to be similar enough to those whom he redeems that he could be both an acceptable substitute to satisfy God's justice and a reasonable example for his followers to live as he did by the same means that he did.

---

[14]My presupposition is that Scripture reveals God as Trinity: God is eternally Father, Son, and Holy Spirit. All discussion of the three persons and their relationships in this study depends on the biblically warranted claim that each of the three persons is fully God, and God is numerically one in his essence. The recognition of the Trinity in Scripture allows for incarnational Christology in that the eternal Son and Logos of God assumed human nature to live in a second condition of existence as a man and die for sinners. I think this trinitarian framework entails the preexistence of Jesus of Nazareth as the Logos and eternal Son of God.

[15]Oliver D. Crisp, "Did Christ have a *Fallen* Human Nature?", *International Journal of Systematic Theology* 6 (2004): 287, makes a similar claim: "Christ is both sinless and yet possesses a human nature affected by the fall. And this makes sense of those biblical passages where Christ is tired, weeps and is sad." Crisp cites Augustine as a witness to this idea in *The Trinity* 13.23.

These five affirmations and denials are an alternative to the traditional ways of categorizing the states of humanity (e.g., pre-fall, unregenerate, regenerate, glorified) and comparing them with Jesus' humanity. Whatever is meant by those in recent centuries who claim that Jesus assumed a *fallen* human nature (e.g., Edward Irving, Karl Barth, T. F. Torrance), I disclaim that term as misleading and prefer the descriptive alternative of these five claims. These claims are minimal and not a comprehensive statement of Christ's humanity, but they are especially relevant for the study.

The study will proceed in the sequence of biblical evidence, historical theology, and a contemporary theological response. Part one, the biblical evidence, (chapters 1-3) will present the biblical evidence for Christ's temptation and sinlessness. The sources of historical theology frequently refer to these biblical passages, so it will help to have these texts clearly in mind as part of being able to understand the subsequent theological formulations. One additional biblical topic that is included here is the Holy Spirit's role in the life of the Messiah. The cluster of passages indicating the Spirit's involvement in Christ is counted by some in the tradition as important to understanding Christ's impeccability and temptation, so we will consider these texts as well.

Part two, the theological models, (chapters 4-9) contain my arrangement of historical research in a models approach (not a history of doctrine *per se*). I will argue that nine main models of Christ's impeccability and temptation are apparent in historical theology (these models are listed on the Abbreviations page). For each period (patristic, medieval, Reformation, modern), I will consider the setting, distinctive features, and representatives of each model. I will also interact with each model by way of an evaluation of its theological adequacy. The continuing development of new models in successive centuries indicates that these theologians deemed earlier answers inadequate, or at least open to improvement. As is normally the case with patristic theology, these early models represent the majority of theological development of this topic and are thus foundational. Models appearing in subsequent periods draw heavily from the four patristic models. Even some of the supposed innovations in contemporary theology are anticipated in one or another of the patristic models. The contemporary discussion of our topic will be included with the modern period (spanning the eighteenth to twenty-first centuries).

Part three, the systematic formulation, (chapters 10-12) is my reflection on Christ's impeccability, temptation, and sinlessness. I have tried to capture the essence of this reformulation in the claim that Jesus was *tempted for us*, that is, however we understand the topic, we cannot lose sight of the way his experiences were endured on our behalf, and with a view to doing things in such a way as would benefit us by supplying what we needed. My goal here is to explain how the biblical claim of a true correspondence between his temptations ours is reasonable, which might seem hard to believe when we keep in mind the sharp differences between Jesus and us (his impeccability and our sinfulness). The likeness of Christ's temptations to our temptations is important to his role as a priest who can both empathize with us credibly (Heb 4:15) and offer us help in the midst of our temptations (Heb 4:16)—help that he has proven to be effective in his own human adventure.

My goal is to draw valuable assistance for the followers of Jesus from the study of the theological models. As we make our way through life waylaid by temptations of all sorts, my hope is that we will be encouraged, inspired, and helped by Jesus who has walked this path ahead of us. With his battle-proven help ready at hand, we may advance in salvation from one day to the next (by his grace and for his glory).

BIBLICAL EVIDENCE

CHAPTER 1

The Temptation and Sinlessness of Jesus

The different explanations given in the models of Christ's impeccability and temptation are caused partly by two factors. First, models follow from divergent interpretations of the biblical texts related to Christ's human moral life. Second, models weigh some texts more heavily in relation to others in systematic formulation. The models are explanations of the biblical data in light of each historical period's setting and concerns. The models appeal to six sorts of biblical texts. These Christological passages variously deal with Christ's deity, humanity, temptation, sinlessness, the relevance of his human experiences for redemption, and his empowerment by the Holy Spirit. Chalcedonian Christology has established the interpretation of the first two sorts of biblical texts by affirming that Jesus Christ is fully God and fully man. In agreement with this tradition, we will bypass the first two sorts of biblical texts and take a fresh look at the remaining four sorts of the biblical evidence for Christ's moral life. This chapter will explore the evidence for Christ's temptation and sinlessness. (I will consider the evidence for the relevance of temptation and sinlessness for salvation and the role of the Holy Spirit in the subsequent chapters.)

Biblical Evidence for Christ's Temptations in His True Humanity

The central term denoting Christ's temptation is πειράζω ("I tempt, I test"), used in two senses by the New Testament and extrabiblical Greek writing. The positive sense of πειράζω is the action to test or discover the truth about something or someone by affliction (e.g., 2 Cor 13:5; 1 Pet 1:6). The negative sense of πειράζω is to tempt someone to sin, to solicit to evil (e.g., Mark 1:13; 1 Cor 10:13).[1] Determination of the sense depends on context. Some New

---

[1] Raymond E. Brown, *Death of the Messiah, from Gethsemane to the Grave: A Commentary on the Passion Narratives in the Four Gospels*, Anchor Bible Reference Library (New York: Doubleday, 1994), 1:159. Cf. Walter Bauer, *A Greek-English Lexicon of the New Testament and Other Early Christian Literature*, ed. and trans. William F. Arndt, F. Wilber Gingrich, and Frederick W. Danker, rev. and ed. F. W. Danker, 3rd ed. (Chicago: University of Chicago Press, 2000), s.v. "πειράζω"; "πειρασμός".

Testament occurrences of πειράζω contain both senses as two sides of one experience: God *tests* Jesus to prove his obedience while Satan simultaneously *tempts* Jesus to draw him into sin.² We will consider the clearest temptation texts from Hebrews and the Gospels, and then an assortment of other examples from the Gospels.

Jesus' Temptation in Hebrews 2:17-18

(17) ὅθεν ὤφειλεν κατὰ πάντα τοῖς ἀδελφοῖς ὁμοιωθῆναι,
 ἵνα ἐλεήμων γένηται
 καὶ πιστὸς ἀρχιερεὺς τὰ πρὸς τὸν θεὸν
  εἰς τὸ ἱλάσκεσθαι τὰς ἁμαρτίας τοῦ λαοῦ.
(18) ἐν ᾧ γὰρ πέπονθεν αὐτὸς πειρασθείς,
 δύναται τοῖς πειραζομένοις βοηθῆσαι.³

(17) Consequently, he was obligated to be made like his brothers in all respects,
 so that he might become merciful
 and a faithful high priest in things pertaining to God
  to make propitiation for the sins of the people.
(18) For in what he himself has suffered he was tempted,⁴
 he is able to provide help to those being tempted.

The broader context of the epistle to the Hebrews demonstrates Jesus Christ's priestly superiority to the mediation of angels (1:1—2:18), Moses (3:1—4:16), and the Aaronic priesthood (5:1—10:25). Within this context, Hebrews 2:17-18 connects Christ's purpose as a mediatorial priest with his entrance into humanity (cf. Gal 4:4-5). The passage focuses on Christ's superior priesthood in two priestly tasks of dealing with the people's sins and compassionately

---

²Theological determinations about the impossibility that Jesus could be tempted to sin must be submitted to the contextual use of the term, including uses that are applied to the Christian experience of temptation (Heb 2:17-18; 4:15). Jesus is sympathetic to their temptations because of having been tempted himself. One example of not having followed the context to determine meaning is H.P. Owen, "The Sinlessness of Jesus", in *Religion, Reason and the Self*, ed. Stewart R. Sutherland and T.A. Roberts (Cardiff: University of Wales Press, 1989), 123, who objects to the idea that Jesus was tempted to do evil (a minority view) and thus prefers the translation of *tested* or *tried* in every instance of πειράζω despite traditional translations of *tempted*.

³The Greek text for this and all subsequent New Testament quotations is from *Novum Testamentum Graece*, ed. Eberhard and Erwin Nestle, 27th ed., rev. Barbara Aland and Kurt Aland et al. (Stuttgart: Deutsche Bibelgesellschaft, 1993).

⁴NIV, NASV, ESV, RSV, NLT, NKJV, and AV have *tempted*. NRSV and NEB have *tested*.

giving help to people who are faced with temptations to sin.⁵

Incarnation and human life experience are the constitutive means by which Jesus became a priest. To be an effective priest, he was "obligated" (ὤφειλεν, 17a) to become a man. His incarnation equipped him with the full range of human experiences sufficient to make him merciful towards the people as their priest. The Son's entrance into creaturely existence—his own human life—is partly for this purpose (notice the ἵνα clause in 17b, "so that") of becoming merciful because of his first-hand experiences. The writer emphasizes the total identification between Jesus and the readers in terms of their humanity.⁶ The relevant sign of Christ's merciful character from having been made like his brothers is his experience of suffering (18a). This vulnerability to suffering also formed the context for his temptations (2:18; cf. 4:15; 5:7-9; 12:2-3).⁷ Furthermore, his specific experiences of temptation are the existential, first-hand basis for his ability and compassionate inclination to give help to those suffering temptations just as he did. Geerhardus Vos observes the relation between Christ's suffering of temptations and the compassion with which he regards his people:

> Because Christ's sufferings were not sufferings in general, but specifically temptation-sufferings, sufferings which became for him a source of temptation, therefore He can succor those who are in an analogous situation, *i.e.*, tempted to sin by their sufferings. The aorist participle πειρασθείς has a causal force and assigns the temptation-aspect of His sufferings as the ground for His ability to succor.⁸

The parallel between Christ's temptations and the readers' temptations specifies his likeness to them in the way that is most relevant to their pressing concern: temptation to apostasy as a way to avoid suffering because of the Christian confession.⁹ This parallel implies that Jesus was not merely tested for a positive outcome of his faithfulness to God, but, like the readers, he was also tempted to turn away from God's will and thereby avoid the suffering he faced in his human life. Christ's relevance to them is based on his experience of withstanding temptation to sin. His suffering to the ultimate extent of his agony

---

⁵Paul Ellingworth, *The Epistle to the Hebrews: A Commentary on the Greek Text*, New International Greek Testament Commentary, vol. 53 (Grand Rapids: Eerdmans, 1993; reprint, 2000), 186.
⁶William L. Lane, *Hebrews 1-8*, Word Biblical Commentary, vol. 47A (Dallas: Word, 1991), 64.
⁷Lane, *Hebrews 1-8*, 66. "The incarnation exposed the Son to the conflicts and tensions of human life, which were climaxed by the suffering of death in a final act of obedience to the will of God."
⁸Geerhardus Vos, "The Priesthood of Christ in the Epistle to the Hebrews", *Princeton Theological Review* 5 (1907): 582.
⁹Ellingworth, *Hebrews*, 80.

in the cross is compared as a greater measure to the readers' suffering (cf. 12:1-4), so his offer of compassionate aid to resist their temptations is substantial. He is able to help other people because he has experienced the human situation of suffering and temptation. He was truly tempted, and because of this he can truly offer help to others being tempted as he was. Therefore, Christ's experience of temptations to sin in likeness to their temptation constitutes his priestly sufficiency to lend divine aid to human beings. This point is reiterated as the letter goes on.

Jesus' Temptation in Hebrews 4:15

Οὐ γὰρ ἔχομεν ἀρχιερέα
    μὴ δυνάμενον συμπαθῆσαι
        ταῖς ἀσθενείαις ἡμῶν,
    πεπειρασμένον δὲ
        κατὰ πάντα καθ' ὁμοιότητα
        χωρὶς ἁμαρτίας.

For we do not have a high priest
    who is unable to empathize
        with our weaknesses,
    but one who has been tempted[10]
        according to all the same ways,
        without sin (as the result).

Hebrews 4:15 develops the earlier theme of 2:17-18 about Jesus' likeness to the people he saves. As in 2:17, the phrase "according to all" (κατὰ πάντα) in 4:15 denotes the sameness or likeness of Christ's solidarity with the readers in a common experience of human suffering and temptation.[11] Oscar Cullmann notes the relation between Jesus' true humanity and his temptation: "This statement of Hebrews, which thus goes beyond the Synoptic reports of Jesus' being tempted, is perhaps the boldest assertion of the completely human character of Jesus in the New Testament."[12] Cullmann is right since 4:15 deepens the claim of 2:17-18 that Jesus' empathy as a compassionate priest is based on his fully human experience of temptations. Hebrews 4:15 adds depth with two further points that specify the likeness of Jesus' temptation to the readers' experience.

First, Christ's solidarity with the readers' common humanity includes his ability to *empathize* with their *weaknesses*. The present tense of the verb ("able

---

[10]NASV, NIV, ESV, RSV, NKJV, NLT, and AV have *tempted*. NRSV has *tested*.
[11]Ellingworth, *Hebrews*, 269.
[12]Oscar Cullmann, *The Christology of the New Testament*, trans. Shirley C. Guthrie and Charles A. M. Hall (London: SCM, 1959), 95.

to", δυνάμενον, complemented with the aorist infinitive, "empathize", συμπαθῆσαι) indicates the present suffering of Christ alongside the readers, that is, empathy in an existential sense of solidarity with them, not merely psychological sympathy.[13] The author establishes the correspondence between the readers' "weaknesses" (ἀσθενείαις, which refers to their temptations) and the "sameness" of Christ's temptations (ὁμοιότητα).[14] Jesus identifies with the readers' experience by his own experience of the human weaknesses that are common to all: vulnerability to physical, emotional, and relational suffering.[15] Jesus himself describes the weakened human condition of his disciples (and perhaps his own experience) as vulnerable to temptation this way when he says in Gethsemane that the spirit is willing to do right, "but the flesh is weak" (ἡ δὲ σὰρξ ἀσθενής, Matt 26:41; Mark 14:38).[16] The weaknesses are most likely the general, non-sinful, frail, and passible human condition shared by Jesus and the readers.[17] Hebrews 5:7 reiterates Christ's share in this general human condition of weakness "in the days of his flesh" (ἐν ταῖς ἡμέραις τῆς σαρκὸς αὐτοῦ) with special focus on Christ's experience of weakness during his distresses at Gethsemane and at Golgotha.[18]

The weaknesses are most likely not the sinful weaknesses of a propensity to sin because such meaning would set a difference between Jesus and the readers when the author's emphasis is on Christ's likeness to them. Jesus, having been "born of a woman, born under the Law" (Gal 4:4) bears a human body that

---

[13]Cleon L. Rogers, Jr. and Cleon L. Rogers, III, *The New Linguistic and Exegetical Key to the Greek New Testament* (Grand Rapids: Zondervan, 1998), 525.

[14]Rogers and Rogers, *Linguistic and Exegetical Key*, 525, "The word [ὁμοιότης] emphasizes exact correspondence."

[15]Cullmann, *Christology*, 95. "The author of Hebrews really thinks of the common temptations connected with our human weakness, the temptations to which we are exposed simply because we are men. 'In every respect as we are' refers not only to form but also to content." Also in view may be the common human susceptibility to sickness, grief, and death, the emotional and physical suffering of life, all of which are likely consequences of the fall (Rom 8:18-21).

[16]Notice that the main force of the Synoptic meaning of *flesh* is not the orientation against God as in some of Paul's usage (e.g., Rom 8:7-8) because the contrast here is with *spirit* in terms of power versus susceptibility, not moral depravity. The meaning here is perhaps more in line with Paul's description in 1 Cor 15:38-57 of the power of the resurrection mode of life in contrast with the weakness and mortality of the present mode.

[17]Lane, *Hebrews 1-8*, 114. "The emphatic statement . . . implies that he was susceptible to all the temptations that are connected with the weaknesses inherent in the frailty of humanity." Harold W. Attridge, *The Epistle to the Hebrews*, Hermeneia, vol. 53 (Philadelphia: Fortress, 1989), 140, identifies the weaknesses as general human weakness and especially those that make people susceptible to sin.

[18]Attridge, *Hebrews*, 149, agrees that σαρκὸς denotes the general conditions of his humanity in common weakness, including vulnerability to death. Cf. Ellingworth, *Hebrews*, 287, agrees that *flesh* in Hebrews 5:7 is not ethically pejorative as in Paul.

"suffers from the effects of the fall because it is generated from the physical substance of Mary."[19] The difference of Christ's not having these weaknesses would contradict the emphasis in 4:15 (and 2:17) on his likeness to the readers and ability to sympathize with them because of a common experience.[20] If the weaknesses are sinful in the sense of the readers' weakness in sin that Jesus does not have, then the qualifier that he was tempted "without sin" (χωρὶς ἁμαρτίας) would have to mean that his temptations were of a different sort than those the readers experienced. Instead of marking Jesus' difference from the readers, the author's argument depends upon the common human experience shared by Jesus and the readers (cf. 2:17).

Being able to empathize with their weaknesses is a specific mark of Christ's similarity of being made like human beings in all respects, as was declared earlier in Hebrews 2:17 (ὁμοιωθῆναι, "being made like").[21] Christ's ability to empathize with the readers' weaknesses that make them vulnerable to temptation depends upon his having been tempted "according to all the same ways as they are" (κατὰ πάντα καθ' ὁμοιότητα). The parallel relation shows that he was tempted like them because he had weaknesses as they do. Despite his being the Son of God, he is yet a priest who endured a full human experience in temptability. This solidarity in temptations is set emphatically with a double negative (οὐ . . . μή . . .) against the background of his greatness as the Son of God (4:14).[22] The description of his temptations in relation to the readers' includes both the extent of his lifelong temptations, "in all the ways" (κατὰ πάντα), and the similarity of those temptations to what other humans normally experience (καθ' ὁμοιότητα, "according to the likeness", or "in the same ways"). The extent of his temptations matches the extent of theirs.

A second point added in 4:15 (beyond what was declared in 2:17-18) is that Christ's temptations were "without sin" (χωρὶς ἁμαρτίας). The unqualified use of the phrase "according to all" (κατὰ πάντα) in 2:17 is qualified when it appears in 4:15 by the addition that his temptations were *without sin*. This qualifier restricts the likeness of Jesus' temptations to the readers' temptations in one respect. One interpretation of this restriction presupposes that there are

---

[19]Oliver D. Crisp, "Shedd*ing* the theanthropic person of Christ", *Scottish Journal of Theology* 59 (2006): 349. Crisp helpfully distinguishes a share in the effects of the fall (which seem to be necessary for the experiences of suffering and death) from a share in original sin (his sinless human soul was created out of nothing, and not from Mary).

[20]Vos, "Priesthood of Christ", 583. Ellingworth, *Hebrews*, 268, notes that other occurrences in Heb 5:2, 7:28, and 11:34 indicate the ineffectiveness of the Old Testament priests.

[21]Cf. Rom 8:3, Paul writes that Christ was sent in the *likeness* (ὁμοιώματι) of sinful flesh; in Phil 2:7, Paul declares that Jesus was made in the *likeness* (ὁμοιώματι) of men.

[22]Lane, *Hebrews 1-8*, 114. Cf. Vos, "Priesthood of Christ", 582-83. "The γὰρ at the opening of verse 15 is intended to guard against the mistaken inference, as if the exalted nature and position of the heavenly high priest detracted in any way from His sympathy with men in their miserable state as sinners."

two sorts of temptations: some inwardly generated by sin, and some externally generated without sin. This interpretation is that Christ's temptations did not originate from inward sin; his likeness to others is only in the external, non-sinful sort of temptations.[23] This interpretation undermines the main emphasis of 4:15 and 2:17 that Christ's ability to empathize and give help is because of the exact likeness of his temptations to what the readers are experiencing. Were this true that there are two categories of temptations (sinful and sinless, or, in other terms, internal and external), this would be the only passage in Scripture that affirmed such a notion.[24]

The other interpretation of the phrase *without sin* is that for all Christ's likeness to the readers in being tempted in all the same ways as they are, his distinction is that he never sinned as the result of temptation.[25] According to this second interpretation, Christ's empathy with the readers' experience is based on his close solidarity with them by his own experience of all the same sorts of temptations. This view fits with the movement of 4:14-16 to resolve the paradox that despite his dissimilarity as the Son of God, Jesus is fully qualified as a compassionate priest because of his human similarity to the readers.[26] Moreover, the author's exhortation to seek help in temptation ("let us always come near", προσερχώμεθα, 4:16, cf. 2:18) depends on understanding *without sin* as his perfect result after having endured all the same kinds of temptations.[27]

---

[23]Some examples of this view include John Calvin, *The Epistle of Paul the Apostle to the Hebrews and the First and Second epistles of St. Peter*, trans. William B. Johnston, ed. David F. Torrance and Thomas F. Torrance, Calvin's New Testament Commentaries, vol. 12 (Grand Rapids: Eerdmans, 1963), 56; B. F. Westcott, *The Epistle to the Hebrews*, 2nd ed. (London: Macmillan, 1892), 107; Lewis Sperry Chafer, *Systematic Theology* (Dallas: Dallas Seminary Press, 1948) 5:83; James O. Buswell, Jr., *A Systematic Theology of the Christian Religion* (Grand Rapids: Zondervan, 1962), 2:59.

[24]If we consider all the statements in Scripture about temptation, they are uniformly broad and all-inclusive in ways that exclude excuses for being tempted in a particular way or somehow beyond the help of God to resist the temptation: Matt 6:13 //; Matt 26:41 //; 1 Cor 10:13; Heb 2:17-18; 4:15; Jas 1:13-15; 2 Pet 2:9. The consistent message of Scripture seems to be that temptation is a single thing, not a twofold reality (I will argue for a an all-inclusive definition of temptation in chapter 9).

[25]Some examples of this view are Martin Luther, *Commentary on Psalm 22*, trans. Henry Cole, *Select Works of Martin Luther*, vol. 4 (London: Simpkin and Marshall, 1826), 362-63; Elllingworth, *Hebrews*, 269; Lane, *Hebrews 1-8*; 114; Attridge, *Hebrews*, 140; Wolfhart Pannenberg, *Jesus—God and Man*, 2nd ed., trans. Lewis L. Wilkins and Duane A. Priebe (Philadelphia: Westminster, 1977), 355.

[26]On the first interpretation of *without sin* as an inward, originating temptation, the paradox would be deepened by Jesus' difference from the readers in the way he was tempted, only externally, but not internally from sinful desire.

[27]Rogers and Rogers, *Linguistic and Exegetical Key*, 525, note helpfully that the same word προσερχώμεθα appears in the Septuagint for the priestly approach to God, and that

Jesus is able to help because he has succeeded against the same temptations in his own life as a man. He continues to be a compassionate priest eager to offer his help because he knows the struggle of temptation by having lived through it himself. Moreover, his sinlessness (cf. 7:26) is the proof of his success and ability to give help to those being tempted as he was.

In Hebrews 2:17-18 and 4:15, Christ's temptation to sin is essential to the author's argument to reassure the readers of the Lord's competence and eagerness to help them as the all-sufficient priest. Consequently, in 4:16 the author exhorts the fearful audience to continue trusting in Christ and relying on his ever-present help because he understands their needs by his past personal experience of what they presently experience in weaknesses, suffering, and temptations. With these declarations about Jesus' temptations in mind, we now turn to the accounts of specific temptations in the Gospels.

Jesus' Temptation in the Wilderness

The three temptations addressed to Jesus by Satan at the onset of his messianic ministry are the first cases mentioned.[28] However, these are not the only temptations to sin that he experienced.[29] The wilderness temptations receive special treatment in the Synoptic tradition because of their redemptive-historical significance (Jesus stands in for Adam and Israel). Matthew and Luke's accounts tell the same three temptations as a prologue to Christ's ministry. Mark, who omits the details of the temptations, elaborates on the three wilderness temptations in the context of Jesus' ministry as the paradigmatic challenges of hostile forces that continually assailed him.[30] The effect of Mark's presentation is to demonstrate Christ's progressive struggle against temptations, a struggle that did not cease with his return from the desert but characterized his entire ministry from start to finish.

The Synoptic accounts emphasize the significance of Christ's temptations in

---

the present tense "emphasizes that the privilege [of drawing near to Christ] is always available".

[28]Some scholars have questioned the traditional claim that Satan is a personal adversary of God and his people. I take the biblical revelation for Satan (including references to the devil and the serpent) at face value in agreement with the traditional view.

[29]N. T. Wright, *Jesus and the Victory of God* (Minneapolis: Fortress, 1996), 458, helpfully observes that since temptations are a private experience, we only know about these temptations because Jesus must have told his disciples about the entire battle.

[30]Richard Dormandy, "Jesus' Temptations in Mark's Gospel: Mark 1:12-13", *Expository Times* 114 (2003): 187, argues persuasively that Mark's careful use of πειράζω in the wilderness account and then only three other times (8:1-13; 10:1-12; 12:13-17) in events that match the wilderness temptations shows these key temptations throughout Jesus' ministry. Mark's emphasis shows in the way he has withheld using πειράζω in other triple tradition accounts where Matthew and Luke have it. I think Matthew and Luke have added it while following Mark to write for their own purposes.

the wilderness with Satan as both a type of Adam's trial in the Garden of Eden and Israel's forty years of wandering between Egypt and the conquest of Canaan.[31] Jesus recapitulates the history of Adam and Israel as the second Adam (cf. Rom 5:12-21; 1 Cor 15:21-22, 45) and true, faithful Servant of God. Luke's emphasis seems to be the typological fulfillment in line with Adam because he inserts his genealogy account between the Jordan baptism and the temptations.[32] An Adamic background would suggest that the three temptations matched the three aspects of the temptation offered to Eve: the lust of the eyes, the lust of the flesh, and the pride of life (Gen 3:6, cf. Josh 7:21; 1 John 2:16). Matthew and Mark point additionally to the Israel-Christ typology.[33] In contrast to both types, Jesus succeeds where his precursors failed; he is the new head of the race, the second Adam and true vine of God's people who brings the eschatological salvation that renews the fallen creation.[34]

As with Israel's wilderness experience and Adam's trial in Eden, Jesus, as the messianic Son, is confronted primarily in his relationship to God as his Father.[35] Birger Gerhardsson makes a good case for this covenantal theme in all

---

[31]In addition to Satan's direct address with temptations regarding food and power to be had by disobeying God, Mark's reference to the wild beasts suggests a parallel with Adam, though reversed as a hostile setting compared to the paradise of Eden. The forty days and quotations from Deuteronomy suggest the parallel with Israel in the wilderness. An allusion to the preparations of Moses and Elijah with forty-day fasts may also be in view. In Moses' case, the fast was *without food or water* on the occasion of writing the new tablets (Exod 34:28, cf. Deut 9:18; Moses had an earlier forty-day encounter with God, Exod 24:18).

[32]Biblical typology is the rich literary pattern of progressive revelation by which *persons* (e.g., Adam, Moses, and David), *events* (e.g., the Edenic temptation and Israel's journey in the wilderness), and *institutions* (e.g., Passover and Israel's sacrificial system) were laid down by God in advance to point forward to their fulfillment in Christ. These types are the deep roots of Christ's ministry as foretold by metaphors or parallels in the Old Testament and Israel's history.

[33]The Adamic-typology is clear in Mark's reference to the wild animals, reminiscent of Adam in Eden. Interpreters noting the Israel-typology are D. A. Carson, *Matthew*, in vol. 8 of *The Expositor's Bible Commentary*, ed. Frank E. Gaebelein and J. D. Douglas (Grand Rapids: Zondervan, Regency Reference Library, 1984), 111; and G. H. P. Thompson, "Called-Proved-Obedient: A Study in the Baptism and Temptation Narratives of Matthew and Luke", *Journal of Theological Studies*, n.s., 11 (1960): 7-9.

[34]Cf. Wayne A. Grudem, *Systematic Theology* (Grand Rapids: Zondervan, 1994), 537. "In these temptations in the wilderness and in the various temptations that faced him through the thirty-three years of his life, Christ obeyed God in our place and as our representative, thus succeeding where Adam had failed, where the people of Israel in the wilderness had failed, and where we had failed (see Rom. 5:18-19)."

[35]Wright, *Jesus*, 458, has a similar idea that the struggle is about the nature of Christ's vocation and ministry. Jesus is tempted to doubt what God has called him to do at his Jordan baptism and take the easier path to fulfilling his vocation as the Messiah without suffering.

three temptations, setting Christ's temptations against the background of Israel's wilderness trial (told in Deuteronomy 6-8).[36] However, notwithstanding their redemptive-historical significance, Christ's temptations in the wilderness are also the same kinds of temptations that befall all people who seek to follow God: temptations that challenge human fidelity to God with the enticement to turn away in sin.[37] God's intention is to test Jesus as proof of his faithfulness; Satan's intention is to tempt Jesus into ruin, as happened previously with both Adam (with Eve) and Israel.

The first temptation (Matt 4:3-4; Luke 4:3-4) occurs when Satan exploits Christ's hunger for food.[38] Jesus is especially temptable because he is a true man with bodily needs for food. Satan tempts Jesus to provide bread for himself miraculously. Underneath this surface of the temptation is the enticement to be discontented with what God had provided for Jesus. This temptation corresponds to at least four places in the Old Testament background: first, Genesis 3:6, where Eve's assessment of the forbidden fruit as good for food is made in the midst of the abundant provision by God elsewhere in the garden, second, Israel's discontentment with the divinely-provided manna, as in Numbers 11:1-6, third, the Old Testament promises that God provides food for his children,[39] and (possibly) fourth, the temptation or lust of the flesh in 1 John

---

[36]Birger Gerhardsson, *The Testing of God's Son: (Matt 4:1-1 and Par) An Analysis of Early Christian Midrash*, trans. John Toy (Lund, SWE: CWK Gleerup, 1966), 26. He notes that the term for *test* is a covenant word normally used within the covenant relationship in the Old Testament. The contextually defined meaning is "a testing of the partner in the covenant to see whether he is keeping his side of the agreement." I do not agree with Gerhardsson's assumption that the biblical temptation accounts are Christian midrash.

[37]Gerhardsson, *Testing of God's Son*, 79. "We note here [Heb 4:14-16] the epithet 'Son of God' and the fact that the temptations of Jesus are not specifically messianic ones but are of the same kind as ours (the people of God), and the phrase 'in every respect'. . . . The passage in Hebrews is a significant witness to the way in which an early Christian 'author' thought of the temptations of Jesus; and we know that his thought follows the same lines as those of the synoptic author (M): Jesus was tempted in everything, as we are, yet he was without sin." Gerhardsson designates merely the author of Matthew, not a personal reference (which I think is more skeptical than is necessary).

[38]G. H. Twelftree, "Temptation of Jesus", in *Dictionary of Jesus and the Gospels*, ed. Joel B. Green and Scot McKnight (Downers Grove, IL: InterVarsity, 1992), 823, notes that Matthew's order of the second and third temptations could be his redaction to fit the climax of his Gospel on the mountain in 28:18, but Luke's redaction is more likely to reverse the order (Q?) and fit his emphasis in Luke-Acts on Jerusalem and the temple. We will follow Matthew's order as the slightly more plausible historical pattern.

[39]W. Schneider, C. Brown, *New International Dictionary of New Testament Theology*, ed. Willem A. VanGemeren [CD-ROM] (Grand Rapids: Zondervan, 1997, 2002), s.v. "Temptation". They cite Old Testament examples of the promise: Pss 23:1; 33:18f; 34:10; 37:19; 104:27f; 145:15; 146:7; Deut 2:7; 28:1-14; Neh 9:21. The authors also note helpfully the principle in Matt 7:9 that no reasonable father will give his son a stone

2:16.[40] Had Jesus succumbed to this temptation, his discontentment and self-reliance would have been a failure of covenantal trust in God who led him into the wilderness. To accept an attitude of discontentment as Satan proposed would have been to rebel against the regulation of God's word and the leadership of the Holy Spirit who had guided him into the wilderness. A misuse of Christ's powers to provide miraculously for himself is part of the temptation, but the primary element is a sin in Christ's relationship to God (by which I mean here as his human, creature-to-Creator relationship, and not so much his eternal, filial relationship to the Father as the Son and Logos).[41] The basic idea is a temptation that depends on Christ's bodily needs for food (after nearly starving for forty days) and his psychological need for assurance of his identity in view of the present difficulties he is experiencing that would seem to deny a special, filial relation to God. Jesus is really a man, and his human needs make him susceptible to temptation in a way that would not be possible for the eternal Son apart from incarnation.

The second wilderness temptation is to test God's protection of Jesus by recklessly imperiling himself with a leap from the temple heights (Matt 4:5-7; Luke 4:9-12). Satan tempts Jesus to confirm his identity as the Son by obligating God to fulfill his covenantal pledge to protect his own, just as he pledged to Israel (Deut 8:14ff.).[42] This temptation also possibly corresponds to Eve's prideful desire for wisdom, what John calls the pride of life (if the triad in 1 John 2:16 reflects the Edenic triad). The appeal to human pride is certainly a temptation that is common to all people. Satan aims the temptation according to Christ's special identity and difficult circumstances of apparent abandonment by God. The temple locale especially emphasizes the proximity of God's presence and his promise of protection.[43] Satan's provocation depends upon the existential assurance of Christ's special identity that would be confirmed if he received divine protection from bodily harm, as promised in the psalm that Satan quotes. Against this temptation, and without denying the truthfulness of the promise, Jesus sets all of these questions back in the proper perspective of his relationship to God in total obedience.[44]

The third temptation is to seize power to rule on his own, independently of God's promise and provision, all to be possessed simply by meeting the

---

when he asks for bread—and how much more can God be counted upon to provide for his children.

[40]I am indebted to Professor Bruce A. Ware for pointing out the correspondence between the Edenic temptations, the triad in 1 John 2:16, and Christ's wilderness temptations.

[41]Gerhardsson, *Testing of God's Son*, 44-52. Carson, *Matthew*, 113. Michael J. Wilkins, *Matthew*, NIV Application Commentary, vol. 37 (Grand Rapids: Zondervan, 2004), 158.

[42]Wilkins, *Matthew*, 160.

[43]Darrell L. Bock, *Luke 1:1-9:50*, Baker Exegetical Commentary on the New Testament, vol. 39, pt. 1 (Grand Rapids: Baker, 1994), 380.

[44]Bock, *Luke 1:1-9:50*, 382.

condition that he worship Satan (Matt 4:8-10; Luke 4:5-8).[45] This temptation directly pulls at Jesus to forsake God for the power, possessions, and honor of the world kingdoms—and this without having to endure the suffering ordained as the means (cf. Acts 4:27-28). Israel frequently succumbed to this temptation of forsaking God in idolatrous attempts to gain material blessings and security. This temptation may correspond to Eve's desire for the fruit that she saw as a delight to her eyes, or, in the phrase of 1 John 2:16, the desire of the eyes— meaning the desire to possess what is not given by God. In Christ's temptation, the nations were promised to him as the Messiah (e.g., Ps 2:8), but the cross was his appointed means to receiving them (cf. Matt 28:18). Jesus surmounts the temptation by reaffirming his proper place as an obedient man in relation to God, and cites Scripture to underline his obligation of exclusive worship owed to the Creator.

In each case, the three temptations that Satan presented to Jesus are enticements to sin in terms of his mode of life as a man in relationship to God. The temptations have a specific appeal to Jesus because of his unique role as the Messiah. God's purpose in the wilderness was to test Jesus by means of Satan's temptations[46] (which, as with many things God does, seems counter-intuitive and antithetical, as in using poison to serve as the cure for a disease). The wilderness accounts are important markers of Christ's triumph over Satan in redemption. The redemptive-historical implication of Christ's reversal of Adam's fall is that Jesus begins a new start for humanity that is victorious over temptation to sin (the theme of recapitulation).[47] Instead of failing as Adam did, Jesus relied on Scripture to refute Satan in each case. The three wilderness temptations are also typical of the appeals that Jesus experienced throughout his years of ministry.[48] A further soteriological value is that the wilderness accounts demonstrate Christ's true humanity: he was tempted as only a true man can be attacked. We have seen Scripture note the importance of these temptations as those experiences that constituted him to be the compassionate priest for others (Heb 2:17; 4:15). The soteriological values of recapitulation and (eternal) priestly ministry would seem to be impossible unless we conclude from these accounts that Jesus was truly tempted to sin.

Moreover, these accounts indicate the human limitations within which Jesus was both tempted and responded to his provocateur. Christ replied to Satan's temptations with the words of Scripture as a man living under the authoritative word of God. The importance of this is that Satan intended that Jesus respond by first a display of divine power, and then by a deed that would precipitate a powerful divine rescue. The text is silent about whether these divine displays

---

[45] Bock, *Luke 1:1-9:50*, 376.
[46] R. T. France, *The Gospel of Mark*, New International Greek Testament Commentary, vol. 38 (Grand Rapids: Eerdmans, 2002), 85. Wilkins, *Matthew*, 155.
[47] Wilkins, *Matthew*, 157.
[48] Dormandy, "Jesus' Temptations", 183-87.

were possible for Jesus to execute or evoke (in the second case). Instead, Christ's response in ways proper to his manhood tells that he resisted these temptations within his human limitations. These are paradigm examples of his temptations at the onset of his public ministry, and they suggest that all of his resistance to temptation was fought within his limitations as a man (especially in the absence of any evidence to the contrary). The separate theological question of whether or not he could have resorted to other, divine means of resistance should not distract from the inference that, by all appearances indicated in the temptation accounts, it does not seem that Jesus resorted to inherent divine powers as his means of resisting temptation. Had he done so, he would hardly be a reasonable example for us to follow. Furthermore, we can remember another helpful distinction between the related questions of *why he could not sin* (impeccability) and *why* (or *how*) *he did not sin* (sinlessness).[49] It seems safe to conclude that, so far as the evidence from the wilderness temptations shows, Christ's intrinsic divine power of impeccability (if he possessed such power) was not the reason (or, the means and method) why he did not sin.

Jesus' Temptation in Gethsemane

GOSPEL ACCOUNTS

Between the wilderness and Gethsemane, Jesus' ministry was characterized as "my trials" of an undefined number (πειρασμοῖς μου, Luke 22:28). These trials prepared him for the final temptation and test of his obedience in the events of his passion. Jesus was tempted in Gethsemane to abandon his role as savior, to save himself instead, and to avoid the supreme suffering of bearing the world's sin.[50] The temptation to avoid this imminent, vicarious punishment was the appeal of a choice to disobey his Father's will as the way to take a detour from his suffering. This temptation brought together a conflict of desires between Christ's relationship with God and his own creaturely desire for self-preservation. Moreover, Satan's role to tempt Jesus away from the cross cannot be ignored either, and the devil's assault on the second Adam (here, in a

---

[49] I am indebted for this helpful distinction to Bruce A. Ware, "Fully God Fully Man: Revisiting the Impeccability, Temptations, and Sinlessness of Christ", a paper presented at the 59th Annual Meeting of the Evangelical Theological Society, San Diego, CA, 16 November 2007.

[50] E. David Willis, *Calvin's Catholic Christology: The Function of the So-Called Extra Calvinisticum in Calvin's Christology,* Studies in Medieval and Reformation Thought 2 (Leiden: E. J. Brill, 1966), 90, thinks this was Christ's greatest temptation: "His temptation in the Garden of Gethsemane was all the greater than any temptation we know; for we do not have such dominion and our routes of escape are more limited. Our disobedience rests in our use of what power of escape we do have; Christ's obedience rested in his refusal to use the unlimited powers of escape at his disposal in order to take up what we have attempted to evade."

garden, as before, in Eden) no doubt added to the intensity of the temptation.[51]

The four Gospels give a varied picture of Christ's temptation in Gethsemane. Luke's account is textually uncertain and includes a unique and important element (to be discussed below). Mark and Matthew's accounts are close to each other at the relevant points in this discussion about Gethsemane as a temptation for Jesus.[52] I will follow the double tradition in Mark's gospel (Mark 14:32-42 // Matt 26:36-46) and then consider Luke's account. John's account gives another impression entirely distinct from the Synoptics, so I will discuss this separately, and first in order.

In John's Gospel, Jesus briefly experienced intense inner turmoil in advance of going to Gethsemane ("my soul is troubled", 12:27; "he was troubled in

---

[51] Most scholars seem to agree that Satan tempted Jesus in Gethsemane to avoid the cross, as at earlier times in his ministry, cf. Peter's attempt to block Jesus from his death (Mark 8:31-33). Initially, I thought this was not the case because it would have been self-defeating for Satan to deter Jesus from the cross since he was also involved in Judas' motivation to betray Jesus that same night (Luke 22:3, 21; John 13:26-30). According to 1 Cor 2:8 (cf. Ps 2:2; Acts 2:26), Satan seems to be included among the rulers of the world (demonic and human) who would not have crucified Jesus had they understood the wisdom of God to accomplish redemption and Satan's downfall by means of Christ's death. Luke 22:3 clearly connects Satan with Judas's betraying activity, so it seems that getting Jesus to the cross, not away from it, was Satan's strategy to destroy him. Moreover, Luke 22:31-32 presents Christ's continuing power over Satan's destructive intentions concerning the sifting of Peter throughout the events of Christ's arrest and trial. Nonetheless, Robert L. Saucy helped me to see that while it is possible that Jesus could have been tempted to avoid the cross because he feared the punishment for sin (i.e., Satan's activity was not necessary for Jesus to feel tempted in this way), it is also likely that Satan was assaulting Jesus on two fronts—both to attack him at the point of his obedience to the Father's will in relation to the cross, and, should that approach fail, to defeat Jesus through the cross. Thus, I agree with Brown, *Death of the Messiah*, 1:160-61, who identifies *the power of darkness* noted at the arrest of Jesus (Luke 22:53) as evidence of Satan's continuing activity in the betrayal (through Judas), arrest, and crucifixion of Jesus, and (in agreement with the majority of interpreters) I can add that Satan has been simultaneously tempting Jesus to avoid the cross. The typology of the tree in Eden and the cross (cf. 1 Pet 2:24, cf. the parallel of one sin and one act of righteousness in Rom 5:18) is clear that the events of the cross (anticipation, suffering, resurrection) are God's decisive reversal of Satan's victory in Eden (cf. 1 Cor 15:21-23, 54-56; Heb 2:18).

[52] If Markan priority is right, then it appears that Matthew's redaction is slight. He replaces Mark's stronger term that Jesus experienced *shocked distress* (ἐκθαμβεῖσθαι, Mark 14:33), with the milder term that Jesus was *full of sorrow* (λυπεῖσθαι, Matt 26:37). Matthew seems to have a problem with Jesus' fearful distress perhaps because it is too low a view of Jesus, so Matthew has edited Mark by using the term for the sorrow (from Mark 14:34) twice. There is a clear trend in Matthew and Luke (again, assuming Markan priority) to minimize Mark's presentation of Jesus' emotions by either substituting milder terms for the strong words or omitting them entirely.

spirit", 13:21).[53] John records that Jesus consoles his disciples in their distress at his final words (14:1, 27), but was himself resolute to the apparent exclusion of any temptation or serious struggle against disobedience (or, at least none worth mentioning). Once in Gethsemane, John comments that Jesus is fully aware of what is happening when the soldiers arrive, that he knew all things had come upon him (18:4). Whereas the Synoptic accounts emphasize Christ's struggle to submit to God's will, John's account presents Jesus embracing the cup of wrath with unwavering fortitude to the point that he commands Peter to sheathe his sword and cease intervening for him (18:10). Perhaps because John was aware of the Synoptic accounts of Christ's temptations in the wilderness and Gethsemane (or for other reasons), John simply does not care to repeat the facts of Christ's temptations.[54] John's mention of Christ's inner turmoil at two points during the eve of his crucifixion show at least the severity of spiritual and intensely internal pain in Christ's experience, even if the temptation aspect is not emphasized. John's picture of Christ is that the Lord is freely marching to his doom in the cross.

Mark presents the prayerful struggle in Gethsemane as an explicit account of Christ's temptation. Jesus warns the three disciples with him to "pray that you may not enter into temptation" (Mark 14:38). Christ's explanation of the danger reflects his own struggle against temptation in the weakness of his flesh, as he says, "the spirit is willing, but the flesh is *weak*" (ἀσθενής, cf. "our weaknesses" in Heb 4:15, ἀσθενείαις ἡμῶν).[55] This is explicit evidence for Christ's struggle against temptation within the limits of his humanity. The probability that Jesus is describing his own struggle against the temptation to avoid the vicarious punishment for sin is increased by the description in Mark 14:33 of his experience as "shock and intense distress" (ἐκθαμβεῖσθαι καὶ ἀδημονεῖν).[56] According to Mark 14:34, Jesus laments that "my soul is distraught to the limit of death" (περίλυπός ἐστιν ἡ ψυχή μου ἕως θανάτου)

---

[53]*Troubled* (ταράσσω) is also used in John 11:33 (Christ's distress at Lazarus's tomb).

[54]This description of the differences of John's account from the Synoptics is not to suggest a conflict or even that John did not know the Synoptic accounts (indeed, on my view, John was present for the actual events with Jesus and he was present when the apostolic stories about Christ's life and teaching were translated into Greek shortly after Pentecost, that is, what became the fixed, normative oral tradition reflected in Mark and followed by Matthew and Luke).

[55]Brown, *Death of the Messiah*, 1:198-200. "Jesus himself is in turmoil, while praying and facing *peirasmos*; he wants their watching and praying to accompany him. An interpretation of 'the spirit is willing, but the flesh is weak' should not exclude Jesus." Cf. Donald A. Hagner, *Matthew 14-28*, Word Biblical Commentary, vol. 33B (Dallas: Word, 1995), 783. "The lesson of Jesus' experience is thus applied to the disciples." Notice also that Luke repeats this warning against entering temptation twice in 22:40, 46, but without mentioning the weakness.

[56]France, *Mark*, 582, translates the terms this way.

in his misery because of his impending suffering.⁵⁷ The specific reason for Christ's dread is not given,⁵⁸ but it is probable that Jesus was aware at this point that his suffering would include his death and having to bear the curse for sin (cf. Matt 20:17-19; Isa 53). Jesus speaks of death as his internal experience of such sorrows that threaten to tear him apart.⁵⁹ His shocked and distressed anticipation of the suffering in connection with death and judgment for the world's sin is also the likely cause of those emotions that threatened to destroy him.⁶⁰

Christ's initial prayer is that his Father would spare him from the vicarious punishment symbolized by the cup (Mark 14:36).⁶¹ Then Jesus reaffirms his desire for God's will instead of and above all of his own wishes to avoid the suffering.⁶² In the context of this fear that is provoked by the anticipation of his suffering, Mark and Matthew depict Jesus as tempted to turn away from his Father's plan.⁶³ Ultimately, however, he submitted his will as a man to God's will.

Luke 22:43-44 is textually uncertain and the passage differs from Mark and Matthew.⁶⁴ Strangely, Luke omits their account of Christ's suffering when

---

⁵⁷France, *Mark*, 582-83. France uses the phrase *being stretched to the limit*. Matthew has the same phrase as Mark.

⁵⁸Hagner, *Matthew*, 782.

⁵⁹John R. Donahue and Daniel J. Harrington, *The Gospel of Mark*, Sacra Pagina Series, vol. 2 (Collegeville, MN: Liturgical, 2002), 407.

⁶⁰France, *Mark*, 583. Cf. Wilkins, *Matthew*, 841, "His overwhelming sorrow reveals a heart broken almost to the point of death itself, because he knows that he will experience his Father's forsakenness." Brown, *Death of the Messiah*, 1:155, suggests both options of (1) the deathly provocation of his sorrow and (2) the intensity of sorrow that brought Jesus close to death, cf. Ps 55:5.

⁶¹Hagner, *Matthew*, 783.

⁶²Bock, *Luke 9:51-24:53,* Baker Exegetical Commentary on the New Testament, vol. 39, pt. 2 (Grand Rapids: Baker, 1996), 1759. Bock explains that the closing affirmation of the prayer makes "it clear that Jesus' request is less significant than his desire to do God's will".

⁶³Wilkins, *Matthew*, 841. "Jesus is facing a real temptation, the most severe of his life."

⁶⁴Joseph A. Fitzmyer, *The Gospel according to Luke (X-XXIV)*, Anchor Bible, vol. 28A (Garden City, NY: Doubleday, 1985), 1444. Verses 43-44 that mention the presence of angels are missing from some manuscripts. Fitzmyer prefers the shorter reading over the longer because there is no Synoptic parallel, it is against Luke's tendency to note emotions, and the longer text is absent from the oldest copy, P⁷⁵. Darrell Bock, *Luke 9:51-24:53*, 1764, counters each of Fitzmyer's objections to defend the longer reading: "The angel's ministry looks like evidence of the original text since it is hard to explain why a copyist would insert these verses. The absence of a parallel and the issue of Christology raised in the remark makes inclusion the more difficult reading, though the decision is not absolutely clear." Also on the side of the longer reading, Joel Green, "Jesus on the Mount of Olives [Luke 22.39-46]: Tradition and Theology", *Journal for*

elsewhere Luke's two volumes emphasize Jesus as the Suffering Servant through allusions to Isaiah and a direct quote of Isaiah 53:12.[65] Nevertheless, Luke's choice to depict a different perspective of Christ's struggle includes the presence of angelic support to strengthen him for the task. Christ's need for angelic help and the description of profuse sweat generated by his exertion in prayer surely entail an intense emotional and volitional turmoil that is consistent with Matthew and Mark.[66]

Another slight difference in Luke is that the note of warning—that the disciples pray so as not to succumb to temptation—is repeated twice in Luke's account (22:40, 46). This doubling of the warning heightens the tension of Jesus' struggle to obey in the face of his desires to shrink back. Despite the differences among the other accounts, Luke's account agrees with the emphasis in Mark and Matthew that Gethsemane was an intense event of human temptation for Christ.

To sum up, when the Synoptic accounts are combined with the resolve expressed in John's account, we have this sequence. Jesus is filled with fearful anticipation (as the meaning of the cup of wrath dawns upon him), he feels distress with reluctance (it is not his desire to suffer), and then he continues to seek God. Then Jesus receives divine assistance in the form of angelic presence (cf. the appearance of angels at the conclusion of his wilderness temptations, Matt 4:11 // Mark 1:13). Finally, Jesus triumphs in his resolve to obey despite the cost. Jesus struggled as a man alongside his disciples, and he did the same thing in response to temptation that he told them to do (pray for help). All that we have is evidence of a struggle experienced and met entirely within the limits of his humanity, without any apparent recourse to inherent immunity to sin (if he was impeccable).

---

the Study of the New Testament 26 (1986): 37, argues that vv. 40-44 are inexplicable as a redaction; instead, Luke must have had some other source besides Mark.

[65] Green, "Jesus on the Mount of Olives", 42; Jerome H. Neyrey, "The Absence of Jesus' Emotions–the Lucan Redaction of Lk 22,39-46", *Biblica* 61 (1980): 154. Neyrey argues that Luke's omission is according to the Stoic view of *grief* (λύπη) as an evil passion that leads to fear and defeat. On Neyrey's view, Luke's version instead portrays Jesus with the virtue of obedience wrested forcefully in his combat against temptation, which he overcomes through "sweat-like blood of exertion". Green, "Jesus on the Mount of Olives", 32-33, 38, disagrees, saying that Jesus' struggle was not against λύπη, but against satanic opposition, and the objectionable Stoic term is not in the text anyway (περίλυπος is the term in the parallels, not λύπη). Green also points to Luke's tendency of avoiding doublets as a better explanation for omitting Mark 14:33-34 in preference for another tradition that expresses Luke's emphasis on prayer (Luke 22:43-44).

[66] Bock, *Luke 9:51-24:53*, 1761-62. Brown, *Death of the Messiah*, 1:185, agrees that the sweat was not bloody, but only that the profuse sweat resembled the free flow of blood.

HEBREWS 5:7-8
(7) ὃς ἐν ταῖς ἡμέραις τῆς σαρκὸς αὐτοῦ
       δεήσεις τε καὶ ἱκετηρίας
              πρὸς τὸν δυνάμενον σῴζειν αὐτὸν ἐκ θανάτου
              μετὰ κραυγῆς ἰσχυρᾶς καὶ δακρύων
  προσενέγκας καὶ εἰσακουσθεὶς ἀπὸ τῆς εὐλαβείας,
(8) καίπερ ὢν υἱός,
    ἔμαθεν ἀφ' ὧν ἔπαθεν τὴν ὑπακοήν

(7) In the days of his flesh
    prayers and supplications
        to the one who was able to save him out of death
        with great sobs and tears
  he offered and he was heard because of his godly fear.
(8) Although he was the Son,
    he learned, from the things he suffered, obedience.

In relation to Gethsemane, Hebrews 5:7-8 gives further explanation about Christ's struggle to obey God in the face of his temptation to avoid suffering by disobeying God.[67] The description in Hebrews broadly includes the entire passion sequence and other suffering in Christ's life, not simply the single event of his anguish in Gethsemane. However, the Gethsemane experience is surely included as one of the events within the broad description in Hebrews 5:7-8 of Jesus' true and relevant human experience that constitute him a "high priest" (ἀρχιερεύς, v.10; cf. 2:17; 4:15).

Hebrews 5:7-8 introduces the theme of Christ's suffering in relation to his progress in obedience with the generalizing statement of the temporal context: "in the days of his flesh".[68] This statement draws together his entire human life while the passage also alludes to the specific suffering in his passion. The emotional distress and struggle to submit his wishes as a man to God's will are at least reminiscent of his Gethsemane prayers if not directly parallel to those

---

[67] Brown, *Death of the Messiah*, 1:231-33, agrees that Heb 5:7-10 corresponds to both Gethsemane, and the crucifixion as well. Ellingworth, *Hebrews*, 286, is skeptical about 5:7-10 as a biographical reference to a specific event in the passion sequence. He thinks the description more likely relates to the broader pattern of Christ's life in humiliation and exaltation that culminated in the crucifixion. France, *Mark*, 581, thinks Gethsemane probably does lie behind Heb 5:7-10.

[68] Cf. a similar summary in Phil 2:8 of Christ's entire human life as his human obedience to God that culminated in the cross. John Piper drew my attention to this in his lecture, "Justification and the Diminishing Work of Christ", The Crossway Lecture at the 59th Annual Meeting of the Evangelical Theological Society, San Diego (14 November 2007). This seems to be a Pauline theme, since Rom 5:12-21 bears the same focus on Christ's entire life as one act of human obedience for righteousness, culminating in the cross.

offered with "great sobs and tears" (κραυγῆς ἰσχυρᾶς καὶ δακρύων). For the readers of Hebrews, having been told about Christ's empathy for them in being tempted (2:17-18; 4:15), they receive a vivid reminder from his earthly life that his experience of suffering was not minimized or mitigated by his deity. Christ's successful, obedient struggle against temptation is set before the readers as the example and motivation for their own struggle against the temptation to apostasy (cf. 12:1-4). Just as for them now, Jesus was called by God to obedience with the suffering of the cross, and in a much greater way.[69] Hebrews 5:7-8 recalls the severe degree of his temptation despite his Sonship so that the audience can find courage in Christ's example.

Jesus' development in obedience through suffering—"he learned, from the things he suffered, obedience" (v.8; ἔμαθεν ἀφ' ὧν ἔπαθεν τὴν ὑπακοήν)—is his progress throughout his life experiences to be constituted for the official role of priest.[70] The final position of "obedience" and the addition of the definite article (*the* obedience) emphasize the particular obedience that God required of him "in the days of his flesh", an obedience that could only be accomplished by the Son as a man.[71] I think it is right to see here that what Jesus accomplishes is a specifically human obedience that was originally required of Adam (cf. Rom 5:19), and can now be credited to the new humanity in Christ for justification as a gift of righteousness (Rom 5:17). By his obedience that culminates in choosing to go to the cross, Jesus reverses disobedient humanity to reclaim in himself the original design of creation and humanity.

Moreover, we have seen above that the suffering and struggle to obey was constitutive for him to become the compassionate priest who can empathize with his people in terms of their temptation (cf. 2:17; 4:15). The suffering that sets a context for temptation in Jesus' life and the readers' lives is purposeful. This means that even Christ's prayer, offered to the God, the one who could "save him out of death" (σῴζειν αὐτὸν ἐκ θανάτου), was that he would be rescued with divine support in the midst of his death—not a prayer that Jesus

---

[69] Vos, "Priesthood of Christ", 584. Lane, *Hebrews 1-8*, 121-22.

[70] Vos, "Priesthood of Christ", 589. Vos is right that the development is official, not ethical, *contra* Susan R. Garrett, *The Temptations of Jesus in Mark's Gospel* (Grand Rapids: Eerdmans, 1998), 107, who claims that Mark's account of Jesus shows that he developed morally from double-minded struggle to eventual single-minded commitment; and *contra* Ronald Williamson, "Hebrews 4:15 and the Sinlessness of Jesus", *Expository Times* 86 (1974): 4-8, who argues that Jesus achieved perfected obedience of sinlessness only at the end of his life, not that he had it innately from the beginning.

[71] Rogers and Rogers, *Linguistic and Exegetical Keys*, 526. This is not to deny that the Son obeys the Father in an eternal trinitarian relationship. Indeed, the sending of the Son by the Father for incarnation shows his eternal, *ad intra* trinitarian obedience.

would be protected entirely from peril.[72] The difference of this prayer from Christ's prayer in Gethsemane, where he asked for another way besides his imminent peril ("if it is possible", εἰ δυνατόν ἐστιν, Mark 14:35//), is not a contradiction because Hebrews 5:7 underscores his plea for help to endure the suffering.

Also distinct from the Gethsemane accounts are the *great sobs and tears* of Hebrews 5:7. This description certainly reflects the anguish of his prayers on the night before his death, but "sobs and tears" may refer more precisely to his suffering on the cross. The Gospels tell of no loud cries and tears in Gethsemane, but the Gospels bear clear evidence that Jesus screamed with loud shouts and cries at Golgotha.[73] Furthermore, Christ's final prayer of surrender into the Father's hands (Luke 23:46) seems to fit the Hebrews 5:7 prayer for support as he entered into death.[74] As was the case throughout his life, Christ's suffering during the crucifixion was likely a context for his temptation in a severe, maximal degree. This possibility of his temptation while suffering on the cross is reinforced by the way Hebrews 5:7-8 functions as an exhortation for the readers in context of their temptation.

Therefore, Hebrews 5:7-8 corresponds to both Christ's suffering in Gethsemane and Golgotha. Gethsemane is clearly a context of temptation because of the way the Gospels note Christ's warnings about temptation to his disciples. Golgotha is a likely context for his temptation because of the way Hebrews 5:7-8 employs his suffering there as an example of his having experienced concrete temptation in a maximum degree that makes him able to sympathize with the troubled audience. Moreover, Martin Luther and John Calvin mark the crucifixion as the scene of Jesus' greatest temptation (see below; however, many contemporary interpreters do not see Golgotha this way).

Jesus' Temptation during the Crucifixion

The obvious temptation during the crucifixion is the threefold mockery of Jesus by passersby, priests and soldiers, and the two criminals dying alongside him (Mark 15:29-32 and parallels).[75] The mockers deride Jesus with taunts that he

---

[72]Vos, "Priesthood of Christ", 585. Attridge, *Hebrews*, 150. Ellingworth, *Hebrews*, 288. The foreshadowing of this rescue is in Luke's account of Gethsemane that includes the strengthening support of the angel in response to Jesus' prayer (Luke 22:43).

[73]Wilkins, *Matthew*, 894-95, has a helpful list of seven cries of Jesus from the cross. Brown, *Death of the Messiah*, 1:232, notes the likeness between the cries of Heb 5:7-8 and Golgotha.

[74]Brown, *Death of the Messiah*, 1:230. Brown's observation is helpful. "The emphasis that Hebrews places on Jesus' blood and sacrifice means that being saved from death cannot mean that he was spared dying. Rather Jesus was spared from being conquered by death, as in 2:14."

[75]Brown, *Death of the Messiah*, 2:985-1000.

should save himself and prove his claims that he is the Messiah and Son of God. These taunts are of the same sort that Jesus heard earlier as Satan's first temptation in the wilderness, that Jesus comfort himself by transforming stones into bread. Certainly this derision during the hours of Christ's suffering under divine wrath for sin and the pains of crucifixion was an invitation to turn away from God's will and give himself relief. Nonetheless, Martin Luther and John Calvin infer a much more serious temptation during the crucifixion than the common taunts and mockery of disbelief that Jesus had heard for years, if not his whole human life.

Luther affirms that Jesus was tempted to blaspheme God when he felt cursed and abandoned by God during the crucifixion.[76] Calvin similarly affirms that a temptation was presented to Christ when he felt the opposition of God as Judge against him.[77] As the preeminent righteous sufferer, Jesus may have been in the position of Job, who was tempted by his wife (perhaps voicing his own temptation to despair) that he should curse God and die (Job 2:9). But Job, like Jesus after him, refused to curse God for the evil he suffered (Job 9:10). Considering Jesus, Luther and Calvin have in view the intensity of Christ's anguish, dread, and horror in bearing the sin of the world while the torture of crucifixion broke his human life. However, these affirmations are impossible to verify. Scholars are at least willing to agree that Christ's cry in the vernacular Aramaic of Psalm 22:2 (MT) expresses his feeling of having been abandoned by God.[78] This pain of abandonment, as with all suffering, is the context for temptation to sin. Raymond Brown explains the meaning of Christ's cry:

> Darkness has covered the earth; there is nothing that shows God acting on Jesus' side. How appropriate that Jesus feel forsaken! His "Why?" is that of someone who has plumbed the depths of the abyss, and feels enveloped by the power of darkness. Jesus is not questioning the existence of God or the power of God to do something about what is happening; he is questioning the silence of the one whom he calls "My God". . . . Feeling forsaken as if he were not being heard, he no longer presumes to speak intimately to the All-Powerful as "Father" but employs the address common to all human beings, "My God".[79]

---

[76]Martin Luther *Psalmus XXI* (22), *D. Martin Luthers Werke: Kritische Gesamtausgabe* (Weimar: Harmann Böhlaus Nachfolger, 1912), 5:611, 33; 5:612, 19. (All page numbers to critical editions of Luther's writing refer to this series, abbreviated WA.) Cited by Marc Lienhard, *Luther: Witness to Jesus Christ,* trans. Edwin H. Robertson (Minneapolis: Augsburg, 1982), 118.

[77]John Calvin, *Commentary on a Harmony of the Evangelists*, trans. William Pringle, Calvin's Commentaries, vol. 3 (Edinburgh: Calvin Translation Society; reprint, Grand Rapids: Baker, 1996), 318.

[78]Wilkins, *Matthew*, 902. Hagner, *Matthew*, 844. France, *Mark*, 652. Donahue and Harrington, *Mark*, 450-51.

[79]Brown, *Death of the Messiah*, 2:1046.

Another possibility is the correspondence between his cry of *why?* and Hebrews 5:7-8.[80] This text points along the course of Christ's lifelong progress in obedience to God within the context of suffering. His obedience culminates with his suffering in the crucifixion and simultaneous bearing of the punishment for sin. Because Hebrews 5:7-8 is set in a context to commend Jesus as an example in resisting temptation, it may be that the writer pictures Jesus still struggling to obey during the crucifixion.[81] Jesus had been strengthened to face and succeed in this final, ultimate test by the collective experiences of tests throughout his life. Therefore, the cry that echoes Psalm 22:2 (if considered among the *strong sobs and tears* in the prayer for ultimate deliverance out of death Heb 5:8), is more likely a sign of the temptation that Luther and Calvin claimed Jesus felt. Some of the many martyrs in redemptive history have no doubt felt this same sort of temptation as they endured violence at the hands of sinners as Jesus did (cf. Heb 12:3-4). Jesus was truly tempted, even to the final moments of his mortal life (and despite his having come to a firm resolve to obey in Gethsemane, before he was arrested).

The Relational Setting of Christ's Temptations

We have seen several specific cases of Christ's temptations. In addition, it will help to consider his experience as a man in relationships with others because these too likely constituted many other temptations that are common to humanity. Examples from the Gospels are the Jews' demand for a sign from heaven,[82] Peter's opposition to Jesus for talking about suffering while at Caesarea Philippi,[83] the Pharisees' trap about the legitimacy of divorce,[84] the

---

[80]Brown, *Death of the Messiah*, 1:230-32; 2:1047.

[81]But this may be only one aspect. In John's gospel, Jesus is presented as a man totally in command of the situation by giving orders from the cross to his followers.

[82]Mark 8:1-13; Matt 12:38-39 // Luke 11:16, 29; Matt 16:1-2a, 4. These and the subsequent references of listed in this sentence are drawn from the study by Jeffrey B. Gibson, *The Temptations of Jesus in Early Christianity*, Journal for the Study of the New Testament Supplement Series 112 (Sheffield: Sheffield Academic, 1995), 21-23. Dormandy, "Jesus' Temptations", 185, argues that this temptation is Mark's way of elaborating on the first of Jesus' three temptations in the wilderness, here transposed as the temptation to fulfill the people's demands and confirm his identity. This occurs in proximity to the theme of a miraculous provision of food.

[83]Mark 8:27-33; Matt 16:13-23.

[84]Mark 10:1-12 // Matt 19:1-12. Dormandy, "Jesus' Temptations", 185, argues persuasively that the temptation in Mark matches the second wilderness temptation to prove his messiahship by recklessness in the face of Herod's recent divorce. John the Baptizer was arrested and executed for the very offense of criticizing Herod's divorce and remarriage.

malicious query about paying taxes to Caesar,[85] the test question about the requirements for attaining eternal life,[86] the loaded question about the greatest commandment,[87] and the treacherous demand for a verdict on the woman caught in adultery.[88] Many of these examples use the specific term for temptation (πειράζω) in some form. In each case, we should see that the negative sense of *temptation to sin* is at least partially in view (and not merely the sense of *testing*) because the questioners are antagonists attempting to waylay Jesus and cause his failure (that is, they are not aiming to help him prove his success and identity, which would be the positive meaning of *testing*).

These frequent traps, though different from the challenges to sin that were offered by Satan, are all assaults on Christ's sense of identity and significance (imagine having to bear that truth and convince others that you, a mere human being, are the divine Messiah!). Jesus faces these opponents as a man among others; he is enmeshed in a daily life social network and thereby susceptible to attacks from others (and also blessings). All of the examples represent the voices of skepticism and hostility that entice Jesus (however weakly or strongly) to doubt and prove his identity and, in these ways, to take matters into his own hands instead of following the will of God. In this way, the examples of temptations that occur in Christ's interactions with his human critics echo Satan's temptations as the subversive suggestions that Jesus does not stand in special relationship to God and that he is not who he thought he was (or, that he should adjust his self-concept and mission to be an insurrectionist as some demanded).

Jesus faced other temptations within the setting of his human relationships. In the social context of his home life at Nazareth, people who knew Jesus while growing up derided him in a way that, however slightly or strongly he may have felt it, became the temptation to think of himself as merely Joseph and Mary's son, the unimportant brother of his sisters and brothers who were among them, and certainly not a prophet of God or the promised Messiah.[89] The temptation to perform several miracles to awaken their faith in him and prove himself to them may have had continuing appeal beyond the incident noted in Mark 6:5-6.[90] This temptation to prove himself to people who disbelieved his

---

[85]Mark 12:13-17 // Matt 22:15-22 // Luke 20:20-26. Dormandy, "Jesus' Temptations", 186, explains Mark's version as corresponding to the third wilderness temptation by the same theme of worshipping God or Satan in context of the relationship to Rome.
[86]Luke 10:25-26.
[87]Matt 22:34-40.
[88]John 7:53-8:11. Note: the textual evidence does not support an affirmation that this is a Johannine account, but the passage should probably be accepted as historically authentic while its absence from the first several centuries of the manuscript tradition and several placements make it mysterious.
[89]Luke 4:22; Matt 13:55-57; cf. John 6:42.
[90]Ralph A. Letch, *Temptation and Freedom: The Temptations of God* (Harrow, UK: Eureditions, 1978), 47-48.

claims may have been typical throughout his ministry. Even during the crucifixion the crowd called for him to save himself and come down off the cross to prove that his claims were true (Matt 27:40).

Jesus had no refuge from critics in his hometown or in his home. His own brothers mocked his vocation and tempted him to make a public relations gala in Jerusalem at the very time that his enemies in Judea were seeking to kill him (John 7:1-9). Setting their doubts against his own confidence about who he was and what relationship he had with God, Christ's treatment by his brothers likely provoked him to the further temptation that he deviate from God's guidance, doubt his identity and mission, and shrink back entirely from his mission. Or, he may have been tempted to retaliate against their treatment of him, similar to the way that James and John offered retaliation by calling down fire from heaven in vengeance against a particularly disrespectful Samaritan village (Luke 9:54).

The temptation suggested by the relationship with his brothers was also echoed by the crowds who wanted to make him king according to the Jewish hope of a political deliverer (just as Jesus himself was aware that he was fulfilling those same Old Testament promises that fueled the mob's enthusiasm, e.g., Matt 5:17).[91] Van Iersel's observation is helpful to point out the relational dynamics of these trials that were repeated throughout his ministry:

> It is evidence how common and normal these temptations were. Jesus, like other people, was usually led into temptation by his surroundings – in fact by his relatives, his followers and his adversaries. The main feature of these temptations was . . . a question of method. They simply asked Jesus to act as they expected the Messiah, whom he pretended to be, to act.[92]

More examples of his temptations could easily be multiplied from the accounts of Christ's intense anger and frustrations in his relationships with people. His wrath burned against their misuse of the Temple cult to exclude worshippers at the Temple, their sham use of the sacrificial system to give themselves license for sin, their hard hearts that valued Sabbath regulations above caring for people, and his own disciples' exclusion of children from getting near to him.[93] In these examples Jesus clearly restrained himself from

---

[91] Letch, *Temptation and Freedom*, 50. John 6:15 (after feeding the 5,000); John 12:13-15 (during his final entry to Jerusalem).

[92] B. Van Iersel, *The Bible on the Temptations of Man*, trans F. Vander Heijden (De Pere, WI: St. Norbert Abbey Press, 1966), 50. Wright, *Jesus,* 458, agrees that the temptation to be a Messiah of popular expectation was strong: "We cannot doubt that Jesus was constantly tempted to share, and act in accordance with, the mindset of most Jews of his day. He cannot have been indifferent to the plight of his fellow Jews, as they were systematically crushed, economically, politically and militarily, by Rome. The temptation to be the sort of Messiah that many wanted must have been real and strong."

[93] Mark 11:15-18; 3:1-5; 10:14.

sinning in his anger (cf. Eph 4:26), and the accounts suggest that he struggled in some way with the temptation to do something wrong. Beyond these examples, we can assume that Jesus endured four other sets of temptations as part of being a (sinless) human being.

In his relationship with God, Jesus likely faced temptations to disobey God's written requirements from the time of his early childhood to the end of his earthly life. Christ likely faced the temptation to be frustrated and anxiously fearful about God's plans that imperiled him from the start with Herod's wrath at his birth. He could have been tempted to be resentful and doubtful of God's care because his family had to flee to Egypt and then limp along without Joseph after some years in Nazareth.[94]

In his relationship with the created world, he possibly had to face temptations of greed and gluttony (however mildly), even as he was accused of being a glutton and a drunk (Matt 11:19), in addition to the prospect of stealing things he needed or wanted for himself or others. Satan's suggestion in the wilderness that Jesus turn stones into bread to satisfy his hunger implies a sort of stealing as the misuse of powers to satisfy his bodily hunger (even though the existential hunger to confirm his special identity may have been more acute).

In relationship to women, Jesus possibly faced temptations to his sexuality because this is a normal and legitimate need for humans, as shown in Paul's instructions to some ascetic-leaning Christians about sex in marriage (1 Cor 7:1-9). Christ's record of sinlessness—despite the devoted attention of several married and unmarried women (Luke 8:2-3)—indicates that he had the gift of celibacy that Paul mentions, but this does not mean that the gift entails no internal turmoil without any effort to maintain his obedience to God. Instead, Jesus (as Paul and others) likely had the gift of a special desire for God that he could set against his natural desire for full bodily-relational union with a woman (and thereby repel whatever temptations he felt).[95]

Also, Jesus was possibly tempted to please people by performing for them in

---

[94] It seems that Joseph died some time before Christ's ministry began, perhaps when Jesus was a teen since there is no mention of Joseph during Jesus' ministry and Jesus had the responsibility for his mother that he passed off to John (John 19:26-27).

[95] This is not to say that Jesus experienced *lust* in the sense of desiring illicit sexual expression, which seems to be a distinctly sinful sort of desires. On my view (with the majority of the tradition), Jesus had no sinful desires because he was not only sinless, but also free from original sin and its corruption. I doubt that all temptations in relation to sexuality are necessarily lust and thereby sinful temptations, but probably most of the sexual temptations experienced by people other than Jesus are sinful, stemming from a lustful, corrupt desire. In no way do I mean to condone or excuse the lustful sorts of desires, or suggest that Jesus experienced these as part of a temptation. I will have more to say about this in Part Three.

ways that deviated from God's plan.⁹⁶ This was repeated in Satan's well-chosen offer of the kingdoms of the world, in Pilate's query about Jesus' kingship (John 18:35-37), and in the excited anticipation of the imminent kingdom that Christ's disciples expressed after his resurrection (Acts 1:6).⁹⁷ This sort of people-pleasing temptation in many varieties seems to have been present throughout his life. The frequent disappointment of disciples and the crowd in his failure to bring in the political dimensions of the eschatological kingdom probably corresponds to Christ's frequent temptation to be disappointed in them. He may have been tempted to the point of feeling disdain and unbounded frustration with his followers, and hatefully despising those who mocked him out of fear, envy, and unbelief. Peter seems to commend Jesus for restraint from sinful retaliation when he was cruelly abused (1 Pet 2:23).

Finally, in relationship within himself he possibly felt the temptations to disbelieve what he had been told about who he was (audibly confirmed from heaven at his Jordan baptism)—that the Scriptures he studied really referred to him uniquely and that he was God-incarnate, God the Son who had been sent in mission to be the Savior.⁹⁸ As for the audience of Hebrews 10:36-39, who needed warning against shrinking back from faithfulness in enduring suffering, Jesus too may have been tempted at times to ignore God's call and shrink back to self-preservation. The existential struggle of having to trust God for defining his identity and direction in life entails a temptation to recoil from faith as the unknown, unseen, and humility-requiring dependence on the invisible God. He may have felt the pull to back away from God to reliance on self or others who are seen and known tangibly. Christ's struggle to entrust himself to God in Gethsemane and again on the cross do not seem to have been the first occasions

---

⁹⁶An illustration of this sort of situation is the wedding in Cana (John 2:3-4) when Jesus clearly did not want to get involved, but his mother implored him to fix the problem. This occasion was not a temptation to sin; however, the example shows the way people may have appealed to him at other times to do something that would have been against his Father's plan.

⁹⁷Letch, *Temptation and Freedom*, 80-81.

⁹⁸The matter of Jesus' self-consciousness is very speculative. Clearly, by age twelve he was aware of his unique identity and significance (Luke 2:41-51). It seems that his awareness developed (in a non-adoptionistic sense) so that even though he was fully God the Son always, he came to understand this progressively in his consciousness as a man. How that awareness was regulated may have been by the Father and the Spirit's influence, but we are beyond the limits of verification here. Mark 13:32 and Matt 24:36 are often raised as evidence of Jesus' incomplete or limited human knowledge, especially since the objectionable phrase in Matthew's version (*nor the Son*, οὐδὲ ὁ υἱός) was omitted in many early copies and patristic citations. Nonetheless, R. T. France, *Mark*, 544, is right that the subject of the pericope is eschatology, not Christology. The emphasis of the statement is on the unpredictability of the time of Jesus' return since it is the Father's plan, not on the specifications of Jesus' human intellectual capacities.

of such struggle; probably these were just the greatest in a pattern of having to do so repeatedly throughout his life (cf. Heb 4:15; 5:7-8).

Conclusion

Theologically, the biblical evidence for Christ's temptations to sin in context of his true humanity is varied. The temptations recorded in the Gospels at the beginning and the end of his public ministry bracket the entire range of other temptations that he experienced. The Gospels relate certain temptations and suggest others in the setting of his relationships in a true human existence. Hebrews 2:17 and 4:15 clearly affirm these specific and general references to Jesus' temptations as the similar kinds and extent of temptations that Jesus experienced. Hebrews 5:7-8 further recalls the intense, maximum degree of psychological hardship that Jesus endured. The intended readers of that letter are similarly tempted and therefore need the assurance that the Savior is both sufficient and ably compassionate to aid them in holding to a dangerous confession of faith in Christ who suffered to the same extent and degree as they do. Taken together, the evidence of Hebrews and the Gospels for Christ's many temptations is set forth clearly. Unless skeptics are willing to admit that Jesus only pretended to suffer and be tempted, theologians must recognize the reality of his temptations and the varied forms and forces of them in his experience.

The temptations of Jesus are evidence of his true humanity in likeness to others whom he saves. He was tempted as a man and he resisted his temptations as a man. In no New Testament example of his temptation is Christ's divine power indicated as the means of his resistance to temptations. Of course, this silence does not mean that he was unable to use innate divine powers to enhance his weakened humanity or that he never did so, but none of the evidence indicates that he ever did. Being the Godman, Jesus may have been able to rely on his divinity at some point, but the New Testament portrayal of him throughout his temptations does not support that theological inference. To the contrary, the only means of Jesus' resistance noted clearly in the accounts are Scripture (in the wilderness), his open communication with his Father through prayer (in Gethsemane), the support of angels, and the (potential, but failed) assistance of his closest friends. Based on the available evidence for his life, the best explanation is that Jesus experienced and resisted his temptations within the limits of his humanity.

Biblical Evidence for the Sinlessness of Jesus

Even with the claims of some theologians that Jesus was able to sin, only very rarely has any theologian questioned Christ's sinlessness and affirm that he actually sinned.⁹⁹ Empirical demonstration from Scripture of the contrary claim—that he was sinless—would not likely be convincing since the biographical data available for scrutiny in the Gospels are incomplete, especially about the early years of his life.¹⁰⁰ Nonetheless, the New Testament evidence grounds Christ's sinlessness in the soteriological claims about him as the holy, perfect, and righteous Son of God who can deal with sins because he is sinless. These claims are uncontroversial because of the clarity of their presentation in Scripture. However, we briefly consider a representative portion of the New Testament evidence because of the relationship between the claims of Christ's sinlessness and his temptation. Orthodoxy has traditionally held that both claims are true.

Luke-Acts

Luke 1:35 recounts how the angel told Mary that her holy child would be called the Son of God. The child would be born as the result of the creative power of God in divine conception.¹⁰¹ The Holy Spirit conceived Jesus in Mary's womb as a holy child. The attribute of "holiness" (ἅγιος) indicates two aspects. First, Jesus is set apart for special service. Second, because he is the Son of God, the emphasis is on his character as divinely pure in the sense of separateness from sin and complete righteousness.¹⁰² Luke repeatedly includes references to Jesus as the holy or righteous one (Acts 2:27; 3:14; 4:27; 7:52; 13:35). This attribute of holiness entails his sinlessness. Luke 1:35 is representative of the many New Testament passages that assert Christ's moral purity from sin as part of declaring his holiness or righteousness.

---

⁹⁹An example of this egregious claim is Nels Ferré, *Christ and the Christian* (New York: Harper & Row, 1958), 110-14. The supposed sin is Jesus' anxiety and lack of trust in the Father, which Ferré counts as the sin of unbelief. I think a better way is to interpret Jesus as struggling in his faith, exerting his faith against the contrary evidence of his imminent suffering.

¹⁰⁰David G. A. Calvert, *From Christ to God: A Study of Some Trends, Problems and Possibilities in Contemporary Christology* (London: Epworth, 1983), 44, observes, "There is simply not the [historical] evidence available – neither a list of sins Jesus did not commit, nor a description of his human goodness in such detail that would enable the historian to draw the probable conclusion of his sinlessness." Nonetheless, as a mediating theologian, Carl Ullmann, *The Sinlessness of Jesus: An Evidence for Christianity*, 7th English ed., trans. Sophia Taylor (Edinburgh: T & T Clark, 1882), has tried to do just this by using Jesus' ethical record in the Gospels as an apologetic argument for his deity.

¹⁰¹Bock, *Luke 9:51-24:53*, 123.

¹⁰²Bock, *Luke 9:51-24:53*, 123.

The Gospel of John

John retells the claims Jesus makes about his own sinlessness.[103] In 8:29, John gives a statement by Jesus that the Father is continually present with him. The proof of this presence is the actions of Jesus that are always pleasing to the Father. This claim that he always does what pleases God entails Christ's sinlessness in the same way that holiness or purity does.[104] Within the narrative, Jesus strengthens his declaration of sinlessness by challenging his opponents to convict him of sin (8:46). John records no response from Christ's opponents, implying that they who were most eager to find some fault with Jesus could not answer his challenge. One apparent exception to this is in John 9 when the Pharisees' dim misperception of Jesus as a sinner (9:24) is presented in context of their spiritual blindness. The man whom Jesus had healed from lifelong blindness is the one who refutes the Pharisees by citing the proof of the miracle that gave him sight (9:31-33). In terms of John's presentation of Jesus and the Pharisees, their claim against him fails obviously in a way that exaggerates their own blindness and sin in contrast to Jesus' sinlessness that is attested by his ability to perform the special miracle (9:40-41). Christ's claim stands out unopposed as the bold revelation of his sinlessness and the mark of his clear conscience and innocence of all sin before God.[105]

Later in the narrative (14:30-31), Jesus again tells about his purity from sin when he explains that Satan has no power over him: "in me he has nothing" (ἐν ἐμοὶ οἰκ ἔχει οὐδέν). The implication is that because Jesus has never sinned, he is not vulnerable to Satan's influence through sin.[106] Instead of being swayed by the ruler of the world, Jesus remains free to do "just what my Father commands".[107] Christ's distinction from others who are under Satan's thrall through sin entails his sinlessness, just as he declared this about himself in third-person reference earlier, "unrighteousness is not in him" (ἀδικία ἐν αὐτῷ οὐκ ἔστιν, 7:18). Therefore, Christ's own statements represent the Evangelist's plain evidence for the sinlessness of Jesus.

---

[103]While acknowledging the controversies about authorship, composition history, and audience for Fourth Gospel, the traditional view seems most compelling that the author is John, the beloved disciple, the son of Zebedee, writing independently of the Synoptics in the locale of Ephesus at a late date in the 90s. Similar controversies about the authorship of 1 Peter and 1 John notwithstanding, the traditional view of the authors as the apostles Peter and John seem most reasonable and has been ably defended by others.

[104]Leon Morris, *The Gospel according to John*, rev. ed., New International Commentary on the New Testament, vol. 40 (Grand Rapids: Eerdmans, 1995), 402.

[105]Morris, *John*, 412.

[106]The intended meaning here could be even stronger that Jesus is unable to sin, but we cannot be sure of that claim by this statement alone.

[107]Morris, *John*, 585.

2 Corinthians

Paul argues a common New Testament theme that Jesus' sinlessness was a requirement to justify sinners by his self-sacrifice. Christ's ability to bear the sins of others depends on his sinlessness. In 2 Corinthians 5:21, Paul declares that Jesus is the one "who knew no sin" (μὴ γνόντα ἁμαρτίαν). He never gained the knowledge of sin by personal experience of sinning at any time in his life.[108] Being free of sin himself, Jesus could be "made sin" (ἁμαρτίαν ἐποίησεν) for others in the substitutionary, vicarious sense that he bore the punishment for their sins.[109] Other New Testament passages reiterate this theme of Jesus' sinlessness as a necessity for making reconciliation between humanity and God.[110]

Hebrews

As argued earlier, the phrase *without sin* is written in Hebrews 4:15 to distinguish Christ's only difference in having experienced temptation in all the same ways as those common to humanity. Hebrews exhorts the readers to resist sin as Jesus has, he is the model of having been tempted as they are, yet he never caved in or gave up. He is the object and pattern of faith for them as one who never sinned despite his temptations.

His example of sinlessness in the face of numerous temptations is also the ground of his unique sufficiency as a priest who does not need to offer sacrifices for himself as Levitical priests do (7:26-28). Jesus is "separated from sinners" in two ways. He is separate in the qualitative, moral sense of separation by his sinless purity despite his intercession (denoted by the three adjectives of purity that precede this: "holy, innocent, undefiled"). He is separate in the spatial sense of his removal from the sphere of sinners to his exaltation in heaven. Together, both senses support Christ's unique sufficiency as a priest for the readers.[111] Therefore, because he is sinless, Jesus can offer himself (9:11-14) as the definitive, sinlessly pure, and all-sufficient sacrifice for

---

[108] Murray J. Harris, *The Second Epistle to the Corinthians*, New International Greek Testament Commentary, vol. 43, pt. 2 (Grand Rapids: Eerdmans, 2005), 450, notes that the meaning of γνόντα (*he knew*) follows the classical Greek usage for "knowledge gained by personal participation". Harris also observes that the articular aorist participle is timeless, denoting not merely Jesus' pre-existent condition, but also his earthly and continuing condition.

[109] Even critical scholars recognize that 2 Cor 5:21 alludes to the Old Testament sin offering (e.g., Lev 4:8, 20-21). Hans-Josef Klauck, "Sacrifice and Sacrificial Offerings", trans. Reginald H. Fuller, in *Anchor Bible Dictionary*, ed. David Noel Freedman (New York: Doubleday, 1992), 5:888.

[110] E.g., John 1:29; Gal 3:13; Heb 7:26-28; 9:14; 1 Pet 3:18; 1 John 3:5.

[111] Craig R. Koester, *Hebrews*, Anchor Bible, vol. 36 (New York: Doubleday, 2001), 367.

the sins of others.

Hebrews 5:7-8 has seemed to some as telling a moral progress to sinlessness and not simply greater feats of Christ's obedience.[112] On the contrary, Hebrews 10:5-10 tells that Jesus began his human life in this pattern of sinless fidelity to God, having come into the world to do God's will.[113] His progress and completion as the obedient Son and priest do not constitute moral development; this would contradict the earlier assertion of his sinlessness (4:15). Instead, the progress is in terms of his becoming equipped to function as a compassionate priest. Moreover, the idea of progress from being a sinner to becoming a sinless savior is self-contradictory in terms of the main theme of assurance argued in Hebrews. Christ's unique sufficiency as the priest who can mediate for others depends upon his complete sinlessness. He himself can mediate for others because he stands righteous in relation to God. Any sin early in life or later would compromise this standing and his consequent ability to mediate for others.

1 Peter

Isaiah 53 supplies the metaphor of the Suffering Servant as an unblemished, spotless lamb that Peter applies to Jesus. In a similar way to Hebrews 5:7-8, 1 Peter 1:18-19 underscores that Christ's moral perfection is necessary to his efficacy as a substitutionary sacrifice.[114] His sinless purity also supports the exhortation that the readers strive to be similarly flawless and faultless in a way consistent with the holy God who called them (1:15-16) and the Holy Spirit who sanctifies them (1:2).[115]

Peter goes on to emphasize the sinlessness of Jesus, presenting him as the pattern the readers should follow closely (2:22) by copying his righteous response as the Suffering Servant (Isa 53:9). Christ's sinlessness indicates his perfect innocence. His suffering was undeserved, just as that unjust suffering that Peter's readers are called by God to endure (2:21). Even when suffering his unjust trial and crucifixion, Jesus continued to demonstrate his sinlessness by entrusting himself to God instead of sinfully taking revenge by his speech or action (2:23-24).[116]

First Peter 3:18 repeats the sacrificial theme of 2:21-24 that Christ is "the

---

[112]E.g., Williamson, "Hebrews 4:15", 4-8.

[113]Koester, *Hebrews*, 283-84, notes that Hebrews portrays sinlessness as obedience to God, even when God calls his sons to suffer innocently. Sin is apostasy that must be resisted by the obedience of faith. Jesus' exemplary obedience (5:8) is his faithfulness to do God's will (10:5), and thus his sinlessness.

[114]Peter H. Davids, *The First Epistle of Peter*, New International Commentary on the New Testament, vol. 56 (Grand Rapids: Eerdmans, 1990), 73.

[115]John H. Elliott, *1 Peter*, Anchor Bible, vol. 37B (New York: Doubleday, 2000), 355.

[116]Elliott, *1 Peter*, 529.

righteous one" who died "for the unrighteous" (δίκαιος ὑπὲρ ἀδίκων). Therefore, the familiar New Testament theme of Christ's sinlessness as a redemptive necessity is expanded to exhort readers to follow the example of his sinlessness even when suffering innocently as he did to the utmost.

1 John

The redemptive necessity that Jesus must be sinless to deal with the sins of others is repeated in 1 John 3:5. John restates two statements in the Fourth Gospel to mark Jesus' sinlessness. First, the epistle describes Jesus as the one who "takes away sins" (τὰς ἁμαρτίας ἄρῃ), which is an echo of John the Baptizer's declaration in the Gospel about the lamb "who takes away the sins" (ὁ αἴρων τὴν ἁμαρτίαν, John 1:29). Second, 1 John 3:5 grounds Jesus' efficacy to save from sin by saying emphatically that "sin is not in him" (ἁμαρτία ἐν αὐτῷ οὐκ ἔστιν). This restates Jesus' statement in John 14:30 that Satan has nothing in him. The epistle also emphasizes Christ's sinlessness with the positive claims that he is "righteous" (2:29; 3:7) and "pure" (3:3).[117]

Conclusion

This summary of representative New Testament evidence for the sinlessness of Jesus shows the emphatic, varied, and clear presentation of the claim. More could be said to connect the New Testament affirmations with Old Testament predictions and typology that the Messiah must be sinless.[118] No exhaustive data of Christ's life is available for study to test the claim of his sinlessness positively or negatively. Instead, the clear declaration of his sinlessness by the New Testament is the necessary and sufficient ground for the traditional theological claim. As with the traditional claim that Jesus was truly tempted, so also the claim that he was sinless must not be denied in light of the New Testament evidence reviewed here. Furthermore, the biblical evidence suggests that Christ did not have what subsequent theology has termed original sin because the Holy Spirit specially wrought the Son's incarnation as a virginal conception.[119]

---

[117]Stephen S. Smalley, *1, 2, 3 John*, Word Biblical Commentary, vol. 51 (Waco, TX: Word, 1984), 157.

[118]Jonathan Edwards, *Freedom of the Will*, ed. Paul Ramsey, vol. 1 of *The Works of Jonathan Edwards* (New Haven: Yale University Press, 1957), 281-89, gives eleven proofs for the impeccability of Christ, most of which are based on a redemptive necessity that if he could sin, the promises and plans of God would be voided. Zabriskie, "The Impeccability of Christ", 160-89, argues much the same way as Edwards for the necessity of Christ's impeccability because of Christ's person, the Old Testament promises, and the redemptive necessity that the Messiah be sinless forever.

[119]The concept of original sin is intended here to include original guilt and the consequent original corruption as members of Adam (Rom 5:12-21). Cf. Oliver D.

Despite the clarity, one question not addressed by Scripture in an obvious way is *how* Jesus achieved sinlessness, whether by his inherent deity, the Holy Spirit, a combination of these, or some other means. This question requires the theological formulations presented in the historical chapters. Theological models attempt to explain what remains unclear in Scripture. One place where Scripture comes near to this question is Luke 1:35, but this applies narrowly to Christ's start in human life. Moreover, his purity at conception is attributable to the involvement of the Holy Spirit, who similarly effected a miraculous conception for Christ's cousin John (though without purity as the result).

Without diminishing Jesus' holy uniqueness in relation to John and the rest of humanity, the evidence for his sinlessness stresses the praiseworthiness of his achievement, a true example. To be an example, inherent divine power cannot have been the active cause of his sinlessness. Of course, his divinity could have been the actual factor determining his sinlessness, but the New Testament examples stress the humanness of his purity as a restart of humanity by proper obedience to God. His sinless purity is to be imitated by other humans. His sinlessness is the humanly achieved result after having been truly tempted, and he resisted within human limitations.

Crisp's helpful argument for this connection of guilt and corruption in "Did Christ have a *Fallen* Human Nature?", 278.

CHAPTER 2

The Relevance of Temptation and Sinlessness

In this chapter, we will return to several passages discussed above because they tell of Christ's sinlessness and temptations in terms of their soteriological value for human beings. The three topics are his empathy, his pattern for others to live obediently as he did, and his efficacy as a substitutionary sacrifice. The first two points of relevance depend on the authenticity of Christ's temptation; the third depends on the reality of his sinlessness.

Empathy and Help

The author of Hebrews 2:17-18 and 4:15-16 stresses the relevance of Christ's experience for the readers' immediate situation of temptation. In 2:17-18, the Lord's entrance into a vulnerable human mode of life and his temptations were the necessary equipment to constitute him as a compassionate priest for the people. Because he has endured the suffering and temptation in all the ways that the readers experienced them (4:15), Jesus can offer help to others as the priest who understands their situation and is thus able to provide effective support (4:16).

The relevance of Christ's temptations also shows in these two passages as persuasive power to win the readers' trust in Jesus as priest, despite the suffering that accompanies their continued faith in him. He is uniquely sufficient (he is the divine Son compared to the angels) and he is specially and humanly compassionate (he is a perfect man compared to Moses and the Levites). Christ's exaltation as the Son of God does not remove him from being able to empathize compassionately with the readers' situation. On the contrary, he has totally identified with them in their situation of suffering and temptation. Therefore, the relevance of his temptation experiences is that these form him to be compassionate and able to help others endure their own temptations. He came into solidarity with them in temptation so that they can be in solidarity with him to resist it successfully.

If Christ's temptations are diminished or denied, then his compassion and help as priest are lost. His temptations are necessary to convince suffering believers like those first addressed by the letter to the Hebrews that obedience to God is possible even in the midst of severe suffering and temptation. Hebrews 5:7-8 recalls the actual, lived example of Christ's persistence to obey despite his suffering. His obedience demonstrates his success against temptations, and for all time his experience constitutes his ability to help others (2:18; 4:16). He is also inclined to help because he knows from experience what others suffer. He is able to help because he is the God-man who relied upon divine support provided to all faithful followers. The evidence of Jesus' confrontation with Satan's temptations in the wilderness and Gethsemane showed that Christ relied on the Scriptures and prayer as a true man trusting God. He suffered and resisted temptations on the same terms as others—within his human limitations. Therefore, Jesus' temptations are necessary to his relevance of supplying help to others when they are tempted, and to point the way of hope to refuse temptations as he did.

The Pattern to Copy

Jesus is the object of faith and the pattern to copy in living faithfully as he did. His human (active) obedience is emphasized in the specific context of resisting temptations. The reasonableness of his pattern is urged to readers in Hebrews 4:15 and 5:7-8, where we saw his obedience as a real possibility for others who suffer the temptation to turn away from God's will. The emphasis continues in Hebrews 12:1-3 and 1 Peter 2:21-25, where Christ's pattern is commended to Christians living in the midst of suffering and temptation.

Jesus: The Pattern to Copy in Hebrews 12:1-3

(1) Τοιγαροῦν καὶ ἡμεῖς τοσοῦτον ἔχοντες περικείμενον ἡμῖν νέφος μαρτύρων,
    ὄγκον ἀποθέμενοι πάντα καὶ τὴν εὐπερίστατον ἁμαρτίαν,
    δι᾿ ὑπομονῆς τρέχωμεν τὸν προκείμενον ἡμῖν ἀγῶνα
(2)   ἀφορῶντες εἰς τὸν τῆς πίστεως ἀρχηγὸν καὶ τελειωτὴν Ἰησοῦν, ὅς
    ἀντὶ τῆς προκειμένης αὐτῷ χαρᾶς
    ὑπέμεινεν σταυρὸν αἰσχύνης
    καταφρονήσας ἐν δεξιᾷ τε τοῦ θρόνου τοῦ θεοῦ κεκάθικεν.
(3)   ἀναλογίσασθε γὰρ τὸν τοιαύτην ὑπομεμενηκότα
    ὑπὸ τῶν ἁμαρτωλῶν εἰς ἑαυτὸν ἀντιλογίαν,
ἵνα μὴ κάμητε ταῖς ψυχαῖς ὑμῶν ἐκλυόμενοι.

(1) Consequently, because we have so great a cloud of witnesses around us,
    we must put off every weight and the entangling sin,
    so that we must run with endurance the race set before us
(2)   by focusing on the founder and completer of faith,
    Jesus, who,

because of¹ the joy set before him,
endured a cross disregarding the shame
and he has sat down at the right hand of God's throne.
(3)   For think of such a one as he who has endured hostility
by sinners in himself,
so that you may not become weary, fainting in your souls.

Hebrews 12:1-3 focuses the readers' hope and inspiration on Christ's pattern of endurance in the life of faith. Just as they face perils as part of their trust in Jesus, he himself faced and persevered through perils on their behalf. He is the greatest inspiration and example to their faithfulness, having demonstrated in his own life the perseverance to which God now calls these troubled readers to imitate.

Based on the prior argument that Christ is superior to Judaism and that the heroes of Israel's history endured in faith (towards Jesus), the readers are exhorted to endure their suffering by getting rid of all opposition to their faith so that they do not become weary or fainthearted in their diligence to live by faith. Beginning with the strong summary indicator—"Consequently" (Τοιγαροῦν, 1a)—Hebrews 12 brings the argument of the entire book to a climax. This climactic exhortation is the answer to the readers' implicit question: "What shall we do about the persecution that we are about to suffer?" Structurally, the author marks off this passage by reinforcing the initial summary marker (Τοιγαροῦν) with the purpose clause of 12:3b ("so that", ἵνα). The author reminds the readers to consider their own situation within the broader scope of history and the examples of faithfulness in Israel's history, the life of Jesus, and the work of God to sustain his people through worse perils than the readers currently experience.

The argument proceeds by first comparing the faith of the witnesses of Hebrews 11 to the readers' faith that is hindered with "weights" (ὄγκον, 1b).²

---

¹The sense of ἀντί is controversial in this passage (*because of* vs. *instead of*). A brief discussion with references to several proponents on each side is in Daniel B. Wallace, *Greek Grammar Beyond the Basics* (Grand Rapids: Zondervan, 1996), 367-68. Wallace does not take a side. William L. Lane, *Hebrews 9-13*, Word Biblical Commentary, vol. 47B (Dallas: Word, 1991), 413, argues for the substitutionary sense of ἀντί: *instead of* the joy of heaven, he came to die; the Son forsook his joy (cf. Phil 2:6-7) to bring others into the kingdom of God. Ellingworth, *Hebrews*, 641, Koester, *Hebrews*, 524, and most modern translations take ἀντί here as anticipatory: *because of* the joy of the salvation of believers—the joy, glory, and salvation are the anticipated prize of the race for which the Son advanced to the cross. On either view, Jesus is the inspiring example to the readers for remaining faithful to God in the face of suffering and temptation.

²In terms of the broader argument of the book that suggests the readers are Jewish Christians tempted to return to Judaism as a way to avoid persecution for a confession of Christ, these *weights* are most likely the tempting alternative of salvation through the cultic rites and Mosaic law of Judaism.

The "cloud of witnesses" is evidence that many others have endured far worse suffering than the readers have, but these ancestors persisted in faith. The point is that the readers also can endure, but they must do as others have by ridding themselves of their own weighty distractions and the sin of unbelief by which they hinder themselves from faithfulness.[3] Such weights will cause them to "become weary" and "faint in your souls" (3b). The athletic imagery conveys the obvious problem of running a race while carrying weights. Similarly, the readers' continued faithfulness to Christ becomes increasingly difficult when they look back to the distractions of misplaced hopes in the institutions of the Mosaic Covenant instead of looking to Jesus as the object of their faith.

Then the author exhorts the audience based on the example of Jesus' faithful endurance on the cross. The readers must persevere in their God-given circumstances by looking to the model of endurance and considering his inspiring example of faithfulness.[4] The author argues from lesser to greater by comparing the audience's life of faith to the life demonstrated by Jesus. The letter earlier alluded to Christ's suffering and obedience (2:17; 4:15; 5:7-8), then brings these to culmination (12:2-3) with reference to Jesus' ultimate act of faithfulness in his crucifixion (cf. 12:4, "to blood"). The readers must contend with their *weights* of the temptations to sin; Jesus had to contend with the sinners who betrayed, arrested, falsely accused, and executed him. The author uses nearly identical terms for the readers' entangling "sin" (ἁμαρτίαν, 1b) and the "sinners" (ἁμαρτωλῶν, 3a)[5] who afflicted Jesus, using the wordplay to create the impression that Christ is their example for resisting sin—and he experienced much more severe persecution and attendant temptations than what the readers face. Jesus, having endured not only all that they have in temptations (4:15), and on the same terms of human limitation in their weaknesses (2:17), has endured so much more suffering as the ultimate

---

[3]Lane, *Hebrews 9-13*, 409, disagrees that *the sin* is specific as apostasy, but refers to all sorts of sins that cause problems for Christians. However, Heb 3:13 seems to focus on this as the particular sin causing trouble for the readers. Either way, the importance of Jesus as an example in turning away from sin to faith remains central.

[4]That Christ is the one who *completes* the life of faith implies God's sovereign ordering of events that contribute to the sanctification of believers. This is harmonious with Paul's statement in Rom 8:28-30. T. E. Pollard, *Fullness of Humanity: Christ's Humanness and Ours*, The Croall Lectures 1980 (Sheffield: Almond, 1982), 81, argues persuasively that the *faith* of Heb 12:2 is Jesus' faith. As a real man, Jesus had to exercise faith in the tradition of the examples of faith in chapter 11. This interpretation strengthens the emphasis of the passage on Jesus as the example of faithfulness in the face of temptation.

[5]A dual reference for "sinners" is likely to include not only the Romans and Jews who actually crucified Jesus, but also the readers of Hebrews because his punishment was for their sins too.

model for endurance in faith.⁶ He demonstrates that obedience is possible for them just as it was for him; therefore, the readers must persist in faith with endurance by finding their strength, hope, and inspiration in Jesus.

Structurally, several features reinforce the emphasis on Jesus as the model of faithfulness. The author places Jesus' name in the final, emphatic position of the second clause (1c-2b).⁷ "Endurance" (ὑπομονῆς, appearing three times in 1c, 2c, and 3a), is the repeated, thematic key to the exhortation to endure as Jesus did. This pattern follows the structure of the passage that is centered on Jesus' endurance.

The readers must persevere by looking to Jesus both because he is the inspiring model who pioneered and triumphed in the life of faith for them, and because he is the empowering goal of their faith. The main exhortation to obedience comes in the form of an athletic metaphor, "we must run" (τρέχωμεν, 1c),⁸ and is grounded on Jesus' example of faithfulness. This imperatival urgency is reinforced by the command to "think of" or "set your minds on" Jesus' example (ἀναλογίσασθε, 3a). The structural marker—"For" (γάρ, 3a)— that accompanies this imperative to focus their attention on Jesus makes the transition between focus on the ascended Christ, seated in ultimate authority (2d), and returns the readers' attention to considering his endurance of suffering (3a). Looking at what Jesus endured in his obedience with suffering, the readers must take inspiration and motivation—"so that you do not become weary" (ἵνα μὴ κάμητε, 3b), that is, for the purpose of enduring their own suffering of smaller proportions.⁹ Since Christ has already gone ahead of them and completed the course of faithfulness (1c), the readers can find encouragement by continuing to follow him, despite their temptations to turn away. Jesus is not only the one to be grasped by faith for salvation; he is also the human-scale model of ultimate endurance in it, demonstrating a choice of obedience to God despite the cost.

The author also provides God's perspective on the suffering and sanctification that the readers fear to endure: Jesus has already made their endurance a possibility and success by his own endurance in their stead. While the readers are concerned about being able to continue forward in the race, the author assures them that the entire race belongs to Christ who is the "founder" (ἀρχηγόν, 2a) and "completer" (τελειωτήν, 2a) of faith. Their success in perseverance does not depend upon their efforts alone or even primarily, but upon the surety of Christ's salvation of them and the help he offers to them.

---

⁶Lane, *Hebrews 9-13*, 405. Ὑπομονῆς (endurance) and cognates are repeated in 12:1c, 2c, 3b; cf. 10:32, 36; 12:7.
⁷Ellingworth, *Hebrews*, 641.
⁸The mood of the verb is subjunctive, but it has the force of an exhortation in context of warnings and the mounting intensity of life-and-death urgency in the letter.
⁹ Ἵνα + subjunctive indicates the purpose of looking to Jesus for results in their own struggle.

If Jesus had not been tempted in the severe ways depicted in the Gospels and Hebrews, then his value as an example for obeying God would be lost. Hebrews 12:1-3 makes use of Christ as the ultimate model of faithful obedience to God within the context of his lifelong suffering and temptation that culminated in the crucifixion. Without his likeness to the readers in temptations to sin (2:17; 4:15), the exhortation to follow Jesus' example in obeying God within human limitations loses its force. Christ's relevance as an example in 12:1-3 depends on his experience of temptation as the struggle to obey God instead of disobeying in the context of his suffering (cf. 5:7-8). Therefore, to diminish or deny the severity and reality of Jesus' temptations undermines his value as an example in faithfulness.

Jesus: The Pattern to Copy in 1 Peter 2:21-25

(21) εἰς τοῦτο γὰρ ἐκλήθητε,
    ὅτι καὶ Χριστὸς ἔπαθεν ὑπὲρ ὑμῶν
        ὑμῖν ὑπολιμπάνων ὑπογραμμὸν
        ἵνα ἐπακολουθήσητε τοῖς ἴχνεσιν αυτοῦ,
(22) ὃς ἁμαρτίαν οὐκ ἐποίησεν
    οὐδὲ εὑρέθη δόλος ἐν τῷ στόματι αὐτοῦ,
(23) ὃς λοιδορούμενος οὐκ ἀντελοιδόρει,
    πάσχων οὐκ ἠπείλει,
    παρεδίδου δὲ τῷ κρίνοντι δικαίως·
(24) ὃς τὰς ἁμαρτίας ἡμῶν αὐτὸς ἀνήνεγκεν
    ἐν τῷ σώματι αὐτοῦ ἐπὶ τὸ ξύλον,
    ἵνα
        ταῖς ἁμαρτίας ἀπογενόμενοι
        τῇ δικαιοσύνῃ ζήσωμεν,
οὗ τῷ μώλωπι ἰάθητε.
(25) ἦτε γὰρ ὡς πρόβατα πλανώμενοι,
ἀλλὰ ἐπεστράφητε νῦν ἐπὶ τὸν ποιμένα καὶ ἐπίσκοπον τῶν ψυχῶν ὑμῶν.

(21) For to this you have been called,
    because Christ also suffered for you
        leaving a pattern for you
        so that you may follow in his footsteps,
(22) who did not sin
    nor was found deceit in his mouth,
(23) who when being insulted he did not return insults,
    when suffering he did not threaten,
    but gave up to the one who judges righteously
(24) who, our sins he himself bore
    in his body on the tree,

> so that
>> to sins we might die
>> to righteousness we might live,
> for by his wounds you were healed.
> (25) For you were like sheep going astray
>> but now you have returned to the Shepherd and Guardian of your souls.[10]

In 2:21-25, Peter points to Christ's conduct as one who suffered innocently and now serves as the pattern of life for domestic slaves (2:18-20) and the entire Christian community (2:13-17) in the context of their unjust suffering. The principle is that God calls his people to suffer things they do not deserve. God also honors his people when they endure undeserved suffering (2:19-20) and readily speak for him in spite of their mistreatment (3:13-16). Peter especially applies the principle to slaves, writing that they are called by God to suffer unjustly in their particular vulnerability to undeserved harsh treatment. Nonetheless, Peter's appeal to Jesus as the pattern of such a call universalizes the principle for all Christians.[11] Peter stresses that all Christians who follow Jesus have been called by God "to this" (2:21), that is, called to suffer unjustly while responding honorably in spite of their suffering, just as Jesus did.[12] Such suffering is part of their identification with Christ.

Christ is the preeminent case of someone who suffered innocently.[13] He is the "unblemished and spotless lamb" (1:19) who bought them in salvation.[14] Peter applies Isaiah 53:9 to Jesus to demonstrate that he, though sinned against, had not sinned in word or deed to deserve what he suffered (2:22).[15] Peter then

---

[10]This structural layout is adapted from Elliott, *1 Peter*, 511.

[11]In Peter's view, all Christians are "slaves of God" (θεοῦ δοῦλοι, 2:16). Karen H. Jobes, *1 Peter*, Baker Exegetical Commentary on the New Testament, vol. 56 (Grand Rapids: Baker Academic, 2005), 192, notes that Peter joins ethics to theology by using Christ as the paradigm for Christian conduct. Slaves in the ancient world were particularly vulnerable to beatings, false accusation, being deprived of children and the opportunity to marry, and wrongful death because they had no rights.

[12]Thomas R. Schreiner, *1, 2 Peter, Jude*, New American Commentary, vol. 37 (Nashville: Broadman and Holman, 2003), 141.

[13]An Old Testament parallel of the righteous sufferer is Job. Jesus' difference is that he alone was perfect in respect to sin and obedience to God, cf. the stress on his perfection in 1 Pet 1:19.

[14]Davids, *1 Peter*, 73, notes that the combination of Old Testament terms indicates the complete purity of Christ as a sacrifice.

[15]Jobes, *1 Peter*, 194, notes four clear quotations and four allusions to Isa 53 in 2:21-25 as the clearest identification of the suffering servant with Jesus in the New Testament. Peter has his own translation of Isaiah's "violence" (חמס), which has the moral meaning of *doing wrong*. The LXX has "lawlessness" (ἀνομίας). Peter's translation of חמס as "sin" (ἁμαρτίας) emphasizes the innocence of Jesus in a way that is consistent with the meaning in Isa 53. The Servant is undeserving by his actions and words of the

reminds his readers that when insulted and afflicted Jesus did not retaliate, but instead entrusted himself to God (2:23c; cf. 2:20). Peter emphasizes Christ as the pattern of faith for when people suffer unjustly, even to the extent of the crucifixion and bearing punishment for the sin of the world (2:24). The reference to the crucifixion in 2:24 confirms the prophecy in Isaiah that corresponds to the Gospel accounts of Jesus' silence before his abusers.[16] Jesus' refusal to lie as a way of avoiding suffering—"nor was found deceit in his mouth" (2:22b)—contrasts starkly with Peter's own regrettable lies by which he avoided the possibility of suffering for having known Jesus.[17] Peter reiterates this exhortation in the specific way of not telling lies after having warned his readers to turn away from *deceit* in 2:1 and then he reminds them again in 3:10. Christ's example of innocence cited in 2:22 is central to Peter's repeated charge that the readers follow that pattern despite their unjust suffering.

Moreover, Christ's innocence in contrast to the normal human response and Peter's own failure is that Christ's suffering was not only undeserved, but he also suffered vicariously for what others deserved—"for you" (ὑπὲρ ὑμῶν, 2:21b). The use of Jesus as the example of this righteous response contradicts the normal human response of feeling justified for self-defense to retaliate when people have been mistreated unjustly.[18] Against this desire for retaliation, Peter points to Christ as the definitive model of one who went a different way. By his death, Christ makes others able to follow him in this different way as they copy his conduct in faithfulness to God.[19] Therefore, Peter reminds his readers that since they have been spared the suffering that they deserve for their sins, they must not tell lies to dodge the lesser suffering to which God calls them as his witnesses.

Christ's suffering was efficacious to heal the readers from their own sinful corruption (2:24) so that they can now copy his pattern by making his attitudes and actions their own. As the "pattern" (ὑπογραμμόν, 2:21c), that is, the template for their attitudes and actions, the readers must learn the forms and motions of righteous living by tracing over Christ's attitudes and actions with

---

punishment he suffered. Jesus' fulfillment of this point of the prophecy depends on his sinless, unjust suffering.

[16] Elliott, *1 Peter*, 530. E.g., Mark 14:61; 15:5 and parallels.

[17] The Gospel tradition about Peter's three denials that he knew Jesus, and his later three-fold restoration after the resurrection would have been well-known to Peter's readers (e.g., Mark 14:66-72). Peter's denial is one of the few passages common to all four Gospels. Peter was likely closely involved with the early translation of the Gospel accounts into Greek for the Jerusalem Hellenists, and likely insisted on the inclusion of his denials.

[18] Elliott, *1 Peter*, 531. The conventional wisdom is that people stop bullies by standing up to them, sometimes forcefully.

[19] Elliott, *1 Peter*, 528.

their own.[20] Peter's metaphor of the template refers to the models that children used to learn to write letters and draw basic forms, tracing over the patterns as guidelines.[21] Similarly, Peter exhorts his readers to imitate Christ's actions as the guidelines for their own actions—especially when they are tempted to sin because of unjust suffering and persecution (cf. 4:1-6). The relevance of Jesus' suffering is thus twofold, constituting both their redemption by which the readers have returned to God (2:24-25) and the "pattern" or template for them to copy him by not sinning even when they are mistreated.

Christ's suffering wrought their salvation from sin for the purpose that they "live to righteousness" (2:24c). He not only gives them the guidelines by his own life, but Jesus enables them for the purpose that they "follow in his steps" (2:21d).[22] Jesus' faithfulness in suffering to accomplish salvation makes possible the readers' faithfulness after his pattern. Peter thus answers the possible objections from his audience that mere sinners cannot possibly surmount the common response to injustice by responding instead with a blessing (cf. 3:8-12).[23]

The relevance of Jesus as the pattern for Christians is that instead of sinning when he suffered unjustly, Jesus gave himself into God's care (cf. the exhortation that the readers do the same, 4:19).[24] If Jesus had not suffered and experienced the temptation to respond in self-defense or take revenge, then he could not be the pattern as Peter commends him for Christians who suffer the insults and unjust abuse by others. Christ's value as a template of sinlessness in the midst of all sorts of suffering and even to the extreme degree of his passion is relevant because he really endured that suffering. Christ's temptations are implied by the reminder in this account that he did *not* return insult for insult, he did *not* threaten those who tortured him, and he did *not* lie as a way of avoiding pain. Certainly, the readers of 1 Peter were tempted to do these things, but against that common human impulse for self-preservation Peter commends the pattern that Jesus laid down for them in his own conduct. To diminish or deny Christ's temptations in this case (i.e., the temptation to retaliate against his abusers or avoid pain by lying) would diminish his relevance as the pattern for Christians to copy.

---

[20]Elliott, *1 Peter*, 527. Vv. 22-23 explain that Jesus' actions are guidelines established for them to learn his responses despite unjust suffering.

[21]Bauer, *A Greek-English Lexicon of the New Testament*, s.v. "ὑπογραμμός".

[22]Elliott, *1 Peter*, 528. Elliott gives the helpful analogy of a father walking ahead of his son in the deep snow so the boy can follow by stepping into the packed footprints.

[23]This claim that the readers' ability to endure their suffering patiently and even respond to insults and evil with a blessing entails the important point that is elaborated by the author of Hebrews: Jesus' solidarity with common humanity makes him a peer among them who enables others to live as he did.

[24]Jobes, *1 Peter*, 197.

The Sufficient Sacrifice

The soteriological relevance of Christ's sinlessness is that his ability to make the sacrifice depends upon his purity as the offering and intercessor of the New Covenant. Examples show throughout the Bible. In the New Testament, Jesus' ability to take away sin requires his sinlessness. This was noted in the discussion of 2 Corinthians 5:21 (above). The necessity of his purity is also suggested in Hebrews 7:26-28, where Christ's difference from the Levitical priests is applied to the difference of his service for others. The other priests must offer sacrifices for their own sins before they can intercede for others.[25] Jesus, being "holy, innocent, undefiled" (7:26), can by his death "offer himself once for all" (7:27; cf. 9:12, 28; 10:10) as the only effective priest with a truly sufficient sacrifice to redeem others.[26] Plainly, the relevance of his sinlessness is that such purity is essential to his priestly role in redemption. Without it, he cannot save.

This redemptive requirement that Hebrews makes explicit is in continuity with the Old Testament promises about the necessary sinlessness of the Messiah. An example is the way Jeremiah 23:5-6 connects the Messiah's righteousness with his kingly rule in justice and righteousness. David's descendant is called the "righteous branch" who will "do justice and righteousness" in the land. Jeremiah 33:15-16 repeats the same relation between the righteous character of David's branch and the righteousness and justice that he will accomplish worldwide. A similar idea is in Isaiah 9:7 and 11:1-5.

Isaiah 53:9-12 connects the Messiah's righteous sinlessness to his efficacy as a sinless sacrifice that redeems the people from sin.[27] As the guilt offering that takes away the guilt of the people (53:10b), the Messiah had to be the righteous one who could justify others (53:11b). Although he was innocent and righteous, the Messiah "bore the sin of all" (53:12e). In Old Testament context, the purity of a Passover sacrifice and sin offering is established by the requirements given, for example, in Exodus 12:5 and Leviticus 22:17-25, with reaffirmation by Yahweh's censure in Malachi 1:6-14. To be acceptable to God, the offerings must be spotlessly *perfect* and *complete* in the sense of *unblemished* and *without defect* as a metaphor for moral purity and

---

[25]Lane, *Hebrews 1-8*, 194, notes that the daily offerings were not the annual Day of Atonement service of the high priest. The point is the contrast between the efficacy of a sinless priest and those others who cannot even come before God to intercede for others without frequently offering sacrifices for their own sins.

[26]Ellingworth, *Hebrews*, 727. The offering is his life poured out through death, cf. 9:11-14; 25; 10:1-15.

[27]The identifications of the Suffering Servant of Isa 53 with the promised Messiah and the fulfillment by Jesus Christ are controversial. However, the clear identification of Jesus with the Servant by quotations and allusions to Isaiah 53 in 1 Pet 2:21-24 confirms the traditional interpretation that I present here.

blamelessness.[28] In the divinely ordained sacrificial mechanism of the temple cult, the physically pure animals were accepted as a metaphorically pure substitutes and coverings for the sins of the people. Christ's sinlessness fulfills this Old Testament typology and the promises of a sinless and righteous Messiah who saves the people.

Therefore, in canonical perspective, Christ's sinlessness is doubly relevant for his role as the self-sacrifice of redemption and for his role as the righteous king establishing justice throughout the earth. Any model that diminishes (or denies) Christ's sinlessness also causes a problem for these essential points of his soteriological relevance.[29]

Conclusion

The biblical evidence for the relevance of Christ's temptation and sinlessness confirms that each is necessary for salvation. His relevance in empathizing with and giving help to others who struggle against temptations to sin depends on his lived experience of the same degree and extent of temptations as they experience. His relevance as the pattern for other people to copy in resisting temptation to sin likewise requires that he had to be tempted as they are. Not only did he have to be tempted as they are, but it seems further that he, if he is to be empathetic and a model for others in resisting temptation, must have achieved sinlessness within his limitations as a man. Finally, his sinlessness is also redemptively necessary for him to offer a sufficient sacrifice for the sin of the world. The biblical evidence for his true temptation, sinlessness, and the relevance of each for salvation are mutually implicative.

---

[28]Cf. the moral sense in Gen 6:9, where Noah is called "righteous, blameless". 1 Tim 6:14 and Jas 1:27 are examples that demonstrate the way the New Testament explains the Old Testament metaphor of physical perfection and bodily wholeness as moral purity.
[29]That is, he cannot be the sacrifice as required by God's justice if he is not sinless.

CHAPTER 3

Jesus and the Holy Spirit

As we will see below in the historical chapters, several models of Christ's impeccability and temptation account for his sinlessness in terms of some sort of empowering grace by the Holy Spirit. Other sorts of grace may be simply the gift of divine presence or provision, but *empowering grace* is the divine gift of assistance to enable a person in a particular way, such as some sort of ministry or to remain faithful in the midst of persecution. This idea of empowerment is usually derived from biblical evidence. We will consider this evidence for the role of the Holy Spirit in the life of the Messiah, both in the Old Testament prophecies and the New Testament fulfillment (revealed in Christ's life). This topic is controversial in recent theology,[1] with a long history beneath it.[2] In my

---

[1] The main issue is whether or not Christ's experience of the Holy Spirit is typical for others who receive the Holy Spirit from Jesus. Interpreters are further divided about whether the Holy Spirit's primary role is to empower Jesus and others for preaching and miracles, to commission people in ministry, or to guide believers. Pentecostal interpreters usually argue that Jesus was empowered by the Holy Spirit primarily to preach the gospel and perform miracles, in parallel to the claim that the Spirit's empowerment of Christians is to do the same. For a survey and critique from a charismatic perspective, see Max Turner, *The Holy Spirit and Spiritual Gifts: In the New Testament Church and Today*, rev. ed. (Peabody, MA: Hendrickson, 1998). For a critique of the Pentecostal view from a non-charismatic perspective, see James D. G. Dunn, *Jesus and the Spirit: A Study of the Religious and Charismatic Experience of Jesus and the First Christians as Reflected in the New Testament* (1975; reprint, Grand Rapids: Eerdmans, 1997).

[2] The controversy over the Spirit's role in the life of Jesus goes back at least to the fourth century debate between two prominent church leaders, Nestorius of Constantinople and Cyril of Alexandria. Cyril's ninth anathema against Nestorius was included in the declarations of the Third Ecumenical Council (Ephesus, 431) and the Fourth Ecumenical Council (Chalcedon, 451). At the Sixth Ecumenical Council (Constantinople II, 553), the Council additionally condemned Theodoret for countering Cyril's anathemas regarding this point. Cyril's anathema against Nestorius reads: "If any man shall say that the one Lord Jesus Christ was glorified by the Holy Ghost, so that he used through him a power not his own and from him received power against unclean spirits and power to work miracles before men and shall not rather confess that it was his own Spirit through which he worked these divine signs; let him be anathema." Philip Schaff and Henry Wace, eds, *The Seven Ecumenical Councils*, NPNF[2], 14:214-15.

view of the Old Testament messianic prophecies, the Spirit primarily equips the Messiah to rule as king for God while also fulfilling a prophetic task of proclamation. In my view of the New Testament fulfillment in Christ's life, the Spirit is associated with Jesus directly and indirectly. Jesus was conceived by the Holy Spirit (Luke 1:35), he was driven by the Spirit into the wilderness to be tempted by Satan (Mark 1:12), he performed miracles of healing by the Holy Spirit (e.g., Luke 5:17), he cast out demons by the Spirit of God (Matt 12:28), and Christ's general activity of "doing good and healing all who were oppressed by the devil" is connected with his possession of the Holy Spirit (Acts 10:38). Among these diverse pneumatological data, we will focus on the ethical aspect of the Spirit's role in the life of the Messiah because of the way this role corresponds to the topic of Jesus' temptation and sinlessness.

Old Testament Promise of the Messiah

Old Testament pneumatology emphasizes the way the Spirit of God equips individuals for the prophetic and ruling tasks in Israel (including judicial, legislative, executive, priestly, and military tasks, as in the time of the judges). The Spirit equips the Messiah for his prophetic task of proclamation by putting the words of God in his mouth (Isa 59:21). Other prophetic tasks of performing miracles should not be excluded from the Messiah because of Christ's many miracles that obviously match the miracles of Israel's prophets, particularly Elijah and Elisha (cf. Jesus' self-designation as a prophet in Luke 4:25-27). Parallels in the ministry of the prophets and Jesus are the acts of controlling nature, raising the dead, multiplying food, and healing leprosy. Moreover, the Messiah of Isaiah is a prophet like Moses, leading the people in a new Exodus of salvation.[3]

However, Old Testament messianic pneumatology focuses on the Spirit's provision of equipment for the Messiah to govern for God as the eschatological king. This kingly role is prominent with pneumatological features in Isaiah 11:1-10, 42:1-9 (applied to Jesus in Matt 12:17-21), 50:4-11, and 58:6. Isaiah 61:1-11 expands the kingly theme with a prophetic task to proclaim and establish a comprehensive vision of eschatological salvation, which is important because Jesus identifies himself and his ministry with this pneumatological, messianic passage (Luke 4:16-21). Isaiah 61 combines the prophetic and kingly tasks in the single mission of bringing divine salvation (the blessing of God's rule by which he rescues his creation).

My interest in the Holy Spirit's role is the way that these Old Testament passages emphasize the ethical equipping of the Messiah, a man empowered by the Spirit in ways that form his character in righteousness.[4] Thus equipped by

---

[3]Turner, *Holy Spirit*, 33.

[4]The identification of the Servant with the Messiah in Isaiah is controversial. Most critical scholars reject the idea. In Isaiah, the Servant refers alternately to Israel, an

the Holy Spirit, the Messiah is able to establish God's righteousness at every level of the created order.

Pneumatological Christology[5] *in Isaiah 11:1-5*

(1) Then a branch will proceed from the trunk of Jesse,
    and a sprout from his roots will bear fruit.
(2) And the Spirit of Yahweh will remain upon him,
    A   the Spirit of wisdom and understanding
       B   the Spirit of counsel and strength
          C   the Spirit of knowledge and the fear of Yahweh.
(3)   C` And he will delight in the fear of Yahweh,
       B` and not by seeing with his eyes will he judge
    A` and not by hearing with his ears will he decide;
(4)   B`` but he has judged the poor with righteousness
    A`` and he has decided for the afflicted of the earth with equity
          D   and he has struck the earth with the scepter of his mouth,
          D` and with the breath of his lips he has slain the wicked.
(5)   E   And righteousness is the belt around his waist,
          E` and faithfulness the belt [around] his mid-section.[6]

In Isaiah, the promise of a Messiah-Servant first appears in 7:14 and becomes

---

individual (such as Cyrus), and the Davidic Messiah. In Isa 61, as in Isa 11:1-10 and 42:1-4, the Servant is an individual who represents Israel since the mission is directed to Israel, and the speaker's voice is singular—"upon me" (עלי, 42:1a). Jesus applies Isa 61:1-3 and 58:6 to himself in Luke 4:16-21, making the interpretation of a Servant-Messiah synthesis clear. Isaiah develops both the Servant and Messiah themes and combines them in Isa 61; the Servant-Messiah is the eschatological prophet-king who both proclaims and establishes the salvation depicted in Isaiah 58-61.

[5]Some of the recent literature on the Holy Spirit's role in the life of Jesus uses the phrase *Spirit Christology* as an alternative to what has been labeled *Logos Christology*. Logos Christology marks the divine element in Christ as the Son of God. Some using the phrase Spirit Christology deny that Jesus is identical with the eternal Logos, and affirm the Adoptionistic view that the man Jesus was adopted by God and empowered by the Spirit to function as the Messiah, as in G.W.H. Lampe, "The Holy Spirit and the person of Christ", in *Christ, Faith and History: Cambridge Studies in Christology*, ed. S. W. Sykes and J. P. Clayton (Cambridge: Cambridge University Press, 1972), 111-30. Others using the phrase Spirit Christology have no intentions of Adoptionism, but simply intend to count the empowering role of the Spirit to the Son of God in his human life. To avoid confusion, I prefer to use the phrase *pneumatological Christology* for the meaning that the divine messiah was fully God (the eternal Logos and Son of God) who received empowerment from the Holy Spirit according to his human nature.

[6]My translation for this passage follows the Hebrew text from the *Biblia Hebraica Stuttgartensia*, ed. K. Elliger and W. Rudolph, 5th rev. ed. (Stuttgart: German Bible Society, 1997). I have not provided the Hebrew text because of the formatting is chaotic.

clearer as the chapters unfold to depict the Messiah as a ruler and prince of peace in 9:1-7. The cause for hope in his rule appears in 11:1-10, where Isaiah writes that the Spirit of God will specially equip the Davidic descendant for his task to rule for God in righteousness and justice.[7] In each of the three pairs of the Holy Spirit's endowments of 11:2, the synthetic parallelism of the two terms constitutes one quality (a *hendiadys*). The results of these three endowments are the Servant's ruling actions of 11:3-5. The global effect of the Servant's ruling actions is the restoration of the world order, signified by the peaceful relationships among the wild and domestic animals (11:6-7), between animals and people (11:8), and, finally, peace among people in Jerusalem and throughout the world (11:9) that looks to the Messiah in his glory of a righteous reign (11:10). Our concern is specially the three-fold pneumatological endowment and results in the Servant's actions (11:2-5).

The first two pairs in 11:2 are gifts for two kingly tasks that are closely related: decision-making and judging. In the first pair, "wisdom" and "understanding" (A) are the Servant's endowments to enable his righteous decision-making in civil and military matters for the benefit of the people.[8] This decision-making task is reiterated in 11:3 (A`) and 11:4 (A``). In the second pair of 11:2, "counsel" and "strength" (B) are the king's equipment for his task as judge. The judicial task is reiterated by the descriptions of the Servant's judging actions in 11:3 (B`) and 11:4 (B``). Both tasks are pneumatological in the endowments and the unusual manner of the Servant's decision-making and judging according to a transcendent standard of righteousness and equity (11:4; B``, A``), not simply according to what he sees (11:3; B`) or by what he hears (11:3; A`). Therefore, the Servant's decisions and judgments are righteous and just because the Spirit who remains upon him specially bonds the Servant in relationship to God.[9]

The Holy Spirit's empowerment for ruling by uncommon wisdom and leadership was also the case for Saul (1 Sam 10:10) and David (1 Sam 16:13) when each had been chosen by God to be king. The Spirit equipped them to be leaders of the people for God. This divine empowerment was evident in David's life even before he came to the throne. People recognized the effect of the Spirit's presence in terms of his valor, prudence, and the general sense that God was with him in a special way (1 Sam 16:18). Similar examples of the

---

[7]Joseph Blenkinsopp, *Isaiah 1-39*, Anchor Bible, vol. 19 (New York: Doubleday, 2000), 265. "It seems that all the charismatic endowments listed converge on the tasks of the equitable administration of justice (3-5). That this was viewed throughout the Near East and beyond as the primary responsibility of the ruler is abundantly in evidence."

[8]Alec Motyer, *The Prophecy of Isaiah* (Downers Grove, IL: InterVarsity, 1993), 122. John D. W. Watts, *Isaiah 1-33*, Word Biblical Commentary, vol. 24 (Waco: Word, 1985), 172.

[9]I interpret Isa 11 as depicting Christ's earthly reign at his return (cf. Ps 2; Ps 110; Zech 14; Rom 11:26-27; 1 Cor 15:23-28; Rev 20:1-10), which is startling to consider that even his eschatological existence as the Godman is pneumatological.

Holy Spirit's empowerment for a governing role are Moses and Solomon.[10] In the case of the Messiah-Servant of Isaiah 11, the people can take assurance in this man's reliability and competency as God's eschatological king because of the pneumatological equipment that ground his righteous rule. (This would have been especially comforting in view of the failures of Israel's kings.)

The third pair of Spirit's endowments in 11:2 points to the religious-ethical life of the king (the formation of his character) who obeys God above all other considerations.[11] The third gift is the most important in the passage because, as Solomon and Saul proved by their sinful folly, without the ethical formation of conformity to God's heart, the king might still turn away despite his gifts of wisdom and strength. Structurally, this gift is emphasized at the chiastic center of the passage (11:2; C; 11:3; C`).[12] The king will serve Yahweh faithfully because of his firsthand, relational "knowledge" of Yahweh and his worldview as oriented by his reverential, religious "fear of Yahweh" (C) caused by the Holy Spirit. The two terms in the pair point to the single quality of the king's ethical formation to be the righteous servant able to accomplish the righteous rule and justice of God. The second term of his *fear* confirms that the *knowledge* is the relational, devotional, and personal knowledge-*of* God, which includes the objective and merely theological knowledge-*about* God. The Servant's action of doing justice is dependent upon his being as a man conformed to God's will.[13] Isaiah 11:4-5 elaborates the Servant's righteousness and faithfulness (E, E`) that are the ethical basis for his righteous action (D, D`). The shift to perfect tense (D, E, E`) expresses the completed action of these verbs as the surety of Yahweh's righteousness established on earth by his Spirit-endowed Servant.

Because of the presence of the Spirit to equip the Servant with the ethical

---

[10]Moses had several ruling functions as God's leader of the people: judging their disputes, ordering their lives with laws for every area of life, and commanding them in battle. When the Moses motif is taken up and applied to Jesus in the New Testament accounts and commentary, these additional functions must be included, even as Jesus' foretelling of his return shows generally that his primary function will be to rule (cf. 1 Cor 15:24-28; Rev 20:6). The Spirit's provision for Solomon is implicit in the statements that God gave him uncommon wisdom to rule the people for God (e.g., 1 Kgs 4:29-34; 5:12). However, unlike the Messiah, Solomon failed by plunging the nation into idolatry instead of leading them to faithfulness.

[11]In Old Testament perspective, religion and ethics are integrated so that devotion to God is obedience to him in all attitudes and action towards God, the world, and other people.

[12]I am aware that the middle part of a chiasm is not always structured that way for particular emphasis, and many times the first and last parts are most important. In this passage, however, I think the structure and ideas point to the same conclusion of an emphasis on the Messiah's life with God.

[13]Cf. Heb 10:5-7 applies this statement in Ps 40:7-8 to Jesus: "I have come . . . to do your will, O God".

formation necessary for righteous rule, the promised king would be conformed to God in obedience. This ethical quality is what Saul lacked in his regrettable reign by which he lost his kingship through repeated disobedience to God. By contrast, David's most notable distinction and singular greatness was his character formation to become a man who obeyed God: David was "a man after [God's] own heart" (1 Sam 13:14).[14] As David's descendant, the Servant-Messiah of Isaiah 11 exemplifies this godly character in a surpassing way because the Spirit of God causes this inward conformity to God's will.

Godliness in ethical action in faithfulness to God is the preeminent quality that Yahweh values in his king. This importance shows in the emphatic final position of this third pair of attributes in Isaiah 11:2.[15] In the Old Testament wisdom tradition, the *fear of Yahweh* is the precondition and basis for wisdom—the practical knowledge of how to successfully accomplish tasks and, most of all, to live well.[16] The importance of the Servant's character formation under the influence of the Spirit also shows in the context of Isaiah 11:1-10, which forms a chiasm that emphasizes Yahweh's righteousness and justice that the Servant has been equipped to bring about for Israel.[17]

The inward, ethical emphasis of the Spirit's work had become primary in the developing pneumatology as revelation progressed in the expanding canon of the Old Testament. John Oswalt comments on this trend in Isaiah 11:2: "To say that God's spirit was upon someone became almost a code phrase for saying that the person was acting out of a capacity which was more than merely human. This phrase came to be applied supremely to capacity for ethical behavior."[18] Oswalt notes Ezekiel 36:25-27 as proof of this trend, where the main effect of the indwelling Holy Spirit in the New Covenant is the new heart by which God's people will finally obey him.

Moreover, the centrality of the heart in God's assessment of human life and in the theological explanation for human action is an abundant biblical theme that integrates religious and ethical life in the single concept of obedience to God.[19] Accordingly, the Servant promised in Isaiah 11 will be a great king because of the Spirit of God who remains upon him for his ethical formation to be a man after God's own heart, as David had been—and in a way greater than David was. Because of God's Spirit remaining upon him, the Servant will be a

---

[14]Stephen's application of this passage to David in his speech in Acts 13:22 confirms the identification.

[15]The ethical dimension is the single condition of the covenant in the repeated promise of blessing should the king obey Yahweh's law (e.g., Ps 89:30-32). The priority of character transformation shows in the way that Solomon's wisdom without sufficient character development failed him as he turned to idolatry.

[16]E.g., Job 28:28; Ps 111:10; Prov 1:7; 9:10; 15:33.

[17]Watts, *Isaiah 1-33*, 171.

[18]John N. Oswalt, *The Book of Isaiah: 1-39*, New International Commentary on the Old Testament, vol. 20 (Grand Rapids: Eerdmans, 1986), 279.

[19]E.g., Gen 6:5; Prov 3:5-6 and 4:23.

man who knows and obeys Yahweh unswervingly, thus assuring the people that his righteousness and justice is grounded in a Spirit-endowed ethical life. In New Testament (partial) fulfillment of Isaiah 11, Jesus' purity (Luke 1:35b) and development in wisdom, stature, and favor with God and men (Luke 2:40, 52) are based on the pneumatological righteousness of Isaiah 11:1-4 and confirm the ethical orientation of the Spirit's role for the Messiah-king.[20]

Pneumatological Christology in Isaiah 42:1-9[21]

As with Isaiah 11, the Servant in 42:1-9 has the Spirit from Yahweh as an effective enablement for his ruling task of bringing justice to the nations, i.e., God's salvation. Isaiah 42:1 reiterates the Spirit's ethical role in the life of the Servant-Messiah to "uphold him" for the result that he will rule with right judgments. This idea of God's promise to work closely in the life of the Servant is repeated in 42:6 in the statements that God will take him by the hand and safeguard him to enable the fulfillment of the appointed purposes.

Also as in Isaiah 11, 42:1 connects the Servant with the Spirit of God in a relationship of endowment to accomplish God's justice by ruling the entire earth (vv. 1, 3, 4). Yahweh puts his Spirit on the Servant to enable him for the task of viceroyalty (cf. Gen 1:26). A Spirit-enabled reign of justice is the beneficial, renewing rule of God over the whole earth in a comprehensive salvation (e.g., release from blindness and imprisonment, v. 7). This description of the task further expands the judicial, administrative, and strategic aspects of kingdom rule that were emphasized in Isaiah 11.[22] The Servant's function is in continuity with other Isaianic references to an individual Servant (11:1-9; 16:5), making it clear that the Servant is an individual who represents Israel, not a collective Israel.[23] The statement of display in 42:1 ("Look!" or, "Behold!") indicates the commissioning of a divinely appointed ruler[24] (a point that is obvious even for scholars who discount this passage as a reference to Jesus[25]).

Matthew's application of Isaiah 42:1-9 to the life and ministry of Jesus (12:15-21) is important in at least three ways. First, Matthew confirms that

---

[20]Turner, *Holy Spirit*, 24. Cf. Sinclair B. Ferguson, *The Holy Spirit* (Downers Grove: InterVarsity, 1996), 43, "Luke 2:52 is the fulfillment and application of Isaiah 11:1-3a".

[21]The exegetical and lexical particulars are not so significant here (and in Isa 61:1-3) as in the other passages reviewed thus far. I am including these briefly because they emphasize and clarify the themes established in Isa 11:1-10.

[22]John N. Oswalt, *The Book of Isaiah: 40-66*, New International Commentary on the Old Testament, vol. 20 (Grand Rapids: Eerdmans, 1998), 108.

[23]Oswalt, *Isaiah: 40-66*, 110. Also, an individual is in view since Matthew refers this passage to Jesus in Matt 12:15-21.

[24]Oswalt, *Isaiah: 40-66*, 109.

[25]Joseph Blenkinsopp, *Isaiah 40-55*, Anchor Bible, vol. 19a (New York: Doubleday, 2000), 210, and John D. W. Watts, *Isaiah 34-66*, Word Biblical Commentary, vol. 25 (Waco: Word, 1987), 116-18, take Isa 42:1-9 as referring to Cyrus.

Jesus is the Servant in view (however ambiguous the text in Isaiah may seem). Second, Matthew reminds us to see the emphasis on the Servant's faithfulness (Isa 42:3b) as fulfilled in Christ's human obedience to God (Jesus is the faithful Son, cf. Matt 17:5). Additionally, the rest of the Isaiah passage not included by Matthew is characteristic of the Christ's comprehensive salvation that characterized his ministry: revelation of God and deliverance of sinners from bondage (Isa 42:6b-7, which seems to be the bondage that results from sin, cf. John 8:34; Rom 6:17). Third, Matthew's arrangement of his narrative places the quotation of Isaiah 42:1-3 just before a passage in which the people wonder if Jesus is the Messiah (Matt 12:23) and the Pharisees denounce him as an agent of Beelzebul (12:24). The response that Jesus gives fits with the use of Isaiah 42:1-3 because Jesus clearly identifies his ministry of healing (Matt 12:15) and exorcism (12:22, 28) with the empowerment of the Holy Spirit. The Spirit's role is so obvious that the Pharisees have committed an unforgivable sin to deny his presence in Christ's ministry. In terms of Isaiah 42 alone (and with Isa 11 in mind), we might think of the Spirit's empowerment of the messianic Servant for governing the world for God. We can see additionally that the Spirit enabled the works of Christ's first advent in his roles as prophet and priest (cf. Matt 12:28; Heb 9:14). Accordingly, the ethical orientation of Isaiah 42 (with the emphasis on faithfulness and the Servant's perseverance despite opposition, cf. 42:4) seems in view as well. There is a strong emphasis on the assuring providential care of God for the Servant,[26] and this close presence of God seems best as the ethical role of the Holy Spirit declared in 42:1.

Pneumatological Christology in Isaiah 61:1-3

The commissioning and endowment of the Servant-Messiah for a specific task of bringing God's comprehensive deliverance is repeated in Isaiah 61, adding a prophetic role to the continuing emphasis on a kingly role. In the near context of Isaiah 59:21, the endowment of the Messiah with God's Spirit and word for mediating salvation has been repeated (from Isa 11, 42). While continuing to sound the justice-governance theme from Isaiah 11 and 42 (cf. 61:8, 11), Isaiah 61 develops the salvation theme of release (from Isa 42:7). Isaiah 61 tells that *proclaiming* (a task repeated twice for emphasis in 61:1, 2) and *effecting release* are the two major emphases of the Messiah's work to bring the good news—he is the herald who brings God's restorative, renewing kingdom rule. This primary task of bringing the good news of salvation is elaborated by the clauses that follow: *to bind up, to proclaim, to comfort,* and *to grant salvation* with the result that the people will be transformed, an effect that points to the glory of God (v. 3).

Christ's application of these verses to himself in Luke 4:18-21 confirms what seems to be Isaiah's synthesis of the Messiah and the Servant of

---

[26]Motyer, *Isaiah*, 320.

Yahweh.[27] As the ministry of Jesus made clear, the prophet who heralds the kingdom reign is himself the good news because he makes actual the era of salvation that he proclaims.[28] When Jesus quotes Isaiah 61:1-2 in Nazareth (Luke 4:18-19), he further clarifies about this passage that *the year of favor* (emphasis on a long time, presently occurring in Christ's ministry) and *the day of vengeance* (a brief time) are separated into his two advents by which he comes first as Servant-savior and then returns as conqueror-ruler.[29] Confirmed by Christ's self-designation with this passage (and his ministry of words and deeds), Isaiah 61:1-3 depicts the Servant's task as a herald and bearer of the promised eschatological deliverance for which God has equipped him with the Holy Spirit.[30] Thus, this Spirit-equipped Servant brings the reign of God into the present evil age, displacing oppression with the eschatological release of God's righteous kingdom. This passage is important because of the way that the prophetic and kingly themes are brought together, and that Jesus defines himself in light of Isaiah 61:1-2. Integral to both the themes and Jesus' self-understanding of his ministry is the endowment of the Spirit for a role of empowerment and (if I have followed all the evidence correctly) ethical support for accomplishing a faithful life under God.

Conclusion

My aim has been to recall the messianic pneumatology of Isaiah, and demonstrate that within this picture there is a strong orientation of the Holy Spirit to an inward, ethical formation of the Messiah. I have not included Isaiah 50:4-5 because the explicit pneumatological aspect is absent. Nonetheless, this passage implies the similar details of Yahweh's empowerment of the Servant in ethical ways. In connection with the other evidence we have seen for the Spirit's role in the Messiah's life, it seems best to see the Servant's testimony to mean that because he has been equipped by God's Spirit, he can support the weary, he is awakened to learn and hear God's word, and he is consequently obedient instead of rebellious (Isa 50:4-5). Sinclair Ferguson makes a similar observation about the pneumatological and ethical orientation of Isaiah 11:1-3; 42:1 and 50:4-5 in his synthetic interpretation of these passages: "The convergence of these various strands of the Old Testament suggests that the

---

[27]Oswalt, *Isaiah 40-66*, 563; Motyer, *Isaiah*, 499.

[28]Oswalt, *Isaiah 40-66*, 564.

[29]Motyer, *Isaiah*, 500. But notice that these are primary emphases, not mutually exclusive roles since some conquest is apparent in the first advent as Jesus drives out many demons and authorizes his disciples to do so during his first advent. Similarly, when Jesus returns more recognizably as conqueror, he will also have a continuing servant role as the ruler, serving both humanity and God by his ministry of comprehensive justice.

[30]The context of Isaiah 59-66 is clearly eschatological.

ministry of the Spirit to Jesus during the 'hidden years' was intimately related to his understanding of God's word and his sensitivity and obedience to it as he came to recognize its significance for his own life."[31] Vos agrees that an inward, ethical orientation is in view here: "The Spirit furnishes the official equipment of the Messiah (Isa 11:2, 28:6, 42:1, 59:21), *in which the Spirit affects the Messiah's subjective religious life.*"[32]

We have seen that Isaiah tells of the Spirit's empowerment of the Servant both for his function as prophet, proclaiming the good news of God's release from bondage of many sorts, and for his role as the Davidic king, ruling the earth with God's justice. These functions are given together as the proclamation and establishment of God's renewing, life-giving rule, and the Spirit of Yahweh is prominently noted as the inward effective principle given to empower the Messiah to rule for God. We can infer from the testimony of Hebrews 9:14 that the Spirit's endowment also enables the Messiah to do the priestly work of propitiation told about in Isaiah 52:13-53:12, (a priest-sacrifice, cf. Mark 10:45; 15:33-39; 1 Pet 2:22-25).

When we consider this evidence in light of our topic and the New Testament accounts of Christ's temptations, we can see that the Holy Spirit's ethical role is important to guide and influence Christ's character development and resistance to sin as a man.[33] We should expect that the New Testament would elaborate the Old Testament evidence for the role of the Spirit in the Messiah's life.

New Testament Fulfillment of the Messiah

The New Testament is clear that the Holy Spirit was pervasively involved in the Messiah's life, particularly for his inward character formation to be the man who was tempted and yet remained sinless. Christ's birth, growth, and ministry are each associated with the special action of the Holy Spirit. We will limit the discussion to the ethical aspect of the Holy Spirit's involvement.

The Holy Spirit and Jesus' Conception, Birth, and Early Life

Matthew and Luke tell of the Spirit's role in the special births of Jesus and John the Baptizer, signaling by the flurry of Holy Spirit's activity surrounding these

---

[31] Ferguson, *Holy Spirit*, 44.
[32] Geerhardus Vos, *The Pauline Eschatology* (Grand Rapids: Eerdmans, 1953), 161. Emphasis added.
[33] Ferguson, *Holy Spirit*, 52. Ferguson comes to a similar conclusion: "The fact that Jesus was the Man of the Spirit is, therefore, not merely a theological categorization; it was a flesh-and-blood reality. What was produced in him was fully realized human holiness. He was the incarnation of the blessed life of the covenant and of the kingdom-beatitudes which are its fruit."

two births that the eschatological fulfillment of the promised salvation has begun.³⁴ The Holy Spirit is the creative agent that brings about the Son's entrance into human life by means of Mary's formless seed and void womb (recalling the Spirit's similar creative role in the formless and void world of Genesis 1:2).³⁵ Despite Christ's difference from John, Luke's comparison of the two boys' development suggests that the divine Son was not only brought into his incarnation by the Holy Spirit in purity, but also that he was accompanied by the Spirit from his conception onward in the same or a greater way than John was filled by the Spirit (Luke 1:15).³⁶ This *a fortiori* comparison of the two boys is apparent when Luke notes Jesus' development twice (2:40, 52) but mentions John's growth only once (1:80). Luke's note that Jesus was "filled with wisdom" and had "the grace of God upon him" (2:40) indicates the spiritual or religious-ethical growth in Jesus' awareness of God and an experience of God's presence with him in some sense. This recalls the wisdom, understanding, counsel, strength, knowledge and fear of Yahweh that are the Holy Spirit's gifts to the Servant in Isaiah 11:2.³⁷ Luke's use of a passive participle in 2:40 tells that Jesus was "being filled with wisdom" (πληρούμενον σοφίᾳ). This is likely an implied reference to the Holy Spirit who was continuously with Jesus (a divine passive).³⁸ Luke strongly implies the Spirit's involvement by adding, "and the grace of God was upon him". The two statements of wisdom and grace may indicate Jesus' growth in his understanding of God's will, spiritual growth along with his physical growth.³⁹ Thus, Luke 2:40 and 2:52 describe the fulfillment of the promise in Isaiah 11:1-2 that the Holy Spirit would form the ethical life of the Messiah and equip him for ministry.

---

³⁴Ferguson, *Holy Spirit*, 22. Zacharias, Mary, Elizabeth, and Simeon are all filled by the Spirit to prophesy about Jesus and John, besides the many angelic visitations and star in the night skies that drew the Magi.

³⁵Raymond E. Brown, *Birth of the Messiah: A Commentary on the Infancy Narratives in Matthew and Luke* (Garden City, NY: Doubleday, 1977), 314.

³⁶Gerald F. Hawthorne, *The Presence and the Power: The Significance of the Holy Spirit in the Life and Ministry of Jesus* (Dallas: Word, 1991), 89. "When Luke says that John the Baptist was filled with the Spirit before his birth, we should assume that this was true of Jesus also." This interpretation is consistent with the Isa 42:6b promise that Yahweh would hold the Servant's hand and watch over him.

³⁷Bock, *Luke 1:1-9:50*, 274. Bock thinks that reference to the grace of God indicates his moral growth. In view of Luke's emphasis on the Spirit in Luke-Acts, I take his intention in this passage to be reference to the Holy Spirit.

³⁸Commonly, a passive verb of unusual action not attributed to anyone is a depiction that should be attributed to God. See Hawthorne, *Presence and the Power*, 99. Hawthorne's interpretation of Luke 2:40-52 is that "God was even then in the process of graciously fitting Jesus out with those special powers requisite for the unique role he was to play in redemptive history" (101).

³⁹Bock, *Luke 1:1-9:50*, 254.

The relevance of this evidence for interpreting Christ's temptation and sinlessness should be clear. The Holy Spirit's role in the life of Jesus included upholding him in the midst of temptation so that he would choose right instead of wrong. If right, this means that Jesus struggled against temptation within the limits of his humanity, and he employed only the means of resistance that were available to him as a man. In this way he could truly experience temptation and become empathetic and an example for others. The key factor of the Spirit's role is that, in the New Covenant work of the Spirit the promised indwelling and empowerment is available to all believers. If the Spirit worked to form and develop Christ's character to be consistently obedient to God, then Christ's life in the Spirit forecasts the possibilities for Christians (for whom he is the template of life in the Spirit).

The Holy Spirit and Jesus' Baptism

At Christ's Jordan baptism the Holy Spirit descended to him in a visible way (Mark 1:10 and par.) to indicate that his entire ministry is under the influence of the Holy Spirit and in obedience to God the Father. The event is clearly eschatological since John the Baptizer recognizes Jesus as the Servant of Isaiah because of the Spirit that rests upon him (John 1:33).

One question is disputed as to whether the Spirit descends upon Jesus to empower him, to commission him, or merely to confirm for him and John that Jesus is the Messiah.[40] The occasion of the water baptism, a significant metaphor of spiritual purification, guides our interpretation of the event to connect the Spirit with the eschatological salvation of cleansing (Ezek 36:25-27). This is the same subject that John preached about in his call for a baptism of repentance and his prophecy of the Greater One who was to come and bring a greater baptism of true spiritual cleansing and renewal by means of the eschatological Spirit (Mark 1:7-8).[41] Moreover, in Luke's account, Simeon has already recognized Jesus as the Messiah (Luke 2:26-32), so the descent of the Spirit and the word of affirmation from heaven probably mean something else than that Jesus became the Anointed One at the Jordan. It seems that the Spirit and the voice signify an endorsement and confirmation of Jesus for his mission as the Messiah sent from heaven.[42] Also, we should see the anointing with the Spirit in continuity with others in Israel's history whom God empowered and

---

[40]Pentecostals who find evidence for a two-stage experience of the Holy Spirit (in which Spirit baptism comes subsequent to one's conversion and regeneration with the indwelling Spirit) typically count Jesus' Jordan baptism as his reception of the Spirit's empowerment for *ministry*, having already received the Spirit for *relationship* at his conception.

[41]Robert A. Guelich, *Mark 1-8:26*, Word Biblical Commentary, 34A (Dallas: Word, 1989), 25, 33.

[42]Bock, *Luke 1:1-9:50*, 344.

audibly commissioned to propel them in particular missions. This sign is especially important in Mark's account because he has no infancy narrative to establish Christ's relation to God as Matthew and Luke do.[43]

The significance for our topic is that the Holy Spirit is active in Christ's life in a variety of ways that were necessary to him in some sense. Because of his entrance into the limitations of a true humanity, he was in need for internal and external confirmations from God. The Spirit was not superfluous to him as a man, and especially for his life with God, formed with the character of obedience and delight in the fear of the Lord. The Spirit's role in confirming Christ's identity and marking him out at the Jordan baptism is also important to set Jesus up for being tempted in the wilderness by Satan.

The Holy Spirit and Jesus in the Wilderness

All three of the Synoptics tell that the next step after the Holy Spirit's descent and the voice from heaven is that the Spirit propelled Jesus into the wilderness (Mark 1:12 and par.). This agreement on the Spirit's initial role as a guide for Jesus should count as an additional clue for the interpretation of the Spirit's overall role from this point in Christ's life forward. Under the Spirit's direction, Jesus faces temptations by the devil in the wilderness by responding with Scripture. The Spirit's ethical role to test Jesus by subjecting him to temptation as preparation for his public ministry is implicit. Interpretations of the Spirit's role as limited to commissioning for official ministry or merely empowerment for preaching and miracles are inadequate in light of this emphasis on the Spirit's guidance by which he "propelled" Jesus into the wilderness (ἐκβάλλει, Mark 1:12) as part of a program to strengthen him through testing. And we should assume that Jesus experienced continual support from the Spirit, a man's dependence on God, which relationship seems to be the point of Luke's note that Jesus returned from the wilderness full of the Holy Spirit (Luke 4:1, an echo of being filled with wisdom in 2:40, 52).[44]

---

[43]Joseph A. Fitzmyer, *The Gospel According to Luke (I-IX)*, Anchor Bible, vol. 28 (Garden City, NY: Doubleday, 1981), 229.

[44]What I am calling pneumatological Christology has a minority of interpreters sharing the same view of the Spirit's presence with Jesus during his wilderness temptations. Cf. John Owen, *Discourse on the Holy Spirit*, ed. William H. Goold, vol. 3 of *The Works of John Owen* (London: Johnstone & Hunter, 1850-53; reprint, Edinburgh: Banner of Truth Trust, 1965), 174-75. "By [the Holy Spirit] was [Jesus] *guided, directed, comforted, supported*, in the whole course of his ministry, temptations, obedience, and sufferings. . . By his assistance was he carried triumphantly through the course of his temptations unto a perfect conquest of his adversary." Also, Hawthorne, *Presence and the Power*, 139, "Thus at the outset of his ministry Jesus is depicted as overcoming the evil one who stands in opposition to the work of the kingdom ([Luke] 11:19, 20) through the all-sufficient energizing power of the Spirit of God." Turner, *The Holy Spirit and Spiritual Gifts*, 29-30, "The final 'temptations' echo Israel's in the wilderness but, while they

The Holy Spirit and Jesus' Ministry

In Luke's account (4:16-21) Jesus defines his ministry and his relationship to the Spirit as the eschatological fulfillment of promises in Isaiah and elsewhere. Jesus confirms this relationship and his identity when he quotes parts of Isaiah 61:1-2 and 58:6 in the Nazareth synagogue. The point of the two Isaiah texts is to emphasize the fulfillment in Jesus and his mission of "proclaiming release" that would characterize his entire ministry ("release" is repeated by adding the phrase from Isa 58:6).[45] By choosing Isaiah 61:1-2 instead of 42:1 or 11:1-2, Jesus emphasizes the prophetic dimension of the Messiah's work, and mutes the more dominant king-over-the-earth role that is prominent in the other passages (along with the phrase, "day of God's vengeance", which Jesus stops short of mentioning). Jesus further marks his relation to the Spirit in his first advent as primarily a prophetic one by recalling the deeds of prophets Elijah and Elisha after he explains that he fulfills the Isaiah promise (Luke 4:24-27).[46] This does not mean that Jesus sees himself fulfilling only a prophetic role in his first advent because deliverance as the royal Messiah is as much his task as proclamation of the good news (just as Moses was a prophet, deliverer, and ruler).[47] Luke affirms this bi-vocational mission by hurrying to tell that after Nazareth rejected him with scorn, Jesus delivered a man from the harms of a demon in Capernaum, where even the demon recognized that Jesus was the Holy One of God (4:31-35), and all the people were amazed at Christ's unique authority (4:36-37). Clearly, Jesus both proclaims and brings the promised eschatological deliverance in the power of the Spirit.

'rebelled and grieved his Holy Spirit' there (Isa. 63:10), the new representative of Israel remains faithful and overcomes the tempter. Luke does not specify whether this is because the Spirit affords Jesus new depths of charismatic wisdom and insight, which is the basis of the hoped-for Messiah's redoubtable righteousness (*1 Enoch* 49:2-3; *Pss. Sol.* 17:37; 18:7; 1QSb 5.25; *Tg. Isa.*11:1-2, etc.), but such is probably to be inferred – for to what else could the redactional statement that he was led 'in the Spirit', *during* this period of temptations, otherwise reasonably refer?" Graham A. Cole, *He Who Gives Life: The Doctrine of the Holy Spirit* (Wheaton, IL: Crossway, 2007), 160, "In the power of the Spirit, Jesus is all that Israel should have been as God's son and all that Adam should have been as God's son. In other words, Jesus is the true Israel and the true Adam. Clearly the temptations are not only a Christological moment but also a pneumatological one."

[45]Joel B. Green, *The Gospel of Luke*, New International Commentary on the New Testament (Grand Rapids: Eerdmans, 1997), 209-10. Bock (*Luke*, 405) concludes that Jesus likely used both passages in the actual setting, even though a mixing of texts was unusual. On the other hand, we should not be concerned about a Lucan redaction here because this is his common practice according to the standards of his day to summarize speeches and provide their essence while adding emphasis through careful structural emendation. The entire account is brief with a dramatic tone.

[46]Fitzmyer, *Luke*, 530.

[47]Bock, *Luke*, 407.

One of the clearest passages that relates the Spirit's role to Christ's ministry is the exorcism in Matthew 12:28 (cf. Luke 11:20). Jesus attributes his power to the Holy Spirit, and in Matthew's account this immediately follows the quote of Isaiah 42:1-4 to show messianic fulfillment (Matt 12:9-21), emphasizing that the Spirit is associated with Christ's work of proclaiming release from sin's bondage.[48] Less clear is the meaning of the Spirit's involvement in the exorcisms: was it merely empowerment of the prophet or a sign of Christ's ministry as the arrival of God's kingdom deliverance, or was it both?[49] As with the Spirit's descent at the Jordan baptism, the Spirit's association with Jesus in exorcism marks him as the Messiah because the Synoptics emphasize the deeds themselves more than the Holy Spirit as the source of them (John drops out the pneumatological aspect completely to show Christ's oneness with the Father instead).[50] Thus, the Spirit's empowerment has an identifying function to clarify Christ's works as messianic fulfillment and as telltale pointers to his mission in light of Isaiah's prophecy.[51]

An interpreter who participated in the ministry of Jesus is Peter (as presented by Luke), who explains Jesus' action throughout his ministry with a pneumatological emphasis. Peter's summary of Christ's ministry (Acts 10:38) connects the Holy Spirit with the entire range of Jesus' work in power, from his "doing good" to his "healing all who were oppressed by the devil", adding the explanation, "for God was with him". Along with empowerment, the ethical orientation of the Spirit's role seems to be in view here since the last phrase of

---

[48]Donald A. Hagner, *Matthew 1-13*, Word Biblical Commentary, vol. 33a (Dallas: Word, 1993), 343. Luke's disagreement with Matthew is difficult since it is unlikely that Luke would have changed a Q reading of "by the Spirit" to "by the finger of God" purely to support his prophet-like-Moses motif. More likely is that the original was "finger" that Matthew changed to fit Jesus' fulfillment of Isaiah 42.

[49]Daniel J. Harrington, *The Gospel of Matthew*, Sacra Pagina Series, vol. 1 (Collegeville, MN: Liturgical, 1991), 187.

[50]Gary M. Burge, *The Anointed Community: The Holy Spirit in the Johannine Tradition* (Grand Rapids: Eerdmans, 1987), 99. "We noticed in our examination of Jesus' works of power that the Johannine Christ is not a pneumatic. His miracles are revelatory and make glory evident rather than power. Thus they are christological in that they express who Jesus is instead of what he bears. In addition this Johannine theme serves a oneness christology in which we can say that the works of power do not reveal the power of the Spirit but the presence of the Father. . . . It appears that the role of the Spirit is somewhat preempted by the presence of the Father in Johannine christology."

[51]Burge, *Anointed Community*, 67, explains, "Exorcisms and miracles did not conclusively prove that Jesus bore the Spirit. They were portals through which the presence of the Spirit might be viewed. They pointed to who Jesus was and demanded a response from the view in the light of this revelation." The pneumatological factor in the exorcisms is also John Owen's interpretation of the exorcisms (*Holy Spirit*, in *Works* 3:174): "It was in an especial manner by the power of the Holy Spirit he wrought those great and *miraculous works* whereby his ministry was attested unto and confirmed."

Acts 10:38 is a Septuagintal idiom for God's guidance and protection.[52] Also significant in this passage is the connection between the Spirit and power, which Hawthorne counts throughout the many occurrences in the Synoptics as an implicit reference to the Spirit.[53] But it is important to count the evidence in Luke-Acts for power as based upon Christ's own authority and person, and not by the Holy Spirit alone (Luke 4:36; 5:12, 17; 6:19; 8:46; 9:1; 10:19; Acts 3:12, 16; 4:7).[54] It is difficult to say which is primary, the Spirit's empowerment of Jesus, or the Spirit's signification of Jesus as the Messiah, showing that God is with him, since these are as two sides of a single coin.

Nonetheless, my goal in this section has been to recall the inward, ethical orientation of the Spirit's role in Jesus, and particularly in his experiences of temptation. There is less evidence in this last section than in others, but the picture is consistent of a pneumatological-Christology in which the Holy Spirit is pervasively involved in Christ's life. Evidence seems clear for the outward deeds by the empowerment of the Spirit, and contributes to the overall picture of Jesus' need for the Spirit for guidance and living a godly life. Of chief importance for this study is the inward, ethical orientation and support during temptation as a possible explanation for how Jesus resisted temptation and achieved sinlessness within the limits of his humanity (as an example for others).

Conclusion to the Biblical Evidence

The Old Testament and New Testament evidence for the role of the Holy Spirit in the Messiah's life are fully harmonious and mutually illuminating as the promise and initial fulfillment.[55] Isaiah 11:1-5 shows that the Holy Spirit is an empowering associate of the Servant-Messiah for both his roles as prophet and king.[56] The ethical-religious aspect of the Servant's gifts from the Holy Spirit

---

[52]Luke Timothy Johnson, *The Acts of the Apostles*, Sacra Pagina Series, vol. 5 (Collegeville, MN: Liturgical, 1992), 193. He notes these examples: Gen 21:20, 22; 39:2; Exod 3:12; Isa 58:11. (The Septuagint is the Greek translation of the Old Testament that was favored by the early church.)

[53]Hawthorne, *Presence and the Power*, 154-55. He also argues that *authority* is an implicit reference to the Spirit (156-60), making a reference to the Spirit either explicit or implicit on nearly every page of the Gospels.

[54]Bock, *Luke*, 344.

[55]I am aware that some details of this interpretation of promise and fulfillment in the already-not yet scheme are disputed. Some interpreters do not see Old Testament promises of an actual messianic kingdom on the earth that is distinct from the progress of the gospel in the present ministry of the Church.

[56]The two vocations here are additional to the third role as priest (Mark 10:45; Heb 9:14); however, this priestly role was not clear in the Isaianic passages that connect the Spirit with the Servant's work. Moreover, the priestly vocation is certainly implicit in light of Jesus' ministry and the testimony of Hebrews that he offered himself *through*

indicates an important role that corresponds to Jesus' sinlessness despite his many temptations. Gospel evidence for the ethical aspect of the Holy Spirit's involvement with Jesus is important data for Christ's moral life that fulfills the Old Testament promises with his concrete experiences of temptation and righteous action.

I have rehearsed the biblical evidence for Christ's temptation, sinlessness, and the relevance of each for salvation. Most interpreters agree that, based on this evidence, Jesus experienced temptations in the context of his earthly human life, within his human limitations, and especially those that were reported during the years of his ministry. My argument from this evidence will be to say further that Jesus struggled against temptations in a way that made him credibly compassionate towards others who experience the same basic sorts of struggles. His main difference from others is that he never sinned in all his temptations (not to deny his original sinlessness, just to discount this as the main difference).

Furthermore, the biblical evidence warrants the traditional theological inference that Christ did not have original sin (because the Holy Spirit specially wrought the Son's incarnation in a sinless human nature).[57] As the result, Jesus is *holy* from the moment of conception by the Holy Spirit (Luke 1:35), and yet he battled temptations within his human limitations and vulnerabilities to emerge sinless from each conflict. His sinlessness is relevant to his efficacy as the perfect priest who can completely deal with the sins of the people. Despite his difference of being sinless, Scripture commends Christ to others as the pattern to copy in resisting temptation to sin. Scripture is also clear that Jesus himself offers help for people to imitate his pattern of obedience.

Finally, Scripture tells of an ethical aspect of the Holy Spirit's role in Christ's life. This role is announced in the Old Testament promises as the equipment of the eschatological king who establishes divine righteousness and salvation. This role is concretely fulfilled in the conception, development, and adult life of Jesus even before he comes to his throne.

Scripture does not resolve the difficulties that arise when theologians affirm the conclusions of Christ's temptation and sinlessness together with the conclusions that he is fully God and fully man. One difficulty is that, being divinely impeccable and (as God) unable to be tempted, Christ's experience of true temptation to sin seems impossible. But he could not have faked the

---

the eternal Spirit. Lane, *Hebrews 9-13*, 240, agrees that because this section in Hebrews alludes to Isaiah, the unique reference to the Spirit in connection with Jesus' self-sacrifice is a reference to the Holy Spirit and his sustaining empowerment in the deed.

[57]Oliver D. Crisp, "Shedd*ing* the theanthropic person of Christ", *Scottish Journal of Theology* 59 (2006): 348-49, suggests that God created Christ's human soul out of nothing, having derived from Mary only the "raw materials" for Christ's human body, for the result of a sinless human nature. The traditional idea is that the Holy Spirit sanctified Christ's human nature as part of preparing it for incarnation in sinlessness.

temptations because such deception would have been impossible for him. Moreover, if he had merely pretended to wrestle against temptations that were otherwise unreal for him, then the relevance of his experiences would be lost. He could be neither a compassionate priest nor an example from his having struggled within a human frame of life as others do. His relevance depends upon the authenticity of his temptations. Any satisfactory model of Christ's impeccability and temptation must reconcile his full divinity with the authenticity of his temptations to sin.

Another difficulty is that, being divinely unable to do otherwise than good, Christ's example for resisting temptation to sin seems diminished. Divine impeccability (or, necessary goodness) seems to make Jesus no more realistic of a pattern to copy than God himself, the eternal, transcendent Creator. Of course, God is an example to be emulated by his people as the *moral ideal* (e.g., Matt 5:48; Eph 5:1), but the special relevance of Christ's example in sinlessness is that in him people have a *peer ideal* with a human scale of life to copy.[58] Christ is God come-alongside-us to show us human life in a godly mode. In Christ, God has fully and humbly demonstrated the possibility and pattern of an obedient life in the midst of suffering and temptation to sin.

I have passed over the biblical data for Christ's full divinity and humanity by assuming the interpretation of Scripture as reached by the orthodox tradition. The claim for his full humanity is implicit in the evidence we have seen for his temptation, sinlessness, and the relevance of each. The claim for his full deity must be kept in mind among the conclusions from the biblical evidence because this is what causes difficulties of his praiseworthiness, ability to be an example for humans, and the compatibility of his impeccability with true temptations. All this evidence must remain in mind as we turn to consider the theological models of Christ's impeccability and temptation.

---

[58]Richard Sturch, *The Word and the Christ: An Essay in Analytic Christology* (New York: Oxford, 1991), 188-90.

THEOLOGICAL MODELS

CHAPTER 4

Patristic Models (Part 1)

In this chapter, I argue that patristic theologians formulated several discernible models of Christ's impeccability and temptation as part of the larger task of Christological reflection. I will expound the main contributions without chronicling the historical developments of doctrine. This is not the place for a critique of patristic Christological models or the conciliar judgments of what constitutes heresy and orthodoxy about Christ. Instead, my goal is simply to uncover the main models of Christ's impeccability and temptation that will inform a contemporary statement of the doctrines.[1] If right, the summary of these models will show the progress of patristic model construction towards greater clarity and theological adequacy.

The historical evidence suggests four main models of explaining Christ's impeccability and temptation.[2] I have given them brief descriptive labels and numbers as follows: M1, Sinless by Inherent Impeccability, M2, Sinless by Deification, M3, Sinless by the Divine Hegemony, and M4, Sinless by Empowering Grace. Both orthodox and unorthodox formulations are included so that we may learn from these varied attempts to explain the biblical data (despite their problems).[3] We will consider each model's main features,

---

[1] Some theologians of dubious reputation such as Apollinaris, Origen, Nestorius, and others are included because of their attention to this specific issue of impeccability and temptation, but others such as Paul of Samosata, Arius, and Pelagius are so problematic that they are unhelpful and thus excluded (e.g., diminishing the deity of Christ and the force of sin).

[2] I am adopting a models approach to the theological evidence. The purpose is to discern the best explanation of the theological teaching of Scripture through sorting and evaluating the different ways that theologians have approached particular topics. After describing a distinct approach or set of explanations on a topic, we can evaluate strengths and weaknesses of the model, and test how well it fits the biblical revelation. A models approach aims to make explicit the distinct perspectives in the theological tradition and invites readers to get beyond their own perspective to see other approaches. Two examples are the books by Avery Dulles, *Models of the Church: A Critical Assessment of the Church in all its aspects* (New York: Doubleday, 1974), and *Models of Revelation* (New York: Doubleday, 1983).

[3] While not exhaustive of all the patristic writers and all their writings, this study is an attempt to cover thoroughly the breadth of theology for the period. Based on what I have examined, it does not seem that extending the study in depth and breadth further would

representatives, and an evaluation. First, however, we must review the relevant features of the background of patristic theology.

Background to the Patristic Models

Some difficulties should be kept in mind when considering patristic theology. First, theologians often do not treat the topics of Christ's impeccability and temptation thoroughly or systematically. More often the case is that writers allude to a model as part of discussing a biblical text or a theological topic that is more pressing, such as the coherence of divine impassibility and Christ's suffering. We must rely on hints and suggestions of the models as these things show up in the patristic discussions of biblical texts, the incarnational union, salvation, and refutations of what were perceived to be heretical Christological formulations.

Second, in their comments that are relevant to our topic, patristic theologians are not always consistent. They can be read to support more than one model, and even read in ways that seem contradictory. An example of this ambiguity was at the Sixth Ecumenical Council (Constantinople III, 681-82), which was called to resolve the dispute about whether there is one will and active energy in Christ, or two wills. Proponents of the one will view (Monothelitism) appealed to passages from writings of the early fathers for authoritative support of their own position.[4] Proponents of the two will view (Dyothelitism) appealed to many of these same passages. Some of the problem in the debate of the Sixth Council was anachronism because disputants had to impose the question of Christ's will upon the writings of early centuries when this issue was not a concern. Similarly, the matter of Christ's impeccability was a question taken up with more precision in later times than in the early centuries.[5]

Nonetheless, it should not count against the accuracy of our study if it seems

---

yield more models than what I have reported here. As will show in the notes, I am indebted to Aloys Grillmeier (and his collaborators) for providing the leads to a great many of the relevant patristic sources.

[4]Jaroslav Pelikan, *The Spirit of Eastern Christendom (700-1700)*, vol. 2 of *The Christian Tradition: A History of the Development of Doctrine* (Chicago: University of Chicago Press, 1974), 69. The monothelites brought three volumes of quotations in support of their view. Both sides accused the others of quoting out of context and rewriting texts to suit their claims better.

[5]Pannenberg, *Jesus*, 355-59, notes that the sinlessness of Jesus appears "in the Eastern declaration to the Nicene Creed", in Cyril's tenth anathema (Ephesus, 431) and in the Chalcedonian definition (451), but that a conclusion on Christ's impeccability did not appear in a conciliar confession until 553 (Constantinople II). Pannenberg seems to have in mind the charge against Theodore of Mopsuestia that he taught Christ was impeccable after the resurrection. Also, it has been noted by Galot, *Who is Christ?*, 384, that the impeccability of Christ was explicitly affirmed by the Council of Florence (1431) in the statement that Jesus was conceived without sin, and remained so from birth to death.

that some patristic writers can be read in support of more than one model of Christ's impeccability and temptation. Instead, we find that some representatives supply material to more than one model because they are attempting more than one way to explain the biblical data. Two examples of trying for more than one model are Origen and Augustine (see below). This is not to say that these theologians are inconsistent, or that they changed their views over time (though they may have, as Nestorius seems to have done). By including one or another theologian as a representative of a model is also not to say that he totally disagrees with the other models and does not support them in any sense as truthful (but in some cases there was clear and mutual disagreement, as in the fifth century dispute between Cyril of Alexandria and Nestorius). Despite these difficulties, the early models were clear enough to provide starting points for theologians in later periods (as we shall see, below).

Third, another difficulty is that while the writings of the orthodox are preserved relatively well, others who innovated in ways that may be helpful for our study have not been retained with the same care, if at all. Indeed, the writings of so-called heretics such as Nestorius, Theodore of Mopsuestia, Theodoret, and Apollinaris survive only minimally. Often what remains are only the fragmentary citations of their writing in the works of their opponents as memorials of error, remembered only so that readers may be warned against these mistakes.

Fourth, it will be apparent that the models are similar to one another because all contributors accept the three key factors: Christ's actual sinlessness, his true temptations, and his divine impeccability. The different models are formulated because theologians dispute how these three factors should be related to one another, to other factors of soteriology, and to relevant details of Christology.

Finally, the four models are not mutually exclusive of each other. Some models have significant agreement because of presuppositions that are common to all contributors, such as these four: the Nicene faith, the soteriological requirements that link Christ's person with his work, the response to heretical proposals (e.g., Arianism, Apollinarianism), and the assumptions of patristic philosophical theology that developed in its Hellenistic setting.[6] We will review each of these presuppositions briefly as part of orienting our understanding to the patristic theology that so fruitfully produced four models of Christ's impeccability and temptation. We should keep in mind that what proceeds is not a history of the doctrines but a models approach to excavate and evaluate the main attempts to work out explanations of the theological teaching of Scripture on these topics.

---

[6]E.g., the stock theories of physical union supplied by Stoic philosophers and Aristotle, and a particular view of divine impassibility (see below).

Common Presuppositions

THE NICENE FAITH

The models developed in the patristic period presuppose the Nicene faith from the creed that Christ is *homoousios* (same nature) with God the Father.[7] This foundational Christological and trinitarian idea entails Jesus' preexistence as the divine Son and a monotheistic view of God as triune Father, Son, and Holy Spirit. This claim was defended against the Arian proposal that denied the full deity of Christ by saying the Logos is merely a glorious creature. For the orthodox, Christ's preexistence and divine nature are commonly noted as the *divine spirit*, often used as a way of protecting the monotheistic concept of God alongside affirming the deity of Christ. An early example of this method of predicating Christ with deity in a nuanced formula is the way Clement of Alexandria calls Jesus the "spirit incarnate" (πνεῦμα σαρχούμενον) and he does not mean the Holy Spirit.[8] Similarly, Hilary of Poitiers used the terms *spirit* and *power* as synonyms for the divine substance shared by the Son and the Father, and for the divine nature in Christ.[9] Accordingly, patristic agreement on this idea about Christ (which was formally declared at the Council of Nicaea I, 325) accounts for some of the similarity of the models of his impeccability and temptation. Indeed, it is because of this basic claim of Nicene faith that nearly all agreed that Jesus was impeccable. Since God is impeccable, and Jesus is fully God, then Jesus must be impeccable also.

SOTERIOLOGICAL REQUIREMENTS

All orthodox contributors to the models agree that Jesus had to be fully God and fully man to save humanity because these theological ideas are apparent in the biblical revelation. This idea is connected with the Nicene faith that it must be right to confess Jesus as fully God (not a creature, as the Arians proposed) since only God can save us. Soteriological and Christological concerns are seen to be mutually determinative, and especially so during this period.[10] For example, when Apollinaris countered Arian Christology by saying the Logos took the place of a human soul in Christ, the orthodox reacted by clarifying that

---

[7]Frances M. Young, "Christological Ideas in the Greek Commentaries on the Epistle to the Hebrews", *Journal of Theological Studies*, n.s., 20 (1969): 151.
[8]Clement of Alexandria *Paedagogus* 1.6.43.3, ed. M. Marcovich, Supplements to Vigiliae Christianae, 61 (Leiden: Brill, 2002), 28.
[9]Paul C. Burns, "The Christology in Hilary of Poitiers' Commentary on Matthew" (BLitt thesis, Oxford University, 1977), 74-75. "Spiritus, as the divine element in Christ, is often seen as the source of divine power and operation in Christ." Burns gives as examples Hilary's comments on the blasphemy of the Spirit in Matt 12:31, where in each case Hilary explains that the insult is against the divine nature, not the person of the Holy Spirit.
[10]Young, "Christological Ideas", 162. "The formulation of both Trinitarian and Christological definitions was directly caused by soteriological beliefs."

Christ's full humanity, alongside his deity, must not be denied (because salvation depends on his humanity as well as his deity).[11] Since many in the early centuries of the patristic period understand salvation as healing or deification,[12] they agreed that Christ had to be fully God if he was to raise humanity in its deification (through union to the divine nature in him). The often repeated axiom of Gregory Nazianzen, "The unassumed is the *unhealed*" (ἀθεράπευτον),[13] expresses this common idea that the salvation of humanity requires God's taking up of all that humanity is (to heal it).[14] Salvation, as the orthodox understood it, was something that only God could do, so Jesus had to be fully God (he had to have power over death and the devil, Heb 2:14; 1 John 3:8). Moreover, Jesus also had to be a man, not only for the deification of humanity but because of the biblical witness to his priestly sacrifice and sympathetic intercession (Heb 2:17-18), the example of his godly life (1 Pet 2:21), and his role as the second Adam overturning the first Adam's sin (Rom 5:19). Many patristic teachers recognized that Christ's weaknesses, temptations, and death were signs of his full humanity (e.g., Matt 4:2; Heb 4:15, 1 Cor 15:3) and necessary to his work of saving us. Thus, because of this common patristic emphasis on the basic soteriological requirements (deification, healing, giving an example, etc.), the explanations of Christ's impeccability and temptation tend to come out in similar ways (despite important differences).

OPPOSITION TO HERESIES

Orthodox theologians agree with one another in their opposition to the heretical formulations of Gnostics, the Arians, and individuals such as Apollinaris. The polemical stance is evident in the titles of many theological writings, e.g.,

---

[11] Maurice Wiles, *The Making of Christian Doctrine* (Cambridge: Cambridge University Press, 1967), 106. "On the one hand was the conviction that the saviour must be fully divine; on the other was the conviction that what is not assumed is not healed. Or, to put the matter in other words, the source of salvation must be God; the locus of salvation must be man."

[12] Those who are associated with the exegetical methods of Antioch (e.g., Diodore of Tarsus, Theodore of Mopsuestia, Nestorius) are generally an exception to this view, as noted by Joanne McWilliam Dewart, *The Theology of Theodore of Mopsuestia* (Washington, DC: The Catholic University of America Press, 1971), 149.

[13] Gregory Nazianzen *Epistle* 101.7, *ad Cledonium* Patrologia Graeca (Paris: J. –P. Migne, 1837) 37:181. Hereafter, volumes will be listed as PG.

[14] Anthony Meredith, *The Cappadocians* (Crestwood, NY: St Vladimir's Seminary Press, 1995), 113, notes that the Hellenistic setting was likely influential in the theological development of this concept of salvation as healing in conjunction with biblical evidence that suggests the concept (Isa 53:5; Matt 13:15; 1 Pet 2:24; Heb 12:13). Meredith cites examples of Origen, *On Jeremiah* 1.16, *Against Celsus* 4.72, *On First Principles* 2.10.4-6, and Gregory of Nyssa, *Catechetical Oration* 8 and 26 as having taken over the idea of salvation as healing from Plato *Gorgias* 477A, 480C.

Against the Arians, *Against Marcion*, *Against Heresies*, and *Against Celsus*.[15] The doctrines of Christology were forged partly by means of the fires of these challenges as theologians answered them from the biblical evidence for Christ's deity by his miracles, preexistence, and soteriological efficacy. For example, how were they to answer the problem that Arius raised about the possibility of suffering and change for the Logos incarnate (having united to a mutable human nature)? The challenge called for a response and defense of the truth. The difficulty in countering these heresies shows in the way that Gregory of Nazianzen equivocated when he interpreted John 11:33, arguing one way against the Arians, and then replying differently (using the Arian interpretation of John 11:33) to refute the Apollinarians.[16] Heresy evoked the formation of polemical Christology, and nearly everyone took up the fight to resist the same heretical proposals.

For his part, Apollinaris constructed his Christological model specifically in opposition to the problem raised by Arians of the mutability of the Logos in the Incarnation, which entailed the possibility of sin (if Jesus possessed a human mind and will, he was susceptible to sin).[17] Apollinaris's solution was to eclipse the human soul in Christ. Consequently, this formulation provoked other theologians to defend the biblical evidence for Christ's full humanity. Scripture and theology require that Christ's humanity must include a rational human soul, a human will, and the full susceptibility to weaknesses of hunger, suffering, incomplete knowledge, and death.

Fear of the heretical formulations like these thus drove all the orthodox in a common direction (despite all their differences), sometimes leaving behind a few ideas that have since been reconsidered. One example of a discarded idea is the widespread fear of Adoptionism (Jesus was a mere man adopted by God and empowered by the Spirit). This fear was provoked by the proposals of Paul of Samosata, Arius, and others who argued that Jesus experienced progressive empowerment from God, not that he was essentially and eternally divine. By this fear of adoptionism, most theologians were resistant to *pneumatological Christology*, a formulation that emphasizes the empowering role of the Holy Spirit in Christ's life and ministry (cf. Acts 10:38). An example of the resistance to pneumatological Christology shows in Cyril of Alexandria's ninth anathema, which is included in the documents of Third Council (Ephesus, 431):

---

[15]The authors of these writings in order are Athanasius, Tertullian, Irenaeus, and Origen.

[16]Donald F. Winslow, "Christology and Exegesis in the Cappadocians", *Church History* 40 (1971): 391-92. Winslow notes the example of John 11:33 as one among many where Gregory of Nazianzen accuses the Apollinarians of construing Jesus' question about where Lazarus was laid as a marker of Jesus' humanity (*Epistle* 102), then Gregory uses the passage to argue for divine and human levels to Jesus' action (*Oratio* 29.20).

[17]Kelley McCarthy Spoerl, "Apollinarius and the Response to Early Arian Christology", in Studia patristica 26, ed. Elizabeth A. Livingstone (Leuven: Peeters, 1993), 421.

If any man shall say that the one Lord Jesus Christ was glorified by the Holy Ghost, so that he used through him a power not his own and from him received power against unclean spirits and power to work miracles before men and shall not rather confess that it was his own Spirit through which he worked these divine signs; let him be anathema.[18]

Aloys Grillmeier notes that Cyril's view (motivated by fear of pneumatological Christology) was the norm:

> Cyril of Alexandria was not successful in allocating a sufficient function to the Spirit in the interpretation of the baptism of Christ. Dread of the Arian position hindered him from doing this. Because the divine Logos is present in Christ by nature, Cyril's Christ does not need the grace of the Spirit for himself. He receives it only for us.[19]

The limited evidence for the person of the Holy Spirit in Scripture, and the dangers of heretical formulations of dynamistic Adoptionism repulsed most theologians from considering a real role of the Holy Spirit in Christ. The opposition to reckoning the Holy Spirit's person and activity was so sharp that a conciliar creed was necessary at the Second Council (Constantinople I, 381), to affirm the Holy Spirit's place within the Godhead (as developed in reaction by Gregory of Nazianzen to those called the "Spirit-fighters"). Similar opposition to development of doctrines related to the Holy Spirit occurred in the East, as Maurice Wiles observes:

> Cyril of Jerusalem declared in his Catechetical Lectures delivered about A.D. 350 that it is enough to acknowledge the identity of the gifts of the Father and of the Holy Spirit, but that the nature and the substance of that Holy Spirit are not proper subjects of inquiry. Ten years later the attention of Athanasius was called to a group of Egyptian Christians who, while accepting the full divinity of the Son, spoke disparagingly of the Spirit as a creature; as a result of their errors he found himself forced to launch out on just such an inquiry into the nature of the Spirit as Cyril had discouraged, even though he had no clear terminology in which to discuss his subject-matter with any measure of precision. But the Tropici, as this Egyptian group were named by Athanasius, were not alone. There were others all over the Eastern world who followed a similar line of thought. They readily

---

[18]Cyril of Alexandria *Apologeticus Contra Theodoretum Pro XII Capitibus* 9 (ed. J. Auberti, PG 76 [1859]: 429C, trans. Henry Percival, NPNF², 14: 214-15. The spectre of Montanism as a community encouraging private revelations by the Spirit also discouraged pneumatological formulations of a dynamic work of the Spirit in Christ.

[19]Aloys Grillmeier, in collaboration with Theresia Hainthaler, *Christ in Christian Tradition*, trans. John Cawte and Pauline Allen (Louisville: Westminster John Knox, 1995), 2.2:303.

acknowledged the Son's divinity but, with varying degrees of definiteness, rejected any suggestion of the Spirit's godhead.[20]

Thus, the shadows of Arius and other heretics haunted theologians to form common presuppositions in opposition to the lurking dangers of pneumatological Christology. The influence of these ideas on explaining Christ's impeccability and temptation was expressed in a pervasive exclusion of the role of the Holy Spirit in Christ, and a united resistance to any claims to that effect (such as by Theodore of Mopsuestia and Nestorius).

THE HELLENISTIC PHILOSOPHICAL SETTING

The philosophical setting of the Hellenistic world provided influential norms for patristic theologians together with their allegiance to the teaching of Scripture.[21] Among these norms are the negative views of *passibility* (to be caught and affected by emotion and suffering) and *ignorance* because, for philosophers of the day, these traits seemed to entail sin of some sort. If they entail sin, then they are improper for God. If these traits are improper for God, then they cannot be true of God incarnate.

Divine Impassibility

Hellenistic philosophers had an entirely dim view of emotions as being opposed to reason and right action. Stoic philosophers identified passions as diseases of the soul. This generally accepted philosophical conception was begun by Plato and developed by the Stoics: the soul is a two-level house with emotion dwelling below (an unfortunate concomitant of embodiment) and reason residing above. As the supreme Mind, God is "above joy and sorrow".[22] Right reason must rule the passions. For example, Plutarch classes grief and passion as detestable sins in company with fear and lust, and Philo associates grief with punishment for sin and an indication of guilt.[23]

Consequently, the theology that develops in this setting is that God must be devoid of emotions and suffering, eternally undisturbed in the ideal of divine impassibility.[24] Christian theologians affirmed the same, as in Nestorius's

---

[20]Wiles, Making of Christian Doctrine, 32.
[21]Young, "Christological Ideas", 160-61. "As we have frequently noted, Nicene orthodoxy as it was understood within the framework of contemporary philosophical theology made the Christological problem essentially insoluble."
[22]Abraham J. Heschel, The Prophets, 2 vol. in 1 (Peabody, Mass: Prince, 2000), 2:31.
[23]Cited in Jerome H. Neyrey, "The Absence of Jesus' Emotions–the Lucan Redaction of Lk 22,39-46", Biblica 61 (1980): 155-56. Neyrey notes Diogenes Laertius and Cicero as other examples of impassibility in Stoic philosophy.
[24]T. E. Pollard, "The Impassibility of God", Scottish Journal of Theology 8 (1955): 353-64, argues that the Greek idea of divine impassibility is one of several dubious gifts to Christian theology. Kevin Vanhoozer, First Theology (Downers Grove, IL: InterVarsity, 2002), 74, observes the effect of Stoic views of impassibility on Christian theology:

statement: "the Godhead is not susceptible to passion".[25] To affirm that God is susceptible to passion would mean he is "susceptible to modification or alteration as the result of the operation of an alien, external agency",[26] which, of course, contradicts the biblical picture of God's sovereignty, transcendence, and immutability. Thus, it must be that God is impassible.

The problem for Christian theologians is that their affirmation of divine impassibility is difficult to reconcile with the suffering of Jesus, as reported in the New Testament. An example of the difficulty is Origen's commentary on Matthew, where he explains away the evidence of Christ's emotions of anguish in Gethsemane.[27] Origen introduces a distinction between being vulnerable to the anguish and actually experiencing it. The state of initial vulnerability to passion, the *pre-passion state* (προπάθεια), is as if one is on the doorstep of the intense emotional experience. This vulnerable state was distinguished from *passion* (πάθος) as the state experienced after the soul becomes imbalanced and caught by the full emotion of anguished fear. Passion was thought to lead necessarily to being susceptible to sin, which was unthinkable regarding Christ because he was also God.[28] As with Origen, Christian theologians commonly believed that a necessary relation exists between passibility and evil, reinforcing the belief that God incarnate cannot be passible any more than God can be passible.[29]

The Hellenistic presupposition of divine impassibility further complicates Christological formulation because patristic theologians assumed that human

---

"Where the Bible appears to ascribe emotion or suffering to God, the tradition quickly concluded that such language must be figurative. . . . For the Stoics and the whole eudaemonist tradition of antiquity, happiness is a matter of uninterrupted bliss. The wise person is one who learns how not to be disturbed by changes in the world. The wise person lacks pathos: he or she is without passion, is impervious to changes that would overturn the rule of reason."

[25] Nestorius *Second Letter to Cyril*, in *The Christological Controversy*, trans. and ed. R. A. Norris (Philadelphia: Fortress, 1980), 137. Hence, Nestorius's strict distinction of Christ's two natures to prevent the human passibility from affecting the divine nature.

[26] R. A. Norris, *Manhood and Christ: A Study in the Christology of Theodore of Mopsuestia* (Oxford: Clarendon, 1963), 5. I am indebted to my student Chad Glazener for this reference.

[27] Cited by Benjamin B. Warfield, *The Person and Work of Christ*, ed. Samuel G. Craig (Philadelphia: Presbyterian and Reformed, 1950), 138 n.120. Warfield gives a translation of Origen's comment on Matt 26:37, which seems to match the Latin text of Origen, *Commentaria in Evangelium secundum Matthaem* (ed. C. and C. Vicentii Delarue, PG 13 [1857]: 1741).

[28] Aloys Grillmeier, *Christ in Christian Tradition*, trans. John Bowden, 2nd ed. (Atlanta: John Knox, 1975), 1:363.

[29] Another example is Gregory of Nyssa *Against Eunomius* 6.3, where he writes that passions are a diseased condition of the will that tend to sin; Jesus had only a natural sort of passions that are different from those of fallen humanity so he could be passible without also being sinful.

actions are necessarily passive, and thereby vulnerable to fluctuation and evil, in contrast to the active, impassible, and good motions of God. An example is John of Damascus:

> Thus if, because the divine motion is action, the human is passion, then it will definitely follow that, because the divine nature is good, the human will be evil. Conversely, because the human motion is called passion, the divine is called action; and because human nature is evil, the divine will be good.[30]

This extension of the basic starting point to view passibility negatively caused great difficulty for explaining a divine incarnation of Jesus Christ who is both fully God and fully man—and as a man who suffered in his temptations. Indeed, temptation does not seem to have been possible unless he was passible.

As the solution to the problems of passibility for the God-man, patristic theologians developed various ways of attributing passibility to Jesus. One solution was to predicate suffering only of Christ's humanity, thereby protecting his divine impassibility as the eternal Logos. By this method, theologians could predicate passibility and impassibility to his two natures in a double predication model. Another solution was to predicate suffering and impassibility to Jesus as the single subject of his two natures. These approaches of reduplicative predication have been critiqued in recent years,[31] but they were satisfying to patristic theologians.[32] Passibility seems to be important to temptation (especially in a situation like Gethsemane, anticipating the cup of wrath), so the reckoning of this as part of explaining Christ's impeccability and temptation is an added difficulty for patristic theology.[33]

---

[30]John of Damascus *De Fide Orthodoxa* 3.15, trans. Frederic H. Chase, Jr., in *Saint John of Damascus: Writings*, Fathers of the Church 37 (New York: Fathers of the Church, 1958), 312. (All volumes in the Fathers of the Church series will be abbreviated FOC.)

[31]Thomas V. Morris, "Reduplication and Representational Christology", *Modern Theology* 2:4 (1986): 319-27. Morris primarily interacts with a contemporary defender of the reduplicative strategy (R. T. Herbert), but his charge is a blanket criticism that reduplicative predication is inadequate to explain the incarnation.

[32]E.g., Gregory of Nazianzen *Oratio* 29.20 (PG 36 [1858]: 100C). Hilary *Tractatus In LIV Psalmum* Patrologia Latina (Paris: J.-P. Migne, 1844), 9:348B. Hereafter, volumes in this series will be given as PL. Contemporary Christologists (despite Morris's challenge) can be found to favor the traditional solution as well, e.g., O'Collins, *Christology*, 233-34, Brian Hebblethwaite, *The Incarnation: Collected Essays in Christology* (Cambridge: Cambridge University Press, 1987), Kathryn Tanner, *Jesus, Humanity and the Trinity* (Minneapolis: Fortress, 2001), 16, and (cited by Morris) R. L. Sturch, "God, Christ and Possibilities", *Religious Studies* 16 (1980): 81-84.

[33]For a recent study of divine impassibility with a special focus on the Incarnation, see ch. 5 of Robert G. Lister, III, "Impassible and Impassioned: Reevaluating the Doctrines of Divine Impassibility and Divine Relationality", PhD diss., The Southern Baptist Theological Seminary (2007).

The Knowledge of God Incarnate

Another philosophical concept influenced by the Hellenistic setting that complicates matters for Christological formulation is the assumption that ignorance entails or at least possibly leads to sin. Underlying this assumption was the idea that decision-making depends on knowledge; thus, knowledge determines moral action.[34] This theory means that ignorance causes sin, an assumption that causes trouble for Christians who read the Gospel suggestions of Christ's ignorance of the time of his return (e.g., Mark 13:32) and ignorance regarding other information for which he has to ask questions to know the facts (that is, questions asked for information, not simply as part of teaching or to evoke a response, e.g., John 11:34). Many patristic theologians denied any ignorance in Christ because they believed that ignorance entailed a liability to sin.[35] As part of protecting the sinlessness (and the impeccability) of Jesus, patristic writers were driven by the assumptions of their setting to some sort of nuance regarding ignorance in Christ. Examples of this trend are Jerome, Augustine, Basil, and John Chrysostom.[36] Theodosius is an example of those who affirmed Christ's ignorance as a predication of his assumed humanity.[37] Others such as Gregory of Nyssa, Themistius, Athanasius, and Cyril of

---

[34]John J. O'Keefe, "Sin, *apatheia* and Freedom of the Will in Gregory of Nyssa", in Studia patristica 22, ed. Elizabeth A. Livingstone (Leuven: Peeters, 1989), 52-53. This presupposition is termed the intellectualist theory of action. O'Keefe explains: "Because they perceived the world as fundamentally knowable through reason, and because they saw this world as conforming to certain predictable standards . . . the Greeks naturally concluded that proper moral behavior was the natural product of correct knowing. Conversely, error and failure had little to do with a failure of the will, but a great deal to do with ignorance of the good and the true."

[35]Grillmeier's comment, *Christ*, 2.2:363-64, is helpful: "Ignorance (*agnoia*) was already seen by the ancient Greeks in relation to moral evil, indeed as the font and reason for false moral decisions. Thus with regard to Christ, if ignorance were to be conceded in him, his 'sinlessness' would be undermined."

[36]Jerome, *Dialogue against the Pelagians* 32, in *Saint Jerome: Dogmatic and Polemical Works*, trans. John N. Hritzu, FOC 53 (Washington, DC: The Catholic University of America Press, 1965), 278-79; Augustine *De Trinitate* 1.12.23 (ed. W. J. Mountain, Corpus Christianorum Series Latina [Turnhout: Brepols, 1968] 50:61-62), hereafter volumes in this series will appear with the abbreviation CCSL; Basil *Ep.* 236 *ad Amphilochius*, in *Saint Basil: The Letters*, vol. 3, trans. Roy J. Deferrari and Martin R. P. McGuire, Loeb Classical Library (Cambridge, MA: Harvard University Press, 1930), 387-405; John Chrysostom *In illud: Pater si possible est* 1 (ed. D. Bern de Montfaucon, PG 51 [1859]: 31), cited by Camillus Hay, "St John Chrysostom and the Integrity of the Human Nature of Christ", *Franciscan Studies* 19 (1959): 304.

[37]Theodosius of Alexandria *Tome to Empress Theodora* 337-339, in *Monophysite Texts of the Sixth Century*, ed. and trans. Albert Van Roey and Pauline Allen, Orientalia Lovaniensia Analecta 56 (Leuven: Peeters, 1994), 51.

Alexandria affirmed Christ's ignorance as a marker of his full humanity,[38] despite the reservations that many had about the Arian use of John 11:34 and Mark 13:32 to undermine orthodox claims (that is, Arians pointed to these passages as proof that Jesus was not fully God).

Stock Theories of Physical Union

The Stoic philosophers and Aristotle reasoned five theories for how two things could be united together.[39] Christian theologians generally agreed on one or more of these theories for explaining the union of deity and humanity in Christ. The same widely popular analogies for union appear frequently in the patristic Christological writings in East and West: fire and iron are united when the iron is heated to share the burning property of the fire, a drop of vinegar is absorbed in the ocean, and wine is mixed with water. In Wolfson's evaluation, the Fifth Council (Constantinople II, 553) specifically ruled out what he labels *Stoic union by confusion* (union by mixing two things) in connection with the views of Apollinaris and Eutyches, and the Council authorized what Wolfson calls *Aristotelian union by predominance* (union by synthesis of a greater and a lesser).[40] Wolfson defines the union of predominance as two things that interrelate in unequal ways such that the greater element is united to the lesser element, as form is to matter, without corruption of either component.[41] An example of this union is combining equal parts of water and wine, where the compound acts like the wine because wine is the stronger element that predominates over the water.[42] Wolfson's claim is that the orthodox agreement showed not only in the conciliar anathema but in the patristic Christological

---

[38]Gregory of Nyssa *Antirrheticus adv. Apollinarem* 11, 14, 24, 32, cited by J. H. Srawley, "St Gregory of Nyssa on the Sinlessness of Christ", *Journal of Theological Studies* 7 (1906): 435; Themistius was the Alexandrian founder of the Agnoetae movement in opposition to those who denied Christ's ignorance (noted by Van Roey and Allen, *Monophysite Texts*, 18); Grillmeier's comment (*Christ*, 1:315) on Athanasius: "Athanasius displays a general tendency to weaken the character of certain of Christ's inner experiences which might be attributed to a human soul so as to dissociate the Logos from them from the start. Thus Christ's anguish was only 'feigned', and not real anguish; his ignorance was not real ignorance, but only an *ignorantia de jure*, which was proper to the human nature from the start"; Cyril of Alexandria *Thesaurus, assertio* 22 (ed. J. Auberti, PG 75 [1859]: 369B).

[39]These are analyzed by Harry Austryn Wolfson, *Faith, Trinity, Incarnation*, vol. 1 of *The Philosophy of the Church Fathers*, 3rd ed. (Cambridge, MA: Harvard University Press, 1970), 372-486. In his summary, the five theories of union are: composition, Aristotelian mixture, Stoic mixture, Stoic confusion, and Aristotelian predominance.

[40]Wolfson, *Faith, Trinity, Incarnation*, 417-18.

[41]Wolfson, *Faith, Trinity, Incarnation*, 385.

[42]Wolfson, *Faith, Trinity, Incarnation*, 377-78. Wolfson's citation from Aristotle is *De Gen. et Corr.* 1.10.322a, 9-10s.

writings as well, despite the problem of multiple uses for key terms of union.[43] Furthermore, Wolfson notes that two innovators, Theodore of Mopsuestia and Nestorius, departed from the mainstream at exactly this point in their rejection of the analogies of mixture, confusion, and predominance out of preference for a union of conjunction,[44] as with the union of two things by their surface contact with each other.[45]

Wolfson's analysis is helpful as far as it goes, but requires some nuance. The evidence of patristic Christological discussions shows a further distinction in the relation of Christ's two natures and his impeccability and temptation.[46] The union of predominance in its application to Christ's sinlessness as a man could be seen as subdivided in two ways: first, by *predominance of nature*, by which the divine nature transformed the human nature to be like it in impeccability, i.e., divine nature over human nature, and second, by *predominance of the person*, by which the divine Logos supervenes over his human existence to resist human weaknesses sinlessly. These two ways of union by predominance will be seen later to characterize two models of Christ's impeccability and temptation (M2 and M3). All of this is to say that the Stoic and Aristotelian supply of widely used terms and analogies were a common background for theologizing about the union of two natures in Christ.

These four sets of common presuppositions—the Nicene faith, soteriological requirements, opposition to heresies, and the philosophical setting—influence the Christological models in general, and they specifically inform the early models of Christ's impeccability and temptation. Two other background topics relevant to the models of impeccability and temptation are the divergent Christological tendencies and the geopolitical setting of the patristic Christological debates. Whereas the foregoing presuppositions account for the similarities of the models, these next topics partly show how different models of Christ's impeccability and temptation developed according to theological tendencies.

Divergent Theological Tendencies

The two primary schools of thought that are opposed to each other during the patristic period have been generally described as the Alexandrian and

---

[43] Wolfson, *Faith, Trinity, Incarnation*, 386.
[44] Wolfson, *Faith, Trinity, Incarnation*, 451-63.
[45] Wolfson, *Faith, Trinity, Incarnation*, 379.
[46] However, the further distinction that I propose is in spite of the way patristic writers use the stock terms and analogies of physical union equivocally, a point that Wolfson admits (Wolfson, *Faith, Trinity, Incarnation*, 386).

Antiochene schools.[47] Many scholars have identified these two distinct schools of thought in the fourth and fifth centuries (as labeled by historians according to the geography of these two prominent cities, Alexandria in North Africa and Antioch in Syria). As it concerns Christology, the Alexandrian model is typically described as emphasizing the union of the Incarnation. The Logos-Son of God became incarnate by uniting a human nature to himself; thus, the model is often called *Word-flesh* (to emphasize the union to a human nature). The Antiochene model is commonly described as an emphasis on the integrity of the two natures, and is often called *Word-man* because of the insistence that Jesus is a true human being united with the Word of God (emphasizing the union to a specific man).

Nonetheless, these traditional labels have been critiqued.[48] There seem to be many exceptions to the standard typology that the Alexandrian and Antiochene labels are not as useful as once thought. A more accurate approach is to distinguish these schools of thought in terms of exegetical methodology instead of Christology. The labels of *unitive Christology* and *divisive Christology* have been suggested to categorize the basic tendencies among patristic theologians.[49] Unitive Christology emphasizes the single subject of the Logos-Son, who is the one person in Christ. Divisive Christology marks a duality of the subjects of each of Christ's two natures, divine and human (as in Nestorianism). Divisive Christology was eventually viewed as unorthodox in the fifth and sixth centuries.[50] Thus, we can see that (for example) John Chrysostom was typically Antiochene in his exegetical method, but distinctly unitive in his Christology (that is, he agreed closely with Cyril of Alexandria to emphasize a single subject of the Incarnation).[51]

So, we are still concerned with two schools of thought (though not

---

[47]I am simply noting the turmoil and dominant trends that are the setting for developing models of Christ's impeccability and temptation. This summary is the barest of comments that one could say about patristic Christological models.

[48]The traditional ordering in these labels has been critiqued as superficial, reductionistic, and inadequate by R. A. Norris, "Christological Models in Cyril of Alexandria", in Studia Patristica, vol. 13, pt. 2, ed. E. A. Livingstone, Texte und Untersuchungen, 116 (Berlin: Akademie Verlag, 1975), 255-68.

[49]These labels are explained in Ashish Jacob Naidu, "The Doctrine of Christ as it Relates to the Christian Life in John Chrysostom's Homilies on the Gospel of John and Hebrews", PhD thesis, University of Aberdeen (2005), 198-201. Naidu also notes that Alexandria was much more organized than Antioch as a center of teaching, and thus, a school of thought.

[50]The divisive Christology label is not intended to include orthodox formulations that emphasize the integrity and authenticity of Christ's two natures more than stressing their union. Instead, the label is for proposals that are unorthodox because they violate the union of God incarnate (as in the case of Nestorius and, before him, Theodore of Mopsuestia).

[51]Naidu, "The Doctrine of Christ", 201.

necessarily coinciding as distinct Christologies) that we can summarize in terms of their differences. These exegetical tendencies that sometimes influenced Christological formulation can generally be stated in this way. Theologians associated with the Alexandrian school of thought interpreted Scripture in a twofold way, frequently preferring the higher or allegorical meaning (typological, symbolical, or spiritual meaning) of the text, but this does not mean a denial or disregard of the literal, historical meaning.[52] This preference for the higher meaning was consistent with the Platonic philosophical trends preferred in Alexandria.[53] The Christologies produced by thinkers such as Origen, Athanasius, Apollinaris, the Cappadocians, and Cyril of Alexandria tended to emphasize the unity of the Incarnation (possibly at the risk of diminishing the full integrity of his humanity).[54] Also, a consistent concern among Alexandrian writers and unitive Christology is for salvation by deification, the assumption of a generic human nature into union with the divine nature of the Logos.[55]

Theologians associated with the Antioch emphasized grammatical exegesis (though not to exclude typological meanings) and the premises of what resembled an Aristotelian worldview (by which God and absolutes were understood through the empirical world).[56] Theologians associated with Antioch such as Theodore of Mopsuestia, Nestorius, and Theodoret of Cyrus typically emphasized the human example of Christ's life as a distinct experience from the impassible Logos who could not share in the passible

---

[52]Naidu, "The Doctrine of Christ", 38-40.

[53]Maurice F. Wiles, "The Doctrine of Christ in the Patristic Age", in *Christ for Us Today*, ed. Norman Pittenger (London: SCM, 1968), 87. "The Platonic approach, according to which humanity as such is a more fundamental and more real concept than individual man, provided a framework of thought within which it seemed possible to make the essential Alexandrian affirmation of the subjecthood of the divine Logos throughout without destroying the humanity of Christ, or even reducing it in any really significant respect." Cf. David F. Wells, *The Person of Christ* (Westchester, IL: Crossway, 1984), 101, and Johannes Quasten, *Patrology: The Golden Age of Greek Patristic Literature* (Utrecht: The Newman Press) 2:122 (cited in Naidu, "Doctrine of Christ", 64-65).

[54]Young, "Christological Ideas", 161, in critique of Cyril of Alexandria's views: "It must be regarded as a form of Docetism to say: the Logos cannot have suffered; the flesh suffered but it was so united to the Logos that the possibility of its giving way or succumbing to temptation and sin is not a real one." Cf. Meredith, *Cappadocians*, 110-11.

[55]Alister E. McGrath, *Historical Theology* (Oxford: Blackwell, 1998), 51-55.

[56]Wells, *Person of Christ*, 102; Dewart, *The Theology of Theodore of Mopsuestia*, 149. However, Naidu, "The Doctrine of Christ", 66, explains, "Chrysostom, like other Antiochenes, had little respect for the teaching of the philosophers, and often criticized their philosophical assumptions." So, the Aristotle vs. Plato dichotomy will not necessarily hold as a neat distinction between Antioch and Alexandria.

humanity in any way.[57] Moreover, writers associated with Antioch emphasized the moral aspect of Christ's specific human obedience. He is a true man who serves as an example for others to imitate his obedience. Accordingly, those interpreters following a divisive Christology counted a role of the Holy Spirit in the life and ministry of Christ (and in connection with achieving sinlessness as a man), in sharp contrast to the method of unitive Christology (which preferred to count the role of the Logos in Christ instead of the Holy Spirit).[58] With these theological and exegetical tendencies in view, we can note that the divergences in patristic theological trends were influential in formulating different models of Christ's impeccability and temptation.

Geopolitical Setting

From the political side, the Roman emperors frequently meddled in church affairs for the sake of unifying the empire on doctrinal grounds. Emperors called all of the seven ecumenical councils (no doubt in unwitting accordance with God's providence). Political leaders sought the aid of church leaders and alternately installed or exiled Christian teachers to promote imperial interests with the assistance of the church. From the ecclesiastical side (though to a lesser degree), church leaders invited imperial involvement to promote and secure ecclesial unity in the midst of doctrinally based divisions. A threat to both church and state was the rising power of Persian and Arab forces encroaching from the East.

Within the church geopolitical structure, leaders had established the bishop of Rome as the dominant ecclesial authority in the West, while leaders at Alexandria vied with those leaders at Constantinople for ascendancy in the East. This rivalry became enflamed when Nestorius, a proponent of divisive Christology, gained the patriarchate of Constantinople (and was subsequently opposed by Cyril of Alexandria, who defended unitive Christology).[59] Jaroslav Pelikan explains how this geopolitical mixture influenced patristic theological formulations: "Even more than the christological controversies before Chalcedon the continuing debate after Chalcedon was shaped by nontheological factors, ranging from mob rule and athletic rivalry to military promotions and

---

[57]Wiles, "The Doctrine of Christ", 88; Meredith, *Cappadocians*, 110-11.
[58]See above for the discussion of pneumatological Christology.
[59]Donald Fairbairn, *Grace and Christology in the Early Church*, Oxford Early Christian Studies (New York: Oxford University Press, 2003), 6. Fairbairn notes that Nestorius pushed the teaching of his teachers, Diodore of Tarsus and Theodore of Mopsuestia, through the work of many monks in Constantinople. Whereas Cyril had ignored such teaching before Nestorius's patriarchate, the combined factors of doctrine and politics seemed to have roused Cyril to denounce to the Antiochenes' teaching.

the domestic intrigues of the imperial household."[60] Nonetheless, the attendant circumstances to the Christological models of the patristic period need not detract from the theological achievements that developed amidst the presuppositions and influences that we have reviewed. In my view, God has sovereignly worked through the mixed motives and flawed ecclesiastical processes. The result of messy circumstances can be seen as the gift to the church of God's progressive illumination of the theological teaching of Scripture.

Four Models in the Patristic Period

We will proceed through the descriptions and representatives of four main models of Christ's impeccability and temptation as they can be recognized in the inferential, suggestive way that each writer's thoughts can be discerned. The four models in their briefest labels are: M1, Sinless by Inherent Impeccability, M2, Sinless by Deification, M3, Sinless by the Divine Hegemony, and M4, Sinless by Empowering Grace. For convenience, I will refer to these models using the abbreviations of M1, M2, M3, and M4. The labels summarize the way each model explains how the impeccable Savior achieved human sinlessness (despite his temptations). Impeccability is variously appealed to as a factor in the models, but this is a theological idea. In the forefront of patristic theology is contending with the biblical revelation that Jesus was tempted and sinless. Theology concludes from Nicene doctrine that, being fully God, Jesus was impeccable. Some models explain Christ's sinlessness in terms of impeccability, but this is only one version of the basic concern to explain how Jesus experienced temptation and came through it perfectly, without sin.[61] Along with presenting each model, I will briefly evaluate each explanation for its theological adequacy, and especially in view of the relevant biblical evidence that we have already considered.

M1: Sinless by Inherent Impeccability

DESCRIPTION OF M1

The first model is the general claim that Christ's sinlessness was caused by his inherent impeccability as God. By his divine nature as the eternal Logos and Son, Jesus was immune to sin even in his human experiences. The distinctive of this model is the emphasis on Christ's preexistence to his incarnation as the

---

[60] Jaroslav Pelikan, *The Emergence of the Catholic Tradition (100-600)*, vol. 1 of *The Christian Tradition: A History of the Development of Doctrine* (Chicago: University of Chicago Press, 1971), 266-67.

[61] Later theology, as we will see in later chapters, takes up the concern of how Jesus could be tempted and achieve sinlessness despite his impeccability.

Logos who becomes incarnate as a man.[62] Because Christ is God before the Incarnation, and God cannot sin, then Christ cannot sin even when he is tempted as a man because he is divinely impeccable. This claim follows the Nicene theology that Jesus is fully God.

This inherent impeccability model is the early answer to the problem posed by the Arians that since a man would have a mutable will with susceptibility to sin, and God cannot be mutable or sin, then Christ the man could not also be fully God (eternally and essentially divine). The simple answer of M1 is that despite his incarnation in humanity and the experiences of temptation, Jesus Christ could not sin because he is divine as the preexistent Logos. His sinlessness is a necessity of his deity. Proponents do not specify whether this is a necessity of his divine nature or because he is a divine person who wills perfectly by his holiness. Theologians affirm simply that because Christ is the divine Lord, it was logically impossible for him to sin.[63]

To sum up, the primary question of M1 is this: What was it about Jesus that distinguished him from other men? M1 gives the answer by a philosophical deduction: God cannot sin, and Jesus is the divine Son, so Jesus was sinless because of his inherent impeccability (as God). The rationale of the model is that Christ's sinlessness is a necessity of his divine impeccability.

REPRESENTATIVES OF M1

Tertullian, Augustine, and Origen are examples of M1.[64] These three articulate the common explanation that the divine impeccability of the Logos is the efficient and material cause of Christ's human sinlessness.

Tertullian (ca. 155–220) insists that the normally sinful humanity was emptied of sin when assumed by Christ so that his was a sinless, transformed humanity.[65] That explains his initial state of sinlessness as a man. Tertullian elsewhere affirms the M1 idea that Christ's sinlessness is based on his deity, explaining that just as God alone is without sin, so also Christ is the only man

---

[62] Origen's variation of Christ's preexistence as a perfect human soul is idiosyncratic, but at least Origen is in agreement with the preexistence idea (see below).

[63] A summary statement of the patristic idea in M1 is given by Jacques Dupuis, *Who Do You Say I Am? An Introduction to Christology* (Maryknoll, NY: Orbis, 1994), 129: "If Jesus were to commit sin, God would be the author of sinful actions, which is a contradiction." See also Thomas C. Oden, *The Word of Life,* vol. 2 of *Systematic Theology* (San Francisco: Harper & Row, 1989), 254. Oden summarizes this general patristic view that I am calling M1: "If God does not will contrary to God's will, and if sin is to act counter to God's will, then the God-man would not sin." Unfortunately, Oden provides no sources for his summary of this argument.

[64] The dates given for the early fathers are sometimes disputed as historians disagree by a few years about birth and death dates. Chronology is not an important aspect in this study, so I have used dates that are generally reported by what seem to be reliable historical studies (while acknowledging that more careful study could be done).

[65] Tertullian *De Carne Christi* 16.780-81 (ed. J. -P. Migne, PL 2 [1866]: 826).

without sin.[66] For Tertullian, Christ's sinlessness is an entailment of his deity, and no other explanation than this is given for how Jesus remained sinless.

Augustine (354–430) represents M1 with a clear declaration in his sermon on the temptations that Jesus endured: "That Christ was the conqueror there, why should we be surprised? He was almighty God."[67] M1 is indicated by the way Augustine counts Christ's deity as the cause of his victory. Augustine also affirms that Christ's sinlessness was caused in some (undefined) way by his exceptional constitution, being God and man. He writes that the uniqueness of Christ's human life without sin is attributable to this fact: "in His nature [Jesus is] not man only, but also God, in whom we could prove such perfection of character to have existed."[68] The plain logic of the model shows in the connection between the (impeccable) deity of the Son and the sinless human action of Jesus Christ as a direct result. This is not all Augustine has to say on the subject because his thought follows other models besides M1.

Origen (ca. 184–ca. 253) follows the M1 principle of a preexistent cause of Christ's human sinlessness.[69] He also deviates from others by employing the Platonic doctrine of preexistent human souls in understanding of the Incarnation (which is contrary to Scripture).[70] Origen writes that the preexistent human soul assumed by the Logos became immune to the possibility of sin because this soul chose to cling to the Logos. The result was that "what formerly depended upon the will was by the influence of long custom changed

---

[66]Tert. *De Anima* 41.3 (ed. J. H. Waszink [Amsterdam: J. M. Meulenhoff, 1947], 57). "Solus enim deus sine peccato et solus homo sine peccato Christus, quia et deus Christus." My interpretation of Tertullian is different than Wolfhart Pannenberg's interpretation of the same passages in *Jesus—God and Man*, 356. Pannenberg denies that Tertullian views Christ's sinlessness in terms of "a special disposition of his nature".

[67]Aug. *Sermon* 284.5 (PL 38 [1863]: 1292, trans. Edmund Hill, *Sermons 273-305A: On the Saints*, vol. III/8 of *The Works of Saint Augustine* [Hyde Park, NY: New City, 1994], 91).

[68]Aug. *On the Spirit and the Letter* 1, in *Saint Augustine's Anti-Pelagian Works*, trans. Peter Holmes and Robert Ernest Wallis, rev. Benjamin Warfield, *A Select Library of the Nicene and Post-Nicene Fathers of the Christian Church*, First Series, ed. P. Schaff (New York: Christian Literature Co., 1886), 5:84. Hereafter, NPNF[1].

[69]Pannenberg, *Jesus*, 356, claims Origen was the first to argue for the impeccability of Christ when others had commonly affirmed his actual sinlessness. This may be the case, but Clement should also be counted as one of the earliest to affirm Christ's impeccability, if not the first (see M2, below).

[70]Melvin E. Lawrenz, *The Christology of John Chrysostom* (Lewiston, NY: Edwin Mellen, 1996), 22. "Origen reflected the prevailing Platonism of his native Alexandria in the soteriological presuppositions that underlie his Christology. All souls have pre-existed, and God used the one soul that did not fall away—that of Jesus—to be united with his Logos or Wisdom which in turn became united with human flesh thus providing a way of redemption for the race." Cf. Or. *In Canticum Canticorum* 2.8 (ed. C. and C. Vincentii Delarue, PG 13 [1857]: 126C).

into nature".[71] Origen's idea is that the human soul merited its assumption by the Logos, and the miraculous birth in a human body was the divine action to secure that impeccability which the human soul had merited, "so that the soul may be able to remain without having tasted evil".[72] Few accepted Origen's notion of a merited assumption by the Logos,[73] and others readily condemned it.[74] Nevertheless, Origen affirmed the generally recognized idea of M1 that Jesus was "incapable of all evil because he was the divine Word."[75]

EVALUATION OF M1: SINLESS BY INHERENT IMPECCABILITY

M1 becomes an umbrella for other patristic models (M2-M4) by the basic M1 affirmation of Christ's intrinsic impeccability as God. Further development of these models beyond the simplicity of M1 will take up the questions about the compossibility of certain biblical details—the Son's incarnation in the likeness of sinful flesh (Rom 8:3), Christ's sinlessness as a human example (1 Pet 2:21-22), his sympathy for human sinners (Heb 4:15), and the accounts of his own struggle as a man to obey God (Luke 22:40-44).

M1 is important as early evidence that patristic writers understood Scripture and theology to require an impeccable Christ. M1 supplies a plausible explanation for Christ's success in all his temptations: he could not be defeated because of his divine impeccability, so in every temptation he did in fact emerge victorious and sinless. The primary concern of M1 is to uphold the full deity of Christ, demonstrated in the sinless perfection of his human life. Soteriology and Christology are bound together with the doctrine of God (God is impeccable, so Christ is impeccable and thereby sinless).

Nonetheless, we find that patristic theologians formulated other models, which indicates that M1 was theologically inadequate. I recognize that the formulation of multiple models does not entail that a prior model was theologically deficient, but I think that in this case the subsequent developments do indicate the theological inadequacy of M1. Moreover, even when considered apart from other models, M1 is theologically inadequate in several ways.

We can begin an evaluation by seeing how the model explains an actual case of Jesus in temptation. According to M1, Jesus, when struggling in Gethsemane

---

[71] Or. *De Principiis* 2.6.5, in *Origens Werke*, vol. 5, *De Principiis*, ed. P. Koetschau, Die grieschischen christlichen Schriftsteller der ersten drei Jahrhunderte 22 (Berlin: Academie, 1913), 145; trans. G. W. Butterworth (London: S.P.C.K., 1936), 112-13.

[72] Or. *Contra Celsum* 1.33 (ed. M. Marcovich, Supplements to Vigiliae Christianae 54 [Leiden: Brill, 2001], 35).

[73] An exception is Evagrius Ponticus, who developed Origen's preexistent soul application in Christology by which the preexistent human soul in Christ is "the seat of moral decisions and of sinlessness" (Grillmeier, *Christ in Christian Tradition*, 1:379).

[74] E.g., Augustine denounces the idea of merit in the incarnational assumption repeatedly, as in *Enchiridion* 36 and *Letter 187*.

[75] Or. *Celsum* 4.15 (229).

to embrace the cup of wrath, finally resisted the temptation to turn away from his suffering because he was God. His deity was the (unspecified) power that enabled him to turn aside from temptation. He could not have chosen any other path than the cross because of his deity. More than that, he chose the cross (he did not turn away in sin) because, in some undefined way, his deity was in play to influence and determine his human choice in the face of his fiercest temptation. The struggle, therefore, seems to have been much less intense on the M1 account than the story might otherwise suggest (Christ's profuse sweating, repeated pleas for relief, being deeply troubled in soul, and receiving angelic assistance). His distress was caused by the anticipation of suffering, but the choice to drink the cup is one that his deity finally determined for him. Jesus chose to employ his deity (whether passively or actively?) that enabled him to obey as a man. Jesus did not simply choose to obey. In saying, "Not my will but your will be done", Jesus has actually declared that he has relied on divine power to carry him to obedience. Jesus eventually met his temptation with a divine counterforce (impeccability), not human obedience. Nearby, Peter, James, and John were being tempted alongside Jesus, having been called along to support him in prayer. He urged them to pray that they would not enter into temptation. Meanwhile, Jesus himself was counting down the moments until he would employ his deity with overwhelming causal force that determined his human obedience.[76]

One part of the M1 explanation is right: the ultimate outcome of Christ's temptation was never in doubt (he was unable to sin because of his deity). But this is distinct from the question about *how* Jesus got to that outcome (sinlessness as an achievement). On this second question M1 seems to be theologically inadequate for the way the model explains his sinlessness in terms of his impeccability. If this had been true, Jesus seems to have endured a vastly different experience of temptation than what other humans do, and this undermines his relevance.

I see at least four problems. First, because the M1 picture is that Jesus was struggling to wait until he employed his impeccability (or whatever it was of his deity that fortified his perfect obedience), this does not seem to be an experience of temptation at all. He is not struggling between right and wrong choices because the entire process is overshadowed by the larger reality that, in the end, he is not going to struggle at all, but simply will opt for his deity. Thus, M1 does not adequately account for the basic item of Christ's true temptation in a way that is like ours (a struggle of the tempted one between right and wrong choices with their opposite outcomes).

---

[76]The causal relation is a bit like the way Kazantzakis, in his *Last Temptation*, implausibly describes Jesus as being afflicted by an invisible force with a painful, talon-like gripping of his skull numerous times (as if a great bird attacked him) to divert him forcefully from his desire of pursuing his childhood playmate, Mary Magdalene (romantically, to be a husband to her).

Second, having transposed the meaning of Christ's temptation into a unique experience of *how long to wait until employing deity?*, M1 consequently proves its further inadequacy to account for the relevance of Christ's temptation and sinlessness. His obedience as a man is not a reasonable pattern for other humans, in the same way that a man flying an airplane over Mt. Everest is not a reasonable example for others to climb the peak on foot. The possession and employment of deity to surmount his temptation disqualifies Christ from being a reasonable pattern of how to resist temptation. Furthermore, the use of deity to repel temptation does not fit the accounts in Hebrews 2:17-18 and 4:15-16 that Christ can empathize with others in their struggles of temptation because of his first-hand experience. On the M1 account, his experience is totally unlike theirs, and his empathy is consequently hollow. Whatever help he might offer others cannot be the same that he employed himself. Again, advice shouted from the airplane above might not be effective or credible for the man struggling on the snowy slopes below.

Third, M1 is theologically inadequate because the model fails to explain the significance of Christ's victory over temptation. The marvel of God's rout of the devil is that the incarnate Son regained lost ground on the same terms within the limitations of his frail humanity, just as the first Adam. The victory of the second Adam is empty if M1 is the fullest explanation we may give for Christ's triumph over Satan's temptation. Were M1 true, Christ's obedience would not be a human obedience learned through suffering (Heb 5:7-8) or a human faithfulness that God counts as a gift of righteousness to believers for justification (Rom 5:17-19).

Finally, M1 does not explain how impeccability becomes a shareable property in Christ's human nature communicated from his deity. Is this deification, by which the human nature of Jesus is elevated to function in perfection because of union with the divine nature? Proponents of two other models seem to take their starting point with M1 and address this point of its inadequacy. Both M2 and M3 offer explanations of how divine impeccability is communicated to Christ's humanity for the result of sinlessness.

Therefore, the inherent impeccability model, though including an important truth that Jesus could not sin, is theologically inadequate for explaining Christ's impeccability, temptation, and sinlessness.

M2: Sinless by Deification

DESCRIPTION OF M2

The question asked in M2 is this: How does the union of Christ's divine nature with his human nature make him sinless as a man? The answer given is that his sinlessness is the result of the deification of his human nature by his divine nature. Deification is the process by which human nature can share in or acquire divine attributes by grace to counteract the effects of the fall. The deity in Jesus energizes his humanity, deifying and strengthening it against natural human weaknesses. The theory of salvation by deification deals especially in terms of transforming the common plight of human mutability and susceptibility to sin. The Logos assumes and deifies the human nature of his incarnation to heal and restore it for others as immutable and impeccable.[77] The deification of Christ's humanity by his divinity is a relation between the two natures that is a type of deification and future sinlessness for all who obey God and enjoy salvation through sharing in the divine nature of the Logos (2 Pet 1:4).

M2 depends on the deification concept to explain that Christ's divine nature is the efficient cause of the human impeccability, which is then the material cause of Christ's human sinlessness. Some proponents assert the unity of the two natures so strongly that the incarnational union is often summarized with the maxim: "One incarnate nature of the Son" (μίαν τὴν τοῦ υἱοῦ φύσιν σεσαρκωμένην).[78] M2 does not approach the heresy of Eutychianism (that Christ's humanity is absorbed by his deity) because due regard is made for the ongoing reality of his full humanity and divinity. However, the union has real effects for his human nature. Since union to the Logos has deified the humanity in Christ, it is a humanity that is kept sinless by union with the divine nature. The moral immutability and impassibility of the Logos constitute the moral immutability and impassibility of his human nature.[79]

As in M1, the deification model affirms that the divine impeccability of the Logos is the main factor securing and transforming Christ's moral life as a man; thus, sin is impossible for Christ (and he is consequently sinless). Temptations never threaten him, just as a bar of heated iron cannot admit cold because of its union to the fire. Unlike M1, the deifying union of M2 specifies the way that Christ's divine nature affects his humanity for the result of a sinless life. The general principle of necessary sinlessness in M1 is defined in M2 as the deification of Christ's humanity by transforming union to his divinity. His humanity becomes deiform. Proponents of M2 would deny any substantial change to his human nature (just as iron remains substantially unchanged when united to fire). Nonetheless, the effect of the union is that Christ's humanity is made impeccable (just as white-hot iron receives the

---

[77]Wiles, *Making of Christian Doctrine*, 109, "Cyril of Alexandria with his Platonist background similarly saw the incarnation as an assumption of humanity in general rather than as the becoming of a man. Thereby they could interpret Christ as divinizing mankind as a single entity."

[78]Cyr. *Epistola* 44 *ad Eulogius* (PG 77 [1859]: 225B). Lionel R. Wickham, ed. and trans., *Cyril of Alexandria: Select Letters*, Oxford Early Christian Texts (Oxford: Oxford University Press, 1983), 62-63, notes that this phrase appears in a series of quotes from Athanasius, but that scholars have generally assigned it to Apollinaris.

[79]Leontius of Jerusalem *Adversus Nestorianos* 1.6 (PG 86 pt. 1 [1860]: 1425D). Cited in Patrick T. R. Gray, "Leontius of Jerusalem's Case for a 'Synthetic' Union in Christ", in Studia patristica 18.1, ed. Elizabeth A. Livingstone (Kalamazoo, MI: Cistercian Publications, 1985), 151.

burning properties of fire that heated it).[80]

Representatives of M2 tend to rely upon something like the Aristotelian theory of union by predominance—a union of two things that are unequal; the lesser part is strongly influenced by the greater, thereby bonding the two while they remain distinct from each other. In this understanding of the incarnational union, the lower, weaker human nature in Christ becomes influenced by the greater, dominating divine nature to which it is united. In other words, in a union by predominance, the divine nature transforms the human nature to become impeccable without substantially changing from being truly human.[81]

Important to M2 is the communication of attributes from the divine nature to the human nature through their union. In this communication of attributes from one nature to the other, divine attributes are shared with the humanity of Christ. Alternately, the otherwise untemptable Son of God can experience temptations by single-subject predication (the predication of attributes from his human nature to the person, the single subject of the Incarnation).[82] Despite his temptability as a man, Jesus is also impeccable by his deiform human nature. Unable to fall in sin, Jesus is nonetheless tempted for the instruction of humanity.

REPRESENTATIVES OF M2

Clement of Alexandria (ca. 150–215) is one of the first to express M2.[83] Clement writes that Christ is "sinless" (ἀναμάρτητος) and "passionless in soul" (ἀπαθὴς τὴν ψυχήν) because he is the Son of the Father and God the Logos

---

[80]Wolfson, *Faith, Trinity, Incarnation*, 380-81, identifies this analogy of fire and iron as typical of the Stoic view of a mixture of two things, without mutual corruption, but the two can be unmixed and do not constitute a *tertium quid*, just as water that has been mixed with wine can be drawn out by an oiled sponge. Similarly, heated iron, when removed from the fire (though having become temporarily softened and hot), is quickly shown to be hard iron as it was before.

[81]I do not mean to say that proponents of the deified humanity model consciously subscribed to the Aristotelian theory of predominance, just that there seems to be a strong affinity between this theory and the sort of union that is implied by those writers grouped together in this model.

[82]Grillmeier, *Christ in Christian Tradition*, 2.2:287, distinguishes double predication (distinguishing the attributes of the two natures, and sometimes as communicated from one nature to the other) from the more common single-subject predication (the predication of the divine and human attributes to the single subject of the union). A representative statement is Cyril of Alexandria's view, interpreted by John Anthony McGuckin writes in the introduction to *St Cyril of Alexandria: On the Unity of Christ* (Crestwood, NY: St Vladimir's Seminary Press, 1995), 40, "The person of the Logos is the sole personal subject of all the conditions of his existence, divine or human."

[83]*Paedagogus* was written ca. 190, as noted in the introduction to *Clement of Alexandria: Christ the Educator*, trans. Simon P. Wood, FOC 23 (New York: Fathers of the Church, 1954), xi.

who possesses "the nature of God" (τῷ σχήματι θεός).⁸⁴ At first glance, this seems like M1. However, Clement also explains the divinizing elevation of Christ's humanity by communication of the divine "impassibility" (ἀπάθεια) to his humanity.⁸⁵ Thus, Clement explains that Christ's humanity is the "heavenly flesh sanctified" (ἁγιαζομένη σὰρξ οὐράνιος).⁸⁶ For Clement, impassibility was the highest ethical ideal, the moral likeness of God.⁸⁷ Accordingly, he exhorts his readers to follow Christ's example of being free from human passions in their own striving against temptations.⁸⁸ For Jesus, however, the divine attribute of impassibility is determinative of his human action of sinlessness (or, positively, righteousness and faithfulness to God). Clement understands the divine attribute of impassibility to be the single answer to the question of why Jesus could not sin, and the question of why Jesus did not sin. Thus, Christ's sinlessness is explained by the deification of his assumed humanity.

We have seen Origen's views above as a representative of M1. More examples of his thought show that Origen also saw Christ's sinlessness in terms of M2—the result of the deifying union of his human nature with the divine nature. An example already noted shows this (though with reference to the soul as preexistent) as Christ's human soul having been changed through union to the Logos to become insusceptible to moral change and thus impeccable.⁸⁹ Origen supports this claim with the well-known analogy of fire and iron, saying that once the iron has received the fire into it thoroughly, the metal becomes fire with the same burning property and cannot admit cold so long as it remains united to the fire. Similarly, the soul of Christ was deified in union with the Word so that it had the same immunity to change and evil.⁹⁰ Using typically allegorical exegesis to establish Christ's impeccability, Origen takes the poetic phrase "anointed with the oil of gladness" from Psalm 45:7 as a Christological description of the way that the essence of God filled Christ's human soul. Origen states plainly that the presence of the divine Word with the human soul of Christ causes that human soul to be uniquely "incapable of sin" (*peccati incapax fuit*).⁹¹ In *Contra Celsum*, Origen expresses his view of the transforming union without specific reference to Christ's sinlessness. More important to Origen is the transformation as a general purpose for salvation: "For Christians see that with Jesus human and divine nature began to be woven

---

⁸⁴Clem. *Paed.* 1.2.4.1-2 (3-4).
⁸⁵Clem. *Paed.* 1.2.4.1-2 (3-4).
⁸⁶Clem. *Paed.* 1.6.43.3 (28).
⁸⁷Salvatore R. C. Lilla, *Clement of Alexandria: A Study in Christian Platonism and Gnosticism* (Oxford: Oxford University Press, 1971), 277.
⁸⁸Clem. *Paed.* 1.2.4.1-2 (3-4).
⁸⁹Or. *De Prin.* 2.6.5 (145).
⁹⁰Or. *De Prin.* 2.6.6 (145).
⁹¹Or. *De Prin.* 4.1.31 (354).

together, so that by fellowship with divinity human nature might become divine, not only in Jesus, but also in all those who believe."[92] The theme of a universal humanity deified in Christ shows up here as the soteriological emphasis of M2. Elsewhere in *Contra Celsum*, Origen affirms Christ's humanity as changeless and incapable of evil because of the divine Word.[93] Finally, Origen also defends the virgin birth on the basis that the human body assumed in the Incarnation had to be miraculous and extraordinary to prevent sin from contaminating the human soul.[94] To sum up, Origen relates the factors of divine impeccability, temptation, and human sinlessness through an elevation of Christ's humanity by deification.

Hilary of Poitiers (ca. 300–368) exemplifies M2 when he describes the commingling of the natural predicates in Christ's divine-human life:

> Taking upon himself the weakness of our flesh, and remaining both his and ours, he performs, prays, professes, looks for all those things that are ours in such a way that those things which are his own are also *commingled* with them: at one time he speaks as a man, because he was born as a man, suffered and died as a man; at another time he speaks completely as God the Word.[95]

This example can be read two ways, both as a communication of attributes between the two natures (commingling of attributes), and as the single-subject predication of the attributes to the one person. Hilary is not as clear as we would like. He recognizes the reality of Christ's humanity in the wilderness temptations, where Christ overcomes the devil as a man and reverses Adam's defeat.[96] Hilary also emphasizes the progressive exaltation of Christ's humanity, as Grillmeier observes: "[Hilary] sees this mixing of divine and human in all of the earthly activity of Christ, until finally the Godhead is fully revealed and the humanity of Christ is virtually overwhelmed by the Godhead."[97] Commenting on Psalm 53, Hilary affirms the result of a commingling that causes Christ's human immunity to sin: Jesus "is not liable" to the anger, hatred, greed, and shame that are "common failings of human

---

[92]Or. *Cels.* 3.28 (174; trans. Henry Chadwick [Cambridge: Cambridge University Press, 1953; reprint, 1965], 146).
[93]Or. *Cels.* 4.15 (229).
[94]Or. *Cels.* 1.33 (35). Unfortunately, in Origen's view this is the preexistent human soul, but he still expressed the basic idea of M2 that there was a transformation of the assumed humanity by the divinity to be sinless.
[95]Hilary *Tractatus In LIV Psalmum* (PL 9 [1844]: 348B), trans. Grillmeier, *Christ in Christian Tradition*, 1:400.
[96]Burns, "Christology in Hilary", 141.
[97]Grillmeier, *Christ in Christian Tradition*, 1:400. Burns, "Christology in Hilary", 163, concurs: "Christ also experienced in himself the progress from humility to glory. So to that extent he does share our condition and could be at least an example for our progress. But there is evidence in the Commentary that Christ is more than just an example."

instability".⁹⁸ Hilary has sin in view as part of these common failings because he follows this statement by saying that Christ is unique in his sinlessness of perfect obedience despite being persecuted (and he specifies the persecution of Christ in 1 Pet 2:22-24). In *De Trinitate*, Hilary gives another example of Christ's humanity as divinely constituted to be impassible, which entails impeccability because of the widely assumed connection between passibility (susceptible to the passions) and sin:

> That flesh, that is, that Bread, is from Heaven; that humanity is from God. He had a body to suffer, and He suffered: but He had not a nature which could feel pain. For His body possessed a unique nature of its own; it was transformed into heavenly glory on the Mount, it put fevers to flight by its touch, it gave new eyesight by its spittle.⁹⁹

Hilary sees the humanity of Christ as elevated to be unable to sin because of deification, or the progressive glorification that finally showed in fullness at the transfiguration. With respect to our study, this suggests M2 by which Jesus was tempted to sin but his deity made him impeccable as the heavenly man.

One example from Didymus the Blind (ca. 313–ca. 398) shows the tendency of unitive Christology for M2 (typically but not exclusively associated with theologians from Alexandria). Didymus comments on 1 Peter 2:21 that the cause of Christ's sinlessness is that he is good by nature, by contrast to Christians who are merely good by grace.¹⁰⁰ The distinction that Didymus makes here between Christ's natural, inherent goodness and others' goodness by grace is important because Peter commends Jesus as an example for his readers to follow as they face the temptations that come with persecution. However, Didymus reasons that Christ was able to experience temptation in his humanity because his human soul does not share in the immutability and impassibility of the divine nature.¹⁰¹ Didymus uses the concept of a pre-passion state as that moment of human experience just prior to the full instability of the state of passion, which entails liability to sin.¹⁰² Christ's human soul can

---

⁹⁸Hil. *Tractatus In LIII Psalmum* 6 (PL 9:341A). Anger et al. are in the preceding context.

⁹⁹Hil. *De Trinitate* 10.23 (PL 10 [1845]: 363A, trans. E. W. Watson and L. Pullan, ed. W. Sanday, A Select Library of the Nicene and Post-Nicene Fathers of the Christian Church, Second Series, ed. P. Schaff (New York: Christian Literature, 1887-94; reprint, Grand Rapids: Eerdmans, 1955), 9:188. Hereafter, NPNF².

¹⁰⁰Didymus of Alexandria *Enarratio In Epistolam 1 S. Petri.* (ed. J. -P. Migne, PG 39 [1858]: 1767D).

¹⁰¹Adolphe Gesché, *La christologie du 'Commentaire sur les Psaumes' découvert à Toura* (Gembloux: Éditions J. Duculot, 1962), 135.

¹⁰²Grillmeier, *Christ in Christian Tradition*, 1:363. He notes that the remains of *Commentary on the Psalms* found at Toura in France (1941) may be inauthentic, but they were written by somebody from the same time and region as Didymus.

experience the stresses of temptation at the level of the pre-passion state without the dangers of actual failure, as in Didymus's comment on Psalm 39:2: "Now as the soul which Jesus took is something other than the Trinity, it is by nature created to endure *propatheia* [pre-passion] and the beginning of amazement."[103] Therefore, Didymus makes a way to see how Jesus could experience temptation despite his inability to sin. Didymus's formulation is less clear to represent M2 than others are, but it is plain at least that he explains Christ's sinlessness in terms of a distinct goodness of the human nature as derived from the divine nature (which indicates M2).

Another Alexandrian, Athanasius (328–373), represents M2 by his emphasis on Christ's "deified humanity" (ἐθεοποιήθη ἄνθρωπος) for the deification of all. This shows in his comment that the power of the Logos "destroys" (ἀνήλωται) the sinful corruptions of the flesh for Christ and others so that they may share in his eternal life to be "immortal and incorruptible" as he is.[104] Athanasius suggests that the transformation in Christ is a microcosm for the universal humanity because Jesus has broken the power of sin in human nature through union to the divine Word. Christ's humanity is consequently made sinless: "the all-holy Word of God . . . being incorruptible, vivified and purified [ἐκαθάριζεν] the mortal body. For Scripture says: '*He did no sin, nor was deceit found in his mouth.*'"[105] Thus, Athanasius connects the divine incorruption and purification causally with Christ's sinlessness. This connection shows that even though the main concern is death,[106] the problem of sin is still important in Athanasius's soteriology. In his view, God has solved both problems by means of a universal human nature that the divine nature of the Logos deifies in Christ. Therefore, Athanasius reasons that the Logos accomplished a sinless human life and our deification by enhancing his human nature to be impeccable.

Basil of Caesarea (ca. 330–379) reflects the Cappadocians' concern with human passibility because of the outcome of sin. Basil distinguishes between the natural passions that Christ assumed, and those "passions" that arise "from wickedness" (ἀπὸ κακίας πάθη).[107] The transformation of his humanity must

---

[103]Didym. *Commentary on Psalms* Text 18.1.4-5 (ed. Gesché, *La christologie du 'Commentaire sur les Psaumes'*, 135); trans. Grillmeier, *Christ in Christian Tradition*, 1:363.

[104]Athanasius *Oratio III contra Arianos* 33 (ed. B. de Montfaucon, PG 26 [1857]: 393B).

[105]Ath. *De Incarnatione* 17, in *Contra Gentes and De Incarnatione*, ed. and trans. Robert W. Thomson, Oxford Early Christian Texts (Oxford: Clarendon, 1971), 177, italics in trans.

[106]Cf. Pelikan's observation, *Emergence of the Catholic Tradition*, 285-86, "Despite their fundamental differences, the theory of the hypostatic union and the theory of the indwelling Logos both concentrated on death rather than on sin."

[107]Basil *Epistle 261*, in *The Letters*, trans. Roy J. Deferrari and Martin R.P. McGuire, Loeb Classical Library [1934], 4:80.

eclipse the evil passions because they are unworthy of Christ's divine purity.[108] Basil sees this transformation in an incarnational union by which the divine nature in Christ absorbed his humanity.[109] By this sort of deifying union, the divine nature destroys both death and sin in Christ's humanity to make it immortal and impeccable—"not liable to sin" (μήτε ὑπεύθυνον ἁμαρτία).[110] His human sinlessness was thus caused by his divine impeccability as a deification of human nature that Christians will share in through union with Christ (2 Pet 1:4).

Gregory of Nyssa (ca. 335–ca. 394) represents M2 with his strong emphasis on deification. This transformation by communication of attributes is clear when he says that the humanity in Christ "does not remain in its own properties" (οὔτε... ἐν τοῖς ἑαυτῆς ἰδιώμασιν) after being unified with "the heavenly impassibility" (οὐρανοὺς ἄνοδον).[111] The humanity of Christ is "transformed into divine power" (τὴν θείαν δύναμιν μεταστοιχειώσας), having been invested with power which specifically blocks the sin that normally arises in the human will.[112] The deification continues in a progressive exaltation of Christ's humanity by absorption in the divinity, illustrated by the well-known image of a drop of vinegar mixed in an endless ocean.[113] Gregory's primary concerns are to defend the completeness of Christ's humanity (proven by his temptations, along with other markers of true humanity[114]) and the union of two natures in Christ.[115] Nonetheless, this union cannot take place unless by transformation that eclipses the human passibility with divine impassibility because of the tendency of passibility to sin.[116] Therefore, Gregory's view of Christ's impeccability, temptation, and sinlessness expresses M2 as the divine impassibility and purity that divinizes the Lord's human nature to be

---

[108] Basil *Epistle 261*, 4:80.

[109] Basil *Epistle 261*, 4:82.

[110] Basil *Epistle 261*, 4:82.

[111] Gregory of Nyssa *Antirrheticus Adversus Apollinarem* 42 (ed. J. -P. Migne, PG 45 [1858]: 1253B).

[112] Gr. Nyss. *Epistola III ad Eustathia et Ambrosia* (PG 46:1021A).

[113] Gr. Nyss. *Ad Theophilum Adv. Apoll.* (PG 45:1276CD). Wolfson (*Philosophy of the Church Fathers*, 381-82, 398) notes that this image was not original with Gregory, but came from stock usage by the Stoics, as in Stobaeus *Ecologae* 1.17, and was typically used to indicate the theory of union that Wolfson calls Stoic mixture of two things that can be unmixed. The mixture is not a *tertium quid*, but there is reciprocal corruption (or, transformation) of each component. This seems to fit Gregory's view of the union and explains why he used the vinegar drop image so frequently as he did.

[114] Srawley, "Gregory of Nyssa on the Sinlessness of Christ", 435. Other markers of his true humanity are Jesus' ignorance, growth in knowledge, fearing death, and having a sense of abandonment by God.

[115] Srawley, "Gregory of Nyssa on the Sinlessness of Christ", 434.

[116] Gr. Nyss. *Contra Eunomium* 6.3 (PG 45:721B).

impeccable.[117]

Cyril of Alexandria (378–444) gives many examples of M2 because of his soteriological concern for the deification of a universal humanity in Christ (similar to the Cappadocians and Athanasius).[118] Cyril writes about the need for deification of Christ's humanity in relation to sin: "As God he wished to make that flesh which was held in the grip of sin and death evidently superior to sin and death."[119] This example fits M2 closely by affirming that the divine nature of the Logos enhances his assumed humanity to make it naturally impeccable. Cyril insists on Christ's impeccability as a man who is not subject to sin as others are.[120] He is not even subject to temptation, but his temptations were given by God's love for the sake of other humans who are tempted and need to know how to resist these dangers.[121] Cyril argues that the union of the divine nature with the human nature in Christ was a transformation that he likens to dyeing textiles: the Logos effectively immersed his human soul in the divine "immutability" (ἄτρεπτον) in the same way that wool is set in a bath of dye.[122] The purpose of this deification was to make the humanity of Christ more powerful than sin by means of the divine immutability.[123] In light of this view of Christ's humanity as enhanced by his divinity to be impeccable, Cyril was shocked to hear that some people thought sin was a possibility for Jesus. For Cyril, it was so obvious from Christ's sinlessness that no danger existed for him

---

[117]Grillmeier's assessment, *Christ in Christian Tradition*, 1:376, of Gregory's view says as much: "Christ's humanity, then, is not simply dissolved in the Godhead. It has reality, but no longer its earthly *idiomata*. Everything that makes the 'universal human physis' the human hypostasis or the human individual or the 'person' is done away with and replaced by the divine characteristics, wisdom, power, holiness, impassibility. As there are only divine *idiomata* in Christ (i.e. in the humanity of Christ), there is no longer any cause to speak of two Sons. The human element in Christ is no longer shown in natural properties. . . . All is filled with the glory of the Godhead."

[118]McGuckin, *St Cyril*, 35, explains this view: "Cyril understands that the incarnation of God as man is not a static event, but rather the pattern and archetype of a process. He points to the seamless union of God and man in the single divine person of Jesus, truly God and man at one and the same time, founded on the single subjectivity of Christ, as not merely a sacrament of the presence of God among us, but a sacrament of how our own human lives are destined to be drawn into his divine life, and transformed in a similar manner. In short, for Cyril the manner of the incarnation is analogous to the manner of the sanctification and transfiguration of Christ's disciples."

[119]Cyr. *OTI EIS O KRISTOS* 718.28-32, in *Cyrille D'Alexandrie, Deux Dialogues Christologiques*, ed. and trans. G. M. de Durand, Sources chrétiennes 97 (Paris, Éditions du Cerf, 1964), 316; trans. McGuckin, *St Cyril*, 55.

[120]Cyr. *OTI EIS O KRISTOS* 744.37-39 (402).

[121]Cyr. *OTI EIS O KRISTOS* 754.22-26 (434).

[122]Cyr. *De Incarnatione unigenitii* 691.27-30, in *Cyrille D'Alexandrie, Deux Dialogues Christologiques*, Sources chrétiennes 97:230.

[123]Cyr. *Oratio Ad Theodosium* 54.26-30, ed. Eduardus Schwartz, *Acta conciliorum oecumenicorum* (Berlin: Walter de Gruyter, 1927), 1.1-4:54.

in being tempted to sin.[124] Instead of peccability, Cyril's view was that salvation required that Christ be impeccable, and explained it in terms of what I have summarized as M2.

Leo the Great (400–461) represents M2 in the Latin West. In his influential *Letter to Flavian* (the *Tome*), Leo is ambiguous when he affirms that the inviolable nature of divinity was united to passible humanity, causing an increase to the humanity, possibly explained in context as the way Christ was protected to remain "without inborn sin" (*sine sorde peccati*).[125] Leo's view is that temptations did not assault Christ in his purified humanity,[126] just as the two natures were mixed with each other[127] for this incarnational result. As with Cyril, Leo's view of Christ's temptations is that these were merely permitted by God for the sake of those who needed an example.[128] Leo affirms a true, full humanity in Christ; however, this is a humanity that has been perfected by communion with Christ's deity.

A final representative of M2 is Leontius of Jerusalem (d. 538).[129] Leontius argues that in the incarnational union, only the attributes (*idiomata*) of the two natures are transformed; the natures themselves remain unmingled.[130] This is the way he explains the deification of human nature as a universal assumed and elevated in Christ.[131] By taking up human nature in the union, the unassailable Logos deifies his human nature to protect it from the devil, sin, and death.[132] This "deification" (ἐκθεώσεως) is a fulfillment and re-creation of the humanity by making it share in the divine nature.[133] Moreover, Leontius sees the actual

---

[124]Cyr. *Adversus Anthropomorphitas, epistola ad Calosyrium* 18 (ed. J. Auberti, PG 76 [1859]: 1120D).

[125]Leo Magnus *The Tome of Pope Leo the Great*, ed. E. H. Blakeney, Texts for Students 29 (London: S.P.C.K., 1923), 24.

[126]Leo Mag. *Ep.* 35.3 *ad Julianum* (ed. Petro Fratibus Ballerinis and Hieronymo Fratibus Ballerinis, PL 54 [1865]: 809A).

[127]Leo Mag. *Sermo* 23.1 (PL 54:200A).

[128]Leo Mag. *Sermo* 39.3 (PL 54:264C).

[129]Some have identified Leontius of Byzantium with Leontius of Jerusalem (Leontius H.), but I trust the conclusion of Grillmeier, *Christ*, 2.2:274, and David Beecher Evans, *Leontius of Byzantium: An Origenist Christology*, Dumbarton Oaks Studies 13 (Washington, DC: Dumbarton Oaks Center for Byzantine Studies, 1970), 1-2, 141-42, that the two should be distinguished. Evans seems right to mark the similarities in their thought and language as from Leontius H. having responded to Leontius B. as among his opponents in *Adversus Nestorianos* (long attributed to Leontius B., as in Migne), and he is replicating Leontius B.'s arguments to refute him.

[130]Grillmeier, *Christ in Christian Tradition*, 2.2:295-297.

[131]Leontius of Jerusalem *Adversus Nestorianos* 1.6 (ed. Migne, PG 86 pt. 1 [1860]: 1425D).

[132]Leontius of Jerusalem *Adversus Nestorianos* 1.47 (PG 86 pt. 1:1505D).

[133]Leontius of Jerusalem *Adversus Nestorianos* 1.18 (PG 86 pt. 1:1468C). Cited by Gray, "Leontius of Jerusalem's Case", 152. Gray comments that this passage tells, "a sharing in the essence of the Word as well as a sharing in His being." Gray notes that

sinlessness of Christ as a proof of his deity,[134] which also means that his impeccable deity has caused his human sinlessness. Though different from some others in his formulation, Leontius expresses M2 while emphasizing the integrity of the natures—particularly the freedom of Christ's humanity (i.e., Christ's freedom as a man, according to his human nature).[135]

EVALUATION OF M2: SINLESS BY DEIFICATION

The primary concern of M2 is to protect the unity of Christ's deity and humanity (which is consistent with unitive Christology). The impassibility of the divine nature is seen to be endangered by the passibility of the human nature (and the consequent susceptibility to sin). Thus, M2 formulates a deifying, elevating union between the two natures in Christ, resulting in his impeccable sinlessness. The incarnational union is a paradigm for human salvation in Christ's own person because he unites human nature to deity for the results of sanctifying, renewing, and empowering that lower nature for all believers.

I think M2 is a better, more developed model than M1. The number of patristic proponents should commend the model to us, since it seems to have been an adequate explanation for their purposes throughout many centuries. Unlike M1, M2 gives an explanation of *which* aspect of Christ's deity caused his sinlessness (and *how*), specifying the energizing of the human nature in deification.

Impassibility was the particular divine attribute emphasized by Clement of Alexandria and Gregory of Nyssa that caused Jesus' sinlessness. However, had this been true, impassibility would seem to have excluded temptation entirely (not just sin). If Jesus lacked the ability to suffer or feel the pull of temptation to some sin as a possible good, then it does not seem that temptation would have been possible for Jesus. Indeed, some sort of passibility seems necessary for Jesus if he was to have the experiences that are described in the Scripture (and for God too, if the concept of divine passibility is qualified properly).[136] So, versions of M2 that specify deification according to impassibility seem

---

this is a rare term for divinization (ἐκθεώσεως), but not one that is unattested elsewhere (153).

[134]Leontius of Jerusalem *Adversus Nestorianos* 4.37 (PG 86 pt. 1:1705C). Cited by Grillmeier, *Christ in Christian Tradition*, 2.2:300.

[135]The development of emphasizing Christ's human freedom is noted by Grillmeier, *Christ in Christian Tradition*, 2.2:300, who takes this as extremely important in the progress of doctrine. He lauds this emphasis as particularly harmonious with modern Christological reflections that stress the true humanity of Christ.

[136]Abraham Heschel's theology of pathos (*The Prophets*, 2:1-11) seems right to describe God's dynamic relationship with humanity, by which God passionately participates in history. Yet, there is some sense in which God remains transcendent to his creation and untouchable by it. I am indebted to Robert G. Lister for this distinction in his "Impassible and Impassioned".

unhelpful and inadequate because such cannot account for temptation.

The deification model contributes something that should not be missed by the account of Christ's humanity as somehow having been affected by union with the divine nature. At this point it may be best to consider M2 as giving part of the answer to the dilemma of impeccability and temptation, that is, explaining precisely *why* Jesus could not have sinned. (The other part is explaining *how* Jesus did not sin in a way that he remains an example, becomes empathetic, and is praiseworthy for the achievement.) M2 may provide some light along the lines of what John of Damascus formulated as nature-perichoresis.[137] Nature-perichoresis is the asymmetrical penetration of Christ's human nature by the divine nature (by omnipresence) without an actual communication of divine attributes or the transformation of the human attributes.[138] When the Damascene addresses the question of Jesus and temptation, he appeals to what I have termed M3 (below), but his formulation of nature-perichoresis seems to express the main idea of M2, that is, something of the divine nature was specially (uniquely) present and active in Christ's human nature in a way that prevented him from sinning. Despite what Jesus may have experienced (or feared?) as a possibility of sin, the hypostatic union (by which he remained fully God while he became fully man) seems to require some sort of divine restriction from sin.[139] M2 explains this restriction as the result of deification, the energizing of Christ's human nature through union to his deity. An absolute of the deifying union is that Jesus was unable to sin. Were Jesus to be in danger of failing against temptation purely on the basis of his human efforts, the perichoresis of the divine nature penetrating his human nature would have functioned as a sort of steel backbone of impassibility to his human will, fortifying the natural faculty to resist the temptation and embrace obedience. In this way, M2 may provide a reasonable account of Christ's impeccability according to deification of the nature-perichoresis sort.

Where M2 seems to fall short as theologically inadequate is in the way the model explains *how* Jesus resisted sin. Two of the same critiques noted above with M1 (diminishing the temptation and the validity of Christ's victory) could be repeated here because both M1 and M2 explain Christ's sinlessness in terms of his impeccability (or, for Gregory of Nyssa and Clement of Alexandria, the impeccability that results from impassibility). Both models affirm that Jesus did not sin because he could not sin. Thus, if we consider how M2 works as an

---

[137] John of Damascus, *De fide orthodoxa* 3.7, cited by Oliver D. Crisp, *Divinity and Humanity* (Cambridge: Cambridge University Press, 2007), 20.

[138] Crisp, *Divinity and Humanity*, 24-27. Crisp has helpfully developed the concept as he finds it in John of Damascus. Crisp is careful to distinguish that the penetration of Christ's human nature by the divine nature is a much greater degree than the penetration that can be said of God's sustaining involvement in all creatures.

[139] More can be said, but suffice it here to say that it is impossible for God to sin, so God incarnate is unable to sin. See chs 10-12 below, Systematic Formulation.

explanation of Christ's temptation in Gethsemane, it seems that at most M2 can tell why a failure never could have occurred, but not why Jesus was able to choose to obey rather than shrink back from God's will.

According to M2, Jesus, when struggling in temptation to avoid the cup of wrath, finally resisted by means of the energized, deified power of his humanity. Through union with his divine nature, divine energy produced something inherent in his humanity and steeled him to resist sin indefectibly. As a man, Jesus feels the strain of his fear and his anticipation of suffering, right alongside his three friends (who are overwhelmed and fail to watch with him in prayer). His distress is real, but he feels something else rising within him to meet the challenge—a firm resolve of his human will, made impassible or impeccable by union to his divine nature—and he casts himself on the side of obedience. As a man, he chooses right, denies his human desire to evade the suffering, and faithfully submits himself to God's will. Here, as in his other temptations, he has triumphed against the appeal of a sin by means of his fortified, deified human nature that enjoys the strength of the divine nature to which it is welded. Jesus knows he is weak in his flesh, but he is able to exert that nature to obedience because his humanity has been strengthened and energized through union with his deity. The outcome was never in doubt (a contrast with the disciples' experiences at the same time, and Peter's repeated failure), but Jesus struggled against his temptation as a man nonetheless.

Unlike M1, M2 does not explain Christ's victory by means of his having resorted to his deity as a supernatural, external-to-his-humanity weapon or shield. M2 places the impervious divine support within Christ's humanity, and he withstood the temptation on that basis. Deification elevated and fortified his human nature without changing it. But this enrichment seems to undermine Christ's experience and achievement. If we repeat the analogy (from M1) of ascending Mt. Everest on foot, the effect of deification is as if Jesus has relied on performance-enhancing drugs to climb the mountain in his human nature (which is significantly closer to common human experience than flying in an airplane overhead). His deified humanity and the quality of his temptations are what glorified humanity experiences (if glorified humanity is still subject to temptation in the new creation). He enjoyed a power within his humanity that others do not, so how could he understand as a first-hand experience what it is to be tempted in a human nature and struggle against sin? If his human nature is strengthened to resist temptation, then he feels only a small twinge of the strain against him. Thus, the relevance of his temptation is diminished because his experiences are too different to make him truly empathetic with others, or reasonable as a model for them to follow. M2 makes it difficult to see how Jesus and his temptations are like ours because, he, unlike us, possessed a divine ingredient that proved most decisive in his victory over temptation.

Proponents might argue that this same deification is possible for all believers (thus, Jesus has opened the way for Christians to share in the divine nature after his pattern), but they do not argue this way (they posit deification by grace, not by nature), and there are problems with arguing for a deification analogy to Christ's experience anyway. The limitation that deification set on how much strain of temptation Jesus felt seems far different from the (apparently) frail humanity possessed by Adam in which he is (apparently) easily overcome by Satan in Eden. No such deification seems to have been available for Adam, yet Christ's battle with Satan in the wilderness seems explicitly orchestrated by God as a recapitulation of that first struggle in the cosmic war between God and Satan in Eden. Instead of recapitulation, if M2 is right, Jesus faced and defeated Satan's temptations as the fortified Son, not simply as the faithful Son who exhibits prototypical obedience for all believers. M2 is not able to account for the frailty of Jesus within his humanity, having faced and triumphed over temptation within the same sort of human nature that is common to Adam and the rest of humanity (i.e., without deification). In other words, M2 depicts Jesus as having cheated through using the internal effects of deification (analogous to using performance-enhancing drugs in sports), which I think is false. If Jesus possessed an unequal advantage of deification in temptation relative to the rest of us, then the praiseworthiness of his triumph (as the second Adam) and his example for others (as the pattern for faithfulness) may be called into question. It seems that if deification were the cause of his sinlessness, this would have also precluded the struggle necessary to Jesus learning empathy (Heb 4:15) and obedience through that suffering (Heb 5:7-8).

Moreover, Scripture does not specify anything like deification in the actual means Jesus employed in resisting temptation, or as the means that believers are exhorted to rely upon as assistance for meeting their temptations.[140] Instead, the only clear reference to deification that I am aware of (2 Pet 1:4) is the fulfillment and completion of salvation, synonymous with glorification, and is not specified as the generative means of progressing in salvation on this side of glory.[141] The problem of marking Christ's difference from others because of deification is also suggested by the way two proponents of M2 (Cyril, Leo) believed that his temptations were expressly (and only?) for giving an example to others, a sort of *how to* practicum on temptation, not that any temptation was for Jesus a real and unavoidable assault that truly tested his human moral mettle.

Proponents of M2 could argue that deification for Christ occurs by the Holy Spirit, and a parallel sort of deification by grace is available to believers. This is not the way they have explained the deification of Christ's human nature. On

---

[140] The argument from silence is not best, but I think here it is at least good because specific things are mentioned in Scripture (e.g., prayer, community, the Holy Spirit, angels) as the support accompanying Jesus in his temptations, while the idea of deification is never indicated in this connection.

[141] I think the deification in view is relational engagement with God. Psalm 82:6 might be considered in regard to deification, but even here the concept is a status of those engaged by God relationally, not an ontological transformation of their nature.

the contrary, Cyril, for one, was extremely hostile to the suggestion that the Holy Spirit had this sort of role.[142] Thus, in M2, the role of the Holy Spirit for the Messiah's spiritual life and ministry was counted as superfluous because the divine nature of the Logos deified his human nature.[143]

Therefore, I find M2 to be theologically inadequate to explain how Jesus did not sin. The causative force of deification in his human nature raises too much difference between Jesus and the rest of humanity (unnecessarily) and cannot be harmonized with the relevance of his temptation that Scripture highlights. Patristic contemporaries of M2 proponents also seem to have found the model lacking because two other models were formulated during the period as alternate explanations. These are presented in the next chapter.

---

[142]See above, ch. 3, n. 2 for Cyril's anathema against all who counted a dynamic role of the Holy Spirit in Christ. I assume that this anathema is to guard against Adoptionism.

[143]This is the critique of a patristic contemporary, Theodore of Mopsuestia (see M4, below), in *Fragmenta Dogmatica, ex libris contra Apollinarium* (PG 66 [1859]: 996B). According to G. J. Reinink, "Quotations from the Lost Works of Theodoret of Cyrus and Theodore of Mopsuestia in an Unpublished East Syrian Work on Christology", in Studia patristica 33, ed. Elizabeth A. Livingstone (Leuven: Peeters, 1997), 565, Theodore charged that many had obscured or ignored the Holy Spirit's involvement in the life of Jesus. The quotations noted by Reinink are from Theodore's *De Incarnatione* 5 and 12. Unfortunately, Reinink does not give the text, reference, or translation that is the basis of his claim that Theodore was critical in this way.

CHAPTER 5

Patristic Models (Part 2)

As noted above, two additional models were formulated during the patristic period for explaining Christ's impeccability, temptation, and sinlessness. For each model, I will describe the distinctive features, survey several representatives of those features in chronological progression, and then evaluate the model's theological adequacy.

M3: Sinless by Divine Hegemony

DESCRIPTION OF M3

The question asked in M3 is this: How does Christ's *operation* in two natures result in his sinlessness as a man? The answer given is that the divine Logos directs his humanity sinlessly in all the actions of his human experience. Like M2, M3 explains Christ's impeccability and resultant sinlessness in temptation by means of the predominance of his deity over his humanity. Different from M2 is the way that M3 explains this predominance as *personal* and *volitional* hegemony, not *natural* predominance of M2 (i.e., the deifying enhancement of humanity by a divine attribute). The predominance of M3 is the Logos's leadership of his humanity to resist his temptations sinlessly. Christ's sinlessness is not a necessity of his human nature; it is a necessity of his divine will.[1] The Logos is the active, efficient cause of his human sinlessness. The impeccable Logos directs his assumed humanity in sinless action by his prevailing divine will. Jesus can be tempted as a man, but he cannot sin because

---

[1] The question of whether the will is a faculty of the person (as in Monothelitism, the view that Christ has only one will to operate his two natures) or a faculty of the nature (as in Dyothelitism, the view that Christ has two wills, one that is proper to each nature) was resolved at the Sixth Council (Constantinople III, 681) in favor of Dyothelitism. I think the representatives of M3 uniformly assume Dyothelitism (that is, even those who have not explicitly declared it because they lived in a time when it was not questioned). Alongside the greatest defender of Dyothelitism in the seventh century, Maximus the Confessor, a fourth century example is Gregory of Nazianzen's statement: "[Christ's] human will cannot be opposed to God, seeing it is altogether taken into God; but conceived of simply as in our nature" *Fourth Theological Oration*, in *Christology of the Later Fathers*, ed. Edward R. hardy, vol. 3, The Library of Christian classics (Philadelphia: Westminster, 1954), 185.

he is the divine Son who will never choose to sin. His human will is subordinate and submitted to his divine will.[2] Consequently, Christ's attitudes and actions as a man are elevated and deified *de facto* because of the overriding will and choice of the agent-operator. In answer to the question of how did Jesus remain sinless in the face of temptations, M3 proponents point to the will of the divine person who is master of the human nature he has assumed. The single-subject predication of all Christ's attributes to his person—*viz.* temptability of his humanity and impeccability of his deity—secures the unity of the incarnation. In contrast to M2, M3 has no room for a substantial transformation or deifying fortification of Christ's humanity. Instead, M3 explains Christ's sinlessness as a fulfilled and perfected human operation. Emphasis on the recapitulation of a human victory over Satan and temptation demonstrates the godly life of Jesus as a human example for Christians to follow. Emphasis on the integrity of the two natures possessed by the divine Logos shows the concern that the union has not substantially modified the human nature he assumed. Instead, the hegemony of the Logos over his humanity leads to the mirroring of divine attributes without changing human nature. M3 pictures an *enabling* communication of divine leadership instead of the *transforming* communication of deifying divine attributes (as in M2). Important to advocates of M3 are at least three features: the likeness of Christ's humanity to common humanity, the example that Jesus demonstrates for others, and his achievement of sinlessness as a human accomplishment in the face of temptations. Some representatives of M3 suggest the idea that Christ's humanity is instrumental in fulfilling the redemptive plan, and the Logos directs his manhood as his tool. Moreover, Christ's incarnational action occurs without his human nature becoming different from the nature in which other human beings must struggle against temptations to sin. His human nature is the same, temptable stuff as ours. The only difference is the sinlessness of his actions. Thus, if others follow Christ's example, they may live towards sinless ends as he did, employing his methods as their own vital means of obedience.

REPRESENTATIVES OF M3

The earliest theologian to suggest M3 is Irenaeus of Lyons (130–200). He insists on the divine use of the assumed humanity in an instrumental way, which fits his view of Christ's whole life as a redemptive recapitulation as the second Adam.[3] Irenaeus opposed the Gnostics' mistaken ideas about Christ

---

[2] Cf. the conclusion of the Sixth Council that Jesus has two wills, as noted by Dupuis, *Who Do You Say I Am?*, 114. "Constantinople III [681] affirmed in Jesus an authentic human will and action not contrary to, but perfectly submitted to, the divine will."

[3] Irenaeus *Adversus haereses* 5.24.4 (ed. Migne, PG 7 [1857]: 1188C). Irenaeus's view of recapitulation is helpfully summarized by M. Steiner, *La Tentation de Jésus dans L'Interprétation Patristique de Saint Justin a Origéne* (Paris: Libraire Lecoffre, 1962), 201: "The recapitulation is the restoration of humanity lost in Adam, the final links in

(i.e., that Christ did not have a physical body, but only seemed to be a man) to argue instead for the likeness of "the Lord's flesh" with "our flesh".[4] This claim of the essential likeness suggests that Irenaeus also opposes the idea of M2 that Christ's humanity was transformed to be deiform. Irenaeus has a concern to be able to affirm Christ's sinlessness without setting that moral achievement as a marker of his natural difference from the rest of sinful humanity.[5] In his view, the Logos aided Christ's assumed humanity to conquer his temptations to sin. Irenaeus explains that the authenticity of Christ as a true second Adam required that he exercise *reserve* or *rest* his divine powers to permit human temptation: "The Logos remained quiescent during the process of temptation, crucifixion and death, but aided the human nature when it conquered, and endured, and performed deeds of kindness, and rose again from the dead, and was received up into heaven."[6] M3 shows in Irenaeus's insistence on Christ's human victory that reverses the human defeat of Adam. Jesus obeys the law as a man, and answers Satan's temptations in the wilderness through nothing else but by quoting Scripture (thus demonstrating the example for others to follow).[7]

Tertullian suggests M3 (in addition to M1) when he writes that Jesus struck down his temptations by abstinence, possibly meaning a volitional mastery of

---

which Adam let himself be enclosed by Satan." Steiner notes that the links are the three temptations and death, which are paralleled in Adam and Christ.

[4]Iren. *Haer.* 5.14.3 (PG 7:1162C). The Gnostics favored Docetism, the heresy that denied a physical, bodily aspect to Christ's human nature (he only seemed to be a man, but was actually a spirit only), because they believed in a complete dichotomy between spiritual and material reality. God could not have entered into a true, bodily human existence because the material world is subject to change and corruption, which is incompatible with the way they understood the nature of God to be impassible, immutable spirit.

[5]Iren. *Haer.* 5.14.3 (PG 7:1162C).

[6]Iren. *Haer.* 3.19.3 (PG 7:941; trans. Adolf von Harnack, *History of Dogma*, vol. 2, trans. Neil Buchanan [Boston: Roberts Brothers, 1897], 284). This quotation and the concept of veiling the divine nature is repeated approvingly by Calvin, *Comment. in Harm.*, Luc. 2.40, *Ioannis Calvini Opera quae supersunt omnia*, ed. Wilhelm Baum, Eduard Cunitz, and Euard Reuss, Corpus Reformatum (Brunswick, NJ: C. A. Schwetschke and Son, 1892; reprint, New York: Johnston Reprint Corp., 1964), 45:104. All page numbers to volumes of critical editions in this series will be given with the abbreviation CO. (I will return to the idea of quiescent deity when we get to Calvin, below).

[7]Iren. *Haer.* 5.21.1 (PG 7:1179BC). A similar emphasis on Jesus' triumph over Satan in the wilderness by biblical logic shows in Justin Martyr *Dialogus Cum Trypohone* 125.4 (ed. Miroslav Marcovich [Berlin: Walter De Guyter, 1997], 286). Justin (ca. 100-165) sees Jesus' human resistance to Satan as the typological fulfillment of Jacob's struggle with God, *Isra El*, and the parallel between Jacob's injury and Christ's death. Justin does not have more material that indicates his part in one model of Christ's impeccability and temptation or another (from what I could find).

the weak cravings of the flesh.⁸ Christ's corporeal humanity is a necessary instrument for the redemptive work of the Son, so Tertullian emphasizes the similarity of Christ's authentic humanity to common humanity.⁹ In his opposition to the Gnostics, Tertullian argued for the reality of Christ's sinless humanity in essential likeness to the sinful flesh of Adam and others.¹⁰ Harnack observes that Tertullian "distinguished what Christ did as man from what he did as God in order to prove that he was not a *tertium quid*", which is consistent with the M3 emphasis on the integrity of the natures.¹¹ Accordingly, Tertullian matches the trends of thought that constitute M3 in the way that he insists on the human example and the likeness of Christ's flesh to other human beings. Nonetheless, Tertullian's alignment with M3 is not as clear as some others are.

Apollinaris of Laodicea (ca. 310–390, "the Younger") shows the danger of going too far with M3.¹² More than many others, Apollinaris forms his Christological model in response to the problem of Christ's passible, mutable, and temptable humanity.¹³ Apollinaris thought that deity and humanity could not exist together in one person in their entirety, believing that two complete natures always entail two persons. Conflict between the two souls was inevitable (each soul having a mind and a will). Apollinaris proposes the Word as the intellectual replacement for the human mind. When charged that he had diminished Christ's humanity and made it unlike normal humans, Apollinaris responded that Jesus was only "found as a man" (Phil 2:8) and so was different from humans in part. But Apollinaris also saw this as necessary that Jesus have a divine rational soul because the theologian asserted that a free human will is necessarily subject to sin. Instead, the Christ of Apollinarianism had an immutable, divine will because the Logos operated in place of the human

---

⁸Tert. *De Baptismo* 20.20-24 (*Tertullian's Homily on Baptism*, ed. and trans. Ernest Evans [London: S.P.C.K., 1964], 42-43).
⁹Tert. *Adversus Marcionem* 5.14.1-2 (*Against Marcion*, 2 vols., ed. and trans. Ernest Evans [Oxford: Clarendon, 1972], 597-99).
¹⁰Tert. *De Car.* 16.780-81 (ed. J. -P. Migne, PL 2:826).
¹¹Harnack, *History of Dogma*, 2:283. This seems to indicate that he would be opposed to a transformation model. Unfortunately, Harnack does not document the basis for his assessment.
¹²Despite the similarity between Apollinarianism and Eutychianism (both are unitive Christological types that diminish the humanity of Jesus), I think that Eutyches would have agreed more with M2 on the basis of the type of relation between the divine and human natures as completely mingled. Extant writings of Eutyches do not indicate his thoughts on the topic of the impeccability and temptation of Christ. For Apollinaris, the issue in his formulation is human susceptibility to sin, so I include him here despite his denial of a full humanity in Christ (the Logos took the place of a human soul, so there is no created human soul in Christ, meaning mind and will).
¹³Apollinaris's Logos Christology truncated Christ's humanity to protect his deity from the taint of a wayward human will. J.N.D. Kelly, *Early Christian Doctrines*, 5ᵗʰ rev. ed., (London, Adam & Charles Black, 1960), 289-97.

mind.¹⁴ Thus, Apollinaris explains that in Christ the unconquerable divine Logos directs the flesh and actions of Jesus in a sinless human life, using the concept of *energies*, which I take to mean the powers of choice and will:

> According to Scripture, the complete man is not pure of sin in the present life, because of his inability to make his own energies coincide with the divine energies, and that is why he is not free from death. Therefore, God, having united himself to human flesh, retains the purity of his own energy, since he is a spirit not subject to psychical and carnal affections and governs the flesh in its carnal inclinations in a divine and impeccable way.¹⁵

This is an instrumental view of the humanity in Christ. The eternal Word drives his humanity in a divine way, fulfilling it as the *leading* or *ruling principle* of the assumed humanity (which just means a human physical body). Apollinaris sees this rule as soteriologically necessary, as in his claim:

> Therefore, the human race is saved not by the assumption of an intellect and of a whole human being but by the assumption of flesh, whose nature is to be ruled. What was needed was unchangeable Intellect which did not fall under the domination of the flesh on account of its weakness of understanding.¹⁶

Therefore, Apollinaris views the incarnational union as the Logos joined to a body, having displaced what exists in us as a human soul (including the substitution of his divine mind and will for a human mind and will), thereby securing the human sinlessness of Christ and salvation by the hegemony principle of M3.

Gregory of Nazianzen (ca. 325–389) is a Cappadocian representative of

---

¹⁴Meredith, *Cappadocians*, 111-12, explains that impeccability was one of the two primary motivations for Apollinaris: "The sinlessness of Christ derived from his being a vehicle of the divine nature, which *could not* sin. Unity and sinlessness were the main props upon which the Apollinarian picture of Christ rested." Cf. the comment by Spoerl, "Apollinarius and the Response", 427, "Apollinarius specifically constructed his heterodox tripartite Christological model, in which the Saviour is composed of divine (and thus necessarily ἄτρεπτος [immutable]) Word, a human animal soul and human flesh, to make it respond more adequately to the early Arian positing of a created, τρεπτός [mutable] Word incarnate in Jesus Christ, who was theoretically, if not actually, vulnerable to sin."

¹⁵Apollinaris of Laodicea *H KATA MEROS PISTIS* 30.13-16 (in *Apollinaris von Laodicea und Seine Schule I*, ed. Hans Lietzmann, Texte und Untersuchungen [Tübingen: J. C. B. Mohr, 1904; reprint: Hildesheim, New York: Georg Olms, 1970], 178-79), trans. in Jean Galot, *Who is Christ? A Theology of Incarnation*, trans. M. Angeline Bouchard (Chicago: Franciscan Herald, 1981), 231.

¹⁶Apollinar. *Fragments*, 76, trans. in Norris, *The Christological Controversy*, 109.

M3.[17] Gregory asserts that Christ was tempted as a man, but he triumphed as God, thus, Gregory gives full account of the reality of each nature in two sets of experiences.[18] The signs of M3 show in the way Gregory emphasizes Christ's human struggle and victory over temptations in comparison with Paul's struggles. According to that likeness between Jesus and other human beings, Gregory counts Christ's struggle through fasting as an important aspect in his victory over temptation.[19] This suggests that it is the *personal* effort that Jesus exerted against temptation, and not simply the divine power of an unwavering nature. When Gregory declares that Christ's deity was unassailable in temptation, it seems best to interpret him to mean that Jesus always succeeded because he is the divine Logos leading his humanity to perfection.[20] Frederick Norris also observes this hegemony idea of M3, "Nazianzen develops thematically the dominance of Jesus Christ's divinity."[21] This domination or hegemony is also expressed in the way Gregory defines Christ's human will as deified so that did not oppose the will of God,[22] as in this statement: "His Human Will cannot be opposed to God, seeing it is altogether taken into God; but conceived of simply as in our nature, inasmuch as the human will does not completely follow the Divine, but for the most part struggles against and resists it."[23] The divine will of Christ prevails and leads his human will in obedience. Therefore, Gregory stresses the unity of the two natures in Christ, and a view of salvation as deification (ideas common to M2), but Gregory's comments on Christ's temptations suggest that the Logos achieves the victory of human sinlessness as the leading principle in the incarnation (an M3 formula).

John Chrysostom (344–407) shows the features of M3 in his descriptions of Christ's temptations. Chrysostom writes that Christ's sinlessness must be a demonstration of what is possible in human flesh as the example of victory over

---

[17] It may be possible to sort Gregory with M2, with an emphasis on the divine nature instead of the person of the Logos, but I have sorted him (with some reservation) in M3 because he has much more regard for the struggle Jesus experienced (as in M3), and the M2 formulation seems to count this less.

[18] Gregory of Nazianzen *Oratio* 29.20 (PG 36 [1858]: 100C).

[19] Gr. Naz. *Oratio* 14.3 (PG 35 [1857]: 861B).

[20] Gr. Naz. *Oratio* 24.9 (PG 35:1180B), cf. *Oratio* 29.20.

[21] Frederick Norris, *Faith Gives Fullness to Reasoning: The Five Theological Orations of Gregory Nazianzen*, intro. and comm. Frederick W. Norris, trans. Lionel Wickham and Frederick Williams, Supplements to Vigiliae Christianae 13 (Leiden: Brill, 1991), 156.

[22] Demetrios Bathrellos, *The Byzantine Christ: Person, Nature, and Will in the Christology of Saint Maximus the Confessor*, Oxford Early Christian Studies (Oxford: Oxford University Press, 2004), 141.

[23] Gr. Naz. *Or.* 30.12, trans. Charles Gordon Browne and James Edward Swallow, NPNF², 7: 313.

temptation.[24] This means a triumph through the divine nature would not count soteriologically. For Jesus to be a true human example for his people and truly sympathetic to them without compromising his divine immutability, he must suffer the human weaknesses and surmount them by his divine will. Chrysostom explains this M3 sort of predominance in the following statement, using the literary device of Christ's first person perspective:

> I have never left the assumed humanity unharmonized with the divine operation, (acting) now as man, now as God, both indicating the nature, and bringing faith to the economy; teaching that the humbler things are to be referred to the humanity, and the nobler to the divinity, and by this unequal mixture of actions, interpreting the unequal union of the natures, and by (my) power over sufferings, declaring that my own sufferings are voluntary; as God, I curbed nature, supporting a fast for forty days, but afterwards, as man, I was hungry and tired; as God I calmed the raging sea, as man, I was tempted by the devil; as God, I expelled devils, as man, I am about to suffer for men.[25]

In this quotation, the experiences *as God* and *as man* frequently refer to the natures, but the emphasis on the unifying, single subject (*I*, the person) of the experiences emphasizes the agency and will of the Logos adventuring in his earthly life. Camillus Hay agrees that there is in Chrysostom a personal focus of the attributions quoted above, as he explains Chrysostom's formulation: "Christ acts as a man, but these human actions are controlled by the Divine Person in such a way that they bring faith to the economy without overshadowing the divine nature."[26] Hay also concludes that Chrysostom "nowhere affirms the presence of a human will in Christ", which fits with an overall view of the divine predominance.[27] In his method of harmonizing the divine and human actions of Jesus, Chrysostom protects his soteriological commitments to divine immutability and to Christ's human example in temptation.[28] Therefore, when read along with others who come to similar

---

[24]John Chrysostom *In Epist. Ad Hebraeos. Cap. IV. Homil. VII* (ed. D. Bern de Montfaucon, PG 63 [1860]: 63.75).

[25]Chrys. *In quat. Lazarum* (PG 50 [1859]: 643.647; trans. in Hay, "St John Chrysostom", 310).

[26]Hay, "St John Chrysostom", 310.

[27]Hay, "St John Chrysostom", 309. Of course, the lack of an affirmation of Christ's human will does not mean Chrysostom was a Monothelite (Jesus had only one will, not two), but the absence of mention seems to be explained by the dominant emphasis on the divine Subject of the incarnation. If pressed, Chrysostom probably would have affirmed that Christ certainly has two wills, but that his human will was surrendered or perfectly obedient to his divine will (an explanation that became common, as in the conclusion defended by Maximus the Confessor, and the Sixth Council [Constantinople III, 681]).

[28]Cf. Naidu, "The Doctrine of Christ", 226, who agrees that Chrysostom underscores Christ's example for Christian life (a major feature of M3): "As a noble champion who

conclusions, Chrysostom can be sorted along with the proponents of M3.

Jerome (ca. 347–420) is not as clear on this topic as we would like,[29] but he indicates his tendency to the M3 explanation of Christ's temptation in his homily on Psalm 16.[30] Jerome interprets verse seven as a prophetic type of Christ's anguished temptation in Gethsemane, explaining that the kidneys in the passage "metaphorically represent the innermost thoughts of the self, which the divine Word controls, enabling Christ to anticipate and endure his suffering without emotional disturbance".[31] Jerome suggests that Jesus was tempted in his humanity as a redemptive pattern for others, but when he discusses the wilderness temptations, Jerome is unclear about how the Lord won his victory in his humanity.[32]

Augustine represents M3 when he describes the human will of Christ as subservient to the divine will during the Gethsemane temptation.[33] Similarly, Augustine specifies that there is a human mind in Christ, but this too is taken up and supervened by the Logos,[34] which hegemony is necessary to protect him from the human ignorance that would entail sin (as many believed). Augustine thus suggests the divine hegemony model, and opposes the transformation concept of M2. He affirms, "Divinity is not changed into the creature, so as to cease to be Divinity; nor the creature into Divinity, so as to cease to be creature."[35] However, Augustine has more detailed thoughts on the topic, and represents M4 much more strongly than M3 (or M1, above).

Another Latin theologian, Leo the Great, represents M3 because he insists

---

has withstood the rigors of testing and affliction in his human experience, Christ has become our example. Christians must be willing to take up the cross and follow him, because he was willing to do so in the first place. Christ not only identified with us in his human nature by entering brotherhood with us, he also experienced the pain of suffering."

[29]Cf. Grillmeier's comment (*Christ in Christian Tradition*, 1:402): "Jerome did not treat christology in such detail and depth as Hilary. There is still no consideration of the way in which God and man are one in Christ."

[30]Jerome *Tract. psal. XV* (in *Opera Pars II: Opera Homiletica*, ed. G. Morin, CCSL 78 [1953], 376-77). Jerome follows the LXX numbering; it is Psalm 16 in English versions.

[31]Quoted and trans. in Richard A. Layton, "From "Holy Passion" to Sinful Emotion: Jerome and the Doctrine of *Propassio*", in *In Dominico Eloquio, In Lordly Eloquence: Essays on Patristic Exegesis in Honor of Robert Louis Wilken*, ed. Paul M. Blowers et al. (Grand Rapids: Eerdmans, 2002), 286-87. This seems to be a complicated (and inadequate) way of affirming impassibility despite the evidence for Jesus' suffering.

[32]Jerome *Homily* 76 (II), in *Homilies of Saint Jerome*, vol. 2, trans. Marie Liguori Ewald, FOC 57 (Washington, DC: The Catholic University of America Press, 1966), 132.

[33]Aug. *2 Enarratione In Ps.* 32 (1).2 (in *Enarrationes in Psalmos I – L*, ed. E. Eligius Dekkers and Johannes Fraipont, CCSL 38 [1956]: 248).

[34]Aug. *Enarr. In Ps.* 3.3 (*Enarrationes in Psalmos I – L*, CCSL 38:8).

[35]Aug. *De Trin.* 1.7.14 (ed. W.J. Mountain, CCSL 50:46; trans. Arthur West Haddan, NPNF[1] 3 [1956]: 24).

on the integrity of the two natures in Christ. Leo can account for the full humanity in Christ only by subordinating it to the ruling divine will especially in terms of sin and passibility. Leo writes: "For he had no opposition in his flesh, nor did the strife of desires give rise to a conflict of wishes. His bodily senses were active without the law of sin, and the reality of his emotions being under the control of his Godhead and his mind, was neither assaulted by temptations nor yielded to injurious influences."[36] Despite the evidence for Leo's alignment with M2 (noted above), this example shows the variety of his ideas (as with Augustine) by which Leo also thinks of Christ along the lines of M3.

Leontius of Byzantium (485–543) defends Chalcedonian Christology and suggests some features of M3. Leontius writes that for Christ to be an example to follow, his humanity could not be transformed, but had to be weak like other human beings.[37] Grillmeier observes that the hegemony of the divine will in the incarnational union is Leontius's way of guaranteeing the sinlessness of Christ.[38] Leontius argues that since passibility normally entails vulnerability to sin, Christ kept himself from sin as a man by the will of the Logos, as in this statement on the role of the divine will:

> When the flesh bears the sufferings that are natural to it, the Logos with many others sends it control over the passions. For the 'physical bond' of the Logos with the flesh is inseparable and absolutely insoluble. To be free from suffering was not possible for the body in every respect. For it [his humanity] had this freedom from suffering not from the union as such, but from the will of the one united (Logos), who disposed of this according to the moment and the need.[39]

The hegemony of the divine will over the assumed humanity preserves the integrity of the weaker nature by leading it to fulfillment. Leontius writes, "Supernatural [powers] do not abrogate natural ones; rather, they lead it onwards, and set them in motion to be able to do those things [proper to them], and to receive in addition the power to do what lies above them."[40] Thus, Leontius explains the sinlessness of Christ in terms of his divine will.

Maximus the Confessor (580-662) defended two wills in Christ and

---

[36]Leo Mag. *Ep.* 35.3 *ad Julianum* (ed. Ballerinis, PL 54 [1865]: 809A; trans. in Grillmeier, *Christ in Christian Tradition*, 1:535).

[37]Leontius B. *Contra Aphthartodocetas* (PG 86 pt. 1:1348D-1349D).

[38]Grillmeier, *Christ in Christian Tradition*, 2.2:218.

[39]Leontius B. *Contra Aphthartodocetas* (PG 86 pt. 1:1332B; trans. Grillmeier, *Christ in Christian Tradition*, 2.2:218).

[40]Leontius B. *Contra Aphthartodocetas* (PG 86 pt. 1:1333B; trans. in Brian E. Daley, "'A Richer Union': Leontius of Byzantium and the Relationship of Human and Divine in Christ", in Studia patristica 24, ed. Elizabeth A. Livingstone [Leuven: Peeters, 1993], 263 n.100).

formulated his model along the lines of M3.[41] The choice of the Logos (which Maximus sees as the choice of the agent or hypostasis, not simply the divine will) was to align his human will to the divine will. Maximus understood Christ as a microcosm of salvation, and the pattern for all people to conform their wills to the divine will.[42] Maximus explains that Christ's human willing is divinely shaped, moved, and deified in the elevation of its operation of harmony and concurrence with the divine will, as in the example of Christ's struggle in Gethsemane:

> He was in truth and properly a human being: to this his natural will bears witness in his plea to be spared from death. . . . And again that the human will is wholly deified, in its agreement with the divine will itself, since it is eternally moved and shaped by it and in accordance with it, is clear when he shows that all that matters is a perfect verification of the will of the Father, in his saying as a human being, 'Not mine, but your will be done,' by this giving himself as a type and example of setting aside our own will by the perfect fulfillment of the divine, even if because of this we find ourselves face to face with death.[43]

Christ's sinlessness, for Maximus, is the willing obedience to God by the Logos according to the will in his human nature. This was possible and necessary because Christ's human will has received its fulfillment through the divine will, having been anchored to God's will for true freedom of the creaturely will.[44] While Maximus is concerned to draw a parallel between Christ's sinlessness and the glorified deification of the human will in believers so that they (by grace) will not sin,[45] his analysis of Christ's human willing rests upon the choice of the Logos to bow his human will to God's will. The will itself does not choose, but the person possessing the will chooses and enacts his choices by means of the will, and sinlessly so, as Maximus writes: "But as for the Savior's willing according to his human nature, even though it was natural, it was not bare like ours, any more than his humanity as such is, since it has been perfectly deified above us in union, because of which it is actually sinless."[46]

---

[41]Maximus could be interpreted along the lines of M2 in some ways because of his emphasis on deification. However, I have sorted him with M3 because of the emphasis on a personal choice of the Logos, which is different from the primarily natural influence of the divine attributes on the human nature in M2.

[42]Ian A. McFarland, "'Willing Is Not Choosing': Some Anthropological Implications of Dyothelite Christology", *International Journal of Systematic Theology* 9 (2007): 6.

[43]Maximus the Confessor *Opuscula Theologica et Polemica 7* (PG 91:80C-D), trans. Andrew Louth, *Maximus the Confessor* (London: Routledge, 1996), 186, cited in McFarland, "Anthropological Implications", 14. Cf. *Opusc.* 1, 32A; *Opusc.* 3, 45C, cited in Bathrellos, *Byzantine Christ*, 161, n. 356.

[44]McFarland, "Anthropological Implications", 15.

[45]McFarland, "Anthropological Implications", 18.

[46]Maximus *Opuscula Theologica et Polemica 20* (PG 91:236D), trans. McFarland, "Anthropological Implications", 11.

The deification or shaping of the human will by the divine will is the result of a hypostatic or personal choice of the Logos, and by which choice he was willingly impeccable as a man:

> The human will of God [incarnate] . . . having received being in unity together with God the Word, had a motion that was without hesitation but had instead fixed motion in accordance with the natural appetite or will; or, to speak more precisely, there was in him an unmoving condition in accord with his absolutely pure, completely deified subsistence in God the Word.[47]

Maximus labored to preserve the consubstantiality of Christ's human will with our will, while properly distinguishing them as two modes of human willing (ours is fallen, or *gnomic*, in being cut adrift from conformity to God, Christ's is *natural* and unfallen and permanently anchored to God's will).[48] His formula ends up roughly following the lines of M3 by explaining the sinlessness of Christ as a human achievement, though one wrought by the leading choice of the divine Logos to conform his human will to the divine will repeatedly.[49]

The final representative of M3 is John of Damascus (ca. 675–754). The Damascene argues that Christ's human will followed his divine will, willing in subordination to the divine will.[50] By this volitional divine hegemony, Christ could assume natural passibility for a true humanity without allowing his emotional sensibilities to become controlling influences on his divine will, and hence vulnerable to sin.[51] In his humanity, Jesus could suffer all the pains of hunger, thirst, grief, fear of death, agony in suffering, and the Devil's temptations, and yet, having been tempted for us, Jesus could also conquer them for us.[52] He could conquer in his weak, passible humanity because of enrichment from his deity. This is deification without transformation, a divine operation of the human nature without mingling the natures—just as fire heats steel to carry or share in the power to burn without changing the nature of the steel.[53] The Damascene resists the idea of transformation to protect the integrity

---

[47]Maximus *Opuscula Theologica et Polemica 1* (PG 91:32A), trans. McFarland, "Anthropological Implications", 12, n. 32.

[48]McFarland, "Anthropological Implications", 8-12. Maximus has been criticized for marking off too much of a distinction between Christ and us, but see McFarland's helpful defense.

[49]Cf. Pannenberg, *Jesus*, 349-50 n. 49, summarizes Maximus's view that Jesus possessed freedom though conformity to the divine will.

[50]John of Damascus *De Fide Orthodoxa* 3.18 (in vol. 2 of *Die Schriften des Johannes von Damaskos*, ed. P. B. Kotter, Patristische Texte und Studien, Band 12 [Berlin: Walter de Gruyter, 1973], 158). John of Damascus's dyothelite position is clear in 3.13, 14.

[51]John of Damascus *De Fide Orthodoxa* 3.20 (Kotter, 163).

[52]John of Damascus *De Fide Orthodoxa* 3.20 (Kotter, 162).

[53]John of Damascus *De Fide Orthodoxa* 3.17 (Kotter, 156). Apollinaris also noted this analogy in *Fragments*, 128, trans. in Norris, *The Christological Controversy*, 111.

of the natures. He also emphasizes the value of Jesus as a model of obedience for believers, he who became what they are to restore their obedience by his own exemplary life.[54] John of Damascus therefore represents M3 by relating the divine strength and human weakness through the dominance of divine will over his humanity to live sinlessly as a man.

EVALUATION OF M3: SINLESS BY DIVINE HEGEMONY

Much more reckoning of the human element in Christ's temptation and sinlessness shows up in M3 than in M1 and M2. M3 explains Christ's sinlessness as having been secured by his deity, though in a way that does not override or transform his humanity. The primary concerns are to explain Christ's life as a soteriological pattern by his recapitulation of Adam and the submission of his human will to the divine will as an example for believers to follow. M3 strongly emphasizes the unifying, leading role of Christ's person and divine will as part of affirming the close likeness of Christ's humanity to common humanity.

I think M3 shifts the focus away from properties or attributes of the divine and human natures to the person who is Christ and the Logos.[55] This double-natured, double-willed person is the one who was tempted and triumphed as a man. Christ's human will is truly human (though perhaps not fallen if Maximus is right), and enjoys no special powers that are not also available to other humans. What Jesus does enjoy is the ability to make a choice to harmonize his human will to his (and God the Father's) divine will, and thereby choose by the will in full freedom of concurrence with God's will despite temptations to the contrary. M3 involves the human will of Christ to achieve sinlessness while all the time the finite will is impeccable by conformity to the divine will.[56] The model is also attractive because M3 connects the reasons for the temptations closely to the biblical relevance for Christ's temptation: Jesus provided an example for resisting sin, became sympathetic to others, and demonstrated a human life fully submitted to God. Other people helped by grace may imitate Christ's example by submitting their wills to God's will, and thereby flee sin.

If we consider how M3 contributes to our understanding of Christ's struggle in Gethsemane, inadequacies of the model show up. Praying amidst the olive trees, Jesus is caught between the fearful inclination of his human will to flee

---

[54]John of Damascus *De Fide Orthodoxa* 3.1 (Kotter, 108). Christ's example of obedience was a typically (though not exclusively) Antiochene emphasis that shows in John Chrysostom, Theodore Mopsuestia, and Nestorius.

[55]Many of the proponents of M3 surveyed above follow a unitive Christology, which can have the liability of so much emphasis on the union that the moral freedom and humanity of Christ is swallowed up in the deity of the Logos.

[56]The exception on this key point among M3 representatives is Apollinaris, who denied a human will and mind in Christ because the Logos took the place of these to guarantee that all of Christ's willing would be impeccable.

his imminent suffering that nearly overwhelms him ("If there is any other way; yet not what I will") and his human desire to obey God ("Let your will be done"). The second desire is provided by his choice to conform to God's will (concurrence), and thus he, the single subject of his two natures, enacts the choice for this perilous desire instead of the desire to break away from God's will (and avoid his peril). His disciples witness the man's resolve as he rises to meet his enemies, and the human decision has been struck for obedience. The assistance Jesus has received for his frail human will has come from God, and he commended his disciples to seek the same sort of assistance to their wills (that they must pray so as not to enter into temptation). The Logos has enacted a triumph of human obedience against temptation to sin. Because the choice resides in the Logos (not simply in the human will), the outcome was never in doubt. The Logos immutably chooses right (divinely), and would never do otherwise than choose with the Father and the Holy Spirit that the Son suffers the cup of wrath. All that remained was for the Son to will as a man to obey God. Jesus, unlike his disciples, succeeds because he has aligned his human will with the divine will (concurrence), which thus enables him to want something (obedience) above his own desire to avoid suffering. The advantage of one's will being led by the divine person and shaped by the divine will enables Jesus to do as a man what no others were able to do—obey God perfectly from start to finish.

The M3 account makes it difficult to see how a single being (the theanthropic person) can genuinely suffer temptation when his human will is perfectly anchored to, supervened by, and deified in concurrence with God's will. The problem of temptation seems to be much more the existential struggle to enact that choice of conformity to God's will instead of disobedience. This is contrary to the struggle with temptation as it appears in M3, in which victory comes by a choice that is antecedent to all human willing from a position outside the human frame of experience and possibly assisted or dominated by the presence of a divine will. The model rightly stresses the person as the ultimate, responsible agent for moral actions (and distinct from the natures which the person instantiates), but where is the struggle for the divine person if the human will is inexorably concurrent with the divine will? How can a human will that is antecedently conformed to the divine will be tempted in a way that constitutes some recognizable temptation experience and struggle that might be sufficient for Christ's empathy for others and his demonstration for them of a reasonable way out? M3 seems inadequate to these aspects of biblical revelation.

A second critique can be leveled particularly at Maximus's analysis of Christ's human will and the human willing common to the rest of us. Maximus argued that Christ's human will is a different mode (*tropos*) of human willing.[57]

---

[57]Dorner's critique of the M3 sort of Dyothelitism championed at the Sixth Council knocks proponents for wrongly diminishing the human will: "They again contrived, by

Christ's human will is not fallen (*gnomic*) with the plight of deliberation between options in the way that ours is, but Christ's is a human will in essence (i.e., it is a human will, and not a divine or angelic will) that operates in the *natural* mode of concurrence with God's will.[58] For Maximus, the natural mode is the unfallen state of the human will, and the great hope for deified, glorified humanity. However, it is difficult to see how temptation could ever occur if a *natural* will does not deliberate between options, and only the *gnomic* will is addressed with sinful options.

M3 does explain how sinlessness can become achievable for others (at least occasionally) because the concurrence of wills in Christ is possible for others by grace in deification. The deification concept, however inspiring for describing Jesus as a pattern of glorification by grace, remains troubling. I have difficulty seeing how deification and the absolute concurrence of his human will with the divine will satisfies Christ's struggles in our sort of experience and avoids a virtual Apollinarianism (the human initiative in M3 fades into the glory of the divine will that supervenes it). Deification in the complete sense realized for Christ's human will seems to exclude temptation, since what sin can be presented to a divine, divinized, or deiform will as a desirable good? Will we continue to experience struggle and temptation when we are glorified?[59] While the wilderness temptations seem to show ready responses and a tone of fixed resolve in Jesus, the temptation in Gethsemane seems much more of a struggle that is echoed by Hebrews 5:7-8 and serious struggle seems

---

means of unexpected addenda, to give to the will of the divine such predominance, that the human will was degraded from the position of a free, to that of a merely operative, power . . . constituting little more than a point of transition for the all-decisive divine will" (J. A. Dorner, *Doctrine of the Person of Christ*, II. I. 168), cited in Harry Johnson, *The Humanity of the Saviour: A Biblical and Historical Study of the Human Nature of Christ in relation to Original Sin, with special reference to its Soteriological Significance* (London: Epworth, 1962), 199. I do not share Johnson's conclusion that Christ assumed a fallen human nature. The distinction of *gnomic* and *natural* may or may not be right—I am not sure if it is right to say that Christ's human willing lacked all deliberation, that is, that the natural will is devoid of deliberation (cf. pre-fall Adam), and the whole struggle or weighing of multiple options is not simply a fallen *gnomic* mode of the will.

[58] McFarland, "Anthropological Implications", 8, cites the criticism of Maximus on this point by Raymund Schwager, *Der wunderbare Tausch: zur Geschichte und Deutung der Erlösungslehre* (München: Kösel, 1986), 157-58.

[59] I hope not, but perhaps there is some enduring value in temptations for sinless, glorified people. Bruce A. Ware has suggested to me that we may well continue to be tempted in glory, though impeccably so (in parallel to Christ's impeccability and temptation), and this will be to the glory of God that we may continually choose him freely forever. If true, this might entail that the ascended Christ remains temptable presently as well, though the occasions for him and us would be greatly reduced. Millard J. Erickson, *Christian Theology*, 2nd ed. (Grand Rapids: Baker, 1998), 1011, gives an opposite view that temptation will be entirely removed from us in glory.

necessary to satisfy the empathy-building experiences noted in Hebrews 4:15.

Finally, deification or leadership of the human will by the Logos seems inadequate for giving a real example in triumphing over temptation. In M3, Christ's human will is immutably conformed to the divine will. Instead, the Gospels present Jesus employing several means of grace, which would seem to have been superfluous for a Logos-led human will or a deified human will. According to M3, Jesus uniquely directs his human will in concert with an immutable divine will. The instrumental relation of his humanity to his personal choice and divine will is more like a theophany than an incarnation because the role of his human will is so greatly reduced to little more than an assent to divine volition. Such reduction counts against both Christ's function as an example and an empathetic priest because he does not seem to be engaged with temptations, despite how the biblical accounts may portray him. These inadequacies are perhaps the sorts of things perceived by others who formulated M4, which brings Jesus much closer to us than M1-M3 dared.

M4: Sinless by Empowering Grace

DESCRIPTION OF M4

The question asked by M4 is this: How was Jesus sinless as a man in a way that he can be a true human example for others? The answer given is that Jesus relied upon divine grace, which worked with his human will and empowered him to live sinlessly as a man. Christ's sinlessness was the result of cooperation between divine grace and his human will to choose right in the face of temptation. The divine nature of the Logos kept Jesus from sin (as in M1-M3, he was impeccable), but Jesus kept himself from sin as a man who has learned to obey God.[60] Christ's human obedience was *not* due to his inherent divine power (M2) or the immutable divine will (M3). Instead, M4 counts Christ's sinlessness as having been achieved by the man through empowering grace, which preserves his true humanity (with real human freedom) and allows him to be an example for Christians in their struggles against temptation. Christ's empathy for others is authentic because he has suffered in the same ways that they do in temptation. Having come into solidarity with them in human vulnerability and temptations, Jesus can also lead his people out of their troubles through the enablement of divine grace that was decisive for his own victory. Accordingly, M4 includes a distinctive view of divine grace as *empowering assistance*.[61] This view of grace as empowerment and aid is distinct from the usual patristic view of divine grace as divine presence, as in

---

[60]One proponent who did not affirm Christ's impeccability was Theodore of Mopsuestia. See the discussion below for his view that Christ did not become impeccable as a man until after the resurrection. Theodore was condemned for this view at the Fifth Council (Constantinople II, 553), over a century after his death.

[61]Fairbairn, *Grace and Christology*, 52, 166.

Fairbairn's summary of the M4 idea of grace: "God gives people those gifts (power, aid, and cooperation) that they will need in order to advance from the age of mortality to that of perfection [i.e., sanctification]."[62] Jesus, having been empowered by grace as a true man, is thus seen as the example and prototype of God's work to empower Christians in sanctification. In view of the biblical evidence for Christ's ignorance, weaknesses, struggles to obey, dependence on divine help, and the corresponding exhortations that Christians must imitate his obedience, the model infers that empowering grace accounts best for these phenomena. The eternal Logos lived as a man fully vulnerable to temptation, but he achieved sinlessness through empowering grace (not his own divine power) so that he could be a true man, example, and encouragement to others.

REPRESENTATIVES OF M4

Theodore of Mopsuestia (ca. 352–428) is the earliest clear representative of M4; others preceding him at Antioch may have contributed to the formulation also.[63] Theodore agreed with most others that Christ was impeccable and immutable as a man, but Theodore uniquely claimed that Christ did not become so until *after* the resurrection. Before the resurrection, Christ needed the empowering grace from the Holy Spirit to resist temptations and struggle for moral virtue.[64] Theodore summarizes his pneumatological Christology: "Christ had need of the Spirit in order to defeat the devil, to perform miracles and to

---

[62]Fairbairn, *Grace and Christology*, 28.

[63]Possibly Diodore of Tarsus (d. 394) was another early proponent of M4, but what remains of his writing does not show his thoughts on our topic. His agreement with other divisive Christology priorities (such as double predication and the integrity of the humanity in Christ) implies that he would agree with this model more than the others. Rowan A. Greer, "The Antiochene Christology of Diodore of Tarsus", *Journal of Theological Studies*, n.s., 17 (1966): 329, notes that Diodore was influential for Theodore of Mopsuestia and Nestorius by his emphasis on two subjects of attribution in the incarnation.

[64]The Fifth Council (Constantinople II, 553) anathematized anyone who defends Theodore's doctrine that Christ progressed in good works by means of the grace of the Holy Spirit to become immutable and impeccable after the resurrection (*Concilium universale Ephesenum*, ed. Eduardus Schwartz, *Acta conciliorum oecumenicorum* 4.1 (1971): 219; trans. in NPNF[2] 14:315, Canon 12). Theodore mentions impassibility and immutability that are Christ's after the resurrection in *Treatises Against Apollinarius*, 3, frag. 10 in vol. 2 of *Theodore of Mopsuestia on the Minor Epistles of S. Paul*, ed. H. B. Swete (Cambridge: Cambridge University Press, 1882; reprint, Westmead, UK: Gregg, 1969), 317-18, and in *Catechetical Commentary on the Nicene Creed*, ed. Mingana, A., (Woodbrooke Studies V), Cambridge: W. Heffer and Sons, 1932, cited in Rowan A. Greer, *Theodore of Mopsuestia: Exegete and Theologian* (Westminster: Faith, 1961), 50. The minority view of an emphasis on the help of the Holy Spirit to Christ will reappear in the work of John Owen, Edward Irving, Lewis S. Chafer, and, more recently, Gerald F. Hawthorne, Alan Spence, Max Turner, and Wayne Grudem (among others).

receive (divine) instruction as to the activities he should undertake."[65] Theodore argues that if Christ did not need this help of divine grace (that is, if he was all-sufficient with inherent divine power in his humanity), then the indwelling of the Holy Spirit was *superfluous* for him. Theodore sees a necessary role for the Holy Spirit in Christ; he observes that other theologians had overlooked this role.[66] Theodore believed that for others an acknowledgment of the Spirit seemed to imply that the Spirit was greater than the Logos.[67] The concept of grace can mean all divine activity, including both the will of God and his providence; however, Theodore identifies divine grace with the indwelling and empowerment of the Holy Spirit in Christ.[68] Theodore affirmed that by this grace the Logos always kept the assumed man from sin (M1, M3), but this enrichment of impeccability is in the background and not an active factor in Christ's achievement of sinlessness until after the resurrection.[69] This is the helpful distinction between the questions of *why Jesus could not sin* and *why Jesus did not sin*, answering the second question with empowering grace. Accordingly, Theodore emphasized that in the wilderness temptations Jesus had to struggle as a man, not as God, and is therefore an example for others:

> If as God Jesus overcame the devil, it was no great accomplishment for him to defeat the apostate angel whom he himself had made. Nor is this victory to be ascribed to his humanity alone. But by long-suffering, he prevailed over him as man, teaching us that it is not through miracles but by long-suffering and patient

---

[65]Theodore of Mopsuestia *Fragmenta Dogmatica, ex libris contra Apollinarium* (PG 66 [1859]: 996B); trans. Boris Bobrinskoy, "The Indwelling of the Spirit in Christ: 'Pneumatic Christology' in the Cappadocian Fathers", *St Vladimir's Theological Quarterly* 28 (1984): 61.

[66]Basil is an exception because of his defense of the Spirit's role in the redemptive economy. Basil *De Spiritu Sanctu* 16.39; trans. Bobrinskoy, "Indwelling of the Spirit", 61: "Every operation was accomplished (in Christ) with the cooperation of the Holy Spirit."

[67]This is the claim of G.J. Reinink, "Quotations from the Lost Works of Theodoret of Cyrus and Theodore of Mopsuestia in an Unpublished East Syrian Work on Christology", in Studia patristica 33, ed. Elizabeth A. Livingstone (Leuven: Peeters, 1997), 565.

[68]Rowan A. Greer, *The Captain of Our Salvation: A Study of the Patristic Exegesis of Hebrews*, Beiträge zur Geschichte der biblischen exegese 15 (Tübingen: J.C.B. Mohr (Paul Siebeck), 1973), 195. Greer gives a good example from Theodore's commentary on John 1:16.

[69]Thdr. Mops. *Catechetical Homilies* 7.13 (*Les Homélies Catéchétiques de Théodore de Mopsueste*, trans. and intro. Raymond Tonneau in collaboration with Robert Devreesse, Studi e Testi 145 [Vatican City: Bibliotec Apostolica Vaticana, 1949], 181); cited by Francis A. Sullivan, *The Christology of Theodore of Mopsuestia*, Analecta Gregoriana 82 (Rome: Apud Aedes Universitatis Gregorianae, 1956), 252.

endurance that we must prevail over the devil and that we should do nothing merely for show or for notoriety's sake.[70]

The freedom of Christ's human will is important for Theodore because this gives moral reality to Jesus' choices for the good instead of evil.[71] Theodore develops his idea of grace as *power* or *aid* given to Christ that is analogous to the way God empowers other human beings.[72] Still, Theodore distinguishes Christ from other humans. Jesus is uniquely gifted with grace in a degree of divine assistance that is greater than all others because of the incarnational union.[73] Christ's exemplary life is the result of grace in a way that has not transformed him to be superhuman.[74] Jesus is a perfect human who is unique in his attainment of righteousness because of the special operation of grace in his life, as Rowan Greer explains: "His sinlessness, his virtual omniscience and omnipotence—these remain human, but they differ radically from moral and prophetic gifts bestowed upon others. The unique operation of God's grace explains the unique humanity of the Man."[75] Theodore also emphasizes Christ's human struggle in cooperation with divine grace as an achievement that is relevant for the rest of humanity:

> The Lord was more troubled, and struggled harder, with reference to the passions of the soul than with reference to those of the body. He mastered the pleasures by a more powerful rational process, while the Deity manifestly mediated and assisted him towards righteousness. So it is that the Lord is perceived to open war against these [passions of the soul] especially. Undeceived by the lust for riches

---

[70] Thdr. Mops. *Fragment* 20, in *Mattäus-Kommentare aus der griechischen Kirche*, ed. Joseph Reuss (Berlin: Akademi-Verlag, 1957), 103; trans. Manilo Simonetti, *Matthew 1-13*, Ancient Christian Commentary on Scripture: New Testament, vol. 1a (Downers Grove, IL: InterVarsity, 2001), 60.

[71] Thdr. Mops. *De Incarnatione* 14 (PG 66:989D); cited by Joanne M. Dewart, *The Theology of Grace of Theodore of Mopsuestia*, The Catholic University of America Studies in Christian Antiquity 16 (Washington DC: The Catholic University of America Press, 1971), 75-76. Dewart notes that for Theodore, a true moral choice and the reality of Jesus' temptations entail the possibility of sinning.

[72] Fairbairn, *Grace and Christology*, 52.

[73] Thdr. Mops. *De Incar.* 7 (ed. Swete, *Theodore of Mopsuestia*, 2:298). Theodore's term is "cooperation", συνέρηειαν. We may wonder if Theodore's Christology is Adoptionistic. Nonetheless, Theodore affirms that the incarnation was a union with the assumed man from the beginning, in the womb (*De Incar.* 7 [PG 66:976D]). At least two of his recent interpreters have defended him as orthodox on this point. See Dewart, *Theology of Grace*, 79, and Greer, *Theodore of Mopsuestia*, 63-64, and *Captain of Our Salvation*, 212.

[74] "Moreover, the grace given the Man does not change his nature, however much it affects the capacities of his nature." Thdr. Mops. *De Incar.* 2 (ed. Swete, 291-92; trans. Greer, "The Analogy of Grace", 94).

[75] Greer, "The Analogy of Grace", 96.

and untempted by the desire for fame, he conceded nothing to the flesh. It was not for him to be overcome by such as these.[76]

Theodore clarifies the concern of M4, how could Jesus be an example if he triumphed simply as God? He could not. Instead, the value of his life as an example is that Jesus struggled to his obedience as a man, according to the same scale of life as believers live. Writing against the Apollinarian denial of a human soul in Christ, Theodore highlights Jesus' true struggle and relevance:

> However, if he had not possessed a soul, but (rather) it is the Deity which was victorious—none of the things accomplished would have been to our profit. For what likeness is there between Deity and the human soul with respect to perfection of activity? And the Lord's struggles would appear not to be of profit for us, but to have taken place for the sake of (empty) show. And if it is impossible to say this, it is certain that those things were done for our sakes, and (that) he instituted a greater battle against the passions of the soul, a lesser against those of the flesh.[77]

Therefore, Theodore of Mopsuestia demonstrates key features of M4 by his emphasis on the example, human freedom, need for grace, and struggle of Christ in his humanity to resist sin and obey perfectly. Theodore, in a minority opinion, counted a role for the Holy Spirit providing divine help to Jesus as a man, and thus Theodore sought to preserve Christ's human freedom and the analogy empowering grace in Christian experience.

Already noted as a representative of M1 and M3, Augustine should be sorted with M4 as the view that he favored most (and in spite of the way that the ideas of M4 were attacked in the East[78]). Augustine's conflict with Pelagius forced the bishop of Hippo to develop his doctrines of sin and grace with important formulations for understanding grace in relation to Christ's sinlessness and Christian sanctification.[79] First, Augustine argues for the unique and original sinlessness of Jesus at his conception. One motive is to affirm Christ's start in purity (while maintaining against Pelagius that all others are born sinful).[80]

---

[76]Thdr. Mops. *De Incar.* 15.3 (ed. Swete, 2:311; trans. R. A. Norris, Jr., *Manhood and Christ: A Study in the Christology of Theodore of Mopsuestia* [Oxford: Clarendon, 1963], 206).

[77]Thdr. Mops. *De Incar.* 15.3 (2:311; trans. Norris, *Manhood and Christ*, 206).

[78]Joanne M. Dewart, "The Christology of the Pelagian Controversy", in Studia patristica 17.3, ed. Elizabeth A. Livingstone (Leuven: Peeters, 1993), 1241, observes that Augustine was unaware of the "christological storm brewing in the east" where Cyril of Alexandria rallied the orthodox against the ideas of grace the assistance of the Holy Spirit to support Christ.

[79]Peter Brown, *Augustine of Hippo* (Berkeley: University of California Press, 1967, 2000), 355.

[80]Aug. *Contra Duas Epistulas Pelagianorum* 4.2.2, ed. Karl F. Urba and Joseph Zycha, Corpus scriptorum ecclesiasticorum latinorum (Vindobonae: F. Tempsky, 1913; reprint:

Another motive in graced-conception that is both virginal and enacted in purity by the Holy Spirit is to secure the purity of Jesus from corrupt desires that normally accompany fallen sexuality and procreation.[81] Second, Augustine develops the concept of empowering grace. He notes the differences and similarities of empowering grace in Christ and other human beings. Comparing Adam and Jesus, Augustine writes that Jesus was given greater grace that made him able to overcome the "will of the flesh" by the "will of the spirit".[82] But when comparing Christ to the elect, Augustine affirms that this empowering grace is "the same grace in the man Christ" as the grace that is in the elect. The difference is that in Christ grace empowered him so that even as a true man, Jesus "had no ability to sin" (impeccability).[83] This is remarkable, and agrees with Theodore's formulation of an analogy of grace: the empowering grace that enabled Jesus to continue sinlessly throughout his human life is the same grace that is available to others by the Holy Spirit.[84] However, because of the similarity of empowering grace for Jesus and Christians (and with due regard for differences), Augustine can preserve Christ's unique impeccability alongside affirming Christ's value as a pattern for others. Because Jesus lived by empowering grace to achieve his sinlessness in the face of temptations, he can be an example and "through giving help", he can assist those who struggle with temptations to sin.[85] Augustine emphasizes that grace enhanced Christ's freedom of will in his humanity by making him unable to serve sin.[86] Augustine thus sees the twofold operation of grace in Jesus as specially securing his sinlessness at birth (a prominent role of the Holy Spirit), and then Jesus conquers his temptations by empowering grace.

Nestorius (ca. 386—451) represents M4, following his teacher Theodore of Mopsuestia on some aspects of this topic (as elsewhere).[87] Nestorius affirms that Jesus was impeccable: "He was in that [divine] nature which sins not". However, Nestorius also claims that Jesus, in his humanity, "kept himself

---

New York: Johnson Reprint, 1962), 60:521. Hereafter, all volumes in this series will be listed as CSEL.

[81] Aug. *Contra Julianum Pelagianum* 5.15.57 (ed. J. -P. Migne, PL 44 [1865]: 793), cited in Dewart, "Christology of the Pelagian Controversy", 1233.

[82] Aug. *De Correptione et Gratia* 31 (PL 44:935). Perhaps the Holy Spirit, cf. n. 188.

[83] Aug. *Enchiridion* 11.36 (CCSL 46 [1969]: 70).

[84] Aug. *Enchiridion* 11.36 12.40 (CCSL 46:72). Grace is defined as the gift of the Holy Spirit that became natural to Christ in his humanity so that sin could not be admitted.

[85] Aug. *De Trin.* 4.13.17 (CCSL 50:183).

[86] Aug. *De Praedestinatione Sanctorum* 15.30 (PL 44:982). This is a much different explanation for impeccability than what he has said elsewhere (with M1 and M3).

[87] Fairbairn, *Grace and Christology*, 61, concludes, "The similarity of Nestorius' starting point to that of Theodore, the congruence between what he does write about salvation and Theodore's idea of the two ages, and the consistency of his technical christology with Theodore's all suggest that Nestorius was operating from the same basic understanding of grace."

without sin"[88] (an echo of Theodore here). *How* Jesus kept himself from sin is less clear. Nestorius affirms that it was not by natural impeccability that Jesus did not sin (*contra* M2). Instead, Nestorius claims that the Son "took a nature which had sinned, lest in taking a nature which was not subject unto sins he should be supposed not to have sinned on account of the nature and not on account of his obedience."[89] Nestorius repeats the divisive Christology of Theodore to emphasize Christ's obedience as a man. Only in this way could Nestorius see that Jesus could give a pattern of life by his own example.[90] The feature of empowering grace does not appear in extant materials of Nestorius (from what I could tell), but he was condemned by Cyril of Alexandria and the Third Council (noted above, in ch. 4) as one of those who say Christ was glorified and work powers by the Holy Spirit, and not simply by his inherent power as the Logos.[91] Nestorius was also criticized severely for these M4 views by John Cassian, who accused Nestorius of saying that Christ was assisted in his humanity by the Holy Spirit: "The whole of your blasphemy then consists in this: that Christ had nothing of himself: nor did he, a mere man, as you say, receive anything from the Word, i.e., the Son of God, but everything in him was the gift of the Spirit",[92] and, "You will have it that the Holy Ghost gave assistance to the Lord Jesus Christ as if he had been feeble and powerless: and that he granted those things to him, which he was unable to procure for

---

[88]Nestorius *Liber Heraclidis* 2.1.295-298, in *The Bazaar of Heracleides*, ed. and trans. G. R. Driver and Leonard Hodgson (Oxford: Oxford University Press, 1925), 213.

[89]Nestorius *Liber Heraclidis* 1.1.68 (63). In speaking of a "nature which had sinned" Nestorius most likely means that Christ took from humanity with true susceptibility to temptation and sin, not that his human nature was sinful or that he had some sort of glorified human nature. The accent is on Christ's obedience, not that he was guilty or impaired by sin.

[90]James Bethune-Baker, *Nestorius and His Teaching: A Fresh Examination of the Evidence* (Cambridge: Cambridge University Press, 1908), 123. "To Nestorius it seems that the moral purpose of the Incarnation is frustrated unless the incarnate Word of God underwent a genuine human experience, and he argues against every doctrine of His Person which seems to debar Him from being a real Example and Pattern of a genuinely human life."

[91]Cf. Bobrinskoy, "The Indwelling of the Spirit", 61, makes the broad critique that Nestorius allowed too great a role for the Holy Spirit in Christ. Unfortunately, Bobrinskoy does not give examples to substantiate his judgment.

[92]John Cassian *De Incarnatione Domini Contra Nestorium* 7.17 (ed. Michael Petschenig, CSEL 17 [1888]: 373, trans. Grillmeier, *Christ in Christian Tradition*, 1:471). Grillmeier notes that Cassian did not comment on Christ's humanity significantly: "Cassian draws a very empty picture of the humanity of Jesus." Fairbairn (*Grace and Christology*, 166) confirms this with his view of Cassian's idea of grace and Christology: "It is significant that he discusses co-operation or divine aid only when considering the monk's efforts to strive after virtue; he never mentions these ideas when discussing Christ."

himself."[93] Of course, these are attacks by two of Nestorius's critics, and so perhaps they are not the best basis for reconstructing his theology. Nonetheless, Nestorius exemplifies M4 by his own words about Christ's neediness in the authenticity of his humanity: "While he was poor in everything and was violently drawn away by the opposite, he in nothing deviated from the purpose of God, although indeed Satan made use of all these things to remove him far from the purpose of God."[94] Nestorius has not been clearer than this (at least not in the materials available to me). At best it seems that he can be counted as a proponent of some major features of M4, but he has not given us a good articulation of the model.[95]

Like Nestorius, Theodoret of Cyrus (ca. 393–457) follows Theodore of Mopsuestia's teaching in a way that suggests M4 (and divisive Christology). Theodoret argues for the integrity of the natures (and denies a communication of attributes to the unifying Logos-subject) to protect the impassibility of the Logos and the weakness of the man, which then allows for counting an important role of the Holy Spirit.[96] Theodoret argues that it was not *as God* that Jesus fought against and defeated the devil in the wilderness, but *as a man*, a claim that excludes M1 and M2.[97] Christ's moral triumph was by human wisdom, not by divine power.[98] Nonetheless, Theodoret is not specific that Jesus had divine assistance of grace to enable him to conquer temptation.

---

[93]Cass. *De Incar.* 5.12 (321-22; trans. Grillmeier, *Christ in Christian Tradition*, 1:471).
[94]Nest. *Lib. Her.* 1.1.70 (63).
[95]Cf. the summary of the central idea in Nestorius's Christology by John A. McGuckin, *St. Cyril of Alexandria The Christological Controversy: Its History, Theology, and Texts*, Supplements to Vigiliae Christianae 23 (Leiden: E. J. Brill, 1994), 161. "The Logos binds himself to the man Jesus in an unassailably intimate union, without destroying any of the free capacities of the human life he graces with his unlimited power and presence." Notice the M4 emphasis on human freedom that is not abrogated by incarnational union.
[96]Joseph M. Hallman, "The Communication of Idioms in Theodoret's *Commentary on Hebrews*", in *In Dominico Eloquio, In Lordly Eloquence: Essays on Patristic Exegesis in Honor of Robert Louis Wilken*, ed. Paul M. Blowers et al. (Grand Rapids: Eerdmans, 2002), 373.
[97]Theodoret of Cyrus *De Incarnatione* 15 (PG 75: 1444A), cited in Klaus-Peter Köppen, "The Interpretation of Jesus' Temptations by the Early Church Fathers", *Patristic and Byzantine Review* 8 (1989): 43. Migne has mistakenly attributed this to Cyril of Alexandria. (Theodoret's place reference of Cyrus is also written as Cyrrhus.)
[98]Thdt. *De Providentia, Oratio* 10 (ed. J. L. Schulze, PG 83 [1859]: 752C-753A, cited in Klaus-Peter Köppen, *Die Auslegung der Versuchungsgeschichte unter besonderer Berücksichtigung der Alten Kirche* 4, *Beiträge zur Geschichte der biblischen Exegese* [Tübingen: J. C. B. Mohr, 1961], 79-80). The same trend to preserve the integrity of Christ's humanity shows in Theodoret's commentary on Hebrews. Frances Young, "Christological Ideas", 158, writes: "The person is divided but the real humanity given the chance to prove itself without being overridden by the all-embracing power of the Divinity."

Theodoret mentions the power of the Holy Spirit, however, which suggests his affinity for the principle of empowering grace in M4. Furthermore, Theodoret seems to favor M4 because he defended Nestorius against Cyril's ninth anathema by affirming the role of the Holy Spirit in Christ's humanity. The anathema addressed the role of the Holy Spirit as an external power used by Jesus to work divine signs of miracles and exorcisms. In response, Theodoret quoted three messianic passages that tell the Holy Spirit's role of empowerment for Christ to proclaim and deliver God's saving rule, and Christ's own testimony that he cast demons out by power of the Holy Spirit.[99] Therefore, Theodoret represents some key features of M4 because of his emphasis on the role of the Holy Spirit as an external power in the life of Christ, and by his insistence on the authenticity of Christ's human achievements in the struggles of temptation.

A final representative of M4 is Leontius of Jerusalem. Leontius explains that the impeccability of Jesus was caused by the coordination of his human will and the Logos, described as "the divine nature being given through the Holy Spirit in Christ".[100] In this M4 feature, Leontius preserves the human freedom of Jesus that participates in the divine grace so that the Savior can be a model for other humans. Leontius understands divine grace not in terms of aid or power, but as the leading principle that gives freedom to Christ's humanity.[101] Leontius's formulation also fits M2 (see above) and M3 because of the way he sees a closeness of operation between the divine and human aspects in Christ. In fact, Leontius's Nestorian opponents objected to his formula as a denial of Christ's human achievement of sinlessness, having been caused by the divine nature.[102] Nonetheless, Leontius's innovation that fits M4 is the way he sees *grace* as the hypostatic union of Christ's humanity to the Logos, and this grace protects Jesus from Satan, sin, and death.[103] The effect of the union is Christ's human sinlessness, but this is a result coordinate with Christ's human freedom as the necessity of grace, not of nature (cf. M2). Leontius is different from the Antiochene proponents of M4 in that his meaning of grace is the presence of the divine nature, not simply the power or aid given by God.[104] His formula could be seen as a hybrid of M2, M3, and M4 (which indicates the originality of his thought in a post-Chalcedonian theological environment). I have sorted

---

[99]The passages are Isa 11:1-2; 42:1; 61:1-3; Luke 4:18-21; Matt 12:28. Theodoret of Cyrus, quoted by Cyr. in *Apologeticus contra Theodoretum pro XII capitibus* (PG 76 [1859]:429D-431D; trans. NPNF² 14: 215-16).

[100]Leontius H. *Adversus Nestorianos* 19 (PG 86 pt. 1:1484D). Cited in Grillmeier, *Christ in Christian Tradition*, 2.2:295-300.

[101]Leontius H. *Adversus Nestorianos* 19 (PG 86 pt. 1:1485A).

[102]Leontius H. *Adversus Nestorianos* 19 (PG 86 pt. 1:1505AB).

[103]Leontius H. *Adversus Nestorianos* 19 (PG 86 pt. 1:1505CD).

[104]Fairbairn, *Grace and Christology*, 166, sees the usual patristic view of grace as God's gift of himself, as here in Leontius, in contrast to Theodore of Mopsuestia's view of grace as divine aid or power given as some*thing*.

Leontius with M4 because the important features for Leontius are also important features in M4, i.e., a way to protect Christ's human freedom as an example for others through the empowering presence of grace.

EVALUATION OF M4: SINLESS BY EMPOWERING GRACE

M4 stresses the integrity of Christ's two natures in the union. Consequently, the primary concerns in M4 are to protect the divine nature from being diminished by union with the human, and to protect the human nature from being enriched by union with the divine. Christ's weak humanity requires the aid of divine grace by the Holy Spirit. Related to this concern is the interest in Christ's sinlessness as an example that others can imitate by similar help of empowering grace. M4 affirms that Jesus was impeccable (though Theodore would not have said so) and that he resisted temptation as a man in a way that others can follow his pattern.

Two problems are associated with M4 because of the theologians who favored the model. First, Theodore of Mopsuestia denied the impeccability of Christ before the resurrection. This is unacceptable in terms of the unity of the Incarnation, just as Chalcedonian Christology has interpreted the biblical revelation properly. Theodore is the exception among M4 proponents, so we can see that his aberration is not essential to the model. Indeed, those later in the tradition who re-use the model do not follow Theodore on this point.

Second, M4 has affinity with divisive Christology, including the extreme form of Nestorius that was condemned. However, Augustine and Leontius both align with unitive Christology. Later proponents of M4 and pneumatological Christology have been able to avoid the problems of divisive Christology (e.g., John Calvin, John Owen).

I think that if we leave to the side the denial of impeccability in Theodore and the excessively divisive Christology in Theodore and Nestorius, M4 is the best patristic proposal for Christ's impeccability and temptation. This judgment is supported by the way that others in the medieval, Reformation, and modern periods have repeated the distinctive idea of M4 that Christ fought his temptation by the help of empowering grace. The evidence that continued formulation developed some or all the aspects of M4 also indicates that, in its patristic form, the model was not quite theologically adequate for later theologians, and had to be adjusted.

At least two reasons for favoring M4 should be mentioned. First, M4 follows the biblical evidence for Christ's temptations closely with a reasonable theological explanation for how Jesus could truly experience these trials—he suffered them in his humanity without the intrusion of his deity. This explanation alone (of the orthodox proposals thus far in the history) secures his true empathy with others who are not God incarnate as he is, and the reasonableness of his pattern in sinless victory requires some sort of limitation to struggle within human means (as in M4).[105] The biblical evidence for these two points of practical relevance from Christ's temptation seems to require an explanation like M4.

Second, the model's account for Christ's success as based on the empowering grace of the Holy Spirit (or otherwise provided by God) satisfies the difficult factor of Jesus' human freedom (despite the incarnational union with his divine nature) and builds the analogy to Christian experience receiving the same Holy Spirit from the risen Lord. Jesus has provided both the path and the means to walking through life as he did, and by employing that means instead of his inherent deity, Jesus became constituted through his experiences with empathy for others, fully qualified to be their priest to help them in the time of need when they are tempted (Heb 4:16).

Accordingly, in Gethsemane, M4 pictures Jesus feeling the strain of temptation in his human will and consciousness.[106] In his human awareness and desires, he perceives the imminent darkness and suffering that is the cup of God's wrath. Everything in him as a man rightly desires to flee that experience of being forsaken by God. Jesus is relying on the ever-present help of the Holy Spirit to him as a man, and he is thus able to pray to God, making known his wish even as he commits himself to obedience: "Not my will but your will be done". His distress is so fierce and dark that Jesus needs and receives the visible, tangible reassurance of God's empowering presence in the form of an angel to strengthen him in the choice of obedience.[107] The three disciples there with him are overcome in the dread that they probably do not even understand. Jesus pleads with them to endure with him, and he urges them to find help to surmount their temptation to abandon him by the same means of empowering grace that he has experienced. They must pray for help that they will not enter into temptation. Then, Jesus, having received the help he sought in his fiercest moment of need as a man, knows that he has crested the top of his temptation, as coming over a steep mountain, and he now can proceed with resolve to face the pain of his choice. He has freely willed by his human will to obey God's terrible command, and Jesus can freely give himself up for arrest, ridicule,

---

[105] A later innovation, the kenotic theory, formulated in various ways beginning in the nineteenth century, proposed a contraction or self-limitation of the powers of the divine Logos to the scale of a limited human existence for incarnation. This theory was seen to provide an alternate way of guaranteeing the true empathy of the Godman in solidarity with humanity.

[106] I am assuming the traditional view of two minds and wills in Christ, according to his two natures. Patristic and contemporary proposals to relocate the mind and will in the person (Monothelitism) instead of in the nature (as in Dyothelitism) have not persuaded me. Monothelitism raises more problems than the proposal solves, particularly the problem of a temptable divine will and a distinct, created, substantial human soul as a necessary component of Christ's humanity.

[107] That is, if Luke's account of the angel is authentic in 22:43. I think the arguments are better for authenticity than those against it.

injustice, and the combined terror of his physical and existential suffering as a man forsaken by God and tortured by men. His disciples are later able to take courage from Christ's example, being confident that he truly suffered temptation in the ways that they do. They know he understands, and that he demonstrated the way out by reliance on the grace of the Holy Spirit. Peter would later commend Christ's example to suffering Christians that they must willingly endure their pain without retaliating in sin, but instead they must entrust themselves to God just as Jesus did (1 Pet 2:21-25).

One problem I see with M4 is that the model may seem excessively complicated, especially by comparison with the simplicity of M1-M3. Nonetheless, the complex reality of the incarnation and a temptable Godman may require a complicated explanation. M4 affirms Christ's impeccability by his deity (at least in Augustine's formulation), but sets this aside as not having been the causal factor in his sinlessness. This formula allows for empowering grace as a moral factor in Christ; however, the formula raises the question of how the force of divine impeccability was not a factor in Christ's temptations. How does the divine nature *not* affect Christ's moral life? How is the divine nature *restrained* so that Jesus is truly limited in the weakness of his humanity with need for grace from the Holy Spirit? M4 affirms that Christ was always impeccable because he was fully God, but the failure to explain *how* this was so, without allowing any causative significance to Christ's divine will or nature for overcoming sinfulness is a weakness of the model. The distinction between the questions *why Jesus could not sin* (divine impeccability) and *why Jesus did not sin* (human effort with the help of empowering grace) seems to need some additional feature to show how they can both be true simultaneously.[108] This is the main theological inadequacy of the model that I will address with help from formulations of Calvin and Luther.

Why was the empowering grace model not favored in its day? Church councils held at Ephesus (431), Chalcedon (451), and Constantinople (553) that repeatedly condemned the eastern proponents of M4. Theodore of Mopsuestia, Nestorius, and Theodoret of Cyrus were charged with emphasizing Christ's humanity and the action of divine grace so much that the divisive Christology obscured due regard for his deity. Antiochene proponents of divisive Christology were fond of referring to Christ's humanity as "the assumed man" (but this is not the case with Augustine).

Moreover, we have already seen how pneumatological Christology was suspect because of fears of Adoptionism. M4 explains Christ's unique sinlessness in terms of grace that is similarly operative in other people. So, does the model reduce Jesus to a mere man who is specially empowered by divine

---

[108]Perhaps this was the problem Theodore sought to resolve by denying impeccability until after the resurrection. However, the idea of a peccable Christ ignores the ontology of the Godman who remains impeccable in whatever state he enters, human or otherwise, because God is immutably good.

grace to function as the adopted Son of God? I think the proponents are clear to exclude adoptionism (especially Augustine!). The model seems acceptable and orthodox if we consider that Christ's essential likeness to humanity (he is truly human, and thus can be a pattern of being empowered by the Holy Spirit) and his essential difference from humanity (he is truly God) as two of the orthodox markers of describing his identity properly. What remains to be done is to explain how such empowering grace works in Christ and others.

Finally, M4 recognizes a significant, ongoing role for the Holy Spirit in the incarnation. M4 counts the Spirit as providing grace to Christ's humanity in a way that matches the biblical evidence the Messiah's earthly life and the analogous role of the Holy Spirit in the lives of Christians. To patristic theologians these were risky ideas, but a few theologians have favored a pneumatological aspect to the incarnation since the Reformation (and especially in recent decades).

Conclusion

In the patristic period, we have seen that common presuppositions—the Nicene faith, soteriological requirements, opposition to heresies, and the Hellenistic philosophical setting—influenced the development of four models of Christ's impeccability and temptation. The models also overlapped on two-nature Christology, deification, divine impassibility, and theories of physical union. M1, Sinless by Inherent Impeccability, was the baseline affirmation of Christ's human sinlessness as caused by his inherent divine impeccability. M2, Sinless by Deification, explained the relation between Christ's divine impeccability and his human temptability and sinlessness as caused by an elevated, deified humanity. M3, Sinless by the Divine Hegemony, counted the predominance of Logos's will over his human nature as the cause of Christ's sinlessness. M4, Sinless by Empowering Grace, explained that Jesus could be an example in his temptations and sinlessness as a man who was helped in an external way by divine grace through the Holy Spirit. The resources that the patristic theologians passed on are rich in the different ways of explaining Christ's impeccability, temptation, and sinlessness as a subset of the interaction of deity and humanity in the incarnational union. We will see that few advances will be made beyond what the patristic thinkers developed in these four models. We will consider these advances in the medieval, Reformation, and modern periods.

CHAPTER 6

The Medieval Model

Patristic theology provides the broad and deep foundation for theology in the subsequent periods of the church. Theologians in the medieval period construct their formulations of Christ's impeccability and temptation using the foundational models of the patristic period.[1] Theologians re-use patristic concepts in new settings by combining elements from the patristic models to form modified versions that explain the biblical and philosophical data more adequately. I argue that in the medieval period, the aggregate formulation of a model of Christ's impeccability and temptation is M5, Sinless by Created Grace.

Background to the Medieval Model

The medieval theologians repeated the main patristic conclusions about Jesus: one person in two natures, fully human and fully God, and without confusion, change, division, or separation of the natures (Chalcedonian Christology). Most theologians agreed that the subsistence theory of the incarnational union is the right one (i.e., the divine person subsists in two natures and from two natures, more generally known as the hypostatic union).[2] There is also continued consideration of the *assumptus homo* theory that the Word assumed a certain man for incarnation, and the *habitus* theory that God became man in a way that is analogous to a man putting on clothing.[3] What dominates the medieval

---

[1] I do not include theology from the churches of the Eastern tradition beyond the patristic period because this is not a historical theology and I am interested in the most important contributions as building blocks, not merely as matters of historical development of the doctrines, however valuable such a historical study would be. As far as I know, the Eastern tradition seems to follow the deification theology of M2. M3 may be favored as well.
[2] Walter Henry Principe, *William of Auxerre's Theology of the Hypostatic Union*, vol. 1 of *The Theology of the Hypostatic Union in the Early Thirteenth Century*, Studies and Texts 7 (Toronto: Pontifical Institute of Mediaeval Studies, 1963), 10. Principe notes Albert the Great, Bonaventure, and Thomas Aquinas as examples of the general acceptance of the subsistence theory.
[3] Walter H. Principe, *Alexander of Hales' Theology of the Hypostatic Union*, vol. 2 of *The Theology of the Hypostatic Union in the Early Thirteenth Century*, Studies and Texts 12 (Toronto: Pontifical Institute of Mediaeval Studies, 1967), 206. Abelard

discussion are the attributes of humanity and deity that were present in Christ in view of his status as the divine Son and his work as the savior of humanity.[4] All theologians agreed that Jesus had to be sinless and could not have sinned because he was God, and such sin would have voided his work as savior. This agreement repeats the patristic M1, Sinless by Inherent Impeccability. All agreed that for his work as savior, Jesus had to be capable of dying and experiencing the weaknesses and suffering common to all (but not sinful desires). Medieval theologians maintained the distinction between Christ's two natures by carrying forward from Augustine the idea of created grace that filled in divine knowledge for Christ's humanity. Such knowledge seemed fitting for medieval theologians because Jesus was God, his divine knowledge enabled him to fulfill his work as savior, and his divine knowledge did not compromise his role as a human savior.

Medieval theologians had less concern than patristic writers did about the tension between the theological conclusion of Christ's impeccability and the biblical evidence for his true temptation (partly because the medieval writers diminish the force of the temptations). The philosophical simplicity of M1 continued to be satisfying as an explanation of Christ's sinlessness.

The troubles that come to the forefront in the medieval period were how to account for Christ's merit in terms of his human freedom, and how much of the normal human defects he possessed in his assumed human nature. These troubles seemed to follow the medieval emphasis on Christ's deity in wide metaphysical distinction from, and in contradiction to, his finite humanity. Consequently, their problem was how to account for Christ's humanity in terms of the strong affirmation of his divinity. Even so, they recognized the necessity that Christ's humanity included the normal human freedom that is requisite for earning merit, and he possessed the normal human weaknesses that are necessary for redemptive tasks of satisfaction and providing an example in resisting temptation.

---

favored the *habitus* theory to preserve the immutability of God in the hypostatic union with the assumed humanity as accidental to the Son. This view was also called nihilianism because many thought it entailed that the humanity of Christ was non-existent apart from the union.

[4]Isaak Dorner, *The History of the Development of the Doctrine of the Person of Christ*, trans. W. L. Alexander and D. W. Simon, Clark's Foreign Theological Library, third series (Edinburgh: T. & T. Clark, 1878) I, 1:83-84. "The *second* period [after the first four centuries] advances to the problem for which the first has furnished the data, and works on these data. These are: the elements which belong to the concept of the Divine, and the elements which belong to the concept of the human, whose difference is comprised in the duplicity of the Natures. Setting out from this distinction, it has to investigate the *How* of the unity of both in the Person of Christ; for the *That*, or the actual existence of this unity, remains the first presupposition, always present, as vouched for by faith." Notice that *duplicity* here means *twofold*, not *double-dealing* in the sense of deception.

The human weaknesses or *defects*—suffering, ignorance, temptation to sin, bodily weaknesses, and death—were thought to be a problem because they are contradictory to deity as understood in medieval theology.[5] The medieval solution was to use the Savior's job description to sort which defects Jesus needed and which ones he did not need for fulfilling his redemptive tasks.[6] By this soteriological criterion, medieval theologians elevated the humanity of Jesus in a way that satisfied their metaphysical concerns about the compossibility of humanity with deity (resulting in a divinized humanity in Christ). Such maximizing of Christ's humanity also minimizes his likeness to common humanity wherever sin and its effects are concerned (i.e., corrupt desires, ignorance, deformities). Therefore, instead of the patristic axiom, *the unassumed is the unhealed*, the dominant medieval presupposition seems to be that Christ's humanity must be *high enough for incarnation and low enough for redemption*.[7] In this statement, *high* denotes the glorified features of Christ's humanity to make it as fitting as possible for union with the divine Son (e.g., perfect knowledge). *Low* denotes the defects necessary for accomplishing redemption (e.g., possibility for satisfaction through death and temptability for providing an example of obedient humanity).

The medieval model of Christ's impeccability and temptation is an aggregate of the patristic models with some elements made prominent in accordance with their particular soteriological concerns. The new setting for medieval theologians includes feudal ideas of justice and the penitential discipline of a Church constituted by a priestly hierarchy that mediated salvation through the sacraments, especially confession and the mass.[8] Also

---

[5]Dorner, *History*, I, 1:83-84, observes the medieval and patristic emphasis on Jesus' divinity: "Now it is a feature of the dogmatic thinking of the time before the Reformation, that in it the Divine element had a onesided preponderance."

[6]Marilyn McCord Adams, *What Sort of Human Nature? Medieval Philosophy and the Systematics of Christology*, The Aquinas Lecture 1999 (Milwaukee: Marquette University Press, 1999), 96-97. In her view, the soteriological tasks that define Jesus' job description are "for making satisfaction, for earning merit, for conquering the devil, for furnishing an inspiring role model." I am indebted to Adams for pointing me to many of the medieval sources used in this chapter.

[7]Adams, *What Sort of Human Nature,* 95: "Such 'top-down' pressure to endow Christ's humanity with maximal perfection is reinforced by the 'bottom-up' thrust of soteriological considerations." Dorner, *History*, I, 1:83-84, notes that in the first four centuries of the church, theologians wrestled with the question of *how* the divine and human natures in Christ are related. As reflection continued through the medieval period, theologians predominantly worked out the question of *what* elements belong to Christ's divine and human natures. This work tended to prejudice the divinity in Christ over his humanity until the Reformation theologians regained a place for speaking fully about Christ's humanity.

[8]Sydney Cave, *The Doctrine of the Person of Christ* (New York: Charles Scribner's Son's, 1925), 128.

part of the new setting is the charge from Jewish and Muslim philosophers that a divine incarnation is false teaching (incoherent) and blasphemous because of the metaphysical distance between the infinite Creator and a finite created nature.[9]

Medieval theologians correlated their soteriological concerns to Christ's person and work as redeemer. On one side is the necessity of Christ's sinlessness for him to make satisfaction for sins, paying a debt of humanity that only God can pay. Because God made satisfaction by means of an assumed human nature that is peccable, that nature had to be reconstituted *im*peccable to protect the Logos from predication of a moral failure by the exchange of attributes with his human nature (*communicatio idiomatum*).[10] On the other side of Christ's work is the concept of merit as a reward for some good action.[11] His death is the supreme act of merit that earned humanity's salvation as the reward of eternal life. For merit earning to be possible for an impeccable Christ, medieval theologians stressed the reality of his temptation and his freedom of choice. They opened up space for this freedom and temptation by recycling the patristic concept of empowering grace in Christ's humanity (from M4). Medieval use of this concept in Christological models expanded the M4 idea of grace into two sorts of grace: the grace of union and created grace (infused), to be explained below.

With this background in mind, I will describe M5 and evaluate the model for its theological adequacy. This presentation of one model for the medieval period does not mean that all contributors agree on all the details of their Christological affirmations (indeed, they do not). I recognize that there are important differences among the many formulations and nothing like a consensus beyond embracing Chalcedonian Christology and its entailments (such as Dyothelitism).[12] However, on the topic of Christ's impeccability and temptations, what is apparent to me is that the formulations do run along similar lines and converge in what I am summarizing as M5. Moreover, I did not find enough difference among the Christological proposals as relates to this specific topic to form multiple models for the period. Distinct Christological models may have a common approach to multiple elements (indeed this is to be expected for all models following Chalcedonian Christology). Perhaps the

---

[9]Adams, *What Sort of Human Nature*, 95.

[10]Adams, *What Sort of Human Nature*, 96. "Because God is not, cannot be a sinner, neither can there be any insubordinate defection of will in the human nature God assumes."

[11]Adolf von Harnack, *History of Dogma*, trans. Neil Buchanan (Boston: Little, Brown, and Co., 1899), 6:190, 277. Harnack notes that Peter Lombard brought merit into the foreground, and, with regard to merit, reproduce Augustinianism with a semi-Pelagian view of free will (*Sententiae* 2.24 C, 27 G, 26 G, 27 J, 41 C).

[12]Richard Cross, *The Metaphysics of the Incarnation: Thomas Aquinas to Duns Scotus* (New York: Oxford University Press, 2002), has demonstrated the variety of medieval Christological views and notes some points of consensus among them.

special concerns of the medieval period for merit, grace, freedom, and fascination with integrating metaphysical principles from philosophy (philosophical theology) drove theologians in a similar direction on this special question. Moreover, the rough uniformity on this relatively minor question of Christ's impeccability and temptation may have been influenced by the scholastic pedagogy. Peter Lombard's *Sentences* were used as the framework for theological training. Following the *Sentences*, theologians learned to give a primary place to patristic ideas through repetition, collection, and interpretation. In other words, while divergent Christological models are present in medieval theology, there is a commonality of opinion concerning this topic. Two contemporary theologians have argued for a rough medieval consensus on the closely related topics of Christ's humanity and impeccability.[13]

Description of M5: Sinless by Created Grace

The medieval model is distinct from the patristic models as a harmony of them, using materials developed in the earlier period to construct a model for the medieval setting and concerns. Classified in our study as M5, Sinless by Created Grace, the medieval formulation appropriates the patristic models in specific ways. M1, Sinless by Inherent Impeccability, continues as the umbrella presupposition for M5 that Jesus, being God incarnate, is impeccable because God is impeccable.[14] From M2, Sinless by Deification, M5 develops the concept of Christ's elevated, deiform humanity, though in the medieval context this means the glorification of his human soul (mind, will, emotion). The glorification of Christ's soul, or, to use the medieval terms, the fullness of grace

---

[13]Marilyn Adams (see n. 6, above) has argued for common claims on the topic of Christ's human nature among five influential medieval theologians in her published Aquinas Lecture. Wolfhart Pannenberg also concludes that there was a medieval consensus on Christ's impeccability. In his *Jesus—God and Man*, 2nd ed., trans. Lewis L. Wilkins and Duane A. Priebe (Philadelphia: Westminster, 1977), 358-59, Pannenberg writes: "This question [of impeccability] was hotly discussed in twelfth-century Latin Scholasticism, especially with respect to the meritorious character of Jesus' sinless obedience. They came to agree on his impeccability as a gracious sinlessness, not attributed to the human nature or derived directly from the hypostatic union or the hegemony of the divinity over the humanity in Christ. The scholastic view was of a community of natures within the hypostatic union, by which gracious sinlessness left the ability to be tempted and the meritorious capacity of Jesus' human will untouched." Notice that two of the other three options Pannenberg mentions are descriptions of M2 and M3.

[14]E.g., Anselm *Cur Deus Homo* 2.10, in *Opera omnia ad fidem codicum recensuit*, vol. 2, ed. F. S. Schmitt (Edinburgh: Thomas Nelson & Sons, 1946), 106; Peter Lombard *Sententiae* 3.12.3.1, in vol. 2 of *Libri IV Sententiarum,* 2nd ed. (Grottaferrata: College of St. Bonaventure, 1916), 602.

and the beatific vision, is the medieval equivalent of the patristic emphasis on deification. M3, Sinless by Divine Hegemony, has a place in M5 as the harmony of divine and human wills in Christ, a concurrence by which his human will is submitted to his divine will in a way that preserves Christ's human freedom of will and the possibility of merit. Medieval theologians formulated several ways of harmonizing the two wills in Christ, but M3 was a popular way to secure his impeccability. M4, Sinless by Empowering Grace, contributes the idea of divine grace as given to Christ's humanity to be the means of transforming his human nature. Such elevation is necessary for his humanity to be sufficiently deiform for incarnation and as the proper instrument for redemption. While the patristic idea of grace in M4 was empowerment throughout the process of Christ's life, the medieval construction uses the grace concept as an initial infusion of godliness (created, finite grace appropriate to finite human nature) and as the *means* to the *end* of the transformation affirmed in M2. In other words, M4 counted grace as divine assistance; M5 counts grace as a divine gift in a way tantamount to the divine presence with all its transforming effects that mimic M2. As the aggregate, eclectic appropriation of patristic models, the medieval model also includes an emphasis on human merit as initiated and enabled by grace in a way that preserves both human freedom for merit and divine initiative to give the necessary help that is the source of all merit.

In brief, M5 pictures Christ's humanity as transformed by grace and ruled by the divine will to live sinlessly in a way that Jesus can earn merit by his freedom and be an example for others. Christ demonstrates how human life should be lived with the help of divine grace. The question asked by M5 is this: How could Christ's humanity be deiform in impeccability and also remain temptable for redemption? The M5 answer is that grace given in the soul secures Christ's absolute sinlessness (impeccability) while his body remains an avenue of temptation.

We will explore the two parts of this model, impeccability and temptation. The first part has the three ways of explaining Christ's impeccability, stressing created grace at the core of the medieval formulation. Created grace is the active factor in sinlessness as Christ's meritorious human achievement. Because of this stress, I have labeled the model according to that feature. The second part is an analysis of temptations in terms of the relevance of Christ's experiences for redemption.

First Part: The Impeccability of Christ

In expansion of M1, medieval theologians develop three ways that Jesus was impeccable and thereby did not sin. The three lines of argument that secure his sinlessness are transformation by grace, hegemony of the divine will, and the moral necessity of unity in his person and work. These arguments deal with the medieval question about *how high* Christ's humanity had to be for divine incarnation, with the answer that his human nature must be trebly impeccable.

TRANSFORMED BY GRACE

Medieval theologians combine ideas of deification (M2) and empowering grace (M4) to explain Christ's humanity as partly glorified by grace at the start of its existence. The medieval concept of grace, however, is different from the patristic formulations in M4. One explanation for this difference may be the shift from Neoplatonic philosophy in the background of Augustine's thought to the increasing use of Aristotelian categories in medieval theology.[15] In medieval theology, this means a shift from the M4 meaning of grace as *empowerment* to the M5 meaning of grace as *a created disposition in the human soul*. A related idea is the medieval emphasis on grace as the source of merit. Medieval theologians take the idea of grace-as-empowerment from M4 and develop this concept into the grace of union, created grace, and the grace of the beatific vision. All three are important for the impeccability and sinlessness of Christ.

With this development of grace as a multifaceted concept, medieval theologians can affirm the two natures of Christ, account for the authentic fullness of each nature, and satisfy the problems of a metaphysical distance between his infinite (divine) and finite (human) natures. Grace is the way that Christ's humanity can be appropriately elevated to be deiform (e.g., possessing omniscience in his humanity) while remaining recognizably human (albeit glorified in aspects of his soul). Also, grace is the way to satisfy the Chalcedonian requirements—two natures without confusion, change, division, or separation—and at the same time satisfy medieval requirements that Christ's humanity be as deiform as possible to be compatible for a divine incarnation. By these three developments, M5 forms three factors of Christ's impeccability that, in turn, cause his sinlessness as a man.[16]

---

[15] J. Patout Burns, "Grace", in *Augustine Throughout the Ages: An Encyclopedia*, ed. Allan D. Fitzgerald (Grand Rapids: Eerdmans, 1999), 391. Burns gives helpful summary of this conceptual shift: "Augustine's reliance on Neoplatonic philosophy [particularly the emanationism by which being, power and operation are continuously communicated from the highest to lowest levels in the hierarchically ordered universe], however, meant that the conceptual foundations of his teaching were significantly different from the Aristotelian categories used in the scholastic elaboration of his thought and the self-conscious biblicism of the Reformers' rejection of that medieval development."

[16] Reginald Garrigou-Lagrange, *Christ the Savior: A Commentary on the Third Part of St. Thomas' Theological Summa*, trans. Bede Rose (St. Louis and London: Herder, 1950), 411. "The Thomists and other theologians generally assign three causes for Christ's absolute impeccability. These are: (1) the grace of union; (2) fullness of inamissible habitual grace by reason of its connection with the grace of union; (3) the beatific vision."

The Grace of Union

The grace of union is the gratuitous honor and access to divine grace given to the Lord's human nature by virtue of its union to his deity.[17] Medieval theologians relate the grace of union to other graces in Christ as the basis for his human nature to receive the fullness of created grace and the beatific vision.[18] Thomas Aquinas (1225-1274) describes the created grace in Christ as the effect of the grace of union, just as the sun causes light in air.[19] Moreover, the grace of union has an effect in Christ's life to prepare his humanity to be pure from original sin for union with the Son (i.e., conception by the Holy Spirit; Luke 1:35).[20] Impeccability for his human nature is one effect of the union, giving moral fortitude and moral perfection from the first moment.[21]

By the grace of union, Christ's humanity is also prepared in purity to bear the further grace needed to make his humanity a receptive nature for divine gifts. Unlike the earlier formulation of M2, M5 maintains a clearer distinction of the human nature from the divine. The union with the Son of God does not deify Christ's human soul (as in M2). Instead, as a recipient of grace in the same way as other humans receive grace, Christ's human nature becomes deiform, worthy and usable for the Son without violating the distinction of his humanity from his divinity as an authentic human nature.[22] Instead of receiving deification as the communication of divine attributes directly to the humanity in a natural transfer (M2), medieval theologians posit created grace.

Created Grace

Created grace or habitual grace is the infusion of grace into Christ's human soul

---

[17] A. B. Bruce, *The Humiliation of Christ: In Its Physical, Ethical, and Official Aspects*, 4th ed. (Grand Rapids: Eerdmans, 1955), 77. Bruce has Thomas in view here. W. H. Principe, "Some Examples of Augustine's Influence on Medieval Christology", in *Collectanea Augustiniana: Mélanges T. J. Van Bavel*, ed. B. Brunin, M. Lamberigts, J. Van Houtem (Leuven: Leuven University Press, 1990), 963, notes that Augustine's idea of the grace of union is that Jesus did not merit the Incarnation in an Adoptionistic sense, but that God initiated and accomplished the Incarnation wholly by grace, in parallel with the way a person becomes a Christian by grace. Medieval theologians developed this idea into "a starting point for their speculations about the grace of union in Christ".

[18] Principe, "Some Examples of Augustine's Influence", 964. Principe cites Peter Lombard, *Sent*. 3.4.2 as an example of abundant medieval reliance on Augustine, e.g., *Enchir*. 12.40, 13.41.

[19] Thomas Aquinas *Summa Theologiae* 3.7.13.c, in *The Grace of Christ*, ed. Liam G. Walsh, vol. 49 of *St Thomas Aquinas Summa Theologiae* (London: Eyre & Spottiswoode; New York: McGraw-Hill, 1974), 50. All volumes in this edition of *Summa Theologiae* will be abbreviated *ST* with the page numbers and translator.

[20] Principe, "Some Examples of Augustine's Influence", 965.

[21] Principe, *Alexander of Hales*, 169-70. Principe cites *Glossa* 1.8.14 as an example.

[22] Aquinas *Summa Theologiae* 3.7.1, reply 1 (ed. Walsh, *ST* 49:8).

because of union to the Word. God creates grace in the human soul, so this grace is a finite gift in proportion to Christ's finite human nature.[23] Created grace is distinct from the personal presence of the Holy Spirit.[24] Jesus had this gift of grace as the divine empowerment in his humanity to the greatest degree because of his proximity to the source of grace and because of his role as the fount of grace for the rest of humanity.[25] By this grace Jesus remained sinless.

Thomas follows Augustine and John of Damascus to deny the transfer of attributes from one nature to the other in Christ. Thomas claims that the attributes proper to each nature are predicated of Christ in those natures.[26] Consequently, created grace is necessary as an alternate way to inform and elevate Christ's humanity for divine use in redemption. Created grace influences Christ's human will to be conformed to the divine will, which insures his impeccability, since the divine will cannot sin (cf. M3).[27]

Created grace also gives Jesus complete knowledge, protecting him from the ignorance that entails or at least leads to sin.[28] One example is Anselm of Canterbury (1033-1109), who claims that Jesus was omniscient in his humanity from the beginning of his earthly existence.[29] Thomas agrees, but he allows for growth in Christ's human knowledge (cf. Luke 2:52).[30] This growth is the

---

[23] Aquinas *Summa Theologiae* 3.7.11 (*ST* 49:38-42).

[24] Walsh, comment in *Grace of Christ*, *ST* 49:6.

[25] Aquinas *Summa Theologiae* 3.7.9 (trans. Walsh, *ST* 49:33). "For the soul of Christ received grace so that it could be passed on, as it were, from him to others. Hence he required the maximum grace; just as fire, which makes things hot, is itself the hottest thing of all." Cf. Paul Gondreau, "The Humanity of Christ, the Incarnate Word", in *The Theology of Thomas Aquinas*, ed. Rik Van Nieuwenhove and Joseph Wawrykow (Notre Dame: University of Notre Dame Press, 2005), 260.

[26] Aquinas *Summa Theologiae* 3.16.4-5 (*The One Mediator*, ed. Colman E. O'Neill, *ST* 50 [1965]: 16-22).

[27] Adams, *What Sort of Human Nature*, 30. Adams cites Bonaventure *Sententiae* 3.13.1.2, c; ad 2, 3, 5.

[28] Principe, "Some Examples of Augustine's Influence", 964. "With respect to Christ's human knowledge, Augustine's most profound influence on western theology was through his viewing ignorance as the cause and also the result of sin. . . . Following his lead, theologians in the west rejected ignorance in Christ and by the same token found it difficult to see any growth in Christ's human knowledge other than by his concrete experience of what he already knew." Exceptions to this trend are Thomas and Scotus, who affirm Christ's omniscience as the Logos and his progressive growth to omniscience in his humanity (see below).

[29] Anselm *Cur Deus Homo* 2.13 (ed. Schmitt, 2:112, 26-27).

[30] Aquinas *Summa Theologiae* 3.9.1 (ed. Walsh, *ST* 49:82-86); 3.12.2 (*ST* 49:138-40). Cf. Kevin Madigan, "Did Jesus 'Progress in Wisdom'? Thomas Aquinas on Luke 2:52 in Ancient and High-Medieval Context", *Traditio* 52 (1997): 191. Thomas's argument is that the normal human capacity to abstract knowledge from experience would not be denied Christ's full humanity, and he eventually attained omniscience on this order of his knowing, in addition to his infused omniscience.

progress of his learning by normal human perception and reasoning alongside his infused knowledge that was given in full (impossible to increase) as created grace from the beginning of his existence.[31] Thomas explains the twofold knowledge as knowing the same things in two ways (divine and human).

According to the concept of created grace, medieval theologians picture Christ's human soul as effectively deified (cf. M2).[32] They add the nuance that this grace comes indirectly to Christ's humanity as a created act of God in the same way as for all in the church. The result is his impeccability because he had this gift of grace in a maximal way. Similar to this parallel relation of created grace for Christ and others is the beatific vision.

The Beatific Vision

The beatific vision is the second effect of the grace of union that makes Christ impeccable. The beatific vision is the unending, relational experience of seeing God in heaven that the redeemed will possess as part of the final, glorified state of humanity.[33] The medieval theory is that Christ enjoyed this beatific vision from the beginning of his human experience, in advance of his glorification and return to heaven. John Duns Scotus (1266-1308) writes: "Christ, in the first instant of his union with God was beatified, and beatitude removed from him all the ability to sin."[34] The beatific vision cancels the need for Jesus to have faith and hope while providing him with maximal empowerment and gifts by the Holy Spirit.[35] Influential here is the patristic idea of M3 that Christ recapitulates all the states of humanity, and the beatific vision is Christ's share in glorified humanity.[36] The glorified status of Christ's human soul entails his impeccability as a man since the only way to lose the beatific vision is to sin. Just as God prevents this possibility for saints in glory, so also God prevented Christ from sinning.[37] Two ideas relevant to the model of Christ's impeccability

---

[31] Aquinas *Summa Theologiae* 3.21.1 (ed. O'Neill, *ST* 50:120-22).

[32] David F. Wells, *The Person of Christ* (Westchester, IL: Crossway, 1984), 119-20.

[33] Richard Cross, *Duns Scotus*, Great Medieval Thinkers (New York: Oxford University Press, 1999), 150.

[34] John Duns Scotus *Ordinatio* 3.12, q. unica (fol. 152vb); text and trans. Allan Wolter, "John Duns Scotus on the Primacy and Personality of Christ", in *Franciscan Christology: Selected Texts, Translations, and Introductory Essays*, ed. Damian McElrath, Franciscan Sources 1 (St. Bonaventure, NY: The Franciscan Institute of St. Bonaventure University, 1980), 143.

[35] Aquinas *Summa Theologiae* 3.7.3-5, 7 (ed. Walsh, *ST* 49:12-20, 24-26).

[36] Adams, *What Sort of Human Nature*, 18. Adams notes that Peter Lombard takes this concept of Christ's recapitulation of human history from Boethius (without citation) in four aspects: (1) pre-fall immunity from sin, (2) post-fall punishment and defects for sin, (2) redeemed fullness of grace, (3) glorified inability to sin and direct contemplation of God. Adams cites Lombard *Sent.* 3.15.2.

[37] Adams (*What Sort*, 76-77) explains that this is Duns Scotus's view, citing *Quaestiones in Lib. III. Sententiarum* 3.12, q.u, n.2, in *John Duns Scotus: Opera Omnia*, vol. 7, part

and temptation follow from the view that he had the beatific vision.

First, the beatific vision is a glorified aspect of Christ's humanity, touching his soul but not his body. Christ's beatific vision allows him to be tempted and earn merit for right actions because his human soul is the interface between the deity and the body of Christ, where *propassiones* (pre-passions) remained despite the beatific vision.[38] *Propassiones* are the natural desires that do not sway the will to choose sin; they are an experience felt by the agent before the onset of real instability and struggle between desires and the will.

Second, the medieval reasoning about Christ's impeccability by way of grace and the beatific vision means that his humanity, though glorified, remains like common humanity, and there is no contradiction between his human freedom and impeccability. Scotus has a minority opinion about God's power, but he expresses the general view that the work of divine grace in Christ's humanity is logically possible for other humans also to enjoy grace and the beatific vision: "God in his absolute power can confer such grace on another nature [other than Christ's], whether assumed or perhaps not assumed."[39] This preservation of Christ's human freedom by means of an *indirect* divine work of grace (i.e., not simply within the hypostatic union) secures both his full humanity and his ability to earn merit—despite Christ's impeccability. This is in contrast to a simply *direct* transfer of impeccability from his divine nature to his human nature (within the hypostatic union).

To sum up, the beatific vision, created grace, and the grace of union elevate Christ's humanity to be impeccable on the same terms (though to a greater degree) as God is thought to do for the elect in final glorification (making them

---

1, ed. Luke Wadding (Lyon: Laurence Durand, 1639; reprint, Hildesheim: Georg Olms, 1968), 254. Cross (*Duns Scotus*, 149) explains the general medieval view of the beatific vision: "According to Catholic doctrine, the saints in heaven enjoy the beatific vision for ever, such that they cannot lose this vision. One way in which—if it were possible—the beatific vision would be lost would be if such a saint were to sin. So the saints in heaven must be impeccable." Scotus's explanation for how this works is that God removes the opportunity for the will to choose to refrain from loving God. Cross continues, "Retaining the *power* for opposites—even without the opportunity for exercising this power—is sufficient for freedom. Because the determining agent is metaphysically superior (God), so a metaphysically superior agent can affect the actions of an inferior agent without interfering with the inferior agent's nature—and thus without interfering with its causal powers. And this, according to Scotus, is how we explain the impeccability of the saints enjoying the beatific vision in heaven" (150-51).

[38] Alexander of Hales *Glossa* 3.18.2, cited in Principe, *Alexander of Hales*, 207. Philipp W. Rosemann, *Peter Lombard* (Oxford: Oxford University Press, 2004), 136, notes that the distinction between *passions* and *propassions* also appears in Peter Lombard, so that Jesus can be said to have experienced genuine fear and sadness but only as *propassion*, not in a way of *passion* that disorders the soul and leads the soul away from God.

[39] Duns Scotus *Ord.* 3.13.4, n.8, ed. Wadding, 7.1:267; cited and trans. in Cross, *Duns Scotus*, 124.

impeccable forever).[40] Other aspects of Christ's transformation by grace are the ways his human nature is elevated to have some but not all the defects of normal humanity.

Grace and Normal Human Weaknesses

The elevation of Christ's humanity by grace has "top-down pressures" in medieval theology.[41] These pressures are the requirements of what medieval theologians think are fitting for divine incarnation in human nature and the so-called unfitting defects that follow from finitude and sin. This formulation to explain that Christ's humanity is transformed by grace is the attempt to account for Christ's humanity as *high enough* in capacity and fittedness for incarnation. As noted above, one example of a normal human defect that medieval theologians consider unfit for Christ's humanity is ignorance (incomplete knowledge). They agree that Christ's knowledge was complete (omniscience), and the indications in the biblical revelation for his ignorance and growth in knowledge meet with elaborate explanations to make them consistent with the claim that he was omniscient (whether divine or human; Thomas allows that Christ grew to his human omniscience).[42]

Another normal human attribute that, in medieval theology, must have been eclipsed by transforming grace in Christ is original sin and its corruptive effects on desires (he must be free of both the guilt and the corruption of sin).[43] Consequently, his temptations could only have occurred through external appeals, and not at all from internal desires or sinful lusts as is the case for the rest of humanity. Thomas is representative of the description of Christ's temptation: "Furthermore, although he did not have to cope with attacks from within due to the spark of sin, he did undergo attack from outside, both from the world and the devil. In conquering these he merited the crown of victory."[44] Thomas reasons that Christ's human freedom was limited in his will as presented with many good options but no sinful options because he could never desire evil: "Although Christ's will is determined towards what is good, it is still not determined to this or that particular good thing. Thus for Christ, as for the blessed in heaven, choice meant use of a free will confirmed in good."[45] This means that Jesus was determined by grace to will only the good, but not specifically *which* good among many possibilities, giving him the freedom of will (the ability to enact choices freely, which is consistent with impeccability), though not the freedom for opposites (good and evil), and Christ's freedom

---

[40]Garrigou-Lagrange, *Christ the Savior*, 411.

[41]Adams, *What Sort of Human Nature*, 95.

[42]Madigan, "Did Jesus 'Progress in Wisdom'?", 191.

[43]Lombard *Sent.* 3.15, c.1, (Grottaferatta ed., 2:613.96); Aquinas *Summa Theologiae* 3.14.1, 3 (ed. Walsh, 49:170-176, 180-182); 3.15.2 (49:194-196).

[44]Aquinas *Summa Theologiae* 3.15.2, c (ed. and trans. Walsh, *ST* 49:196-197).

[45]Aquinas *Summa Theologiae* 3.18.4, c (ed. and trans. O'Neill, *ST* 50:76-77).

anticipates the glorified life of all redeemed humanity. These affirmations about Christ's temptations and freedom are intended to account for his sinlessness and explain the specific ways of how grace transformed his humanity to be impeccable.

By contrast, Christ had other normal human weaknesses that enabled him to merit redemption because these do not contradict the fullness of his human virtue by grace or endanger his sinlessness. Medieval theologians repeat this category of natural defects from the patristic period—death, hunger, thirst, and bodily weakness. These are the consequences of sin that Jesus assumed voluntarily.[46] Notice that these are all bodily defects; the transforming grace in the soul of Jesus precludes any defects from encroaching upon his soul (e.g., ignorance and corrupt desires). For Peter Lombard, true passions are also thought to be excluded from Christ's emotional experience,[47] but Thomas argues that Jesus had real movements of *sinless passions* that never threatened to tear him away from God (as may happen with sinful passions).[48] Therefore, Christ's human nature had only those defects of normal humanity that fit with a divine incarnation, but grace transformed his humanity to be free of all other defects in a way that constituted him impeccable in his humanity. And this is just the first of three ways in M5 that Christ is impeccable as a man.

IMPECCABLE BY HEGEMONY OF THE DIVINE WILL

The medieval model takes up M3 from the patristic period to secure Christ's sinlessness by the rule of the divine will over his human will. This is clear in Peter Lombard, who argues that Christ's defeat of the devil required determinative divine involvement: "And so that man may win, it is necessary that God be in him, who renders him immune from sins."[49] Because the context here is temptation, the factors must be volitional. So, the divine factor must be understood as the divine will that fortifies his human will against sin.

In a more nuanced discussion, Anselm accounts for Christ's human freedom together with his impeccability by saying that Jesus possessed both *the ability to sin* (e.g., the power to speak the words of a lie) and the *inability to will to sin* (e.g., he would always maintain his moral integrity and never actually choose to

---

[46] Aquinas *Summa Theologiae* 3.14.4 (ed. Walsh, *ST* 49:184). Following John of Damascus, Thomas explains that Christ assumed only those defects necessary for making satisfaction for sin. The categories of defects are: (1) natural defects from original sin that are compatible with the perfection of knowledge and grace, (2) natural defects that are incompatible with perfection, such as ignorance, inclination to evil, moral inability to do good, (3) personal defects caused by people in particular cases, such as leprosy, epilepsy, blindness, and obesity.

[47] Lombard *Sent.* 3.15, c.2, secs 1-3 (Grottaferrata ed., 2:614.98-99).

[48] Aquinas *ST* 3.15.4c, cited by Gondreau, "Humanity of Christ", 268-69.

[49] Lombard *Sent.* 3.19.2, cited and trans. in Rosemann, *Peter Lombard*, 138-39.

speak a lie, since his divine will would never choose to lie).[50] Anselm argues that Christ's obedience is the act to conform his human will to the divine will, and this is a free movement of his human will. This is a fullness of freedom in full liberty to obey God, not simply a limitation of freedom *from* being able to will sin. The ultimate incapability for sin (because of the divine will) cancels Christ's human power to sin without limiting his human freedom because all of his choices are based on a prior, all-determining choice that he has made to obey (even if that choice is based on the prior and eternal act of his divine will).[51] With his human freedom preserved, Christ's human obedience is also meritorious (even if he could not have chosen otherwise with his human will!).

Thomas explains that Christ felt the desire to will according to his human nature against the divine will in his plea to avoid the pain overshadowing him in Gethsemane.[52] However, this non-sinful discord occurs at the level of desires, not choice (and only momentarily). Christ's human *sensual will* naturally shrank back from imminent pain, but his *rational will* was always conformed to the divine will. This active conformity is the choice to will in relation to the will of another, which Thomas observes is what commonly happens when two friends agree: each one wills something in relation to the will of the other person.[53] Moreover, Christ's human will was determined to align with the divine will because this human will was in a divine hypostasis (this is similar to Anselm's view).[54] Thomas explains that human willing is normally a natural relationship between body and soul, "But in Christ this natural relationship lay under the control of his divine will."[55]

The problem that Thomas and Anselm are addressing is the freedom of Christ's human will in concert with his divine will (the traditional orthodoxy of Dyothelitism is presupposed, Christ had two wills according to his two natures). Thus, the formulation allows for Christ to earn merit by his active choice of a particular good through his human will. The human act is not determined by the divine will, but remains free while submitted to the divine will perfectly and voluntarily. Nonetheless, neither Anselm nor Thomas allows that Jesus could choose to will humanly against the divine will as regards sin.

---

[50]Anselm *Cur Deus Homo* 2.10 (ed. Schmitt, 2:106-07). Cf. Adams, *What Sort of Human Nature*, 13, "It is *Christ's own* Divine will that controls *His own* human will."

[51]Dániel Deme, *The Christology of Anselm of Canterbury* (Aldershot, UK, and Burlington, VT: Ashgate, 2003), 190-91.

[52]Whose divine will does Christ struggle against in his humanity? In Gethsemane, Jesus attributes the divine will to God the Father, and Thomas understands this as the same divine will possessed by Jesus (*Summa Theologiae* 3.18.5-6). What the Gospels depict as an interpersonal struggle of Jesus to obey the Father is understood by Thomas as simultaneously an intrapersonal struggle within Jesus the God-man, choosing to submit his human will to his divine will (which is also the will of God the Father).

[53]Aquinas *Summa Theologiae* 3.18.5-6 (ed. O'Neill, *ST* 50:76-84).

[54]Aquinas *Summa Theologiae* 3.18.1, d (*ST* 50:68).

[55]Aquinas *Summa Theologiae* 3.14.1, b (ed. and trans. Walsh, *ST* 49:175).

The conformity of his human will to the divine may be something that Jesus chose freely, but he also chose to submit necessarily, just as God's own freedom of necessity is to will his goodness and he can never will to sin. In other words, the Thomistic view is that Christ and God alike have *psychological liberty* (real freedom to choose among several good options without being determined to any one in particular) without having *moral liberty* (the unconditioned freedom to choose among good or sinful options).[56]

A stronger affirmation of divine hegemony is clear in Scotus, who points to the hegemony of the divine will in Jesus as parallel to the divine hegemony over all the elect. God is a superior agent who determines the contingent, created wills of both the elect and Jesus while preserving their self-determination.[57] The difference between the elect and Christ is that his human will is always conformed to his divine will in a way that the elect will only experience when they have been glorified.

Scotus and the other theologians cited show that the medieval model retains the patristic M3 by which the humanity of Jesus is an instrument moved by the divine will. The medieval adjustment in assembling M5 is to explain Christ's impeccability alongside his freedom of will, all the while holding to divine volitional hegemony that secures Christ's indefectible and meritorious human willing. There remains one more M5 aspect of Christ's human impeccability.

IMPECCABLE BY MORAL NECESSITY

The third way that M5 secures Christ's impeccability is by the moral necessity of his personal union and his redemptive work. These two ways secure Christ's moral liberty impeccably as the freedom fulfilled to fully obey God, exclusive of all sin.

First, the moral necessity that he be impeccable by his personal union to the impeccable Logos is a related point to both the grace of union and the divine hegemony noted above. Anselm allows that Jesus possessed the power to sin, but he adds that Jesus was unable to sin because such an act would have contradicted the holiness that he possesses in his humanity from his divine nature.[58] This consequent necessity of impeccability for Jesus, as for the righteous angels, is because he and they *initially* chose holiness, thus they deserve praise. As in M1, Jesus, being the divine Logos who is impeccable, is unable to sin in his human nature that is otherwise capable of sin (if considered as broken apart from the Logos). M5 develops the person-nature distinction so that the possibility of sin for Christ's human nature as abstracted from the personal union is bound and overruled by the moral or personal necessity of his

---

[56] Garrigou-Lagrange, *Christ the Savior*, 458.

[57] Adams, *What Sort of Human Nature*, 77.

[58] Anselm *Cur Deus Homo* 2.10 (ed. Schmidt, 107-08).

divine impeccability.[59]

Second, M5 explains Christ's impeccability in terms of the moral necessity of his work in redemption. Thomas uses the criterion of the savior's job-description to rule out sin in Christ in three ways. (1) Jesus could not make satisfaction for the sins of others if he owed a debt for his own sins, because God does not approve of gifts of the wicked. (2) Sin is unnecessary for proving the truth of human nature, so Jesus was able to be without sin and remain able to prove his true humanity. (3) Jesus could not be an example of virtue if he sinned.[60]

Therefore, the necessity of Christ's sinlessness by his moral impeccability and his redemptive work is a third explanation in M5 for his impeccability. This affirmation is part of the answer to the medieval question about his human nature being *high enough* for divine incarnation. Christ is impeccable as a man because of created grace, the influence of the divine will over his human will, and moral necessity of his incarnational union and redemptive tasks. Alongside the threefold argument for Christ's impeccability, M5 develops four questions related to his temptability. This second part deals with the medieval question about Jesus' humanity being *low enough* for his redemptive tasks (i.e., the defects voluntarily incorporated in his human nature, above).

Second Part: The Temptability of Christ

Medieval theologians labor to account fully for the New Testament revelation of Christ's true human experience of temptation. They understood that Jesus was tempted despite his impeccability and divine immunity to all temptation. Seeking to reconcile this problem, M5 explains Christ's temptability as an external, voluntary condition, and relates it to his freedom, merit, and example for others.

EXTERNAL TEMPTATIONS

Thomas gives an example of the typical distinction between temptations that arise internally, from sin, and temptations presented externally by the world and the devil.[61] From this he argues that Jesus was only tempted in an external way by the world and the devil, but not at all by the flesh, which was thought to entail internal, sinful desires.[62] Thus, Jesus experienced only one of the two categories of temptations that are common to humanity, just those temptations

---

[59]Adams, *What Sort of Human Nature*, 19, 40, 76-77, notes that Abelard, Lombard, and Scotus each recognize Christ's impeccability by his person, despite his otherwise peccable human nature.
[60]Aquinas *Summa Theologiae* 3.15.1 (ed. Walsh, *ST* 49:190).
[61]Aquinas *Summa Theologiae* 3.41.1, c (*The Life of Christ*, ed. Samuel Parsons and Albert Pinheiro, *ST* 53 [1971]: 72).
[62]Aquinas *Summa Theologiae* 3.15.2, c (ed. Walsh, *ST* 49:196).

which are externally generated. The natural defects such as weakness, death, hunger, and thirst do not appear in the medieval model as occasions of Christ's temptations.[63] Furthermore, Thomas gives four reasons for the temptations that come to Jesus externally by Satan, emphasizing how they are voluntary and undertaken on behalf of others: strengthening people against temptation, warning people that temptations come to all, teaching by his example how to overcome the devil's temptations (by quoting Scripture), and giving people confidence in his mercy to help them.[64] Anselm agrees with the voluntary aspect, explaining that Jesus merely submitted to being tempted as a redemptive task, just as the suffering he experienced throughout his life on earth was voluntary.[65] So, he freely enjoined temptation, but only those of the external sort.

FREEDOM

A medieval move not considered in the patristic models is to wonder about the peccability of Christ's humanity in abstraction from the hypostatic union. Anselm raises this question as a mark of Christ's human freedom (but he quickly explains that the human will always submitted to the divine will). Peter Abelard (1079-1142) goes further to claim that the ability to sin and the ability not to sin are essential to human nature. His view is that Christ's humanity, when considered apart from the union (*in abstracto*) was both able to sin and able not to sin, a condition which is necessary for moral virtue. However, because of the incarnational union Jesus was humanly not able to sin.[66] Likewise, Bonaventure (ca. 1217-1274) affirms that Jesus had the freedom to choose opposites (a freedom that belongs to pre-fall humanity), but concluded that Christ's simultaneous possession of a glorified human soul elevates his freedom to be exclusively surrendered to God, making him not able to sin.[67] On a different tack, Scotus boldly admits that Christ's humanity was able to sin but became transformed to be *not* able to sin as an effect of the beatific vision (not simply by the incarnational union):

> I say that the nature which he assumed was of itself peccable and able to sin, because it was not beatified by reason of its union and it had free will, and thus

---

[63]Instead, these are occasions for his merit and example of virtue, as part of his redemptive task. Anselm *Cur Deus Homo* 2.11 (ed. Schmitt, 2:11); Aquinas *Summa Theologiae* 3.14.4, b (ed. Walsh, *ST* 49:184-86).

[64]Aquinas *Summa Theologiae* 3.41.1 (ed. Parsons and Pinheiro, *ST* 53:72).

[65]Anselm *Cur Deus Homo* 2.12 (ed. Schmitt, 2:112).

[66]Abelard *Ep. ad Roman.* 1, cited in Augustus Neander, *General History of the Christian Religion and Church*, 1st American ed., trans. Joseph Torrey (Boston: Crocker & Brewster, 1851), 4:496.

[67]Bonaventure *Sententiarum Librum* 3.12.a.2, q.2, c ad 2, 3, 4, *Commentaria in Quaturo Libros Sententiarum Magistri Petri Lombardi,* in *Opera omnia* (Quaracchi: College of St. Bonaventurae, 1887), 269. Cited by Adams, *What Sort of Human Nature*, 40.

was able to choose in either of two ways. But it was because of beatitude that it was confirmed in the first instant so that it became impeccable in the same way as the other blessed [in glory] are impeccable.[68]

The medieval recognition in these examples is that Christ's humanity was low enough to be like that of common humanity in having the ability to sin when tempted, but beatification raised his humanity to be impeccable. Thus, in M5 the likeness of Christ's humanity to common humanity in susceptibility to sin is only the same freedom when considered apart from the union, that is, theoretically separated from the eternal Word and the benefits bestowed upon his human soul by divine grace. Jesus demonstrates the highest possibilities of a glorified humanity endowed with transforming grace, but his humanity was enriched far beyond the normal human experience.

MERIT

A major medieval concern is that Jesus was able to merit humanity's salvation despite his inability to disobey the Father or do other than live a perfect human life. Adams summarizes the medieval view that causes a problem for Christology: "Beatitude normally closes an agent's merit-earning career."[69] For Scotus, the possibility of Christ's merit is simply a divine exception in the divinely-mandated code of salvation, since all salvation is a free divine act and God could accept whatever he determined as meritorious.[70] Thus, according to Scotus, Jesus could merit rewards by fasting, watching, and prayer.[71] Generally, medieval theologians mark Christ's death as the main meritorious act that earns justification and eternal life for the elect.[72] We saw earlier that Anselm solved

---

[68]Scotus *Ord.* 3.12, q.u. (fol. 152vb); text and translation in Wolter, "John Duns Scotus", 182.
[69]Adams, *What Sort of Human Nature*, 78.
[70]Scotus *Ord.* 3.12, q.u, n.2 (ed. Wadding, 7.1:254). Scotus's formulation of the acception theory, *acceptatio*, is that God has set the terms autonomously for what he would accept as a meritorious work worthy of a reward. The common view was that Christ's work has infinite value because he is an infinite person acting through the finite instrument of his humanity; Scotus denied this and reasoned instead that by God's power and freedom he has accepted the finite sacrifice as the full payment for sin. Scotus's view should also be distinguished from *acceptilatio*, according to which under Roman law a debtor could be freed without payment if the creditor is willing to consider the debt paid. Both terms are helpfully defined by Richard A Muller, *Dictionary of Latin and Greek Theological Terms: Drawn Principally from Protestant Scholastic Theology* (Grand Rapids: Baker, and Carlisle: Paternoster, 1985), 18-19.
[71]Reinhold Seeberg, *History of Doctrines in the Middle and Modern Ages*, in vol. 2 of Text-Book of the History of Doctrines, trans. Charles E. Hay, rev. ed. (Philadelphia: Lutheran Publication Society, 1905), 154. Seeberg notes further that Scotus specified that Christ's merit was finite in keeping with his finite human nature.
[72]Cross, *Duns Scotus*, 129. E.g., Aquinas *Summa Theologiae* 3.48.1 (*The Passion of Christ*, ed. Richard T. A. Murphy, *ST* 54 [1965]: 74.

the problem of Christ's impeccability and merit-earning (which entails his human freedom) by arguing that Christ made a human choice for holiness and conformity to the divine will in advance of his subsequent choices.[73] Thus, M5 includes the ability of Christ to earn merit as a man despite impeccability.

THE EXAMPLE FOR HUMANITY

Like M4, M5 emphasizes Christ's purpose as a pattern of how to live, and to do so as a model of grace-assisted humanity in all the God-given capacities.[74] As part of this role, the divine Son assumed some so-called normal human defects as a way to demonstrate humility and patience for others.[75] Jesus was thereby able to demonstrate a pattern of resisting temptation and obeying God to the fullest. Anselm explains that this demonstration was part of Christ's job-description:

> For who can say how necessary and wise a thing it was for him who was to redeem mankind, and lead them back by his teaching from the way of death and destruction into the path of life and eternal happiness, when he conversed with men, and when he taught them by personal intercourse, to set them an example himself of the way in which they ought to live? But how could he have given this example to weak and dying men, that they should not deviate from holiness because of injuries, or scorn, or tortures, or even death, had they not been able to recognise all these virtues in himself?[76]

The medieval emphasis on Christ's grace-enhanced humanity (from M4) makes his value as the example of virtuous living relevant despite his wide differences of enjoying the maximal perfection in grace that does not occur for the elect until they enter glory.

In M5, Christ exemplifies a mode of human life that was low enough to need created grace and resembles the suffering of common human experience to encourage others' obedience after his pattern. Anselm shows this point with reference to the way Christ's obedience in a death he assumed voluntarily (a true self-sacrifice because his death was undeserved, unlike martyrs) is an example of the obedience to God that others should have when faced with persecution and suffering:[77] "Do you not perceive that when he bore with gentle

---

[73] Anselm *Cur Deus Homo* 2.10 (ed. Schmitt, 2:106-7). According to Anselm, this is the same principle by which the righteous angels earned merit by a first choice that determined all subsequent choices.

[74] Adams, *What Sort of Human Nature*, 42.

[75] Bonaventure *Sent.* 3.15.1, q.1, d (Quaracchi ed., 3:331). Cited by Adams, *What Sort of Human Nature*, 41.

[76] Anselm *Cur Deus Homo* 2:11 (ed. Schmitt, 2:111-112); trans. Sidney Norton Deane, *St. Anselm: Proslogium; Monologium; An Appendix in Behalf of the Fool by Gaunilon; and Cur Deus Homo* (Chicago: Open Court, 1903), 259.

[77] Deme, *Christology of Anselm*, 198.

patience the insults put upon him, violence and even crucifixion among thieves that he might maintain strict holiness; by this he set men an example that they should never turn aside from the holiness due to God on account of personal sacrifice?"[78] Part of Anselm's point here is that obedience to God is possible because Jesus demonstrated this way of life for others to the utmost. The example Jesus gives of perfect obedience is a life given *for others* in self-sacrifice to endure his entire (voluntary) suffering and culminates in death—all from a motivation of love.[79]

To sum up, the picture of Jesus in M5 is that his glorified humanity is adjusted to be just *low enough* to satisfy these requirements indicated by the biblical data for his temptation. His humanity must be such that he could be tempted externally, suffer pains and death, sympathize with others in their temptation, and be the pattern for others to imitate.

Evaluation of M5: Sinless by Created Grace

The medieval synthesis of patristic models is important for its reformulation of the earlier concepts in to meet new concerns (especially those raised by philosophical theology of medieval scholasticism). A major concern of M5 is to reconcile the metaphysical distance between Christ's two natures in view of what was necessary for redemption and what human attributes were suitable for divine incarnation. The answer in M5 draws from each of the patristic models. The result is a complicated explanation of Christ's sinlessness in connection with grace. Grace enables and transforms his humanity to be trebly impeccable and yet be able to earn merit, be tempted, and provide an example of right living for Christians. We have seen that two prominent contributions are the medieval idea of created grace and the preservation of Christ's ability to earn merit despite enjoying the beatific vision with impeccability.

I think M5 is a rich restatement of some of the best theology received from the patristic writers, and the model is particularly strong on the concerns of M3 and M4 to preserve the value of Jesus as the example of a man helped by grace to live righteously. However, the inclusion of other elements undermines both these concerns to make the model theologically inadequate. Others have recognized the inadequacy by the ways that both Protestant and many Catholic theologians have abandoned a key element innovated in M5 (the beatific vision).[80]

The model picks up the concern of M2 as part of fortifying the theological claim of Christ's impeccability, but an objection may be raised against the way M5 explains impeccability. If Christ's humanity was impeccable by the divine

---

[78]Anselm *Cur Deus Homo* 2.18 (ed. Schmitt, 2:127); trans. Deane, *St. Anselm*, 279-80.
[79]Deme, *Christology of Anselm*, 205.
[80]O'Collins, *Christology*, 207, 257, Jacques Dupuis, *Who Do You Say I Am?* (Maryknoll, NY: Orbis, 1994), 118; Galot, *Who is Christ?*, 353-57.

nature as some sort of energizing or glorifying relation by virtue of the union (a communication of divine attributes to the human nature), then how could any temptation and his achievement of sinlessness have occurred in conjunction with the divine immunity to temptation and sin? In other words, if the divine nature is counted as somehow being involved in Christ's humanity as an active presence to prevent sin from occurring, then the entire experience of temptation and struggling to choose right for sinlessness would seem to be precluded as well. By analogy, if by raising a metal shield (the divine nature) I prevent a fatal sword stroke from stabbing me (sin), the raised shield also prevents the lesser blows (temptation) that I might have deflected by my own sword, body armor, or some deft movement. In relation to sin and temptation, the divine nature functions as a sort of shield, and, if raised against the possibility of sin, the possibility of temptation is necessarily prevented as well (since the divine nature is immune to temptation no less than sin, Jas 1:13).

A way out might be to argue that the divine nature is provisionally unexpressed in Christ's humanity, and would only be employed should Christ be in danger of failure on the terms of his human defenses alone. In this case, the divine shield is not raised, and only potentially would have functioned as a cause of his impeccability and sinlessness, but the shield never became necessary because Jesus managed on other means. Nonetheless, M5 does not take this way out and explains instead that Jesus was partially glorified with created grace (a divinizing effect of the divine nature on the human nature for impeccability).

Another reason for the inadequacy of M5 is the dichotomy of human temptation into internal and external temptation. M5 limits the extent and degree of Christ's temptations as only external, from the world and the devil, but not internal from his human existence (as is common to the rest of us). This means that Christ's experience of temptation is only partly comparable to the common human experience. This reduction of the shared experience of temptations corresponds to a reduction in his relevance for empathy with others and his example to them for facing temptation victoriously. Moreover, according to M5, his temptations were experienced merely as demonstrations for the benefit of others, and he did not experience them as the necessary conjuncts of authentic human existence. By analogy, the billionaire's attempt at empathy with the homeless masses by choosing to spend a week living on the street with them is mitigated by the voluntariness and brevity of her condition. All through the privation and suffering she remains fully conscious that she may return to her comforts of home and wealth whenever she pleases, and the humiliation of street life is not something that holds her as a condition of grimy and soul-debilitating existence. For Jesus, his human existence is entirely voluntary, but the necessity of his temptations seem to be inescapable in a way that seems different from the M5 account of them as merely didactic and demonstrative. If he is to recapitulate Adam and Israel's temptations in victory, then it seems that he would have to suffer as an internal experience of struggle in temptation, just as they did. Credible empathy and effective recapitulation seem to require true solidarity with us. M5 denies this can be so.

The internal-external distinction of temptations has become traditional even to the present day, but the division into two categories of temptation causes trouble for any attempt to explain Christ's empathy and example for those who experience an entirely different category of temptations (i.e., internal) than he did. If Jesus is only relevant in empathy and example for the temptations that are external, having originated from demons or other people tempting us, then what are we to do with the vast majority of our temptations that arise from within us? How can Jesus be relevant for temptations that are based on malformed and corrupt desires? This is not to say that we must imagine that Jesus experienced sinful desires if we are to think of him as relevant for us, but that the internal-external distinction does not allow him to be relevant to us. Instead, as I will propose later in my observations about temptation, it seems more adequate to say that all temptations are both internal and external, and a better distinction is to sort temptations that are sinless (i.e., not arising from sin, as in the desire for food) from those that are sinful (i.e., arising from sin, as in the desire for heroin), recognizing that Jesus knows only the sinless sort. M5 properly assigns only sinless temptations to Jesus, but errs by sorting all of his temptations as external. The language of Hebrews 4:15 ("he was tempted in all ways we are") seems to exclude an internal-external distinction that wrongly protects Jesus from ever having experienced the majority of ways that sinful humans are tempted. That is, if *tempted in all ways* should be taken to mean categories of temptations, then we should say Jesus experienced all of them with us. The internal-external distinction, having been raised to protect Christ's difference from sinful humanity, causes a problem with Hebrews 4:15 and the two important points of practical relevance in Christ's having been tempted for us (his empathy and example), both of which are based on his actual experience that reasonably corresponds to ours.

A related problem of M5 is positing created grace in Christ's humanity as the empowerment by which he achieved sinlessness. The analogy of grace in Christ and Christians (following M4) is helpful for understanding Jesus as the pattern for Christians to follow (because they receive similar empowering grace). I think M5 is on the right track, but takes the enrichment of grace too far for the model to be adequate theologically. Christ's experience with the transforming enrichment of created grace glorifies his soul and sets his human experience so distant from common human experience that M5 reduces his value as an example and his ability to empathize with others. Christ's differences from others are so great that even his human limitations are mitigated after the infusion of created grace. His embodiment and finite nature may resemble common humanity outwardly and in important ways of exercising created faculties of perception, emotion, mind, and will, but M5 revisions his human soul in a way that makes his inward experience seem categorically different from the rest of humanity (Jesus is human, but he is so different a sort of human being that he may no longer be able to function for others as a reasonable model).[81]

The concept of created grace is itself deficient because according to this idea the action of grace has been divorced from the Holy Spirit and made into a numinous mechanism deposited in the human soul. This picture seems far different (and impersonally magical) from the accounts in the New Testament of dynamic personal movements of the Holy Spirit in Christ and the early church. The created grace idea threatens to make grace relatively autonomous of the Holy Spirit's personal involvement.[82]

The M5 formulation of the beatific vision is a flaw that is recognized by some contemporary Roman Catholic Christologists who deny that Jesus possessed this pre-resurrection glorification.[83] This beatific vision of God that belongs to glorified humanity is difficult to reconcile with the Gospel reports of Christ's occasional experiences of emotional distress (e.g., John 11:33; 12:27; 13:21) and especially his experience of being forsaken by God during the crucifixion. Such internal distresses seem to have been important components of Christ's temptations as his inner anticipation of the suffering he humanly desired to avoid. To preclude internal distress in the way M5 does seems wrong, especially when Scripture is clear on these details of his experience (e.g., Heb 5:7-8). If he was tempted for us, then there must be something to how his temptations were like ours.

Consequently, according to M5, in the Gethsemane temptation on the eve of the cross, Jesus was not really so distressed and torn apart in his soul as the Gospels might seem to present him. He is full of the knowledge (omniscience) of all the exact details regarding his temptation, arrest, and death, and knows even that he will be praying in a cyclical way to his Father before finally voicing the foregone conclusion of his human alignment to the Father's will. He withdraws with his three closest friends to pray in Gethsemane, but he experiences the struggle as merely something presented to him from the outside, and perhaps he is pressed by Satan in a last recap of the trial in the wilderness. In no sense does Jesus feel the press and internal appeal of this temptation to choose another way than embracing the cup of wrath. Having always known how this event would come out, he feels his human desires for self-preservation and to flee pain, but nothing more has just now dawned upon

---

[81]Adams, *What Sort of Human Nature*, 98-99, makes a similar objection, and suggests instead that an incarnation in a fallen human nature (having to struggle against actual sins and the inward corruption of sin) would be much more inspiring of hope than incarnation in a glorified humanity as the medievals envisioned. I do not share her conclusion, but I agree that a human nature closer to what we experience (i.e., not glorified in soul) is closer to the truth and necessary for motivating Christians by his authentic example and empathy.

[82]I thank Matt Jenson for alerting me to this critique.

[83]See n. 80.

his human consciousness in perceiving and fearing—just now in prayer—the full blast of the wrath he is called upon to face. Instead, having eternally chosen to conform his human will to his divine will, his struggle with temptation to shrink back from the cross is simply a countdown to the point at which he will rest on his divine will to carry his human will through the struggle and the pain. He has acted freely to obey, but it is the freedom as of water *freely* flowing through a pipe (the divine will)—no other true option is available to him. All the while, because Jesus is omniscient, he is fully aware of not only his deity but also his impeccability. He knows that in this struggle, just as in every earlier trial, his menu of available choices is always filled with a single item of whatever God has chosen for him. Perhaps the fact that he is considering a temptation in his human consciousness is an amazing thing in itself, for how can he be tempted when he knows he cannot sin? And yet, his disciples see the profuse sweating on his face and they feel the dread of his decision. He turns to them with command that they pray for assistance not to succumb to their temptation, but all the while he enjoys the fullness of created grace pulsing through his humanity. Jesus is aware of his temptation, but the danger is always distant.

M5 has proven unsatisfactory for these and perhaps other reasons. The changes in settings of the Reformation and modern periods also called for continued reformulation of models of Christ's impeccability and temptation.

CHAPTER 7

The Reformation Model

The theological upheavals of the sixteenth century did not bring about new understanding of Christ's impeccability.[1] Concerning Christ's temptation, the Reformers argued repeatedly for the severity of Christ's experiences. In doing so, they were careful to reflect on Christ's person and work within the traditional boundaries of the Chalcedonian Definition.[2] Whether by allegiance to Chalcedonian Christology or biblical theology, Christology of the Reformation had some common main lines despite some divergences. Moreover, Christological formulation during the Reformation continues to be interwoven with soteriology, as in earlier theology.

Nonetheless, the new setting of the Reformation period raised some new concerns for its theologians. In general, the emphasis of Renaissance humanists on classical sources facilitated theological renewal through attention to Scripture (*Sola Scriptura*) and the writings of the patristic fathers. The Reformers reacted to the Roman Catholic doctrine of transubstantiation (the Eucharist elements are transformed into Christ's flesh and blood) and the claim that Jesus lived out his life and ministry in a human nature that was glorified in many ways.[3] The Reformers also clashed with one another when they set out their theology of Christ's presence in the Lord's Supper. Two main streams of Christology would later develop in the sixteenth century, following the leads of Luther and Calvin.[4]

Despite this doctrinal schism regarding Christ's presence in the Eucharist,

---

[1]Ullmann, *Sinlessness of Jesus*, 19. "We find this dogma enunciated by [the Reformers]: only we discover in their writings no minute discussion of [impeccability], or attempt to demonstrate its truth; for to them it appears to have been not a position requiring proof, but an immediate certainty, an irresistible intuition, something far above mere logical demonstration."

[2]Wells, *Person of Christ*, 122. "Luther and Calvin as biblical theologians affirmed a Christology which was in full accord with Chalcedon; indeed, the Chalcedonian Definition became an important element in the creedal literature of most of the Reformation churches."

[3]E.g., Luther's view that Jesus actually felt abandoned and cursed by God (he did not possess the beatific vision), noted by Adams, *What Sort of Human Nature*, 97.

[4]Bruce, *Humiliation of Christ*, 82. Of course, a thorough historical study would include much more than just Luther and Calvin as representative of a Reformation model. Our goal here is to get the main contributions from the period on the specific topic.

the towering contributions of Martin Luther (1483-1546) and John Calvin (1509-1564) hold in common a sixth model of Christ's impeccability and temptation. Similar to the ways that we have seen differences and agreements among contemporaries in earlier periods, Luther and Calvin exhibit common concerns about Christ's impeccability and temptation while they clearly disagree on other aspects of Christology (i.e., whether Christ's humanity could receive the divine property of omnipresence after the resurrection, which Calvin and the Reformed denied). In view of the divergence, the agreements of Luther and Calvin on the specific topic of Christ's impeccability and temptation are all the more remarkable. Moreover, the Eucharistic Controversy concerned Christ's post-resurrection existence, *the state of exaltation*, which Lutherans distinguished from *the state of humiliation* (the period from Christ's conception to his resurrection).[5] This means that the disagreement in Christological models concerns the state of the risen Christ; we are concerned here with how Luther and Calvin understood the *ante mortem* (pre-death) existence of Christ, during which time he was tempted and achieved sinlessness. I will argue that the two Reformers share enough in common on this topic to be sorted together in what I describe as the Reformation model. (They are not so different on this topic that they could be sorted into two models.)

The primary distinction of Reformation Christology from the medieval formulations is a renewed and emboldened emphasis on the humanity of Jesus as the locus of human salvation.[6] The prominence of Christ's human nature is a major concern for the Reformers that shifted their thinking to develop a distinct model of Christ's impeccability and temptation. This and other differences

---

[5]Bruce L. McCormack, *For Us and Our Salvation: Incarnation and Atonement in the Reformed Tradition* (Princeton, NJ: Princeton University Press, 1993), 5. Some have judged that Calvin and Luther both favored unitive Christology. McCormack notes that Calvin's Christology belonged to the Alexandrian-Cyrillian type, despite Calvin's antipathy for what seemed like Eutychianism in the Lutheran claim of post-resurrection ubiquity of Christ's humanity (p. 8). Calvin's preference for the unitive Christology of Cyril (and Chalcedon) is harmonious with Luther's general affinity for Alexandrian Christology, noted by Marc Lienhard, *Luther: Witness to Jesus Christ,* trans. Edwin H. Robertson (Minneapolis: Augsburg, 1982), 28. I am indebted to Lienhard for many specific citations in Luther's works.

[6]"Taught by Scripture, the Reformers attached great significance to the humanity of Christ because it relates so plainly and categorically to his mediatorial work." Geoffrey W. Bromiley, "The Reformers and the Humanity of Christ", in *Perspectives on Christology: Essays in Honor of Paul K. Jewett,* ed. Marguerite Shuster and Richard Muller (Grand Rapids: Zondervan, 1991), 86. Bromiley cites evidence of this special emphasis on Christ's true humanity in the Lutheran, Reformed, and Anglican confessions (88). This is also the opinion of Dorner, *History*, I.1:84, "[The Reformation was] a real transition-point in the history of the world, inasmuch as it, by resuming the truth taught in the old time, opened a free course for the right knowledge of the human side [of the doctrine of Christ]."

from earlier models flow from the innovations of Luther and Calvin that correspond to the new setting and concerns of the Reformation period. Additionally, as with M5, the Reformation model draws much material from earlier models. We will describe M6, note the repetition of earlier models, explore the innovations of M6, and evaluate the model's theological adequacy.

M6: Temptable by the Human Eclipse of Divine Power

Description of M6

M6 asks this question: How was Christ, God the Son, able to live in redemptive solidarity with us in our temptable weaknesses? The answer given is that he voluntarily condescended to the limits of a human nature such as we are, and veiled his deity with that vulnerable humanity for our redemption. God's power upholds Christ's experience in human weakness. The divine Son's ability to condescend in humiliation is itself an expression of God's power, and M6 thus recognizes a larger role for the Holy Spirit to facilitate Christ's experience in his humanity, thereby becoming vulnerable to suffering in a sinful world. Two perspectives are offered. First, Christ's deity was concealed, as if it were set in the *background* to his humanity, accomplishing the Incarnation and underlying his humanity, so that Jesus could be tempted as a man in all sorts of ways while remaining unable to sin.

Second, Christ's humanity was taken up by the Son as the visible covering or concealment of the totality of his existence when he comes into the world as one man among us. Consequently, Jesus was truly limited in his knowledge as a man, grew in knowledge, experienced fears, anxiety, and a whole life of temptations and sufferings through his human body and soul. Most patristic and some medieval theologians thought this sort of internal suffering was impossible for the Godman. By contrast, a primary concern in M6 is to emphasize Christ's relevance as the pattern, brother, and ally for other human beings who suffer temptations in a fallen world. Christ's solidarity is as a brother with others in his own humanity, a comradeship and identification made possible only by the eclipse from display of his divine majesty with his human weakness.

M6 follows the biblical statements about Christ's voluntary humiliation to take on a second mode of existence as a temptable, passible man while remaining fully God. The Reformers find this doctrine of divine condescension as a biblical theme (e.g., John 1:14; Phil 2:6-7). The logic of this condescension to allow his true humanity a full expression in divine incarnation is that the majesty of the divine nature had to move behind his humanity, out of view in his earthly existence, so that God the Son could meet the requirements of redemption. As a man he had to live, suffer pains and temptations, and die for the sins of the world. By this logic of Christ's humanity eclipsing his deity in a soteriological formula, the Reformers' explanation of the biblical evidence implies that his divine impeccability is concealed in the background to his human temptability. Metaphors for describing this logic are that the deity of Christ is *veiled* or *concealed* by the humanity, *laid aside* from being used, and *quiescent* or *reposed* to allow the full expression and experience of the Son in his humanity. If we see all the metaphors together, the divine powers are not only hidden beneath the human weakness (though potentially operative), but they are also not in operation in ways that would compromise the authentic finitude of the human nature in Christ.

By contrast with the concern of M5 to protect the deity of Christ from the corruptions and indignities of human frailty, M6 reverses this concern to protect his human nature from divine interference (whether by deification through a communication of attributes, beatific vision, or otherwise) that might have prevented authentic human experience (e.g., temptation, suffering, weakness, death).[7] In the medieval theology of M5, the concern was how God could deign to come so *low* to be incarnate in a human nature with the defects shown by Christ because of the metaphysical distance between God and humanity and all the indignity of created frailty and finitude. The pressing M5 question of *how low did God condescend in incarnation* is replaced in M6 by the claim from the biblical data that *thus did Christ condescend fully as one of us, a true man who suffered for us*. The Reformers explain that this descent to the likeness of sinful humanity took place with no detraction of the Son's dignity and power (no loss of deity), but the condescension was an expression of divine power motivated by his love and pity for the lost.[8] An authentic and temptable humanity in Christ is recognized in M6 as the necessary equipment for Jesus to be a human mediator between sinful humanity and the righteous God.

In short, M6 affirms Christ's temptations as part of the redemptive necessity that Christ must be fully human in solidarity with humanity to save the world. His divine nature did not dilute the force of his suffering within the limits of his human nature. His impeccability, divine will, and other divine attributes did not prevent him from feeling the strain of his temptations to sin. He was so vulnerably human that he needed divine support to hold him up. His human sinlessness was a way of life grounded in his purity from original sin, but he lived obediently by the divine assistance of grace and the Holy Spirit. He never ceased to be impeccable as the divine Son, but this attribute did not interfere with his ability to be fully temptable in his humanity. In other words, M6 marks

---

[7] As far as I know, Luther's claim of ubiquity for Christ's human nature in the Eucharist was not repeated as a claim for the communication of some divine attribute that might preclude temptation and sin, or that miraculously enabled Jesus to surmount these.

[8] John Calvin *Institutio Christianae religionis* 2.16.12, in vol. 3 of *Joannis Calvini Opera Selecta,* ed. P. Barth and W. Niesel, 2nd rev. ed. (Munich: Chr. Kaiser, 1959), 497.31-33. (All page numbers for the critical edition of the *Institutes* refer to this edition, abbreviated *OS*.)

the cause of Christ's impeccability (his deity) as distinct from the cause of his sinlessness (his human effort by grace). M6 explains these facts in terms of the human eclipse of the divine power.

Recycled Elements

M6 repeats three elements from earlier models. These are Christ's inherent impeccability as God the Son (M1), the divine assistance of empowering grace (M4), and the purity of Christ's human nature from original sin (M5).[9] Examples of each of these from Luther and Calvin show their dependence on tradition despite the renewal that the Reformers introduce.

INHERENT IMPECCABILITY

M6 continues the traditional recognition of M1 as the philosophical deduction from Christ's deity that he is impeccable. Luther affirms this when he writes in *The Freedom of a Christian* that because Christ is God and man in one person, he cannot sin, because "his righteousness, life, and salvation are all

---

[9]Purity at conception is an Augustinian idea that was appropriated for M5. As for M3, the divine hegemony concept was already muted somewhat in the medieval model that changed it to more of a volitional harmony. In Luther and Calvin the M3 idea does not appear in connection with Christ's sinlessness (as far as I am aware). Luther also recycles M2 as part of his assertion of the ubiquity of Christ's humanity *post resurrection*, which is irrelevant to the temptation that occurred *ante mortem*. Luther's battle to defend the real presence of the risen Christ's ubiquitous humanity in the Lord's Supper brings out his claim that by the incarnational union, Christ's two natures exchange attributes. In the particular application to the Eucharistic controversy, this means that the real presence of Christ's humanity is hypothetically possible in terms of the ubiquity of his humanity as communicated from the divine nature. Luther's innovation is to affirm a fully symmetrical and reciprocal exchange by which even the suffering of the human nature is ascribed to the divine nature. Alasdair Heron, "Communicatio Idiomatum and Deification of Human Nature: A Reformed Perspective", *Greek Orthodox Review* 43 (1998): 372, notes that Luther's formulation of a symmetrical communication between the natures is unprecedented in patristic and medieval theology. Luther also contradicts his own innovation by arguing that Christ's humanity was not transformed by sharing the divine attributes, as in the Roman Catholic teaching of transubstantiation (Luther, *De captivate Babylonica ecclesiae praeludium*, in D. Martin Luthers Werke: Kritische Gesamtausgabe Band 6 [Weimar: Hermann Böhlaus Nachfolger, 1888], 511, 34-36, hereafter volumes from this series are abbreviated WA and the volume number). We should emphasize that the transfer of ubiquity to Christ's human nature from his divine nature is a *post resurrection* condition of Christ in the state of exaltation, and has no bearing on our question of Christ's impeccability, sinlessness, and temptation. Moreover, in fairness to Luther, his affirmation of the ubiquity of Christ's humanity was a proposal to explain the possibility of the real presence in the Lord's Supper. Without the Eucharistic Controversy, he might not have proposed his strange doctrine of Christ's post resurrection ubiquitous humanity at all.

unconquerable, eternal, omnipotent".[10] Commenting on John 1:10, Luther marks Christ's sinlessness as the only difference between the savior and us, and he explains that Christ was free of sin because he was very God.[11] In his comments on Hebrews 7:26, Luther explains that Christ is fit to be a priest because he is untainted, having no inner filth (sin) of his own as believers do, and so their sins do not contaminate him when he redeems them.[12]

Calvin gives a similar explanation by saying that Christ's sinlessness is a requirement for him to be a mediator before God for humanity, with the biblical proof given that Jesus sanctifies his own humanity (John 17:19) for the sake of others.[13] This implies that holiness is an inherent attribute for him because Calvin clarifies that Jesus does not need sanctification for his deity.[14] Calvin also explains John 17:19 as indicating the inherent sense of Christ's holiness because his sanctification is *for others* and not acquired for himself.[15] Calvin's suggestion of M1 is less forceful compared to Luther's overt declarations, yet both indicate that M1 is a background presupposition for the formulation they hold in common as M6.

EMPOWERING GRACE

The Reformers repeat the idea from M4 that Jesus needed the grace of gifts from the Holy Spirit to enhance his human nature. The multiform concept of grace in M5 is not repeated in M6 as the surety of Christ's sinlessness because the Reformers seem to be more concerned with Christ's vulnerable, *low* humanity than with his divinely empowered immunity to sin. As an example, Luther affirms the continual work of the Holy Spirit in Christ from his conception onward, moving Christ from time to time in an increasing way throughout his life (Luke 2:40).[16]

Calvin mentions the gift of the Holy Spirit to Christ as a mark of his true humanity because the deity of Christ does not need the divine enrichment and equipping that the Holy Spirit gave him to fulfill his mediatorial office as

---

[10]Martin Luther *Tractatus de libertate christiana*, WA 7 (1897): 55; trans. *The Freedom of a Christian*, in *The Career of the Reformer*, vol. 1, *Luther's Works*, American Edition, vol. 31, ed. Helmut T. Lehmann, trans. W. A. Lambert, rev. Harold J. Grimm, 327-378 (Philadelphia: Muhlenberg, 1957), 351-52. (Henceforth all references to volumes in this series will be abbreviated LW.)

[11]Luther *Auslegung des ersten und zweiten Kapitels Johannis in Predigten 1537 und 1538*, 1.10, WA 46 (1912): 598.

[12]Luther *Commentariolus in epistolam divi Pauli Apostoli ad Hebreos* 7.26, WA 57.3 (1939): 194.

[13]Calvin *Inst.* 2.15.6, *OS* 3:480, 1-3; 481, 6-10.

[14]Calvin *Inst.* 2.13.1 (*OS* 3:450, 4-6), 2.13.4 (*OS* 3:457, 16-20).

[15]Calvin *Inst.* 2.17.6, *OS* 3:514, 30-34.

[16]Luther *Evangelium am Sonntag nach dem Christtage, Luk. 2, 33-40*, WA 10.1.1 (1910): 446.

teacher.[17] In Calvin's comment on Acts 10:38, he identifies Christ's miraculous powers with the power of the Holy Spirit, who was given to Christ as his anointing from the Father.[18] Calvin has arrived at the concept of empowering grace and closely identified it with the Holy Spirit as a personal operation of divine aid hinted at in M4.

PURIFICATION FROM ORIGINAL SIN

Medieval theologians had embraced Augustine's idea about original sin and the operation of grace in Christ's humanity, and M6 likewise affirms that the Holy Spirit purified Christ's humanity from original sin at his conception. For the Reformers, this purity at conception is the single difference of Jesus' human nature from the rest of humanity (of course, his human nature is also uniquely united to the Logos, but as a human body and soul considered side by side with other human beings, Christ's humanity is truly human).[19] The Reformers frequently comment on the Lord's initial purity from original sin as a work of the Spirit and the initial ground of his sinlessness. Luther connects Christ's purity with the virgin birth as the work of God to purify both Mary and Jesus.[20] Calvin affirms Jesus' purity from original sin but denies that Mary had the same purity.[21] Calvin further denies that Christ's innocence (being untainted by original sin) resulted from the virginal conception as the means of his purity. Calvin argues instead that the special action of the Holy Spirit is the sole cause of Christ's purified human nature.[22] Nonetheless, the significant point is the Luther-Calvin agreement that Christ's sinless life was established at the outset by his having been miraculously purified by the Holy Spirit from original sin.

M6 draws these three elements from earlier models. New elements added by Luther and Calvin are important contributions that constitute a distinct model of Christ's impeccability and temptation. These innovations culminate in the two Reformers' common support for a dominating new Christological element: the divine power is in the background to allow the full demonstration of Christ's humanity, now set on display before the watching world. The relevance of this point to our topic is that Christ's divine impeccability is counted paradoxically alongside his human temptability. His temptations are true, unmitigated by his

---

[17]Calvin *Inst.* 2.13.1 (*OS* 3:450, 1-5), 2.15.2 (*OS* 3:473, 17-22), 2.15.5 (*OS* 3:477, 3-14).
[18]Calvin *Commentarius in Acta Apostolorum*, 10.38, CO 48 (1892): 245.
[19]E.g., Luther *Auslegung des ersten und zweiten Kapitels Johannis in Predigten 1537 und 1538*, 1.14, WA 46:634.
[20]Lienhard, *Luther*, 118. One example cited by Lienhard is Luther, *Evangelium in der Christmess, Luk. 2, 1-14*, WA 10.1.1:68, 2.
[21]Calvin *Inst.* 2.13.4, *OS* 3:457, 8-20.
[22]Richard A. Muller, *Christ and the Decree: Christology and Predestination in Reformed Theology from Calvin to Perkins*, Studies in Historical Theology 2 (Durham, NC: Labyrinth, 1986), 28. "He rejects any explanation of sinlessness as a result of the virgin birth: the central issues for Calvin is that Christ is a true man, 'in the likeness of sinful flesh,' but sanctified by the Holy Spirit."

deity, and his sinlessness is valid, achieved by his action as a man (not directly by his deity). For his humanity to be true and full in all the aspects reported in the Gospels and as are required for redemption, Christ's actual sinlessness had to be caused by something other than the force of his divine attributes. In other words, M6 explains Jesus' suffering in weakness and temptation as the veiling of divine power (a factor that otherwise would have prevented such vulnerability and suffering). Always in the background, his deity was eclipsed (unchanged but inoperative in his human life) to allow the possibility of temptation without allowing the possibility of sin. The divine powers were not communicated to the human nature in ways that would have cut off Jesus' authentic human life. We will see this and other new elements in Luther and Calvin that constitute M6.

New Elements in Luther

Luther develops two Christological elements that relate to a model of Christ's impeccability and temptation. First, Luther boldly affirms the temptation experience of Christ as including vulnerability and suffering in his body *and soul*. Second, Luther explains the true and fully human experience of Christ as having occurred by means of living with his divine power in the background.

TEMPTATION IN BODY AND SOUL

Luther affirms that Christ's temptations were not merely in his body (by natural vulnerability to hunger, thirst, fatigue, and death) but that he also suffered temptations in his soul, like the rest of humanity (e.g., fear, anxiety, and sadness).[23] Christ's only difference was that he was sinless, not that he suffered less than other people do or only partly what others suffer.[24] Luther claims that Jesus' temptations were much stronger, and more lethal in every way than what others experience.[25] Jesus had to endure these internal temptations to be a substitute for sinners, the one punished with God's wrath against sin. Thus,

---

[23]Luther, *Commentary on Psalm 22*, in *Select Works* IV, 360, "Christ himself suffered the dread and horror of a distressed conscience that tasted eternal wrath."

[24]Luther lists Christ's natural human frailties in his comment on John 1:10 (Luther *Auslegung des ersten und zweiten Kapitels Johannis*, WA 46:598). Luther does not comment specifically on Heb 2:18 or 4:15 in his lectures on Hebrews, but in his *Sermon on St. Matthias' Day* (1525) he explains Matt 11:29 in terms of Heb 4:15: "And Christ makes a special point of saying here that he is gentle. It is as though he were saying: I know how to deal with sinners. I myself have experienced what it is to have a timid, terrified conscience (as the letter to the Hebrews [4:15] says, he "in every respect has been tempted as we are, yet without sinning)." Luther *Am tage Matthie des hailigen Apostels Euangelion Mathei*, WA 17.2 (1927): 396, 15-18; trans. John W. Doberstein, *Sermons 1*, LW 51 (Philadelphia: Muhlenberg, 1959), 131.

[25]Luther *Psalmus XXII* (21), WA 5 (1892): 635, 27. Cited in Lienhard, *Luther*, 148 n. 60.

Jesus had to feel in himself the guilty sense of their terror with a conscience stricken by the accusation of the Law: "The blows with which God strikes [against Christ] because of sins are not only the pain of death, but also the fear and the terror of a troubled conscience, which feels the eternal anger and behaves as though it were eternally abandoned and rejected from the face of God."[26] Commenting on Psalm 22, Luther writes about the wide range of Christ's internal experience: "In Christ there coexisted both the highest joy and the deepest sorrow, the most abject weakness and the greatest strength, the highest glory and the lowest shame, the greatest peace and the deepest trouble, the most exalted life and the most miserable death."[27] For Luther, the deepest trouble for Jesus occurred on the cross, when Jesus "felt in his conscience that he was cursed by God."[28] Luther thinks this experience of being forsaken by God provoked Jesus to be tempted to blaspheme God for abandoning him as a creature (not answering his cry as God had done in the past for the fathers of Israel).[29] This intensity of his temptation is a level of suffering in Christ's soul that medieval theologians denied because of their view that Jesus possessed the beatific vision. Gogarten comments regarding Luther's uniqueness on this point: "There is no theology before him, nor apart from Kierkegaard, any after him that so makes the tempted Christ into the object and ground of faith."[30] Luther writes: "One must believe that he was subjected to all the temptations, as a pure and true human being."[31] Luther thus praises Christ for suffering on behalf of sinners in his own despairing sorrow. Moreover, Luther argues that this suffering against the torment and temptations could not have been possible for Christ unless he deprived himself of the divine power that would have precluded his human pain.

HUMAN EXPERIENCE IN THE FOREGROUND

Luther is able to emphasize Christ's full humanity and the ferocious reality of his temptations by explaining that the Son's divine power had been set in the background to allow Christ's experiences as a man to occur. Luther focuses on Christ's struggle in his humanity against the temptation to blaspheme God when Jesus was cursed and abandoned in the cross. In his dereliction, Christ suffered his lethal vulnerability to the devil, death, hell, and the consequent

---

[26]Luther *Ps. XXI* (22), WA 5:603, 14, trans. Lienhard, *Luther*, 116.
[27]Luther *Ps. XXI* (22), WA 5:602, 22-25; trans. Lienhard, *Luther*, 119.
[28]Luther *Ps. XXI* (22), WA 5:603, 34; trans. Lienhard, *Luther*, 118.
[29]Luther *Ps. XXI* (22), WA 5:604, 32; 605, 9; 610-13. Cited in Lienhard, *Luther*, 118.
[30]Fredrich Gogarten, *Luthers Theologie* (Tübingen: 1967), 63, cited and trans. in Lienhard, *Luther*, 147 n. 54.
[31]Luther *Operationes in Psalmos* WA 5:387, 27; cited and trans. Lienhard, *Luther*, 148 n. 59.

temptations to curse God for abandoning him to these horrors.[32] Luther declares bluntly that Jesus was deprived of God's help in the cross.[33] This deprivation was a necessity of redemption because Jesus had to be unassisted by divine power to be able to take up the full consequences of sin and be immersed in death in his humanity and reverse the devil's conquest of Adam.[34]

Elsewhere than his commentary on Psalm 22, Luther explains the condescension of the Son of God to the limits of a human existence: "And in fact He was forsaken by God. This does not mean that the deity was separated from the humanity . . . but that the deity withdrew and hid. . . . The humanity was left alone, the devil had free access to Christ, and the deity withdrew its power and let the humanity fight alone."[35] The Son could only be passible as a man by this raw exposure unmitigated by his deity.

Moreover, the human eclipse of the divine power in Christ's life as a man was not only in the cross; this eclipse occurred normatively throughout Jesus' life so that he could live as a true man. Luther affirms that Jesus "was a man who did not know certain things," and again, "the humanity of Christ did not know all things."[36] Luther writes that the Incarnation was a humiliation and full entrance into a temptable human experience that was made possible by Christ's having put off the form of divine majesty, by which he means Christ put on the form of human vulnerability that eclipsed his divine power:

> [The form of a servant] means that Christ divested or emptied himself, that is, acted as though he laid his Godhead aside, and would not use it. . . . Not that he removed it or could put it off or remove it, but that he put off the form of the divine majesty, and did not behave as God, which he truly was. Just as he did not put off the form of God so that one would not feel or see it, for then there would be no form of God there, but did not make use of it, did not make a display of it against us, but much rather served us with it.[37]

---

[32]Luther *Epistel auss den Palmtag. Philippen. 2*, WA 17.2:244, 19. "In which he submitted himself not only to human beings, but also to sin, death, and the devil and bore all this for us." Trans. Lienhard, *Luther*, 192 n. 48.

[33]Luther *Ps. XXI (22)*, WA 5:601, 14, 19. Cited in Lienhard, *Luther*, 115.

[34]Luther, *Commentary on Psalm 22*, in *Select Works* IV, 359. Luther explains that to be immersed in death means to be involved in "death, darkness, ignorance, lies, sin, malice, weakness, sorrow, confusion, dismay, desperation, damnation, and all evil".

[35]Luther *Predigten des Jahres 1537, Nr. 40* (Ps. 8:5), WA 45 (1911): 239, 32-40; trans. Jaroslav Pelikan, in LW 12, ed. Jaroslav Pelikan (Philadelphia: Muhlenberg, 1955), 126-27.

[36]Luther *Predigten Luthers gesammelt von Joh. Boliander* (1519-1521), *De Centurione*, WA 9 (1893): 556, 30-32, trans. in Lienhard, 191 n. 28; Luther *Epistel am Christtag, Hebr. 1, 1-12*, WA 10.1.1:149, 6-7; trans. Lienhard, *Luther*, 170.

[37]Luther *Epistel auss den Palmtag. Philippen. 2*, WA 17.2:243, 2-11, trans. Bernhard Lohse, *Martin Luther's Theology: Its Historical and Systematic Development*, trans. and ed. Roy A. Harrisville (Minneapolis: Fortress, 1999), 229.

Luther's explanation is that Christ's emptying is in terms of the exclusive action, use, behavior, and display of his human weakness on earth, without ceasing to be fully divine in any way (just obscuring his divine power from mitigating his human life).

Because Calvin comes to a similar conclusion, the two Reformers together distinguish M6 primarily at this point of their agreement about the restraint or withholding of divine power to allow a place for Jesus' human experience in the foreground of his earthly experience and temptation. This point is especially relevant for a model of Christ's impeccability and temptation because by means of it the Reformers discern a way to affirm fully two paradoxical truths without diminishing either one. They affirm the full weight of the biblical data about Christ's weakness in temptation alongside affirming the full power of his divine impeccability. Jesus could be tempted in every way as the rest humanity (Heb 4:15), though he could not sin as others do. The empathy and example of Jesus for others because of his experience are protected without diminishing his full deity (as Chalcedonian Christology and Scripture demand). We now turn to Calvin's formulation the same elements in a radical vision of Jesus in M6.

New Elements in Calvin

Calvin develops three Christological contributions that (along with Luther's) constitute the distinctive features of M6. Most important is the point (noted already with Luther) in Calvin's affirmation that Christ's human experience was made possible by the quiescence or veiling of the divine power in the background to display his humanity in the foreground of his earthly experience. Two other contributions support this main point. First, Calvin (like Luther) emphasizes the authenticity and example of Christ's humanity that is temptable and vulnerable in body and soul. Second, Calvin discerns a role of the Holy Spirit in the Incarnation to keep Christ's human nature pure through all his temptations as a pneumatological operation of divine power in the life of the Messiah.

HUMAN EXPERIENCE IN THE FOREGROUND

Calvin explains that Christ's temptation was only possible by a voluntary eclipse of divine power in the background to demonstrate his human weakness in the foreground. David Willis gives a helpful summary of Calvin's view: "This full humanity was enabled by the Eternal Son's emptying himself in the sense of freely concealing himself and withholding the exercise of his powers through the flesh to which he was fully joined. The *kenosis* was the concealment, not the abdication, of the Eternal Son's divine majesty."[38] Calvin

---

[38] E. David Willis, *Calvin's Catholic Christology: The Function of the So-Called Extra Calvinisticum in Calvin's Christology,* Studies in Medieval and Reformation Thought 2

mentions this concealment idea frequently as the *veiling* of the divine power with the human nature, as in Calvin's comment on Philippians 2:7, "Christ, indeed, could not renounce His divinity, but He kept it concealed for a time, that under the weakness of the flesh it might not be seen. Hence He laid aside His glory in the view of men, not by lessening, but by concealing it."[39] Calvin repeats this veiling idea in the *Institutes* when discussing the same passage, explaining the *kenosis* in Paul's theology as an addition of human nature and involving no loss of deity:

> His object is not to show what kind of body Christ assumed, but that, when he might have justly asserted his divinity, he was pleased to exhibit nothing but the attributes of a mean and despised man. For, in order to exhort us to submission by his example, he shows, that when as God he might have displayed to the world the brightness of his glory, he gave up his right, and voluntarily emptied himself; that he assumed the form of a servant, and, contented with that humble condition, he suffered his divinity to be concealed under a veil of flesh.[40]

Accordingly, Bruce McCormack concludes that this idea of God the Son displaying himself in the limitation and beneath the veil of flesh is "the heartbeat of Calvin's thought."[41]

Calvin sharpens his use of the veiling concept as the explanation for how Jesus could be tempted to sin. In his explanation of Jesus' intense internal distress, told in John 12:27, Calvin writes that the divine nature had to be restrained so that Christ could suffer even his anticipatory emotions of fear about the punishment he would experience in the cross. Calvin explains the restraint as the suppression of the divine nature so as not to exert its force.[42] As the result of this suppression, Christ was able to suffer fully within the vulnerability and pains of his humanity, and without retreating to his divine immunity when faced with his greatest temptation in the cross.[43] Similarly, Calvin explains that the wilderness temptations (and Christ's temptations throughout his life) were opportunities allowed only by the temporary desertion of the angels, "when God's grace, though present, lay hidden from Him,

---

(Leiden: E. J. Brill, 1966), 80. The kenosis concept is from the verb in Phil 2:7, *he emptied*.

[39] Calvin *Commentarius in Epistolam ad Philippenses,* 2.7, CO 30 (1895): 26, trans. T. H. L. Parker, *The Epistles of Paul the Apostle to the Galatians, Ephesians, Philippians and Colossians,* Calvin's Commentaries, vol. 11 (Grand Rapids: Eerdmans, 1965), 248.

[40] Calvin *Inst.* 2.13.2 (*OS* 3:450, 20-451, 1), cf. 2:14.3 (*OS* 3:461, 17-19), trans. Beveridge, *Institutes,* 410. In *Inst.* 2.16.17 (*OS* 3:504, 27-31), Calvin also uses this veiling idea for the present status of Christ's kingdom as a humiliated form that will give way to its full demonstration of majesty and power when Christ returns.

[41] McCormack, *For Us and Our Salvation,* 7.

[42] Calvin *Commentarius in Evangelium Ioannis,* 12.27, CO 47 (1892): 291.

[43] Willis, *Calvin's Catholic Christology,* 79.

according to the perception of the flesh."⁴⁴ Thus Calvin connects the veiling concept specifically with allowing Christ's temptability and suppressing the help from his divine power. With divine power set in the background to his human experience, Calvin sees Jesus as having become vulnerable to passibility and temptation that are otherwise impossible for God.

In Calvin's view, the greatest temptation culminated in Christ's suffering in the cross, and for this (as well as in other temptations) the divine power had to be set in the background and suppressed to allow Jesus' human experience in all weakness to be unmitigated by deity. Jesus fully experienced his temptations inwardly, which was consistent with the full display of his authentic humanity outwardly. Calvin explains that in the cross, the divine power of the Spirit "veiled itself" (*occultavit*) to allow a place for Christ's human weakness to suffer the "temptation out of pain and fear."⁴⁵ The suppression of divine power allowed him to fulfill his redemptive role of suffering, and necessarily so because, Calvin explains, "the mystery of our salvation could not have been fulfilled otherwise."⁴⁶ Clearly, this divine concealment must occur for the Godman to experience death according to his humanity. Calvin extends the necessity "divinity resting" (*quiescente divinitate*) in the background even for Jesus to experience the grief and internal torment of temptation that he endured along with death.⁴⁷

THE INTEGRITY OF HIS TEMPTABLE HUMANITY

Calvin explains that in the incarnational union, the authenticity of Christ's human nature was preserved from the elevating, transforming effects through union with the divine nature. The need for this was so that Christ could suffer temptations on the same terms that are common to other human beings. Calvin reverses the typically Antiochene (or, divisive Christology) motive of distinguishing the two natures to protect Christ's deity from degradation in the

---

⁴⁴Calvin *Commentarius in Harmonim Evangelicam*, Matth. 4.11, CO 45 (1891): 137; trans. A. W. Morrison, *A Harmony of the Gospels Matthew, Mark and Luke*, Calvin's Commentaries (Grand Rapids: Eerdmans, 1972), 1:143.

⁴⁵Calvin *Inst.* 2.16.12, *OS* 3:499.2-5. Willis, *Calvin's Catholic Christology*, 84, notes that Calvin gives multiple accounts of the divine power displayed in Jesus' life: "There is no clear indication as to the identity of the divine power of Jesus to which Calvin gives so much weight. Is that power the efficacy of the Second Person which makes itself experienced beyond the confines of Christ's flesh, or is it in fact the Holy Spirit himself: Calvin has no set phrase for denoting the divine power at Jesus' disposal. He usually restricts his descriptions to the effect of that power, sometimes calling it the divine Spirit of Christ, the power of the Holy Spirit, Christ's divine or secret power, or Jesus Christ's spiritual power."

⁴⁶Calvin *Comment. in Harm.*, Matth. 26:37, CO 45:719; trans. Morrison, *Harmony*, 3:147-48.

⁴⁷Calvin *Comment. in Harm.*, Luc. 2.40, CO 45:104. Calvin quotes Irenaeus approvingly here on the concept of deity resting. So, it is not a new idea.

union (especially passibility). Instead of guarding the deity, Calvin's motive is to show how Christ's human temptability has been protected from divine interference. Stephen Edmondson explains Calvin's point:

> The separation of natures is what ensures the lowliness of this flesh – Christ's humanity is fragile, weak, and anxious only as it remains separate from his divinity and can experience reality in a human manner. Christ knows our weaknesses only because his human nature is truly and fully human, not safeguarded from the travail of human experience by his divinity, but immersed in such travail as his divinity refuses to exert any ameliorating influence over him. Calvin emphasizes the separation of the two natures in Christ primarily so that Christ can share our condition. [48]

This distinction supports what Calvin notes as Christ's relevance as an example and his ability to provide help for other humans suffering temptations.[49] Calvin affirms that Jesus' genuine humanity meant that he was so vulnerable to temptation in his human weakness that he prayed for divine support to resist the temptations (within the limits of his humanity).[50]

As part of preserving the integrity of Christ's humanity and his suffering in temptation, Calvin affirms an ancient teaching that the divine Logos was not limited to the constraints of his human nature. Calvin argues that *the Logos exists beyond the flesh*, that is, the Word of God is not limited to his incarnate presence on earth as a man, but continues simultaneously to exist omnipresent in all power (*Logos extra carnem*).[51] By this appropriation of an idea that was

---

[48] Stephen Edmondson, *Calvin's Christology* (Cambridge: Cambridge University Press, 2004), 119-120.

[49] Calvin *Commentarius in Epistolam ad Hebraeos*, 2.17, CO 55 (1896): 34-35. I should also note that in his comment on Heb 4:15, Calvin takes "without sin" to mean that Jesus was not tempted from within as from an inward sinfulness (Calvin, *The Epistle of Paul the Apostle to the Hebrews*, trans. William B. Johnston, ed. David F. Torrance and Thomas F. Torrance, Calvin's New Testament Commentaries, vol. 12 [Grand Rapids: Eerdmans, 1963], 56). I have argued above in chapter 1 that "without sin" in Heb 4:15 refers to the outcome or result of Christ's temptations. Calvin's idea is right as a theological claim that Jesus, having no sin, was not tempted sinfully according to sinful desires, but Heb 4:15 does not teach this.

[50] Calvin *Comment. in Harm.*, Matth. 26.46, CO 45:728.

[51] Calvin *Inst.* 2.13.4, *OS* 3:458.5-13. Heiko Augustus Oberman, "The 'Extra' Dimension in the Theology of Calvin", in *The Dawn of the Reformation*, ed. Heiko Augustus Oberman (Edinburgh: T & T Clark, 1986), 249, summarizes Calvin's view of the so-called *extra calvinisticum* (the label was affixed to Calvin by Lutherans who disputed it): "The *extra calvinisticum* serves to relate the eternal Son to the historical Jesus, the Mediator at the right hand to the sacramental Christ, in such a way that the 'flesh of our flesh' is safeguarded. Rather than hiding secret divine resources, which mark a divide between the incarnate Christ and fallen man, the *extra calvinisticum* is meant to express both the reality of the *kenosis* and the reality of the Ascension."

common in patristic and medieval theology,[52] Calvin can affirm that Christ is fully human without giving up any of Christ's deity. Calvin's use of the traditional formula allows him to explain how the divine nature could be in the background to Jesus' human experience without being a factor that transforms his human nature to a glorious state invulnerable to suffering or weakness (or, deified and glorified by the union to deity). Had his humanity been deified in this way (as in M2), he would be irrelevant as an inspiring and reasonable example of an authentic human life. Calvin argues that Christ's human temptability was preserved in all vulnerability because the Reformer maintains a continuing distinction of the human existence from the divine nature that was beyond Christ's humanity (i.e., not limited to or merged with his humanity). This explanation is Calvin's way of affirming Christ's unchanged possession of deity in the traditional way and also accounting for Christ's human vulnerability. Thus, Calvin can say of Jesus in Gethsemane: "[Christ] was struck with fright and seized with anguish, and so compelled to shift (as it were) between the violent waves of trial from one prayer to another."[53] We see here that, Calvin counters any move to diminish the depth and severity of Christ's temptations in body or soul because he affirms Jesus' full and true humanity, as he warns any who might lessen the truly visceral struggle: "People who exempt Him from feeling temptations make Him Victor without a fight. And it is quite forbidden to suppose that He made a pretence, when He complained of mortal sadness in His soul. The Evangelists do not lie when they recorded that He was overcome with sorrow and in great fear."[54] This sort of claim is very close to Luther and far from M5.

Therefore, Calvin, in agreement with Luther, affirms the intensity of Christ's suffering in temptation because of the biblical evidence (despite the theological paradox), and he does so in a way that recognizes the integrity of Christ's human nature. A further step of explanation for the temptable and sinless human life of Jesus is Calvin's recognition of the Holy Spirit's role in the Incarnation.

---

[52]Willis, *Calvin's Catholic Christology*, 60, demonstrates that the so-called *extra calvinisticum* was taught almost universally in patristic and medieval theology, as shows in abundant examples he provides from Origen, Theodore of Mopsuestia, Athanasius, Cyril of Alexandria, Augustine, Peter Lombard, Thomas Aquinas, and Gabriel Biel. A noteworthy example is Leo the Great's *Tome to Flavian*: "So it is that God's Son enters this lower world. He descends from his heavenly throne and is born with a new kind of birth in a novel order of existence, yet without departing from the glory of his Father... While continuing to be beyond time, he begins to exist from a point in time. Veiling his measureless majesty, the Lord of the universe assumes the 'form of a slave'." Letter XXVIII.4, trans. Charles Lett Feltoe, NPNF², 12:41.
[53]Calvin *Comment. in Harm.*, Matth. 26.39, CO 45:721; trans. Morrison, *Harmony*, 3:149.
[54]Calvin *Comment. in Harm.*, Matth. 26.39, CO 45:724; trans. Morrison, *Harmony*, 3:152.

THE HELP OF THE HOLY SPIRIT

Calvin emphasizes the Holy Spirit's role of helping Christ to remain pure from sin throughout all his temptations. Willis comments on Calvin's view of the Holy Spirit in Christ:

> One of the strengths of Calvin's Christology and of his Pneumatology is his representation of the person and work of Christ in constant reference to the Spirit, and the reality and work of the Spirit in constant reference to Christ. Calvin's Christology is of course a 'Spirit-Christology' in the sense that it is so much a *Filioque-Christology* he never loses sight of the role of the Holy Spirit in the Incarnation. . . . Part of the force of the 'extra Calvinisticum' in Calvin's thought is that it makes Pneumatology integral to Christology and so affords a Christology more properly Trinitarian than would otherwise be the case.[55]

This pneumatological emphasis properly recognizes a trinitarian dimension to Christ's impeccability and temptation, just as Jesus' entire life as Messiah is a trinitarian operation of divine power, not simply God the Son fulfilling an incarnational task. Calvin explains that in the Synoptic account of the wilderness temptations, Luke's special reference to the Holy Spirit's fullness in Christ means that Jesus was given grace and power to face Satan's temptations. Calvin then compares Jesus to Adam. Like Adam, Jesus had the same human weakness in temptability that made him needy for the Holy Spirit. Unlike Adam, who was merely able not to sin (*posse non peccare*), Jesus was "so defended by the power of the Spirit, that Satan's darts could not reach him."[56] That is, reach him in a final, defeating way, not that Jesus did not feel the temptations. This explanation of empowering grace given by the Holy Spirit is tantamount to impeccability, because Jesus experienced Adam's vulnerability but the Holy Spirit was a new unconquerable factor guaranteeing Christ's sinlessness and the salvation of sinners. In considering Christ's temptations on the eve of his death, Calvin notes again the divine factor of empowerment that supported Jesus in an external way and not from within himself: "With prayers and tears He gained new strength from heaven: not that lack of strength had ever made Him waver, but in the weakness of the flesh, which He had freely assumed, He wished to wrestle in anguish, in painful and hard combat, that in His own person He might win the victory for us."[57]

By contrast to other models that counted Christ's enriched ability to withstand his temptations in Gethsemane, Calvin explains that the disciples failed there "because they are not yet sufficiently possessed of the power of the

---

[55] Willis, *Calvin's Catholic Christology*, 82-83. John Owen will develop this further in the next century, as we will see below.

[56] Calvin *Comment. in Harm.*, Matth. 4.1, CO 45:130-31; trans. Morrison, *Harmony*, 1:136.

[57] Calvin *Comment. in Harm.*, Matth. 26.46, CO 45:728; trans. Morrison, *Harmony*, 3:156.

Spirit."[58] Jesus prescribed that they pray for help to resist temptation, just as he has himself been praying and then received the visible form of divine aid when angels appeared to strengthen him. Calvin explains that the angels generally represent visible divine aid, and especially so for Christ in Gethsemane: "Though it is the Spirit of God alone who supplies courage, there is no objection to God using His angels as servants. We may infer the enormity of suffering that Christ endured, when God had to give Him aid in visible form."[59] The presence of angels indicates the weakness of his vulnerability and his heavy reliance upon divine aid to meet the adversity within his human limits.

Therefore, Calvin supports his picture of Christ as radically temptable despite his impeccability. The role of the Holy Spirit is a gift from the Father to empower Jesus in his humanity through all his temptations. Calvin's insistence on the authenticity of Christ's human nature, unmitigated by the greatness of the Son's divine power, further explains the ferocity of Christ's temptations.

Evaluation of M6: Temptable by the Human Eclipse of Divine Power

Luther and Calvin contribute their emphasis on the truly temptable humanity of Christ. They add that this authentic and severe temptability became possible for Jesus by the veiling of his divine power with his human weakness. The Reformers' innovations that form M6 are distinctive among the earlier models while drawing several useful elements from them. M6 reverses the trend of earlier theology that emphasized Christ's deity overshadowed by his humanity. The Reformers asserted bold conclusions from the biblical evidence for Christ's temptations.

M6 offers two new solutions to old problems. First, the M6 principle of Christ's veiled deity explains the difficulty of how to relate his two natures in view of the evidence for his temptations and weakness. I think M6 has followed the biblical text properly to a complicated explanation of a complex reality (i.e., a divine incarnation with impeccability and temptation). Scripture tells of some mysterious sort of a limitation of divine power within the Incarnation (e.g., Jesus is not omniscient or omnipotent as a man), and temptation would otherwise be impossible for the Godman were this not the case. With deity veiled from human perception and prevented from mitigating Jesus' own human experience, the God the Son was able to suffer temptation in a way that is reasonably relevant for all those who do not possess deity as he does. This seems right because Scripture marks Jesus' humanity and temptations as his equipment to become a merciful mediator and a genuine, reasonable human example to follow.

---

[58]Calvin *Comment. in Harm.*, Matth. 26.41, CO 45:725; trans. Morrison, *Harmony*, 3:153.
[59]Calvin *Comment. in Harm.*, Matth. 26.42, CO 45:726; trans. Morrison, *Harmony*, 3:154.

M6 affirms the internal distress of Jesus' temptations as constitutive of his empathy for others because he felt the way we do. Because Jesus became merciful and a pattern to copy by his own credible experiences, M6 is right to say Jesus truly struggled within human limitations without relying on his divine powers as a shield or way of escape. Never does Scripture mark inherent divine powers as Christ's means of resisting temptation, and always noted are the humanly available means of divine aid through Scripture, prayer, the Holy Spirit, and angels as the help for him to fight out his obedience.

M6 maintains the tension between Jesus' divine impeccability and human temptation by affirming the support of the Holy Spirit as the active, guaranteeing factor in his human achievement of sinlessness. In this way, M6 explains how Christ's effort is praiseworthy and motivational for those who follow his example. Suffering Christians may be reversed from despair by knowing that he suffered in all the ways as they suffer in temptation and he offers them help that proved effective for him (cf. Heb 4:16).[60] Because M6 affirms that Christ was not insulated from the strains of human temptations, his example is that much more credible and generates hope to obey God as he did.

Moreover, I think that the veiling principle enhances the theological adequacy of M6 to balance the strong emphasis on Jesus' humanity by an equally strong emphasis on his full deity and impeccability as the ultimate ground of his sinlessness. The emphasis on Jesus' susceptibility to temptation through divine concealment protects the integrity of his natures from corruption and enrichment, in alignment with the Chalcedonian definition.[61] The genius of the veiling principle is to explain how Jesus entered into mediatorial solidarity through his human limitations.

Second, M6 deals with the problem of Christ's humanly achieved sinlessness in terms of the empowering grace of the Holy Spirit.[62] The abundant biblical evidence for the Spirit's role is best explained this way (otherwise, why would God the Son need help from God the Holy Spirit unless the Son truly lived according to severe human vulnerability on earth?). M6 explains the role

---

[60]This is not to say that Jesus had a sinful set of temptations that go with being a fallen creature, but that his temptations were real struggles that match or compare with the difficulties that other human beings experience.

[61]Luther is possibly equivocal on this point because of the Eucharistic controversy, and only with reference to the divine attribute of ubiquity. But notice that his innovation of the ubiquity of Christ's humanity is counted for the post-resurrection life of Christ. Luther did not say Jesus was ubiquitous as a man during the days of his humiliation (as far as I know). Moreover, Luther affirmed the integrity of Jesus' humanity in opposition to transubstantiation. Luther's emphasis on Jesus' suffering within the limits of his humanity during his temptations shows his concern to maintain the integrity of the natures (even if the ubiquity doctrine is inconsistent with this concern).

[62]Or, stated positively, his righteousness for perfect obedience to God as a man, e.g. Rom 5:17-19; Phil 2:8, which is essential to justification of the ungodly by a gift of righteousness, one man's for all who share in him.

of the Holy Spirit in Christ's earthly life as the mode of divine support for him as a man tempted to sin. The emphasis on Christ's role as the Spirit-empowered mediator in solidarity with the people's weaknesses supports the reasonableness of his pattern for their sanctification. This pneumatological involvement fits together with the analogous presence of the Holy Spirit in believers for sanctification: the same Holy Spirit who assisted Jesus in his humanity enables Christian sanctification in conformity to Christ. Moreover, the pneumatology of M6 is a conjunct of the radical human weakness of Jesus, which was necessary because of his setting in redemptive history, whereby he achieves salvation by means of suffering the full consequences of sin and reversing the devil's defeat of Adam. Jesus only does this as a true man, and the needed assistance of the Holy Spirit underlines his limitation to battle as a genuine human being and second Adam.

The M6 picture of Jesus in Gethsemane includes the ferocity of his temptation and his complete vulnerability to it. Jesus in Gethsemane is a man stricken to the core and haunted with the prospect of divine wrath and the desperate possibility of escape. Jesus has come to the end of himself in his human abilities. He has called along three witnesses to his torment, his three closest friends, Peter, James, and John. He has asked for their support and told them of his struggle, that he is sorrowful even to the point of feeling that great powers are tearing him apart, to the point of death. He feels nearly overcome by the horror set before him. He imagines the full terror of being forsaken and cursed as a creature by God. All of his life experiences and the ongoing help of the Holy Spirit have prepared him for these last anguished steps in the marathon of his of obedience, a march that will end in the greatest possible suffering before he sees victory. Yet he is, even now, conflicted between ardent desire to embrace obedience with suffering, and the mounting, fearful desire to flee the impending doom. His terror competes with his awareness of the oft-comforting consciousness that he is the eternal Son of God. He feels only human fear, human uncertainty, and human vulnerability to the test. His theology and thoughts have narrowed into the tunnel of one pulsating imperative. To the side, he feels the pull to escape it. His choice is never in question because he has always obeyed God in everything, but he struggles with the question nonetheless. He appeals repeatedly for some alternative way that would allow him to escape while remaining home with his Father. But no relief comes. He faces only the dreadful anticipation of nearly total abandonment by his God. Even his friends who have just pledged to die with him have fallen away into their sleep. There are visible signs of his torment. His effort in prayer breaks out great drops of sweat on his face. His friends hear his loud sobs and cries for help from God. They perceive him entirely gripped in his doom, as a man, and with no hint of divine power glimmering before them. Deity is utterly concealed, and no such divine shield protects Jesus from having to fight his inner conflict. They see him appealing to God, receiving help from God with the momentary appearance of an angel, and they hear his grieving, gut-ripping prayer of human submission to God. (Yet, the worst was still to come, since even angelic support would be removed from him when on the cross. Even now, the trial in Gethsemane is preparatory for that final and greatest temptation in cursed abandonment by God.) Resignation, in the end, comes at the cost of everything he has, and he leans heavily on the glimpse of external help given him at last. The disciples are entirely overwhelmed so that they continue to fall sleeping, only to wake finally into the nightmare of soldiers, arrest, trial, and the complete devastation of all their hopes in the crucifixion. Seeing him suffer later in the sequence that culminates in his final despairing cry of a creature forsaken and cursed by God on the cross, the disciples have no room left for their dream that Jesus is the Son of God, much less the Messiah of Israel. Weeks later, having passed beyond despair and now looking backward in hope of glory because of his resurrection, they are convinced of his agony and take courage from his solidarity with them. Memory of his distresses in genuine creaturely limitation now power their endurance in like manner of blood and pain, knowing all the while that he truly knows their turmoil and provides ready help that supported him in his lifelong conflicts. Such is the gory and glorious picture of Jesus in temptation according to M6, which I find to be largely adequate theologically as an explanatory model.

One shortcoming of M6 is that the mechanism of veiling remains unclear. How does the veiling of Jesus' deity with his humanity work? Does the concealment of deity mean divine powers are inoperative? The Reformers might have replied that it is enough to discern what Scripture reveals without pressing into needless speculation about the metaphysics of the hypostatic union. I think that Calvin, like M4 proponents before him and a minority opinion in Reformed theology after him, has already suggested the seed of a reasonable explanation. I will take this seed up as part of my proposal (Part Three).

I think M6, even with the silence of the Reformers on speculating about the veiling concept, is the best model of Christ's impeccability and temptation so far. The best elements of M4 are repeated (whether because of M6 dependence on M4 or a common way of reading the relevant biblical texts properly), and the additional element of the veiling concept in relation to Jesus' experience of temptation provides a much more reasonable understanding of the biblical accounts than previously given in the tradition. My proposal will rely heavily upon M6 while drawing additionally from proposals offered in the period that follows to the present day. Three models try new features to explain old paradoxes.

CHAPTER 8

Modern Models (Part 1)

As with earlier models, the modern period has its distinctive background that influenced Christology with new settings and questions for which the traditional answers no longer seemed adequate. This inadequacy of traditional theology for the modern mind is especially true for the way theologians explained about Christ's impeccability, temptation, and sinlessness. After the Reformation, the developments in Christology formed three distinct models of Christ's impeccability and temptation. I will briefly review the relevant background of the modern period, including two responses to the modern situation in Christology, and then describe and evaluate three distinct modern models of Christ's impeccability and temptation. The common theme of these models is the humanization of the Logos. One theologian has called the modern Christological opinion as the end of Docetism because of taking the full humanity of Christ more seriously than ever before.[1]

Background to the Modern Models

John Macquarrie describes the modern shift of Christological emphasis from deity to humanity: "The classical christology that had stood so long . . . was increasingly subject to criticism. Both its historical content and its doctrinal formulations were now in doubt . . . Jesus Christ was being humanized."[2] The modern Christological trend, in opposition to the patristic and medieval emphasis on the deification of Christ's humanity, has been to explain Christ's deity as having been humanized for incarnation. Picking up from the Reformers' reassertion of Christ's authentic humanity, modern theologians have been especially interested in Christ's experiences of suffering and temptation because these validate his true humanity and mark his solidarity with us. Marilyn Adams has also observed the modern trend that reverses the priorities of earlier Christology to stress the humanity of Jesus:

> All our medieval authors were committed to the infallible truth of Holy Scripture. Yet, they inherited from the patristic period a flexible hermeneutic that enabled

---

[1] D.M. Baillie, *God Was in Christ: An Essay on Incarnation and Atonement* (New York: Charles Scribner's Sons, 1948), 11.
[2] John Macquarrie, *Jesus Christ in Modern Thought* (London: SCM, 1990), 235.

them to harmonize by creative interpretations that explain away. Luke 2:52 is made to stand with claims of beatific vision, the knowledge of vision, or habitual omniscience. Hebrews 2:18 and 4:15 are made compatible with impeccability and right reason's invincible control. *By contrast*, early twentieth century theologians were eager to read the Gospels as an historical record. Many of them preferred to establish their Christological baseline with the Synoptic career and passion narratives, and Hebrews 4:15; to make "like us except for sin" their first approximation; and to design for Christ as normal an *ante-mortem* [pre-death] human nature as possible given that sin must be taken away. In effect, *they reversed the Anselmian burdens of proof*, placing the onus instead on any who wish to assign Christ's human nature special advantages or perfections that would lift Him out of the rough and tumble of our *post-lapsum* [fallen] world.[3]

Whereas the Christology that was formulated up to and throughout the post-Reformation period grew out of the Chalcedonian definition of two natures in Christ, many theologians in the modern period have rejected the traditional definition outright.[4] Traditional orthodoxy and Christology in particular were subjected to the new canons of authority raised by the Enlightenment.[5] This exaltation of reason as independent from divine revelation and traditional Christian orthodoxy has been described as a turn from a theocentric worldview to an anthropocentric one.[6] Philosophers and theologians have rejected traditional Christology as no longer tenable in the new rationalistic worldview because they judged the central claim, "Jesus is the Son of God", to be irrational.[7] The abandonment of the theocentric, revelation-dependent, and tradition-oriented worldview allowed new possibilities for Christologies that

---

[3] Adams, *What Sort of Human Nature*, 99. Emphasis added. For her part, Adams is sympathetic to this shift and commends a revisioning of Jesus in a fallen human nature (98).
[4] Donald Macleod, "The Christology of Chalcedon", in *Jesus the Only Hope: Yesterday, Today, Forever*, ed. Mark Elliott and John L. McPake (Fearn, Ross-shire: Christian Focus, 2001), 77-82. Macleod defends Chalcedonian Christology against the critiques he perceives in modern theology.
[5] McGrath, *Historical Theology*, 221. "The Enlightenment criticism of traditional Christianity was based upon the principle of the omnicompetence of human reason." *Die Aufklärung*, the Age of Enlightenment, developed a rationalistic worldview during the seventeenth and eighteenth centuries and continues as the so-called modern period. Major shifts in thought about political theory, nature, education, theology, and science followed from the Enlightenment exchange of authority for knowledge based on revelation and tradition for the new authority for knowledge based on reason.
[6] H. R. Mackintosh, *The Doctrine of the Person of Jesus Christ* (New York: Charles Scribner's Sons, 1942), 247-49.
[7] McGrath, *Historical Theology*, 223-24, notes that David Hume's *Essay on Miracles* (1748) swept aside the New Testament proofs for Jesus' deity based on miracles and eyewitness testimony. Other critics added to the radical skepticism that unverifiable New Testament events and the eyewitness testimony for them could not warrant the traditional claims about Jesus.

were *rationalistic* (Immanuel Kant), *humanistic* (Friedrich Schleiermacher), *idealistic* (Georg Hegel), and *kenotic* (Gottfried Thomasius).[8]

One result of the new anthropocentrism for Christology was the heightened interest in the humanity of Jesus, continuing the Reformers' discovery, and especially in terms of Jesus as a common man much like one of us.[9] This interest was developed through the approach of studying Jesus as a self-conscious human individual with a biography and experiences like any other culturally and historically conditioned human being.[10] Scholars presupposed that Jesus was a regular man (much like themselves), and they interpreted the Gospel evidence of Jesus' life in terms of their own observations and experiences. The results were published as low Christologies that diluted his uniqueness and redemptive significance as the Godman. Many of the nineteenth century biographies presented the man from Nazareth as merely a man like others (not a Godman), and many of these historical Jesus studies eclipsed his miracles, claims for his sinlessness, and evidence of his divine nature.[11] Interest in the social and cultural world of Jesus' life flourished in the modern period, along with corresponding disinterest in his significance and identity as God incarnate.[12]

The modern trend of emphasizing the humanity of Jesus flowed directly out of the Reformation re-discovery of his solidarity with humanity in temptable weakness and suffering to redeem sinners. However, the anthropocentric worldview of modern theology upset the Reformers' balance of Jesus' likeness to and difference from the rest of humanity. With some exceptions, the trend in

---

[8]Macquarrie, *Jesus Christ in Modern Thought*, 235.

[9]David G. A. Calvert, *From Christ to God: A Study of Some Trends, Problems and Possibilities in Contemporary Christology* (London: Epworth, 1983), 3-5.

[10]Calvert, *From Christ to God*, 3-5. Calvert notes that Marxist scholars have been particularly influential for reconstructing Jesus' biography in terms of socio-historical forces.

[11]Fisher H. Humphreys, "The Humanity of Christ in Some Modern Theologies", *Faith and Mission* 5 (1988): 5. The critical approach is that the gospels do not give us access to the historical Jesus because the stories are just myths to convey religious ideals. An example is D. F. Strauss, *The Life of Jesus Critically Examined*, 4th ed. [1835], trans. George Eliot, ed. Peter C. Hodgson, Lives of Jesus Series (Philadelphia: Fortress, 1972), 238-39. Strauss claims that Jesus did not have a sinless development from childhood and confessed his own sins at the Jordan baptism (Strauss cites a statement from the Gospel of the Hebrews that Jesus confessed his own sins). Strauss reasons that Jesus must have sinned and made his confession because, "According to Matt. iii.6, John appears to have required a confession of sins previous to baptism; such a confession Jesus, presupposing his impeccability, could not deliver without a falsehood."

[12]Humphreys, "The Humanity of Christ", 6-7, summarizes the anthropological interest of the lives-of-Jesus projects: "Yet it was characteristic of the writers of the lives of Jesus that they often made the case of Jesus' historicity and humanity at the expense of his deity." An example noted by Humphreys is Ernest Renan, *The Life of Jesus* (1863).

modern Protestant theology has been to erode Christ's deity and consider him as merely a great man.[13] As never before, some modern theologians have not only denied his impeccability but they have also questioned Jesus' sinlessness.[14] One example of these novel ideas is Carl Ullmann's nineteenth century defense of Jesus' sinlessness as a proof of his deity.[15] Ullmann argued against those who denied Christ's sinlessness (and, by implication, his deity), but agreed with the trend to deny Christ's impeccability.

In response to these critical revisions to and departures from traditional doctrine, many theologians have reasserted and defended the pre-modern orthodoxy of old. Other theologians have responded to the critical approach with innovations for a rapprochement alongside of the commitment to remain within the boundaries of Chalcedonian Christology. These two sorts of responses contribute additional features to the background of the three modern models.

Reassertion of the Traditional Models (M1-M6)

Among the many theologians that could be cited, the representatives included here maintain the traditional formulations about Christ's impeccability and temptation.[16] They also take up the modern accent on the true humanity of Jesus and recognize his real condescension to human limitations of mind, temptability, and other weaknesses such as fear and distress. This emphasis comes from the M6, which reversed the tradition in M5 and denied that Jesus was deified by grace. Perhaps because of this reversal, the distinctive features of M5, Sinless by Created Grace, do not show in the Protestant tradition. The principle of grace in M5 is perhaps generally voiced in M6 that Christ's sinlessness was empowered by grace as the divine aid for his human nature,

---

[13]Calvert, *From Christ to God*, 3-5, notes that the traditional description of Jesus as the Second Person of the Trinity is unintelligible to many because of the rising antipathy for traditional God-language in an increasingly secular age.

[14]G. C. Berkouwer, *The Person of Christ*, trans. John Vriend (Grand Rapids: Eerdmans, 1955), 255. "On the basis of the intensity of the temptation people whittled away at the absoluteness of Christ's sinlessness." Peccability was a minority view (cf. Theodore of Mopsuestia), but the suggestion that Jesus had sinned was never considered until the modern period. Bavinck, *Reformed Dogmatics: Sin and Salvation in Christ*, 313 n. 226, notes that Kant, Fichte, Strauss, and Renan all objected to Jesus' sinlessness.

[15]Carl Ullmann, *The Sinlessness of Jesus: An Evidence for Christianity*, 7th English ed., trans. Sophia Taylor (Edinburgh: T & T Clark, 1882), 163. "On the assumption that Jesus was a true, a real man, it cannot of course be denied that it was possible for Him to sin. This possibility is directly involved in human nature, in so far as is to be morally developed."

[16]Dates are given for theologians living before the twentieth century; thereafter, the publication dates within the twentieth century are given for a rough chronological context.

including the gift of the Holy Spirit. Some contemporary Roman Catholic theologians have specifically maintained the created grace idea of M5.[17]

The theologians included here in chronological order represent the conservation of the traditional models throughout the modern period. This brief survey demonstrates the continuing influence of earlier models in modern theology despite the bold departures from tradition. The diversity of opinions on the topic continues in Protestant theology (just as in Roman Catholic theology) despite the embrace of earlier models.[18] By including one or another theologian as a representative of an earlier model, I do not claim that proponents reflect a conscious dependence upon the tradition, only that the earlier formulations are still considered adequate in the modern setting (whether these theologians have arrived at formulations independently or through drawing on traditional theology).

M1: SINLESS BY INHERENT IMPECCABILITY

Jesus could not sin because he was God. M1 is a minority report in modern theology because the tradition has raised questions that require more explanation than M1 delivers. Nonetheless, the basic idea still shows up and, for many church members in conservative denominations, M1 remains satisfying for its simplicity and high Christology. American Presbyterian Loraine Boettner (1943) writes along the lines of M1 that Jesus could not sin because "in His essential nature He was God, and God cannot sin."[19] More recently, Scottish theologian Donald Macleod (1998), argues that "the impeccability of Christ . . . rests not upon his unique endowment with the Spirit nor upon the indefectibility of God's redemptive purpose, but upon the fact that he is who he is."[20] M1 remains an adequate formula for these contemporary theologians to explain Christ's impeccability, but not his temptation and sinlessness. A common feature in modern theology is to ground impeccability in the divine nature and then credit Jesus with sinlessness according to some other means (see below for the way Macleod does this by appeal to M4).

M2: SINLESS BY DEIFICATION

Jesus could not sin because of the divine nature. Modern theologians repeat the principle from M2 that Christ's deity supported and enabled his humanity to be sinless by natural necessity. Puritan luminary John Owen (1616-1683) grounds

---

[17]E.g., Ralph Del Colle, *Christ and the Spirit: Spirit-Christology in Trinitarian Perspective* (New York: Oxford University Press, 1994).

[18]Galot, *Who is Christ*, 385. "The impeccability of Jesus has been generally accepted in Catholic theology, but there has been no agreement as to the reason why." Not even M5 is a dominating presence in contemporary Roman Catholic theology.

[19]Loraine Boettner, *The Person of Christ* (Grand Rapids: Eerdmans, 1943), 125.

[20]Donald Macleod, *The Person of Christ*, Contours of Christian Theology (Downers Grove, IL: InterVarsity, 1998), 229-30.

Christ's sinlessness in the essential goodness of the Son of God. Discussing the life and ministry of Jesus, Owen writes that the divine nature is the immediate principle of all the outward acts of God,[21] and that Jesus exercised the holy properties of the divine nature "in moral duties of obedience", including the property of infinite goodness.[22] Lutheran theologian John Adam Scherzer (1628-1683) affirms M2 as one of several proofs for Christ's impeccability: "Christ never sinned, nor was He even able to sin. We prove the statement that he was not even able to sin, or that He was impeccable . . . he who is both holy by His origin, and is exempt from original sin, who can never have a depraved will, and constitutes one person with God Himself is clearly impeccable."[23] Two influential German theologians, Friedrich Schleiermacher (1768-1834)[24] and Isaak Dorner (1809-1884),[25] restate the M2 principle that the hypostatic union of humanity with the divine nature made Jesus impeccable. American Presbyterian theologian William G. T. Shedd (1820-1894) repeats M2 in his explanation of Jesus' impeccability as having been supported by his divine omniscience, omnipotence, and immutable holiness. Shedd adds that there was special divine aid provided for Jesus' human nature in all his temptations (as in M4).[26] Dutch Reformed theologian Herman Bavinck (1854-1921) counts Christ's true temptation as a man as not having been "made redundant or vain" by his divine inability to sin. Instead, Bavinck points to M2 as the divine ground of impeccability. Any claim that Jesus could sin entails the blasphemy that God could sin and the error that the union of divine and human natures in

---

[21] John Owen, *The Glory of Christ*, ed. William H. Goold, vol. 1 of *The Works of John Owen* (London: Johnstone & Hunter: 1850-53; reprint, Edinburgh: Banner of Truth Trust, 1965), 225.

[22] Owen, *The Glory of Christ*, in *Works*, 1:175. These statements are puzzling when considered along with Owen's strong emphasis on the empowering work of the Holy Spirit, as in the summary statement in *Holy Spirit*, in *Works*, 3:175, "Now, all the voluntary communications of the divine nature unto the human [nature of Jesus] were, as we have showed, by the Holy Spirit." We will return to Owen's pneumatological emphasis as part of the continuing prominence of M4, below.

[23] John Adam Scherzer, *Systema Theologiae*, 389. Cited in Heinrich Schmid, *The Doctrinal Theology of the Evangelical Lutheran Church,* trans. Charles A. Hay and Henry A. Jacobs, 3rd rev. ed. (Philadelphia: United Lutheran Publication House, 1899; reprint, Minneapolis: Augsburg, 1961), 302.

[24] Friedrich Schleiermacher, *The Christian Faith*, ed. H. R. Mackintosh and J. S. Stewart, 2nd ed. (Edinburgh: T & T Clark, 1928), 413, 415. An oddity is that Schleiermacher also denies that Christ was really tempted at all, calling the temptation accounts unhistorical (382).

[25] Isaak A. Dorner, *System of Christian Doctrine*, in *God and Incarnation in Mid-Nineteenth Century German Theology*, trans. and ed. Claude Welch, A Library of Protestant Thought (New York: Oxford University Press, 1965), 267.

[26] William G. T. Shedd, *Dogmatic Theology*, ed. Alan W. Gomes, 3rd ed. (Phillipsburg, NJ: Presbyterian and Reformed, 2003), 660-62.

Jesus could be broken.[27] Similarly, Reformed theologian Louis Berkhof (1939) argues that sin was impossible for Christ because of "the essential bond between the human and divine natures."[28] More recently, American theologian Wayne Grudem (1994) repeats M2, explaining simply that the union of Christ's two natures prevented the possibility of sin.[29] British philosopher Richard Swinburne (1994) also favors M2, because Christ's humanity was "connected enough with the divine nature so that Christ does no wrong."[30] In each of these examples, the M2 idea of the natural necessity of Christ's divine nature in union with his human nature secures his impeccability despite his incarnation and temptations of all sorts.

As with the modern restatement of M1, proponents of M2 frequently appeal to the model as a sort of backstop or shield of the divine nature that is coordinate with Christ's human ability to achieve righteousness by resisting all his temptations as a true man. A typical analogy of M2 is that just as a metal wire by itself may be bent easily (human nature), a wire that is welded to an anvil (divine nature) cannot be bent.[31] One exception is the M2 proposal of Gordon Lewis and Bruce Demarest (1990) that Jesus may have used his divine powers intermittently to surmount some temptations: "Even though ordinarily he chose not to rely on his own divine abilities, in the fiercest moments of temptations he could have and may have resorted to his divine powers."[32]

M3: SINLESS BY DIVINE HEGEMONY

Jesus could not sin because he is the impeccable Word who became flesh. The divine hegemony model continues in modern theology in the claim that Jesus remained sinless by subjecting his human will to the divine will. Jonathan Edwards (1703-1758) repeats M3 when he argues that Christ's human will was "conformed to the will of the Father" and was thus "infallibly, unalterably and unfrustrably determined to good, and that alone."[33] Philip Fisk summarizes Edwards's view: "It is precisely this habit of the heart of Jesus to incline to the Father more and more throughout his life that is the key to understanding the

---

[27]Bavinck, *Reformed Dogmatics: Sin and Salvation in Christ*, 314-15.
[28]Louis Berkhof, *Systematic Theology*, 4th ed. (Grand Rapids: Eerdmans, 1939), 318.
[29]Wayne A. Grudem, *Systematic Theology* (Grand Rapids: Zondervan, 1994), 539.
[30]Richard Swinburne, *The Christian God* (New York: Oxford University Press, 1994), 208.
[31]I owe this to Clyde Cook.
[32]Gordon R. Lewis and Bruce A. Demarest, *Integrative Theology* (Grand Rapids: Academie Books, 1990), 2:346. If this were the case, Jesus' relevance as an example for others would be undermined since Scripture has the fiercest trials in view as the basis for Christ's empathy with us (Heb 5:7-10 recalls Gethsemane, in context with bold statements of the temptations in Heb 2:17-18 and 4:14-16).
[33]Jonathan Edwards, *Freedom of the Will*, ed. Paul Ramsey, in vol. 1 of *The Works of Jonathan Edwards* (New Haven: Yale University Press, 1957), 289-90. Edwards gives special attention to the topic of Christ's impeccability, offering eleven proofs.

source of the impeccability of the human soul of Jesus Christ."[34] The conformity of his human will to the divine will through maturation is counted as a reasonable explanation for Jesus' true development and freedom in his full humanity, complete with the free choice of a finite, creaturely human will (though one that is supervened by his divine will).

William Shedd's support for M3 shows in his claim that "impeccability depends upon the will." Shedd applies this principle to Christ: "the divine will so strengthened the human will, that no conceivable stress of temptation could overcome Jesus Christ and bring about the apostasy of the second Adam."[35] Shedd explains what he calls the *coaction* of the two wills, such that Christ's divine will and human will may alternately lead when Jesus performs divine or human actions. The ultimate compatibility and harmony of the two wills is grounded in the dominance of Christ's divine will over Christ's sinless human will.[36] Shedd is concerned to avoid the monothelite heresy (the claim that Christ possessed only one will for both natures) and to preserve Christ's impeccability. Shedd's M3 account of Christ's dual volition (Dyothelitism, the orthodox view that Christ possessed two wills) is consistent with the theologian's repeated insistence that the divine nature was the root and base of Christ's theanthropic person.[37]

More recently, American theologian Donald Bloesch (1997) presents M3 as he writes that Christ's human nature "is subordinate to his divine nature" in a submissive relation of wills that gives him "true freedom" and grounds "the purity of his commitment" which totally excludes conquest by temptation.[38] Similarly, Jesuit theologian Gerald O'Collins (2002) criticizes an M2-type explanation of Christ's sinlessness and suggests instead an M3-type formula by the accent on the divine, personal hegemony: "Could a divine person, in his incarnate state, have possibly sinned? If God is necessarily and *de iure* impeccable, the same should hold true of the Logos incarnate as Jesus of Nazareth."[39]

These examples show that Christ's impeccability is a necessity of his divine hegemony over his human will and temptable nature. A difference in the

---

[34]Philip J. Fisk, "Jonathan Edwards's *Freedom of the Will* and his defence of the impeccability of Jesus Christ", *Scottish Journal of Theology* 60 (2007): 319.

[35]Shedd, *Dogmatic Theology*, 662-63.

[36]Shedd, *Dogmatic Theology*, 657.

[37]Shedd, *Dogmatic Theology*, 660-63. Notice that Shedd appeals to M3 for impeccability, and then M2 for sinlessness. See the detailed critique of Shedd's account of how an impeccable Christ could be tempted, Oliver D. Crisp, "William Shedd on Christ's Impeccability", *Philosophia Christi*, 9 (2007): 165-88.

[38]Donald G. Bloesch, *Jesus Christ: Savior and Lord*, vol. 4 of Christian Foundations, (Carlisle, UK: Paternoster, 1997), 73.

[39]Gerald O'Collins, "The Incarnation: The Critical Issues", in *The Incarnation: An Interdisciplinary Symposium on the Incarnation of the Son of God*, ed. Stephen T. Davis, Daniel Kendall, and Gerald O'Collins (Oxford: Oxford University Press, 2002), 15.

modern use of M3 from appeals to M1 and M2 is that M3 is seen to explain two questions—*why* Jesus was impeccable and *how* Jesus achieved sinlessness.

M4: SINLESS BY EMPOWERING GRACE

Jesus did not sin because of the Holy Spirit's help. John Owen (noted above, M2) presents a rich account of M4 that empowering grace given by the Holy Spirit enabled Jesus to fulfill his perfect human moral action.[40] Owen writes that the "fulness of grace was necessary unto the human nature of Christ . . . as unto his own obedience in the flesh", by which Owen means that grace was the lifelong empowerment provided by the Holy Spirit.[41] This M4 account upholds the distinction of the human nature from the divine, as Owen explains that the Holy Spirit provided Jesus with grace according to his human nature, just as he was a true man with authentic limitations and temptations:

> Now, in the improvement and exercise of these faculties and powers of his soul, he had and made a progress after the manner of other men; for he was made like unto us "in all things," yet without sin. In their increase, enlargement, and exercise, there was required a progression in grace also, and this he had continually by the Holy Ghost.[42]

Owen concludes from Luke 2:40 and 2:52 that Jesus' developing wisdom and character is pneumatological because such working was forecast in the messianic prophecies of Isaiah 11:2-3, 42:1-4, 50:4-9, and 61:1-3. Owen explains that Holy Spirit's close involvement in Christ's human experience covered everything the Messiah did, and suggests a joint agency of Jesus and the Spirit in the achieved human obedience: "The glory of the human nature, as united unto the person of the Son of God, and engaged in the discharge of his office of mediator, consists alone in these imminent, peculiar, ineffable communications of the Spirit of God unto him, and his powerful operations in him."[43] Owen has Christ's *obedience-through-temptations* especially in view when he specifies the Holy Spirit's empowering assistance for the entire course of Christ's perfect human life:

---

[40]Owen, *Holy Spirit*, in *Works*, 3:168-88.

[41]Owen, *Holy Spirit*, in *Works*, 3:170. Cf. Scherzer, *Systema Theologiae*, 389, "He to whom the Holy Ghost has been given without measure, is also holy and just without measure, and therefore cannot sin." Cited in Schmid, *Doctrinal Theology*, 302.

[42]Owen, *Holy Spirit*, in *Works*, 3:169.

[43]Owen, *Holy Spirit*, in *Works*, 3:186. This is surely in continuity with the joint agency of the Spirit and believers described as the life in the Spirit (Gal 5:16, 25), and being filled with the Spirit (Eph 5:18). Owen states the principle of continuity between the work of the Spirit in Christ to the work of the Spirit in Christians (3:188), and develops his account of the Spirit's work in relation to the believer thereafter.

By him [the Spirit] was he [Christ] directed, strengthened, and comforted, in his whole course, —in all his temptations, troubles, and sufferings, from first to last; for we know that there was a confluence of all these upon him in his whole way and work, a great part of that whereunto he humbled himself for our sakes consisting in these things. In and under them he stood in need of mighty supportment and strong consolation. This God promised unto him, and this he expected, Isa. xlii. 4, 6, xlix. 5-8, l. 7, 8. Now, all the voluntary communications of the divine nature unto the human were, as we have showed, by the Holy Spirit.[44]

Owen has carried forward Calvin's claims for the Spirit's work throughout all of Christ's life and ministry (not merely a miraculous conception and a few exorcisms by the Spirit). Accordingly, Owen counts Christ's acts of obedience to God as partially pneumatological works. The pinnacle of temptation and obedience was experienced in the cross, and even here Owen can count the obedience of Jesus according to Hebrews 9:14 as pneumatological, having been "*wrought* in him, this he was wrought unto, *by the Holy Spirit*; and therefore *by him* he offered himself unto God."[45] Considering the totality of Owen's views on Christ's impeccability and temptation, we have seen that Owen appeals to M2 for impeccability, and then explains Christ's sinlessness as a positive human achievement according to M4 (through dependence upon the empowerment of the Holy Spirit). In this way, Owen argues that Jesus has set down a pattern for his followers to live by the same means of the Spirit's resources that are provided by the risen Lord to his church.[46]

Somewhat differently from Owen, Jonathan Edwards (noted above in his appeal to M3 as explanation for Christ's active sinlessness) appeals to the Holy Spirit to explain Christ's impeccability. As the first of his eleven proofs for Christ's impeccability, Edwards argues that the work of the Spirit was to support Christ in impeccability as a man, which repeats M4 in part. Edwards's proof is that the Holy Spirit was promised to uphold the Messiah (Isa 42:1-8), and this was applied to Jesus in Matthew 12:18, implying "a promise of his being so upheld by God's spirit, that he should be preserved from sin . . . and

---

[44]Owen, *Holy Spirit*, in *Works*, 3:175.

[45]Owen, *Holy Spirit*, in *Works*, 3:179. Emphasis added. Bruce, *Humiliation of Christ*, 125, notes that the construction is typical of Reformed Christology.

[46]Cf. on Owen's pneumatological Christology, Sinclair B. Ferguson, "John Owen on the Spirit in the Life of Christ", *Fire and Ice Sermon Series* (accessed on 8 May 2008 at http://www.puritansermons.com/), 6-7, and Alan Spence, "Christ's Humanity and Ours: John Owen", in *Persons, Divine and Human: King's College Essays in Theological Anthropology*, eds Christoph Schwöbel and Colin E. Gunton (Edinburgh: T. & T. Clark, 1991), 88, 97. Also, Alan Spence has just contributed a monograph on Owen's pneumatological Christology, *Incarnation and Inspiration: John Owen and the Coherence of Christology* (London: T. & T. Clark, 2007). Unfortunately, I became aware of this book too late to be able to incorporate it here.

from being overcome by any of the temptations."⁴⁷ This is missing the typical M4 emphasis on empowering grace for achieving obedience, but Edwards's account shows that he thinks the Holy Spirit is part of the explanation for how the Godman remained sinless despite his temptations as a man (though not in the way his near contemporary Owen thinks).⁴⁸

More recently, Richard Sturch (1991) shows the continuing modern embrace of M4: "I can see no reason to doubt that grace, the work of the Holy Spirit on Jesus' life, was the direct source of His sinlessness."⁴⁹ Similarly, Macleod presents a pneumatological account very close to Owen's (he quotes Owen approvingly) and connects this empowerment with Christ's achievement of sinlessness.⁵⁰

These examples represent a fraction of the contemporary popularity for pneumatological Christology along the lines of the M4 (Christ's sinlessness was achieved by means of the Holy Spirit's influence in his life).⁵¹ What was once a minority model in the tradition has become a common view in recent decades of evangelical theology. Pentecostal and charismatic interpreters have been particularly enthusiastic to emphasize the analogy between Christian life in the Spirit and Christ's reliance on the Spirit in a way that repeats M4. Nonetheless, contemporary proponents give no indication that they are aware of the ancient formulations of M4 that were first articulated by Theodore of Mopsuestia and Augustine. Some re-inventing of the M4 wheel has occurred in

---

⁴⁷Edwards, *Freedom of the Will*, Works, 1:281-82.

⁴⁸W. Ross Hastings, "'Honoring the Spirit': Analysis and Evaluation of Jonathan Edwards' Pneumatological Doctrine of the Incarnation", *International Journal of Systematic Theology* 7 (2005): 293-97, compares the pneumatological Christology of Edwards and John Owen, and concludes that Edwards's view is the Spirit's role as bonding the two natures and protecting the Son from corruption, not so much empowering him as a man in moral progress of obedience (as in Owen). Hastings argues that the difference is in a Cappadocian model of the trinity (Owen) versus an Augustinian model (Edwards).

⁴⁹Sturch, *The Word and The Christ*, 261.

⁵⁰Macleod, *Person of Christ*, 195-96, 220.

⁵¹See also Robert Lewis Dabney, *Syllabus and Notes of the Course of Systematic and Polemic Theology*, 2ⁿᵈ ed. (St. Louis: Presbyterian Publishing Company of St. Louis, 1878), 471. Augustus H. Strong, *Systematic Theology*, 3 vols. in 1 (Philadelphia: Judson, 1907), 677, 703. Louis Berkhof, *Systematic Theology*, 4ᵗʰ ed. (Grand Rapids: Eerdmans, 1939), 335. Lewis Sperry Chafer, *Systematic Theology*, vol. 5 of 8 (Dallas: Dallas Seminary Press, 1948), 80. Thomas C. Oden, *The Word of Life, Systematic Theology*, vol. 2 (San Francisco: Harper & Row, 1989), 246. Gerald F. Hawthorne, *The Presence and the Power: The Significance of the Holy Spirit in the Life of Jesus* (Dallas: Word, 1991), ch. 4. Hawthorne's book is the most extensive study I know of since John Owen (strangely, Hawthorne neglects Owen). Grudem, *Systematic Theology*, 539. Macleod, *Person of Christ*, 195-96, 220. M.E. Osterhaven, "Sinlessness of Christ", in *Evangelical Dictionary of Theology*, 2ⁿᵈ ed., ed. Walter A. Elwell (Grand Rapids: Baker Academic, 2001), 1109.

modern theology since many have overlooked Calvin and Owen as well (particularly Hawthorne seems to have overlooked them). The (apparently) independent discovery of M4 further commends the model that has seemed theologically adequate for so many interpreters that have been based in different theological traditions.

M6: TEMPTABLE BY THE HUMAN ECLIPSE OF DIVINE POWER

Remaining what he was as God, Jesus was truly tempted as a man. The emphasis on the Holy Spirit in the Reformation model is partly represented by those noted above as repeating M4. However, the specific insistence of Luther and Calvin on the concealment of deity with humanity to allow Jesus' temptations is much less attested in modern theology than M4. After the Reformation, M6 seems to have continued only in Reformed theology. Lutheran development explored *kenoticism*, the idea that the Logos gave up certain divine attributes to become incarnate, and, alternately, the deification of Christ's humanity from his conception.[52]

On the Reformed side, Scottish theologian A. B. Bruce (1831-1899) summarizes the teaching (citing Ursinus as a representative) that Christ "concealed His divinity in the state of exinanition",[53] and "the divine nature also wills this obedience [of Jesus as a man], and conceals its power and glory, not repelling from the human nature death and ignominy, yet sustains that nature in torment."[54] Bruce concludes approvingly that Reformed Christology recognizes the reality of Christ's temptations as having been possible and viscerally real because of divine restraint. Moreover, Bruce reports that the consistent Reformed claim is that Jesus achieved sinlessness through temptation not by means of the impervious divine nature (as in M1-M3) but by the Holy Spirit who aided him. Bruce's quotation of his fellow Scotsman Prof. M'Lagan (no detail is given about this theologian) expresses M6 vividly, marking off that the work of the divine nature through the Holy Spirit is

> not to raise Christ's suffering nature to such a height of glorious power as would render all trial slight and contemptible; but to confer upon it such strength as would be infallibly sufficient, but not more than sufficient, just to bear Him through the fearful strife that awaited Him, without His being broken or destroyed,—so that He might thoroughly experience, in all the faculties of His soul and body, the innumerable sensations of overpowering difficulty, and exhausting toil, and fainting weakness, and tormenting anguish, though by the Holy Ghost preserved from sin,—and might touch the very brink of danger,

---

[52] Macleod, *Person of Christ*, 198.
[53] Bruce, *Humiliation of Christ*, 120.
[54] Bruce, *Humiliation of Christ*, 123, quoting *Admonitio Neostadtiensis* (1581) sec. 5.

though not be swept away by it; and feel all the horror of the precipice, but without falling over.[55]

The two concepts of M6 are thus reiterated: divine restraint to allow full vulnerability to temptation, and the corresponding aid to meet the challenge as a true man but support of the Holy Spirit.

Another witness who gives evidence confirming Bruce's conclusion is Francis Turretin (1623-1687). The Swiss theologian repeats the veiling idea, noting there was in Christ limitation of the divine nature as concealed by the veil of the flesh. The Holy Spirit was involved to provide wisdom for the human nature of Jesus progressively.[56] However, Turretin does not explain the temptation of Christ this way.

Bavinck comes closer to M6 in his summary of the Reformed teaching that the Lord

> laid aside the divine majesty and glory, the form of God, in which he existed before the incarnation, or rather concealed it behind the form of a servant in which he went about on earth; and that . . . during his humiliation he never for a moment used his divine power and divine attributes to please himself and to defeat his enemies.[57]

The reality and relevance of Christ's humanity, temptation, and sinlessness are thus preserved because Jesus existed in the state of humiliation, with an eclipse or concealment of his deity. Bavinck also counts the role of the Holy Spirit as decisive in Christ's ongoing freedom from sin throughout his earthly life (not simply that his sinlessness was caused by purification at his conception), which repeats the pneumatological empowerment of M6.[58]

Although he does not go all the way to M6, Scottish theologian Donald Baillie (1948) repeats the M6 emphasis on Christ's true temptation that was unmitigated by his impeccability.[59]

G. C. Berkouwer (1955) defends the principle of M6 in light of the modern concern for Christ's true humanity: "When Reformed theology spoke of concealment, it was always thought of in reference to the darkness of the way of suffering. Hence Reformed exegesis or dogmatics did not, by speaking of concealment, cast a shadow upon the confession of Christ's true humiliation."[60] Similarly, Bloesch affirms the Reformed veiling idea of M6 against kenotic

---

[55]Bruce, *Humiliation of Christ*, 270-72. Bruce cites Dods, *On the Incarnation of the Eternal Word*, 299-300 as the source for the quote from a sermon of Prof. M'Lagan.
[56]Francis Turretin, *Institutes of Elenctic Theology*, trans. George Musgrave Giger, ed. James T. Dennison, Jr. (Phillipsburg, NJ: P & R, 1994), 2:351.
[57]Bavinck, *Reformed Dogmatics: Sin and Salvation in Christ*, 432.
[58]Bavinck, *Reformed Dogmatics: Sin and Salvation in Christ*, 292-95.
[59]Baillie, *God Was in Christ*, 14-15.
[60]Berkouwer, *Person of Christ*, 361.

theories: "The divine attributes are not renounced by Christ but are concealed in the humiliated Christ." Bloesch also connects Jesus' sinlessness with the presence of the Holy Spirit from his conception.[61]

Macleod (noted above in M1 and M4) quotes Luther and Calvin as twin witnesses to the M6 principle of veiling the divine glory to preserve the true human experience.[62] In this way of eclipsing his deity, Christ's human experience could be truly excruciating, since the Reformers took the cross to be the fiercest point of his temptation. Macleod then repeats the second element of M6 (an echo of M4), that it was by Christ's reliance on the Holy Spirit that he was able to surmount temptation:

> The power which carried the world, stilled the tempest and raised the dead was never used to make his own conditions of service easier. Neither was the prestige he enjoyed in heaven exploited to relax the rules of engagement. Deploying no resources beyond those of his Spirit-filled humanness, he faced the foe as flesh and triumphed as man.[63]

As with the other models, these examples show that several contributors to modern theology have retained M6 as theologically adequate.

To sum up, this survey demonstrates that in the face of critical revisions to traditional Chalcedonian Christology, many theologians in the modern period have repeated the earlier models (often combining them or assigning them to specific aspects of explanation). The historical evidence yields a mixed conclusion on the continuing adequacy of the models since no consensus has formed and three more models continue to be developed to the present day. One last stop on the way to these three models is to consider briefly a modern question that has captivated Christologists and influenced the theology of Christ's temptation, impeccability, and sinlessness.

Innovation: Did Jesus Possess a Fallen Human Nature?

Alongside the conservative response to modern attacks on traditional Christology has come a second response of a rapprochement with the critical revisions through Christological innovation. The innovation is to claim that Christ's humanity was *fallen* and sinfully corrupted just like the rest of humanity. Proponents retain many aspects of traditional orthodoxy (specifically, that the Chalcedonian definition is regulative for Christology) alongside the argument for Jesus' fallen human nature. This innovation meets the modern concern to close the distance between Jesus and the rest of (fallen) humanity. Theologians have thus extended the M6 emphasis on the visceral severity of Christ's temptations and suffering to frame Jesus in terms of a fallen

---

[61]Bloesch, *Jesus Christ*, 61, 73.
[62]Macleod, *Person of Christ*, 217-18.
[63]Macleod, *Person of Christ*, 220.

human nature that we possess. However, many contributors have been careful to affirm that because Jesus was God and not merely a fallen man, he won redemption for sinful humanity by means of that fallen flesh and never actually sinned. Influential proponents throughout the period have been Edward Irving (1792-1834), Karl Barth (1956), Thomas Torrance (1965), and Wolfhart Pannenberg (1977).[64]

Like those noted above as conserving or sounding echoes of traditional models, most innovators maintain a Chalcedonian, two-natured Christology and the sinlessness of Jesus. However, not all affirm Christ's impeccability.[65] The traditional consensus has been that the Logos assumed a human nature with the consequences of sin (physical defects assumed for redemption, such as the vulnerability to pain and death). This assumed nature was not sinful in any sense of being guilty or morally and physically corrupt (unlike the post-fall humanity that is both guilty and corrupt in Adam).[66] Possibly the new way of describing Christ's humanity is unduly exaggerated by the use of the term *fallen* that is normally associated with original sin.[67] The motive for using the

---

[64]These four are only representative. Many contemporary theologians could be cited since the topic continues to be discussed in numerous journal articles. Peculiar is the claim of Harry Johnson, who connects peccability with a fallen human nature in Christ in his published thesis, *The Humanity of the Saviour: A Biblical and Historical Study of the Human Nature of Christ in relation to Original Sin, with special reference to its Soteriological Significance* (London: Epworth, 1962), 51, 119. The result is that Johnson's definition of temptation sharply undermines the force of the original temptation of Adam and Eve.

[65]Edward Irving is not clear on Christ's impeccability, only his sinlessness. Barth affirms Christ's impeccability in terms of M1, M2, and M3; Pannenberg denies it. Karl Barth, *Church Dogmatics* 1.2, trans. G. T. Thomson and Harold Knight, ed. G. W. Bromiley and T. F. Torrance, *The Doctrine of the Word of God* (Edinburgh: T & T Clark, 1956), 147-59; *Church Dogmatics* 4.2, trans. G. W. Bromiley, *The Doctrine of Reconciliation* (1958), 91-93. Barth responded to a specific question on this point, as recorded in *Karl Barth's Table Talk*, ed. John D. Godsey, Scottish Journal of Theology Occasional Papers 10 (Edinburgh: Oliver and Boyd, 1963), 68-69. Pannenberg, in *Jesus*, claims that Jesus' human freedom was constituted by an indefectible union to the Father's will, which follows M3 (349), however, Pannenberg explicitly denies Jesus' impeccability as part of denying the virginal conception (361-64).

[66]Thomas G. Weinandy, *In the Likeness of Sinful Flesh: An Essay on the Humanity of Christ* (Edinburgh: T & T Clark, 1993), disputes this interpretation of a traditional consensus and gives historical argument from patristic and medieval sources to support his claim that Jesus took a fallen human nature. Nonetheless, Weinandy specifically denies that Jesus had original sin or concupiscence (98-99). This seems to blunt the claim of a fallen human nature and dissolve the innovation semantically to another way of saying Jesus was vulnerable to pains and struggle as a sinless man.

[67]Crisp, "Did Christ have a *Fallen* Human Nature?", 270, observes that several Eastern Orthodox theologians have taken this position on Christ's humanity. Crisp argues that the problem of fallenness is that it entails sinfulness. However it may be defined, the

term seems to be to affirm Jesus' experience of a weakened, suffering humanity in solidarity with those he saves, and not merely having come in a deiform or partially glorified humanity as many patristic and medieval theologians argued (cf. M2, M5).[68] Innovators use the term *fallen* to emphasize the inwardness of Jesus' temptations, in solidarity with the rest of fallen humanity.[69] They argue that Christ enters the human stage in a vitiated condition and conquers sin in his own person on the way to winning redemption for all. Their claim is that Jesus battled in his sinful flesh *just like ours* to accomplish his sinlessness and holiness as a heroic, exemplary, and intensely *human* moral achievement.[70] However, the innovators are ambiguous in their definition of Christ's *fallen* human nature.[71] Some affirm that the Holy Spirit purified Christ's fallen humanity from original sin at conception (a traditional interpretation based on Luke 1:35).[72] Most innovators suggest that the meaning of Christ's fallen human nature is his redemptive significance for the rest of humanity, recalling the patristic Christological axiom, *the unassumed is the unhealed*, as the requirement that Jesus bore a fallen human nature, just like us, to save us through his restoration of it. His was a spoiled humanity, one that has been wrecked by sin like the rest of humanity.[73] His human nature was fallen

---

original corruption of fallenness cannot be separated from original guilt. Compare the same conclusion by Bruce, *Humiliation of Christ*, 255, that *fallen* human nature must mean a body and soul tainted with original sin. Also, I question how the term *fallen* can be used without the idea of humanity as separated and alienated from God (Gen 3; Eph 2:1-5) in a spiritual death needing reconciliation to live properly in relationship to God. If *fallen* is to mean humanity as separated from God, then it seems wrong to see this as true for Christ to be cut off from grace and God's ordering influence on Christ's human nature.

[68]Mackintosh, *Person of Jesus*, 276-77.

[69]Barth, *Church Dogmatics* 1.2, 158.

[70]Edward Irving, *The Orthodox and Catholic Doctrine of Our Lord's Human Nature, Tried by the Westminster Confession of Faith* (London: Baldwin and Craddock, 1830), 66-67, cited by Graham W. P. McFarlane, *Christ and the Spirit: The Doctrine of the Incarnation According to Edward Irving* (Carlisle, UK: Paternoster, 1996), 147.

[71]A weakness noted by Crisp, "*Fallen* Human Nature", 271. According to McFarlane, *Christ and the Spirit*, 142-43, Irving defines fallen humanity as solidarity in Adam and "participating collectively in Adam's fall" and "solidarity in humanity under the power of sin."

[72]E.g., Edward Irving, *The Opinions Circulating Concerning Our Lord's Human Nature* (Edinburgh: John Lindsay, 1830), 6-7; cited by McFarlane, *Christ and the Spirit*, 140. Weinandy, *Likeness of Sinful Flesh*, 98-99. Barth, *Church Dogmatics* 1.2, 156. An exception is Pannenberg, *Jesus*, 362, who claims that the idea of a purified humanity in Christ contradicts the New Testament. I disagree with Pannenberg on this point.

[73]Weinandy, *Likeness of Sinful Flesh*, 18.

because this is the only sort of human nature that exists.[74] The new claim is that, being just like us, Jesus was tempted both outwardly and inwardly, and that he thus conquered sin internally in his own fallen nature. By incarnation in fallen human nature, Jesus has racial solidarity with the rest of humanity fallen in Adam, but without having become a sinner himself. In this way, the innovators affirm the traditional claims and adjust them for a rapprochement with the modern emphasis on Christ's sameness with common humanity.[75]

The outcome of this innovation for our question is that some proponents of a fallen human nature claim that Jesus was able to sin. His temptations were fully on level with ours in that he was truly in peril and able to choose against God (just as Adam was, just as we are). Moreover, other modern theologians have agreed that the traditional claim of Jesus' impeccability should be set aside because this seems to contradict the claim that he genuinely suffered temptation as a man.[76]

The growing modern skepticism about Christ's deity and impeccability, and the modern emphasis on Jesus' psychology and relevance as a man have converged in the three modern models. The result is a common theme that Christ's temptations exhibit the humanization of his deity. The explanation in the first of the three models, M7, is that Christ's divine impeccability was humanized so that he is able to sin just as we are. M8 and M9 are two explanations of how Christ's *knowledge* of his impeccability was humanized so that he could be tempted genuinely (while remaining impeccable). Several proponents of each of the three modern models count the Holy Spirit as Christ's effective means to resist his temptations (cf. M4, M6).

M7: Temptable by the Humanization of Divine Impeccability

Description of M7

Jesus could be truly tempted as a man because he had surrendered his divine impeccability. The modern concern in M7 is to emphasize more than earlier

---

[74]Irving, *The Collected Writings of Edward Irving in Five Volumes*, ed. Rev. G. Carlyle (London: Alexander Strahan, 1864), 5:115, cited by McFarlane, *Christ and the Spirit*, 141.

[75]A full engagement with the question of a fallen human nature in Christ is beyond our focus here, but I have provided my view in the Introduction, where I listed five assertions about Christ's authentic human nature. I think these are defensible as claims but will not take the time here to duplicate the work of Crisp ("A *Fallen* Human Nature?") and Macleod (*Person of Christ*, 224-30) who have refuted the challenges to the traditional view.

[76]E.g., T. A. Hart, "Sinlessness and Moral Responsibility: A Problem in Christology", *Scottish Journal of Theology* 48 (1995): 40. "The traditional christological insistence upon the *non posse peccare* [not able to sin] appears in effect to rob Jesus of that moral freedom which allows his temptation to be viewed as genuine."

models the internal, intensely visceral, and severe moral struggle that Jesus experienced in his temptations.[77] For many modern theologians, this struggle requires that he possessed the so-called freedom to sin, just as the rest of us are able to sin (he could commit sin). Christ's distinction is that he remained sinless by his consistent exercise of the ability not to sin. In the traditional terminology, Jesus was both *posse peccare* (able to sin) and *posse non peccare* (able *not* to sin), just as Adam before the fall (and those who are regenerated in Christ because they are no longer enslaved to sin, Rom 6:1-23). For this unique accomplishment of sinlessness, Jesus is a morally praiseworthy savior and a proper, authentic example for humanity. His relevance as a pattern for us depends upon the close likeness of his human experience to that of other human beings. He entered into true solidarity with humanity in the struggle against sin.

If Jesus had relied on divine impeccability overtly or even if he had possessed (but did not use) impeccability during his time on earth, then his advantaged position nullifies the reports of his struggle against temptation to sin. The explanation given is that impeccability entails a foregone conclusion of sinlessness, which, on such advantaged terms, is not an achievement worthy of praise but a sham.[78] No struggle against sin means no victory has been won. By contrast with traditional models, M7 explains how Christ's fight was real, keeping with the biblical evidence of his real struggles in temptation.

The question asked and answered in M7 is this: how was the eternal Son of God able to suffer temptations truly and relevantly as an exemplary man? The answer given is that the Son humanized his divine impeccability to be tempted truly as a man. Humanization of the divine attributes is Christ's noble humility to condescend to a condition of existence that is beneath his rights as the Son of God. He descended to the role of a servant within the human limitations that were necessary for redemption. M7 praises Christ for limiting himself to reveal God and redeem lost humanity at great personal risk and cost.

All proponents of the three modern models (M7-M9) agree that without some sort of humanization to make him vulnerable to sin's appeals, Christ's temptations cannot be relevant for the rest of humanity. Proponents of M7 assume that being impeccable necessarily reduces the force of his temptations (or excludes them entirely) because Jesus never would have had to struggle against them. If he could not fail when tested by the appeals of sin, then his

---

[77]Marguerite Shuster, "The Temptation, Sinlessness, and Sympathy of Jesus: Another Look at the Dilemma of Hebrews 4:15", in *Perspectives on Christology: Essays in Honor of Paul K. Jewett*, ed. Marguerite Shuster and Richard A. Muller (Grand Rapids: Zondervan, 1991), 199, observes the inadequacy of defining Jesus' temptation as merely an external testing that touches no internal struggle.

[78]David Werther, "The Temptation of God Incarnate", *Religious Studies* 29 (1993): 49-50, argues that Jesus cannot be praiseworthy if he possesses necessary goodness (impeccability) because his divine nature always prevented him from forming wrong intentions. Praise is not due to someone who could not have done otherwise than good.

having passed the tests is irrelevant for the rest of humanity. Instead of temptation-nullifying impeccability, M7 explains his temptations as real and relevant contests because he could have failed the test (Jesus could have sinned). M7 thus resolves the perceived contradiction between divine impeccability and human temptability by reasoning that the divine attribute had been subordinated to the human attribute of peccability (because true human experiences of freedom and temptation are incompatible with impeccability).

Proponents argue that only in this way of becoming peccable (able to sin) could Christ's humanity be true and his temptations real. By humanizing his deity so he may become peccable as a man, Jesus could be tempted and achieve his sinlessness through long and difficult moral struggle. Having fought a real struggle, he became the example for other human beings who contend with temptation. Jesus remains fully God, but he humanized his divine impeccability to make possible his true humanity.

Proponents define Christ's humanity and temptation based on what can be observed and experienced by the rest of humanity. All known human beings from Adam to the present day are able to sin; so essential humanity and temptation must include the ability to sin. As a true human who experienced true temptation, Jesus must share the ability to sin (or, the deficiency of power with possible failure to do right). This shift from the traditional orthodoxy parallels a trend among some philosophers of religion who argue that even God is capable of sin.[79] Hints of the peccability trend showed during the medieval

---

[79]The typical move of divine peccabilists is that the statement—"God cannot sin"—is a logical necessity about the assertion (*de dicto*) and not a metaphysical necessity of the properties of God (*de re*), by which they affirm that if the person who is *God* (office) should sin, he would cease to hold the office of *God*. See Nelson Pike, "Omnipotence and God's Ability to Sin", in *Divine Commands and Morality*, ed. Paul Helm (Oxford: Oxford University Press, 1981), 68; Bruce Reichenbach, *Evil and a Good God* (New York: Fordham University Press, 1982); Stephen Davis, *Logic and the Nature of God* (Grand Rapids: Eerdmans, 1983); Vincent Brümmer, "Divine Impeccability", *Religious Studies* 20 (1984): 203-14; W. R. Carter, "Impeccability Revisited", *Analysis* 44 (1985): 52-55; Keith E. Yandell, "Divine Necessity and Divine Goodness", in *Divine and Human Action: Essays in the Metaphysics of Theism*, ed. Thomas V. Morris (Ithaca, NY: Cornell University Press, 1988), 313-44; Robert F. Brown, "God's Ability to Will Moral Evil", *Faith and Philosophy* 8 (1991): 3-20. At least one theologian has agreed with this view, Mark W. Elliott, "The Way from Chalcedon", in *Jesus the Only Hope: Yesterday, Today, Forever*, ed. Mark Elliott and John L. McPake (Fearn, Ross-shire: Christian Focus, 2001), 124: "logically the choice is there for God". This denial of God's necessary goodness calls into question God's immutability, among other essential attributes and key biblical evidence noted by Thomas Morris, "The Necessity of God's Goodness", in his *Anselmian Explorations: Essays in Philosophical Theology* (Notre Dame, IN: University of Notre Dame Press, 1987). Most scholars agree that part of the definition of *God* is his moral purity; some (such as Morris, with whom I agree) go further and affirm that God is morally pure essentially in the *de re* sense, and not just in the *de dicto*, official sense that to remain *God*, Yahweh must never sin.

period when Anselm and Abelard considered that, in abstraction from the incarnational union, Christ's human nature was peccable. Nonetheless, and despite the earlier views that harmonized human moral struggle with impeccability (cf. M4-M6), the way that M7 rejects M1 to affirm Christ's actual peccability has been extremely rare in the tradition. I will present representatives of M7 according to the two basic premises that lead to the conclusion that Jesus, since was human and truly tempted, must have been peccable.[80]

TRUE HUMANITY REQUIRES PECCABILITY

Breaking away from tradition, proponents of M7 affirm that because true humanity is capable of sin, and Jesus was truly human, then Jesus was capable of sin. Philip Schaff (1819-1893) is representative of this M7 premise:

> His sinlessness was at first only the *relative* sinlessness of Adam before the Fall; which implies the necessity of trial and temptation, and the peccability, or the possibility of sinning. Had he been endowed from the start with *absolute* impeccability, or with the impossibility of sinning, he could not be a true man, nor our model for imitation: his holiness, instead of being his own self-acquired act and inherent merit, would be an accidental or outward gift, and his temptation an unreal show. As a true man, Christ must have been a free and responsible agent: freedom implies the power of choice between good and evil, and the power of disobedience as well as obedience to the law of God.[81]

To maintain the orthodoxy of the Chalcedonian definition and the validity of the biblical evidence for Christ's humanity, many accept the presupposition that his freedom to sin is a necessary entailment of his true humanity. Adam, the original human being, possessed the capacity to commit sin. Jesus, being a genuine human being and the second Adam, was capable of sin but he never sinned because he exercised his ability *not* to sin (as Adam could have before the fall). Along with Schaff, other modern theologians who exemplify this axiom of M7 are Lutheran theologian Carl Ullmann (1796-1865), Presbyterian Charles Hodge (1797-1878), and, more recently, Anglican John Macquarrie (1990).[82] These proponents clearly affirm Christ's sinlessness, but they deny

---

[80] Oliver D. Crisp, "Was Christ Sinless or Impeccable?" *Irish Theological Quarterly* 72 (2007): 168, labels what I have termed M7 as *the sinlessness view*, the claim that Jesus was merely sinless but not impeccable. Crisp's defense of the traditional impeccability view and critique of the sinlessness view are helpful contributions.

[81] Philip Schaff, *The Person of Christ: His Perfect Humanity a Proof of His Divinity* (New York: George H. Doran, 1913), 35-36.

[82] Macquarrie, *Jesus Christ in Modern Thought*, 397. A premodern proponent during the post-Reformation period is Remonstrant theologian Simon Episcopius (1583-1643), whose position is noted disapprovingly by Edwards, *Freedom of the Will*, in *Works*, 1:289.

the traditional claim of his impeccability because of the perceived contradiction to his true humanity. Their definition of humanity stipulates what must be true for Jesus, as Hodge notes simply: "If He was a true man He must have been capable of sinning."[83] Ullmann, a zealous defender of Christ's sinlessness, argues: "On the assumption that Jesus was a true, a real man, it cannot of course be denied that it was possible for Him to sin. This possibility is directly involved in the nature of man as a being who is made subject to moral laws, and who is therefore free."[84] The presupposition that Christ's divine impeccability and human nature are mutually exclusive is assumed to be one of the modern Christological dilemmas. The solution given in M7 is to humanize Christ's divine impeccability with the human freedom to sin.[85] This solution seems to be confirmed by the reality of his temptation, which is the second premise of M7.

TRUE TEMPTATION REQUIRES PECCABILITY

Christ's real temptations entail his peccability, just because *temptation* means that the one who is tempted is able to fail. Without the ability to give in to temptation, in no sense can we believe that temptation could have occurred. Trevor Hart's comment is representative:

> If we draw that line in such a way that it removes from Jesus all possibility of sinning, are we not thereby precisely robbing him of the experience of being 'tempted in all things as we are'? Is the genuine potential for sin not analytic in some way in the very notion of temptation? Certainly it would seem to be basic to human temptation as we know and experience it.[86]

This is the presupposition that Christ's temptations as reported in the New Testament are valid if and only if he could have sinned. Actual temptation for all other human beings has the perilous possibility of sin. Since this is the case for all humanity, so it must have been the case for Jesus (who was *tempted as we are tempted*). For some interpreters, the range of Christ's temptation in

---

[83] Charles Hodge, *Systematic Theology* (New York: Scribner, Armstrong, and Co., 1873; reprint, New York: Charles Scribner's Sons, 1898), 2:457.
[84] Ullmann, *Sinlessness of Jesus*, 196.
[85] A further step by a few theologians is to argue that being a true human being entails that Jesus was *not* sinless. Examples are John A. T. Robinson, *The Human Face of God* (Philadelphia: Westminster, 1973), 89-93 (cited by Paul Gondreau, "The Humanity of Christ, the Incarnate Word", in *The Theology of Thomas Aquinas*, ed. Rik Van Nieuwenhove and Joseph Wawrykow [Notre Dame: University of Notre Dame Press, 2005], 261), John Knox, *Humanity and Divinity of Christ*, 51, Nels Ferré *Christ and the Christian* (New York: Harper & Row, 1958), 110-14 (cited in Millard Erickson, *Christian Theology*, 2nd ed. [Grand Rapids: Baker, 1998], 736 n. 28).
[86] Hart, "Sinlessness of Jesus", 38.

likeness to others includes the appeals to his sexual desires.[87] His difference is that he did not sin because he never misused that freedom to sin. Instead, Jesus always chose in accordance with his freedom not to sin, and this at great personal cost in his lifelong suffering. The sympathy that Jesus feels for others because of his temptations is only real and credible because he has been tempted with the same vulnerability to actual sin as they have. Examples of modern theologians who affirm Christ's peccability because of his actual temptation and real sympathy for others are Ullmann, Hodge, Millard Erickson (1991), Trevor Hart (1995), Robert Stein (1996), and Elias Dantas (2005).[88] This is the second modern dilemma that real temptation and the traditional claim of Christ's impeccability are incompatible. The solution, as before with the definition of Christ's true humanity, is to reason that Christ humanized his deity with the capability for sin that his true temptation entails.

Modern theologians construct their model of Christ's impeccability and temptation as a way to explain and understand the data of Scripture, theology, and experience. M7 takes up the premises supplied by the modern concerns for the relevance of Christ's true human experience in close likeness to the rest of humanity. The modern taste for a humanized deity in Jesus solves the modern problem of his impeccability and temptation in a way never affirmed by earlier orthodoxy. Moreover, a typical move is to explain that Jesus heroically progressed to impeccability through his sustained vigilance against temptation. Schaff's statement is representative of this view:

> Christ's relative sinlessness became absolute sinlessness by his own moral act, or the right use of his freedom in perfect active and passive obedience to God. In other words, Christ's original *possibility of not sinning*, which includes the opposite possibility of sinning, but excludes the actuality of sin, was unfolded into

---

[87]E.g., John Macquarrie, "Was Jesus Sinless?" *Living Pulpit* 8 (1999): 14-15, affirms Jesus' sexual temptability. Nikos Kazantzakis's novel, *The Last Temptation of Christ*, and Dan Brown's mystery novel, *The Da Vinci Code*, both start from this presupposition that Jesus had normal sexual desires. This assumption is in contrast to the traditional answer of Augustine, who explicitly denies that Jesus experienced the sexual sort of temptations. Augustine's rationale is that sexual desire is transmitted by conception through sexual procreation, which, of course, Jesus lacked (see the Introduction). For discussion of the likelihood of Jesus' sexuality and some sort of temptation (though not lust), see the section in ch. 1, *The Relational Setting of Christ's Temptations*.

[88]These are outstanding examples among many for the period to the present day because they otherwise defend Chalcedonian Christology. Ullmann, *Sinlessness of Jesus*, 196. Hodge, *Systematic Theology*, 457. Millard J. Erickson, *The Word Became Flesh: A Contemporary Incarnational Christology* (Grand Rapids: Baker, 1991), 562-64. Hart, "Sinlessness of Jesus", 38. Robert H. Stein, *Jesus the Messiah* (Downers Grove: InterVarsity, 1996), 110-11. Elias Dantas, "The Incarnation of Christ and its Implications to the Ministry and Mission of the Church", in *Christ the One and Only*, ed. Sung Wook Chung (Grand Rapids: Baker Academic, and Milton Keynes: Paternoster, 2005), 3.

the *impossibility of sinning*, which *cannot* sin because it *will not*. This is the highest stage of freedom where it becomes identical with moral necessity, or absolute and unchangeable self-determination for goodness and holiness. This is the freedom of God, and also of the saints in heaven; with this difference, that the saints obtain that position by deliverance and salvation from sin and death, while Christ acquired it by his own merit.[89]

Historically, we have seen that the Fifth Ecumenical Council (Constantinople II, 553) anathematized anyone who taught what Schaff has claimed, that Jesus progressed from peccability to impeccability (as in the teaching of Theodore of Mopsuestia). Apparently, the ancient ideas have regained favor in M7.

One recent variation on M7 is the proposal of Sam Storms that Jesus was truly able to sin, but the Holy Spirit always kept him from doing so.

Jesus was *peccable* when it came to the *metaphysical potential* for sin in his own human nature (in other words, there was nothing inherent within the person of Christ that made it impossible for him to sin, any more than it was so in the case of Adam), but *impeccable* insofar as it was impossible for the Spirit to fail to energize Jesus' will to depend upon the power that the Spirit supplied.[90]

Storms thereby reduces the risk of any actual sin in Christ by appeal to the Spirit's power, and satisfies the concern in M7 for true humanity and temptation in Christ on the level with us. Similarly, a survey of the blogosphere will show that M7 is a satisfying account of Jesus for at least half of those scholars and others who have posted hundreds of comments and articles e world wide web relating to the topic.[91]

Evaluation of M7

According to the patristic theologians who accepted the anathemas of the Fifth Ecumenical Council (Constantinople II, 553), M7 is a departure from Nicene and Chalcedonian orthodoxy. The bishops specifically anathematized anyone teaching in the way of Theodore of Mopsuestia that Jesus was able to sin before the resurrection, but thereafter was impeccable. Nonetheless, M7 seems compelling for many and the wisdom and decrees of councils may be questioned in view of Scripture. Does M7 follow Scripture better than traditional orthodoxy has recognized?

---

[89]Schaff, *Person of Christ*, 35-36.
[90]Sam Storms, "Could Jesus have Sinned? (2 Cor. 5.21)", posted January 23, 2008 at http://www.enjoyinggodministries.com/article/could-jesus-have-sinned-2-cor-521 (accessed on April 18, 2008).
[91]I have noticed that M7 is also a common view among university students as they come to the topic in my theology classes. They are skeptical that the traditional claim could be true.

The biblical evidence for Christ's genuine humanity and true temptation is expressed boldly in M7. These truths are counted so seriously that proponents have sought to establish them by affirming Christ's peccability. If M7 is right that peccability is a necessary condition for humanity and temptation, then any model that excludes peccability is theologically inadequate.

How does Jesus look according to M7 in Gethsemane? Jesus suffered in ways that are closely comparable to our suffering. Thoughts in his mind may have been: "I have never sinned. I know that I must not. I'm overwhelmed and drowning in my fear! I am pressed out with fear! Father, is there not another way?" He feels the intensity of the struggle and the real danger just as we do. He feels no solace of a divine shield against sin. God truly has taken a risk to set everything in his redemptive plans on the successful faithfulness of the incarnate Son. All creation was plunged into peril because of the first man's failure in the original garden, and now Jesus, as the second man, is gripped by his temptation in the garden of pressed olives. All the biblical descriptions of his suffering with *loud sobs and cries*, the intense grief and feeling of being torn apart by visceral turmoil come into clear view because everything appears to Jesus as it truly is: devastating peril for a man in the thrall of temptation. Nearby, his friends are crushed by the dread and they shrink back to sleep. "Will I fail too?" he murmurs in his soul. He feels his weakness as a man. He suffers the attraction to turn aside from the wrath of God, and, against this pull, he holds to his opposite desire to please God and receive the cup of wrath. "I will not turn away! I will trust! I will obey though he slays me!" At last, he casts his free decision for right. Here, in his greatest fight against sin, death, and the devil, Jesus has entered into the fight of each child of humanity and has struck the beginning of his victory for them as one of them. From Gethsemane to Golgotha, he is resolute and fortified to surrender himself for sin's punishment. His resolve to follow God's will in obedience is the enduring pattern for those who suffer exactly the condition that he entered. His conflict *including the possibility of failure* underlines the greatness and authenticity of his garden victory.

M7 is a compelling view because of the premises that seem so obvious to modern minds, but are they as true as they seem to be? If these premises can be questioned, and if the related objections to the model are valid, then the model can be shown to be theologically inadequate (if not mistaken).

CONTRA: TRUE HUMANITY REQUIRES PECCABILITY

My objection to the premise is twofold. First, the premise wrongly depends upon the assumption that peccability is essential to true humanity. Consubstantiality with humanity (or, possessing a true human nature) does not require that Christ possess peccability any more than that he possess sinfulness, a human father, or an absolute beginning to his existence in time.[92] These attributes are all common for humanity as we know it, but they are not necessary for being a true human. Otherwise, Adam and Eve did not become human until they sinned, and they cannot count as progenitors of true humanity because they lacked human parents. If peccability were necessary for being truly human, then all those who are resurrected to glorified humanity will no longer count as human. In glory, the promise of the absolute end of death entails the end of sin (Rev 21:1-4), which is the basis for the traditional belief that the resurrected righteous will be impeccable. Will they not remain truly human in glory? Of course they will, and the same is so for Jesus. His lack of the attribute of peccability, which is *common* to original and fallen humanity, does not disqualify him from being a true human, so long as he possesses whatever is necessary to true humanity (a rational human soul and human body).[93]

Second, the premise that true humanity requires peccability commits M7 proponents to affirm one of these troublesome options: (1) God is able to sin (peccable), (2) God is impeccable but the Son changed to become peccable as a concomitant to becoming truly human, or (3) God the Son is both impeccable as God and peccable as man, and his peccability trumps his impeccability. I will explore each option that is available to the defender of M7.

Option (1), whether specific to God the Son or the triune God, is a denial of the traditional claim that God is necessarily good (impeccable).[94] Theologically,

---

[92]As in the Arian claim that there was a time when the Logos was *not*. (See the anathemas of the Nicene Creed.)

[93]Morris, *Logic of God Incarnate*, 63-66. Morris helpfully distinguishes common and essential properties of human nature, and the meaning of being merely human compared to fully human, that is, Jesus is able to count fully as a human while possessing more reality than being merely a human (i.e., Jesus is also fully God).

[94]See the defense of God's necessary goodness by Morris, noted above in n. 76. For a recent account of divine impeccability, see John S. Feinberg, *No One Like Him: The Doctrine of God* (Wheaton, IL: Crossway Books, 2001), 288-92. Feinberg helpfully summarizes two approaches. First, divine impeccability is simply the omnipotence of God to act as a morally perfect being. Since any sin would be doing an act that a morally perfect being would not do, sin would be a contradiction, which God does not have the power to do. Second, God possesses the power to do any act, and cannot do acts that would be sins, since such would be impossible because of his moral perfection. I add that if sin is defined as a failure to act properly (and is not viewed as a positive power at all), then God cannot sin because of his perfection in wisdom, power, and goodness never to fail to do right. The Christian tradition is unanimous in recognizing the God of the Bible as one who cannot sin, and thus he is trustworthy and worthy of all worship as the fixed source of goodness. Biblical evidence may not be convincing support for God's *necessary* goodness, but surely Hebrews 6:18 and Titus 1:2, along with James 1:13 mark God's absolute inability to commit sin, and the abundant affirmations of his goodness as everlasting should be sufficient to convince us (e.g., Deut 32:4; 2 Chron 7:3; Ps 34:8; Ps 68:10; Hab 1:13; Mark 10:18 and 1 John 1:5).

the denial of Jesus' impeccability raises problems related to at least three divine attributes. Sin in Christ would contradict his *omnipotence* because, possibly, the case might have been that he would not have fulfilled salvation and sin would have conquered the Son of God. Peccability contradicts his *immutability*, God's ethical fixedness and constancy as the source and standard of goodness, holiness, and righteousness.[95] The possibility that Jesus could ever sin contradicts the divine *truthfulness* because the unconditional promises of God about the certainty of salvation in Christ (e.g., Eph 1:9-12) would be twisted into false statements (and foreknown to have been lies, because God is omniscient). Oliver Crisp agrees that any attribution of peccability to Christ (as in M7) entails a revision of divine peccability. His protest against this move is apt:

> If one revises this divine attribute, it cannot but have implications for other divine attributes (and therefore, for a doctrine of the divine nature). If God is not essentially good, then whence divine holiness, love, compassion or immutability, to give but four of the most obvious examples? It also raises questions about God's worthiness of worship: ought we to worship a being who is only contingently good, and who may choose evil?[96]

In just this brief response to divine peccability, we can see that the path from M7 to option (1) should be abandoned and we ought to take up either another option or a revision of the model.

Option (2), that God the Son changed to become peccable for incarnation, falls under the same critique as option (1), with the special implication for draining most of the meaning out of divine immutability. The notion of a God who changes from entirely good to possibly a sinner describes a different God than the one of Christian belief and the Scriptures. If God is only contingently good, then his immutability and perfection cannot support his promises that are frequently based upon these attributes as certain grounds of assurance (e.g., 2 Sam 22:31; Mal 3:6). A God who is good is *always* good; he does not improve or decline in his perfection because he is self-existent, omnipotent, omniscient, etc. Because the incarnate person known as Jesus of Nazareth is the eternal Logos, he must be immutably impeccable (or, necessarily good). To say otherwise, as in the path from M7 to option (2), means to raise more difficulties with reconciling the proposed revision to our understanding of the divine nature than what M7 proposes to solve (the problem of seeing how an impeccable Godman can be truly tempted). As with option (1), option (2) must be forsaken for another option or the model that leads to it must be revised.

---

[95]For a contemporary defense of divine immutability, see Bruce A. Ware, "An Evangelical Reformulation of the Doctrine of the Immutability of God", *Journal of the Evangelical Theological Society* 29 (1986): 431-46.

[96]Crisp, "Was Christ Sinless or Impeccable?" 186, n. 43. Crisp offers a concise defense of the divine impeccability (184-86).

Option (3), that the Son's impeccability was trumped by his human peccability, is a Nestorian sort of detachment of Christ's human nature from his divine nature. Only by a division of his natures can such self-contradiction occur for the Godman to be peccable. Such separation and division between the two natures seem wrong and unnecessary for the way this undermines the unity of the Incarnation. M7 calls for a redefinition of Jesus along the Nestorian lines by repeating the ancient mistake of ignoring the distinction between *person* and *nature*. Proponents wrongly pit the attributes of one nature against the other nature instead of seeing that the Incarnation means one person possesses two natures without change to either nature. The result is that God the Son did not suffer and die for us, was not tempted and obeyed for us, but only the assumed man has done these things (or, the human nature did them). On the contrary, the importance of Christ's temptations is not merely that he suffered to the same extent and degree as common humanity, but that he was the divine Son who suffered in his humanity to save others as the second Adam who has come from God and *as God in person* to reconcile the human race back to God. The Nestorian problem of M7 shows in Millard Erickson's speculation about what would have happened should Jesus have sinned: Erickson explains that the Logos would have departed from the man just prior to that instant of sin, and what remained would have been a mere human being (yet, a free-standing individual distinct from the Logos).[97] But Christ is God incarnate and acts as a unified Godman possessing and living by virtue of two natures. Anything Christ does as a man he does as a Godman, the Logos. If Christ sins, the Logos sins, and so it cannot be that he is impeccable as God and peccable as man.[98] For M7, the path to option (3) is similarly unfruitful, which calls the model into question as theologically inadequate.

Moreover, if Jesus was peccable during his earthly life, what assurance do we have that he is not still peccable in glory? If he is, then salvation can never be assured to us because, having paid for sins, Christ could yet sometime become a sinner. Were that to happen, he would no longer be able to be a priest for us, and all that he accomplished would eventually be lost as we, now stripped of his constant aid through the Holy Spirit and intercession with God, would inevitably return to the thrall of sin. Therefore, not only is the premise false that true humanity requires peccability, but (as we should expect) adopting this premise introduces drastic problems for our understanding of God.

CONTRA: TRUE TEMPTATION REQUIRES PECCABILITY

Proponents of M7 assume that the ability to sin is bound up in the reality of temptation. For historical perspective, we should remember that only a very

---

[97]Erickson, *Word Became Flesh*, 563-64.
[98]See also Crisp, "Was Christ Sinless or Impeccable?", 183, and Morris, *Logic of God Incarnate*, 146-47.

few have agreed with this idea in two millennia of thinking about Christ. Of course the majority can be wrong, but it is unwise to ignore the way so many have not concluded with M7 that temptation requires peccability.

The importance of this second M7 premise is that we have come to two claims (impeccability and temptation) that some modern theologians think cannot be harmonized. M7 modifies impeccability to fit with temptation, so the meaning of temptation becomes the controlling concept. What then is temptation?

Certainly many temptations involve actual possibilities for the one tempted, but are there some temptations that are just as real but do not involve actual possibilities? As we will see later, M8 and M9 propose that temptation does not require the actual possibility that one can sin for a person to feel truly tempted. Instead, these models propose that at minimum temptation requires a sort of mental or imagined possibility that one can sin (or, temptation requires a lack of certainty about one's inability to sin). When this necessary and sufficient condition is met, then temptations may occur in which the person truly feels tempted, resists successfully, and failure was never a possibility. If either account in M8 or M9 succeeds, then it seems that this peccability premise so important to M7 is at least questionable (if not mistaken). Moreover, I will offer a more detailed definition and explanation of temptation below that is more adequate than the intuition of M7 proponents that temptation requires peccability.

I think the basic alternative of M8 and M9 succeeds, and, if true, then these proposals remove the only redemptive need for peccability in Christ. Of everything that the Savior must accomplish, peccability is unnecessary for fulfilling these tasks. Instead, the possibility that he sins is a tremendous risk that would disqualify him from accomplishing salvation.[99] Were it possible for him to be able to sin as a man, this would be the equivalent of a marathon runner competing while carrying a dozen loosely-pinned grenades in his hands, any one of which could detonate and blow him apart, but none of which was needed for completing his race.

CONCLUSION

The M7 emphasis on Jesus' temptable humanity as necessary to achieving salvation is right, but his impeccable deity as the eternal Son must be emphasized as well. M7 undermines Jesus' full deity by humanizing divine impeccability to human peccability. The premises are questionable, and they lead proponents to a conclusion that involves serious and troubling revisions to

---

[99]The measuring of Christ's humanity according to his redemptive tasks was counted with interest by medieval theologians, as Adams summarizes in, *What Sort of Human Nature?*, 96-97, "Sin is incompatible with the state of glory (*non posse peccare*), and sin is disqualifying for other salient soteriological offices—for making satisfaction, for earning merit, for conquering the devil, for furnishing an inspiring role model."

our understanding of the divine nature. We have seen that peccability causes much more severe problems than what it has been employed to solve, whether vindicating the true humanity or the true temptation of Jesus. In this case, the cure (peccability, that God may become sinful) is worse than the disease (the difficulty of harmonizing temptation with impeccability). I find the model to be theologically inadequate and harmful as a misguided departure from orthodoxy.

Other contemporary theologians agree, and so two alternatives to M7 are offered. They are two paths to the same basic conclusion that some sort of limitation occurred for Christ to be unaware or at least uncertain in his human consciousness regarding his inability to sin. Both models are speculative in the way they extend the veiling idea of M6. Both models share with M7 the modern interest in accounting for the temptation to be authentic, relevant human struggles and harmonious with the Godman's impeccability. We will turn to these similar accounts of the complexity in the next chapter.

CHAPTER 9

Modern Models (Part 2)

Two modern models have been offered as alternatives to the proposal that Jesus must have been able to sin (M7). Both models are complicated as they provide similar explanations of a complex reality, the temptation of the impeccable Godman. Both models meet the modern concern for Jesus' true humanity. The strain of this claim alongside the traditional view that Jesus was impeccable demands theologians to speculate about the mechanics of the hypostatic union and Christ's twofold existence in two very different natures.

M8: Temptable by Kenotic Restriction
Description of M8

Jesus was truly tempted because he temporarily gave up his omniscience regarding his inability to sin. Jesus humanized his awareness of his divine impeccability to the stature of normal human ignorance or uncertainty. This is a voluntary restriction or humanization of divine knowledge that allows true temptation in spite of impeccability. Proponents agree with the basic idea of M7 that Christ's deity had to be humanized so he could experience true temptation. Instead of reasoning that Jesus must have been peccable to be tempted, proponents of M8 affirm Christ's impeccability. Jesus was impeccable, *but he was unaware of this fact when he was tempted.* By humanizing his divine knowledge to the confines of a finite human mind, Jesus was prevented from knowing that he was immune to sin. Without being aware of this, Jesus could be truly human and experience real temptation (while remaining impeccable). At the level of his voluntary confinement to a human mind, the temptations seemed to him as real opportunities to sin. M8 takes Christ's ignorance about his impeccability as a sufficient condition for temptation, and one that preserves his human freedom from being determined by his divine impeccability. He remained impeccable, but his deity did not protect him from suffering the strain of real temptations. According to what he knew at the time of his temptations, he was either unsure of his immunity to sin, or partially persuaded that sin was possible for him. Either way, the setting for a true struggle of temptation was in place for one who is God to be tempted authentically as a man. He was truly tempted as others are through basic needs and innocent desires (e.g., not through lust or greed); consequently, he is a relevant human pattern for resisting sin (cf. 1 Pet 2:21-22).

As in the earlier proposals of M4-M6, proponents of M8 address the concern for Jesus' true humanity that intensifies during the modern period. Also repeated here is the emphasis on empowering grace that aided Jesus as a man. Jesus possessed his divine attributes fully, but he did not live by them in his humanity for the sake of his redemptive tasks. Instead, Jesus could be fully tempted and resist sin within the limits of his humanity as a pattern for others. Here the need for grace from the Holy Spirit is real to support Jesus in his depreciated mode of life as a man (cf. M4, M6). In the modern setting, the material of earlier models is combined with the developing kenotic theories to formulate M8.

Kenotic theory (based on the statement in Phil 2:7 that Jesus *emptied* himself) is the proposal that, in view of the differences between deity and humanity, the Incarnation involved some sort of choice by the Son to give up or limit himself from exercising certain divine attributes that contradict authentic human existence. Originally a Lutheran innovation, early kenotic theory proposed that in light of the Incarnation, the traditional ideas about the divine attributes must be redefined.[1] Gottfried Thomasius (1802-1875) argued that the Son of God gave up the so-called *relative* divine attributes (omnipotence, omnipresence, and omniscience) that are incompatible with true human experience while he retained the *essential* attributes of deity (e.g., love, holiness, and truth).[2] In the UK, Anglican Charles Gore (1853-1932) argued for the kenotic idea that God the Son chose to limit his divine consciousness to allow his true human experience.[3] A limitation of Christ's omniscience is widely assumed because of the Gospel evidence that Jesus did not know certain things (e.g., the time of his return, Mark 13:32), with similar arguments given for the limitation of his omnipresence and omnipotence. Some have modified kenotic theory to say that the Logos gave up the *independent exercise* of his relative divine attributes during his time on earth; thus, Jesus could only exercise his divine powers in conjunction with the Father's will.[4]

---

[1] Ronald J. Feenstra, "Reconsidering Kenotic Christology", in *Trinity, Incarnation, and Atonement*, ed. Ronald J. Feenstra and Cornelius Plantinga Jr. (Notre Dame: Notre Dame University Press, 1989), 135.

[2] Gottfried Thomasius, *Christ's Person and Work*, ed. and trans. Welch, *God and Incarnation*, 70. Relative attributes are those possessed by God in relation to creation, so they are contingent for God as gained when he creates.

[3] Charles Gore, *Dissertations on Subjects Connected with the Incarnation*, 2nd ed. (London: John Murray, 1896), 211. Donald G. Dawe, *The Form of a Servant: A Historical Analysis of the Kenotic Motif* (Philadelphia: Westminster, 1963), 91, writes that Gore used the kenosis idea in 1889 initially to explain how Jesus merely held the erroneous views of his day about the authorship of Old Testament books, and other historical inaccuracies in the Old Testament, because he had limited his divine omniscience to human knowledge.

[4] Augustus H. Strong, *Systematic Theology* (Philadelphia: Judson, 1907), 704.

The relevance of kenotic theory to M8 is that some kenoticists claim that Jesus could be fully tempted because he humanized the knowledge of his impeccability.[5] Scottish theologian P. T. Forsyth (1909) gives a clear example of how kenosis makes sense of Christ's true temptation without surrendering impeccability:

> The infinite mobility of the changeless God in becoming human growth only assumes a special phase of itself. Had the myriad-minded creator of souls no power to live perfectly in the personal and growing form of the souls he made? But sin? There, indeed, we do read a limit. *Non potuit peccare*. But, then, it is at once said, his personality and manhood were not real. But what if it were thus? What if his kenosis went so far that though the impossibility was there he did not know of it? The limitation of his knowledge is indubitable—even about himself. He was not perfectly sure that the cross was his Father's will till the very last. "If it be possible let it pass." Did that nescience not extend to the area of his own moral nature, and so provide for him the temptable conditions which put him in line with our dark conflict, and which truly moralise and humanise his victory when *potuit non peccare*? He knew he came sinless out of each crisis; did he know he never could be anything else? How could he?[6]

Forsyth's presentation of M8 depends on kenotic theory to explain Christ's temptability (while he remained impeccable). Similar reasoning appears in another influential Scottish kenoticist, H. R. Mackintosh.[7] Mackintosh and Forsyth are careful to avoid the problems of earlier kenotic theories that redefined the divine attributes.[8] Both affirm the full deity of Christ with no renunciation of divine attributes (neither the so-called essential nor the relative attributes). Instead, they describe the humanized condition of divine attributes as latent or potential (which is an echo of Calvin's idea of quiescent divinity in M6). These twentieth century kenoticists represent the two concerns in M8 to explain the full deity and full humanity in Christ, especially with respect to his real temptation, and in spite of his impeccability.[9]

---

[5] Thomasius, *Christ's Person and Work*, ed. and trans. Welch, *God and Incarnation*, 67-68.

[6] P.T. Forsyth, *The Person and Place of Jesus Christ* (Boston: Pilgrim, 1909), 300-01.

[7] H.R. Mackintosh, *The Doctrine of the Person of Jesus Christ*, 2nd ed. (1913; reprint, New York: Charles Scribner's Sons, 1942), 480-81.

[8] E.g., Mackintosh, *Person of Christ*, 267-78, disavows the proposals of W.F. Gess and F. Godet to reassign the roles of the Trinity so that the Father carries on the Son's preservation of creation during the state of his humiliation (his earthly life).

[9] Dennis E. Johnson, "Immutability and Incarnation: An Historical and Theological Study of the Concepts of Christ's Divine Unchangeability and His Human Development", PhD diss, Fuller Theological Seminary (1984), 218. Johnson observes that one of the main values of kenotic Christology is to explain Jesus' humanity more adequately in view of the evidence from modern study of the Gospels than the traditional Chalcedonian versions had done.

Gerald F. Hawthorne (1991) is a recent proponent of this so-called modified kenoticism of Mackintosh and Forsyth, and cites both Scots approvingly. Hawthorne agrees that Jesus humanized his deity by limiting himself from exercising his divine attributes while on earth.[10] Hawthorne is important because of his book-length discussion of pneumatological Christology, including a chapter devoted to the temptation. He claims, "Jesus' knowledge was in some way circumscribed."[11] The significance of kenotic limitation for Christ's temptation is that "This view of the person of Christ gives meaning and reality for example, to the temptations he faced. For if indeed it was not possible for him to sin, there is nevertheless the possibility that he was not aware of it."[12]

The step beyond others that Hawthorne makes is the degree of self-limitation and corresponding reliance on the Holy Spirit: "Jesus met and conquered the usurping enemy of God not by his own power alone but aided in his victory by the power of the Holy Spirit."[13] The emphasis here is on Christ's own power as a man and the true need for supplemental power of the Holy Spirit to enable his triumph over temptation. Hawthorne's argument is that Jesus lived dependently on the Holy Spirit in a complete way of self-limited humanization of his divinity. Jesus worked miracles and achieved the moral triumph of his sinlessness entirely by the empowering grace of the Spirit. He even needed the Holy Spirit to give him knowledge of his identity and mission.[14] Representing the modern concerns, Hawthorne combines the twentieth century kenotic explanation with the twentieth century interest in the empowering presence of the Holy Spirit. The result is a kenotic account of the Godman who is truly human and fully tempted with no loss of deity.

Evaluation of M8

M8 explains the true humanity of Jesus, tempted as we are with no advantages of divine impeccability, without giving up on the traditional affirmation that God and Christ cannot sin. The reality of temptation is preserved alongside impeccability because Jesus does not know he is impeccable when he is being tempted. Such knowledge was given up in voluntary, kenotic restriction so that a true incarnation could occur.

How might this M8 formulation have looked in Gethsemane? Jesus faces his horror truly by the kenotic ignorance about his deeper impeccable substance.

---

[10]Gerald F. Hawthorne, *The Presence and the Power: The Significance of the Holy Spirit in the Life of Jesus* (Dallas: Word, 1991), 207-09. Hawthorne explicitly agrees with the kenoticism of Forsyth and Mackintosh.
[11]Hawthorne, *Presence and the Power*, 28.
[12]Hawthorne, *Presence and the Power*, 209.
[13]Hawthorne, *Presence and the Power*, 139.
[14]Hawthorne, *Presence and the Power*, 208.

No divine power courses through him like magic to repel the temptation or its shadow of sin, and no subjective assurance comforts him that the struggle he feels is just a bad dream with no real threat to him. Jesus has suffered hundreds of temptations and passed through each faithfully. He knows the pull and the appeal of sin, and he knows the liberty that he has found whenever he recourses to the difficult obedience of continuing to trust God's word. Christ's own awareness of the struggle is near to the dread that his disciples feel since he and they have no sense of immunity from sin. Jesus prays in real desire that the Father command another plan than the cross. Having cast himself in his humanity dependently upon the working of the Father and the Spirit, Jesus suffers in his deathly distress to embrace obedience as a man. "I might in fact *be able to sin*, but I cannot be certain of that because I am facing real pulls to sin in these temptations. What I must do is resist the sin with all I have available to me and cling to God. Or, it might be that I might in fact *be unable to sin*, but I cannot be certain of that either because I am facing real pulls to sin in these temptations. What I *still* must do is resist the sin with all I have available to me and cling to God."[15] The outcome (from God's perspective) was never in doubt, even as hundreds of confirmations from Scripture attest (the promises of God relating to the success of messianic salvation, all of which would be voided if he sinned) and Jesus' own awareness dawns (before he feels tempted) that God is his surety no matter the threat (as in his confident prayer of John 17). Yet here, within himself and terrified of suffering the wrath of God, his knowledge as a man extends no further than his experiences, perception, and imagination. All these provide no certain proof of his immunity from sin. His startling knowledge and self-understanding that he is the Messiah and Son of God do not mitigate the force of his desire to flee the suffering and he pleads desperately for another way. Before him is the fervent desire to avoid pain through disobedience, and the alternate, ardent and habitual desire to obey his God. When he receives help from God through the Holy Spirit, he finds the ability to resist the temptation genuinely and within the limit of his human nature. From this experience and the rest of his temptations, Jesus has learned obedience through his suffering and become empathetic in the trials of all others who follow him. His empathy and pattern of resistance has immediate relevance for the three disciples who failed where he succeeded, and he has become their faithful priest by entering their condition. His limitation has become their salvation. He has given himself to become the pattern of their hope as they follow him to faithful obedience instead of sin.

---

[15] These are not plausible phrasing of thoughts for Jesus in Gethsemane, but I include them to illustrate the point of uncertainty that M8 proposes as a reasonable and sufficient condition for experiencing temptation. The fictional statements are similar to those given in Psalms 16 and 22 as voiced or contemplated by Jesus: the anguished laments, pleas for help, and statements of confidence regarding God's help to deliver him. With Luther, I think all of Psalm 22 conveys Jesus' inner prayer.

Sam Storms criticizes this account because he is unable to believe in Jesus ignorance or that any practical relevance would remain unless Jesus had been truly able to sin:

> I find it hard to believe that Jesus lacked such self-awareness. Even if he did, we don't, so what benefit is there to us in his having resisted the Devil's overtures? In other words, we find encouragement in Jesus' example only if we know he could have sinned, but didn't (1 Peter 2:21-23). So long as *we* know that his sinning was absolutely impossible, the force of his example is undermined, regardless of what *he* may have known.[16]

Storms has privileged peccability as the necessary condition for real temptation, which, as we have seen in the evaluation of M7, is doubtful. The assertion is that our theological understanding of Jesus' impeccability somehow deflates the reality of his experience and disqualifies him from being a pattern for us. Is this true that our additional theological knowledge changes the relevance of Jesus' experiences for ours? I think the M8 picture of Christ's relevance is no different from the following scenario.

Imagine a realistic, spontaneous fire alarm or emergency drill in which the participants take the signs as real and respond properly to the crisis. They do not discover until afterward that all was an exercise to train them in readiness for the real thing (not simply a routine drill for children). Consider onlookers watching a videotape of the experience at a later time know the whole thing was a drill. We can see that the knowledge of the viewers about the taped experience does not invalidate the experience of the participants, which may include true panic, stress, perceived danger, and active response to the crisis (e.g., they successfully shut down the factory power to prevent an imminent explosion). Moreover, many of the fears and distresses that people experience are in relation to false or misunderstood perceptions, but their fears and trauma are still real to them (as any claustrophobia-sufferer would attest). The M8 account may be difficult for Storms to believe, but his objection is more a matter of subjectively practical adequacy and personal preference, not theological adequacy.

Storms also signals another critique of M8 that Jesus could not have been mistaken or unaware about his impeccability, even when he was struggling through temptation. Because Jesus had definite self-understanding of his consubstantiality with God, and he would have known the clear teaching of the Old Testament that God cannot sin, John Feinberg argues that there is no way Jesus failed to make this logical inference. Instead, Jesus must have had clearly in mind (his human mind) that, being in essential unity with the Father, he was impeccable: "Since Scripture shows that Christ claimed to be God, it is hard to

---

[16] Storms, "Could Jesus have Sinned? (2 Cor. 5.21)". Note that this is an internet post.

see how he could be ignorant of his own impeccability."[17] Feinberg goes on to argue that temptation was still possible for Jesus even with the full knowledge of his impeccability, just as a Christian who is convinced of God's certain promises to preserve him in faith may still be tempted to turn away from the faith.[18]

Storms and Feinberg's critiques apply to a key aspect of M8 (ignorance about impeccability is a sufficient condition for Christ to be tempted) that is shared in M9. I will reply to these critiques below, in the presentation of M9. It may be that both models are theologically inadequate in the face of these two objections. Nonetheless, M8 has an important aspect that distinguishes it from M9 which must be considered.

M8 depends on kenotic theory. Kenotic theory has been subject to criticism in its various forms.[19] Proposals of kenotic theory that require revisions of divine immutability and other attributes are particularly suspicious.[20] To be adequate theologically, any version of kenotic theory employed for M8 must also explain how the temporary limitation of deity for true incarnation did not entail the destruction of Christ's humanity when he *regained* the fullness of his deity when he was glorified in resurrection. If certain divine attributes of omniscience, omnipotence, and omnipresence make a true human existence impossible (and so they must be surrendered for the Son to become a man), then kenotic restriction must be permanent for Jesus to remain a true man in his resurrected life (he is forever the Godman).

The so-called *modified kenotic theory* of Forsyth, Mackintosh, and Hawthorne seems to remain satisfying for some contemporary theologians because the divine attributes are not given up; instead, they explain that Jesus did not exercise them on earth except in conjunction with the Father's will and

---

[17] Feinberg, "The Incarnation", 241. Feinberg engages the proposal of Thomas Morris on this point of Jesus' uncertainty about his impeccability. Since Morris disavows kenotic theory, we will consider his proposal in M9, below.

[18] Feinberg, "The Incarnation", 244. I have agreed with Feinberg on this point until recently. I no longer agree that Jesus' temptation can occur if he is fully convinced that sin is impossible for him.

[19] Bruce, *Humiliation of Christ*, 164-93. Johnson, "Immutability and Incarnation", 218-25. In Johnson's evaluation of kenotic Christology, including Forsyth and Mackintosh, he notes that kenoticists imply that the Son ceased to be God as an entailment of the how they described the contraction of the Son's divine attributes and consciousness. See also the brief critique by Morris, *Logic of God Incarnate*, 93-101.

[20] I have touched on this earlier in connection with the evaluation of M7. Of course, the traditional understanding of certain divine attributes has had a bumpy ride, with, for example, the doctrine of divine impassibility becoming a misunderstood concept after the early centuries and the doctrine of immutability needing to be reformulated in accordance with Scripture. See Ware, "Evangelical Reformulation", and Lister, "Impassible and Impassioned".

by the Spirit's empowerment.[21] The main weakness of the modified version is the speculation in the proposal. Scripture does not exclude the modified kenotic theory, but neither does Scripture give clear support for knowing that kenotic theory is a true account. Moreover, kenotic theory is a theologically novel idea not more than two centuries old, which should make us cautious about it.

A serious weakness of kenotic theory (and, by extension, M8 which depends on it) is the supposed biblical basis for it in Philippians 2:5-11. Without taking on a detailed investigation of this important and widely disputed passage, I note here Macleod's interpretation that the condescension in humility was death on the cross, not incarnation.[22] The passage focuses upon Christ's example of *obedience as a man giving himself for others* (that is, within the frame of his life as a man, and not his example as the eternal Son condescending to human existence). The Son did not lose deity, but took upon himself human existence as the form of a servant.

Additionally, the modified kenotic theory of Forsyth, Mackintosh, and Hawthorne includes the affirmation of Monothelitism (that Christ possessed only one will of the divine Logos).[23] Although M8 does not require Monothelitism, the formulation of M8 with it by these proponents is tainted by the denial of a human will in Christ. I think this denial violates Chalcedonian Christology because Monothelitism falls short of a complete human nature, *body and soul*. Since God cannot be tempted (Jas 1:13), the only way Jesus could have experienced temptation as a man is through a created, substantial human will that was mutable and susceptible to desires that are contrary to God. The Monothelite attractiveness for unifying the Incarnation by positing a single will raises the serious problem for M8 of excluding Jesus from being able to be tempted.[24] Only by incarnation of taking to himself a complete

---

[21]Klaus Issler, "Jesus's Example: Prototype of the Dependent, Spirit-Filled Life", in *Jesus in Trinitarian Perspective*, ed. Fred Sanders and Klaus Issler (Nashville: B & H, 2007), 189-225.

[22]Macleod, *Person of Christ*, 212-17.

[23]Hawthorne, *Presence and the Power*, 212-13. Hawthorne is explicit. Forsyth and Mackintosh each exclude two sets of the faculties of mind and will in Christ (which is tantamount to Monothelitism and Apollinarianism). Forsyth excludes two minds and wills as impossible to believe in light of contemporary psychology, because it is incoherent that one person can know and not know a fact (*Person and Place of Jesus*, 319-20). Mackintosh agrees that two minds and wills are unintelligible for one person. He reasons that it must have been that divine mind was expressed "in a human milieu" (*Person of Jesus Christ*, 469-70).

[24]Despite the long tradition against this teaching, a few contemporary Christologists and philosophers favor Monothelitism. I had earlier been persuaded of a reconfigured form of Monothelitism for a brief time until my first theology teacher, Robert L. Saucy, helped me reverse from heterodoxy. Apollinarianism and Monothelitism were condemned for falling short of accounting for a full, true human nature in Christ. The Sixth Ecumenical Council (Constantinople III, 680-81) specifically addressed

human nature[25] can God the Son experience changeable, passible existence, suffer, be tempted, learn obedience, and achieve righteousness on our behalf as the perfected high priest.

For those who agree with kenotic theory, the M8 explanation for how the impeccable Logos could experience temptation as a man may find this model to be theologically adequate. In my view, kenotic theory is flawed and so the model is theologically inadequate. Nonetheless, the key element of M8 that allows a harmony between impeccability and temptation is also the key element of an alternative model (M9) that avoids kenoticism.

M9: Temptable by Psychological Restriction

Description of M9

Jesus was truly tempted because his full knowledge of his inability to sin was veiled from his consciousness as a man. As noted previously, M9 is parallel to M8 in two aspects while rejecting kenotic theory. First, proponents of M9 are explicit to follow Chalcedonian Christology, which leads them to uphold the inviolable deity of Christ by which he remains impeccable despite incarnation. When Jesus is tempted, never is he able to sin.

Second, M9 is close to M8 in resolving the apparent dilemma of impeccability and temptation by reasoning that a self-limitation, veiling, or eclipse of some sort occurred by which Jesus did not know he was immune to sin when he was tempted. Where M8 appeals to kenotic theory, M9 appeals to modern psychology and analogies for the claim that the Logos was impeccable, but that in his humanity, he did not know it (at least not in a way that would have precluded him from being tempted). Proponents of both models agree that a sufficient condition for temptation is one's uncertainty or ignorance about one's ability to commit the proposed sin. The distinction of M9 is that proponents disavow kenotic theory as the way to explain Christ's ignorance about his impeccability. Unlike kenoticism, proponents of Jesus' psychological restriction claim that Christ lays aside nothing divine to latent, contracted, dependent, or potential status. Instead, M9 explains that Christ's knowledge of his impeccability is present as a subliminal self, or as locked in his divine mind that is subconscious to and thus hidden from his conscious awareness in his human mind. Christ is one person in two natures, and according to his human nature (by virtue of the consciousness he possesses as a man) Jesus is

---

Monothelitism and found that Chalcedonian Christology and the doctrines of redemption and the Trinity required the traditional view that there are two wills in Christ, according to each of his two natures. (Two reasons given were that without a created human will, Christ could not save us, and that Monothelitism was seen to require that there are three wills in the Trinity, and these may be possibly opposed.)

[25] I take the meaning of human nature as body and soul, including the created faculties of mind, will, and emotion.

susceptible to temptations of all sorts because he is blocked from knowing for certain that he is impeccable. Such knowledge is never revealed to his human mind by God (i.e., the Holy Spirit), or perhaps the Holy Spirit precludes him from inferring this conclusion from other evidence, or perhaps Jesus is (through the Spirit's influence) momentarily forgetful of this knowledge in the midst of his temptations. Macleod's observation is helpful here:

> To the angels on the balcony (as to theologians in their armchairs) it may have been perfectly clear that Jesus could never sin. To himself, engaging the devil on the road, the outcome may have been far from clear. Never once, as we observe him struggle with temptation, do we see him deriving comfort from the fact of his own impeccability.[26]

A precursor to M9 is the proposal of British theologian William Sanday (1911), who first applied the conclusions of modern psychology to Christ's incarnational experience.[27] Sanday explained Jesus' deity as *subliminal* to his human consciousness, on analogy with the religious and psychological experience of other human beings. The use of modern psychology and the notion of a subliminal or subconscious mind is not essential to M9, but the analogy has been helpful for some proponents to explain *how* it could have been that an impeccable Godman was truly tempted as a man. Indeed, perhaps this feature of the modern setting allowed philosophers and theologians to speculate in ways that have formulated M9 (and M8 as well).

We should not think, however, that the model is wedded to modern psychology anymore than that the theology of the early Christians was wedded to Greek philosophy because writers employed concepts and helpful terms for conveying Christian revelation. Indeed, Bruce notes that at least one Reformed theologian in the seventeenth century had come to the same conclusion in advance of modern psychology. Bruce summarizes the claim of Hulsius that ignorance and unhappiness were necessary for Christ's work as Savior so that he could fulfill his role in the form of a servant, as in his Gethsemane anguish:

> Rather than admit the agony and the fear in the garden to have been unreal, one may dare to say that, under the influence of extreme perturbation of mind, Christ for the moment forgot the divine decree under which He was appointed, by death to become the Saviour of sinners. Such forgetfulness, according to Hulsius, was not impossible. The knowledge of a decree as to habit is one thing, the actual

---

[26]Macleod, *Person of Christ*, 230.

[27]William Sanday, *Christologies Ancient and Modern*, in *Christology and Personality* (Oxford: Clarendon, 1911). Sanday applied the concept of the subliminal self (the subconscious or unconscious mind) from William James and F.W.H. Myers to divine action in the human soul for us as for Christ, the locus of Deity. This is an Apollinarian type of Christology.

conscious recollection of that knowledge is another thing; the latter, the vehemence of anxiety could take away, though not the former.[28]

With these basic ideas of the model roughly described, we now turn to five contemporary formulations of M9. Among their differences, these representatives agree that impeccable Christ could be truly tempted if he was somehow psychologically restricted (he did not know he was impeccable at the time of his temptations).

Representatives of M9

THOMAS V. MORRIS

American philosopher Thomas Morris (1986) has articulated what he thinks is a philosophically coherent defense of Chalcedonian Christology and the reality of impeccability and temptation without kenoticism.[29] Morris defends the doctrine in the face of objections that Chalcedonian Christology is logically incoherent.

Morris suggests that we may explain the biblical evidence and theological doctrine of two natures by the theory that Christ had two minds, a divine mind and a human mind. Morris proposes that Christ's divine mind contained his human mind. The unity of one person possessing two minds is based in the supervening or containment role of the divine mind in relation to the human mind, with one-way or asymmetrical access to the contents of the human mind. This relationship unifies the two minds and preserves the limited knowledge-contents of the human mind as truly human and truly a possession of the Son (unlike all other human minds that God knows thoroughly, this one is uniquely *his*). According to his human mind, Jesus was unaware that he was impeccable (at least), and he believed (though mistakenly) that he was able to sin. Morris calls this the *epistemic possibility* that allows temptation. This restricted condition of his human mind is sufficient for temptation because "The reality of his temptation does not require the broadly logical, or metaphysical, possibility of what he considers doing. It requires only that the imagined deed not be an epistemic impossibility for him. He must think it possible, and within his power to do. It need not actually be so."[30] Jesus believes that sin may be *possible* for him or, in other words, he does not believe that sin is entirely impossible for him, and thus he can experience temptation in that status of ignorance (at least)

---

[28]Bruce, *Humiliation of Christ*, 131. Unfortunately, Bruce gives only a secondary source for Hulsius's views

[29]Morris, *Logic of God Incarnate*, 92-102, explicitly rejects kenoticism because of two serious defects: first, kenoticism requires an unsatisfactory view of modalities of divine attributes because kenoticism entails that God is not necessarily omniscient, omnipresent, and omnipotent; and, second, kenoticism requires the abandonment of immutability. Morris affirms and defends Chalcedonian Christology as the presupposition of orthodoxy (17-18).

[30]Morris, *Logic of God Incarnate*, 147-48.

or mistaken belief. The humanization of Christ's knowledge by his restriction to a human mind preserves his temptability without canceling his impeccability. Morris explains this restriction as fulfilling the subjective, epistemic condition for temptation:

> Jesus could be tempted to sin just in case it was epistemically possible for him that he sin. If at the times of his reported temptations, the full accessible belief-set of his earthly mind did not rule out the possibility of his sinning, he could be genuinely tempted, in that range of consciousness, to sin. But this could be so only if that belief-set did not contain the information that he is necessarily good. In order that he suffer real temptation, then, it is not necessary that sinning be a broadly logical or metaphysical possibility for Jesus; it is only necessary that it be an epistemic possibility for him.[31]

Morris appeals to an analogy as explanation for how Christ can be impeccable while still experiencing true temptation and making free choices to do right. Morris describes the situation of a man, Jones, who enters a room, closes the door, and remains for two hours with the door locked. He does not know the door is locked. At the end of the time, he rises and goes to the door, which he opens and thus passes the test. Until that moment, the door had been locked and Jones was unable to leave the room during the specified time. His praiseworthiness for freely choosing to remain in the room is preserved even though he was unable to do otherwise. His mistaken belief about the possibility of leaving the room is part of constituting his temptation experience as a real moral struggle to choose right as one desire among his many desires that depend upon his beliefs. Moreover, Morris adds that unbeknownst to Jones, electrodes have been implanted in his brain to prevent him from forming the intention to attempt to leave, but these never activate because Jones chooses freely to remain in the room. Neither the electrodes (which precluded a certain set of intentions by which he might attempt to leave the room) nor the locked door actually caused Jones to remain in the room. He has remained free even though he could be tempted to try to leave because he was unaware of the other factors and believed it was possible for him to leave.[32] This is similar to the way that Jesus, being only able to choose right, also chose right freely when he experienced temptation. He freely chose in accordance with his impeccability, and was not at all constrained or caused by his deity to choose as he did. (Does not the triune God remain free when he chooses to do right, and yet he is precluded from choosing sin?)

Morris does not say that there may be many reasons why Jones may want to leave the room, but for other reasons he chooses to remain in the room, whether to receive a prize or whatever. I think it helps to say Jones has been commanded to enter the room, and Jones has some reasons for wanting to

---

[31] Morris, *Logic of God Incarnate*, 150.
[32] Morris, *Logic of God Incarnate*, 150-51.

leave, for example, the room smells very bad or he has just learned that a close friend is in need of his help.³³ These additional features correspond to Jesus' situation of knowing he was required to fulfill righteousness, suffered the pains for holding to that course (whether by continued starvation in the wilderness or surrendering himself to be crucified), and was genuinely tempted if he chose to obey freely. His freedom is preserved not simply by his always having had the ability to choose otherwise than he did (sin instead of righteousness), but in that he selected his choice in the face of many possible choices that may or may not have seemed desirable or possible for him. In the end, he never chose sin, but these sinful options were still presented to him as desirable and possible—even if he did not fully believe or disbelieve that they were possible for him.

One important feature in Morris's proposal that I should note is that he understands the *epistemic possibility of sin* to be a sufficient condition for true temptation, which means that Jesus, to be tempted, had to hold the false belief that sin was possible for him when, in fact, it was not. Others who argue similarly to Morris in M9 do not agree that Jesus had to believe a lie about his ability to sin. Instead, he may simply have been unsure about his ability to sin.

GERALD O'COLLINS

Jesuit theologian Gerald O'Collins (1995) gives a similar account to explain the supposed dilemma of impeccability and temptation. O'Collins appeals to M9 in the same way as Morris, marking a psychological condition in Christ as sufficient for temptation, and without employing kenotic theory.

> Jesus could be truly tempted and tested, provided that he did not know that he could not sin. If he had known that he could not sin, it would be difficult, if not impossible, to make sense of genuine temptations; they would be reduced to make-believe, a performance put on for the edification of others. It was quite a different situation to be incapable of sin but not to know that.³⁴

The element of Christ's ignorance about his impeccability is repeated here as the sufficient condition for temptation. O'Collins does not go as far as Morris to say Christ must have believed he was able to sin. Jesus was simply unaware. Nothing more is given by O'Collins to explain *how* Christ's ignorance about his impeccability occurred, but the evidence from the Gospels is clear that Jesus did experience a gap in his human knowledge about some things (e.g., the time of his return, Mark 13:32).³⁵ Not all of his questions were strictly for the

---

³³Chris Vinson proposed this modification to Morris's proposal (an unpublished paper).
³⁴Gerald O'Collins, *Christology: A Biblical, Historical, and Systematic Study of Jesus* (New York: Oxford University Press, 1995), 271.
³⁵Raymond E. Brown, in his *Jesus God and Man: Modern Biblical Reflections* (New York: Macmillan, 1967), 102, agrees that Jesus was limited in knowledge and reflected much of the current thought of his contemporaries, viz., he did not possess the beatific vision. Brown cites Cyril of Alexandria (PG 75:369) "We have admired his goodness in

purposes of teaching (e.g., the location of Lazarus's tomb, John 11:34). The knowledge of his impeccability would be just one more detail that was important he *not* know in his human mind so that he could experience true temptation (while remaining impeccable).

RICHARD SWINBURNE

British philosopher Richard Swinburne (1994) also favors M9 as a way to explain how the impeccable Son of God could enter human life and be tempted. Swinburne, interacting with Morris's proposal, marks the cognitive limitation of Christ's human mind as sufficient for experiencing temptation: "Even though he cannot do wrong, he may however, through not allowing himself to be aware of his divine beliefs, be inclined to believe that he may succumb to temptation to do wrong and thus, in the situation of temptation, he may *feel* as we do."[36] Swinburne allows that Christ may have been mistaken about his ability to sin: "someone falsely believing that he can choose what is wrong is indeed in an unfortunate situation which is like our situation of temptation in its psychological aspect."[37] Swinburne adds that Jesus may have been mistaken about many details, such as the dates of the kings of Judah. Swinburne thus agrees with Morris that being mistaken is the sufficient condition for temptation (and without appeal to kenotic theory).

However, Swinburne does not think that Jesus could be tempted to actual sin against God, only tempted to choose a lesser good among many good options, since Swinburne thinks that actual temptation to do wrong is tantamount to what he calls original sinfulness.[38] This account weakens the correspondence between Christ's temptation and what others experience, but M9 is not dependent upon Swinburne's peculiar construal of Christ's temptation.[39] The important thing is Swinburne's agreement that with an epistemic possibility allowed for the tempted one, temptation could still occur despite impeccability.

DONALD MACLEOD

Donald Macleod also disavows the kenotic proposal while suggesting the M9 explanation that Jesus, in his humanity, did not know the whole truth about himself and was thus able to be tempted.[40] Macleod affirms Christ's impeccability in terms of M2 and then reconciles this with the temptations by

---

that for love of us he has not refused to descend to such a low position as to bear all that belongs to our nature, included in which is ignorance."
[36]Swinburne, *Christian God*, 205.
[37]Swinburne, *Christian God*, 205 n. 14.
[38]Swinburne, *Christian God*, 207.
[39]Heb 4:15 is clear that Jesus was tempted as we are, which surely includes temptations to do wrong. The wilderness temptations are plainly acts that are wrong, including the worship of Satan instead of God (idolatry).
[40]Macleod, *Person of Christ*, 209-11.

explaining that Jesus had a humanized (or, truly and exclusively human) point of view:

> It does not follow [from impeccability and sinlessness], however, that when Christ was tempted he was always aware, at the human level, that the Tempter could never conquer him. We know that the devil could, on occasion, put a big *if* against his consciousness of sonship (Mt. 4:3). He would have found it equally easy to question his sinlessness. It would certainly be unwise to conclude that at every single point Jesus was in full possession of the whole truth about himself.[41]

Macleod warrants this explanation with the observation that Jesus' struggles against temptation give no suggestion that he relied on his impeccability. Instead, Christ seems to have relied on the resources that are generally available to all Christians facing temptation. Macleod notes three of these resources: "the company of his fellow-believers (Mk. 14:33), the word of God (Mt. 4:4) and prayer (Mk. 14:35)."[42] Moreover, Macleod repeats the pneumatological emphasis of M4, M6, and M8 by appeal to the Holy Spirit's assistance: "Deploying no resources beyond those of his Spirit-filled humanness, he faced the foe as flesh and triumphed as man."[43] The resulting picture is that Logos, remaining fully God, entered a restricted human existence in which he was dependent on God for knowledge through the Holy Spirit (just as any human),[44] and lived victoriously by his reliance as man upon the assistance God provided. Notice that Macleod marks a gap or eclipse in Christ's knowledge of the truth about himself, not that Jesus believed falsely that he could commit sin.

WILLIAM LANE CRAIG

American philosopher William Lane Craig (2003), noting his dependence on Morris and agreeing with Morris's rejection of kenotic theory, proposes that Jesus experienced a cognitive restriction to his human mind.[45] Craig explains the *mind* in Christ in terms of contemporary depth psychology, so that, as in Sanday's proposal, the full knowledge of the Logos was subliminal or

---

[41] Macleod, *Person of Christ*, 230. See also 168-69, 193-96.
[42] Macleod, *Person of Christ*, 230. I think other means of assistance may have been in play for Jesus as well: angels, the Holy Spirit, and his character formed by habits of obedience, testing, and the pursuit of righteousness.
[43] Macleod, *Person of Christ*, 220.
[44] Macleod, *Person of Christ*, 168-69.
[45] William Lane Craig, "The Incarnation", in J. P. Moreland and William Lane Craig, *Philosophical Foundations for a Christian Worldview* (Downers Grove, IL: InterVarsity, 2003), 604-09, critiques and rejects kenotic theology. Craig's proposal includes what he calls a rehabilitated Apollinarianism and Monothelitism, both of which are troubling formulations (I think he veers away from Chalcedon by failing to recognize a substantial human soul in Christ). However, M9 is not implicated because no other proponent goes down these condemned theological paths.

subconscious to the waking consciousness of Jesus while on earth. Craig appeals to hypnosis and multiple personality disorders as examples of people both knowing and not knowing things about themselves simultaneously. Craig thinks it is reasonable to explain that Jesus was both temptable and impeccable simultaneously because, in his waking consciousness as a man, he did not know he was immune to sin.

> In his conscious experience, Jesus grew in knowledge and wisdom, just as a human child does. One does not have the monstrosity of the baby Jesus lying in the manger possessing the full divine consciousness. In his conscious experience, we see Jesus genuinely tempted, even though he is, in fact, impeccable. The enticements of sin were really felt and could not be blown away like smoke; resisting temptation required spiritual discipline and moral resoluteness on Jesus' part. In his waking consciousness, Jesus is actually ignorant of certain facts, though kept from error and often supernaturally illumined by the divine subliminal. Even though the Logos possess all knowledge about the world from quantum mechanics to auto mechanics, there is no reason to think that Jesus of Nazareth would have been able to answer questions about such subjects, so low had he stooped in condescending to take on human condition.[46]

I should note a few items about Craig's view at this point. First, Craig discusses Morris's two-minds theory and rejects it in favor of Monothelitism (which corresponds to a single divine mind in Christ, as in Apollinarianism).[47] This formulation, though nuanced and qualified carefully by Craig, is not essential to M9. Theologians have repeatedly condemned both Monothelitism and Apollinarianism in the past for violating the full, true humanity of Christ. I strongly disagree with Craig on these points while I agree that a sufficient condition for temptation exists if Jesus was unaware that he was impeccable. Craig raises an important objection to the two minds theory, and we will return to this in the evaluation.

Second, I think a helpful piece that Craig has added is that there was some sort of regulation of Christ's waking consciousness to keep him from error and to illumine him with revelation while Jesus was left in the dark regarding many facts. To be tempted, perhaps he was left (or kept) in the dark regarding his impeccability. I do not agree with Craig's Apollinarianism (Christ has the mind of the Logos as his mind, not a substantial, created human mind distinct from the divine mind), so I prefer to follow Morris's two minds theory (which remains consistent with Chalcedon). As for the regulation of information in Christ's waking consciousness (or, his human mind), Craig does not explain this dynamic. My theologically informed guess is that this sort of role is appropriate to the Holy Spirit, and fully in parallel with evidence for the

---

[46]Craig, "The Incarnation", 612.
[47]Craig, "The Incarnation", 612. He thinks the two-minds theory leads to Nestorianism. I will address his critique of the two-minds theory below in the evaluation of M9.

Spirit's work in Christ and Christian experience. (We have seen this earlier in John Owen, and I will return to this proposal later.)

Third, Craig's appeal to modern depth psychology may be helpful as an analogy, but as noted earlier, this does not mean that M9 is dependent upon modern psychology. One of the dangers of speculation is that we might subordinate theology to one or another discipline, and I am wary of borrowing from psychology or philosophy in a way that leads us away from the canonical revelation of Scripture. The psychological analogy is helpful, but it should not be taken as determinative for M9. Instead, I prefer to make theological guesses at a model according to the best theological evidence based on what God has provided in Scripture (one person in two natures, impeccable and truly tempted for us).

Finally, Craig can be aligned with Macleod and O'Collins to propose Christ's simple ignorance about impeccability; Morris and Swinburne go a bit further to say Jesus held the false belief that sin was possible for him. All five proponents agree that impeccable temptation is reasonable provided some sort of eclipse occurs to limit the tempted one's knowledge.

Evaluation of M9

I have admitted that M9 is speculative and perhaps should not be presented any more strongly than as a possible explanation for how Christ can be both impeccable and truly tempted. Speculation can be dangerous because we are working with logic, analogies, and models instead of drawing directly from divine revelation. Scripture does not tell *how* Jesus was able to experience temptation as a man, so all answers to the question are speculative to one degree or another beyond what Scripture gives. The need for an explanation of the speculative sort has arisen partly because critics of Chalcedonian Christology charge that the doctrine of God incarnate is incoherent. Our concern is to consider the theological adequacy of M9 as a possible explanation that advances our theological understanding (faith seeking understanding, and not that it simply serves an apologetic purpose). At this point we may draw back from fears of speculation and consider model construction as an imperfect and uncertain but reasonable attempt to explain the evidence as best we can. We can further test the model against the evidence, particularly the relevance of Christ's temptation for us, and discover there if the model is theologically fruitful and practically beneficial.

Thus far in the evaluations, I have imagined what Gethsemane may have looked like for each model. However, that depiction of Jesus' experience according to M9 would be very close to M8, so we will not construct a different account here. One possible difference is that Morris and Swinburne see Jesus as (mistakenly) convinced that he was able to sin. I do not know how that feature would be described differently from the struggle between what seem to be live options for Jesus in Gethsemane. Whether he is convinced (mistakenly) he can sin or simply unsure about his abilities, the temptation experience remains the same in that he is a man pulled towards two opposite directions of sin and righteousness. What follows are five objections to M9.

NOT KNOWING IS NOT ENOUGH FOR *US*

The first of two objections that were also noted with M8 is that the practical value of Christ's experiences and achievements for us is cut off if Jesus was unable to sin. The relevance of someone's experience in a virtual or simulated peril is little comfort to someone in an actual peril, even if the simulation aspect is hidden during the test. As noted above, the objection is more of a complaint than charge of theological error. Starting with Scripture and making sense of it in view of what else we know, all interpreters will have to make either the assumption that Jesus could have sinned, and thereby suffered as we do (M7), or that Jesus was unaware of his immunity to sin, and thereby suffered as we do (M8-M9). I think we should protect his incarnational impeccability in view of the theological evidence for divine impeccability, divine ethical immutability, and the unity of God incarnate (according to Chalcedonian Christology). Practically and theologically, there will always be some difficulty in likening Christ's human experience to ours simply because he is different in many ways, impeccability being one aspect among other aspects, such as his preexistence, sinlessness, messianic mission, experience of the Holy Spirit, and unique sense of unity with God as his Father. The claim that Jesus, despite being God the Son, was truly tempted in all the ways that we are may be difficult to believe, but God seems to expect us to embrace and be encouraged by believing so. Moreover, I could multiply counterexamples like the one noted in the evaluation of M8 to demonstrate that it is reasonable for people to be unaware of some aspects of their situation and this does not detract from the reality of their experience or their ability to empathize meaningfully with others who endure actual perils.[48]

HOW COULD JESUS *NOT* HAVE KNOWN HE WAS IMPECCABLE?

The second objection noted above with M8 is that it is inconceivable that Jesus did not know he was impeccable. Jesus would have believed from the Old Testament that God is impeccable, and Jesus clearly believed that he was

---

[48] One contemporary example is the television show, *Survivorman* (first broadcast was 1 November 2004), in which Canadian survival expert Les Stroud intentionally inserts himself in desperate circumstances for an entire week of total isolation so that he is forced to use the available means just as if he had actually been stranded. One thing that distinguishes Stroud from other survivalist shows is that he does all his own camera work. He is utterly stranded, whether cast adrift at sea in a rubber raft or flown into a wilderness and left behind. Maybe he is a bit better off for having chosen the peril and has developed certain skills and knowledge for surviving, but is this not the same as the Son freely coming into the world and assuming human limitations as the second Adam?

essentially one with God, so the logical inference to being convinced of his own impeccability would have been inevitable.[49] I agree that such a conclusion would have been inevitable were it not for a few other considerations.

First, how did Jesus arrive at no false beliefs about physics, astronomy, etc. when he was living out an authentic human life with a potentially fallible human mind among fallible people who believed all sorts of errors about God and the world? Was Jesus constantly having to investigate and test the statements told him by his parents and others? Could Jesus have determined that the world was in fact a planetary sphere in a solar system and not an unmoving platform orbited by the sun? It seems likely that on many questions not touched by Scripture or ancient wisdom (or, in the case of astronomy, misleadingly by ancient wisdom) Jesus would have replied that he did not know for sure. Such measured agnosticism seems likely as the Holy Spirit's regulating work with Christ's fallible human mind to preclude false conclusions and lead him in whatever right conclusions were necessary for his mission. One operation of the Spirit may have been to prevent Christ's normal reasoning from reaching the conclusion that he was impeccable. Instead, the Spirit may have led him to a sort of wilderness of agnosticism and uncertainty about the topic, and Jesus simply had to respond to temptations without knowing for sure if he was vulnerable to sin or not. This ignorance (though not, I think, a mistaken belief) would have been important to preserve Christ's susceptibility to temptation, which was a major part of his mission to earn obedience and fulfill Adam and Israel's vocations.

Second, the Gospels report some gaps in his knowledge, which is consistent with Jesus not knowing that he was impeccable (so that he could be tempted). The credibility of the Gospels as authentic accounts about Jesus shows in the way that these possibly embarrassing details of the clearly professed ignorance of Jesus are reported on several occasions when he asks questions. The presence of these gaps underlines Christ's true humanity, along with the growth in his knowledge as part of normal human development (Luke 2:40, 52). Most bold is the account recorded in Mark 13:32 and Matthew 24:36, where Jesus claims not to know the time of his return, a detail that has been so uncomfortable for some copyists that they omitted his admission of ignorance.[50] The purpose of Jesus' disclosing his ignorance was to end all speculations about guessing the time; instead, he wants them to live in constant readiness.

Similarly, whether Jesus was kept from arriving at knowledge of his impeccability or that he needed revelation to be certain of it apart from empirical verification, I think it is reasonable that this was knowledge or at least certainty that he lacked so that he could remain susceptible to temptation.

---

[49]Feinberg, "The Incarnation", 241-44.
[50]The Nestle-Aland 27th edition of the Greek New Testament cites individual Vulgate manuscripts omit *nor the son* in Mark 13:32; Aleph^1, L, W, f^1, 33, Majority text, Vulgate, Syriac, Coptic, and Jerome omit *nor the son* in Matt 24:36.

There is no necessity for his mission that he arrived at and believed the conclusion that he was impeccable. Instead, his mission would have been undermined if he *did* believe he was impeccable, because to be certain that he could not sin would have set him in a much different sort of experience than others when he considered temptations, and possibly would have cut him off from even being able to experience temptation.[51] Besides, it seems that for human minds *certainty* of the sort that would preclude temptation can only be gained *a priori* through revelation. And, for a human being, revelation of this sort of unusual situation (impeccability) may still be doubtful, just as God may surely reveal the truth, but our sense of that may wax and wane according to changing circumstances. Repeated empirical testing of the theory would seem necessary for indubitable certainty *a posteriori* (which still may lead to a conclusion of probability based on empirical trials, and something less than indubitable certainty). So, perhaps Jesus was confident that having come through numerous temptations sinlessly, *he may have been* impeccable when facing these tests. But to possess human certainty of this may have required that Jesus receive special revelation from God, and, to preserve his susceptibility to temptation, God simply did not give that assurance.

Going a bit more speculative here, the likelihood of Jesus' uncertainty may be corroborated by the devil's uncertainty about Jesus' capability for sin (despite the prophecies, signs, and claims to his messiahship and divine identity). Satan was a close observer of Jesus, and was aware of the messianic prophecies beginning with the word of Satan's own doom told in Genesis 3:15. Satan seems to have been after Jesus from the time of his birth (by means of Herod), but the devil did not count the death of the Messiah as so important that he had to pursue Jesus subsequently until the wilderness three decades later in a rehearsal of the temptation of Adam (in which Adam fell). Satan (most likely) believed that Adam might have been able to fall (as he did himself) because he launched a temptation against Adam and Eve. Similarly, Satan tempted Jesus to bring about his downfall (and the ruin of God's plans in the wilderness) once God had declared Jesus as his son at the Jordan baptism. The devil (most likely) believed that Jesus might have been able to fall (as Adam did) because he attacked Jesus with three calculated temptations in the wilderness so Jesus would disobey and fall. The devil's choice to tempt Jesus indicates at least a partial belief by Satan that Jesus might be able to fall. It does not seem that the

---

[51]Every temptation I can imagine is in relation to things that are actually possible for me, or at least I believe them so, or I am uncertain that they may be possible for me. I cannot imagine being tempted and having to struggle against the desire to commit some action that I simultaneously believe is entirely impossible for me to commit (e.g., the desire to burst into flames by an act of will while I am sitting at my desk). It always seems that some shred of possibility to commit the action in view (or, some shred of uncertainty about the impossibility) accompanies the temptation. I will elaborate on this feature of temptation in my proposal.

devil would have attacked Jesus if he had been convinced that Jesus could not fall (such a defeat for Satan would have been a blow to his pride and would have offered nothing for him to gain from it—How could he succeed against God?). Thus, despite the signs of Jesus' impeccable deity in the messianic promises that required a divine figure, and the declarations of his divine Sonship by God and angels, the devil remained unsure about Jesus. This uncertainty may corroborate the M9 claim that Jesus was uncertain about his capability for sin so that he could be tempted.

A third consideration related to Jesus' certainty is that Feinberg claims that impeccable temptation is reasonable. Feinberg thinks he has demonstrated this claim in the case of a Christian believer who, being convinced theologically that she cannot apostatize because of the promises of Scripture that God's power will preserve her in faith, may yet be tempted to turn away while she is mindful of the impossibility of doing so. I disagree that anyone fully convinced of any impossibility can seriously be tempted from that quarter.[52] For example, Stephen in Acts 7 seems like a good example of full confidence in God that excluded the possibility of his wavering in temptation. The Holy Spirit bolstered his confidence (Acts 6:8 and, when he faced fiercest opposition, 7:55 specify how he was filled with the Holy Spirit), and, together with a vision of Christ in heaven, these seem to have eclipsed his susceptibility to temptation.[53] By God's provision of assurance through the Spirit, the possibility of temptation in that instance is no longer open. Relative uncertainty about a belief, as in being seventy percent sure that the airplane Jane is on will not crash allows thirty percent of uncertainty and the possibility of a temptation to worry about crashing. One hundred percent certainty would exclude any temptation in respect to that issue. In the case of Christ, M9 (and M8 also) propose that for temptation to appeal to him, Jesus had to have at least a shred of uncertainty about his capacity to sin. Feinberg denies this to claim instead that Jesus possessed one hundred percent certainty that he could never sin and still be severely tempted. I think Feinberg's claim strains credibility of a real temptation experience. If Jesus knew for certain that he could not sin, at most he could only be tempted to *wish* that he could do the thing proposed in a temptation (which experience seems less like temptation and more like my contemplation of *wishes* that I could be in two places at once or to know what others are thinking). To sum up, it seems to me that M9 is right that Jesus was prevented from knowing that he was impeccable so that he could be tempted.

---

[52]See n. 51.

[53]This is not to say that all martyrs are exempt from temptation of imminent martyrdom (indeed, the experience is probably analogous to the distress reported for Jesus in his anticipation of the cross). I mean only that Stephen seems to be specially assured by his vision of Christ in heaven, and no shreds of fear or temptation seem to touch him. He is praying for the forgiveness of his murderers—hardly the throes of temptation to defect from Christ or to blaspheme God for handing him over in this sort of execution.

IF JESUS BELIEVED HE COULD SIN, THEN JESUS BELIEVED A LIE

I have noted already that Morris and Swinburne have affirmed that Jesus, to choose freely when he was tempted, had to believe that it was possible for him to sin. The connection between believing a lie and committing a sin through that deception shows in the original human sin (Gen 3). I have trouble seeing how Jesus could hold false beliefs about moral action (his own capacity for sin) while teaching reliably about God's moral requirements. If Jesus was mistaken about the matter of his ability to sin, then what assurance do we have that he was not also mistaken about things he taught us, such as his authority to forgive sins (Matt 9:1-8)?

Crisp also marks this claim as a problem and seems to accept instead the weaker claim that Jesus was simply not aware of his impeccability during the moments of temptation.[54] Three other proponents of M9 (Macleod, O'Collins, Craig) have agreed on this weaker proposal that does not require Jesus to be humanly mistaken and believing a lie, just that he was ignorant or uncertain about this fact. I think this adjustment is right while still meeting the sufficient condition for temptation.

I think Morris's analogies can be modified in line with the weaker claim of ignorance or uncertainty about his impeccability (not false beliefs), and still satisfy the conditions for a true temptation. For example, let us return to the test of a person who must remain in a locked room without knowing the door is locked. Consider a woman, Jane, who may have gone through the test a few times before and even learned from other people that the door was locked for them, or that they got shocked with voltage when they tried to open the door. This time, Jane remains in the room with the door closed, and may consider why she would want to remain in the room, why she would want to leave, and the possibilities of whether the door is in fact locked or not. In the end, having no certainty or sure knowledge that the door is either locked or unlocked, she chooses not to try the door and remain in the room for the time. Her choice was free, she remained uncertain about the actual possibilities available to her, and all the time the possibility of leaving the room was always closed.

Similarly, Jesus may have wondered about the way that others sinned repeatedly but he had no sense of ever having done so himself. When tempted, he was always aware of the desire to obey, and always chose this, but never did he have the certainty that sin was impossible for him. He may have thought it was unlikely, in view of other experiences and assurances of his identity, but could he be *certain* that he was unable in this case? The authentically human

---

[54]Crisp, "William Shedd on Christ's Impeccability", 183-85. However, Crisp also interacts with Morris's view more favorably in "Was Christ Sinless or Impeccable?", 183 n. 32, where he writes: "Christ's temptations make sense only if he believed himself capable of making the alternative choice, and, in some sense, had the capacity to make that choice. Otherwise, as Hart and others rightly point out, the temptations are play-acting."

mindset of: "I do not know, but I am not going to try" allows enough uncertainty for him to wrestle with options of desires leading to sin and face the pressures against his free decision to obey. We see this in Gethsemane when he pleads three times for some other way than that he go to the cross. His impeccability plays no causal role in his free obedience.

Moreover, in his freedom, Jesus had to live by faith to some extent because faith is the epistemological orientation of human beings to truth. Even scientific certainty depends ultimately upon the basic beliefs such as logic and the accuracy of human perception that cannot be verified by an empirical method—these are faith claims. Thus, faith is the intrinsic human mode of knowing, and Jesus had to exercise faith as a man in some sense that is comparable to the faith that others must exercise.[55] While M9 would be theologically inadequate in the form expressed by Morris and Swinburne, the more modest claim of others that Jesus was not mistaken, only agnostic or uncertain, seems acceptable.

THE EPISTEMIC POSSIBILITY OF SIN?

No one has actually challenged this claim in the literature that uncertainty or ignorance regarding one's failure in temptation is a sufficient condition for temptation (as far as I know).[56] Since temptations occur in relation to the beliefs that one has, a mistaken belief (through misinformation or faulty reasoning) or uncertainty of belief seems to allow the same situation as if the person is actually able (metaphysical possibility) to commit the sin she believes she can do or is uncertain about being able to do (epistemic possibility). Morris and Swinburne have argued persuasively for the epistemic situation that is a sufficient condition for temptation. As with other aspects of explaining the Incarnation, we are speculating about two mysteries here: the mystery of the human will and the paradox of God incarnate.

---

[55]Even empirically-based knowledge requires faith in perception and reasoning. Basic beliefs may be provided by God, by which I mean we apprehend truth by faith in God. That Jesus lived by faith is noted by T. E. Pollard, *Fullness of Humanity: Christ's Humanness and Ours*, The Croall Lectures 1980 (Sheffield: Almond, 1982), 81-82. "Jesus is one who lives by faith in God." Pollard claims that *faith* in Heb 12:2 is *Jesus' faith*, cf. the faith of the heroes of Heb 11, not *our* faith as in ESV, RSV. The book of Hebrews bears this claim out by referring to Old Testament texts such as Isa 8:17, "I will put my trust in him"; and the description of Jesus in Heb 12:2 as the pioneer of faith, or, a full obedience of absolute trust in God. Jesus' obedience brings his faith to perfection for having trusted in God all life long. The eschatological prediction of Isa 11 shows the Messiah's faith in the way he will rule based on the Spirit's direction instead of his own perceptive powers of hearing and seeing (Isa 11:2-4).

[56]It may seem that David Werther, "Temptation of God Incarnate", 48-49, has challenged Morris on this point, but Werther actually denies that Morris's analogies allow for epistemic possibility. Werther does not refute the claim that epistemic possibility is a sufficient condition for temptation.

THE TWO-MINDS MODEL IS NESTORIAN

Craig has followed an Apollinarian model because he finds the two-minds theory of Morris to be susceptible to Nestorianism (a divisive Christological model which wrongly counts two personal subjects in Christ, one for each nature). I think the two-minds theory only appears this way if we believe that a mind (whether divine or human) is identical to a person. Instead, two minds are the means by which one the person, the self-conscious agent, possesses and experiences two distinct ranges of consciousness. Chalcedonian Christology affirms that by incarnation, God the Son adds to himself a full human nature, including a finite human mind. From that historical moment forward, God the Son simultaneously knows all things according to his deity, and he learns according to the finite perceptive powers of his humanity. The distinction of *person* from *nature* allows for the unity and distinction so that Jesus, remaining untemptable according to his divine nature, was fully susceptible to temptation according to his human nature (just as he was susceptible to suffering, faith, fear, and death).

If we recognize the difference of God incarnate from normal human experience, we may see a similarity in Jesus' dual consciousness as God and as man in the experience of a bilingual speaker. Remaining one person, the speaker may participate in two distinct linguistic worlds. Participating as a speaker of language A, the person may communicate, think according to the embedded culture inherent in each language, and relate with one group of people according to language A. Likewise, the same speaker participates as a speaker of language B, sharing in the same distinct communication, conceptual frameworks, and relational patterns of language B. Consider the two language systems as analogous to the two minds in Christ, and the one agent who speaks and thinks according to both languages as analogous to the one person of Christ who possesses and thinks according to his two minds. Now, consider how Antoinette, a bilingual speaker, happens to be sharing in a discussion in language A, listening, speaking, and thinking in that conceptual framework. During this discussion, Antoinette receives a text message from a friend who belongs to language B. While continuing to participate in the language A discussion, Antoinette simultaneously reads the language B message on her phone, thinks about and types a response to reply in a text message using the conceptual framework and communication of language B. In this sort of simultaneous multi-tasking that is possible with communication technology, we may have an analogy of the simultaneity of the Incarnation, one person possessing and functioning with two minds simultaneously as God and man.[57]

---

[57]An adjustment to the analogy that might fit broader experience is how many people are able to share in a conversation while reading (which could be frustrating as a divided attention to the conversation partner, but it does mimic a simultaneous and dual cognitive experience). A qualifier is in order here. Despite the clarity of Scripture, Jesus' psychology is not stressed in the Gospels. We should be careful not to reduce him to the

CONCLUSION

M9 focuses on explaining the temptation of an impeccable person. Jesus Christ was unable to sin, but he was able to suffer temptation as a man because he was mistaken or unsure about his capability to sin. His impeccable perfection and acquired empathy with us for having been repeatedly tempted in severe ways can be affirmed as twin truths. Jesus is the focus of our faith salvation and the particular pattern of a true human being who consistently chooses to obey God when tempted to sin.

I should also note that M7-M9 are narrowly focused on particular aspects of the temptation problem. For evaluating the theological adequacy of M9 (as with M7 and M8), I am weighing how the model's suitability for what it affirms—that human temptation can occur for an impeccable Godman, while I recognize that by itself, M9 (no more than M7 or M8) does not give a total picture of Jesus' temptation and sinlessness. That said, I think M9 is theologically adequate for the particular focus it addresses and judge it worthwhile for a broader synthesis that I propose below.

Conclusion to the Theological Models

The variety of the models—each having been conceived as an explanation of the same biblical evidence—suggests that the relevant biblical data does not lock in or determine a particular, exclusive way of thinking about Christ's impeccability and temptation. The same biblical passages can be consistent with more than one of the models. Nonetheless, in my fallible evaluation, each of the models explains the biblical evidence in a way that either limits or undermines one or more aspects of revelation about Christ. For example, M7 diminishes Jesus' deity and denies his impeccability. M9 gives away Jesus' full self-awareness and some proponents suggest that he could have held false beliefs about his moral capabilities. M1-M3, and M5 diminish Jesus' authentic humanity by deifying his human nature or his human operation. M5 and M6 diminish the extent of Jesus' temptations by denying that his flesh was an internal avenue of temptation. M1-M3 diminish the degree of his temptations by setting divine causation in the forefront so that the temptations are merely didactic performances commenced without the pressure and strain that the biblical evidence tells. Thus curtailing Christ's likeness in temptations, M1-M3, M5, and M6 undermine the relevance of Jesus' experiences in temptation and

---

proportions of a self-conscious subject comparable to (fallen) humanity as we experience and observe it. We must remember that Jesus is unique as fully divine and fully human, a divine-human Savior. It is difficult to imagine the experience of one person in two natures with two minds (and wills). Scholars have no way of knowing with certainty what Jesus' human awareness was in relation to his ability to sin, or how he functioned as one person with two minds. God has not told us. Reasonable theological guesses may be fruitful even if we must admit that we cannot know for sure.

sinlessness.

The relation between Jesus' two natures remains a problem for this topic in two ways. First, for models that explain Christ's sinlessness as having been caused by his divine nature or person (M1-M3), the problem is how to explain the relevance of his human experiences for others. If incommunicable deity determined his outcome of sinlessness, then his empathy and example for others are diluted. Second, for models that explain Jesus' sinlessness as having been accomplished within his limitations as a man, without divine necessity playing a factor (M4-M9), the problem is how to explain the restraint of divine causation. For M4-M9 that affirm Jesus' sinlessness as a human accomplishment despite his being divine, the problem remains how to explain such perfection in a way that he is both a reasonable pattern for others and a reliable savior who is sinless forever. These models deny that Christ's divine nature was a causal factor in his sinlessness, but the problem remains how to explain his sinlessness without compromising his uniqueness among others who are merely human. M5 employs the concept of created grace, but the claim that Jesus possessed the beatific vision is implausible (and contradicts Christ's experiences of distress, as in Gethsemane). Created grace also drains out the personal operation of the Holy Spirit's work, with a remainder that seems like a sort of impersonal magical residue. M6 provides the veiling principle as a possible explanation of true human accomplishment, but does not give adequate explanation. In other words, we can easily see how M6 distinguishes the reason Jesus could not sin (impeccability) from the reason he did not sin (grace-empowered resistance to temptation). What is less easy to see is how divine impeccability played no role in his resistance to temptation. This problem was partially addressed by some proponents of M8 and M9 by recourse to the work of the Holy Spirit or kenotic limitation. Finally, M7 purports to solve the problem of M6 by means of ascribing peccability to Christ. This peccability move was shown to violate the incarnational unity and the traditional understanding of the divine nature.

When all things are considered, I have found M9 to be part of the best explanation of the biblical and theological evidence (as we understand it) for Christ's impeccability, temptation, and sinlessness. This is especially so when the formulation is enhanced to employ M2, M4, and M6 for different aspects of the problem. Moreover, the lingering weakness of M6 is the absence of an explanation for *how Christ's deity was veiled* to allow the full, true experience of his humanity. Pneumatological Christology may solve this problem (as proposed by some contributors to M8 and M9).

My response to the nine models of Christ's impeccability and temptation follows in the next chapter. I am not trying to put something entirely new on the table or propose ideas that have never been suggested. Instead, I offer a fresh analysis of temptation and an explanation of the impeccable savior's great task of being tempted for us. I will restate what I have found to be the most helpful theological formulations for explaining this question.

SYSTEMATIC FORMULATION

CHAPTER 10

Jesus Could not Fail

What follows is my response to the biblical revelation and the theological models we have excavated and evaluated up to this point. I will argue for three primary claims and employ the wisdom of several theological models to construct a contemporary picture of Christ's impeccability, temptation, and sinlessness. The questions are complementary to distinguish and encompass the two basic aspects of the picture. The answers must not be merged or exchanged because then we would be trying to fit a round peg into a square hole, and vice versa. Seeing the harmony of all the relevant biblical revelation depends upon recognizing that the way Jesus was unable to sin was *not* the same way that he achieved sinlessness. In this way, we can arrive at a total picture of his impeccability, temptation, and sinlessness.

The first claim is that Jesus was unable to sin because he is the Godman. I will draw upon M1, M2, and M3 as warrants to explain the question of *why Jesus could not sin*. While these models proved theologically inadequate to explain Christ's temptation and sinlessness, they are useful for explaining his impeccability as the answer to the first question (the round peg in the round hole). I will address three common objections related to the first claim.

Second, I will argue that Jesus was truly tempted as we are tempted due to the work of the Holy Spirit. M6 will be the prominent contribution that I will seek to enhance and extend.

The third claim is that Jesus achieved sinlessness as a man helped by grace, not by relying on his divine impeccability. I will draw upon M4, M6, and M9 to explain *how Jesus did not sin* and achieved human righteousness (without the help of his inherent divine powers). I will address two concepts that are helpful to clarifying matters: the meaning of temptation and the Holy Spirit's role in the Messiah's life to enable his temptation and empower his sinlessness (the square peg in the square hole).

Jesus Christ, the Impeccable Godman

In the evaluation of M1, M2, and M3, I argued that all three are theologically inadequate as explanations for how Jesus achieved sinlessness. The models are right and helpful, however, to connect Christ's deity with his impeccability as the ultimate limit on his action as a man so that he never commits sin. This limit is apparent from the perspective of heaven, that is, in God's view and perhaps the watching angels who know that Jesus of Nazareth is the Logos. The limit is a metaphysical impossibility of sin that nonetheless exists without causing or influencing Jesus' free action as a man. The reality of this limit is adequately explained according to M2 and M3. M1 is less adequate to this need because the simple claim that "Jesus could not sin because he is God" begs for the detail of how *being God* limited or excluded what sorts of action he was able to do as a man (no sinful actions, including intentions).[1] Thus, we will focus on M2 and M3 as employed in a particular way for the first question only, *not* as they were originally intended in patristic theology to explain sinlessness as well.

First, according to the union of his two natures (M2), it is impossible that Jesus would be able to act through his human nature in a way that contradicts the necessary goodness (impeccability) of his divine nature. Chalcedonian Christology excludes the separation between the natures that would have to take place for God to sin as a man. Because Jesus is one person uniting the two natures to him, the human nature must be consistent with the impeccability of the divine nature (since both share a common moral reality).[2] Here we need to distinguish impeccability from sinlessness, and affirm that his impeccability is grounded in his divine nature (through deification or nature-perichoresis of the divine nature being present in the human nature without transforming it, see the evaluation of M2) while this union does not cause his sinlessness. The main reason for denying M2 as an account of his sinlessness is that Christ's relevance is severely diminished as a true man suffering temptation and forging ahead of us in obedience. Moreover, Scripture indicates a better explanation for his sinlessness than M2.

Second, according to the personal action of the Logos through his human nature (M3), it is unimaginable that Jesus would be able to act as a man in a way that contradicts his divine will or his Father's command. Jesus was impeccable because he is the eternal Son of God, but, as we saw in the evaluation of M3, if his human conformity to God's will had been the basis and cause of his human sinlessness, then the credibility of his relevance for us would be undermined. His human choices could not have been intrinsically determined and wrought by his divine will if they were to be choices made in our place in a way that we can follow his pattern. His human will must be free to choose right without divine constraint if he is to fulfill redemption as a man.

---

[1] M1 is an example of a bare explanation that can be given and grasped by a child or a new believer, like a first glance at the question that can be satisfied simply. Certainly there is value in such explanations even if they cannot remain adequate for maturing believers who need more detail and can understand complicated accounts of complex reality.

[2] See below for the objection of why impeccability is realized for the human nature in the union, but not other divine attributes of omniscience, omnipotence, etc.

Scripture indicates a more adequate account of his sinlessness than M3 provides.

Therefore, M2 and M3 are properly counted here as resources for explaining Christ's impeccability as a man because of the incarnational union (but not his sinlessness). The models are misleading and inadequate as explanations of his sinlessness because their value is to define why sin was not possible for Jesus, not to specify *how* he freely chose righteousness. (By analogy, we would not say that God is always righteous because he cannot sin, but that he freely chooses to do good according to his will and purposes.) Both models rely upon the same warrants that support the claim that God is impeccable (or, God's necessary goodness) and especially as the conjunct of his omnipotence, immutability, holiness, eternality, and love. As a person who remains essentially impeccable no matter what accidental nature he assumes, the Son of God remained impeccable when he entered the human race as Jesus of Nazareth. I should add that this claim has been the unanimous recognition of Christian tradition until very recently. So, at least on the aspect of claiming that Jesus was unable to sin because he is God (but not that his impeccability was causal for his sinlessness), I am not proposing anything new.

Having become a true man, he is also a unique human being because he is the impeccable Godman. Alongside the numerous likenesses of Jesus as a man to other human beings, impeccability by his deity marks his uniqueness as the man who cannot sin. Despite his need for the Holy Spirit to empower him in sinless action, Jesus is not simply a divinely empowered human, as if he were *merely* a man and nothing else. Jesus is uniquely and *fully* human because he is the eternal Logos and Son of God who assumed the stuff of human nature at the incarnation.[3] Jesus is not merely a human being because his human nature exists in a unique relationship to his divinity that protects him from the danger of normal human peccability. Despite the parallels that are apparent between Jesus' experience of empowering grace and the experience that other people have, Jesus' life can never be explained in terms of being merely a man who enjoyed a greater degree of the Holy Spirit's influence and power. Jesus' human experience was unique as the Godman. Our recognition of his impeccability allows us to see how the integrity of his human nature and divine nature has been preserved—he has not ceased to be impeccable God when we became a temptable man. Corollaries to this point are the soteriological tasks that depend on Jesus' uniqueness as one person who is both a man and the divine Son—revealing God, reconciling humanity to God, and giving the Holy Spirit to the church. When he acts sinlessly as a man, Jesus is simply being true to the whole reality of what he is, and yet these acts are freely chosen according to his life in our frame of experience.

---

[3] The helpful distinctions between *merely* and *fully* as applied to Christ's humanity are from Morris, *Logic of God Incarnate*, 65-67. By "stuff of human nature" I mean a human body and rational human soul, including mind, will, and emotional faculties.

Three common objections may be raised against the claim for Christ's impeccability. For some people, these objections are strong enough to call the claim into question, so I will provide replies to meet the challenges while acknowledging that a certain amount of mystery hangs over the entire topic and some things are just inscrutable to us (but that does not mean our quest for understanding should be abandoned).

Why Impeccable But Not Omniscient, Omnipotent, etc.?

I noted above that among the divine attributes, impeccability somehow stretches across the incarnational union or has an echo in the human nature while it seems that some other attributes do not. For example, Jesus did not express his divine omnipresence, omnipotence, and omniscience in his human course on earth. If he was restricted to corporeal presence, able to suffer and die, and if he was able to be ignorant of certain facts, then why was he not also vulnerable to commit sin (peccable)? The objection has two sides that I will deal with in order: why were other divine attributes blocked or otherwise not carrying over in his human life, and why did impeccability uniquely persist in his human experience?

To distinguish the divine attributes in this way is not to say that the Son gave up these attributes to become incarnate, but that he retained them without using them in his human existence, bearing what seem to be contradictory attributes according to his two natures.[4] The issue is not to say whether or not Jesus possessed these attributes, but whether or not they were present (tacitly, as with impeccability) *in his human nature* by a sort of nature-perichoresis that did not

---

[4]The idea is that contradictory attributes may be predicated of Jesus coherently according to his humanity and according to his deity is argued by O'Collins, *Christology*, 234: "It would be a blatant contradiction in terms to attribute to the same subject at the same time *and under the same aspect* mutually incompatible properties. But that is not being done here. With respect to his divinity Christ is omniscient, but with respect to his humanity he is limited in knowledge. Mutually exclusive characteristics are being simultaneously attributed to him but not within the same frame of reference." The similar idea is stated as *two conditions of existence* by Brian Hebblethwaite, *The Incarnation: Collected Essays in Christology* (Cambridge: Cambridge University Press, 1987). See also Kathryn Tanner, *Jesus, Humanity and the Trinity* (Minneapolis: Fortress, 2001), 16: "Better to think of divinity and humanity not in terms of isolable, discrete qualities that divide up Jesus' life and person, but as what characterize Jesus' life overall, as a whole. Jesus' life as a whole is both divine and human but on different levels or planes of reality, one being the source of the other. Jesus leads a fully human existence but this existence is the result of the assumption of Jesus' humanity by the Word. Because they occur on different planes, so to speak – the leading of a human life on the horizontal plane, the assumption of this whole plane of a human life by the Word on a vertical plane – they neither supplement nor replace one another."

change or deify his humanity. When we say that Jesus remained necessarily good (impeccable) as a man, this is not attributing a positive power to him, but recognizing that all sinful choices were closed to him as a man just as they were closed to him as God the Son. That is much different from saying that Jesus remained omniscient in his humanity, which would mean he could not have failed to know any fact that God knows.

IF IMPECCABILITY, THEN WHY NOT OTHER ATTRIBUTES?

Scripture is clear that the incarnation occurred because the Son, having become the Godman, could only deliver us if he possessed both deity and humanity (Heb 2:14-18). Only God can save us from sin, death, and the devil, but even God can only do so by becoming one of us.[5] As regards his redemptive need to be true God and true man, we can see that, had there occurred a nature-perichoresis or communication of attributes from his deity to his humanity, certain divine attributes would have made redemption impossible (but this is not the case for impeccability, see below).[6] For example, omnipotence would have prevented the Son from suffering the punishment for sin in his human death on the cross. Omnipresence would have been inconsistent with his humanity as a corporeal creature living credibly and truly among others to recapitulate Adam and Israel, to learn empathy by firsthand experience, and to become a pattern for all believers to follow. Omniscience would have precluded him from accomplishing all of the same tasks as omnipresence, and (as I have argued in M9) would have cut him off from being able to experience temptation. If the sufficient condition for an impeccable Christ to be tempted were that he lacks certainty or is clouded from knowing (in his human mind) his capacity for doing sin, then omniscience would prevent him from fulfilling his redemptive tasks. As one person in two natures, Jesus could possess the fullness of both natures, but attributes of the natures cannot be communicated from one to the other without violating the authenticity of each. Chalcedonian Christology marks that there is no change or confusion of the natures. Therefore, adding to him an existence that is finite in power, presence, and knowledge as we are was redemptively necessary, and so these divine attributes had to be veiled or restrained from coming through in his human nature.

---

[5]Effective reconciliation between sinful humanity and God can only take place through the mediation of one who is both God and man. As God, the Son possesses the power, love, and holy innocence to enter the human race freely and blamelessly as savior (he is not implicated with Adam's guilt for sin). In becoming a man, the Son achieves righteousness for us by his perfect human obedience to God, and he can offer himself as the divine-human sacrifice to pay for our sin, one for all. Redemption required his dual possession of humanity and deity, and employing the powers of both natures.

[6]I will only deal with three divine attributes for comparison to impeccability.

WHY THE EXCEPTION FOR IMPECCABILITY?

The exception among other divine attributes seems to be impeccability, which shows up in both natures for Christ. Why is this so? Impeccability need not be a communication from deity to humanity, but is dually present for him because he is one person who must be impeccable in whatever mode of existence he undertakes. Other divine attributes contradict true humanity, but impeccability does not, just as we are confident that in the resurrection, glorified saints will be impeccable forever.[7] Moreover, the alternative of peccability is potentially disastrous for the Son's success in redemption and our understanding of God (as noted above, in the evaluation of M7). A few other things can be said about the uniqueness of sin and morality compared to knowledge, power, and presence.

The vulnerability to do an act of sin (or, alternately, to fail to do right) is not simply a restraint of divine power but is impossible for God as a self-contradiction.[8] Other common human limitations that contradict divine attributes are problematic and seem unfitting for God (such as finite knowledge and local presence), but only sin is part of a moral dimension of reality. Morality is a dimension of human reality that overlaps or shares in God's moral goodness. Thus, human sin always has a reference point in the divine standard of moral goodness that sin violates. Human sin takes place in the setting of this relationship and has ramifications beyond the human sphere of action. The unique transcendence of sin shows in the way that God is obligated by his own moral righteousness to punish human sin and cannot simply ignore evil acts (e.g., Hos 9:9).

When we consider Jesus, sin, and impeccability, we can adopt the helpful distinction that he exists as fully divine and fully human in two frames of reference (simultaneously).[9] Among all his possible experiences in his divine and human frames of reference, sin uniquely transcends the distinction of his two natures in such a way that were Jesus to commit sin as a man, he would implicate God with sin. Conversely, because of the unity of God incarnate, he

---

[7] In the new heavens and earth, sin will be abolished, as indicated by the abolition of the consequences of death, grief, and pain that stem from original sin (Rev 21:4). Unlike the present state of affairs in a fallen creation, the new creation will be characterized by the absence of these consequences because of the absence of sin. This eschatological promise implies the impeccability of glorified believers who will never sin and possibly bring about the conditions of a world wracked with death, grief, and pain as we now have it.

[8] I recognize pre-fall, fallen, and regenerated humanity here as sharing the vulnerability to sin. Fallen humanity is enslaved to sin (unable to do other than commit sin, Rom 6:16-17). The similar ideas are included here of sin as disobedience, rebellion, transgression, and missing the mark of moral perfection in any act, thought, emotion, or intention.

[9] See ch. 7 above for the helpful concept denoted as *Logos extra carnem* and the *extra calvinisticum*.

is completely unable to commit sin because of his necessary goodness as God. Therefore, the idea that God incarnate could rebel against God is incoherent for the same reason that God cannot sin: sin is a violation of God's standard for the conduct of moral agents.

A further problem that marks off sin from other common human weaknesses that are evident in Jesus is that sin is improper and impure for humanity. For example, when we compare the vulnerability to fail to do right (peccability) with finite knowledge that is the vulnerability to fail to know a fact that God knows, it is possible for God incarnate in a human condition of existence to possess human intellect because discursive, finite knowledge is proper and pure by God's design for human beings. Sin (entailed by peccability as a possibility) is neither proper nor pure by God's design.[10] Perfect humanity as demonstrated in Christ is pure from sin (just as glorified humanity is impeccable). Sinfulness became a common human attribute historically with the sin of the first man; this initial sin (and all subsequent sin) was a rebellion against God's design. By contrast, attributes such as limited knowledge and passibility are not morally culpable because they are the normal, created characteristics of finite, contingent creatures. Thus, God the Son could condescend to experience finite knowledge in his human frame of reference, but he could not condescend to commit sin or even be vulnerable to commit such a culpable failure to do right. In other words, righteous human existence (with all of its proper creaturely limitations) is compatible with a divine incarnation, but sinful human existence is not.[11] God cannot tolerate sin, either in a second, assumed condition of existence by incarnation or by his relationship with the human beings he has

---

[10]The same conclusion is recognized by Lewis Sperry Chafer, *Systematic Theology* (Dallas: Dallas Seminary Press, 1948), 5:78. "The contention that Christ *could*, but *would not*, sin is far removed from the contention that Christ *could not* sin. The former either denies his Deity or else dishonors God with the calumnious averment that God is Himself capable of sinning. Again, it must be declared that Christ's human traits which did not involve moral issues could be exhibited freely. The idea might be admitted with certain reservations that he was both omnipotent and impotent, omniscient and ignorant, infinite and finite, unlimited and limited; but it could never be allowed that He was both impeccable and peccable. There are no God-dishonoring elements in human weakness, human pain, human hunger, human thirst, or human limitations with respect to various capacities—even human death may be admitted as a death undergone for others, but not for Himself." Chafer's qualifier on death is important because death is not proper for humanity, but death as a vicarious sacrifice is praiseworthy and is obviously predicable of God in his humanity. Christ's experience of these weaknesses, pains, and death is voluntary and vicarious to redeem a fallen creation, not deserved for personal sin or a share in original sin.

[11]The helpful analysis by Crisp, "Did Christ have a *Fallen* Human Nature?", 270-88, excludes the possibility that the incarnation could involve the Son in the corruption or guilt that come with original sin because corruption of fallen humanity is inseparable from the guilt of original sin.

created. The distinction between the two natures and their distinct frames of reference prevents the contradiction between God's divine omniscience and his human limitation, but no resolution of the contradiction of sin seems possible.[12]

Therefore, the exception of impeccability to be recognized in the Godman's humanity among other divine attributes that are excluded is justified. However, a divine incarnation that does not result in transformation of the human by the divine is difficult to avoid without a special explanation for maintaining the integrity of his two natures. A restraint on the divine powers seems necessary in some way to preserve the integrity of his humanity as an authentic finite nature on our scale. For example, Christ's divine omniscience had to be restrained from his human mind for him to become relevant for other human beings in his empathy and pattern for their experience in temptation. The need for regulation of some sort of boundary between the natures in the union works both ways to prevent the transformation of his humanity (as in Eutychianism, the heresy that the human nature was absorbed by the Son's deity) and the degradation of his deity. The second movement of degrading deity is less plausible because of divine immutability, but in theory, a personal union that is maintained without any flow of attributes in either direction implies some sort of preservation of at least the lesser, mutable nature from being transformed or destroyed in union with the infinite God. I will propose below that the Holy Spirit may have facilitated the prominence of Jesus' human nature and preserved the integrity of his two natures.

If He is Impeccable, How Is Jesus Free?

Medieval and modern theologians have been concerned to preserve Jesus' human moral freedom that in earlier models seems to be limited or diminished by the affirmation of his impeccability. Philosophers of religion are particularly troubled about the compossibility of these two affirmations of impeccability and freedom concerning Jesus and God. For example, Keith Yandell writes that impeccability would cut off Jesus' freedom: "*Being necessarily good* precludes any such scope of freedom."[13] In response, I will argue that impeccable freedom is reasonable for a man and God.

---

[12]Similar contradictions between non-moral divine and human attributes (e.g., omnipotence and impotence, omnipresence and local presence) prove to be only apparent conflicts if the integrity of the two natures in two frames of reference is maintained. See n. 4 above.

[13]Keith E. Yandell, "Divine Necessity and Divine Goodness", in *Divine and Human Action: Essays in the Metaphysics of Theism,* ed. Thomas V. Morris (Ithaca, NY: Cornell University Press, 1988), 333. Cf. Werther, "Temptation of God Incarnate", 47-50; Hart, "Sinlessness and Moral Responsibility: A Problem in Christology", 37-54.

THE POSSIBILITY OF BEING IMPECCABLY FREE AS A MAN

In narrow examples, the combination of impeccability and freedom is not so uncommon among human beings as we might think. We may observe that the physical capacity to commit sin is frequently nullified in practice by the subjective factors of an individual's belief structure and will. The result is that such possible sins are plainly impossible for certain individuals because of the strong stability of the will and character (including one's belief structure). In this way, people may be tempted in relation to these sins (while remaining free) but these individuals are functionally impeccable in relation to those specific sins. For example, a loving mother is *functionally* or *virtually impeccable* in relation to the sin of torturing her children.[14] The action is logically possible but functionally, subjectively, and practically impossible *for her* because of the developed structure of the mother's character and her relation to the children, including all her beliefs, will, and commitments that will restrain her from carrying out the act. No state of affairs exists in which a loving mother in her right mind tortures her young children to death.[15] Such an act can never be justified and perpetrated by a loving mother. Nonetheless, her functional impeccability does not nullify her temptability and struggle against the momentary desires to torture her children, just her practical ability to do so. Many mothers may be exasperated with their children and sin by their intention to commit some harm, but they would never be able to act upon the intention.[16] Thus, the example shows that humans may be constituted unable to perform certain sins (that is, the are unable to fail to do right), and yet remain free and temptable in relation to those evil acts. The freedom may be deep in a person's pattern of choices to commit to another person, as in this case, to love a child.

That Jesus was impeccable is then not so strange or disqualifies him from a normal human experience. He may have developed into a functional impeccability in his humanity and simply experienced this boundary of goodness in a complete, perfected way that others know in a partial way. His capacity for free acts remains intact, but his ability to fulfill them is blocked from within (and this barrier being totally consistent with his divine impeccability but is not caused by it). For example, Jesus may have had the

---

[14]Likewise, loving fathers are functionally impeccable in relation to the same sin.

[15]Some may object that the mother may succumb to the temptation if torturing her children was a necessary condition to save her own life or the world, as in the case of the barbarous, cannibalistic women of northern Israel who devoured their own children during an enemy siege (2 Kgs 6:28-29). In this example, the mothers have fallen from being loving mothers, and loved their own well-being before their children. These unusual exceptions do not disprove the rule in practice that can be multiplied with examples of the way many people do not and will never perpetrate specific evils that are logically possible for them but functionally impossible because of other considerations that are subjective.

[16]Sadly, some mothers do abuse their children, but doing so would mean the mother had ceased to be both a loving mother and one in her right mind.

physical capacity to commit certain sins such as telling a lie, but he was functionally impeccable because of the strong stability of his beliefs, his will, and the dynamic presence of the Holy Spirit that prevented him internally from committing those sins—all within his human frame of reference and without recourse to his divine impeccability. His sinlessness was achieved as a man, even though such was guaranteed but not influenced or determined by his deity.

We can see that Jesus' impeccable temptability was unusual, but not exceptional. He was unable to sin in every way, but many people are normally unable to sin in several ways. For example, a man's fortitude of character may prevent him from committing adultery (though not inhibit him from lust); another man's fear of retaliation may prevent him from stabbing an enemy (though not from relishing the wicked wish and hating the other man). The principle is that impeccability in relation to a specific sin does not disqualify a human being from experiencing temptation to sin and choosing freely to resist it.

Moreover, Jesus' sinlessness includes his never intending to commit sin (unlike the examples above). We must affirm that Jesus was unable to commit even the sins of intention or imagination (e.g., lust and greed). Nonetheless, as a man, Jesus could have been fully unable to sin and yet face the struggle of overcoming his desire for self-preservation (perhaps by turning stones into bread) in preference to his desire to obey God. We see exactly this sort of struggle in Gethsemane, where Jesus feels the press of the temptation with the desire to avoid the punishment for the world's sin. Even the possibility of intending to choose the impossible course of action to flee the cross was absolutely closed to Jesus, but he was tempted thoroughly and had to struggle to choose obedience with suffering instead. We have no evidence that Jesus was constrained to do right, in parallel with the way that Christians are not constrained to believe. However, in each case of the comparison, there is no uncertainty for God regarding both Jesus' righteousness and a Christian's belief while allowing for their significant freedom as human beings.

Therefore, the charge that impeccability cuts off Jesus' freedom is not sufficient to turn us back. On the contrary, we can see that Jesus' impeccable freedom as a man is the model of glorified humanity as forever free and impeccable to share in God's absolute liberty to do only right.

DIVINE IMPECCABILITY AND FREEDOM

The compossibility of Jesus' freedom and impeccability is no different in principle from the problem of freedom and impeccability for God. Critics claim that God is not significantly free if his impeccability restrains him from doing other than the good he does and prevents him from doing evil. For example, Vincent Brümmer charges: "[An impeccable God] would then be more like an infallibly 'constituted' machine, only able to behave in accordance with the way it is made, than like a person freely deciding what to do or not to do."[17] Bruce Reichenbach agrees: "If God's goodness is predicated on the basis of his nature, then the notion of good as applied to God loses its ethical dimension."[18] Nonetheless, this supposed conflict between God's nature and freedom is misleading because God's moral action is what he wills freely in a way that expresses and defines his moral nature.[19] Antonie Vos argues that God has freedom with regard to many things—including morality and goodness—along with his impeccability:

> Nevertheless, from God's essential being as the ultimate moral standard it does not follow that He cannot will and act freely nor that his character works as a constraint. From the infinite set of his real synchronic alternatives only the sinful ones are precluded by the necessary elements of his goodness. On the contingency level of good things and divine commands some goods are synchronically variable and some are diachronically variable too, as the history of the observance of the Sabbath and Sunday shows. So there is no constraint and no lack of freedom; the essence of divine goodness constitutes the value of divine acts and presents marginal conditions by the intrinsic preclusion of God's being unreliable or his being simply evil.[20]

Also helpful on this point is the explanation of Carl F. H. Henry:

> It is obvious enough that unless there is an ultimate ethical tension in the being of God, the Divine nature and will cannot be thought of as in competition with each other, but as morally identical. From this standpoint the good is conformity to God's being and to his will. But the nature of God must not be regarded as necessarily good in the sense that it gains its goodness independently of his will, nor that his good nature determines his will so that the will bows to the good by a sort of pantheistic inevitability. The good is what God wills, and what he freely wills. The good is what the Creator-Lord does and commands. He is the creator of the moral law, and defines its very nature. . . . The moral activity of God is a closer definition of his nature.

Morris notes that among philosophers, most theists favor a libertarian view of freedom (liberty of indifference) such that God is only free (e.g., to keep a promise) if he could have done otherwise (e.g., to fail to keep a promise). Morris argues that God has *significant* freedom—even in a libertarian sense— when God chooses to make a promise (e.g., to give Abraham an heir), and

---

[17]Vincent Brümmer, "Divine Impeccability", *Religious Studies* 20 (1984): 212-13.
[18]Reichenbach, *Evil and a Good God*, 138. Cf. Robert F. Brown, "God's Ability to Will Moral Evil", *Faith and Philosophy* 8 (1991): 13.
[19]Carl F. H. Henry, *Christian Personal Ethics* (Grand Rapids: Eerdmans, 1957), 213.
[20]Antonie Vos, "The Possibility of Impeccability", in *Christian Faith and Philosophical Theology: Essays in Honor of Vincent Brümmer*, ed. Gijsbert van den Brink, Luco J. van den Brom, and Marcel Sarot (Kampen, NL: Kok Pharos, 1992), 237.

when God chooses to fulfill the promise in a particular way (e.g., he could have given Abraham another son than Isaac).[21] The point is that God is free to have done otherwise than as he did in respect to everything in creation because all things that he wills are contingent upon his free decision to create, to sustain, to promise, and to redeem.[22] While all these free choices could have been otherwise, God's choices are consistent with but not necessarily caused by God's goodness. Thus, on a libertarian view of divine freedom, the case seems to be that God has freedom to choose from among several moral actions while evil actions are unavailable to him.

The other option here, the liberty to choose according to one's will and nature, is an easier account of God's freedom and impeccability (as in the quotation of Carl Henry, above). God freely chooses his goodness, and immutably remains so in all his choosing forever.

Those who object that freedom and inability to sin are inconsistent, betray a mistaken assumption that the freedom to will evil is a good thing to have, but few (if any) will admit that the counterexample of freedom to will one's non-existence is a desirable thing to have. Instead, God is greater for his impeccability and not diminished by his inability to do the things that finite creatures can do (such as to will evil, forget thoughts, or scratch his left ear) because the fullness of God's perfection precludes these deficiencies.[23] It may be the case that we are so frail that we may fail to choose and do right, but God never falls short to fail in any action. Peccability is no power, but a shortcoming and degradation of the freedom to choose rightly.

Thus, God's freedom to do many things otherwise than to will evil is consistent with his perfection and essential goodness. The inability of God—and God incarnate—to do otherwise than good does not count against his real freedom to choose good immutably. Brian Hebblethwaite properly draws the parallel between God's impeccable freedom and Christ's impeccable freedom:

> Significant freedom is not always a matter of choice between good and evil. God's freedom is not like that, nor is the freedom of the blessed in heaven who have passed beyond the sphere of temptation. Christ's freedom to act in ways that were always good is to that extent like the freedom of the blessed in heaven. But, unlike theirs, it was exercised on earth and thereby subject to temptation to go astray. Where the rest of us are concerned, there is no guarantee that temptation will always be resisted. . . . But Christ's being who he was, the incarnate Son of

---

[21]Thomas V. Morris, *Anselmian Explorations: Essays in Philosophical Theology* (Notre Dame, IN: University of Notre Dame Press, 1987), 27-29.

[22]According to Gordon Clark, this point is observed by Duns Scotus that God's external acts (but not his acts *ad intra*) contain the possibility of a different choice that might have been made and was not caused by his necessary goodness. Gordon H. Clark, *Thales to Dewey: A History of Philosophy* (Boston: Houghton Mifflin, 1957), 287-88.

[23]Cf. the Anslemian intuition of God's maximal perfection in all great-making properties, elaborated by Morris in *Anselmian Explorations*.

God, did guarantee that temptation, however acute, would be resisted. But that did not make him less than human, any more than the absence of temptation makes the blessed in heaven less than human. To suppose that incarnation involves the real possibility of succumbing to temptation is no more theologically plausible than to suppose that sin belongs to the essence of being human.[24]

If He is Impeccable, How Is Jesus Praiseworthy?

As with freedom, some philosophers question if even God can be both praiseworthy and impeccable, much less Christ. For example, Brümmer writes: "If Yahweh is in this way [by his necessary impeccability] powerless to deviate from his character, he could hardly be praised for not doing so."[25] Stephen Davis agrees: "If God's nature causes or determines him to do good in such a way that doing evil is not in his power, I would conclude that he is not a free and responsible moral agent and thus is not a fit object of the praise and thanks of his people."[26] Nelson Pike suggests that God's goodness is contingent upon dynamic divine freedom because otherwise God would not be morally praiseworthy.[27] Pike's intuition that God is indeed praiseworthy for his goodness requires that God must have been able to do otherwise (commit evil). Thus, Pike concludes that because God cannot be both praiseworthy and impeccable, he must be peccable (contingently good, not necessarily good).

In response, we may recall that a necessarily good God who condescends to create, sustain, and redeem a world is morally praiseworthy for doing all of this freely because he could have done either none of it at all, or all of it differently, and this is compossible with his essential goodness. Thus, God is praiseworthy for the good things he freely chooses to do because nothing obligates him to do any one of them. Indeed, God was alone when he chose to create, so he was entirely free in his solitary goodness.

Moreover, God is also praiseworthy as a model for others who do not share his maximal perfection.[28] He is the ideal of goodness and all else that is worth praising. This second type of praise due to God despite impeccability is readily apparent to Paul Helm: "There could clearly be the praise of admiration and recognition to a God for whom it is logically impossible to do evil. For such a God can be praised for what he is, by analogy with the way in which certain

---

[24]Cf. Brian Hebblethwaite, *Philosophical Theology and Christian Doctrine* (Malden, MA: Blackwell, 2005), 70.

[25]Brümmer, "Divine Impeccability", 213.

[26]Stephen T. Davis, *Logic and the Nature of God* (Grand Rapids: Eerdmans, 1983), 95.

[27]Nelson Pike, "Omnipotence and God's Ability to Sin", in *Divine Commands and Morality,* ed. Paul Helm (Oxford: Oxford University Press, 1981), 68-69. Pike attributes this argument to C. B. Martin, *Religious Belief* (Ithaca, NY: Cornell University Press, 1964).

[28]Joshua Hoffman, "Can God Do Evil?" *Southern Journal of Philosophy* 17 (1979): 218.

human feats or achievements, in art of warfare, or athletics, might be praised quite irrespective of the causal history of these feats."[29]

Thus, it is inappropriate to withhold praise from God because he is necessarily good (or, essentially impeccable), and to withhold acknowledging his necessary goodness for the sake of being able to praise him. Both impeccability and praiseworthiness are appropriate and compossible for God, just as his freedom is consistent with impeccability.

As for God, so also we should affirm the appropriateness of praise for an impeccable Christ. Some philosophers of religion have objected that Jesus' impeccability precludes his praiseworthiness for right actions. If Christ is impeccable, then what merit or praise is due him for choosing right when he was unable to choose sin? Anselm raised and answered this objection in *Cur Deus Homo? (Why the Godman?)* by comparing Christ's praiseworthiness with God and the righteous angels' praiseworthiness despite their inability to sin. His solution was that Christ voluntarily chose holiness, not having been bound by necessity, subsequently maintains his holiness by infinite immutability.[30]

The same arguments for Jesus' freedom and impeccability also support the claim of his praiseworthiness and impeccability. Jesus' choices of right instead of sin are praiseworthy because he chose freely in every case of temptation. He was not constrained to obey. He chose freely to renounce sin and to choose right every time he experienced temptation. For example, in Gethsemane, Jesus was not forced to choose right that entailed drinking the cup of divine wrath. His struggle to renounce his desire to preserve himself from pain was just as real as his struggle to obey (cf. Heb 5:7-9, he learned the difficulty of obedience through his suffering to obtain it). The temptation entailed his freedom to make a choice. Having chosen right freely, Jesus is praiseworthy. Scripture attests Jesus' worthiness of praise for the entire course of his redemptive mission (Phil 2:5-11). Within that course the Father praises him from heaven for taking the first decisive step to fulfill that mission (Mark 1:9-11). His praiseworthiness is two-fold for the great acts he accomplished in redemption and his greatness as the perfect man, head of the new humanity.

Therefore, I think the tradition has been right to uphold Christ's moral freedom, impeccability, and his praiseworthiness for fulfilling all righteousness. The Son of God was not constrained to become incarnate, but freely chose to redeem humanity as the second Adam. Subsequently, according to his humanity, Jesus was not constrained from doing evil but chose what he most wanted at the given moment of his temptation. His choice of right in every temptation was always free despite his inability to choose or intend to choose sin. Jesus was not constrained or coerced to do right, but he always chose freely as a man according to his will and beliefs. That he was unable to fail to choose right is just one aspect of his psychological constitution as a man among others.

---

[29] Paul Helm, "God and the Approval of Sin", *Religious Studies* 20 (1984): 220.
[30] Anselm *Cur Deus Homo* 10.

CHAPTER 11

Tempted as We are Tempted

Now we move to the second claim that Jesus, impeccable because he is fully God and unable to commit sin, nevertheless was able to be tempted as a man through the work of the Holy Spirit.

On the way to this claim, we should consider four questions. First, how are we tempted? Our ability to see the truth of Hebrews 4:15 requires that we first set out clearly what is means that we are tempted in various ways. Then we may compare the ways we are tempted with the ways Jesus was tempted. The difficulty is that once we recognize that Jesus was unable to sin and possessed no corrupt desires as we have, a close comparison seems strained. If we cannot find some meaningful correspondence between Jesus' temptations and ours, then the relevance of his empathy and assistance for us in our time of need is false. I aim to vindicate his relevance in having been tempted for us.

A second question to consider is how temptation works. Spending some time here will help us to see what temptation was for Jesus and for us. The goal is to overcome the problems of seeing how the Godman can be tempted at all, and how his temptations are at all like ours when he is sinless and we are corrupt. The analysis of this question will help to see how one person can be empathetic in temptation with billions of others, just as Scripture declares.

Third, we will draw from the analysis of the two questions above to formulate a definition of temptation that is accurate to Jesus and us. My goal here is to construct a definition of temptation that can include the original, sinless temptation narrated in Genesis 3:1-7, the subsequent sinful temptation common to all, and the sinless temptations of Christ. This definition is intended to be comprehensive to vindicate the truth of the claim in Hebrews 4:15 that some essential commonality of temptation afflicts Jesus and us (despite our corruption and his sinlessness).

Finally, we face the question raised in M6 about how God the Son can be tempted in his earthly life without the interference of his deity. I will argue that the Holy Spirit is closely involved in the Incarnation to enable the Son to be tempted. M9 recognized that some sort of eclipse of divine knowledge was necessary for Jesus to be tempted while he remained impeccable. I propose that the Holy Spirit fulfilled this eclipse. Pneumatological Christology has been developed in Reformed theology intermittently, no doubt because of fears that the heresy of Adoptionism would be thereby restored. So, following on the claim that Jesus is impeccable, we now turn to examining temptation and how Jesus was truly tempted in all the ways as we are.

How We are Tempted

Somehow, as a true man, God the Son experienced the pull of temptation in ways that compare closely with the ways we feel tempted. But his sinlessness (including the lack of sinful desires) seems to set his temptations apart from the rest of humanity since Jesus was never tempted from within, from sinful desires, as we are. Moreover, we know from the Gospel accounts that Jesus was limited to a particular human life, and he did not experience many temptations that come with marriage, parenthood, being a woman, living to old age, etc. How can it be that a perfect Godman was tempted in all the ways as we are? Scripture declares the close correspondence of his temptations with ours as constituting him to be merciful, empathetic, ready to lend help, and providing himself as a pattern for us to follow in righteousness (Heb 4:15), and we aim here to understand how this can be so.

We have seen above that some scholars have understood Hebrews 4:15 to teach a distinction between internal and external temptations. The typical interpretation is that sinners experience temptations arising from sources outside themselves and from the inward source of sinful desires. Moreover, Hebrews 4:15 is taken to teach that Jesus was uniquely tempted without sin as an internal, originating source of his temptations.[1] In my view, this internal-external distinction creates unnecessary problems for interpreting Hebrews 4:15 in context and for comparing Christ's experiences with ours. Instead, I think that most of my temptations arise internally, through my desires, and if *none* of these are comparable to the merely external experiences of temptations for Jesus, then I cannot see how either of his empathy or example are reasonable for us.

One philosopher suggests that temptation may be the defining feature of the human condition.[2] In contrast to God, who cannot be tempted (Jas 1:13), human beings are temptable because of their creaturely weakness, finitude, contingency, and liability to suffering. We must recognize that sinfulness—

---

[1] See the discussion of Heb 4:14-16 in ch. 1. I think it is true that Jesus was not tempted by sinful desires as we are, but that is not what Heb 4:15 teaches. I count passages such as Luke 1:35, John 7:18, 2 Cor 5:21, 1 Pet 3:18, and 1 John 3:5 (see ch. 1) to support the claim that Jesus had no sinful desires. I take sinful desires to be the result of prior sins. Since Jesus never sinned, he could not have had sinful desires. I also think that Rom 8:3 was intended to distinguish the human nature of Jesus from sinful corruption by using the term *likeness*. See the exegesis of Rom 8:3 in Douglas Moo, *The Epistle to the Romans*, New International Commentary on the New Testament (Grand Rapids: Eerdmans, 1996).

[2] A. T. Nuyen, "The Nature of Temptation", *The Southern Journal of Philosophy* 35 (1997): 103.

both from original sin and personal sins—exacerbates the problem of temptability in at least two ways. First, sin is corruptive in a way that weakens the sinner to be more susceptible to further sins. Second, sinners have corrupt desires leading to more sins in addition to the legitimate or innocent desires that lead to sins by satisfaction with the wrong means. Jesus' difference in this respect is that, being sinless (no original and personal sin), he was not subject to the corruption (no corrupt desires). As we will see below, this difference is not of categories of temptations distinguishing Jesus from others, but a difference of person-variability in relation to particular temptations that appeal differently to different people. The point is that human temptability is not from sinfulness (just as Adam, Eve, and Jesus were each tempted without prior sin), but from the factors noted in relation to being a creature, which Jesus fully shared.

Temptation on Five Fronts

Human temptations to sin arise within the matrix of a person's real and imagined needs and desires that correspond to real and imagined satisfaction in relationships with God, the external world, other people, and the self. These four areas of an individual's relationships are spheres of human existence that allow different sorts of temptations to afflict people. Even for the monk in seclusion, temptation is intrinsically relational because the mechanics of temptation are an interaction of relational factors (or, one's relatedness to life).[3] A fifth avenue of temptation is opened when suffering touches us.

TEMPTATION UNDER GOD

First, with respect to God, every temptation to sin is an enticement to be torn away from God.[4] Moreover, every sin has an ultimate setting within a person's creaturely relationship to God as Creator and Judge. The prospect of turning against God by following a temptation to sin arises from the human condition as finite beings with freedom and imagination (but this is no excuse for sin).

---

[3] The relationality that contributes to one's experience of testing (which may include temptation) is also observed by the *Dictionary of Biblical Imagery*, ed. Leland Ryken et al (Downers Grove, IL: InterVarsity, 1998), s.v. "Test Motif". "If we recognize the centrality of the test motif to narrative itself, it becomes virtually impossible to classify the things that test a person. All of life tests us. The external world of nature and weather tests us. Specific people, as well as the entire social environment, test us. Personal relationships test our identity and loyalties, bringing out character traits in the process. It is true, of course, that the Bible tends (as does literature in general) to show characters in extraordinary or unusual situations that test them—a journey, for example, instead of a routine day at home, or a controversial encounter with a personal enemy rather than a conversation with a spouse or friend."

[4] Helmut Thielicke, "The Great Temptation", in *Our Heavenly Father* (San Francisco: Harper & Row, 1960); reprint, *Christianity Today* 29, no.10 (1985): 28.

Reinhold Niebuhr argues that creaturely finitude and freedom together constitute human temptability:

> The situation of finiteness and freedom in which man stands becomes a source of temptation only when it is falsely interpreted. But what is the situation which is the occasion of temptation? Is it not the fact that man is a finite spirit, lacking identity with the whole, but yet a spirit capable in some sense of envisaging the whole, so that he easily commits the error of imagining himself the whole which he envisages?[5]

If Niebuhr is right, we should see that human beings (and presumably angels also, but not God) can be tempted because creaturely finitude and freedom seem to form a tension within the experiencing subject.[6] Niebuhr notes that the tension or anxiety resulting from the paradox of human freedom and finitude is an internal description of the state of temptation.[7] Without the combination of freedom and imagination that allows individuals to consider and be tempted by attractive possibilities, people would not see the opportunity to turn away from God. However, being endowed with freedom and imagination to transcend their divinely ordained limitations, people may consider the untested prospect of another way of life apart from God (that is, their independence from the Creator). Moreover, as finite beings under God's command, human beings are constantly temptable by varied ways of escaping or transcending their limitations through gain of things or status to support their independence. They are tempted to add to themselves and seek to enlarge themselves beyond the constraints of finitude. The sin of this shows in the way they seek independence for the sake of self instead of living for the glory of God (i.e., for which they were made). Thus, finite human beings can imagine their personal transcendence as the temptation to become great and move beyond their divinely ordered status (which is a departure from God to self-destruction).

Creaturely finitude is one aspect of human temptability in relation to God; the created condition of being contingent may be an even more accurate description of human temptability in relation to God.[8] As contingent creatures

---

[5]Reinhold Niebuhr, *The Nature and Destiny of Man: A Christian Interpretation* (New York: Charles Scribner's Sons, 1941), 1:180-81.

[6]I will not speculate on angelic temptation, which must have preceded human temptation and fall. It may be that the temptability of finite creatures is the same sort of thing for everyone, whether angelic or human, but we do not have the information to say so or not.

[7]Niebuhr, *The Nature and Destiny of Man*, 1:182. Niebuhr acknowledges Søren Kierkegaard for the idea of anxiety.

[8]Paul Ricoeur, *Fallible Man*, trans. Charles A. Kelbley (New York: Fordham University Press, 1986), 133-46, critiques the traditional explanation of finitude and argues for the non-necessity of being instead. Ricoeur's proposal that contingency is the condition for fallibility seems more accurate to experience and biblical revelation. Cf. the summary

with an acute sense of their dependence on God, the temptation to turn away from the Creator by a rebellious grasp at independence appeals to the desire for autonomy.[9] The desire may be inexplicable as the dream for life apart from God, the *source* of all goodness and life. At least we can say the desire for autonomy is irrational, just as all sin is fundamentally irrational and self-destructive.[10] These temptations to independence from God may take both the direct form of forsaking God for independence and autonomy through idolatry, and the indirect form of violating the limits that God has established for his creatures' relationships within the natural order.[11]

Humans in the world are bound by their creaturely contingency to recognize God's authority in a relationship of submission to him. From the beginning, God obligated the human race to serve him as viceroy on the earth (Gen 1:26-28), mediating God's rule over the creation in protective and regulative ways that was briefly evident in Adam's work of watching over the garden (Gen 2:15) and naming the animals (Gen 2:19-20). Indeed, the first temptation for humanity occurred in the setting of relationship with God when Satan substituted his lie in place of God's clear declaration that Adam and Eve must obey the ban on the fruit of a single tree. This ban was God's design and limitation for how humans should act in their relationship to a particular tree. Having failed there, humanity needed further obligatory restrictions for their relationships to all created things. Thus, humans are temptable in the setting of their relationship with God because they are feeble in every way (ontologically contingent upon him), and owe God the obedient conduct that he rightly demands as their Creator. God's creation of humanity for special relationship with him is our greatest honor, but with that honor comes our situation of being repeatedly tempted to turn away.

The human condition, then, includes a paradox of glory and temptation because of our special, image-bearing relationship to God. If this is right, we

---

statement that sin is a grasp at autonomy from the Creator observed by Robert L. Saucy, "Theology of Human Nature", in *Christian Perspectives on Being Human*, ed. J.P. Moreland and David M. Ciocchi (Grand Rapids: Baker, 1993), 46: "Scripture consistently sees the origin of sin, whether in the angelic or human realm, in terms of the unexplained use of created freedom to turn against its source in exceeding the limits which the Creator has established for the benefit of the creature (cf. Ezek 28:15)."

[9] Cf. the emphasis on the desire for autonomy in the description of temptation given by Wayne E. Oates, *Temptation: A Biblical and Psychological Approach* (Louisville: Westminster John Knox, 1991), 103: "Temptation is the testing ground between the strivings of the image of God in us and the strivings of our desires to be the masters of our fate, the captains of our souls."

[10] The inexplicable nonsense of sin is the thesis of G. C. Berkouwer, *Sin,* trans. Philip C. Holtrop, Studies in Dogmatics (Grand Rapids: Eerdmans, 1971).

[11] Norman H. Snaith, *Distinctive Ideas of the Old Testament* (London: Epworth, 1944), 60-61, notes the double sense of sin in Old Testament theology as primarily rebellion against God and secondarily the transgression of God's code for human ethical conduct.

should remember that, as a true human being, Jesus shared in this human situation and was tempted as a man in relationship with God. The wilderness temptations seem to have highlighted this relationship and would not have worked otherwise (i.e., he only felt tempted because he had certain obligations to obey God). Thus, if we are right to think that some of our temptations occur with reference to our special relatedness to God, then we can see that Christ's exemplifying this sort of temptation may be one aspect of the meaning of Hebrews 4:15 (i.e., relationship to God is *one* of the ways in which he was tempted in all ways as we are).

TEMPTATION IN THE CREATED WORLD

Second, in relationship to the created world, human beings are created to need and depend upon the world. All people are inescapably frail creatures (we are made of *dust*, Ps 103:14-16) requiring the perpetual, externally supplied life support of food, drink, oxygen, clothing, shelter, sunlight, and more. The temptations that correspond to bodily needs and desires in relationship to the external world afflict humanity constantly, despite the original goodness of both the created world and the human creatures inhabiting it. The severe lack of some needed thing, such as food, brings about suffering and pain for the individual (e.g., weakness, starvation, death). This need for life-support corresponds to the promise of relief, comfort, and well-being that is possible only when eating food, clothing the body, or whatever, satisfies the needs.

The temptations in this relationship can be divided in two sorts. *Legitimate desires* are an internal touch point for the temptation to satisfy a legitimate desire in the wrong way (e.g., hunger satisfied by stolen bread). These desires are sinless and natural just as part of being a human. They are the desires that God created humans to experience.

Corrupt desires are an internal touch point for the temptation to satisfy a corrupt, sinful, and self-destructive desire (e.g., *greed* satisfied by excessive wealth, or *gluttony*, the desire for more food than what one needs). Corrupt desires are the result of sin that disorders the body and soul because the person is alienated from God. By comparison, we can think of *affection* as a legitimate desire for another's care for or attention to oneself, the corruption of affection is *lust*. Lust is the self-focused desire for gratification of oneself *as an impersonal object* by the use of another person as an impersonal object of illicit desire. Lust rises as a self-destructive desire for the use of other people *as objects*, which degrades both their personhood and the order that sexual affection is ordered within the committed love of marriage. (I will focus specifically on the role of desires in temptation below.)

Both the corrupt and legitimate desires in temptation seem to occur as internal experiences of a struggle in relation things in the world environment. Notice that these two sorts of desires form the normative temptations for fallen humanity. We will see below that Jesus was only susceptible to the first sort of desires because he did not possess the corrupt desires that fallen humans possess (i.e., he was not fallen or sinful, so he did not possess *lust*).

As noted above, the variety of temptations in this relationship exists because God has set bounds and prescriptions for human conduct in relation to the natural world of stuff (animals, plants, trees, land, etc.). For example, bestiality, gluttony, and greed are prohibited (even the exploitation of the animals is limited in Exod 23:12, as part of Sabbath regulations). While the world is a habitation designed for humans in a way that corresponds perfectly to their embodiment, the divinely ordered relationship for the ways human beings use the world is also the setting for a multitude of temptations to violate that order.

Being a real man, Jesus was also tempted as an embodied being in relationship to the created world, just as others are. Satan's urging that Jesus provide food for himself after fasting for forty days depends upon Christ's basic need for nutritional sustenance of his body. The category of temptations in relation to the created world is another way of temptation that Jesus experienced in likeness to us.

TEMPTATION WITH OTHER PEOPLE

Third, the social setting of person-to-person relationships constitutes an array of human temptations. In addition to bodily needs, humans have the relational needs for the interpersonal dynamics of love, affection, respect, honor, friendship, companionship, nurture, protection, encouragement, and more. People are tempted to sin in the sphere of their relationships with others both by seeking the wrong means of satisfying legitimate, appropriate interpersonal desires (e.g., the desire for respect by lying about one's experiences), and by trying to get satisfaction for their corrupt interpersonal desires (e.g., the desire for revenge satisfied by attacking an enemy through gossip or violence). Examples of these temptations are commonplace in the ways people abuse and mistreat others instead of respecting and serving for their good as God has ordained. Much of the social, interpersonal evil to which people are tempted combines both relationships of human-to-things and of humans-to-humans. Examples include coveting, greed, theft, slander, deception, property damage, sexual misconduct, persecution, extortion, and assault. These combinations make for misusing things of the natural world in harmful ways against other people. Thus, the needs that people have for other people draw them into interdependent relationships with others by God's design, but this social setting is also the arena for many temptations to sin against that design in relationship to others. People are inescapably oriented towards one another, and yet it is in these relationships that so many virulent temptations arise because of interpersonal needs. Wayne Oates also recognizes the interpersonal, social relationality of temptation:

> [The psychodynamics of temptation] all move on the assumption of the inner self as opposed to the outer self, as opposed to other people. Yet they all assume an interpersonal field of interacting selves. Temptations or inner conflicts arise out of

this field of interpersonal relationships, not merely between the personal world and the material world. They are essentially social in nature.[12]

Likewise for Jesus, living his earthly life as a real man, he also experienced many temptations in his relationships with people. For example, he understands the distrust, rejection, slander, betrayal, assault, and malice by others that may have tempted him to revenge. Jesus knows the temptation to do and say the things that could make him well liked by others. He understands the temptation of a growing boy to disobey his parents when they wrongly blamed him for negligence and pulled him away from enjoying the presence of God and enjoyable theological discourse in the Temple courts. Jesus experienced the close company of men, women, and children who were powerful, weak, outcasts, and honorable. They responded to him with the full range of fawning over him, demanding things of him, bowing to him, and provoking him. Whatever temptations we experience in relation to other people, Hebrews 4:15 seems abundantly truthful that Jesus authentically experienced this third way of temptations just as we do. Such were as inescapable for him as for us.

TEMPTATION AND THE SELF

Fourth, in relationship to the self, individuals have the habitual dynamics of character, moods, emotions, self-concept, and self-awareness. There is opportunity for temptations to pride, distorted body image, despair, happiness, safety, power, achievement, comfort, worth, various illusions, and more. Many of these reflexive, self-oriented temptations are simply the appeals to recapitulate the first human sin of clamoring for one's independence from God. Often these self-referential temptations are based on the problem of seeking to satisfy appropriate desires using the wrong means (e.g., the desire for happiness satisfied through manipulating others to meet one's needs). Other self-referential temptations arise from sinful desires (e.g., the desire to feel superior to others satisfied by manipulating others to make one feel powerful). The issue of temptation in relationship to the self is to see oneself wrongly, according to some false image that is other than God's making, order, and specific call. Human beings face multiform temptations to autonomy for the self, sinful pride, and delusions of power and importance by which sinners violate the proper order of their relationships to God, the world, and other people.

While this relationship of the outer self and inner self or self-consciousness always has a setting in another of the three relationships above, the questions of personal identity and significance make for powerful temptations at this relational level because these have to do with a person's self-awareness. Internal states of being may be either untouched or greatly determined by external relationships, whether these are relations with people, the weather, or chemical substances (e.g., drugs, medications, hormones). At every prospect of

---

[12]Oates, *Temptation*, 77.

sin that contributes to the further distortion of self-awareness or the self-concept, there is vulnerability to self-referential temptation (e.g., to view oneself as greater in worth compared to other people for having accumulated more money than them; to view oneself as inferior to others because of being ugly, ignorant in some ways, or financially poor). This sort of human relationship is difficult to analyze with respect to temptations to sin because no analysts can escape their subjectivity. Nonetheless, the general principle illustrated by the other three relationships seems appropriate here as well—temptation to deviate from God's order for the self-referential relationship. The question in the back of everything is this: will I live as God made me and commands me to live?

Was Jesus tempted in this way? Satan's suggestions in the wilderness pressed especially at this point of Christ's need or at least his desires. Jesus, just having been acknowledged from heaven as God's Son, quickly found himself in the peril of starvation and possibly susceptible to the doubt that his dawning consciousness of being the Son of God and Messiah was a lie.[13] Satan suggested that Jesus force God's hand and thereby confirm his identity as God's Son ("*If* you are the Son of God"). Even if Jesus had no other temptations in relation to himself, these two alone are sufficient to constitute his firsthand empathy for others who face temptations that have to do with self-understanding.

Thus, in every sphere of human life, for Jesus as for us, temptation is that pull on people to act against God and his order for human existence. Hebrews 4:15 reveals that there is a comprehensive correspondence between the ways that we are tempted and the ways Jesus was tempted. I do not mean that the writer of Hebrews had these four ways in mind, but that these four categories help us to see comprehensiveness of the temptations that we suffer and that Jesus experienced for us (to empathize with us and give help to us in following his pattern of obedience). George Painter's observation is apt: "The realm of possible temptation, therefore, is almost infinite, and the impulse to anything whatever, outside the sphere of the right, may lead to evil."[14]

TEMPTATION AND SUFFERING

Alongside these four aspects of human life is one more general category of human temptability: the susceptibility to suffer pain that ranges from moderate discomfort and deprivation to intense, excruciating pain. The prospect of

---

[13] I do not here claim that Jesus only became aware of his divine identity at the Jordan baptism, but that there was some advance and public acknowledgment by God to be challenged by the devil in the wilderness. Jesus seems to have had knowledge of his divine identity as early as age twelve, when he claimed to have a unique relationship with God as his Father (Luke 2:41-52).

[14] George S. Painter, *The Philosophy of Christ's Temptation* (Boston: Sherman, French, and Co., 1914), 136.

suffering in a fallen world creates this avenue of temptation for the promise of relief from pain (or the possible evasion of suffering).[15] Human beings are vulnerable to suffering of many sorts (emotional and physical pain) because of their creaturely contingency and frailty. People are thus open to being tempted to sin by avoiding pain through the wrong means of satisfying their desire for comfort or self-preservation (e.g. stealing bread to escape the pain of hunger; turning away from Christ to escape persecution).[16]

The temptations occasioned by present or imminent suffering are really the pull to sin as a means of relief, which seems truly good to the sufferer (e.g., the legitimate desire to avoid punishment by telling a lie). A biblical example is the book of Hebrews, which addresses the situation where the temptation to turn away from Christ and return to salvation through the Old Covenant has been thrust upon the readers because of their impending persecution for being Christians.[17] The one who is tempted only resists sin by renouncing the reasonable, natural desire to escape from suffering. Such desire for self-preservation is often good, but it can become a means of evil if one chooses self-preservation through sin over the competing desire of clinging to God even when suffering is involved. Thus, trials of all kinds strain people specifically because of embodiment and the relational contingency upon life-support and other needs.

As a true human being who suffered emotionally and physically (e.g., Heb 5:7-8), Jesus was also temptable because of his vulnerability to pain. This is most clear when he was tempted to avoid his drinking the cup of God's wrath (Mark 14:36). Christ's achievement against temptation is supreme in this event; he overcame his desire to avoid pain and chose instead the desire to obey God, come what may.

CONCLUSION: HUMANITY, JESUS, AND TEMPTATION

In summary of these five ways or settings for temptation, we have seen that Jesus experienced all the sorts of temptation that we do. I suggest that these are

---

[15]The conjunction of suffering and temptation is also noted by Marguerite Shuster, "The Temptation, Sinlessness, and Sympathy of Jesus: Another Look at the Dilemma of Hebrews 4:15", in *Perspectives on Christology: Essays in Honor of Paul K. Jewett*, ed. Marguerite Shuster and Richard A. Muller (Grand Rapids: Zondervan, 1991), 205: "Temptation comes when the possibility presents itself of escaping or avoiding suffering (albeit temporarily) *in the wrong way* and with the knowledge that refusing evil will often lead to the increase of earthly suffering."

[16]Dietrich Bonhoeffer, *Creation and Fall: Temptation*, trans. Kathleen Downham, ed. Eberhard Bethge (New York: Touchstone, 1997), 134. Bonhoeffer, well-acquainted with suffering under the Nazi regime, writes that the temptation that is precipitated by suffering (whether serious sickness, poverty, pain, or various deprivations and tortures) is the temptation by a desire for relief from suffering, albeit relief by sinful means of abandoning God or committing some other crime to alleviate one's troubles.

[17]Shuster, "The Temptation, Sinlessness, and Sympathy of Jesus", 203-07.

a helpful picture of the meaning in Hebrews 4:15 that Jesus was tempted in all ways as we are.[18] His differences from the rest of humanity (being an eternal person, fully God, and sinless) did not protect him from experiencing the primary modes of temptation. The authentic correspondence of his experience of temptation to ours cannot be denied. His experience is properly the basis of his empathy and his example for us. Two objections may be raised at this point.

First, what is the point of creating new categories of temptation when Scripture has already provided two such groupings? One account of temptation is the triad in 1 John 2:16, the lust of the flesh, the lust of the eyes, and the pride of life. Certainly these three may correspond to the Edenic temptation and Christ's wilderness temptation, but the practical relevance of his empathy and help for us based simply upon those three epochal temptations is difficult to understand and is not likely to be reassuring or compelling for most because they are too general.[19] Indeed, the author of Hebrews goes beyond them to specify Jesus' temptation in Gethsemane (Heb 5:8-9) and the many temptations of fellow believers in Hebrews 11 who faced deprivations and perils. Moreover, 1 John does not seem intended to provide a comprehensive taxonomy of temptation that would include Adam and Christ.[20] While all our temptations could be grouped into the biblical triad, I think a closer analysis of Jesus' experience and our experience is possible (and desirable), and the five relational aspects of temptation noted above get us further into the details. When we considered these, we found a complete commonality between Jesus and us (despite our sin and his sinlessness).

A second objection to what I suggest as five settings or ways of temptation is that no account is given for the difference between sinless and sinful desires, or, in other words, those temptations that arise from outside (the world and the devil) and those coming from within the individual (the flesh, or, sinful desires). A common explanation is that sinful and sinless sets of temptations are the two basic categories, and Jesus only experienced the sinless sort. I agree that Jesus was tempted sinlessly, but I disagree with this analysis because temptation is deeper and more basic than the typical analysis allows. Sinful desire is not a major part of temptation. Were it true, the common (false) dichotomy undermines how Hebrews 4:15 can be true, since surely most of my

---

[18]Pollard, *Fullness of Humanity*, 80. "Hebrews emphasizes that Jesus was tempted *in every respect as we are*; he is thinking of the common temptations connected with our human weakness, the temptations to which we are exposed simply because we are men."

[19]I must add that Genesis 3 does give the paradigm of sin, and the event is very important for our understanding of temptation. To say, however, that all temptation follows the Edenic pattern would require that the devil is the instigator of all temptation, which I think is false. Paul writes as though temptation is a reality in itself, and does not require the involvement of Satan or one of his agents (1 Cor 10:13).

[20]Reading 1 John 2:16 in terms of Adam, Eve, and Jesus means interpreting the term for *desire* (ἐπθυμία) in a neutral way (ESV), but some translations follow the context to use a negative sense *lust*, sinful desire (RSV, NASB, NIV).

temptations seem to be the sinful sort (since I am thoroughly corrupt and inclined to selfishness and sin). Consequently, Jesus can only empathize with me concerning the comparatively narrow range of sinless temptations that he experienced. Christ's life as a template for living faithfully and resisting temptation is narrowed so that, insofar as I am experiencing sinless temptation, then Jesus is a pattern for me. But when I find myself afflicted with temptations that have some reference to my sin or inborn corruption, I remain on my own without much to inspire me in Christ's example. He does not know my *sinful* temptations because he has never felt them himself.

Instead of following the conventional dichotomy, I think a closer look at temptation needs to be made, and one that proceeds from the premises laid out above regarding the primary settings of temptations, none of which depends upon a prior state of sin or sin's corruption.

How Temptation Works

Temptation is a complex phenomenon. Others have focused on the roles and requirements of a tempter, a temptee (the one tempted), and the object of temptation.[21] The analysis becomes complicated when we think of cases where no tempter is involved, when a temptation occurs for a good outcome (as in testing or training), and when temptations come to all human beings, whether they are sinless (pre-fall, or God incarnate) or sinful.[22] My aim is that through considering the complex aspects of temptation we can see better how Hebrews 4:15 is true that Jesus was tempted just as we are.

We will consider four aspects of how temptation works that have not been discussed adequately in the literature. Simply stated, temptation is the enticement to evil. The obvious factors involved are the tempted person and the tempting prospect of sin (which may or may not be instigated by another

---

[21] J. P. Day, "Temptation", *American Philosophical Quarterly* 30 (1993): 175-81. Nuyen, "The Nature of Temptation".

[22] A common assumption is that glorified humanity is not susceptible to temptation, but Scripture does not say one way or the other. The possibility of ongoing temptation for those in glory is no less reasonable than for the temptation of God incarnate during his earthly life. There may be good God-glorifying reasons that God would allow continuing temptations in glory (without chance of failure, since all sin is excluded from the new creation). Bruce Ware has suggested to me that one reason for temptation to be a continuing condition in glory is to provide the opportunity to glorify God as resurrected saints who continually choose God above all possible deceptions, though they (like Christ) are simultaneously upheld through grace by him impeccably in righteousness. We may wonder if continuing temptation may require the continuation of deception. Deception seems unfitting for the eternal state because who would be forming such lies in their minds and attempting to mislead others by these lies? Since death is ended, then the possility of sin is ended also. How would these deceptions be hatched if no one is able to sin (that is, capable of falling from God's righteousness)?

person, one's own sinful desires, or one's natural desires). I propose that when we look closely, temptation occurs as an internal conflict fomented by both internal factors and external factors. The entire dynamic is further overshadowed and complicated by the dual purposes and person-variability of temptation. Each of these aspects draws our gaze to the occurrence of temptation for the victim, the one who is tempted, so that we can understand temptation as it occurs for us and, perhaps, as it occurred for Jesus who was tempted for us. We will proceed to the four features in this order: the dual purposes, the person-variability, internal factors, and the external factors of temptation.

The Dual Purposes of Temptation

The dual teleology of temptation is that a particular individual's circumstances may be simultaneously a *temptation* to sin and a *test* for sanctification. Biblical translators recognize this by translating the single term in these two ways according to the context.[23] The motive of whoever influences an event determines the event as a test or a temptation, and, a single event may bear both if multiple motives are impressed upon it. For example, God guided Jesus into the wilderness to *test* the Son's faithfulness (Matt 4:1). Simultaneously, the divine test involved subjecting Jesus to the devil's malicious *temptations* to bring about a fall in sin. Positively, God's purpose in arranging for Jesus to face Satan's temptations was to strengthen Jesus by the test at the onset of his public ministry.[24] Negatively, Satan's purpose in suggesting sins to Jesus was so that Jesus would sin just as Adam (and Eve) had in the Garden (Gen 3:1-6). Similarly, Job was repeatedly afflicted in Satan's goal that Job would curse God, having been tempted to do so by his circumstances (including some distorted theology to believe God operates simply according to retribution and reward) and his wife. God's purpose was to bring about the triumph of Job's faithfulness in spite of his afflictions.

God's (positive) purpose in orchestrating (or allowing) a situation that *tests* people for their good (while the situation is simultaneously a temptation) is a frequent biblical theme (e.g., Adam and Eve, Job, Abraham, and Israel). In James 1:2-4, God's purpose seems clear: the difficulties that are causing the readers to feel tempted have been intended by God as tests to purify and form their faith. The readers are told that "whenever various trials may beset you" (ὅταν πειρασμοῖς περιπέσητε ποικίλοις, v. 2) their *trials* function positively as "the testing of your faith" (τὸ δοκίμιον ὑμῶν τῆς πίστεως, v. 3) given to strengthen them by forming endurance for their progressive maturity in

---

[23]E.g., James 1:2 and 1:13-14. This double-duty of the relevant terms is in the Old Testament and the New Testament.

[24]Bruce, *Humiliation of Christ*, 274-80, notes that temptation was necessary to Christ's development to fulfill the role as priest.

perseverance (Jas 1:12).[25] In these tests, God employs the pressures of persecution, deprivation, and other troubles to challenge his people to stretch beyond their present limitations in faith and act like God in their opposition to sin.[26] A biblical metaphor for this transformation is the heat-intensive process of smelting mineral ore by removing the slag from precious gold and silver, as in the summary statement of Proverbs 17:3: "The crucible for silver, and the furnace for gold, and Yahweh's testing for hearts" (cf. the same analogy of refining faith as a smelting process in Isa 1:24-26; Mal 3:1-3; 1 Pet 1:6-7). So, temptations may be experienced as the threat to one's faith, but, when the same experience is considered as the testing of God, the positive purpose may be embraced (exactly as James exhorts his readers in 1:2). Painter observes the positive purpose of these difficult, tempting circumstances for the development of faithfulness:

> It must be evident to all . . . that trial and a proving of ourselves are the absolutely essential conditions of every moral nature for its normal unfolding and development. Life is a warfare, and a survival of the fittest. The giant oak has become strong through the withstanding of the lightning's blast and the winter's storms; so likewise we grow strong in all the relations of our lives by a process of overcoming, and this is peculiarly emphatic in the moral nature.[27]

The *trials* of James 1:2-4 are viewed in a different way in James 1:13. These same trials are described negatively as the occasions of *being tempted* to sin (πειραζόμενος) that are not due to God. Furthermore, James warns against blaming God for circumstances in which people find themselves enticed to sin. On the contrary, God's purpose is only positive for developing his people's faithfulness (Jas 1:12, 16-18). Thus, James assures his readers that they have wrongly construed their difficult circumstances as the occasion for sin (God is not to blame for their temptations and sins). Instead, they ought to take courage from the evidence of God's purpose and joyfully see their hardships as the opportunity for their growth in faithfulness. Moreover, the example in James also shows that at least some (if not most) temptations do not originate with the devil; thus, temptation is not simply a demonic interaction but primarily involves other agents and relationships of the tempted person. In other words, Satan is not essential to temptation.[28]

---

[25]Notice that the shift between positive and negative purposes is contextual, not lexical, since πειρασμός (*test, tempt*) is the term in each statement.
[26]Kees Waaijman, "Temptation: The Basic Theological Structure of Temptation", trans. S. Ralston, *Journal of Empirical Theology* 5 (1992): 89, 92.
[27]Painter, *Philosophy of Christ's Temptation*, 142-43.
[28]The demonic factor in human temptations is thus secondary and partial, always contingent upon one of the four human relationships. Even for those relatively few temptations that involve a demonic agent, his role and malicious power are contingent upon the prior conditions of human temptability in the four settings of life (plus

Regardless of the presence or absence of a demonic tempter, the dual teleology of temptation shows the complexity of temptation. The same experience can be described from two perspectives, and those who feel afflicted are called to respond to the difficulty as a test, for their good, instead of as a temptation, for their ruin in sin. Both purposes overshadow human beings as they stand in relationship to God, whether choosing against him by their sin or aligning with him in their faithful obedience.

Some implications are apparent from the dual teleology as I have described it here. First, temptation is a complicated and possibly mystifying experience. Second, Jesus shared in the complexity, as we see both purposes demonstrated in his testing-temptation in the wilderness. Third, to experience temptation is not itself a sin (since Jesus was tempted sinlessly) and sometimes these afflict us because God is testing us to advance us in salvation (but some temptations are truly our fault, as in a boy who feels tempted to lie because he stole something and wants to avoid getting caught). On the contrary, to feel tempted can be the backside of the opportunity to respond to God's work of renewal by means of difficulties.

The Person-Variability of Temptation

A second aspect of how temptation works is that temptations are relative to the individual who experiences them, or, temptations are person-variable.[29] That is, all temptations are related to the specific and subjective particularity of an individual person. Some people may even be tempted in ways that for others no temptation is felt at all. So, temptation requires a fit between the circumstances and the victim, who must have what Crisp calls "the right psychological configuration" to feel pulled toward the sin in view.[30] This psychological

---

suffering). This partial, contingent role does not constitute a separate category of human temptability, despite the way that some Christians blame the devil for their temptations and sins. By comparison with Satan's temptations of Adam, Eve, and Jesus, the Pauline account of temptation in 1 Thess 3:5; Gal 4:8-9; and Eph 2:1-3 is that Satan works to re-enslave people in sin by exploiting sinful desires (the flesh, a metaphor of our depravity). Clinton E. Arnold, *Power of Darkness: Principalities and Powers in Paul's Letters* (Downers Grove, IL: InterVarsity, 1992), 127-28.

[29]This concept of person-variability is my adaptation from George I. Mavrodes, *Belief in God* (New York: Random House, 1970), 40, where he uses the concept of person variability for the subjective value of arguments for the existence of God. He notes (rightly) that certain arguments may function as *proofs* for some people (they are convinced the argument is true) but not for others. An argument is only a proof if it works to convince the person of the truth. Likewise, a circumstance can only be a temptation if a person feels pulled to sin.

[30]Crisp, "Was Christ Sinless or Impeccable?", 175. Crisp also helpfully uses the idea of temptation as a *pull* on the victim. Nuyen, "The Nature of Temptation", 93, also notes

configuration may include lacking certain internal impediments and possessing certain susceptibilities that allow a particular temptation to engage a person. For example, the availability of narcotics can constitute a fierce temptation for some people because they know and desire the effects of drug use, while others are not tempted at all by narcotics (and they are even repulsed). For the temptation to work, the victim must possess the right psychological configuration of specific knowledge, beliefs, and desires.

If a temptation is going to work, the temptation circumstances must also be person-variable or tailored to suit the victim according to her psychological configuration. Not everyone has the same knowledge, experiences, or desires, so not everyone experiences the same temptations, or, even if they do, they do not always experience temptations in the same way. In other words, all temptations vary in their subjective appeals that are relative to the life circumstances and the psychological configuration of particular individuals. An individual's sensitivity to temptation is similar to what others have observed proverbially about the perception of beauty ("Beauty is in the eye of the beholder") and taste for food ("One man's food is another man's poison"). Both are idiosyncratic, just as for many things in life, temptation included.

Person-variability suggests that temptations correspond to a person's historical-cultural embeddedness, gender, ethnicity, socio-economic status, age, beliefs, and life experience to have a particular and unique force for that person. This match of a specific temptation to an individual shows in the special messianic appeal of Christ's wilderness temptations that were cunningly forceful and uniquely attractive for Jesus expressly because of his status as the Messiah. For any one else, the suggestion to turn stones into bread would seem nonsensical and pose no temptation at all. All others who are not the Messiah lack the psychological configuration to feel the pull. Thus, the person-variability of temptations indicates that temptations depend as much on the experiencing subject as they do on the subject's particular matrix of relationships to God, the world, other people, and the self.

Two things follow from the person-variability of temptation. First, the person-variability of temptations implies that no one can feel another person's temptation in the sense of an identity of experience ("I feel your pain"). But Jesus, because he experienced hundreds (or hundreds of thousands?) of enticements to sin that come naturally with a human life, can say, "I have felt temptation that is like your temptation." He knows firsthand the temptations that come with betrayal, suffering, ridicule, danger, want of food and physical comforts, the sense of abandonment by God and close friends—a whole range of things that come to people in the normal settings of life common to all. Therefore, when Hebrews 4:15 affirms that Jesus was tempted *in all ways as we are*, I take this to mean that he has been tempted in all the ways that are

---

the same idea of a psychological configuration by saying that certain conditions must be met for the victim to feel touched by the temptation.

common to humanity and in his particular experience (which excluded some temptations, such as the pull to steal bread because of the fear that one's child may starve). That he was male and unmarried does not count against his abilities to empathize and offer real help to women and men who experience particular varieties of temptations that are based on their person-variability.[31] For example, Jesus did not need to become a heroin user and feel those particular temptations for him to be able to empathize with heroin users. Jesus has his own intense temptations to draw from for relating to other people. Christ's particularity (even his being the Godman and sinless) does not count against his ability to empathize with any other human being suffering temptations. What matters most is that Jesus was thoroughly tempted in the variety of occurrences in the human setting of his life. These are sufficient to constitute him empathetic and a reasonable pattern for all others in their temptations.[32]

Second, the person-variability of temptation helps us to see that Jesus' sinlessness and total lack of any temptation originating from a sinful desire is just one aspect of his psychological configuration. Instead of setting his temptations in an upper level of sinless temptations separated from a lower level category of sinful temptations, person-variability means that Jesus just had this uniqueness about him that made some temptations ineffective for him. In other words, his sinlessness is no different for his susceptibility to common temptations than my lack of experience with heroin. Just as he would not be tempted by circumstances that might appeal to other men as a temptation to a sinful desire of lust, those men would not have been tempted to turn stones into bread (because they lacked the psychological configuration of believing themselves to be the divine Messiah). Therefore, the person-variability of temptation allows us to see that Jesus is fully within our frame of experience despite his lack of sinful desires. His empathy is valid. His pattern is reasonable.

Internal Factors of Temptation

The third aspect of how temptation works includes beliefs and desires. As part of desires we will have to consider the role of desires in temptation according

---

[31] Two books have sorted what the authors consider to be particularly male and female temptations. Obviously, men and women are different, but the differences are not so sharp that Jesus cannot relate to women, quadriplegics, or anyone else simply because he has not experienced life in the same mode as they do. Mary Ellen Ashcroft, *Temptations Women Face: Honest Talk about Jealousy, Anger, Sex, Money, Food, Pride* (Downers Grove, IL: InterVarsity, 1991). Tom L. Eiseman, *Temptations Men Face: Straightforward Talk on Power, Money, Affairs, Perfectionism, Insensitivity* (Downers Grove, IL: InterVarsity, 1990).
[32] Cf. Bruce, *Humiliation of Christ*, 267.

to James 1:12-15.

BELIEFS

Temptation involves one's beliefs about reality. When tempted, people are pulled to consider what sinful prospects are imaginable or possible in relation to the circumstances of one's life (the outer world or settings of life). To be tempted, a person must be capable of imagining the change effected by choosing the proposed sin.[33] Bernard Ramm observes: "The essence of seduction in temptation is to present the evil as a good."[34] Thus, temptation involves a deception about reality that yielding to temptation (choosing the sin proposed in it) is possibly desirable in place of doing the right action (or, refraining from the sin). The factor of belief shows in the case of Eve, when the devil persuaded her to believe that, contrary to what God had declared, she would not die but become like God if she ate the fruit. Following that false belief, she then proceeded into the sin proposed with the temptation. What shows here is a change of beliefs in the process of being tempted, and a choice made in relation to belief that one holds at the moment of temptation and choice. Similarly, Paul's exposition of human depravity emphasizes the centrality of beliefs in the pattern of human sinfulness because people suppress the truth about God (Rom 1:18) and exchange the truth for a lie (Rom 1:25). For any temptation to be successful, the person must accept (whether consciously or not) some rationalizing deception as the cognitive basis for the choice made for sin.

What seems to be happening is the influence of what Ron Nash calls a person's *scale of values* that is a hierarchy of what we believe to be most important at any given moment.[35] The scale of values is influential at the moment of choice in that a person chooses partly in relation to what thing is most valued at that moment. In Eve's case, she valued becoming like God more highly than she valued obeying God. Our values are constantly shifting and re-sorting within the decision-making process so that people always choose according to the most important value—expressed as a concrete desire such as for eating the fruit to become like God—that they have at the moment of decision. This scale of values varies from person to person, but the principle of choosing voluntarily according to the highest value remains the same for everyone.

Jesus may have had a superior stability of his scale of values than what is

---

[33]Cf. Niebuhr, *The Nature and Destiny of Man*, 1:181-82, explains that the conditions for temptation involve the tension between finitude and freedom, the human power to imagine beyond the current circumstances.

[34]Bernard L. Ramm, *An Evangelical Christology: Ecumenic and Historic* (Nashville: Thomas Nelson, 1985), 81.

[35]Ronald H. Nash, *Life's Ultimate Questions* (Grand Rapids: Zondervan, 1999), 334-38. Nash has derived this analogy from economics.

common for other people, but he still exercised his will as a man according to his beliefs. His will had developed as part of his overall character dynamically influenced by the Holy Spirit, Scripture, people in his life, and the patterns of his choices and experiences in a life of obedience to God. He grew in moral stature of maturity from infancy to adulthood (Luke 2:40, 52) and he learned obedience progressively (Heb 5:8-9). The same formation is possible for other people by God's grace.

Jesus' wilderness temptations especially demonstrate the factor that beliefs play in temptation. In each temptation, Satan proposes a sinful course of action supported by a lie and a false interpretation of Scripture that he has construed as a valid truth-claim. Jesus' responses are counter interpretations of truth-claims that restrict his actions in particular ways and exclude the sins proposed by Satan. Thus, we can say that Jesus never sinned in response to these or any of his temptations because he was never deceived to believe lies as the truth. Jesus never embraced the false beliefs about God, himself, or the world in ways that allowed him to choose against his highest values. Therefore, the factor of beliefs in temptation coordinates a person's beliefs (human mind) with a person's desires (human will) in relation to external circumstances (whether real or imagined).

DESIRES

Internally, a person faced with temptation must choose according to her beliefs between *desires that lead to sin* and *desires that lead to righteousness*. The opposite moral aims of these two sorts of desires entail that they are mutually exclusive sets. For example, Jesus cannot choose his desire that he turn stones into bread and simultaneously choose his desire to continue trusting in God's provision for him.

The first set of desires, *desires that lead to sin*, may be subdivided further into *corrupt desires* and *legitimate desires* that lead to sin.[36] These are two kinds of downward aiming desires that, if chosen, lead the person to sin. Fallen humanity has both types of these desires (corrupt and legitimate). Jesus has only legitimate (sinless) desires that may lead to sin if he had in view a sinful means of satisfaction (e.g., to confirm his sonship by throwing himself from the temple to force God to act on his behalf). These downward desires in Christ are not sinful, but they may lead to sin nonetheless.

The second set of desires, *desires that lead to righteousness*, are alternate, upward, and opposite to the moral aims of the downward desires. The struggle

---

[36]See above for a definition of corrupt and legitimate desires, p. 266. Legitimate desires are also sinless desires that nevertheless may lead to some particular sin. An example of a sinless, natural want is the desire of Jesus to satisfy his hunger by turning stones into bread, which would have been tantamount to sinful discontentment and lack of trust in God's provision for him. By contrast, Israel sinned in the wilderness by complaining about God's provision of manna but not meat.

in any temptation to sin is the choice between desires leading to sin and the antithetical desires leading to obedience. These are the desires that Jesus chose consistently, and they are the desires that God calls all people to choose for life with him through following his ways (cf. Deut 30:19). For any given downward desire, whether legitimate or corrupt, there is an upward desire that is its antithesis and way of escape from sin.

In any particular temptation, the two sets of desires that lead to sin (downward) and righteousness (upward) are mutually exclusive options (hence the struggle). This internal struggle takes place in conjunction with the dynamic of one's personal scale of values in relation to a belief about the situation at hand. The belief may be supplied internally or externally to justify the sin (e.g., the belief that revenge is an appropriate response to an insult).

Jesus could have appropriate, legitimate, and sinless desires to which external circumstances constituted temptations that appealed to him internally.[37] These legitimate desires were conjoined in temptation with sinful means of satisfaction to become desires leading to sin (e.g., the downward desire to preserve his life by avoiding the cross) presented antithetically to his desires for righteousness that involved suffering (the upward desire to obey). Though not so with Jesus, the rest of humanity also has corrupt desires to which temptations appeal and lead to sin (e.g., Judas Iscariot's greed satisfied by stealing money from the disciples' money bag and then betraying Jesus for silver). In both cases, the principle of a conflict between internal desires is the same. Temptation is an internal conflict of desires.[38] The role of desire in temptation is that a desire leading to sin—whether appropriately desiring but with sinful means (e.g., to satisfy hunger with stolen bread) or sinfully desiring (e.g., to satisfy sinful pride by boasting)—is the internal touch point for the external appeal of temptation to pull at the person. The external state of affairs forms the appeal of a temptation that touches an internal desire with the promise of satisfaction.

Internally, at the level of conflicting desires within the will, temptation occurs as a visitation or external intrusion recognized by the self, and the person always chooses (whether consciously or not) to fulfill one desire while

---

[37] Cf. Shuster, "Temptation", 199, agrees that it is inadequate to define Jesus' temptation as merely external testing that touches no internal struggle because the internality of his suffering and inner conflict of desire is evident in Gethsemane and implied by his cry of dereliction from the cross.

[38] André Godin, "Temptation: The Psychology of Temptation", trans. G. J. Schlesselmann, *Journal of Empirical Theology* 5 (1992): 83, gives a psychological definition: temptation is "a conflict in the desire" which entails "a *change*, which prepared the way for a *decision to be made*, influenced by a modification of the external *realities* . . . along the path of *desire-pleasure.*" The reality of temptation as an internal conflict of desires has also been recognized by Bruce, *Humiliation of Christ*, 269, and Nuyen, "Nature of Temptation", 94: "a direct conflict between satisfying the desire for what is offered and satisfying some other desire".

denying the other. The conflict occurs between two desires: the desire leading to sin occasioned by the temptation for a sinful prospect, and a non-sinful desire leading to righteousness (e.g., the desire to please God). Either the person must choose the desire for the tempting state of affairs that entails a proposed sin, or the person must renounce that desire in the choice for the opposite desire leading to righteousness. For example, in Gethsemane Jesus renounced his desire to avoid the suffering of punishment for sin (which desire led to the sin of disobeying God) and he chose instead his desire to obey God.

Commonly, the case in temptation is that many competing motivations complicate the experience with perhaps several sets of antithetical desires, generating what Paul Ricoeur appropriately calls the *dizziness* of human temptability.[39] This metaphor seems especially appropriate as the whirl of factors that distract and disrupt a person in the throes of diverse desires, beliefs, imagined outcomes, and shifting circumstances. All happens much too fast in many temptations to keep track amidst the dizzying confluence of thoughts, perceptions, habits, and desires.

Despite his difference from sinful humanity, Jesus, possessing no corrupt desires at all, was tempted to the same wide extent and dizzying, intense degree as we are by the pull at his sinless desires. Like us though he was sinless, Jesus still had to choose among his sets of antithetical desires—between desires leading to sin and desires leading to obedience. Thus, Jesus' distinction from common humanity as one who did not share in corrupt desires stemming from the total depravity of Adam does not disqualify him from experiencing and triumphing over temptation relevantly as the sinless, empathetic exemplar for others and in their stead (Rom 5:12-21; Heb 4:14-16).

Jesus' true temptation while he remained sinless reminds us that the experience of temptation is not always sinful or blameworthy. Adam and Eve (pre-fall) and Jesus experienced temptation as the moral struggle between right and wrong actions (whether in thought, word, or deed) apart from the prior presence of sin. Jesus additionally remained sinless throughout all of his temptations. Even though all temptations may *feel* to us as though they are sinful (with the sad result that Christians despair of their sin and withdraw from God in shame), many temptations should be properly understood as the struggle within the self between desires leading to sin and desires leading to righteousness that correspond to an individual's relational experience in the world. Temptations are opportunities to seek God's help and may function positively to strengthen one's character in fidelity to God.[40] Temptation provides the opportunity of a choice to be made between desires leading in opposite moral directions. Temptation always entails a personal choice enacted

---

[39]Ricoeur, *Fallible Man*, 139.
[40]Hence the repeated call in Scripture that Christians *rejoice* in all trials (Acts 5:41; Rom 8:37; 2 Cor 12:9-10; Jas 1:2-4; 1 Pet 1:6-9) because these are the means of God's work.

by one's will,[41] even if this ability is impaired by original sin, earlier personal sins (e.g., self-destructive, will-weakening substance abuse), or a particular temptation has come into view as the result of an earlier sin (e.g., stealing bread and then needing to lie as a cover-up). Whatever the case may be, for the Christian, any temptation is the occasion for trust in God through seeking help in the time of need according to the empathy and pattern of Christ in solidarity with us (Heb 4:14-16). God will give help so that a person can choose the desire for righteousness instead of the desire leading to sin in the instance of her temptation.

WHAT ABOUT CORRUPT DESIRE IN JAMES 1:12-15?
Traditional orthodoxy is that Jesus possessed a human will, and this was not a fallen, sinful, or corrupt will with disordered desires. Some might object that since Jesus did not have a fallen human will, he does not share an important category of temptations common to others who tempt themselves by a corrupt will that generates corrupt desires for sin. James 1:12-15 is often taken to teach a self-temptation by sinful desires. This conclusion is matched with the interpretation of Hebrews 4:15 that Jesus was not tempted from within by sinful desires. No doubt this is right that Jesus was not tempted by sinful desires, but I dispute that either passage teaches that there is a set of temptations that arise from within. Instead, James 1:12-15 is better understood to describe the personal responsibility that people have regarding their desires when they feel tempted. Thus, James does not charge people with having tempted themselves, and this is not an inward temptation exclusive of Jesus' experience.

The context in James 1 is God's progressive sanctification of the readers by means of tests of their faith (1:2-4, 12, 17-18). These tests present the choice of life with God as the alternative to death (separation from God). In 1:12, James explains that God's tests are part of a process of three steps for the believer: the test, God's approval, and the result of life. This process of sanctification is set in contrast to the three-step process of sin: a destructive movement from desire (leading to sin), sinful action, and the result of death (1:15).[42] James explains his readers' sin as the end result of the process by which desire carries them away once temptation has been presented (1:14). James uses a fishing metaphor to say that tempted Christians are caught by desires as fish on the barb of a hook and subsequently dragged away to death.

James then changes his metaphor from fishing to birth (1:15-18). He describes how both death and life result from the three-step process of will, conception, and birth. Death is the result when *desire* (personified), in response

---

[41]Ralph A. Letch, *Temptation and Freedom: The Temptations of God* (Harrow, UK: Eureditions, 1978), 42.
[42]Peter H. Davids, *The Epistle of James*, New International Greek Testament Commentary, vol. 55 (Grand Rapids: Eerdmans, 1982), 85. Davids sees this process of life in 1:12 set as a contrast to the process of desire-sin-death in 1:15.

to temptation, *conceives* and *gives birth to sin* (1:15). In an upward, reverse direction, life is the result of three steps by which *God conceives* of believers *by the word* of truth, and then there is *the beginning of a new creation*, or, a renewal of life (1:18; cf. the crown of life result of God's testing in 1:12).

Therefore, James describes the general process of sin and death that involves temptation with desires that lead to sin. People succumb to temptation when they choose their desire that leads to sin in the proposed state of affairs. The testing circumstances and the individual's psychological configuration are the setting for a sin and the corresponding desire that leads to it. By one's choice for a desire that leads to sin, whether the desire is corrupt or legitimate with illegitimate means of satisfaction, the tempted person chooses to engage with and follow the temptation into the sin.

Desire in this psychological configuration is the person's internal susceptibility to an externally occasioned temptation.[43] James tells how sin develops out of the context of temptations by placing the focus on *personal responsibility* for sins that result from temptation,[44] not on a fatalistic *process of temptation*. These temptations to sin coincide with the trials by which God produces a believer's endurance in the choice for life (1:2-4).

On this view, the experience of temptation is not sinful; James only implicates those who sin as the result of temptation that arises in the circumstances of a divinely ordained test. The problem is not the temptation to sin or the desire, but the person's choice for the desire to sin (but this may be an internally habituated choice that no longer feels like a free choice, as in substance abuse). Moreover, this interpretation suggests that James does *not* say that all temptation entails or arises from inward sinfulness, as some interpreters have concluded.[45] Instead, temptation occurs as the perilous opportunity for sin and sin's trajectory of death that is similar to how testing is the fortifying and enriching opportunity for endurance and life (Jas 1:3-4).[46]

---

[43]The term for *strong desire* (ἐπιθυμίας, v.14) is commonly translated negatively in this passage as *lust* (AV, ASV, NASB) and *evil desires* (NIV, NLT). Douglas J. Moo, *The Letter of James*, Pillar New Testament Commentary, vol. 55 (Grand Rapids: Eerdmans, 2000), 74, argues for the negative sense from the context. However, some modern translations convey the meaning without a negative cast as simply *desire* (ESV, NRSV, NKJV). The New Testament and other Greek writing use ἐπιθυμία in three ways, contextually determined. The positive sense of *desire for good things* (e.g., Phil 1:23; Luke 22:15; 1 Thess 2:17), the neutral sense of *strong desire* (Mark 4:19; Rev 18:14), and the negative sense of *desire for something forbidden* (Rom 7:7; 2 Pet 1:4; Col 3:5; 1 Thess 4:5; Gal 5:24; 1 Pet 4:3). This range of meaning is similar to the range of senses for the English term *desire*; BDAG, s.v. "ἐπιθυμία".

[44]Moo, *James*, 75.

[45]Moo, *James*, 75; John Calvin, *The Epistle of James*, trans. and ed. John Owen, Calvin's Commentaries, vol. 22 (Grand Rapids: Baker, 1996), 289.

[46]W. R. Baker, "Temptation", in *Dictionary of the Later New Testament and Its Developments*, ed. Ralph P. Martin and Peter H. Davids (Downers Grove, IL:

This also means that James explains temptation as a general human experience. Sharing in this experience are human beings in all four states of existence: pre-fall, fallen, regenerate, and God incarnate.[47]

Furthermore, as in the traditional view of an internal-external dichotomy of temptations, if *all* temptation occurs *because of* the inner presence of sin or inclination to sin (concupiscence, the corrupt desire from original sin), then it would be the case that Jesus either had sin (which is false) or he had no temptation.[48] Clearly, Jesus had temptation but he did not have sin; this means that at least some temptation is not from sin. In other words, the traditional view of temptation in James 1:12-15 requires that there are two sorts of temptation, internal and external, that are subsets of the general category of temptation. Nonetheless, the question remains whether James 1:12-15 depicts *only* one sort of temptations that arise from within the sinful person (excluding another sort of temptations that arise externally), or whether James describes temptation to sin in *general*. In this latter case, desire is *not* the cause of the temptation but a frequent answer of the sinner to it. Theologically, both options are reasonable because, on the one hand, Jesus was tempted to sin, and on the other hand, there may be temptation that Jesus did not experience because it arises inwardly from sin.

The traditional view sets apart two sorts of temptations (internally sinful, externally sinless). The alternative given here is to explain the differences as different sorts of desires (corrupt desires and legitimate desires leading to sin) that are person-variable because of differing psychological configurations.

InterVarsity, 1997), 1166-70. Baker notes the possible background of Sir 15:11-20 for Jas 1:13-18, indicating that the *yetzer hara* in Old Testament perspective (cf. Gen 6:5; 8:21) is a "buffer between humans' capacity for sin, which comes from being made in God's image, and humans' responsibility for sin, which comes from their own choice to follow their *ye* [inclination]. *Yetzer* may be the vehicle for sin, but it is not sin itself." The resemblance of Sir 15:11-20 to Jas 1 is startling.

[47] A similar New Testament comment on temptation as an experience common to all is Paul's reminder in 1 Cor 10:13. This affirmation of the general, common experience of temptation is not a comfort offered to those afflicted by temptation. Paul counters those among his readers who claimed they were especially bad off in their particular temptations to idolatry (see Anthony C. Thiselton, *The First Epistle to the Corinthians*, New International Greek Testament Commentary, vol. 43 [Grand Rapids: Eerdmans, 2000], 749). The assurance of God's provision for a way to escape temptation minimizes the supposed fatalism that the readers at Corinth share with the readers of James's letter. In each case, Christians are reminded of their responsibility to turn away from sin. In each case, Christians are assured of God's help to resist the temptation. Moreover, Heb 4:15-16 adds the further assurance that Jesus empathizes with tempted Christians in the struggle and offers them true help to resist sin and follow his reasonable pattern of having done so.

[48] For those who claim Jesus took a fallen human nature so that he could be tempted, it should be remembered that Adam and Eve were also truly tempted without sin or concupiscence.

Thus, Jesus' temptation experience is relevantly similar to the temptations that sinful people experience, with variation only according to the person-variability of temptations and the particular desires involved. The greater intensity of his temptations because of his special role, circumstances, and Satanic opposition (see below) more than compensates for any differences of his not having had corrupt desires.

Therefore, James 1:12-15 notwithstanding, the internal dynamic of temptation is the same regardless of one's fallen or unfallen volitional condition. Jesus had to choose between desires leading to sin and desires leading to righteousness in the same way that all others do. Jesus' difference as a man apart from fallen humanity's total depravity and total inability to please God does not disqualify him from achieving human sinlessness in a way that he remains a reasonable pattern for others. On the contrary, we will see below that in a case-by-case comparison of Jesus' temptations with those of some fallen person, the special severity of Jesus' temptations far outweighs the supposed advantages that he had over sinners. Indeed, comparison will show that Jesus was in a far worse position to resist temptation than others are (i.e., believers).[49]

External Factors of Temptation

The internal factors of beliefs and desires are dynamically related to external factors in temptation. This is an alternative account to the common idea that some temptations arise internally, and others arise externally. I argue that all temptation is an internal conflict in relation to the external factors. The clearest distinctions of different temptations should be based on the external factors of life settings, and not on the traditional taxonomy of sinful and sinless temptations. The advantage of taking this view is to narrow the perceived gap between Jesus' experience and our experience in temptation.

First, all temptation is a personal conflict with both internal and external factors. Contrary to the distinction that some have made between internal and external temptations,[50] the case seems to be that all temptations form a bridge

---

[49]We must distinguish here between regenerate and unregenerate humanity. Christ specially delivers regenerate humanity from the power of sin (Rom 6:1-23). By contrast, unregenerate humanity, being totally depraved and totally unable to choose desires leading to righteousness, cannot finally resist temptations to sin, but manage at best to sin less egregiously than they might have otherwise (e.g., perhaps not actively destroying others by crimes and violence, but all the while living solely from a selfish, rebellious resistance to God that tarnishes all the appearance of their moral virtues). Jesus was certainly in a better position than unregenerate humanity, but he remains in a position in relation to temptation that is similar enough if not much worse than regenerate humanity, for whom he is an example of sinlessness.

[50]E.g., Donald G. Bloesch writes in *Essentials of Evangelical Theology* (San Francisco: Harper & Row, 1978), 1:96, that internal temptation presupposes sin, indicating that temptation has roots within the man himself. Bloesch represents a common view that

between an internal desire (whether corrupt or sinless) and the sin-prospect of satisfying that desire in an external state of affairs. Ted Peters observes that temptations do not simply arise internally but press upon the person from the outside: "There is no question that temptation to sin comes to us from beyond ourselves. It is not just an internal affair. Evil is bigger than we are."[51] Temptation seems to be constituted by the correspondence between the external circumstances of life in the world and the internal, subjective awareness of those circumstances in relation to one's desires. The correlation between an internal desire of the person and an external state of affairs can also be compared to a visitation that comes from the outside.[52]

Second, the proposal that this struggle is internal in correspondence to external relationships that occasion the appeals of sin is confirmed by the way the author of Hebrews warns against the straying and hardness of hearts that the disobedient in Israel exemplified (3:7-10). The Israelites are an example to avoid their internal response to the external conditions of their wilderness circumstances. The internal-external interaction also has support in Jesus' exhortation to his disciples that they pray and watch so that they would "not enter into temptation."[53] The temptation is there objectively, but the disciples and Jesus have the internal struggle either to refuse or to enter into temptation.

Therefore, temptation to sin is always an internal experience that is produced by the agent's relational engagement with the external world. The external world that provides the material for temptations may be an imaginative and impossible state of affairs (e.g., fantasizing about assassinating a world leader) or material constituted by the real and possible (e.g., Jesus turning stones into bread). If this description of the struggle in temptation as an internal-external relation is right, then we can explain the description of Jesus' temptations in

---

was also voiced by John Calvin based on an interpretation of *without sin* in Heb 4:15 to mean that Jesus' temptations did not originate from internal sin. Also, we saw in ch. 6 that Thomas Aquinas claimed Jesus was only tempted by the world and the devil, but not by the flesh. Similarly, William L. Banks, *The Day Satan Met Jesus* (Chicago: Moody, 1973), 48, writes, "For Him, temptations could come only from the outside, not from the inside. His holiness then is that which signifies a total absence of any inner fleshly motions of a sin nature." On the contrary, I am arguing that Jesus did experience internal temptation, though not that he was tempted by the flesh in the Pauline sense of a sinful corruption. I do not think that internal temptation is generated by sinful desire in every case. So, just as we experience temptation internally, so did Jesus.

[51]Ted Peters, *Sin: Radical Evil in Soul and Society* (Grand Rapids: Eerdmans, 1994), 25.

[52]B. Van Iersel, *The Bible on the Temptations of Man*, trans. F. Vander Heijden (De Pere, WI: St. Norbert Abbey, 1966), 5, proposes the analogy of a visitation for temptation experiences.

[53]This account is given in Mark 14:38, μὴ ἔλθητε εἰς πειρασμόν. I think that Matthew has intensified teh warning and teh internality of the temptation struggle by adding a prepositional prefix εἰς- (*in*) to the verb to double Mark's single εἰς; Matt 26:41, μὴ εἰσέλθητε εἰς πειρασμόν.

Hebrews 4:15 as truly similar to the temptations commonly experienced by others; *all* temptations are internal-external, and Jesus experienced temptation in this way just as we do.

Externally, the choice presented to the person is between the actual state of affairs and the proposed or possible state of affairs that could be actualized by means of choosing the desire leading to sin. Interrelated with this external situation is the person-variable correspondence of the sinful prospect inherent in the possible state of affairs that appeals uniquely to the tempted individual's psychological configuration (e.g., a heroin user who sees someone drop a wallet will be strongly tempted to keep it as a means to getting dope, a desire leading to sin, and not return the wallet to the owner, a desire leading to righteousness). The person must face the sinful prospect according to the tension between the sinful and non-sinful states of affairs. For Jesus in Gethsemane, this means the tension between avoiding the cross and embracing suffering in the cup of wrath.

The external situation also supplies the material for a sinful target of temptation in relation to an individual's psychological configuration (including one's character), with varying intensity. For example, an honest man will experience a low appeal of temptation to the sins of greed and theft when he sees that someone has dropped a wallet in the parking lot outside a store. But the same man may have great difficulty resisting the temptation to slander his co-worker later that day because, according to his scale of values and beliefs, the belief that getting revenge is justified. By comparison, Jesus' first wilderness temptation to make bread for himself had a high appeal that he felt intensely because the proposed state of affairs appealed was attractive to him in view of his hunger and (likely) desire for assurance of his identity that starvation now called into question.[54] His psychological configuration as the Son of God made that particular sin plausible and tempting for him in a forceful way. To sum up, temptation depends on external circumstances that engage with a person's internal configuration.

Definition of Temptation

People commonly think of temptation as partly sinful, with a significant role of sinful desires. I have sought to show that this does not fit temptation for Jesus, or for Adam and Even before the fall (or, for saints in glory, if temptation continues as a concomitant of freedom). I propose that all temptation (for Jesus and for all others) is intensely internal *and* external to bring about this basic inward conflict among the antithetical desires leading to sin and righteousness. The following definition of temptation collects the features we have explored

---

[54]Nonetheless, we saw in the discussion of Christ's wilderness temptations, the focus primarily had to do with his relation to God, and not simply his hunger for bread. The example is multi-layered.

above:

> Temptation is the internal struggle among a person's beliefs and desires within a particular setting of external circumstances and *pulls* the person to sin as its target.

The advantage of this comprehensive definition allows us to draw direct lines of correspondence between Jesus' temptations and the temptation experiences of believers, according to the claim of Hebrews 4:15 that Jesus' empathy is based on the direct similarity of his experience. This advantage also allows us to draw a direct line between Jesus' resistance to temptation and the possibilities for believers to follow Christ's pattern, according to the claims of Hebrews 12:1-3 and 1 Peter 2:21-25 that Jesus is a reasonable model for human sinlessness. Thus, the definition allows a reasonable explanation of the biblical data for Jesus' relevance in terms of the commonality of human temptation.

Jesus was Tempted for Us

According to the definition of temptation given above, we can trace the experience of Jesus as follows: in Gethsemane, Jesus desires to avoid the punishment for sin (which is a desire that leads to sin) and he desires to obey God (a desire leading to righteousness). Despite his high priority for self-preservation and the possible belief that evading pain may be possible, he chooses to obey God according to his highest value and belief of pleasing his Father. Jesus wants to obey God more than he wants to dodge the pain of being cursed by God. This internal choice occurred dynamically in relation to specific external factors. Jesus' circumstances—with the imminent prospect of suffering the cup of wrath—are countered by the possible, imaginable state of affairs in which he does not drink the cup of wrath. The temptation with its sinful prospect of disobeying God out of a justifiable desire to avoid pain is uniquely fitted (person-variability) to his psychological configuration. No one else could have felt this temptation, or experienced the intensity the way he did because the factors that constituted it to be a temptation for him were both internal and external, and particular to his relationship to God, his special role as the Messiah, and his special awareness of the prospect of his suffering. He suffers the pull and the fear internally as he pleads again and again for a way out. His struggle to obey truly is a fight that involves his beliefs and desires. When his request for a non-sinful escape is not granted, he chooses the only remaining desire that still leads to righteousness (through suffering). His refusal to choose a sinful path is the difficult model for all of us.[55]

Scripture is clear that Jesus' temptations were real in the full range of experiences that were sufficient for him to empathize with all others who are

---

[55] Bolstered by his example, the apostles Peter, James, and John willingly turned down the same path of suffering and martyrdom.

tempted, and he is the reasonable human template of sinlessness for them to resist sin as he did. Jesus could possess legitimate desires and sinless temptations in relation to desires for sinful satisfactions. Jesus had to respond by overcoming his desires without intending or choosing to sin. Jesus' differences of having no corrupt desires or a fallen will do not preclude him from sharing in the common temptation experience of humanity. Temptations related to corrupt desires are person-variable, and do not constitute a distinct set or category of temptations in which Jesus could not share (e.g., internal temptations).

Scripture is also clear that Jesus experienced the full intensity of temptations in his relationships as a man. We have seen that the person-variability of temptation makes comparisons between individual experiences difficult; nonetheless, we may affirm that the relational conditions of Jesus' experiences constituted the greatest possible degree of human temptation and made his temptations much more intense than the rest of humanity's for at least three reasons.

First, in his special role as Messiah, Jesus had the responsibilities and authority of inaugurating the kingdom of heaven and, as a principle greater temptation follows closely on greater power.[56] The pressures he bore as a man because of his role likely made his daily experience in opposition to personal, social, and cosmic evil much more present and pressing. Jesus bore the immense intensity of his temptations as the Messiah by consistently renouncing all the desires for sinful outcomes that afflicted him as a man.

Second, the pressures of temptations that Jesus suffered were compounded because Satan himself was directly provoking him in the wilderness (and possibly at other times, culminating in the cross). His temptations were uniquely set in relation to the cosmic war between God and Satan, as explained helpfully by Sinclair Ferguson:

> His temptations [in the wilderness] constitute an epochal event. They are not merely personal, but cosmic. They constitute the tempting of the last Adam. True, there is a common bond between his temptations and ours: he is really and personally confronted by dark powers. But the significance of the event does not lie in the ways in which our temptations are like his, but in the particularity and uniqueness of his experiences. He was driven into the wilderness as an assault force. His testing was set in the context of a holy war in which he entered the enemy's domain, absorbed his attacks and sent him into retreat (Mt. 4:11, and especially Lk. 4:13). In the power of the Spirit, Jesus advanced as the divine warrior, the God of battles who fights on behalf of his people and for their

---

[56]Letch, *Temptation and Freedom*, 44-46. Human history has abundant examples of the powerful temptations that come to those in power.

salvation (*cf.* Ex. 15:3; Ps. 98:1). His triumph demonstrated that 'the kingdom of God is near' and that the messianic conflict had begun.[57]

So cunning an opponent as Satan directly met Jesus to tempt him, but the evil probably does not engage many others in this personal way. Adam and Eve were defeated this way. The exceptional case of Satan's special attention to Job emphasizes Job's extraordinary virtue in a way that prefigures Satan's direct attacks on Christ. No person can claim to have faced a more difficult temptation experience than what is clearly detailed about Jesus' wilderness temptations in direct contest with the devil.

Third, Jesus uniquely exhausted his temptations in every case by his total resistance and never feeling the relief that comes with surrender.[58] Unlike Jesus, the rest of us experience what Oscar Wilde penned in the thoughts of his character Lord Henry: "The only way to get rid of a temptation is to yield to it. Resist it, and your soul grows sick with longing for the things it has forbidden to itself."[59] By never giving in, Jesus alone has felt the fullest intensity and duration of being tempted to sin, whatever the type and texture of someone's experience that we might compare to his. The intensity of Christ's experience should further be weighed by considering the cost of declining to sin in his final temptation, out of which he made a choice not to escape, but for a level of personal suffering in the curse of God that surpasses what anyone else has ever anticipated or experienced.

This means that even though he was in a better position than regenerate humanity because he lacked corrupt desires, Jesus was in a much worse position because of the special particularity of mission, as an object of diabolical attack, and his complete resistance throughout his life and the excruciating circumstances of his passion. Therefore, what availed him is sufficient for the extremely intense experience of the heroin user and the persecuted Christian—and anyone else—to choose righteously against the temptations with downward desires besetting them forcefully.

The Holy Spirit and the Temptation of God's Son

How can the eternal Son of God, who cannot be tempted *as God*, live as a man in a way that he can be tempted to sin? This question is not unique to temptation, because we can also ask, how can Jesus remain omniscient as God the Son while simultaneously he takes upon himself an existence in which he is limited in his knowledge as man and fails to know things that God knows? I propose that plausibly the Holy Spirit fulfilled a role in the hypostatic union as

---

[57]Sinclair Ferguson, *The Holy Spirit* (Downers Grove, IL: InterVarsity, 1996), 48-49.
[58]Letch, *Temptation and Freedom*, 43.
[59]Oscar Wilde, *The Picture of Dorian Gray* (Franklin Center, PA: The Franklin Library, 1988 [1891]), 24-25.

a bond and boundary to maintain the integrity of each nature as they are fully possessed and expressed by the Son of God. This proposal is consistent with what many theologians in M4-M6 have recognized as pneumatological Christology. I propose that the dual life of Christ, one person in two natures simultaneously, was managed by the Holy Spirit's role to bond and regulate the hypostatic union of God incarnate. This pneumatological involvement was necessary for Jesus to experience temptation because otherwise, he would have known by his divine knowledge and his properly functioning human understanding that he could not do what was proposed to him. Moreover, without a pneumatological restraint or regulation of Christ's divine power from coming through into his human nature, his suffering and death would have been impossible (as in M6).

The Dual Life of God Incarnate and Pneumatological Veiling

Others have found the idea of a dual life for God incarnate to be an adequate and satisfying explanation of Chalcedonian Christology.[60] The concept is helpful for us to see that the eternal Logos exists as fully divine and fully human in two frames of reference.[61] The two frames of reference—or categories of his experience, or modes of existence—are ontologically distinct, with different attributes and rules governing Jesus' action in each setting, frame, or sphere of his action (simultaneously). He exists simultaneously as the one unifying person in two natures, both God the Son from all eternity and a man created within time. He exists eternally as the divine Logos and takes up a second mode of existence temporally in the form of a servant and Son of Man. As the Logos he exists in heaven in the full power of God (transcending creation), and, simultaneously, as the man Jesus he exists on earth in the weakness of humanity (part of creation). With due regard for the unity of the Incarnation, the difficulty remains to preserve the continuing distinction of two sets of drastically different attributes of the two natures. How is this unifying boundary of a dual existence preserved? How is one person unable to be tempted as God, and able to be tempted as man?

---

[60]See above, ch. 7. I am repeating here the long tradition of *Logos extra carnem*, the eternal Logos existed beyond the flesh, that is, remaining what he was as fully God while becoming what he was not as a true human being. He completely took possession of the human nature he assumed for incarnation but was not contained by it. This concept has been pinned on Calvin by Lutherans as the *extra calvinisticum*, but Athanasius, Cyril of Alexandria, Augustine, Leo the Great, Peter Lombard, and Thomas Aquinas all affirm the theological idea. Representing Reformed theology that has carried on this helpful concept, Bruce, *Humiliation of Christ*, 127, writes, "According to this view the Logos had a *double life*, one unaffected by the Incarnation, another in the man Christ Jesus, in which His action is so self-controlled as to leave room for a natural human development involving growth in stature, wisdom, and grace."

[61]See n. 5 above.

As a self-conscious person, the Son of God is able to be limited in his earthly, temporal existence, in a way consistent with a true humanity, while continuing to be unlimited in the full deity of his eternal existence. How can this be? How can one person plausibly grow in knowledge and have limitations on what he knows (consider that Jesus had to ask for information in John 11:34 and confessed his ignorance about his return) while as the eternal Logos he (the same person!) knows completely all things? If we can plausibly see a role for the Holy Spirit to *enrich* Jesus' humanity for the purposes of his messianic mission, then can we not also wonder if the Holy Spirit served to *limit* a flow from Jesus' deity to his humanity and thus preserve his dual life?[62] Such limitation seems to be appropriate for the Logos, who is omnipotent and self-existent, to be able to experience the weakness and contingency of human life with suffering and death. I offer that perhaps the Holy Spirit is the boundary who prevents a flow of properties between the natures because this is appropriate to his role of close involvement in the development of Jesus' human experience (as with all people who obey God).

The proposal of M6 was that Jesus' divine glory *in his earthly mode of existence* was covered by the veil of his humanity in a way similar to how the clouds veil the brightness of the sun. Luther and Calvin perceived that only in this way could the temptation and suffering of Jesus take place, if somehow the divine power was withheld from his humanity. We saw that Calvin explained the *kenosis* of Philippians 2:7 as "the concealment of Christ's divine majesty with the veil of his humanity."[63] The suppression of divine power allowed Jesus to fulfill his redemptive role of suffering, and necessarily so because Calvin asserted, "the mystery of our salvation could not have been fulfilled otherwise."[64] So far so good. The difficulty of this M6 formula is how one

---

[62]Klaus Issler, "Jesus's Example: Prototype of the Dependent, Spirit-Filled Life," in *Jesus in Trinitarian Perspective*, ed. Fred Sanders and Klaus Issler (Nashville: B & H, 2007), 221, suggests the Spirit's role in Jesus' consciousness as a sort of fire wall that regulates his human knowledge of things he knows according to his divine mind.

[63]*Institutes*, 2.13.2; cf. *The Epistles of Paul the Apostle to the Galatians, Ephesians, Philippians and Colossians*, Calvin's Commentaries, vol. 11, trans. T. H. L. Parker (Grand Rapids: Eerdmans, 1965), 248. Cf. E. David Willis, *Calvin's Catholic Christology: The Function of the So-Called Extra Calvinisticum in Calvin's Christology* (Leiden: E. J. Brill, 1966), 80: "This full humanity was enabled by the Eternal Son's emptying himself in the sense of freely concealing himself and withholding the exercise of his powers through the flesh to which he was fully joined. The *kenosis* was the concealment, not the abdication, of the Eternal Son's divine majesty."

[64]Comment on Matt. 26:37, in *A Harmony of the Gospels Matthew, Mark and Luke*, vol. 3 trans. A. W. Morrison (Grand Rapids: Eerdmans, 1972), 147-48. Cf. Stephen Edmondson, *Calvin's Christology* (Cambridge: CUP, 2004), 119-20. "The separation of natures is what ensures the lowliness of this flesh – Christ's humanity is fragile, weak, and anxious only as it remains separate from his divinity and can experience reality in a human manner. Christ knows our weaknesses only because his human nature is truly

person can pull this off without compromising the authenticity of his weaker mode of existence. For example, is it reasonable to consider that Jesus could simultaneously veil his divine knowledge with his human knowledge so that he affirmed truthfully that as a man he did not know the time of his return? Similarly, how could Jesus allow himself to suffer temptation while simultaneously he remained fully aware as the eternal Logos that he could not sin? Of course, our understanding of what is possible for God is dim, and it may be enough for some to stop with the affirmation that the Logos simply did so, became incarnate, and the doing of his two-natured existence remains inscrutable to us.

Nonetheless, it seems to fit better with the rich trinitarian relations and the undivided working of the three persons not to stop but to press on and explain this regulating operation in the hypostatic union as the proper role of the Holy Spirit. This means that the Spirit veiled Jesus' deity with his humanity in the earthly frame or mode of his existence (compare the analogy of being given a memory-blocking drug and then having to give a speech by relying solely upon the words of a teleprompter). Thus, the Spirit's intervention preserved the integrity of Jesus' two natures and the authenticity of his human experience (with all the attendant points of relevance for other human beings so that he can be tempted, bear sin, and be raised from the dead as a man). With his weak, limited humanity fully preserved by the Holy Spirit from transformation (or cancellation) by divine attributes, Jesus can achieve sinlessness, become empathetic, and demonstrate his life as the pattern for others (and be able to die as a substitute). In this way, the Spirit shields Jesus' consciousness as a man from filling with knowledge by his divine mind.

Morris and others have argued for dual or twofold consciousness in Christ.[65] On Morris's account, the unity of the Incarnation (one person with two minds) is plausibly secured because divine mind contains the human mind and possesses one-sided (asymmetric) access to the human contents. What I think needs to be added is that the Holy Spirit regulates this two-fold knowledge and preserves the limitation of the human mental life and personality. Revelation by the Spirit was likely provided to Christ's human mind. We saw that M9 proposed a limit of some sort to Jesus' awareness of his capacity for sin as the sufficient condition for true temptation. I think the evidence for veiling and pneumatological empowerment plausibly supports this eclipse as having been done by the Spirit.[66]

---

and fully human, not safeguarded from the travail of human experience by his divinity, but immersed in such travail as his divinity refuses to exert any ameliorating influence over him. Calvin emphasizes the separation of the two natures in Christ primarily so that Christ can share our condition."

[65]Morris, *Logic of God Incarnate*, 153-62.

[66]Chalcedonian Christology recognizes that the unity of the two natures is that as one person, Christ possesses both natures. However, various formulations of the relation of

The Holy Spirit as the Unifying Bond

By analogy with the role of the Holy Spirit in the Christian's regeneration (John 3:3-8) and ongoing communion with God (Romans 8:13-17), it seems plausible that Jesus' divine-human communion is similarly managed closely by the Holy Spirit.[67] On this view, the Holy Spirit's role in the hypostatic union included forming the union of the two natures and maintaining the distinction between them. Two witnesses to this claim are included just to corroborate what has seemed plausible to me as the proper role of the Holy Spirit and a satisfying explanation for regulating the authentic human life of the Son of God.

First, I find agreement from Jonathan Edwards. He initially argues that "If 'tis by the Spirit of God that the human nature of Christ was conceived, and had life and being, why would we not suppose that 'tis also by the Spirit that he has union with the divine nature?"[68] Edwards additionally argues that Christ was united as Logos to the human nature by the same way that he had divine knowledge as a man—through the Holy Spirit who joined the communion of Christ's two wills and minds.[69] Edwards explains that Jesus implies the Holy Spirit as the bond of his incarnational union in John 10:30-36. Jesus reveals that as the Son he was *sent by the Father* to become incarnate and was *sanctified by the Father* (v. 36), which for Edwards means that since the Spirit is the sanctifier, Jesus says the Father has sent the Spirit to form and unite the humanity to the Logos.[70] Edwards explains further that Jesus' statement follows the charge of blasphemy, that Jesus has made himself to be God (v. 33) when

---

these two natures to each other have raised the problem of a one-way flow of attributes between the two natures, usually from deity to humanity, as in the Lutheran formula with the attribute of omnipresence. The communication of attributes between the natures (*in abstracto*) makes good sense to Lutherans, Eastern Orthodox, and Catholic theologians. I wonder if the appeal of such a model is that were it not for the mediating role of the Holy Spirit that I am proposing here, such communication would occur and dissolve the integrity of the humanity. In other words, the Reformed emphasis on the integrity of the two natures seems to depend upon due recognition of the Holy Spirit's role as we have seen in Calvin, Owen, and Macleod.

[67]Bruce, *Humiliation of Christ*, 127, 130, notes that Lutheran theologian Schneckenburger had argued that the Holy Spirit was the bond of union, the union of two natures in Christ being analogous to the Spirit's work in regeneration to unite the believer to Christ.

[68]Jonathan Edwards, *The "Miscellanies" (Entry Nos. 1-500)*, #487, ed. Thomas A. Schafer, vol. 13 of *The Works of Jonathan Edwards* (New Haven, CT: Yale University Press, 1994), 531. I am grateful to W. Ross Hastings for calling Edwards' pneumatological Christology to my attention in Hastings, "Jonathan Edwards' Pneumatological Doctrine of the Incarnation", 292-97.

[69]Jonathan Edwards, *The "Miscellanies" (Entry Nos. 501-832)*, #513, ed. Ava Chamberlain, vol. 18 of *The Works of Jonathan Edwards* (New Haven, CT: Yale University Press, 2000), 57.

[70]Edwards, *Miscellanies* #624, 154.

he claimed to be one with the Father (v. 30). Jesus' response in v. 36, then, is a revelation of how it happened that he is a man made to be God—by the Holy Spirit's forming and uniting work to incarnate the Son in humanity.[71] In this way, then, Edwards sees that the Logos assumed a human nature by sending (coordinately with the Father's sending) the Holy Spirit to make and unite a human nature to himself, to be the Godman. In an ongoing way, the Holy Spirit was for the Logos the means of his indwelling, possessing, being united to, and empowering the human nature he created for incarnation, as Edwards concludes, "the union of Christ's human nature with the divine is by the Spirit of God."[72] We may wish for more biblical evidence for this claim, but the plausibility of the speculation strikes Edwards as right nonetheless.[73]

Second, Bavinck marks the necessity of the Spirit's role to unite two natures in Christ, and Christ's ongoing communion with the Father according to his life as a man:

> If humans in general cannot have communion with God except by the Holy Spirit, then this applies even more powerfully to Christ's human nature, which had to be unified with the Son in an entirely unique manner. This special union, which far exceeds and differs essentially from the immanence of God in his creatures, the manifestation of God in his people, makes a priori probable and even necessary a very special activity on the part of the Holy Spirit.[74]

The idea of pneumatological union and restraint to regulate an authentic human experience fits well with Christ's relevance as the second Adam and high priest. Having entered a creaturely mode of existence as a true human being, Jesus becomes a pattern of human life under divine influence of the Spirit. An analogy from Jesus' ministry is the way he submitted to the Spirit's guidance for testing. The Spirit directed Jesus into the wilderness where he was bereft of food and community for forty days so he could be assaulted by the devil in an especially vulnerable state. Likewise, the pneumatological restraint of Jesus' deity is the Spirit's limitation for the redemptive program achieved through the Son's authentic humanity. Without some sort of eclipse of Jesus' deity to prevent these powers from being expressed in his human, earthly frame of existence, the weaknesses by which he suffered in an authentic, limited humanity would not have been possible (e.g., temptation, fatigue, limited

---

[71] Edwards, *Miscellanies* #709, 333-35.

[72] Edwards, *Miscellanies* #766, 412.

[73] Without thinking of Chalcedonian and pneumatological Christology, I doubt that Edwards would have seen what he finds in John 10:30-36, but here may be a good example of systematic theology leading the proper interpretation of particular passages of Scripture. I am as yet unsure (but not unconvinced) about Edwards' interpretation, though I think it is consistent with other lines of biblical evidence for pneumatological Christology and the plausibility that the Spirit is the bond of the hypostatic union.

[74] Bavinck, *Sin and Salvation in Christ*, 292.

knowledge, and death). The pneumatological veiling or restraint of deity corresponds to the positive work of the Holy Spirit to contribute ethical formation, guidance, and empowerment that were needed for Jesus to fulfill the messianic tasks within the limited frame of his humanity Luke 2:40, 52; Isa 11:2-3).

A parallel for the pneumatological veiling of Christ's divine nature from display in his human condition of existence is the way that God's work in the church is veiled by the weak, sinful humanity of the people and the flawed ecclesiastical structures we have developed.[75] Like the divine action in the church, the Holy Spirit supervenes Jesus' human experience from conception and throughout his growth and messianic action, supplying what he needs (e.g., guidance, illumination, assurance, power) for his redemptive tasks.

Several advantages commend the proposal of pneumatological veiling of Jesus' deity. First, this proposal explains Jesus' action as a trinitarian operation to coordinate the Father's plan, the Son's mission, and the Holy Spirit's mediating role facilitating the Son's mission. The Gospels indicate trinitarian relations in the Incarnation by the distinct emphases of the Synoptics and John's Gospel. In the Synoptics (especially Luke), Jesus' dependence on the Holy Spirit for guidance and power to fulfill his mission of teaching and healing is presented as a pattern repeated by the church in Acts. In the Gospel of John, Jesus' dependence on the Father for guidance and power is modeled for the church who receives the Holy Spirit from Jesus and is brought into relationship with the Father.[76]

Second, this proposal avoids a divisive Christology by the unitary action of the Son as regulated by the Holy Spirit in his human condition of existence. Jesus has a real, limited, authentic humanity without the incoherence of a self-restriction of his divine attributes. At his ascension, the humanity of Christ remains pneumatological as his ongoing role to bear the Spirit for his people and share the Spirit with them. Isaiah 11 (as one example among many)

---

[75]Calvin *Inst.* 2.16.12, observes that the kingdom of God is presently veiled by the weakness of the flesh in the similar way to how Christ's divine power was veiled with his humanity.

[76]Another who recognizes the parallel of trinitarian operations (i.e., the involvement of the Spirit is attributed to the Father) in the Synoptics and John is Gary M. Burge, *The Anointed Community: The Holy Spirit in the Johannine Tradition* (Grand Rapids: Eerdmans, 1987), 99. "We noticed in our examination of Jesus' works of power that the Johannine Christ is not a pneumatic. His miracles are revelatory and make glory evident rather than power. Thus they are christological in that they express who Jesus is instead of what he bears. In addition this Johannine theme serves a oneness christology in which we can say that the works of power do not reveal the power of the Spirit but the presence of the Father. . . . It appears that the role of the Spirit is somewhat preempted by the presence of the Father in Johannine christology." I should add that John emphasizes Christ's giving of the Holy Spirit to his followers, an idea that is implicit in the Synoptics with the promise that Jesus will baptize with the Spirit (Mark 1:8).

suggests a future eschatological orientation of the Messiah to the Spirit's inward mediation of divine power to Jesus' humanity. The continuing union of the Incarnation remains the Holy Spirit's role.

Third, this proposal upholds Christ's uniqueness. This proposal explains the exercise of the Son's own power (e.g., the authority to forgive sins, to heal those who touch him) in ways that coincide with normal human operation in conjunction with the Holy Spirit. We can say, with Edwards, that when Jesus does divine things by the Spirit, he is the Logos acting as a man by the Holy Spirit he has sent to empower his humanity.[77] Sometimes pneumatological Christology can overlook the distinctions between Jesus and other prophets by overemphasizing the Holy Spirit's role. The idea of pneumatological veiling is entirely a unique operation (despite the analogies) that should preserve Christ's uniqueness among the other pneumatological operations in the lives of those who are not the Messiah (e.g., formation, empowerment, and guidance for all people who obey God, and especially in the New Covenant with the promised outpouring of the Spirit).

To sum up, I propose that Jesus could be tempted despite his impeccability because his divine power was veiled (M6), and his human knowledge was governed so that he lacked certainty about his ability to sin (M9). I suggest that the Holy Spirit did both actions. A third action of the Spirit is more commonly recognized that he also empowered Jesus in sinlessness so it would be a human achievement (not merely a necessity of divine impeccability).

---

[77]Edwards, *Miscellanies* #766, 412. Cf. the Reformed view of Bruce, *Humiliation of Christ*, 125: "Why should not the graces with which the soul of Jesus was enriched be the direct result of the union of the Logos to the humanity; why this roundabout way of communicating spiritual gifts through the Holy Ghost; does not this form of representation tend to make the union of the natures still more external—in fact, to make the divine factor in the union superfluous, and so land us in a purely human personality? . . .The spirit, whose gracious influences were poured into the soul of Christ, was the spirit proceeding from the Logos, His own spirit communicated freely by Himself; and the doctrine that the Logos worked on the humanity of Christ through His spirit, may be taken to mean that the influence of the Logos on the human nature was not physical but moral, not the immediate and necessary effect of the union of natures, but the free, ethically mediated action of the one on the other."

CHAPTER 12

The Perfect Human Life

How did Jesus resist temptation and achieve a perfect, sinless human life? The silence of Scripture on the question leaves us grasping for inferences to synthesize the significance of Jesus' temptation and sinlessness with his redemption, recapitulation, empathy with others, and reasonable pattern for others to follow. We have two options. The first option is that Jesus relied on his divine powers to achieve his sinless, perfect obedience to God. This means he used his deity partially for conquering some temptations or continually to defeat all his temptations. The second option is that his accomplishment was that of a divine person incarnate, but he did not employ his divine power to shield himself from the suffering or to overcome it obediently. I suggest the great unlikelihood of the first option alongside the strong possibility of the other. Had he used his inherent deity, he could not have become relevant for us in his empathy and being a pattern for righteous human life. Had he refrained from doing things as God could and did instead as a man helped by God, then Jesus used the help that is available for other people who follow Jesus.

The Implausibility of Sinlessness by His Divine Power

Some critics have pointed out that a human being who possesses and expresses the attributes of deity is no longer a true human because some of the essential traits of being a human are overwhelmed by the corresponding traits of deity. For example, Jesus would not count as a true human if he exercises the divine traits of omniscience, omnipotence, and omnipresence in his earthly existence. Indeed, many of his human experiences would have been impossible if he had simultaneously expressed certain divine traits while on earth: he could not have learned things, been tempted, suffered pains, or died as a man unless some sort of restraint or eclipse of his divine powers was in place (so, M6).

Consider the temptations of Jesus. The Gospels show the prominence of his human nature and give no hint that he relied on his own divine power as the eternal Son to resist his temptations. The human prominence shows in his human weaknesses that seem impossible without some sort of veiling or restriction of his deity from his human life. We cannot say that his display of weakness was a sham (which is impossible because this would mean he committed a deception), so we must accept his weaknesses as authentic.

Evidence that he did not know certain things, was hungry, fatigued, thirsty, tempted to sin, and felt physical pain and died raises questions about the possibility that his divine power was expressed in his human condition of existence in a continual and full way. Had Jesus walked the earth in the full exercise of his powers as the Son of God, it would be difficult to see how the biblical claims for his human weaknesses (including hunger, thirst, limited knowledge, temptation, fear, and death) and his sympathy with other human beings could be true and credible. Passages such as Hebrews 4:15 and 1 Peter 2:21-25 are written to audiences in desperate need for reassurance that Jesus truly suffered as they suffer, and that the risen Christ offers strength both by his example of human faithfulness and his direct provision of help. Hebrews 5:7-9 specifies that Jesus' being the eternal Son did not shield or exempt him from the difficulties of learning to obey in his suffering. Not only was his deity not an advantage to him alongside the rest of humanity, but without some sort of suppression, all these qualifications as the perfect priest would not have been attained by him.

One possible explanation for his weaknesses and success of perfection is that Jesus' humanity was only intermittently prominent, and the veiling of his divine power temporarily allowed his human weaknesses to be felt. As part of this explanation, Jesus' miracles, supernatural display of knowledge, and evasions of capture until the time of his surrender are attributed to his use of inherent divine powers. However, temptations remain a problem because, if there had been an intermittent restraint or veiling of divine power to allow temptation, then he must also have to overcome his temptation without divine power. No temptation could have occurred for him if his deity had been veiled in one moment, and then unveiled in the next to resist the temptation impeccably. So, divine power cannot be counted as the cause of his sinlessness, and the constancy of his temptations requires the constancy of holding his divine powers at bay. At best (on the view that he used his divine power to fight out his human obedience) he could only be said to have experienced half of temptation, and then he escaped through his deity.

Moreover, other evidence in his life indicates a pervasive role for the Holy Spirit, whom Jesus and the New Testament attributed for the signs and wonders Jesus performed (Matt 12:28; Acts 10:38). The Gospels emphasize the continuity between Jesus' ministry and the earlier ministry of Old Testament prophets by the same Holy Spirit who was to equip the Messiah (e.g., Luke 4:16-27).[1] Thus, the claim that his supernatural works indicate his divine nature are better explained as pneumatological, that is, Jesus is the Son of God anointed in his humanity to be the Messiah in David's line (as in Psalm 2).[2]

---

[1] Luke especially emphasizes Jesus' pneumatological likeness to others, beginning with a comparison *a fortiori* to the development of John the Baptizer.

[2] This is the Synoptic emphasis; John's Gospel emphasizes the Spirit as Christ's gift to his followers.

The combined evidence for his human weakness and the pneumatological dimension of his experience suggests that neither an intermittent nor a constant expression of his divine power in his human condition of existence occurred. This suggestion of implausibility does not necessarily exclude all inherent expression of Jesus' divine power during his earthly life. Such expression could have been the case, but not in ways that mitigated the fullness of his human experiences. His would *not* have been a true humanity if he had escaped suffering and weakness at times by recourse to his deity. Moreover, the New Testament does not present Jesus as relying on inherent divine powers to relieve himself of pain, whether in the midst of temptation, or in his anticipation of and suffering of divine wrath on the cross.[3] The New Testament theme of the divine Son's humiliation (e.g., John 13:3-15; Phil 2:5-11, Heb 2:9-18) and the repeated revelation that God the Son entered the frailty of humanity in a fallen world (cf. Rom 8:3; Heb 4:15) fit better with the affirmation that such divine advantages were not experienced as part of his human life.

This theological fit of a true, unmitigated experience of humanity as we have it (subject to pains and ills in solidarity with us to save us), bereft of divine advantages, is especially clear in contrast with the poor fit between the biblical evidence for Jesus' weaknesses and the traditional explanations. Patristic theology commonly explained that Jesus relied on his divine power to resist temptation.[4] If we think of Jesus' vulnerability to temptation as a man, the entire range of his temptations would be excluded because to have his divine power in play at all in his human life excludes his temptability (Jas 1:13, God cannot be tempted). If, as in some of the traditional views, Jesus had resorted to his divine power to resist temptation, then he could not have become the empathetic exemplar of human sinlessness for other human beings who struggle against temptations (1 Pet 2:21-25; Heb 4:15-16; 12:1-3). His sympathy for others who struggle against temptations large and small would be groundless and hollow. He who would never have known the pain of temptation in a first-person experience could never assure others that he knows their pain. Why would they turn to him for assistance if his means of resisting temptation had been merely his inherent deity and not something that he could make available to them?

Therefore, these items suggest the implausibility that Jesus relied upon his divine power to resist his temptations. This implausibility suggests that we consider other explanations that fit better with the biblical and theological evidence. Fortunately, the theological tradition has provided another option.

---

[3]The transfiguration may have been a display of his divine power, or a glorification by the Holy Spirit (which I think is more likely), but it was not an escape by any means.

[4]E.g., Augustine's explanation, which is typical: "That Christ was the conqueror there, why should we be surprised? He was almighty God." *Sermon 284.5*, in *Sermons 273-305A: On the Saints*, trans. Edmund Hill, vol. III/8 of *The Works of Saint Augustine* (Hyde Park, NY: New City, 1995), 91. Note, however, that Augustine also saw M4.

The Plausibility of Sinlessness by Empowering Grace

M4 and M6 recognized the evidence for the role of the Holy Spirit and various means of empowering grace as necessary and sufficient for Jesus' sinlessness to be a truly human achievement. The high plausibility and theological adequacy of this explanation rests on three premises:

> (1) Jesus' mission was to redeem humanity and provide a reasonable pattern of obeying God by his own human life, and these experiences also equipped him to become empathetic to the needs of others (he was truly tempted as they are).

> (2) The only pattern of a righteous human life that others could reasonably follow is that Jesus relies upon the same resources that may be provided for other human beings.

> (3) Scripture reveals that Jesus relies upon the very same provisions of empowering grace that are given (especially in the age of the Spirit) and repeatedly commended throughout Old Testament and New Testament to all people who obey God.

Thus, Jesus set down the pattern of his life in perfect righteousness for us by relying upon empowering grace, not by using his inherent divine powers as the eternal Son of God. His two-fold purpose was to be tempted and achieve sinlessness for us redemptively *and demonstratively*. Having been provided with his pattern and ready help through empowering grace, we who are regenerated may obey his call to follow him by drawing upon the same empowerment that he provides through the Holy Spirit.[5] Jesus' pattern of life shows that we can live pervaded by divine involvement as he was. Jesus attributed *all* his words and actions to God (e.g., John 5:19, 36; 10:18, 32-38; 12:49-50), just as all people must credit God as the ultimate cause for *all* good words and actions that they do in life (Eph 2:10). We could also say that Jesus demonstrates the life in the Spirit authentically, not superfluously, and that human righteousness is only possible through reliance upon empowering grace.

Pneumatological Christology (by which I mean a pervasive operation of the Holy Spirit to form, develop, and empower the Messiah) seems to be the best explanation for the supernatural aspects of Jesus' deeds (including his miracles

---

[5]By regenerated, I mean those who have been born again by the Holy Spirit to believe in Christ. The persistence of original sin for Christians prevents sinless perfection in this life from becoming a reality. Jesus achieved perfect righteousness, but we cannot (that is why we need him to achieve this for us; we can only be justified the basis of his achievement and never our own acts). Our hope is that we can progress as God leads and empowers us in maturity of righteousness in Christ by the Spirit. Theoretically, others alongside Jesus could receive sufficient divine assistance to live sinlessly (never fail to do right), but the corruption of humanity prevents anyone from doing so in the same full way that Jesus does, just as he receives the Spirit without measure (John 3:34) and does not resist the Spirit as we do.

and sinlessness). Many scholars have argued persuasively for the Holy Spirit's role to bring divine powers to Jesus' humanity, as in Hawthorne's conclusion to a monograph on the topic: "In whatever way the mystery of the Incarnation is finally to be explained, in whatever way one is finally to understand and explain how the divine and human relate to each other in the person of Jesus, one must ultimately take into account the role of the Holy Spirit in resolving this riddle."[6] H. D. McDonald helpfully explains this traditional idea (a minority tradition from M4 and M6):

> The Holy Spirit not only endowed the human nature of Christ with all necessary equipment, but He also caused these to be exercised, gradually, into full activity. During His days in the flesh, Jesus was under the constant and penetrating operation of the Spirit. . . . And since the Holy Spirit is the divine executive of the mighty acts of God, it need not be thought strange that Jesus should have lived His life and fulfilled His divine mission through His power. . . .The Spirit remained with Him throughout His earthly life controlling His mind, will and actions so that He learned from God, acted for God and taught of God unto the fullness of the stature of a perfect man.[7]

Theologically, the Spirit's role to empower Jesus is important for recognizing the authentic humanity of the Savior. His miraculous deeds and knowledge are best attributed to the Holy Spirit's work instead of the inherent power of the Logos because otherwise the Spirit's role would have been superfluous. Instead of a superfluous role, I agree with those who see a necessary role for the Spirit—that Jesus depended the Spirit from start to finish of his earthly life (and after the resurrection, Acts 1:2). Authentic humanity, whether sinless or not, is finite and contingent upon the Creator and his provisions for continuing existence. The Holy Spirit initiated and formed Jesus' humanity in Mary's womb (Luke 1:31-35), guided Jesus' development into manhood (Luke 2:40, 52), led Jesus into the wilderness (Luke 4:1-14), and empowered Jesus' ministry with teaching, exorcisms, and healings (e.g., Matt 12:28). Moreover, Hebrews 9:14 and Romans 1:4 add that even the Messiah's death and resurrection were accomplished by the empowering help of the Holy Spirit. Jesus himself defined his entire ministry from the outset as being under the influence of the Spirit's empowerment (Luke 4:17-21). Luke repeats a similar retrospect on Jesus' ministry in Peter's statements at Pentecost and Caesarea (Acts 2:22; 10:38), emphasizing on each occasion the empowering role of the Holy Spirit. The empowerment of Jesus seems to be intentionally stated as the prototype to the ways the early church was experiencing the Holy Spirit's empowering assistance. Luke highlights the Spirit's role of forming and empowering the Messiah, and then recounts the echoes of the Spirit's work to fill individuals with closely similar effects in the book of Acts (cf. the shape of

---

[6]Hawthorne, *Presence and the Power*, 217.

[7]H.D. McDonald, *Jesus—Human and Divine* (Grand Rapids: Zondervan, 1968), 34-35.

a pneumatological life in John 14—16, Romans 8, Galatians 5, and Ephesians 5:18-21).

The New Testament emphasis on the Spirit's role for Jesus follows a trajectory from the Old Testament, particularly Isaiah 11:1-10.[8] Three observations from this passage support a pneumatological Christology. First, the three-fold equipping of the Messiah for his role as God's king indicates a real need for the Messiah to be assisted in his humanity by the Spirit. In light of the revelation of the entire canon, the evidence for the Spirit's role in relation to God incarnate would otherwise be superfluous, adding deity to deity. Instead of being redundant, we can see the need for empowerment as part of Jesus' task to live a true human life and rule as the Messiah assisted by the Holy Spirit.

Second, the central emphasis of the equipping by the Spirit is internal and ethical, with worldwide ramifications in his righteous rule. The empowerment is not merely for doing the works of God as Messiah, but for living as *the one* who acts in perfect righteousness because of his pneumatological communion with God. The doubled term in Isaiah 11:2-3, "the fear of Yahweh", seems to be related to the righteousness and faithfulness of all the King's actions as world ruler (as described in Isa 11:3-10). We might be tempted to read the supernatural and righteous qualities of his rule according to Jesus' deity, but Isaiah 11 grounds all these effects in the dynamic presence of the Holy Spirit.

Third, the main orientation of this prophecy to salvation history is still in the future, beyond the first advent. Isaiah describes the features of the Messiah's earthly kingdom by which the Davidic king fulfills God's primordial commission to humanity (Gen 1:26) and all the promises that Israel would be a preeminent nation (e.g., Isa 2:1-4). The images of restoration and harmony among animals and people in Isaiah 11:5-10 (repeated in 65:17-25) clearly depict a future reality of kingdom renewal. All this results from the righteous rule of the Spirit-endowed Messiah of Jesse's stump. Nonetheless, the fulfillment of the prophecy is not limited to the future. Luke seems to count partial fulfillment of this empowering presence in Luke 2:40, 52 where the terms he uses for Jesus' exceptional development repeat terms from Isaiah 11:2 (note especially Luke's use of *grace* as a likely reference to the Holy Spirit).

In summary of this claim, it seems especially plausible that the role of the Holy Spirit in the Incarnation included both empowerment with special abilities and guiding the development of Jesus' character as a man. Plausibly, Jesus' communion with God according to his life as a man was mediated and facilitated by the Holy Spirit's ongoing work (just as for all people who obey God). This work began with the conception in Mary and continued throughout Jesus' earthly life as part of preserving the Son's authentic humanity. Jesus' communion with God according to his humanity is a relation that is joined forever by means of the Spirit (a special aspect of the economic Trinity). Mediated by the Spirit, this is a second, created, redemptive relationship that is

---

[8] What follows is a brief rehearsal of the discussion of this passage in ch. 3.

added to the eternal, immediate communion of God the Son and God the Father (in the immanent Trinity). Evidence in Jesus' life further suggests that he relied on empowering grace because of six aspects of help that the Gospels report in the circumstances of his temptations.

Six Signs of Empowering Grace

These six signs of divine assistance are plausibly constitutive of Jesus' sinlessness in coordination with or perhaps by the ethical role of the Holy Spirit in Jesus' development. The case may be that these aspects were individually necessary and jointly sufficient for Jesus' sinlessness.[9] We must not casually ignore the significance of how each is mentioned by the Gospel writers in the context of Jesus' experiences of temptation, and then each is likewise commended elsewhere in Scripture as part of the ethical-religious life of believers (and sometimes noted as the antidote to sin). In order, these are the filling by the Holy Spirit, prayer, visible divine help of angels, God's word, fellowship of the saints, and the momentum of character formed in obedience. Nearly all reflect the dynamic personal presence of the Holy Spirit, but he clearly provides direct help just be being there in Jesus.

FILLING BY THE HOLY SPIRIT

First, promises of undefined support and assurance by the Holy Spirit were reported as abundantly fulfilled in Jesus' experience of guidance, revelation, and joy. We have seen that Isaiah's messianic prophecies indicated a permeating involvement of the Holy Spirit to develop, uphold, and guide the Messiah in a righteous ethical life, not simply to empower him as prophet, priest, and king. We also saw the fulfillment of this multi-faceted pneumatological promise at every stage of Jesus' life and ministry, from conception to resurrection. Being the Messiah, Jesus lived by the help of the Holy Spirit. This help most likely extended to providing for Jesus when he was tempted. This seems especially so in the epochal wilderness temptations that were explicitly described in the Gospels as having been orchestrated by the Holy Spirit and during which time Jesus was described as filled with the Spirit. As a means of empowering grace, the Holy Spirit is himself the gift of assuring support and guidance that may be needed in time of temptation.

Likewise, for those who follow Jesus, God's plan in redemption includes the promise of life in the Holy Spirit. He produces in the believer a life that is conformed ethically to the Spirit's own character as exemplified in Christ (Gal 5:16-26; Rom 8:13-14, 28-29). Life in the Spirit is part of the New Covenant

---

[9]The case may be that these six aspects are not equal in force for Jesus or for believers, e.g., prayer may be more important for resisting sin than community support. Moreover, just as with the person-variability of temptations, the aspects of empowering grace may vary in proportional importance in a person-variable way also.

promise that emphasized the interior working of God on the heart, presumably the ordering of an individual's desires in line with God's will. This life in the Spirit may be synonymous with the New Covenant promise of an internal renewal for Christians by God, placing his law within them, and writing on their hearts (Jer 31:31-33) that are newly given by God (Ezek 36:26-27). This interior renovation is also described as a new source of eternal life from Christ, given within the regenerated person by the Holy Spirit who brings about a new birth (John 3:5-8) that is likened to a fountain of living water (John 4:14; 7:37-39). God's love is active within believers to change them to love him and others (1 John 4:7-21). This means God's love has an ongoing influence on the desires of those who belong to him, converting them from downward desires for selfishness and sin to appropriate upward desires that he has ordained. By comparison with believers, Jesus lived as a man endowed with the Holy Spirit in demonstration of this life of ethical conformity to God's will.[10]

Stephen's martyrdom in Acts 7 may be one example of someone living in the ready help of the Holy Spirit in the midst of intense temptation. Luke has earlier established that the Spirit's involvement in Stephen is particularly evident (repeated four times in 6:3-5, 8, 10). Then, on the brink of Stephen's martyrdom, Luke notes in 7:55-56 that Stephen was full of the Spirit and received a vision of Jesus in heaven. By the Spirit's help, Stephen was thus able to face his death with unwavering confidence in God (7:59) while also praying for the forgiveness of his murderers (7:60), two details that recall Jesus' death (Luke 23:46; 23:34).

ENGAGEMENT WITH GOD THROUGH PRAYER

Second, Jesus was a man of frequent prayer, often for long duration.[11] His special communion with God through prayer seems to have been qualitatively different from what others experience, judging by the frequency, duration, and substance of his prayer life. The substance seems to have been much more conversational than what others commonly experience because when God spoke audibly to Jesus from heaven (e.g., Luke 3:22; John 12:28-30), this seems to be an interaction with which Jesus is familiar. His receptivity to God through conversational prayer also shows in the way God gave him specific instructions as the basis for Jesus' teaching and actions, and his bold assurance that God always hears him.[12] This close relationship through prayer indicates that Jesus enjoyed the relationship of mutual indwelling with his Father that he prayed for his own followers to enter at the end of his ministry (John 15:4;

---

[10]Though we compare Jesus' reception of the Spirit in an analogical sense to the gift of the Holy Spirit for his followers, and without their need for sanctification with respect to sin's corruption.

[11]E.g., Luke's emphasis on this by his frequent reference to Jesus' prayer life in Luke 5:16; 6:12; 9:18, 28; 11:1; 22:32, 41.

[12]E.g., John 5:30; 7:16; 11:42.

17:21). As empowering grace that assisted Jesus in facing temptation, we find that in his struggle in Gethsemane to obey his desire for God's will, Jesus is praying. Moreover, he secludes himself from the twelve, guards himself with the three, and even distances himself from them to gain help from God through prayer. We can only guess, but the suggestion is reasonable that Jesus similarly resorted to the divine help of empowering grace through prayer at other times when he was tempted.[13]

At this point we may consider how empowering grace through prayer or otherwise was beneficial to Jesus in resisting temptation. According to the definition of temptation explained above, the struggles among desires and beliefs provide the opportunity for transcendent assistance. For example, in Gethsemane, Jesus struggled between his natural desire to avoid the punishment for the world's sin, and the desire to obey God and drink the cup of divine wrath. A sovereign God can readily respond to pleas for help by restricting the circumstances of the temptation so that the strain does not become too great, by providing internal and external reminders that God knows will be effective to strengthen the will or fortify the scale of values, or by countering the appeal of escape with the appeal of obedience (cf. Heb 12:2—"for the joy set before him, he endured the cross"). In Jesus' case, we can say that empowering grace surrounded him in temptation experience, giving the inclination and support to pray in his time of need, and reminding him of the deception inherent in the temptation (in this case, perhaps the lie that God should provide some other way of redemption that was less painful). Therefore, empowering grace is the divine assistance to provide what is needed to renounce his desire for escape. At one time the grace is given through a word of assurance in prayer, at another time, the grace is given through a recollection of Scripture and the pneumatological confirmation that Scripture is true (cf. Jesus' responses with Scripture in the wilderness).

Likewise, for those who follow Jesus, the provision of empowering grace through prayer is clear from the repeated emphasis on this biblical theme. Believers are to pray constantly about everything (1 Thess 5:17). Scripture tells a general theme that God will work in the individual who commits himself to God's care.[14] The pattern for prayer that Jesus gave his disciples includes a petition about temptation and the devil's deceptions (Matt 6:13). Peter gives his readers motivation to pray in the midst of temptations by assuring them that God can rescue them especially from temptation (2 Pet 2:9). Hebrews 4:15-16 exhorts the readers to seek God's help in prayer specifically in relation to temptation, and the certain ground for assurance is Jesus' own empathy and success in his own experience of temptation.

---

[13]Cf. Macleod, *Person of Christ*, 230, highlights the value of prayer for Jesus in temptation.

[14]E.g. Prov 3:5; Ps 21:2; 37:4; Rom 8:28-29; 2 Cor 10:5; Phil 2:12-13.

VISIBLE DIVINE HELP OF ANGELS

Third, on at least two occasions of severe temptation, we know that Jesus received empowering grace through the special presence of angels (cf. M6). In Gethsemane, an angel arrived to strengthen Jesus after his first petition (Luke 22:42-43). The account is textually suspect because early manuscripts do not have this, but the concept fits well with other biblical accounts of angelic assistance in times of trial.[15] Also, we find that angels arrived to care for Jesus in the wilderness immediately after Satan left him. This is *after* his contest with Satan, but not necessarily after all of his temptations. Jesus resisted the direct appeals of his desires for comfort that were provoked by Satan, but his temptability apart from Satan remained after the devil's departure. For that time of extreme weakness, as at Gethsemane (if vv. 42-43 are authentic), the angels' assistance was the relational grace ordered by God to preserve Jesus in the midst of his temptations.

As an aspect of empowering grace for resisting temptation, angelic assistance may be a more rare occasion in the life of Jesus and his followers than other aspects, but extreme circumstances perhaps require the rare forms of empowering grace. Indeed, there is a promise of angelic assistance for believers in Psalm 91:11-12, but this is not specifically a promise of help in relation to resisting temptation.[16] However, Scripture tells that God frequently employed angels to assist his people with warnings, guidance, encouragement, and rescue (e.g., Genesis 19; Heb 1:14). Presumably, God would employ the assistance of an angel for a believer facing a fierce temptation (perhaps martyrdom) if that visible form of empowering grace would be effective in God's purpose to uphold the Christian against temptation to sin. In the New Testament, Peter and John were delivered from prison by an angel (Acts 5:17-20), and Peter was rescued a second time by an angel (Acts 12:7-11), so there clearly remains a possibility that God continues to provide help in this visible way. People who face temptations on the point of their death could especially hope in God to provide whatever they needed to follow righteousness with suffering, just as God provided for Jesus in Gethsemane.

ENGAGEMENT WITH GOD THROUGH SCRIPTURE

Fourth, Scripture had an important role in Jesus' ethical fortitude and direct counterstrike to Satan's temptations that were based on deception in the wilderness. Jesus seems to have relied on the empowering grace given through God's word in Scripture.[17] In his three wilderness temptations, Jesus responds in each case by relying solidly on the truthfulness of Scripture as God's authoritative word. Scripture seems to have defined Jesus' teaching, action, and

---

[15] See the discussion of the authenticity of these verses in ch. 1.

[16] Satan used this promise to tempt Jesus in the wilderness, but this was a case of forming the meaning by re-use to provoke Jesus. I do not see temptation in the Psalm's context.

[17] Macleod, *Person of Christ*, 230.

his orientation to God, the created world, other people, and himself. His frequent quotations in reported discourses and teaching indicate his deep and continual immersion in the written word of God to shape his own thoughts and action. Jesus' receptivity to God's word likely formed the basic content for his understanding of and communion with God. We see this in the way he quoted, clarified, and relied upon Scripture so much in his teaching about God and himself.[18] Even his cry from the cross uses the words of Psalm 22:2. Moreover, because temptation involves beliefs and deception, Scripture can function as an important bulwark of truth to sustain a person against temptation—as was the case for Jesus in the wilderness. Christ's replies to Satan are suggestive that the Messiah relied upon the truth of Scripture as the empowering grace and transcendent assistance to resist the downward desires and hold fast to his upward desire in each case. Jesus' demonstration of Scripture illustrates the principle taught in Psalm 119:11 of treasuring God's word as a valuable resource in the fight against temptation to sin. Jesus used Scripture as the counterclaim to his temptation. This is indicative of his simple obedience, what human beings ought to believe (God) when tempted to do otherwise.

Likewise, God promises to renew a person's perception through his word (e.g., Pss 1; 19; 119) and guard his people specifically against sin (Ps 119:11). As a struggle involving beliefs, temptation depends upon some sort of deception that can be routed by the truth given in Scripture. As a transcendent counterclaim to the lies that sinful desires and sinful means of satisfying legitimate desires are good for the tempted one, Scripture is abundantly available as empowering grace by the Holy Spirit (Heb 4:12) to stabilize the believer's scale of values and lay bare the deception of evil. For this reason, Paul exhorts people who have been renewed in Christ (Col 3:1-4) to receive the words of Christ to permeate them (Col 3:16-17), out of which develops the righteous outflow that is equivalent to the life in the Spirit (Eph 5:18-21 is a parallel passage). Peter also commends Scripture for the believer's growth in maturity as part of developing a *taste* and *desperate hunger* for the goodness of God—strengthening the attractiveness of upward desires against desires leading to sin (1 Pet 2:1-3, using the compelling metaphor of nursing infants!).

Finally, God's word his is his personal self-revelation, and so is a accommodated, virtual mode of his personal presence. Made dynamic and effective by the work of the Holy Spirit (cf. Isa 59:21; Heb 4:12), God's word for Jesus was in some sense a way of encountering God as a creature and receiving assistance for his life as a man.

THE COMMUNITY OF FELLOW BELIEVERS

Fifth, Jesus relied upon the empowering grace of assistance from the

---

[18] E.g., in Luke's account, Jesus forecasts entire ministry in the terms of a mixed quotation of Isaiah 58:6 and 61:1-2 that he applies to himself as the fulfillment of Old Testament prophecy (Luke 4:16-21).

community of his fellow believers.[19] In the accounts of his ministry, he is seldom reported to be alone (except to pray), and is normally depicted in close relationships with his chosen disciples and many others. The people who revered him as their teacher were likely an encouragement for Jesus' own continued faithfulness to God, most notably in their confessions of faith in him that he solicited at least once (Mark 8:27-29 par.). Moreover, the devotion showed to Jesus by women on two occasions seems to have been especially important for his own resolve to stay his course despite the growing opposition of his enemies, the defection of his followers, and his own temptations to quit his march to the cross (Luke 7:36-50; John 12:1-8, cf. 11:2). At the beginning of his ministry, Jesus entered the wilderness for forty days bereft of human companions; however, when his final struggle came in Gethsemane, he bade his three closest friends to come and keep watch with him during his time of turmoil (Matt 26:37-46). These various examples of support may be what Jesus had in mind when—in the context of discussing service in the kingdom and temptation by Satan—he acknowledges that his disciples have contributed some help for him, as he says in Luke 22:28, "You are the ones who have remained with me in my temptations."[20] Therefore, the support of other believers seems to have been an important means of assistance for Jesus to resist his temptations (even though they were feeble in themselves). As aspects of God's multi-faceted provision of empowering grace, the assistance given through Jesus' fellow believers may have been decisive, however slight.

Similarly, many biblical exhortations indicate that people should find support in the believing community to help each other practice the habits of obedience that were significant for Jesus in his own struggles against sin (e.g., Gal 6:1-2; Heb 12:12-15). Paul's example was to pray for others regarding their maturity as Christians (e.g., Col 1:9-12). Paul also compares the self-discipline of athletes to the diligence that Christians must practice on the way to becoming stable in virtuous and obedient character (1 Cor 9:24-27; 1 Tim 4:7-8; Heb 10:24-25). The charge that people should entrust themselves to godly leadership (Heb 13:7, 17) and the communal structure of church discipline (Matt 18:15-20) are additional signs that God supports his people to follow Christ by means of corporate church life. This point is also clear in the design of God's empowerment of various church ministries for the good of the people who are then drawn into relational interdependence for the common goal of maturity in Christ (1 Cor 12:4-31).

THE MOMENTUM OF MATURING CHARACTER

Sixth, Jesus had the stable structure of habitual obedience to God that he

---

[19]Cf. Macleod, *Person of Christ*, 230.
[20]Most modern translations use *my trials* instead of *my temptations* here, but the AV and ASV use "temptations." Perhaps both senses of πειρασμοίς are in view, cf. the way that the NASV, NKJV, and ESV translators include a cross-reference to Heb 2:18 and 4:15.

learned over time (cf. Heb 5:7-9).[21] This aspect of empowering grace is the internal formation of Jesus' habits, values, desires, and ethical-religious reflexes in conformity to God by long practice and the Holy Spirit's involvement. Jesus had submitted so regularly to obeying God that by the time of his ministry he describes his own action in words and deeds as completely contingent upon his Father's will.[22] According to John's Gospel, Jesus nearly always defines himself and his mission in relation to his Father as the primary Christological claim, with the result that *Father* as a reference to God occurs 124 times in John (by my count), mostly in Jesus' statements. This constant emphasis in Jesus' consciousness of himself as the Son shows in his lived obedience to his Father.[23] Jesus' obedience had no bounds, as he followed even to point of the facing the horror of death and punishment for sin on the cross (Phil 2:8). He described his mission in terms of glorifying his Father,[24] speaking the Father's words, and doing the Father's works.[25] Such radical obedience was Jesus' active conformity to God's will in responsive relationship; testimony is borne to this in God's repeated declarations of his pleasure with his Son (e.g., Matt 3:17 and 17:5). This habit of obedience may have been orchestrated by the Father and Holy Spirit through progressive tests and life circumstances to use the other aspects of empowering grace to fortify Jesus' character from early childhood (Luke 2:40, 52) in fulfillment of Isaiah 11:3—so that "He delights in the fear of Yahweh" above all else.[26]

Likewise, the momentum for right from habitual obedience to God seems to be an empowerment of grace that God provides for Jesus' followers. Paul

---

[21] I am indebted to Bruce Ware for this suggestion.

[22] E.g., John 4:34; 5:30; 6:38; 7:28; 8:26, 29; 10:32, 37; 12:49.

[23] Cf. the observation of John A. T. Robinson, "Use of the Fourth Gospel for Christology", in *Christ and Spirit in the New Testament*, ed. Barnabas Lindars and Stephen S. Smalley (Cambridge: Cambridge University Press, 1973), 68-69: "Reading the Gospel through at a sitting, one is left with the overwhelming impression of a man whose life was lived in *absolutely intimate dependence* (stressing all three words) upon God as his Father. Everything Jesus was and said and did has its source in this utter closeness of spiritual relationship which he describes as sonship or 'sent-ness'."

[24] John 12:28; 13:31; 14:13; 17:1, 4.

[25] John 14:10, 24; 17:8. Notice that the revealed names of Son and Father indicate the trinitarian relationship *ad intra*, and not merely the *ad extra* economic Trinity. Expressed in Jesus' mission is the eternal functional subordination of the Son to the Father in a relationship of authority and submission of the Son to his Father.

[26] But Jesus' development was not in the mixed way argued by Susan R. Garrett, *The Temptations of Jesus in Mark's Gospel* (Grand Rapids: Eerdmans, 1998), 107, who claims that Mark's account of Jesus shows that he developed morally from double-minded struggle to eventual single-minded commitment. Also unhelpful on this point is Ronald Williamson, "Hebrews 4:15 and the Sinlessness of Jesus", *Expository Times* 86 (1974): 4-8, who argues that Jesus achieved perfected obedience of sinlessness only at the end of his life, not that he proceeded in purity impeccably from the beginning.

explains that character development in the midst of difficulties is sovereignly worked out by God to bring his people to glory in Christ (Rom 5:3-5; 8:17-39). Peter and James echo the same idea that God brings his people to the heights of righteous action by leading through difficult circumstances that train them and mature them with a momentum of obedience no matter the pain (1 Pet 1:5-8; Jas 1:2-18). Finally, the exhortation that parents ought to train their children in the righteous path (Prov 22:6) exemplifies the type of empowering grace by which God builds in his people a momentum of obedience so they can resist temptations.

Conclusion: A Human Triumph of Righteousness for Us

Therefore, Jesus' sinlessness was a truly human accomplishment because (most plausibly) he relied upon empowering grace to sustain and fortify him in his resistance to temptation. The issue in each aspect of empowering grace is that the Spirit's personal assistance is transcendent as the anchor and support to enable the tempted one to hold fast against the deception and struggle of desires, beliefs, and external factors that coordinate with internal factors to create a conflict. Jesus relied on divine help in a maximal way; consequently, the results in his life were maximal in perfect sinlessness (obedience) despite the severity and unique pressures of his temptations. This is important for understanding his achievement of righteousness in our stead. His obedience as a man is authentic in overwhelming reversal of the first man's disobedience (Rom 5:12-21). God counts this humanly achieved perfection as a gift to all who are in Christ, so explanation given here that Jesus' triumph was accomplished without recourse to his inherent deity underlines his heroics. He obeyed perfectly for us *and* as one of us. Perhaps the vicarious aspect requires the authenticity of his limitation. Moreover, despite his achievement of sinlessness and his impeccability, he remains credibly relevant because he relied upon grace of the Spirit that is available to others who are merely human.

We also saw that the same six sorts of empowering grace that were significant in Jesus' fight against temptation are what God commends to Christians as assistance for faithful daily responsiveness to God's leading. Jesus provides for his church the very same grace that was effective for him through the Holy Spirit. The likeness is that in the vulnerability of his assumed humanity, he needed the same empowering grace to vanquish temptations to evil that assaulted him directly throughout his life. For Christ and Christians, empowering grace is not the divine constraint or coercion of individuals to resist temptation. Empowering grace seems to be the divine personal means of enabling and facilitating the voluntary choice of individuals to pursue righteousness. One difference is that Jesus did not need renewal from the corruption of sin. Another difference is that the unique result of Jesus' sinlessness *mirrors* his unique identity as the eternal Son of God. His having received the assistance of empowering grace indicates that he also fought for righteousness as a man, and one who is a pattern for others.

Bruce Ware tells a helpful analogy that conveys the two truths that Jesus was impeccable and Jesus authentically achieved a perfect human life without relying upon his inherent divine power (as some sort of advantage over others who are merely human). A champion swimmer sets out to surpass the world record for an open water distance swim of fifteen miles. The swimmer knows that the strain of swimming for eight hours in turbulent waters can cause his muscles to cramp if he becomes dehydrated and if the lactic acid builds up at a greater rate than his body can dissipate it. A severe muscle cramp during his swim would be fatal if the champion has an off day or ocean currents prove too much for his strength and he cannot keep himself afloat. Knowing this, he allows a boat to follow fifty yards behind him as he swims.

On the day of his test, the champion wades into the surf and launches himself through the waves. He moves slowly away from the shore and passes into open water. As planned, the boat trails behind him and he swims on unaided while those on the boat watch his methodical stroke. Hours and miles pass by and the fatigue is beginning to show. His stroke falters occasionally, and his speed wavers slightly. The champion seems to check his bearing towards the island more frequently. He feels his muscle fibers stiffen, resisting his will to reach the island. He has had to ignore the solace of signaling for help from the boat. Without swimming entirely on his own, he cannot achieve the island swim record. He strains with the last of his lungs and arms to gain the beach. He has done it! A new world record!

All during his swim, the boat had guaranteed that *he could not drown*. Why could he not drown? The boat was always there with people to save him. However, the boat contributed nothing at all towards the champion's achievement of swimming for a new world record. *He did not drown* or fail in his swim because he strained with everything he had as a man in the water, solitary and salt-weary. How did he achieve the record? He swam it victoriously.

And this is so much like Jesus. *He could not sin* because he is the impeccable Son of God. *He did not sin* and *he achieved a perfect human life* because he strained with everything he possessed as a man, including empowerment by the Holy Spirit. Remaining what he was as the impeccable Son of God, he also became the perfect champion of our salvation as Godman.[27]

---

[27] The analogy of swimmer and boat should not be pressed as a model of the incarnational union (it would look divisive). The analogy is intended only to show the distinction between Jesus' true achievement and his true inability to sin. Another analogy is of a whiz math student who takes a difficult math exam. His perfect result is because of his prowess with numbers. The perfect result was guaranteed because he possessed (but did not use) a calculator in his pocket during the entire time of the test. He chose to complete the test by using his mathematical skill, and did so flawlessly.

CONCLUSION

No major church council has ever addressed the question of Christ's impeccability and temptation enjoined here. His impeccability, temptation, and sinlessness are readily affirmed, but there is no consensus on how to relate the three. We have seen why as we reviewed the variety of theological models formulated to meet the question. In the course of excavating and evaluating nine models of Christ's impeccability and temptation, we have seen shifting concerns and approaches that reflected the historical settings of brilliant theologians. Early explanations guarded the impeccability of Christ, and strained to give full account of his temptations. Later explanations reversed the focus to see Jesus' likeness to us as a true man. My response to the historical models has been to carry forward the focus on his authentic humanity without leaving behind Chalcedonian Christology. He is Godman, unable to sin, but truly tempted for us.

I have argued that the humanness of Jesus' sinlessness makes him richly relevant for us. Jesus' reliance on empowering grace is more plausible than relying on inherent deity because this explanation fits the New Testament accounts of his temptations and his practical value as the reasonable pattern for others (with his full, credible empathy). Because Jesus has redeemed his people from slavery to sin and sent them the Holy Spirit, believers stand in nearly the same relation to temptation as Jesus had with the same empowering grace available to enable their faithful obedience to God. Thus, the empowering grace that was effective for his victories over temptation seems to be the same help of the Holy Spirit that is promised for believers. The Holy Spirit's role in the hypostatic union enabled God the Son to enter temptation as a man because he was kept from knowing for certain he was immune to sin. God's provision of aid for Jesus allowed him to experience temptation in a way that constituted him empathetic for others who must struggle in the same human terms that he did. The model of his life for others is as a peer, not merely as the ideal because he limited himself to the resources that God likewise makes available to Jesus' followers. His empathy is credible because the transcendent security of his sinlessness was inevitable but not automatic. Jesus had to fight sin on the same basis that we do.

We have arrived at this set of claims after setting out with many questions in view about the problems of affirming that Jesus was impeccable and truly tempted. We saw the biblical revelation that highlights Christ's temptations and sinlessness. Scripture also makes a clear and vivid correlation between his experiences and the temptations that we suffer. I have argued that Jesus shared *entirely* in our struggle, having been tempted in all the main ways as we are. He was spared no category of temptation that we suffer, and was tested to the same extent and degree (or greater) than any of us faces. Thus, Jesus knows firsthand the severity and desperation we feel when temptation offers us a way out from inconvenience, embarrassment, suffering, or death. Jesus is ready with help that has already been proven in his own tests, and he is compassionate to support us through the Holy Spirit's ever-present and manifold grace. But how does it really matter what we believe about Jesus' impeccability and temptation?

Most people are likely to find that they live by one of three sorts of the models of Christ's impeccability and temptation. First, some will find that, in accordance with M1-M3, they believe Jesus was impeccable, but do not have in mind how he could also truly understand their experiences of temptation and offer them timely help. Consider one illustration as an example. Frank is a Christian who prizes careful thinking about his beliefs. Frank is a hardworking family man who tries to love God and do right. Trained as an electrical engineer, he applies his analytical expertise to understand of Scripture as well. Frank tries to sort out as much as he can from the Bible, but has some gaps that have persistently remained as mildly nagging questions that he and nobody he knows has been able to answer. When Frank thinks about Jesus being tempted, he has difficulty getting around seeing Jesus as God and not being able to sin. When Frank comes to passages about Jesus' temptations, he experiences an unpleasant tension between seeing the inability to sin and the validity of Christ's temptation. When temptations come to Frank, he experiences shame, doubt, and confused frustration at his repeated inability to overcome pride, anger, competition, and lust. Year after year, he does not seem to improve despite his efforts and good intentions. In praying to God, Frank usually stops short of asking for help to face his temptations because he assumes that he is the instigator of them. He concludes that his sinful desires are dragging him down, and he sometimes pleads that God would please just take them away. He wonders if that is just the way it is in a sinful world. More frustrating is that Jesus' example for Frank has become just another sign of his own failure. When he thinks of God the Son living out a perfect life as a man, Frank just feels overwhelmed with a sense of unworthiness and renewed disdain for himself as a failure in the face of his temptations. Sometimes, when he is by himself on a lonely night shift watching over the power plant's systems, Frank wonders if he is not fit for his small roles in church ministry, and he doubts his ability to lead his family as a Christian husband and father. The rift between Jesus and Frank's life is because Frank is unable to see the relevance of Jesus' example and empathy for his own experience. Theology has fallen short of helping Frank to follow Christ. Instead, a fog of disillusionment and frustration has blocked this sincere man's ability to live faithfully. The barrier of the fog is thickened partly by Frank's grasp of belief in Christ's impeccable deity as the way Jesus remained sinless in his human life. Frank's theology cuts Jesus off from having lived the sort of truly human life that Frank has. In this way, believing that Jesus could not sin because he was God has the effect on Frank's practical experience that bright lights have on fog—the murky grey becomes a blinding white cloud. Neither Jesus' temptations nor his sinlessness as a truly human achievement will be apparent to Frank in a way that draws him to follow Jesus' example and appeal for his Lord's help. The result is that Frank suffers daily to fight temptation on his own because he thinks Jesus does not understand what it is to be tempted by internal desires. Frank thinks that he is bound to fail instead of succeed like Jesus because he is not God like Jesus is. When tempted, Frank just does the best he can and never calls out for help or considers Jesus an inspiration and encouragement in any sense. Living for God and family, Frank nonetheless falters on through his temptations all alone.

Moving on from Frank, a second typical sort of model that people live by may be illustrated by George. George talks straight and presses others to be real. He is easily irritated by people who try to dress up uncomfortable and unpleasant beliefs with big words and smooth talk. He talks tough and gruff, but his secret hobby is to draw flowers and paint watercolor landscapes. People were stunned when George was seen at a school carnival painting flowers and designs on children's hands, cheeks, and foreheads. No one thought that someone like George would do anything besides tattoo art. George reads the plain sense of the Bible and calls it like it says. So, George believes something like M7 that he is sure Jesus must have been able to sin. He does not understand how it all works out, but the temptations are just plain there in the Gospels, so Jesus really knows what it is to be tempted to sin. George feels like Jesus knows his situation then, when George comes around a corner into a false accusation against him and he just is not able to hold back from retaliating and setting things right. George does not know how Jesus held back from sin, except maybe that he was God, but George knows it is impossible to do so some times. On the upshot of his theology, George feels that Jesus is real, and really understands what it is to be tempted. The downside is that, though he is unaware of it, George's confidence in God's immutable goodness is something less than full. Without knowing how, his belief that God incarnate could possibly have sinned has worked like a virus that has infected George's belief that God could possibly sin. George is mostly sure God will never change to be an evil God, but the erosion has begun. Then George's right hand was cut off in a factory meat chopper. Where was God? Was this punishment, or was God just not good anymore? George was reluctant to blame God for not treating him fairly, but every time he had the thought to take a pencil and draw something, George's anger and his questioning about God's goodness sharpened a little bit more. Gradually, his confidence about the goodness of God and his promises seeped out each time George heard about some terrible world event. Where was God? Was God still really good? Has the gift of salvation just seemed too good to be true? Years later, George had become unsure about the forgiveness of his sins and hopes of gaining heaven when he died. No longer was he grimly encouraged by Jesus' endurance in temptation with the possibility of sinning. Now George was shadowed with the doubt that Jesus and God were possibly not reliable to do the good to him that everybody talked about the Bible promised. George just could not be sure anymore. And he fared no better against temptation than he ever had.

Finally there is Bob. Bob is a simple man in the best sense of showing no pretense and not being impressed by it in others. This is a helpful trait in Bob's work as a pastoral counselor, laboring to support and guide Christians out of the wreckage of their sins, poor decisions, and the wounds inflicted by others sinning against them. Bob is able to relate to many people as an effective counselor because of his own past forays into drug use, chain smoking cigarettes, and then, when he left tobacco behind, indulging in the comfort of food. Bob understands temptation and failure in a way that he has been able to encourage others out of severe dysfunctions instead of blaming them for their sins. Bob watches over his beliefs with as much care as Frank, and, like George, he takes great solace in the life of Jesus lived as if right alongside of him. The difference of Bob from both men is that Bob has an eye to the mysterious personal aid of the Holy Spirit as in M4 and M6. As a counselor, Bob has sought for guidance and help from the Holy Spirit so he could support others. He knew he was weak in the face of temptations, and he had a hunch that God was able to offer close assistance, just as Bob sought to do in walking through diverse crises and dysfunctions with his clients. Bob is sure that Jesus could not sin, and he is just as sure that somehow Jesus was truly tempted. When Bob paused to think about Hebrews 4:15 and 5:7-9, and the Gospel accounts of Jesus in Gethsemane, he pushed past the plain fact of Jesus' impeccability to gaze at the Lord's desperately human struggle in temptation. Bob felt the tension there, but Scripture was a ready reminder that Jesus, despite being God the Son, really knew what it was to be tempted as a human being. Bob asked himself how Jesus fought his temptations. Slowly and gradually, Bob could see from Scripture that Jesus lived within the limits that Bob had to work with, and Jesus used things that were available to Bob. When he was tempted, Bob's inclination was to feel ashamed and withdraw from God, as if he had sinned just by feeling pulled to retaliate when others provoked him. But Bob was reminded that Jesus was tempted as he was, so that Jesus could lead him out of it. Bob found that just the act of thinking about Jesus when he was assaulted by familiar foes weakened the force of his temptations, and, beyond that, praying for help in the midst of a trial brought him a renewed sense of the ability to set aside his desires that would have led to sin. Bob realized the help of Christ in his time of need (Heb 4:16), and sought for further support through the Holy Spirit's grace. In a similar way to Bob's own vocation to come alongside others and provide support, guidance, and lend them his wisdom and hope, Bob found Scripture to be true that Christ does the same for him by the Holy Spirit. His temptations did not cease, nor did he always succeed against them, but he understood that they were normal challenges for him just as they were for Jesus. To be tempted was not to be in sin. Also, Bob began to see that even in tough temptations there was often a way out that God provided when Bob would call for help. Looking back after several years, Bob could chart crucial tests that God had carried him through, though not without some serious struggle, and shaped his heart in closer allegiance to Christ. His confidence in God's power to help him was matched by his comfort through Christ's true empathy for his struggles. And Bob knew, with growing encouragement despite his frequent failures in sin, that just as Jesus had led the way in his own life, Bob was following him on a difficult road that led to righteousness. And he was sure that even when he faced severe or mild temptations, Bob was not alone and not expected to contend with them alone. In this case, Bob realized the practical hope and help of the theology that Jesus was unable to sin, but he really suffered as a man to become one who can empathize and provide the help we all need in temptation.

Now it is for us, as for Bob, to live through all our trials not alone, but as bolstered by the Holy Spirit and his works of empowering grace. Just as Jesus was tempted for us, we can follow him one fight at a time into eternal life, helped by his ever-present and indwelling Holy Spirit.

Bibliography

Primary Sources

Patristic

Apollinaris *Η ΚΑΤΑ ΜΕΡΟΣ ΠΙΣΤΙΣ*. In *Apollinaris von Laodicea und Seine Schule I*, ed. Hans Lietzmann, 167-85. Texte und Untersuchungen. Tübingen: J. C. B. Mohr, 1904; reprint: Hildesheim, New York: Georg Olms, 1970.
— *ΛΟΓΟΙ*. In *Apollinaris von Laodicea und Seine Schule I*, ed. Hans Lietzmann, 248-49. Texte und Untersuchungen. Tübingen: J. C. B. Mohr, 1904; reprint: Hildesheim, New York: Georg Olms, 1970.
Athanasius *Orationes contra Arianos*. In *Opera omnia quae exstant*, ed. J. -P. Migne, Patrologia Graeca, 26:11-526. Paris: J. -P. Migne, 1857.
— *De Incarnatione*. In *Contra Gentes and De Incarnatione*. Edited and translated by Robert W. Thomson, 134-282. Oxford Early Christian Texts. Oxford: Clarendon, 1971.
Augustine *2 Enarr. In Psalmo* 32. In *Enarrationes in Psalmos I – L*, ed. E. Eligius Dekkers and Johannes Fraipont. Corpus Christianorum Series Latina, 38:247-73. Turnhout: Brepols, 1956.
— *Contra Duas Epistulas Pelagianorum*. In *Sancti Aureli Augustini Opera*, ed. Karl F. Urba and Joseph Zycha. Corpus Scriptorum Ecclesiasticorum Latinorum, 60:423-570. Vindobonae: F. Tempsky, 1913; reprint, New York: Johnston Reprint Corp., 1962.
— *Contra Julianum Pelagianum*. In *Opera omnia*. Edited by J. -P. Migne, Patrologia Latina, 44:641-880. Paris: J. -P. Migne, 1865.
— *De Correptione et Gratia*. In *Opera omnia*, ed. J. -P. Migne, Patrologia Latina, 44:915-58. Paris: J. -P. Migne, 1865.
— *De Praedestinatione Sanctorum*. In *Opera omnia*, ed. J. -P. Migne, Patrologia Latina, 44:959-92. Paris: J. -P. Migne, 1865.
— *De Trinitate (Libri I-XII)*. Edited by W. J. Mountain. Corpus Christianorum Series Latina, 50. Turnhout: Brepols, 1958.
— *On the Holy Trinity*. Translated by Arthur West Haddan. In *Augustine: On the Holy Trinity, Doctrinal Treatises, Moral Treatises*. Revised by Benjamin Warfield and ed. Philip Schaff. A Select Library of the Nicene and Post-Nicene Fathers of the Christian Church, First Series, 3:1-228. Grand Rapids: Eerdmans, 1956.
— *Enarration In Psalmo* 3. In *Enarrationes in Psalmos I – L*, ed. E. Eligius Dekkers and Johannes Fraipont. Corpus Christianorum Series Latina, 38:7-13. Turnhout: Brepols, 1956.
— *Enchiridion ad Laurentium de Fide et Spe et Caritate*. In *Aurelii Augustini Opera*. Corpus Christianorum Series Latina, 46:49-114. Turnhout: Brepols, 1969.

— *Sermon* 284. In *Opera omnia,* ed. J. -P. Migne, Patrologia Latina, 38:1288-93. Paris: J. -P. Migne, 1863.
— *On the Spirit and the Letter.* Translated by Peter Holmes and Robert Ernest Wallis. In *Saint Augustine's Anti-Pelagian Works,* revised by Benjamin Warfield and ed. P. Schaff. A Select Library of the Nicene and Post-Nicene Fathers of the Christian Church, First Series, 5:83-115. Grand Rapids: Eerdmans, 1956.
— *Sermons 273-305A: On the Saints.* Translated by Edmund Hill. Vol. III/8 of *The Works of Saint Augustine.* Hyde Park, NY: New City, 1994.
Basil *Epistle* 236 *ad Amphilochius.* In *Saint Basil: The Letters.* Translated by Roy J. Deferrari and Martin R. P. McGuire. Loeb Classical Library, vol. 3. Cambridge, MA: Harvard University Press, 1930.
— *Epistle 261.* In *Saint Basil: The Letters.* Translated by Roy J. Deferrari and Martin R. P. McGuire. Loeb Classical Library, vol. 4. Cambridge, MA: Harvard University Press, 1934.
Biblia Hebraica Stuttgartensia. Edited by K. Elliger and W. Rudolph. 5th rev. ed. Stuttgart: German Bible Society, 1997.
Clement of Alexandria *Paedagogus.* Edited by M. Marcovich. Leiden: Brill, 2002.
— *Clement of Alexandria: Christ the Educator.* Translated by Simon P. Wood. *Fathers of the Church* 23. New York: Fathers of the Church, 1954.
Cyril of Alexandria *Adversus Anthropomorphitas.* In *Opera quae reperiri potuerunt omnia,* ed. J. Auberti and rev. J. -P. Migne, Patrologia Graeca, 76:1065-132. Paris: J. -P. Migne, 1859.
—*Apologeticus Contra Theodoretum Pro XII Capitibus.* In *Opera quae reperiri potuerunt omnia,* ed. J. Auberti and rev. J. -P. Migne, Patrologia Graeca, 76:315-85. Paris: J. -P. Migne, 1859.
—*De Incarnatione unigenitii.* In *Cyrille D'Alexandrie, Deux Dialogues Christologiques,* ed. G. M. de Durand. Sources Chrétiennes 97:1-301. Paris: Les Éditions Du Cerf, 1964.
— *Epistola 44 ad Eulogius.* In *Opera quae reperiri potuerunt omnia,* ed. J. Auberti and rev. J. -P. Migne, Patrologia Graeca, 77:223-28. Paris: J. -P. Migne, 1859.
— *Epistola 44 ad Eulogius.* In *Cyril of Alexandria: Select Letters.* Translated and edited by Lionel R. Wickham, 62-69. Oxford Early Christian Texts. Oxford: Oxford University Press, 1983.
— *ΟΤΙ ΕΙΣ Ο ΚΡΙΣΤΟΣ.* In *Cyrille D'Alexandrie, Deux Dialogues Christologiques,* ed. G. M. de Durand. Sources Chrétiennes 97:302-55. Paris: Les Éditions Du Cerf, 1964.
— *St Cyril of Alexandria: On the Unity of Christ.* Translated by John Anthony McGuckin. Crestwood, NY: St Vladimir's Seminary Press, 1995.
— *Oratio Ad Theodosium.* In *Concilium universale Ephesenum,* ed. Eduardus Schwartz. *Acta Conciliorum Oecumenicorum,* 1, nos. 1-4: 42-72. Berlin: Walter de Gruyter, 1927.
— *Thesaurus de sancta et consubstantiali Trinitate.* In *Opera quae reperiri potuerunt omnia,* ed. J. Auberti, and rev. J. -P. Migne, Patrologia Graeca, 75:9-656. Paris: J. -P. Migne, 1859.
Concilium universale Ephesenum. In *Acta conciliorum oecumenicorum,* vol. 4, pt. 1, nos. 5-8. Edited by Schwartz, Eduardus. Berlin: Walter de Gruyter, 1971.
Didymus of Alexandria *Enarratio In Epistolam 1 S. Petri.* In *Opera omnia,* ed. J. -P. Migne, Patrologia Graeca, 39:1753-72. Paris: J. -P. Migne, 1858.

Gregory Nazianzen *Epistle* 101, *ad Cledonium presbyterum contra Apollinarum*. In *Opera quae exstant omnia*, ed. J. -P. Migne, Patrologia Graeca, 37:175-94. Paris: J. -P. Migne, 1837.

— *Oratio* 14 *de Pauperum Amore*. In *Opera omnia quae exstant*, ed. J. -P. Migne, Patrologia Graeca, 35:855-910. Paris: J. -P. Migne, 1857.

— *Oratio* 24 *in laudem S. Cypriani*. In *Opera omnia quae exstant*, ed. J. -P. Migne, Patrologia Graeca, 35:1169-94. Paris: J. -P. Migne, 1857.

— *Oratio* 29 *theologica III*. In *Opera omnia quae exstant*, ed. J. -P. Migne, Patrologia Graeca, 36:73-104. Paris: J. -P. Migne, 1858.

— *Faith Gives Fullness to Reasoning: The Five Theological Orations of Gregory Nazianzen*. Translated by Frederick W. Norris and Lionel Wickham. Introduction and commentary by Frederick Williams. Supplements to Vigiliae Christianae 13. Leiden: Brill, 1991.

Gregory of Nyssa *Antirrheticus Adversus Apollinarem*. In *Opera quae reperiri potuerunt omnia*, ed. Morell and rev. J. -P. Migne, Patrologia Graeca, 45:1123-278. Paris: J. -P. Migne, 1858.

— *Contra Eunomium*. In *Opera quae reperiri potuerunt omnia*, ed. J. -P. Migne, Patrologia Graeca, 45:243-1122. Paris: J. -P. Migne, 1858.

— *Epistola III ad Eustathia et Ambrosia*. In *Opera quae reperiri potuerunt omnia*, ed. Morell and rev. J. -P. Migne, Patrologia Graeca, 46:-1015-24. Paris: J. -P. Migne, 1858.

Hilary of Poitiers *De Trinitate*. In *Opera omnia*, ed. J. -P. Migne, Patrologia Latina, 10:9-470. Paris: J. -P. Migne, 1845.

— *De Trinitate*. In *St. Hilary of Potiers: Select Works*, ed. W. Sanday and translated by E. W. Watson and L. Pullan. In A Select Library of the Nicene and Post-Nicene Fathers of the Christian Church, Second Series, 9:40-234. Grand Rapids: Eerdmans, 1955.

— *Tractatus In LIII Psalmum*. In *Opera omnia*, ed. J. -P. Migne, Patrologia Latina, 9:337-46. Paris: J. -P. Migne, 1844.

— *Tractatus In LIV Psalmum*. In *Opera omnia*, ed. J. -P. Migne, Patrologia Latina, 9:346-57. Paris: J. -P. Migne, 1844.

Irenaeus *Adversus haereses*. In *Contra haereses libri quinque*, ed. J. -P. Migne, Patrologia Graeca, 7:433-1221. Paris: J. -P. Migne, 1857.

Jerome. *Tractatus de Psalmo XV*. In *Opera Pars II: Opera Homiletica*, ed. G. Morin, Corpus Christianorum Series Latina 78:364-85. Turnholt: Brepols, 1953.

— *Dialogue Against the Pelagians*. Translated by John N. Hritzu. In *Saint Jerome: Dogmatic and Polemical Works*. The Fathers of the Church 53. Washington DC: The Catholic University of America Press, 1965.

— *Homily* 76 (II). Translated by Marie Liguori Ewald. In vol. 2 of *Homilies of Saint Jerome*. The Fathers of the Church 57. Washington DC: The Catholic University of America Press, 1966.

John Cassian. *De Incarnatione Domini Contra Nestorium*. Edited by Michael Petschenig, Corpus scriptorum ecclesiasticorum latinorum 17:237-391. Vindobonae: F. Tempsky, 1888.

John Chrysostom. *In Epist. Ad Hebraeos. Cap. IV. Homil. VII*. In *Opera omnia*, ed. D. Bern de Montfaucon and rev. J. -P. Migne, Patrologia Graeca, 63:9-236. Paris: J. -P. Migne, 1862.

— *In illud: Pater si possible est.* In *Opera omnia quae exstant,* ed. D. Bern de Montfaucon and rev. J. -P. Migne, Patrologia Graeca, 51:31-40. Paris: J. -P. Migne, 1859.
— *In quat. Lazarum.* In In *Opera omnia quae exstant,* ed. D. Bern de Montfaucon and rev. J. -P. Migne, Patrologia Graeca, 50:641-44. Paris: J. -P. Migne, 1859.
John of Damascus. *De Fide Orthodoxa.* In vol. 2 of *Die Schriften des Johannes von Damaskos*, ed. P. B. Kotter. Patristische Texte und Studien, Band 12. Berlin: Walter de Gruyter, 1973.
— *Orthodox Faith.* Translated by Frederic H. Chase, Jr. In *Saint John of Damascus: Writings.* The Fathers of the Church 37. New York: Fathers of the Church, 1958.
Justin Martyr. *Dialogus Cum Trypohone.* Edited by Miroslav Marcovich. Berlin: Walter De Guyter, 1997.
Leo Magnus. *Epistola* 35 *ad Julianum.* In *Opera omnia,* ed. Petro Fratribus Ballerinis and Hieronymo Fratribus Ballerinis, rev. J. -P. Migne, Patrologia Latina, 54:803-10. Paris: J. -P. Migne, 1865.
— *Sermo* 39. In *Opera omnia,* ed. Petro Fratribus Ballerinis and Hieronymo Fratribus Ballerinis, rev. J. -P. Migne, Patrologia Latina, 54:263-67. Paris: J. -P. Migne, 1865.
— *Sermo* 23. In *Opera omnia,* ed. Petro Fratribus Ballerinis and Hieronymo Fratribus Ballerinis, rev. J. -P. Migne, Patrologia Latina, 54:199-203. Paris: J. -P. Migne, 1865.
— *The Tome of Pope Leo the Great.* Edited and translated by E. H. Blakeney. Texts for Students 29. London: S.P.C.K., 1923.
Leontius of Byzantium. *Contra Nestorianos et Eutychianos.* In *Opera quae reperiri potuerunt omnia,* ed. J. -P. Migne, Patrologia Graeca, 86, pt. 1:1267-398. Paris: J. -P. Migne, 1860.
Leontius of Jerusalem. *Adversus Nestorianos.* In *Opera quae reperiri potuerunt omnia,* ed. J. -P. Migne, Patrologia Graeca, 86, pt. 1:1399-1768. Paris: J. -P. Migne, 1860.
Matthew 1-13, edited by Manilo Simonetti. Ancient Christian Commentary on Scripture: New Testament, vol. 1a. Downers Grove, IL: InterVarsity, 2001.
Maximus the Confessor. *Opuscula Theologica et Polemica 7,* ed. J. -P. Migne, Patrologia Graeca, 91, 1865.
Nestorius. *Liber Heraclidis.* Edited and translated by G. R. Driver and Leonard Hodgson. In *The Bazaar of Heracleides*, ed. G. R. Driver and Leonard Hodgson, 3-381. Oxford: Oxford University Press, 1925.
— *Second Letter to Cyril.* Translated and edited by R. A. Norris. In *The Christological Controversy*, ed. R. A. Norris, 135-40. Philadelphia: Fortress, 1980.
Novum Testamentum Graece. Edited by Eberhard and Erwin Nestle. 27th ed. Revised by Barbara Aland and Kurt Aland, Johannes Karavidopoulos, Carlo M. Martini, and Bruce M. Metzger. Stuttgart: Deutsche Bibelgesellschaft, 1993.
Origen *Commentaria in Evangelium secundum Matthaeum.* In *Opera omnia*, ed. C. and C. Vincentii Delarue and rev. J. -P. Migne, Patrologia Graeca, 13:829-1800. Paris: J. -P. Migne, 1857.
— *Contra Celsum.* Edited by M. Marcovich. Leiden: Brill, 2001.
— *De Principiis.* Edited by P. Koetschau. Die grieschishen christlichen Schriftsteller der ersten [drei] Jahrhunderte 22. Berlin: Academie, 1913.
— *On First Principles.* Translated by G. W. Butterworth. London: S.P.C.K., 1936.
— *In Canticum Canticorum.* In *Opera omnia,* ed. J. -P. Migne, Patrologia Graeca, 13:37-216. Paris: J. -P. Migne, 1857.

Polycarp *The Letter of Polycarp to the Philippians*. Edited and revised by Michael W. Holmes. In *The Apostolic Fathers: Greek Texts and English Translations*, ed. and rev. Michael W. Holmes, 202-21. Grand Rapids: Baker, 1999.

Tertullian *De Anima*. Edited by J. H. Waszink. Amsterdam: J. M. Meulenhoff, 1947.

— *De Carne Christi*. In *Opera omnia quae exstant*, ed. J. -P. Migne, Patrologia Latina, 2:797-836. Paris: J. -P. Migne, 1866.

— *Tertullian's Homily on Baptism*. Edited and translated by Ernest Evans. London: S.P.C.K., 1964.

Theodore of Mopsuestia *De Incarnatione*. In *Opera quae reperiri potuerunt omnia*, ed. J. -P. Migne, Patrologia Graeca, 66:969-90. Paris: J. -P. Migne, 1859.

— *Fragment 20*. In *Mattäus-Kommentare aus der griechischen Kirche*. Edited by Joseph Reuss. Berlin: Akademi-Verlag, 1957.

— *Treatises Against Apollinarius*. In vol. 2 of *Theodore of Mopsuestia on the Minor Epistles of S. Paul*. Edited by H. B. Swete. Cambridge: Cambridge University Press, 1882; reprint, Westmead, U.K.: Gregg, 1969.

— *Catechetical Commentary on the Nicene Creed*. Edited by A. Mingana. Woodbrooke Studies V. Cambridge, UK: W. Heffer and Sons, 1932.

— *Catechetical Homilies*. Translated by Raymond Tonneau in collaboration with Robert Devreese. In *Les Homélies Catéchétiques de Théodore de Mopsueste*, ed. Raymond Tonneau in collaboration with Robert Devreesse. Studi e Testi 145. Vatican City: Biblioteca Apostolica Vaticana, 1949.

Theodoret of Cyrus *De Incarnatione Domini*. In *Opera quae reperiri potuerunt omnia*, ed. J. Auberti and rev. J. -P. Migne, Patrologia Graeca, 75:1419-78. Paris: J. -P. Migne, 1859.

— *De Providentia*. In *Opera omnia*, ed. J. L. Schluze and rev. J. -P. Migne, Patrologia Graeca, 83:355-774. Paris: J. -P. Migne, 1859.

— *Interpretatio Epistolae Ad Hebraeos*. In *Opera omnia*, ed. J. L. Schluze and rev. J. -P. Migne, Patrologia Graeca, 82:673-786. Paris: J. -P. Migne, 1859.

Theodosius of Alexandria. *Tome to Empress Theodora*. Translated by Albert Van Roey and Pauline Allen. In *Monophysite Texts of the Sixth Century*, ed. Albert Van Roey and Pauline Allen. Orientalia Lovaniensia Analecta 56. Leuven: Peeters, 1994.

Medieval

Anselm *Cur Deus Homo*. In vol. 2 of *Opera omnia ad fidem codicum recensuit*. Edited by F. S. Schmitt. Edinburgh: Thomas Nelson & Sons, 1946.

Anselm of Canterbury. *Cur Deus Homo?* Translated by Sidney Norton Deane. In *St. Anselm: Proslogium; Monologium; An Appendix in Behalf of the Fool by Gaunilon; and Cur Deus Homo*, ed. Sidney Norton Deane. Chicago: Open Court, 1903.

Aquinas, Thomas. *The Grace of Christ*. Edited and translated by Liam G. Walsh. Vol. 49 of *St Thomas Aquinas Summa Theologiae*. London: Eyre & Spottiswoode; New York: McGraw-Hill, 1974.

— *The One Mediator*. Edited and translated by Colman E. O'Neill. Vol. 50 of *St Thomas Aquinas Summa Theologiae*. London: Eyre & Spottiswoode; New York: McGraw-Hill, 1965.

— *The Life of Christ*. Edited and translated by Samuel Parsons and Albert Pinheiro. Vol. 53 of *St Thomas Aquinas Summa Theologiae*. London: Eyre & Spottiswoode; New York: McGraw-Hill, 1971.
— *The Passion Christ*. Edited and translated by Richard T. A. Murphy. Vol. 54 of *St Thomas Aquinas Summa Theologiae*. London: Eyre & Spottiswoode; New York: McGraw-Hill, 1965.
Bonaventure *Commentaria in Quaturo Libros Sententiarum Magistri Petri Lombardi*. In *Opera omnia*. Quaracchi: College of St. Bonaventurae, 1887.
Peter the Lombard. *Sententiae*. In *Libri IV Sententiarum*. 2 vols. 2nd ed. Grottaferrata: College of St. Bonaventure, 1916.
Scotus, John Duns *Quaestiones in Lib. III. Sententiarum*. In *Opera Omnia*, ed. Luke Wadding, vol. 7, pt. 1. Lyon: Laurence Durand, 1639; reprint, Hildesheim: Georg Olms, 1968.
— *Ordinatio*. Edited and translated by Allan Wolter. "John Duns Scotus on the Primacy and Personality of Christ." In *Franciscan Christology: Selected texts, Translations, and Introductory Essays*, ed. Damian McElrath, 139-82. Franciscan Sources 1. St. Bonaventure, NY: The Fransciscan Institute of St. Bonaventure University, 1980.

Reformation

Calvin, John. *Commentarius in Epistolam ad Hebraeos*. In vol. 55 of *Ioannis Calvini Opera quae supersunt omnia*, ed. Wilhelm Baum, Eduard Cunitz, and Euard Reuss, 1-198. Corpus Reformatum, vol. 83. Brunswick, NJ: C. A. Schwetschke and Son, 1896; reprint, New York: Johnston Reprint Corp., 1964.
— *The Epistle of Paul the Apostle to the Hebrews and the First and Second epistles of St. Peter*. Edited by David F. Torrance and Thomas F. Torrance. Translated by William B. Johnston. Calvin's New Testament Commentaries, vol. 12. Grand Rapids: Eerdmans, 1963.
— *Institutio Christianae religionis*. In *Joannis Calvini Opera Selecta*, ed. and rev. P. Barth and W. Niesel. 5 vols. 2nd rev. ed. Munich: Chr. Kaiser, 1959.
— *Commentarius in Acta Apostolorum*. In vol. 48 of *Ioannis Calvini Opera quae supersunt omnia*, ed. Wilhelm Baum, Eduard Cunitz, and Euard Reuss, 1-574. Corpus Reformatum, vol. 76. Brunswick, NJ: C. A. Schwetschke and Son, 1892; reprint, New York: Johnston Reprint Corp., 1964.
— *Commentarius in Evangelium Ioannis*. In vol. 47 of *Ioannis Calvini Opera quae supersunt omnia*, ed. Wilhelm Baum, Eduard Cunitz, and Euard Reuss, 1-458. Corpus Reformatum, vol. 75. Brunswick, NJ: C. A. Schwetschke and Son, 1892; reprint, New York: Johnston Reprint Corp., 1964.
— *Commentarius in Harmonim Evangelicam*. In vol. 45 of *Ioannis Calvini Opera quae supersunt omnia*, ed. Wilhelm Baum, Eduard Cunitz, and Euard Reuss, 1-830. Corpus Reformatum, vol. 73. Brunswick, NJ: C. A. Schwetschke and Son, 1891; reprint, New York: Johnston Reprint Corp., 1964.
— *Commentary on a Harmony of the Evangelists*. Translated by William Pringle. Calvin's Commentaries, vol. 3. Edinburgh: Calvin Translation Society; reprint, Grand Rapids: Baker, 1996.

— *A Harmony of the Gospels Matthew, Mark and Luke.* 3 vols. Vols. 1, 3 translated by A. W. Morrison. Vol. 2 translated by T. H. L. Parker. Grand Rapids: Eerdmans, 1972.

— *The Epistle of James.* Translated and edited by John Owen. Calvin's Commentaries, vol. 22. Grand Rapids: Baker, 1996.

— *The Epistles of Paul the Apostle to the Galatians, Ephesians, Philippians and Colossians.* Translated by T. H. L. Parker. Calvin's Commentaries, vol. 11. Grand Rapids: Eerdmans, 1965.

Luther, Martin. *Am tage Matthie des hailigen Apostels Euangelion Mathei.* In *D. Martin Luthers Werke: Kritische Gesamtausgabe,* 17, pt. 2:387-98. Weimar: Hermann Böhlaus Nachfolger, 1927.

— *Sermon on St. Matthew's Day, Matt. 11:25-30.* In *Sermons 1,* trans. and ed. John W. Doberstein. Vol. 51 of *Luther's Works,* ed. Helmut T. Lehmann, 26-32. Philadelphia: Muhlenberg, 1959.

— *Auslegung des ersten und zweiten Kapitels Johannis in Predigten 1537 und 1538.* In *D. Martin Luthers Werke: Kritische Gesamtausgabe,* 46:538-789. Weimar: Hermann Böhlaus Nachfolger, 1912.

— *Commentariolus in epistolam divi Pauli Apostoli ad Hebreos.* In *D. Martin Luthers Werke: Kritische Gesamtausgabe,* 57:97-238. Weimar: Hermann Böhlaus Nachfolger, 1939.

— *Das XVI kapitel Johannes.* In *D. Martin Luthers Werke: Kritische Gesamtausgabe,* 46:1-111. Weimar: Hermann Böhlaus Nachfolger, 1912.

— *De captivate Babylonica ecclesiae praeludium.* In *D. Martin Luthers Werke: Kritische Gesamtausgabe,* 6:484-573. Weimar: Hermann Böhlaus Nachfolger, 1888.

— *Epistel am Christtag, Hebr. 1, 1-12.* In *D. Martin Luthers Werke: Kritische Gesamtausgabe,* 10.1.1:142-79. Weimar: Hermann Böhlaus Nachfolger, 1910.

— *Epistel auss den Palmtag. Philippen. 2.* In *D. Martin Luthers Werke: Kritische Gesamtausgabe,* 17.2:237-45. Weimar: Hermann Böhlaus Nachfolger, 1927.

— *Evangelium am Sonntag nach dem Christtage, Luk. 2, 33-40.* In *D. Martin Luthers Werke: Kritische Gesamtausgabe,* 10.1.1:379-448. Weimar: Hermann Böhlaus Nachfolger, 1910.

— *Evangelium in der Christmess, Luk. 2, 1-14.* In *D. Martin Luthers Werke: Kritische Gesamtausgabe,* 10, 1st half, pt.1:58-94. Weimar: Hermann Böhlaus Nachfolger, 1910.

— *Predigten des Jahres 1537, Nr. 40.* In *D. Martin Luthers Werke: Kritische Gesamtausgabe,* 45:204-64. Weimar: Hermann Böhlaus Nachfolger, 1911.

— *Predigten Luthers gesammelt von Joh. Boliander (1519-1521), Dominica Sebastiani.* In *D. Martin Luthers Werke: Kritische Gesamtausgabe,* 9:554-58. Weimar: Hermann Böhlaus Nachfolger, 1893.

— *Psalmus XXII.* In *D. Martin Luthers Werke: Kritische Gesamtausgabe,* 5:598-673. Weimar: Hermann Böhlaus Nachfolger, 1892.

— *Commentary on Psalm 22.* In *Select Works of Martin Luther,* vol. 4. Translated by Henry Cole. London: Simpkin and Marshall, 1826.

— *Sermon von dem Sacrament des leibs und bluts Christi, widder die Schwarmgeister* (1526). In *D. Martin Luthers Werke: Kritische Gesamtausgabe,* 19:474-523. Weimar: Hermann Böhlaus Nachfolger, 1897.

— *De libertate Christiana.* In *D. Martin Luthers Werke: Kritische Gesamtausgabe,* 7:49-73. Weimar: Hermann Böhlaus Nachfolger, 1897.

— *The Freedom of a Christian*. In *The Career of the Reformer*, vol. 1, *Luther's Works*, American Edition, vol. 31. Edited by Helmut T. Lehmann. Translated by W. A. Lambert. Revised by Harold J. Grimm. Philadelphia: Muhlenberg, 1957.
— *Psalm 8*. In *Selected Psalms 1*, trans. and ed. Jaroslav Pelikan. Vol. 12 of *Luther's Works*, ed. Jaroslav Pelikan, 97-138. Philadelphia: Muhlenberg, 1955.

Modern Sources

Adams, Marilyn McCord. *What Sort of Human Nature? Medieval Philosophy and the Systematics of Christology*. The Aquinas Lecture 1999. Milwaukee: Marquette University Press, 1999.
Althaus, Paul. *The Theology of Luther*. Translated by Robert C. Schultz. 2nd ed. Philadelphia: Fortress, 1966.
Arnold, Clinton E. *Power of Darkness: Principalities and Powers in Paul's Letters*. Downers Grove, IL: InterVarsity, 1992.
Ashcroft, Mary Ellen. *Temptations Women Face: Honest Talk about Jealousy, Anger, Sex, Money, Food, Pride*. Downers Grove, IL: InterVarsity, 1991.
Attridge, Harold W. *The Epistle to the Hebrews*. Hermeneia, vol. 53. Philadelphia: Fortress, 1989.
Baillie, D.M. *God Was in Christ: An Essay on Incarnation and Atonement*. New York: Charles Scribner's Sons, 1948.
Baker, W.R. "Temptation." In *Dictionary of the Later New Testament and Its Developments*, ed. Ralph P. Martin and Peter H. Davids. Downers Grove, IL: InterVarsity, 1997.
Banks, William L. *The Day Satan Met Jesus*. Chicago: Moody, 1973.
Barth, Karl. *Church Dogmatics*. Edited by G. W. Bromiley and T.F. Torrance. Vol. 1, *The Doctrine of the Word of God*. Pt. 2. Translated by G.T. Thomson and Harold Knight. Edinburgh: T. & T. Clark, 1956.
— *Church Dogmatics*. Edited by G. W. Bromiley and T.F. Torrance. Vol. 4, *The Doctrine of Reconciliation*. Pt. 2. Translated by G. W. Bromiley. Edinburgh: T. & T. Clark, 1958.
Bathrellos, Demetrios. *The Byzantine Christ: Person, Nature, and Will in the Christology of Saint Maximus the Confessor*. Oxford: Oxford University Press, 2004.
Bavinck, Herman. *Sin and Salvation in Christ*. Vol. 3 of Reformed Dogmatics. Translated by John Vriend. Edited by John Bolt. Grand Rapids: Baker, 2006.
Berkhof, Louis. *Systematic Theology*. 4th edition. Grand Rapids: Eerdmans, 1939.
Berkouwer, G. C. *Sin*. Translated by Philip C. Holtrop. Studies in Dogmatics. Grand Rapids: Eerdmans, 1971.
— *The Person of Christ*. Translated by John Vriend. Studies in Dogmatics. Grand Rapids: Eerdmans, 1955.
Bethune-Baker, James. *Nestorius and His Teaching: A Fresh Examination of the Evidence*. Cambridge: Cambridge University Press, 1908.
Blenkinsopp, Joseph. *Isaiah 1-39*. Anchor Bible, vol. 19. New York: Doubleday, 2000.
Bloesch, Donald G. *Essentials of Evangelical Theology*. Vol. 1. San Francisco: Harper & Row, 1978.
— *Jesus Christ: Savior and Lord*. Vol. 4 of Christian Foundations. Carlisle: Paternoster, 1997.

Bobrinskoy, Boris. "The Indwelling of the Spirit in Christ: 'Pneumatic Christology' in the Cappadocian Fathers." *St Vladimir's Theological Quarterly* 28 (1984): 49-65.

Bock, Darrell L. *Luke 1:1—9:50*. Baker Exegetical Commentary on the New Testament, vol. 39, pt. 1. Grand Rapids: Baker, 1994.

— *Luke 9:51—24:53*. Baker Exegetical Commentary on the New Testament, vol. 39, pt. 2. Grand Rapids: Baker, 1996.

Boettner, Loraine. *The Person of Christ*. Grand Rapids: Eerdmans, 1943.

Bonhoeffer, Dietrich. *Creation and Fall. Temptation*. Translated by Kathleen Downham. Edited by Eberhard Bethge. New York: Touchstone, 1997.

Bromiley, Geoffrey W. "The Reformers and the Humanity of Christ." In *Perspectives on Christology: Essays in Honor of Paul K. Jewett*, ed. Marguerite Shuster and Richard Muller, 79-104. Grand Rapids: Zondervan, 1991.

Brown, Colin. "The Enlightenment." In *Evangelical Dictionary of Theology*, ed. Walter A. Elwell. 2nd ed. Grand Rapids: Baker Academic, 2001.

Brown, Peter. *Augustine of Hippo*. Berkeley: University of California Press, 1967, 2000.

Brown, Raymond E. *Birth of the Messiah: A Commentary on the Infancy Narratives in Matthew and Luke*. 2 vols. Garden City, NY: Doubleday, 1977.

— *Death of the Messiah, from Gethsemane to the Grave: A Commentary on the Passion Narratives in the Four Gospels*. 2 vols. Anchor Bible Reference Library. New York: Doubleday, 1994.

— *Jesus God and Man: Modern Biblical Reflections*. New York: Macmillan, 1967.

Brown, Robert F. "God's Ability to Will Moral Evil." *Faith and Philosophy* 8 (1991): 3-20.

Bruce, A. B. *The Humiliation of Christ: In Its Physical, Ethical, and Official Aspects*. 4th ed. Grand Rapids: Eerdmans, 1955.

Brümmer, Vincent. "Divine Impeccability." *Religious Studies* 20 (1984): 203-14.

Burge, Gary M. *The Anointed Community: The Holy Spirit in the Johannine Tradition*. Grand Rapids: Eerdmans, 1987.

Burns, J. Patout. "Grace." In *Augustine throughout the Ages: An Encyclopedia*, ed. Allan D. Fitzgerald. Grand Rapids: Eerdmans, 1999.

Calvert, David G. A. *From Christ to God: A Study of some Trends, Problems and Possibilities in Contemporary Christology*. London: Epworth, 1983.

Canham, Michael McGhee. "*Potuit non peccare* or *non potuit peccare*: Evangelicals, Hermeneutics, and the Impeccability Debate." *The Master's Seminary Journal* 11 (2000): 93-114.

Carson, D. A. *Matthew*. In vol. 8 of *The Expositor's Bible Commentary*. Edited by Frank E. Gaebelein and J. D. Douglas, 1-599. Grand Rapids: Zondervan, Regency Reference Library, 1984.

— "The Function of the Paraclete in John 16:7-11." *Journal of Biblical Literature* 98 (1979): 547-66.

Carter, W. R. "Impeccability Revisited." *Analysis* 44 (1985): 52-55.

Cave, Sydney. *The Doctrine of the Person of Christ*. New York: Charles Scribner's Son's, 1925.

Chafer, Lewis Sperry. *Systematic Theology*. Vol. 5. Dallas: Dallas Seminary Press, 1948.

Clark, Gordon H. *Thales to Dewey: A History of Philosophy*. Boston: Houghton Mifflin, 1957.

Coakley, Sarah. "What Does Chalcedon Solve and What does it Not? Some Reflections on the Status and Meaning of the Chalcedonian 'Definition.'" In *The Incarnation*, ed. Stephen T. Davis, Daniel Kendall, and Gerald O'Collins, 143-63. New York: Oxford University Press, 2002.

Cole, Graham A. *He Who Gives Life: The Doctrine of the Holy Spirit*. Wheaton, IL: Crossway, 2007.

Craig, William Lane. "The Incarnation." In J. P. Moreland and William Lane Craig, *Philosophical Foundations for a Christian Worldview*, 597-614. Downers Grove, IL: InterVarsity, 2003.

Crisp, Oliver D. *Divinity and Humanity: The Incarnation Reconsidered*. Cambridge: Cambridge University Press, 2007.

— "Did Christ have a *Fallen* Human Nature?" *International Journal of Systematic Theology* 6 (2004): 270-88.

— "Was Christ Sinless or Impeccable?" *Irish Theological Quarterly* 72 (2007): 168-86.

— "William Shedd on Christ's Impeccability", *Philosophia Christi*, 9 (2007): 165-88.

Cross, Richard. *Duns Scotus*. Great Medieval Thinkers. New York: Oxford University Press, 1999.

— *The Metaphysics of the Incarnation: Thomas Aquinas to Duns Scotus*. New York: Oxford University Press, 2002.

Cullmann, Oscar. *The Christology of the New Testament*. Translated by Shirley C. Guthrie and Charles A. M. Hall. London: SCM, 1959.

Dabney, Robert Lewis. *Syllabus and Notes of the Course of Systematic and polemic theology*. 2nd ed. St. Louis: Presbyterian Publishing Company of St. Louis, 1878.

Daley, Brian E. "'A Richer Union': Leontius of Byzantium and the Relationship of Human and Divine in Christ." Studia patristica 24, ed. Elizabeth A. Livingstone, 239-65. Leuven: Peeters, 1993.

Davids, Peter H. *The Epistle of James*. New International Greek Testament Commentary, vol. 55. Grand Rapids: Eerdmans, 1982.

— *The First Epistle of Peter*. New International Commentary on the New Testament, vol. 56. Grand Rapids: Eerdmans, 1990.

Davis, Stephen T. *Logic and the Nature of God*. Grand Rapids: Eerdmans, 1983.

Del Colle, Ralph. *Christ and the Spirit: Spirit-Christology in Trinitarian Perspective*. New York: Oxford University Press, 1994.Deme, Dániel. *The Christology of Anselm of Canterbury*. Aldershot, U.K., and Burlington, VT: Ashgate, 2003.

Dewart, Joanne McWilliam. *The Theology of Theodore of Mopsuestia*. Washington, DC: The Catholic University of America Press, 1971.

— "The Christology of the Pelagian Controversy," Studia patristica 17.3, ed. Elizabeth A. Livingstone, 1221-43. Leuven: Peeters, 1993.

DeWeese, Garry and Klaus Issler. "Is the Two-Wills / Two-Minds View of the Incarnation Coherent? A Reexamination of the Condemnation of Monothelitism." Paper presented at the annual meeting of Evangelical Theological Society, Toronto, 20 November 2002.

Donahue, John R., and Daniel J. Harrington. *The Gospel of Mark*. Sacra Pagina Series, vol. 2. Collegeville, MN: Liturgical, 2002.

Dormandy, Richard. "Jesus' Temptations in Mark's Gospel: Mark 1:12-13." *Expository Times* 114 (2003): 183-87.

Dorner, Isaak A. *System of Christian Doctrine*. In *God and Incarnation in Mid-Nineteenth Century German Theology*. Translated and edited by Claude Welch, 181-284. Library of Protestant Thought. New York: Oxford University Press, 1965.
— *The History of the Development of the Doctrine of the Person of Christ*. Translated by W. L. Alexander and D. W. Simon. Clark's Foreign Theological Library, 3rd ser. Edinburgh: T. & T. Clark, 1878.
Dunn, James D. G. *Jesus and the Spirit: A Study of the Religious and Charismatic Experience of Jesus and the First Christians as Reflected in the New Testament*. Grand Rapids: Eerdmans, 1997.
Edmondson, Stephen. *Calvin's Christology*. Cambridge: Cambridge University Press, 2004.
Edwards, Jonathan. *The "Miscellanies" (Entry Nos. a-z, aa-zz, 1-500)*. Edited by Thomas A. Schafer. Vol. 13 of *The Works of Jonathan Edwards*. New Haven, CT: Yale University Press, 1994.
— *The "Miscellanies" (Entry Nos. 501-832)*. Edited by Ava Chamberlain. Vol. 18 of *The Works of Jonathan Edwards*. New Haven, CT: Yale University Press, 2000.
— *Freedom of the Will*. Edited by Paul Ramsey. Vol. 1 of *The Works of Jonathan Edwards*. New Haven: Yale University Press, 1957.Eiseman, Tom L. *Temptations Men Face: Straightforward Talk on Power, Money, Affairs, Perfectionism, Insensitivity*. Downers Grove, IL: InterVarsity, 1990.
Ellingworth, Paul. *The Epistle to the Hebrews: A Commentary on the Greek Text*. New International Greek Testament Commentary, vol. 53. Grand Rapids: Eerdmans, 1993; reprint, 2000.
Elliott, John H. *1 Peter*. Anchor Bible, vol. 37B. New York: Doubleday, 2000.
Elliott, Mark W. "The Way from Chalcedon". In *Jesus the Only Hope: Yesterday, Today, Forever*, ed. Mark Elliott and John L. McPake, 95-126. Fearn, Ross-shire: Christian Focus, 2001.
Erickson, Millard J. *The Word Became Flesh: A Contemporary Incarnational Christology*. Grand Rapids: Baker, 1991.
— *Christian Theology*, 2nd ed. Grand Rapids: Baker, 1998.
Evans, David B. *Leontius of Byzantium: An Origenist Christology*. Dumbarton Oaks Studies 13. Washington, DC: Dumbarton Oaks Center for Byzantine Studies, 1970.
Fairbairn, Donald. *Grace and Christology in the Early Church*. Oxford Early Christian Studies. New York: Oxford University Press, 2003.
Feenstra, Ronald J. "Reconsidering Kenotic Christology." In *Trinity, Incarnation, and Atonement*, ed. Ronald J. Feenstra and Cornelius Plantinga Jr., 128-52. Notre Dame: Notre Dame University Press, 1989.
Feinberg, John S. *No One Like Him: The Doctrine of God*. Foundations of Evangelical Theology. Wheaton, IL: Crossway Books, 2001.
Ferguson, Sinclair B. *The Holy Spirit*. Contours of Christian Theology. Downers Grove, IL: InterVarsity, 1996.
— "John Owen on the Spirit in the Life of Christ", *Fire and Ice Sermon Series* (accessed on 8 May 2008 at http://www.puritansermons.com/).Ferre, Nels. *Christ and the Christian*. New York: Harper & Row, 1958.
Ferré, Nels. *Christ and the Christian*. New York: Harper & Row, 1958.
Fisk, Philip J. "Jonathan Edwards's *Freedom of the Will* and his defence of the impeccability of Jesus Christ". *Scottish Journal of Theology* 60 (2007): 309-25.

Fitzmyer, Joseph A. *The Gospel According to Luke I-IX.* Anchor Bible, vol. 28. Garden City: Doubleday, 1981.
— *The Gospel According to Luke X-XXIV.* 2nd ed. Anchor Bible, vol. 28A. Garden City, NY: Doubleday, 1985.
Forsyth, P. T. *The Person and Place of Jesus Christ.* Boston: Pilgrim, 1909.
Foxell, W. J. *The Temptation of Jesus: A Study.* London: S.P.C.K., 1920.
Frame, John M. *The Doctrine of God.* A Theology of Lordship. Phillipsburg, NJ: P & R, 2002.
France, R. T. *The Gospel of Mark.* New International Greek Testament Commentary, vol. 38. Grand Rapids: Eerdmans, 2002.
Gaine, Simon Francis. *'Will There Be Free Will in Heaven?': Freedom, Impeccability and Beatitude.* London: T. & T. Clark, 2003.
Galot, Jean. *Who is Christ? A Theology of the Incarnation.* Translated by M. Angeline Bouchard. Chicago: Franciscan Herald, 1981.
Garrett, James Leo Jr. *Systematic Theology: Biblical, Historical, and Evangelical.* Grand Rapids: Eerdmans, 1995.
Garrett, Susan R. *The Temptations of Jesus in Mark's Gospel.* Grand Rapids: Eerdmans, 1998.
Garrigou-Lagrange, Reginald. *Christ the Savior: A Commentary on the Third Part of St. Thomas' Theological Summa.* Translated by Bede Rose. St. Louis and London: Herder, 1950.
Gerhardsson, Birger. *The Testing of God's Son: (Matt 4:1-1 & Par) An Analysis of Early Christian Midrash.* Translated by John Toy. Lund, SWE: CWK Gleerup, 1966.
Gesché, Adolphe. *La christologie du 'Commentaire sur les Psaumes' découvert à Toura.* Gembloux: Éditions J. Duculot, 1962.
Gibson, Jeffrey B. *The Temptations of Jesus in Early Christianity.* Journal for the Study of the New Testament Supplement Series 112. Sheffield: Sheffield Academic, 1995.
Godin, André. "Temptation: The Psychology of Temptation." Translated by G. J. Schlesselmann. *Journal of Empirical Theology* 5 (1992): 74-85.
Godsey, John D., ed. *Karl Barth's Table Talk.* Scottish Journal of Theology Occasional Papers 10. Edinburgh: Oliver and Boyd, 1963.
Gondreau, Paul. "The Humanity of Christ, the Incarnate Word". In *The Theology of Thomas Aquinas*, ed. Rik Van Nieuwenhove and Joseph Wawrykow, 252-76. Notre Dame, IN: University of Notre Dame Press, 2005.
Gore, Charles. *Dissertations on Subjects Connected with the Incarnation.* 2nd ed. London: John Murray, 1896.
Gray, Patrick T. R. "Leontius of Jerusalem's Case for a 'Synthetic' Union in Christ." Studia patristica 18.1, ed. Elizabeth A. Livingstone, 151-54. Kalamazoo, MI: Cistercian Publications, 1985.
Grayston, Kenneth. "The Meaning of PARAKLETOS." *Journal for the Study of the New Testament* 13 (1981): 67-82.
Green, Joel. "Jesus on the Mount of Olives [Luke 22.39-46]: Tradition and Theology." *Journal for the Study of the New Testament* 26 (1986): 29-48.
Greer, Rowan A. "The Antiochene Christology of Diodore of Tarsus." *Journal of Theological Studies*, n.s., 17 [1966]: 327-41.
— *The Captain of Our Salvation: A Study of the Patristic Exegesis of Hebrews*, Beiträge zur Geschichte der biblischen exegese 15. Tübingen: J. C. B. Mohr (Paul Siebeck), 1973.

— "The Analogy of Grace in Theodore of Mopsuestia's Christology." *Journal of Theological Studies*, n.s., 34 (1983): 82-98.
Grillmeier, Aloys. *Christ in Christian Tradition*. Vol. 1. 2nd ed. Translated by John Bowden. Atlanta: John Knox, 1975.
— *Christ in Christian Tradition*. Vol. 2, pt. 2. In collaboration with Theresia Hainthaler. Translated by John Cawte and Pauline Allen. Louisville: Westminster Kohn Knox, 1995.
Grudem, Wayne A. *Systematic Theology*. Grand Rapids: Zondervan, 1994.
Guelich, Robert A. *Mark 1—8:26*. Word Biblical Commentary, vol. 34A. Dallas: Word, 1989.
Gunton, Colin. *The Promise of Trinitarian Theology*. 2nd ed. Edinburgh: T. & T. Clark, 1991.
Hagner, Donald A. *Matthew 14-28*. Word Biblical Commentary, vol. 33B. Dallas: Word, 1995.
Hallman, Joseph M. "The Communication of Idioms in Theodoret's *Commentary on Hebrews*." In *In Dominico Eloquio, In Lordly Eloquence: Essays on Patristic Exegesis in Honor of Robert Louis Wilken*, ed. Paul M. Blowers, Angela Russell Christman, David Hunter, and Robin Darling Young, 369-79. Grand Rapids: Eerdmans, 2002.
Harnack, Adolf von. *History of Dogma*. Translated by Neil Buchanan. Vol. 2. Boston: Robers Brothers, 1897.
— *History of Dogma*. Translated by Neil Buchanan. Vol. 6. Boston: Little, Brown and Co., 1899.
Harris, Murray J. *The Second Epistle to the Corinthians*. New International Greek Testament Commentary, vol. 43, pt. 2. Grand Rapids: Eerdmans, 2005.
Hart, T. A. "Sinlessness and Moral Responsibility: A Problem in Christology." *Scottish Journal of Theology* 48 (1995): 37-54.
Hastings, W. Ross. "'Honoring the Spirit': Analysis and Evaluation of Jonathan Edwards' Pneumatolgical Doctrine of the Incarnation". *International Journal of Systematic Theology* 7 (2005): 279-99.
Hawthorne, Gerald F. *The Presence and the Power: The Significance of the Holy Spirit in the Life of Jesus*. Dallas: Word, 1991.
Hay, Camillus. "St John Chrysostom and the Integrity of the Human Nature of Christ." *Franciscan Studies* 19 (1959): 298-317.
Hebblethwaite, Brian. *The Incarnation: Collected Essays in Christology*. Cambridge: Cambridge University Press, 1987.
— *Philosophical Theology and Christian Doctrine*. Malden, MA: Blackwell, 2005.
Helland, Roger. "The Hypostatic Union: How Did Jesus Function?" *Evangelical Quarterly* 65 (1993): 311-27.
Helm, Paul. "God and the Approval of Sin." *Religious Studies* 20 (1984): 215-22.
Henry, Carl F. H. *Christian Personal Ethics*. Grand Rapids: Eerdmans, 1957.
Henten, Jan Willem van. "The First Testing of Jesus: A Rereading of Mark 1.12-13." *New Testament Studies* 45 (1999): 349-66.
Heron, Alasdair. "Communicatio Idiomatum and Deification of Human Nature: A Reformed Perspective." *Greek Orthodox Review* 43 (1998): 367-76.
Heschel, Abraham J. *The Prophets*, 2 vol. in 1. Peabody, Mass: Prince, 2000.
Hoffman, Joshua. "Can God Do Evil?" *Southern Journal of Philosophy* 17 (1979): 213-20.

Humphreys, Fisher H. "The Humanity of Christ in Some Modern Theologies." *Faith and Mission* 5 (1988): 3-13.Jobes, Karen H. *1 Peter*. Baker Exegetical Commentary on the New Testament, vol. 56. Grand Rapids: Baker Academic, 2005.

Issler, Klaus. "Jesus's Example: Prototype of the Dependent, Spirit-Filled Life". In *Jesus in Trinitarian Perspective*, ed. Fred Sanders and Klaus Issler, 189-225. Nashville: B & H, 2007.

Johnson, Harry. *The Humanity of the Saviour: A Biblical and Historical Study of the Human Nature of Christ in relation to Original Sin, with special reference to its Soteriological Significance*. London: Epworth, 1962.

Johnson, Luke Timothy. *The Acts of the Apostles*. Sacra Pagina Series, vol. 5. Collegeville, MN: Liturgical, 1992.

Kärkkäinen, Veli-Matti. *Christology: A Global Introduction*. Grand Rapids: Baker Academic, 2003.

Kelly, J.N.D. *Early Christian Doctrines*. 5th rev. ed. London: Adam & Charles Black, 1960.

Klauck, Hans-Josef. "Sacrifice and Sacrificial Offerings." Translated by Reginald H. Fuller. In *Anchor Bible Dictionary*, ed. David Noel Freedman. New York: Doubleday, 1992.

Koester, Craig R. *Hebrews*. Anchor Bible, vol. 36. New York: Doubleday, 2001.

Köppen, Klaus-Peter. *Die Auslegung der Versuchungsgeschichte unter besonderer Berücksichtigung der Alten Kirche*, 4, *Beiträge zur Geschichte der biblischen Exegese*. Tübingen: J. C. B. Mohr, 1961.

— "The Interpretation of Jesus' Temptations by the Early Church Fathers." *Patristic and Byzantine Review* 8 [1989]: 41-43.

Kuhn, Karl Georg. "New Light on Temptation, Sin, and Flesh in the New Testament." In *The Scrolls and the New Testament*, ed. Krister Stendahl, 94-113. New York: Harper & Brothers, 1957.

Lampe, G.W.H. "The Holy Spirit and the person of Christ". In *Christ, Faith and History: Cambridge Studies in Christology*, ed. S. W. Sykes and J. P. Clayton, 111-30. Cambridge: Cambridge University Press, 1972.

Lane, William L. *Hebrews 1-8*. Word Biblical Commentary, vol. 47A. Dallas: Word, 1991.

— *Hebrews 9-13*. Word Biblical Commentary, vol. 47B. Dallas: Word, 1991.

Lawrenz, Melvin E. *The Christology of John Chrysostom*. Lewiston, NY: Edwin Mellen, 1996.

Layton, Richard A. "From 'Holy Passion' to Sinful Emotion: Jerome and the Doctrine of *Propassio*". In *In Dominico Eloquio, In Lordly Eloquence: Essays on Patristic Exegesis in Honor of Robert Louis Wilken*, ed. Paul M. Blowers, Angela Russell Christman, David Hunter, and Robin Darling Young, 280-93. Grand Rapids: Eerdmans, 2002.

Letch, Ralph A. *Temptation and Freedom: The Temptations of God*. Harrow, UK: Eureditions, 1978.

Lewis, Gordon R. and Bruce A. Demarest. *Integrative Theology*. Grand Rapids: Academie Books, 1990.

Lienhard, Marc. *Luther: Witness to Jesus Christ*. Translated by Edwin H. Robertson. Minneapolis: Augsburg, 1982.

Lilla, Salvatore R. C. *Clement of Alexandria: A Study in Christian Platonism and Gnosticism*. Oxford: Oxford University Press, 1971.

Lohse, Bernhard. *Martin Luther's Theology: Its Historical and Systematic Development*. Translated and edited by Roy A. Harrisville. Minneapolis: Fortress, 1999.
Louth, Andrew. *Maximus the Confessor*. London: Routledge, 1996.
Mackintosh, H. R. *The Doctrine of the Person of Jesus Christ*. New York: Charles Scribner's Sons, 1942.
Macleod, Donald. *The Person of Christ*. Contours of Christian Theology. Downers Grove, IL: InterVarsity, 1998.
— "The Christology of Chalcedon." In *Jesus the Only Hope: Yesterday, Today, Forever*, ed. Mark Elliott and John L. McPake, 77-94. Fearn, Ross-shire: Christian Focus, 2001.
Macquarrie, John. *Jesus Christ in Modern Thought*. London: SCM, 1990.
— "Was Jesus Sinless?" *Living Pulpit* 8 (1999): 14-15.
Madigan, Kevin. "Did Jesus "Progress in Wisdom"? Thomas Aquinas on Luke 2:52 in Ancient and High-Medieval Context." *Traditio* 52 (1997): 179-200.
McCormack, Bruce L. *For Us and Our Salvation: Incarnation and Atonement in the Reformed Tradition*. Princeton, NJ: Princeton University Press, 1993.
McDonald, H.D. *Jesus—Human and Divine*. Grand Rapids: Zondervan, 1968.
McFarland, Ian A. "'Willing Is Not Choosing': Some Anthropological Implications of Dyothelite Christology". *International Journal of Systematic Theology* 9 (2007): 3-23.
McFarlane, Graham W. P. *Christ and the Spirit: The Doctrine of the Incarnation According to Edward Irving*. Carlisle: Paternoster, 1996.
McGrath, Alister E. *Historical Theology*. Oxford: Blackwell, 1998.
McGuckin, John A. *St. Cyril of Alexandria The Christological Controversy: Its History, Theology, and Texts*. Supplements to Vigiliae Christianae 23. Leiden: E. J. Brill, 1994.
McIntyre, John. *Theology after the Storm*. Edited by Gary D. Badcock. Grand Rapids: Eerdmans, 1997.
Menzies, Robert P. *The Development of Early Christian Pneumatology with Special Reference to Luke-Acts*. Journal for the Study of the New Testament Supplement Series 54. Sheffield: Sheffield Academic Press, 1991.
Meredith, Anthony. *The Cappadocians*. Crestwood, NY: St Vladimir's Seminary Press, 1995.
Moo, Douglas J. *The Epistle to the Romans*. New International Commentary on the New Testament. Grand Rapids: Eerdmans, 1996.
— *The Letter of James*. Pillar New Testament Commentary, vol. 55. Grand Rapids: Eerdmans, 2000.
Morris, Leon. *The Gospel according to John*. Rev. ed. New International Commentary on the New Testament, vol. 40. Grand Rapids: Eerdmans, 1995.
Morris, Thomas V. *The Logic of God Incarnate*. Ithaca, NY: Cornell University Press, 1986.
— "Reduplication and Representational Christology". *Modern Theology* 2:4 (1986): 319-27.
— *Anselmian Explorations: Essays in Philosophical Theology*. Notre Dame, IN: University of Notre Dame Press, 1987.
Motyer, Alec. *The Prophecy of Isaiah*. Downers Grove, IL: InterVarsity, 1993.

Mühlen, Karl-Heinz zur. "Christology." Translated by Robert E. Shillenn. In *The Oxford Encyclopedia of the Reformation*, ed. Hans J. Hillerbrand. New York and Oxford: Oxford University Press, 1996.

Muller, Richard A. *Christ and the Decree: Christology and Predestination in Reformed Theology from Calvin to Perkins*. Studies in Historical Theology 2. Durham, NC: Labyrinth, 1986.

— *Dictionary of Latin and Greek Theological Terms: Drawn Principally from Protestant Scholastic Theology*. Grand Rapids: Baker, 1985.

Nash, Ronald H. *Life's Ultimate Questions*. Grand Rapids: Zondervan, 1999.

Neander, Augustus. *General History of the Christian Religion and Church*. 1st American ed. Translated by Joseph Torrey. Boston: Crocker & Brewster, 1851.

Neyrey, Jerome H. "The Absence of Jesus' Emotions—the Lucan Redaction of Lk 22,39-46." *Biblica* 61 (1980): 153-71.

Niebuhr, Reinhold. *The Nature and Destiny of Man: A Christian Interpretation*. 2 vols. New York: Charles Scribner's Sons, 1941.

Norris, Jr., R. A. *Manhood and Christ: A Study in the Christology of Theodore of Mopsuestia*. Oxford: Clarendon, 1963.

— "Christological Models in Cyril of Alexandria". In Studia Patristica, vol. 13, pt. 2, 255-68. Edited by E. A. Livingstone, Texte und Untersuchungen, 116. Berlin: Akademie Verlag, 1975.

— *The Christological Controversy*. Philadelphia: Fortress, 1980.

Nuyen, A. T. "The Nature of Temptation". *The Southern Journal of Philosophy* 35 (1997): 91-103.

Oates, Wayne E. *Temptation: A Biblical and Psychological Approach*. Louisville: Westminster John Knox, 1991.

Oberman, Heiko Augustus. "The 'Extra' Dimension in the Theology of Calvin." In *The Dawn of the Reformation*, ed. Heiko Augustus Oberman, 234-58. Edinburgh: T. & T. Clark, 1986.

O'Collins, Gerald. *Christology*. Oxford: Oxford University Press, 1995.

— "The Incarnation: The Critical Issues." In *The Incarnation: An Interdisciplinary Symposium on the Incarnation of the Son of God*, ed. Stephen T. Davis, Daniel Kendall, Gerald O'Collins, 1-27. Oxford: Oxford University Press, 2002.

Oden, Thomas C. *The Word of Life*. Vol. 2 of *Systematic Theology*. San Francisco: Harper & Row, 1989.

O'Keefe, John J. "Sin, ἀπάθεια and Freedom of the Will in Gregory of Nyssa." Studia patristica 22, ed. Elizabeth A. Livingstone, 52-59. Leuven: Peeters, 1989.

Osterhaven, M. E. "Sinlessness of Christ". In *Evangelical Dictionary of Theology*, 2nd ed. Edited by Walter A. Elwell. Grand Rapids: Baker Academic, 2001.

Oswalt, John N. *The Book of Isaiah: 1-39*. New International Commentary on the Old Testament, vol. 20. Grand Rapids: Eerdmans, 1986.

Owen, H. P. "The Sinlessness of Jesus." In *Religion, Reason and the Self*, ed. Stewart R. Sutherland and T. A. Roberts, 119-28. Cardiff: University of Wales Press, 1989.

Owen, John. *The Glory of Christ*. Edited by William H. Goold. Vol. 1 of *The Works of John Owen*. London: Johnstone & Hunter, 1850-53; reprint, Edinburgh: Banner of Truth Trust, 1965.

— *Pneumatologia*. Edited by William H. Goold. Vol. 3 of *The Works of John Owen*. London: Johnstone & Hunter, 1850-53; reprint, Edinburgh: Banner of Truth Trust, 1965.

Painter, George S. *The Philosophy of Christ's Temptation.* Boston: Sherman, French, and Co., 1914.
Pannenberg, Wolfhart. *Jesus—God and Man.* 2nd ed. Translated by Lewis L. Wilkins and Duane A. Priebe. Philadelphia: Westminster, 1977.
Pelikan, Jaroslav. *The Emergence of the Catholic Tradition (100-600).* Vol. 1 of *The Christian Tradition: A History of the Development of Doctrine.* Chicago: University of Chicago Press, 1971.
— *The Spirit of Eastern Christendom (700-1700).* Vol. 2 of *The Christian Tradition: A History of the Development of Doctrine.* Chicago: University of Chicago Press, 1974.
Peters, Albrecht ."Luthers Christuszeugnis als Zusammenfassung der Christusbotschaft der Kirche, II. Teil." *Kerygma und Dogma* 13 (1967): 73-98.
Peters, Ted. *Sin: Radical Evil in Soul and Society.* Grand Rapids: Eerdmans, 1994.
Plantinga, Cornelius, Jr. *Not the Way It's Supposed to Be: A Breviary of Sin.* Grand Rapids: Eerdmans, 1995.
Pike, Nelson. "Omnipotence and God's Ability to Sin." In *Divine Commands and Morality*, ed. Paul Helm, 67-82. Oxford: Oxford University Press, 1981.
Piper, John. "Justification and the Diminishing Work of Christ". The Crossway Lecture at the Annual Meeting of the Evangelical Theological Society, San Diego. 14 November 2007.
Pollard, T. E. *Fullness of Humanity: Christ's Humanness and Ours.* The Croall Lectures 1980. Sheffield: Almond, 1982.
— "The Impassibility of God." *Scottish Journal of Theology* 8 (1955): 353-64.
Principe, Walter H. *Alexander of Hales' Theology of the Hypostatic Union.* Vol. 2 of *The Theology of the Hypostatic Union in the Early Thirteenth Century.* Studies and Texts 12. Toronto: Pontifical Institute of Mediaeval Studies, 1967.
— *William of Auxerre's Theology of the Hypostatic Union.* Vol. 1 of *The Theology of the Hypostatic Union in the Early Thirteenth Century.* Studies and Texts 7. Toronto: Pontifical Institute of Mediaeval Studies, 1963.
— "Some Examples of Augustine's Influence on Medieval Christology." In *Collectanea Augustiniana: Mélanges T. J. Van Bavel*, ed. B. Brunin, M. Lamberigts, J. Van Houtem, 955-74. Leuven: Leuven University Press, 1990.
Quasten, Johannes. *Patrology: The Golden Age of Greek Patristic Literature.* Vols 1-3. Utrecht: The Newman Press, 1975.
Ramm, Bernard L. *An Evangelical Christology: Ecumenic and Historic.* Nashville: Thomas Nelson, 1985.
Reichenbach, Bruce. *Evil and a Good God.* New York: Fordham University Press, 1982.
Reinink, G. J. "Quotations from the Lost Works of Theodoret of Cyrus and Theodore of Mopsuestia in an Unpublished East Syrian Work on Christology." Studia patristica 33, ed. Elizabeth A. Livingstone, 562-67. Leuven: Peeters, 1997.
Relton, Herbert M. *A Study in Christology: The Problem of the Relation of the Two Natures in the Person of Christ.* London: S.P.C.K., 1917.
Ricoeur, Paul *Fallible Man.* Translated by Charles A. Kelbley. New York: Fordham University Press, 1986.
Robinson, John A. T. *The Human Face of God.* Philadelphia: Westminster, 1973.
— "Use of the Fourth Gospel for Christology." In *Christ and Spirit in the New Testament*, ed. Barnabas Lindars and Stephen S. Smalley, 61-78. Cambridge: Cambridge University Press, 1973.

Rogers, Cleon L. Jr., and Cleon L. Rogers, III. *The New Linguistic and Exegetical Key to the Greek New Testament*. Grand Rapids: Zondervan, 1998.

Rosemann, Philipp W. *Peter Lombard*. Oxford: Oxford University Press, 2004.

Sanday, William. *Christologies Ancient and Modern*, in *Christology and Personality*. Oxford: Clarendon, 1911.

Saucy, Robert. "Theology of Human Nature." In *Christian Perspectives on Being Human*, ed. J. P. Moreland and David M. Ciocchi, 17-52. Grand Rapids: Baker, 1993.

Schaff, Philip. *The Person of Christ: His Perfect Humanity a Proof of His Divinity*. New York: George H. Doran, 1913.

Schleiermacher, Friedrich D. E. *The Christian Faith*. Translated and edited by H. R. Mackintosh and J. S. Stewart. 2nd ed. Edinburgh: T. & T. Clark, 1928.

Schmid, Heinrich. *The Doctrinal Theology of the Evangelical Lutheran Church*. Translated by Charles A. Hay and Henry A. Jacobs. 3rd rev. ed. Philadelphia: United Lutheran Publication House, 1899; reprint, Minneapolis: Augsburg, 1961.

Schneider, W., and C. Brown. "Peirasmos". In *New International Dictionary of New Testament Theology*. Edited by Willem A. VanGemeren [CD-ROM]. Grand Rapids: Zondervan, 1997, 2002.

Schreiner, Thomas R. *1, 2 Peter, Jude*. New American Commentary, vol. 37. Nashville: Broadman and Holman, 2003.

Seeberg, Reinhold. *History of Doctrines in the Middle and Modern Ages*. Vol. 2 of *Text-Book of the History of Doctrines*. Translated by Charles E. Hay. Rev. ed. Philadelphia: Lutheran Publication Society, 1905.

Shedd, William G. T. *Dogmatic Theology*. Edited by Alan W. Gomes. 3rd ed. Phillipsburg, NJ: Presbyterian and Reformed, 2003.

Shuster, Marguerite. "The Temptation, Sinlessness, and Sympathy of Jesus: Another Look at the Dilemma of Hebrews 4:15." In *Perspectives on Christology: Essays in Honor of Paul K. Jewett*, ed. Marguerite Shuster and Richard A. Muller, 197-210. Grand Rapids: Zondervan, 1991.

Smalley, Stephen S. *1,2, 3 John*. Word Biblical Commentary, vol. 51. Waco, TX: Word, 1984.

Snaith, Norman H. *Distinctive Ideas of the Old Testament*. London: Epworth, 1944.

Spence, Alan. "Christ's Humanity and Ours: John Owen". In *Persons, Divine and Human: King's College Essays in Theological Anthropology*, ed. Christoph Schwöbel and Colin E. Gunton, 74-97. Edinburgh: T. & T. Clark, 1991.

— *Incarnation and Inspiration: John Owen and the Coherence of Christology*. London: T. & T. Clark, 2007.

Spoerl, Kelley McCarthy. "Apollinarius and the Response to Early Arian Christology." Studia patristica 26, ed. Elizabeth A. Livingstone, 421-27. Leuven: Peeters, 1993.

Srawley, J. H. "St Gregory of Nyssa on the Sinlessness of Christ." *Journal of Theological Studies* 7 (1906): 434-41.

Steiner, M. *La Tentation de Jésus dans L'Interprétation Patristique de Saint Justin a Origéne*. Paris: Libraire Lecoffre, 1962.

Storms, Sam. "Could Jesus have Sinned? (2 Cor. 5.21)". Posted January 23, 2008 at http://www.enjoyinggodministries.com/article/could-jesus-have-sinned-2-cor-521 (accessed on April 18, 2008).

Strauss, D. F. *The Life of Jesus Critically Examined*. Translated by George Eliot. Edited by Peter C. Hodgson. 4th ed. Lives of Jesus Series. Philadelphia: Fortress, 1972.

Strong, Augustus H. *Systematic Theology*. Philadelphia: Judson, 1907.
Stronstad, Roger. *The Charismatic Theology of St. Luke*. Peabody, MA: Hendrickson, 1984.
— *The Prophethood of All Believers: A Study in Luke's Charismatic Theology*. Journal of Pentecostal Theology Supplement Series 16. Sheffield: Sheffield Academic Press, 1999.
Sturch, Richard. *The Word and The Christ: An Essay in Analytic Christology*. Oxford: Clarendon, 1991.
Sullivan, Francis A. *The Christology of Theodore of Mopsuestia*. Analecta Gregoriana 82. Rome: Apud Aedes Universitatis Gregorianae, 1956.
Swete, H. B. "Theodorus (26)." In *A Dictionary of Christian Biography and Literature: To the End of the Sixth Century A.D., with an Account of the Principal Sects and Heresies*, ed. Henry Wace and William C. Piercy. London: John Murray, 1911.
Swinburne, Richard. *The Christian God*. New York: Oxford University Press, 1994.
Taylor, Vincent. *The Person of Christ in New Testament Teaching*. London: Macmillan and Co., 1958.
Teske, Roland J. "St. Augustine on the Humanity of Christ and Temptation". *Augustiniana* 54 (2004): 261-77.
Thielicke, Helmut. "The Great Temptation." In *Our Heavenly Father*. San Francisco: Harper & Row, 1960. Reprint, *Christianity Today* 29, no.10 (1985): 26-31.
Thiselton, Anthony C. *The First Epistle to the Corinthians*. New International Greek Testament Commentary, vol. 43. Grand Rapids: Eerdmans, 2000.
Thomasius, Gottfried. *Christ's Person and Work*. In *God and Incarnation in Mid-Nineteenth Century German Theology*. Translated and edited by Claude Welch, 31-87. A Library of Protestant Thought. New York: Oxford University Press, 1965.
Thompson, G. H. P. "Called—Proved—Obedient: A Study in the Baptism and Temptation Narratives of Matthew and Luke." *Journal of Theological Studies*, n.s., 11 (1960): 1-12.
Turner, Max. *The Holy Spirit and Spiritual Gifts: In the New Testament Church and Today*. Rev. ed. Peabody, MA: Hendrickson, 1998.
— *Power from on High: The Spirit in Israel's Restoration and Witness in Luke-Acts*. Journal for Pentecostal Theology Supplement Series 9. Sheffield: Sheffield Academic Press, 1996.
Turretin, Francis. *Institutes of Elenctic Theology*. Translated by ns. George M. Giger. Edited by James T. Dennison, Jr. Phillipsburg, NJ: P & R, 1994.
Twelftree, G. H. "Temptation of Jesus." In *Dictionary of Jesus and the Gospels*, ed. Joel B. Green and Scot McKnight. Downers Grove, IL: InterVarsity, 1992.
Ullmann, Carl. *The Sinlessness of Jesus: An Evidence for Christianity*. Translated by R. C. Lundin Brown. 6th ed. Edinburgh: T. & T. Clark, 1858.
Vanhoozer, Kevin. *First Theology*. Downers Grove, IL: InterVarsity, 2002.
Van Iersel, B. *The Bible on the Temptations of Man*. Translated by F. Vander Heijden. De Pere, WI: St. Norbert Abbey Press, 1966.
Vos, Geerhardus. *The Pauline Eschatology*. Grand Rapids: Eerdmans, 1953.
— "The Priesthood of Christ in the Epistle to the Hebrews," *Princeton Theological Review* 5 (1907): 579-604.
Vos, Antonie. "The Possibility of Impeccability." In *Christian Faith and Philosophical Theology: Essays in Honor of Vincent Brümmer*, ed. Gijsbert van den Brink, Luco J. van den Brom, and Marcel Sarot, 227-39. Kampen, NL: Kok Pharos, 1992.

Waaijman, Kees. "Temptation: The Basic Theological Structure of Temptation." Translated by S. Ralston. *Journal of Empirical Theology* 5 (1992): 86-92.

Wallace, Daniel B. *Greek Grammar Beyond the Basics*. Grand Rapids: Zondervan, 1996.

Ware, Bruce A. *God's Greater Glory*. Wheaton, IL: Crossway, 2004.

—"Fully God Fully Man: Revisiting the Impeccability, Temptations, and Sinlessness of Christ". Paper presented at the 59th Annual Meeting of the Evangelical Theological Society, San Diego, CA. 16 November 2007.

Warfield, Benjamin B. *The Person and Work of Christ*. Edited by Samuel G. Craig. Philadelphia: Presbyterian and Reformed, 1950.

Watts, John D. W. *Isaiah 1-33*. Word Biblical Commentary, vol. 24. Waco, TX: Word, 1985.

Weinandy, Thomas G. *In the Likeness of Sinful Flesh: An Essay on the Humanity of Christ*. Edinburgh: T. & T. Clark, 1993.

Wells, David F. *The Person of Christ*. Westchester, IL: Crossway, 1984.

Werther, David. "The Temptation of God Incarnate." *Religious Studies* 29 (1993): 47-50.

Westcott, B. F. *The Epistle to the Hebrews*. 2nd ed. London: Macmillan, 1892.

Wilde, Oscar. *The Picture of Dorian Gray*. Franklin Center, PA: The Franklin Library, 1988.

Wiles, Maurice. *The Making of Christian Doctrine*. Cambridge: Cambridge University Press, 1967.

— "The Doctrine of Christ in the Patristic Age." In *Christ for Us Today*, ed. Norman Pittenger, 81-90. London: SCM, 1968.

Wilkins, Michael J. *Matthew*. NIV Application Commentary, vol. 37. Grand Rapids: Zondervan, 2004.

Williamson, Ronald. "Hebrews 4:15 and the Sinlessness of Jesus." *Expository Times* 86 (1974): 4-8

Willis, E. David. *Calvin's Catholic Christology: The Function of the So-Called Extra Calvinisticum in Calvin's Christology*. Studies in Medieval and Reformation Thought 2. Leiden: E. J. Brill, 1966.

Wingren, Gustaf *Man and the Incarnation: A Study in the Biblical Theology of Irenaeus*. Translated by Ross Mackenzie. Edinburgh: Oliver and Boyd, 1959.

Winslow, Donald F. "Christology and Exegesis in the Cappadocians." *Church History* 40 (1971): 389-96.

Wolfson, Harry Austryn. *Faith, Trinity, Incarnation*. 3rd ed. Vol. 1 of *The Philosophy of the Church Fathers*. Cambridge: Harvard University Press, 1970.

Wolter, Allan. "John Duns Scotus on the Primacy and Personality of Christ." In *Franciscan Christology: Selected texts, Translations, and Introductory Essays*, ed. Damian McElrath, 139-82, Franciscan Sources 1. St. Bonaventure, NY: The Fransciscan Institute of St. Bonaventure University, 1980.

Wright, N. T. *Jesus and the Victory of God*. Minneapolis: Fortress, 1996.

Yandell, Keith E. "Divine Necessity and Divine Goodness." In *Divine and Human Action: Essays in the Metaphysics of Theism*, ed. Thomas V. Morris, 313-44. Ithaca, NY: Cornell University Press, 1988.

Young, Frances M. "Christological Ideas in the Greek Commentaries on the Epistle to the Hebrews." *Journal of Theological Studies*, n.s., 20 (1969): 150-63.

Dissertations and Theses

Burns, Paul C. "The Christology in Hilary of Poitiers' Commentary on Matthew". BLitt thesis, Oxford University, 1977.

Johnson, Dennis E. "Immutability and Incarnation: An Historical and Theological Study of the Concepts of Christ's Divine Unchangeability and His Human Development". PhD diss., Fuller Theological Seminary, 1984.

Lister, Robert G., III. "Impassible and Impassioned: Reevaluating the Doctrines of Divine Impassibility and Divine Relationality". PhD diss., The Southern Baptist Theological Seminary, 2007.

Naidu, Ashish Jacob. "The Doctrine of Christ as it Relates to the Christian Life in John Chrysostom's Homilies on the Gospel of John and Hebrews". PhD thesis, University of Aberdeen, 2005.

Sullivan, Thomas P. "On the Temptation of Jesus". PhD diss., University of Massachusetts Amherst, 1993.

Zabriskie, Howard C. "The Impeccability of Christ". ThD diss., Dallas Theological Seminary, 1938.

General Index

Adams, Marilyn McCord 147-49, 153-154, 156, 158-63, 167, 169, 189-90, 216

Adoptionism 2, 53, 86, 87, 142, 143, 261

Anselm 149, 153, 157-59, 161-64, 190, 207-8, 260

Apollinaris 81, 83-86, 92, 95, 103, 120-21, 127-28

Apollinarianism 2, 83, 86, 120-21, 130, 135, 226, 228, 233-34, 242

Arius/ Arian 84, 86, 87, 88, 92, 121, 213

Athanasius 86-87, 91-92, 95, 103, 108, 110, 183, 391

Augustine 1, 7, 10, 83, 91, 98, 99, 100, 124-125, 135-36, 140, 142, 146, 151-53, 175, 183, 200, 210, 291, 301

Baillie, Donald 189

Barth, Karl 9, 11, 203-4

Basil of Caesarea 91, 108-9, 133

Bavinck, Herman 4, 5, 192, 194-96, 201, 295

beatific vision 150-51, 154-55, 161, 164, 167, 169, 172, 177, 190, 243

Bloesch, Donald 9, 196, 201, 202, 285

Bonaventure 145, 149, 153-54, 161, 163

Brown, Dan 1, 2, 210

Brown, Raymond 15, 28-32, 34, 35, 71, 231

Bruce, A. B. 152, 179, 198, 200-1, 204, 207, 225, 228-29, 257, 273, 277, 280, 291, 294, 296

Brümmer, Vincent 207, 256-57

Calvin, John 21, 27, 34-36, 109, 140, 142, 169-76, 179-85, 188, 198, 200, 202, 221, 252, 283, 291-93, 295

Chalcedonian Christology 2, 8, 10, 15, 82, 125, 139, 140, 145, 148, 151, 169, 179, 186, 190, 192, 202, 203, 208, 210, 211, 221, 226, 227, 229, 235, 236, 242, 248, 251, 291, 293, 295, 315

Clement of Alexandria 84, 99, 104-5, 112-13

Craig, William Lane 233-35, 240, 242

Crisp, Oliver D. 10, 20, 46, 77, 103, 196, 203, 204, 205, 208, 214, 215, 240, 253, 275

Cyril of Alexandria 61, 82, 83, 86-87, 89, 91, 92, 94-96, 103, 104, 110, 111, 115, 116, 135-39, 170, 183, 231, 291

deification 81, 85, 95, 97, 102-3, 105-16, 122, 127, 130, 131, 143, 145, 149, 150-52, 172, 189, 200, 248

desires
and temptation 279-84
corrupt 10, 39, 136, 157, 166, 261, 263, 266, 279-84, 288, 290
legitimate 270, 279-80, 284, 288, 309

Didymus the Blind 107-8

divine impassibility 82, 83, 88-90, 109, 143, 225

divine impeccability 5, 6, 83, 98, 100, 102, 103, 106, 109, 142-43, 160, 172, 175, 186, 205-7, 209, 213-14, 222, 236, 247, 256-57, 259, 297

divine peccability 214

Duns Scotus, John 5, 148, 153-55, 159-62, 258

Dyothelitism 82, 117, 126, 127, 129, 141, 148, 158, 186

Edwards, Jonathan 9, 11, 46, 117, 122, 132, 195, 196, 198-99, 203-5, 208, 294-96

epistemic temptation 229-32, 241

extra calvinisticum 182, 184, 252, 281

fallen human nature 6, 10, 11, 89, 127, 128, 130, 136, 136, 167, 182, 186, 190, 202-5, 213, 242, 252-53, 266, 269, 282-5, 288

Feinberg, John S. 9, 213, 224-25, 237, 239

Fifth Ecumenical Council 92, 131, 132, 211

Forsyth, P. T. 221-22, 225-26

Fourth Ecumenical Council 2, 61
see Chalcedonian Christology

Galot, Jean 5, 82, 121, 164

grace 71, 102, 107, 114, 126, 128, 130
created 146, 148-55, 160, 163-68, 193, 243
empowering 61, 131-43, 148, 151, 173, 184, 186, 197, 199, 220, 222, 249, 302, 305, 307-15, 319
of union 148, 151-55, 159

Gregory of Nazianzen 85-87, 90, 117, 121-22

Gregory of Nyssa 85, 89, 91-92, 109, 112, 113

Hart, Trevor 205, 209, 210, 254

Hawthorne, Gerald F. 71, 73, 76, 132, 199, 200, 222, 225, 226, 303

Hilary of Poitiers 84, 90, 106-7, 124

Hodge, Charles 208-10

Holy Spirit 11, 15, 25, 42, 45, 46, 61-77, 87, 88, 96, 115-16, 129, 132-33, 135-43, 153, 154, 167, 171, 172, 174-75, 181-87, 193, 194, 197-205, 211, 215, 220, 222, 223, 228, 233-39, 243-44, 247, 249, 254, 256, 261, 278, 289-319

impeccability of Christ 3-11, 15, 27, 46, 61, 78, 81-85, 88, 90-103, 105, 106, 190, 110, 113, 117-21, 130, 136, 137, 139, 140-65, 168-76, 179, 184-86, 188-217, 297, 312, 315-16, 318, *see chs 9 and 10*

Irenaeus of Lyons 86, 118-19, 181

Irving, Edward 11, 132, 203-5

Jerome 91, 124, 137

John Chrysostom 91, 94-95, 99, 122-24, 128

John of Damascus 90, 113, 127-28, 153, 157

Kazantzakis, Nikos 1, 3, 101, 210

kenotic theory 141, 191, 200, 201, 219-33

Leo the Great 111, 124-25, 183, 291

Leontius of Byzantium 111, 125

Leontius of Jerusalem 103, 111-12, 139-40

Luther, Martin 34, 35, 36, 169-78, 183, 185-86, 200, 202, 282

Mackintosh, H. R. 221, 226

Macleod, Donald 190, 193, 199, 202, 205, 232-33

Macquarrie, John 189, 208

Maximus the Confessor 117, 122, 123, 125-30

Monothelitism 123, 141, 196, 226-27, 234

Morris, Thomas V. 90, 207, 213, 225, 229-42, 254, 257, 258, 293

Nestorius 61, 83, 89, 94, 96, 132, 136-40

Nestorianism 2, 139, 215, 242

Nicene faith 84, 88, 107-9, 211, 213

Niebuhr, Reinhold 264

O'Collins, Gerald 3, 9, 71, 196, 231

Origen 83, 89, 97-100, 105-6

original sin 10, 20, 39, 46, 77, 152, 156, 157, 173, 175, 203, 204, 252, 253, 263, 302

Owen, John 73, 132, 140, 184, 193-94, 197-200, 235, 293

Pannenberg, Wolfhart 21, 82, 98, 99, 127, 149, 203-4

peccability of Christ 4-9, 192, 203, 207-17, 224, 244, 252, 253, 258
Peter Abelard 145, 108
Peter Lombard 148, 149, 154, 155
Pike, Nelson 159

pneumatological Christology 63, 73, 86, 142, 199, 244, 261, 290-97

pneumatological veiling 291-93

recapitulation 23, 26, 115, 118, 128, 154, 165, 166, 251, 268, 299

Sanday, William 228, 233

Saucy, Robert L. 28, 226, 265

Schaff, Philip 208, 210-11

Shedd, William G. T. 194, 196

sinlessness of Jesus, *see ch. 1*

Sixth Ecumenical Council 61, 82, 127, 117, 118, 123, 129, 226

Storms, Sam 211, 224, 225

Swinburne, Richard 9, 185, 232, 235, 240-41

temptation, *see ch. 11*
 and beliefs 278-79
 and desires 279-85
 and freedom 112, 126-28, 131, 134-35, 138-41, 146, 148-50, 155-63, 168, 196, 203, 206-11, 219, 231,

temptation (cont.)
   241, 254-65, 277
   and God 263-66
   and impeccability *see ch. 10*
   and merit 162
   and other people 267
   and peccability 208-16
   and person-variability 275-77
   and suffering 269
   and the created world 266
   and the self 268
   definition of 287-88
   dual purposes of 273-75
   Jesus' experiences of
      Heb 2:17-18 *16-18*
      Heb 4:15-16 *18-22*
      Heb 5:7-8 *32-34*
      in the crucifixion 34-36
      in Gethsemane 27-34
      in the wilderness 22-27
      relative intensity 289-90
      relational setting 36-40
      sexual temptations 1, 39, 210
   relevance of Jesus' for us, *see ch. 2*
      Heb 12:1-3 *50-53*

1 Pet 2:21-25 *54-57*

Tertullian 86, 98, 99, 119-20

Theodore of Mopsuestia 82, 83, 85, 88, 89, 93-96, 116, 128, 131-42, 183, 192, 199, 211

Theodoret of Cyrus 61, 85, 116, 133, 138-39, 142

theological models approach 11, 81, 83

Thomas Aquinas 145, 152-58, 160-61, 182, 183, 285, 291

Thomasius, Gottfried 191, 220

two-minds theory 234, 242

Ullmann, Carl 42, 192, 208, 209, 210

Ware, Bruce A. 25, 27, 130, 214, 225, 272, 310, 312, 313

www.ingramcontent.com/pod-product-compliance
Lightning Source LLC
Chambersburg PA
CBHW071757300426
44116CB00009B/1115